I INFORMATION SYSTEMS

Video training courses are available on the subjects of these books in the
James Martin ADVANCED TECHNOLOGY LIBRARY of over 300 tapes and disks,
from Applied Learning, 1751 West Diehl Road, Naperville, IL 60540 (tel: 312-369-3000).

P9-DMM-842

Database	Telecommunications	Networks and Data Communications	Society
AN END USER'S GUIDE TO DATABASE	TELECOMMUNICATIONS AND THE COMPUTER (third edition)	PRINCIPLES OF DATA COMMUNICATION	THE COMPUTERIZED SOCIETY
PRINCIPLES OF DATABASE MANAGEMENT (second edition)	FUTURE DEVELOPMENTS IN TELECOMMUNICATIONS (third edition)	TELEPROCESSING NETWORK ORGANIZATION	TELEMATIC SOCIETY: A CHALLENGE FOR TOMORROW
COMPUTER DATABASE ORGANIZATION (third edition)	COMMUNICATIONS SATELLITE SYSTEMS	SYSTEMS ANALYSIS FOR DATA TRANSMISSION	TECHNOLOGY'S CRUCIBLE
MANAGING THE DATABASE ENVIRONMENT (second edition)	ISDN	DATA COMMUNICATION TECHNOLOGY	VIEWDATA AND THE INFORMATION SOCIETY
DATABASE ANALYSIS AND DESIGN	**Distributed Processing**	DATA COMMUNICATION DESIGN TECHNIQUES	**SAA: Systems Application Architecture**
VSAM: ACCESS METHOD SERVICES AND PROGRAMMING TECHNIQUES	COMPUTER NETWORKS AND DISTRIBUTED PROCESSING	SNA: IBM's NETWORKING SOLUTION	SAA: COMMON USER ACESS
DB2: CONCEPTS, DESIGN, AND PROGRAMMING	DESIGN AND STRATEGY FOR DISTRIBUTED DATA PROCESSING	ISDN	SAA: COMMON COMMUNICATIONS SUPPORT
IDMS/R: CONCEPTS, DESIGN, AND PROGRAMMING	**Office Automation**	LOCAL AREA NETWORKS: ARCHITECTURES AND IMPLEMENTATIONS	SAA: COMMON PROGRAMMING INTERFACE
SQL	IBM OFFICE SYSTEMS: ARCHITECTURES AND IMPLEMENTATIONS	OFFICE AUTOMATION STANDARDS	SAA: AD/CYCLE
Security	OFFICE AUTOMATION STANDARDS	DATA COMMUNICATION STANDARDS	
SECURITY, ACCURACY, AND PRIVACY IN COMPUTER SYSTEMS		CORPORATE COMMUNICATIONS STRATEGY	
SECURITY AND PRIVACY IN COMPUTER SYSTEMS		COMPUTER NETWORKS AND DISTRIBUTED PROCESSING: SOFTWARE, TECHNIQUES, AND ARCHITECTURE	

INFORMATION ENGINEERING

Book III Design and Construction

A _James Martin_ TRILOGY

THE JAMES MARTIN BOOKS
currently available from Prentice Hall

- Application Development Without Programmers
- Building Expert Systems
- Communications Satellite Systems
- Computer Data-Base Organization, Second Edition
- The Computerized Society
- Computer Networks and Distributed Processing: Software, Techniques, and Architecture
- Data Communication Technology
- DB2: Concepts, Design, and Programming
- Design and Strategy of Distributed Data Processing
- Design of Real-Time Computer Systems
- An End User's Guide to Data Base
- Fourth-Generation Languages, Volume I: Principles
- Fourth-Generation Languages, Volume II: Representative 4GLs
- Fourth-Generation Languages, Volume III: 4GLs from IBM
- Future Developments in Telecommunications, Second Edition
- Hyperdocuments and How to Create Them
- IBM Office Systems: Architectures and Implementations
- IDMS/R: Concepts, Design, and Programming
- Information Engineering, Book I: Introduction
- Information Engineering, Book II: Planning and Analysis
- Information Engineering, Book III: Design and Construction
- An Information Systems Manifesto
- Local Area Networks: Architectures and Implementations
- Managing the Data-Base Environment
- Principles of Data-Base Management
- Principles of Data Communication
- Recommended Diagramming Standards for Analysts and Programmers
- SNA: IBM's Networking Solution
- Strategic Information Planning Methodologies, Second Edition
- System Design from Provably Correct Constructs
- Systems Analysis for Data Transmission
- Technology's Crucible
- Telecommunications and the Computer, Third Edition
- Telematic Society: A Challenge for Tomorrow
- VSAM: Access Method Services and Programming Techniques

with Carma McClure

- Action Diagrams: Clearly Structured Specifications, Programs, and Procedures, Second Edition
- Diagramming Techniques for Analysts and Programmers
- Software Maintenance: The Problem and Its Solutions
- Structured Techniques: The Basis for CASE, Revised Edition

INFORMATION

Book I Introduction
Book II Planning
Book III Design

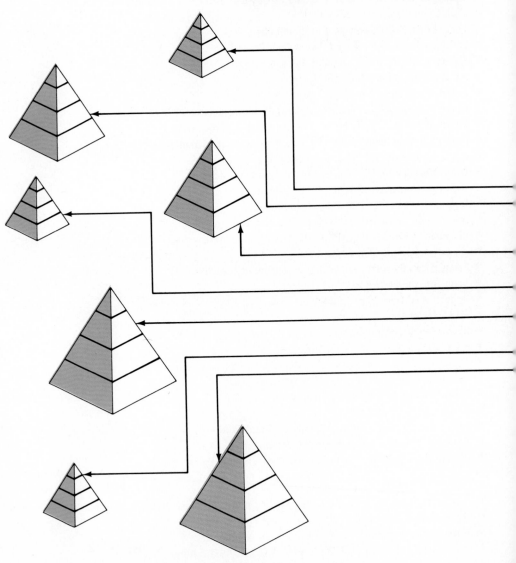

ENGINEERING

and Analysis
and Construction

JAMES MARTIN

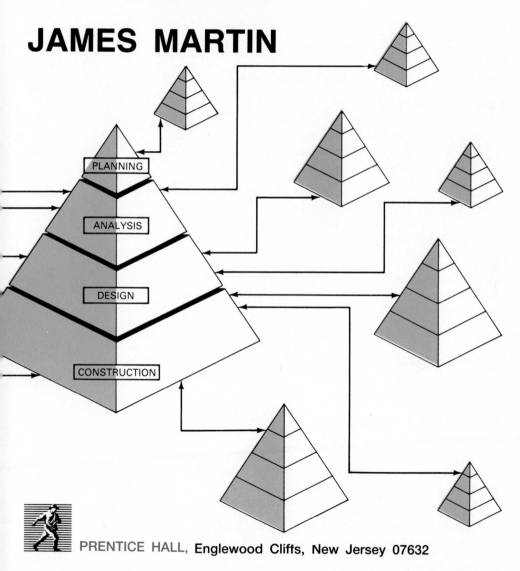

PRENTICE HALL, Englewood Cliffs, New Jersey 07632

Library of Congress Cataloging-in-Publication Data

(Revised for vol. 3)

MARTIN, JAMES (date)
    Information engineering.

    Includes bibliographies and index.
    Contents: v. 1. Introduction—   —v. 3.
Design and construction.
    1. Electronic data processing. 2. System design.
I. Title.
QA76.M3265 1989   004   88-39310
ISBN 0-13-464462-X (v. 1)
ISBN 0-13-465501-X (v. 3)

Editorial/production supervision: *Kathryn Gollin Marshak*
Cover design: *Bruce Kenselaar*
Manufacturing buyer: *Mary Ann Gloriande and Ray Sintel*

Information Engineering, Book III: Design and Construction

Copyright © 1990 by James Martin

Published by Prentice-Hall, Inc.
A division of Simon & Schuster
Englewood Cliffs, New Jersey 07632

The publisher offers discounts on this book when ordered
in bulk quantities. For more information, write:
        Special Sales; Prentice-Hall, Inc.
        College Technical and Reference Division
        Englewood Cliffs, NJ 07632

Printed in the United States of America

10 9 8 7 6 5 4 3

ISBN   0-13-465501-X

PRENTICE-HALL INTERNATIONAL (UK) LIMITED, *London*
PRENTICE-HALL OF AUSTRALIA PTY. LIMITED, *Sydney*
PRENTICE-HALL CANADA INC., *Toronto*
PRENTICE-HALL HISPANOAMERICANA, S.A., *Mexico*
PRENTICE-HALL OF INDIA PRIVATE LIMITED, *New Delhi*
PRENTICE-HALL OF JAPAN, INC., *Tokyo*
SIMON & SCHUSTER ASIA PTE. Ltd., *Singapore*
EDITORA PRENTICE-HALL DO BRASIL, LTDA., *Rio de Janeiro*

TO CORINTHIA

Information engineering is defined as:

The application of an interlocking set of formal techniques for the planning, analysis, design and construction of information systems, applied on an enterprise-wide basis or across a major sector of an enterprise.

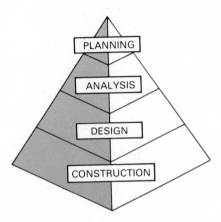

The emphasis is on enterprise-wide planning, modeling, and system design, so sometimes the definition used is

The application of structured techniques to the enterprise as a whole rather than on a project-by-project basis.

Because an enterprise is so complex, planning, analysis, design, and construction cannot be achieved on an enterprise-wide basis without automated tools. Information engineering has been defined with the reference to *automated* techniques as follows:

An interlocking set of automated techniques in which enterprise models, data models and process models are built up in a comprehensive knowledge base and are used to create and maintain data-processing systems.

Information engineering has sometimes been described as

An enterprise-wide set of automated disciplines for getting the right information to the right people at the right time.

INFORMATION ENGINEERING
A Trilogy by James Martin

BOOK II PLANNING AND ANALYSIS

BOOK **III** DESIGN AND
CONSTRUCTION

CONTENTS

4   Diagrams Used in System Design   55

MEETING THE NEEDS OF THE END USER MORE DIRECTLY

PART II

5   User-Oriented Development Techniques   97

6   Prototyping   107

PREFACE

I first used the term *information engineering* in courses conducted in the IBM Systems Research Institute in New York in the early 1970s. The thrust of those courses was that it was necessary to apply top-down planning, data modeling, and process modeling to an enterprise as a whole rather than to isolated projects; otherwise, we could never build a fully computerized enterprise.

Since those days the techniques of information engineering have been greatly refined. Information engineering (IE) is too complex to do with manual techniques. It needs a computerized repository to accumulate and automatically coordinate the mass of detailed information. It needs tools to help in IS planning, data modeling, process modeling, and the translation of these models into working systems. The early tools were crude, but they provided some early experience that led to the refinement of IE techniques.

The full flowering of IE capability had to await the evolution of CASE (computer-aided systems engineering) tools and the use of these tools to drive a code generator. With these tools we create a repository of planning and modeling information in an enterprise, use this as input to a system design workbench, and generate code from the system design.

The staff of James Martin Associates practiced information engineering, using computerized tools, in many corporations. They steadily refined the methodologies that are described in these three books. As with other engineering disciplines, it became clear that IE needs rigor and professionalism; the computerized tools enforce rigor and guide the professional.

Corporations that have gone from top to bottom in IE, in other words, have done the planning, built the data models, and used these to design systems and generate code, have found that they can coordinate their information systems activities, build systems faster, drastically lower their maintenance costs. Once the data models and process models exist, corporations can make competitive thrusts with computerized procedures much more quickly.

The world is becoming an interlaced network of computerized corporations. As electronic data interchange among corporations grows with intercorporate networks, so the windows of opportunity become shorter. We are evolving to a world of just-in-time inventory control, electronic funds transfer, corporations having their customers and retail outlets online, program trading, a computer in one organization placing orders directly with computers in other organizations, and automation of many business decisions. In such a world the corporation in which data processing is in a mess, with spaghetti code, uncoordinated data, and long application backlogs, will not be able to compete. The techniques of information engineering are vital to the competitive corporation.

The future of computing is a battle with complexity. The complexity of enterprises is steadily growing. The complexity of information processing needed in the military and government is overwhelming. We can win this battle with complexity only with automated tools and automated methodologies. The challenge of every IS executive is to evolve as quickly as possible from the mess of old data processing to the building of systems with clean engineering.

Computing needs an engineering discipline with automated tools which enforce that discipline.

James Martin

INFORMATION ENGINEERING

Book III Design and Construction

I **INTRODUCTION**

1 PROLOGUE

Book I of this trilogy discussed the overall principles of information engineering, describing how it applies structured techniques to the enterprise as a whole. It is an extension far beyond software engineering, which applies structured techniques to one project. The span of control of information engineering is typically the span of control of the highest IS (information systems) executive in the enterprise. In a small, medium-sized, or well-integrated large enterprise, the span of control is the entire enterprise. It is probably not possible to build the highly computerized corporation of the future, with computer networks going to every desk, without the integration represented by IE (information engineering).

Information engineering helps to integrate the separate data processing and decision-support systems built by different teams at different times in different places. It does this by employing a common repository of planning information, data models, process models, and design information. It seeks to maximize the value of the systems built in an enterprise, focusing them on the top-management goals and critical success factors. It seeks to automate the work of building and integrating systems. The cost of building systems is substantially lessened by the identification of common data entities, common rules relating to data, reusable design, and reusable code.

Information engineering is illustrated with the pyramid in Fig. 1.1 which has four basic levels: *planning, analysis, design,* and *construction.* The left-hand side of this pyramid relates to data, and the right-hand side relates to activities.

There are four levels of tasks in the implementation of information engineering:

- **Information strategy planning,** which occurs in the enterprise as a whole.
- **Business area analysis,** which occurs when data models and process models

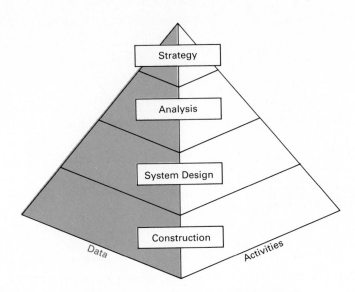

Figure 1.1   The information systems pyramid.

are built for a business area. Different teams may analyze different business areas concurrently.

- **System design,** which occurs with the help of automated tools which employ the information stored in the ISP (information strategy planning) and BAA (business area analysis) process.

- **Construction,** which occurs with the help of automated tools such as code generators which are coupled to the system design tools.

The first two of these levels create a framework within which different teams build different systems at different times. Figure 1.2 illustrates this framework.

Book II was concerned with the framework—the outer, red, part of Fig. 1.2. This book (Book III) is concerned with the design and construction of systems—the inner, black, part of Fig. 1.2. It assumes that the outer framework exists and is represented in an intelligent repository which is part of the information engineering tool set. The framework is often incomplete when design and construction proceeds.

To achieve consistency among separate development activities, the information collected or designed at the four levels of the pyramid are all stored in the repository called the *encyclopedia*. The encyclopedia is an "intelligent" facility which applies many rules to the planning, analysis, and design processes and which helps to drive the automatic generation of code. The encyclopedia rule processing helps to ensure the integrity, completeness, and consistency of the information it is given, with a precision far beyond that possible with manual techniques or text specifications. To emphasize that the encyclopedia is an

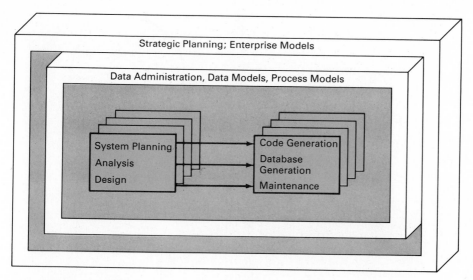

Figure 1.2 The development of individual applications is done within a framework of data modeling and process modeling, which itself relates to strategic planning of how to improve the enterprise with technology.

intelligent facility, it is drawn with a skull-like icon throughout this trilogy of books (Fig. 1.3). It is this intelligent repository, with its automated coupling to tools for planning, analysis, design, and construction, which makes information engineering practical. The encyclopedias used in practice have grown steadily, acquiring more and more knowledge about the plans, models, and systems in corporations committed to information engineering.

The framework in Fig. 1.2 (the top two layers of the pyramid) takes some time to build. Information strategy planning for the enterprise typically takes six months. Business area analysis takes some time for each area of the enterprise, with multiple areas being tackled concurrently. Once the framework is in place, individual systems can be designed and constructed relatively quickly using design automation tools and code generators. The plans and models in the framework are adjusted as systems are built and as the enterprise evolves.

Information engineering is made practical by the use of CASE (computer-aided systems engineering) tools. It is important to choose a tool kit in which the planning, analysis, design, and construction tools are integrated and share the same encyclopedia. The code generator is particularly important; this generates code directly from the encyclopedia and, hence, greatly speeds up implementation.

Information engineering can drastically reduce the systems maintenance costs and difficulties in an enterprise. The tools enforce fully structured design and make designs easy to modify in most cases. New program code is *generated* from the changed design. The tools eliminate the difficult task of investigating

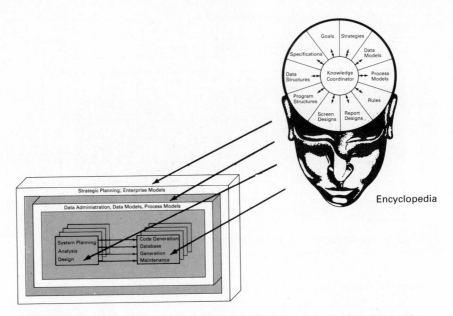

Encyclopedia

Figure 1.3 The encyclopedia interrelates all parts of the information engineering process.

how unstructured, ill-documented programs work and how they can be patched or modified.

System building does not wait until the framework (Fig. 1.2) is completely finished. Systems which directly affect the profit of the business must be built quickly but should be built with CASE tools, which allow quick retrofitting to the information engineering framework as it evolves.

Box 1.1 lists characteristics of information engineering. Book III is particularly concerned with techniques for building systems *rapidly,* and with a high degree of end-user involvement so that they meet the needs of users as well as possible. These are often systems that must *evolve* and should be designed for lengthy ongoing evolution.

Box 1.2 summarizes the benefits of information engineering.

**REPRESENTING
METHODOLOGY
PROCEDURES**

These books are concerned with methodologies. To draw diagrams of methodology procedures, it is appropriate to use the CASE tools with which system procedures are drawn. A data flow diagram, for example, can show a sequence of tasks, some of which are done simultaneously; it can show the inputs to each task and the deliverables. A Gantt chart (with horizontal bars) can also show a sequence of tasks, some of which are done simultaneously, and can set these tasks on to a time scale. An action diagram

BOX 1.1   Characteristics of information engineering

- Information engineering applies structured techniques on an enterprise-wide basis rather than on a projectwide basis.

- Information engineering progresses in a top-down fashion through the following stages:
  Enterprise strategic systems planning
  Enterprise information planning
  Business area analysis
  System design
  Construction
  Cutover

- As it progresses through these stages, IE builds a steadily evolving repository (encyclopedia) of knowledge about the enterprise, its data models, process models, and system designs.

- Information engineering creates a framework for developing a computerized enterprise.

- Separately developed systems fit into this framework.

- Within the framework systems can be built and modified quickly using automated tools.

- The enterprisewide approach makes it possible to achieve coordination among separately built systems, and facilitates the maximum use of reusable design and reusable code.

- Information engineering involves end users strongly at each of the preceding stages.

- Information engineering facilitates the long-term *evolution* of systems.

- Information engineering identifies how computing can best aid the strategic goals of the enterprise.

can provide text relating to sequence of steps with conditions (IF-ELSE), repetition (e.g., DO UNTIL) and mutually exclusive alternatives, escapes, subroutines, inputs, and deliverables. Of these diagram types, the action diagram (with its EXPAND and CONTRACT capabilities) is the most appropriate for showing lists of actions and structured textual descriptions.

Action diagrams are described in Appendix II.

None of the foregoing types of diagrams is completely satisfactory by itself; a combination of them is desirable. If a data flow diagram is used, its blocks should be expandable as action diagram windows. If a Gantt chart is

BOX 1.2   Benefits of information engineering

- Information engineering helps to identify strategic systems opportunities and achieve competitive advantage by building such systems before the competition.
- Information engineering focuses data processing on the goals of the business.
- Information engineering enables an enterprise to get its act together. Different systems are coordinated. The same data is represented in the same way in different systems. There is integration among systems where needed.
- Information engineering manages information so that key decision makers can have the best information available.
- New systems can be built relatively quickly, using power tools, within the IE framework.
- Information engineering gives the capability to change computerized procedures quickly.
- Information engineering facilitates the building of systems of greater complexity and the understanding and control of complex links between systems.
- Information engineering permits the long-term evolution of systems. As systems continue to evolve, they become a vital corporate resource.
- Information engineering makes possible major savings through the use of reusable design and code.
- Information engineering drastically reduces the maintenance and backlog problem in enterprises which have converted old systems to IE form.
- A fully computerized enterprise cannot be built without IE techniques.
- Corporations trapped with manually built systems will become increasingly unable to compete with corporations with full information engineering.

used, its bars should be expandable as action diagram windows. Figure 1.4 shows the combination of a data flow diagram or dependency diagram and action diagram. Figure 1.5 shows the combination of a Gantt chart and action diagram. In a similar way, a combination of a PERT chart and an action diagram could be used.

In a book it is difficult to show windows which can be opened and closed as on a CASE tool screen. Therefore, to simplify the representation of methodology details, they have been shown simply as action diagrams throughout this

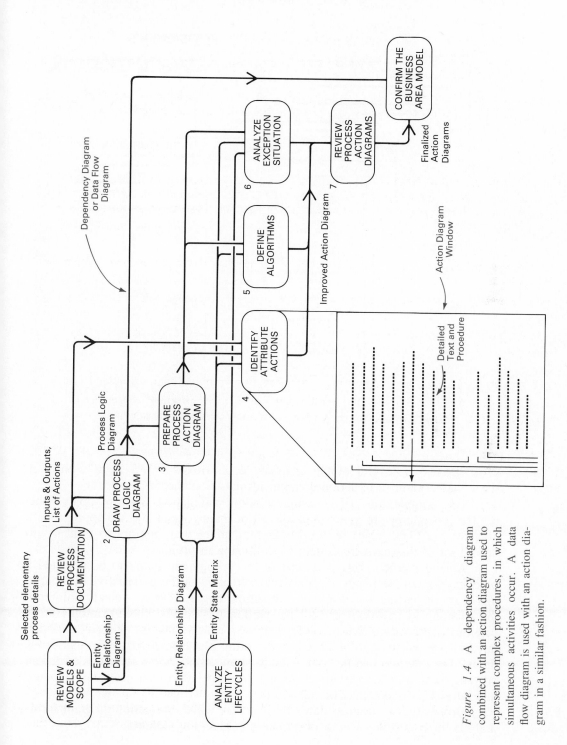

Selected elementary
process details

Inputs & Outputs,
List of Actions

Process Logic
Diagram

Dependency Diagram
or Data Flow
Diagram

REVIEW
MODELS &
SCOPE

1
REVIEW
PROCESS
DOCUMENTATION

Entity
Relationship
Diagram

2
DRAW PROCESS
LOGIC
DIAGRAM

3
PREPARE
PROCESS
ACTION
DIAGRAM

Entity Relationship Diagram

ANALYZE
ENTITY
LIFECYCLES

Entity State Matrix

4
IDENTIFY
ATTRIBUTE
ACTIONS

5
DEFINE
ALGORITHMS

6
ANALYZE
EXCEPTION
SITUATION

7
REVIEW
PROCESS
ACTION
DIAGRAMS

Improved Action Diagram

CONFIRM THE
BUSINESS
AREA MODEL

Finalized
Action
Diagrams

Action Diagram
Window

Detailed
Text and
Procedure

Figure 1.4 A dependency diagram
combined with an action diagram used to
represent complex procedures, in which
simultaneous activities occur. A data
flow diagram is used with an action diagram in a similar fashion.

9

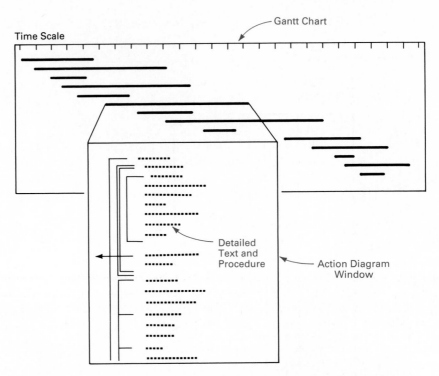

Figure 1.5   A Gantt or PERT chart combined with an action diagram used to represent complex procedures in which simultaneous activities occur.

book. Boxes in several of the chapters (e.g., Boxes 6.3, 7.2, 8.1, and 9.1) show methodologies in action diagram format.

The complexities of showing window navigation in print apply when printed procedures are given to end users or managers. It is often appropriate to give them a Gantt chart or action diagram rather than attempt to print a windowed set of diagrams that might be confusing in print.

All the methodology diagrams in this trilogy are likely to be adjusted in practice to meet the needs of a particular situation or the perspective of a particular team or particular consultant. An action diagram can be quickly tailored to the situation in question, and all the participants can be given printouts of the part of the procedure that involves them. An action diagram editor is a particularly convenient tool for building and editing representations of human procedures. The diagram can be contracted to show an overview or expanded repeatedly to show detailed text or checklists. A large library of procedure modules and tutorial guidance may be maintained.

Box 1.3 lists the procedures in this book which are action diagram format and fits them into the overall information engineering context.

BOX 1.3 Summary of the methodology action diagrams

The IS procedures manual should not be an unchanging paper document, but rather a computerized representation of a family of procedures which can be adapted to the specific requirements of projects. The procedures need to encompass all planning and analysis techniques, and techniques for high-productivity development, such as the use of CASE tools, code generators, fourth-generation languages, prototyping, joint requirements planning, joint application design, time-box techniques, expert systems, design automation, the building of decision-support systems, executive information systems, and new forms of development lifecycles.

All such procedures need to be tailored to the circumstances in which they are used. The tool for representing the procedure should facilitate this tailoring.

It is useful to represent procedures for today's methodologies with action diagrams because much flexibility is needed in adjusting the procedures. An action diagram editor makes it easy to customize the procedures as required. The details represented in action diagrams can be fitted into other CASE diagrams, such as data flow diagrams of methodologies.

```
┌─ Information Engineering Procedures
│  ┌─ The overview model of the enterprise
│  │   o─────────────────────────────o
│  │   | OVERVIEW action diagram |
│  │   o─────────────────────────────o
│  │  ┌─ The organizational chart represented as an action diagram.
│  │  │   o─────────────────────────────o
│  │  │   | Figure 3.2.  Organizational Chart  |
│  │  └   o─────────────────────────────o
│  └
│
│  ┌─ Create Information Strategy Plan for the Enterprise
│  │   o─────────────────────────────────────────────o
│  │   | BOX 2.1.  Procedure for Information Strategy Planning |
│  │   o─────────────────────────────────────────────o
│  │  ┌─ Business-Oriented Strategic Planning
│  │  │  ┌─ Analysis of goals and problems
│  │  │  │   o─────────────────────────────────────────o
│  │  │  │   | BOX 4.1.  Procedure for Analysis of Goals and Problems |
│  │  │  │   o─────────────────────────────────────────o
│  │  │  │  Illustration of goals:
│  │  │  │   o─────────────────────────────o
│  │  │  │   | Figure 4.3.  A Hierarchy of Goals |
│  │  │  └   o─────────────────────────────o
│  │  │  ┌─ Critical Success Factor Analysis
│  │  │  │   o─────────────────────────────────────────o
│  │  │  │   | BOX 5.1. Procedure for Critical-Success-Factor Analysis |
│  │  │  └   o─────────────────────────────────────────o
```

(Continued)

BOX 1.3 *(Continued)*

Technology Impact Analysis
> BOX 6.1. A Detailed Representation of Technological Change
>
> BOX 6.2. A Representation of Business Opportunities
>
> BOX 6.3. Procedure for Technology Impact Analysis

Strategic Information Systems Analysis
> BOX 7.1. Examples of Strategic Systems
>
> BOX 7.2. A Categorization of Strategic Thrusts
>
> BOX 7.3. Examples of Technology for Strategic Thrusts
>
> BOX 7.4. Procedure for Identifying Strategic Systems

For each business area, do a Business Area Analysis
> BOX 11.2. Procedure for Business Area Analysis.
>
> BOX 14.1. The Kernel of Business Area Analysis.

Detailed Data Modeling
> BOX 12.3. Procedure for Data Modeling

Detailed Process Modeling
> BOX 14.1. Procedure for Process Modeling

> BOX 15.1. Preparing for System Design

Book III: Design and Construction

Reusable procedures should be identified wherever possible
> Box 3.1: Identification of reusable procedures

BOX 1.3 *(Continued)*

Joint Requirements Planning (JRP) is used for establishing user
   requirements.
   | Box 7.2: JRP action diagram |

Joint Application Design (JAD) is used for preliminary design.
   | Box 8.1: JAD action diagram |

Prototyping should be used in most systems design
   | Box 6.1: Criteria for Selecting a Prototyping Tool |

   | Box 6.3: Procedure for Prototyping |

   Examples of procedure specifications represented as action diagrams
      | Box 4.1: Action diagrams of procedures |

   Example of a dialog   structure designed with an action diagram
      | Box 4.3: dialog   action diagram |

   Code
      An example of COBOL code on an action diagram
         | Box 4.3: COBOL action diagram |

      An example of PL/I code on an action diagram
         | Box 4.5: PL/I action diagram |

      An example of C language code on an action diagram
         | Box 4.4: C-CODE action diagram |

      An example of fourth-generation language code on an action diagra
         | Box 4.6: IDEAL action diagram |

Timebox techniques are designed for implementing systems quickly
   | Box 9.1: Timebox procedure for rapid development |

(Continued)

BOX 1.3 *(Continued)*

Building decision-support systems needs special procedures.

Box 12.3: Procedure for decision-support system implementation

Tools
  Selection of database management systems

  DBMS action diagram

  Selection of fourth-generation languages and code generators

  4GL's action diagram

Physical design
  Data use analysis

  Box 14.1: Procedure for data use analysis

  Physical database design

  Box 15.1: Procedure for physical database design

  Data distribution analysis

  Box 16.1: Procedure for data distribution analysis

Cultural changes caused by the system need to be planned for.

  Box 17.1: Preparation for cultural changes

Cutover needs careful planning and execution

  Box 17.2: Design for cutover

  Box 18.1: Preparation for cutover

  Box 18.2: Procedure for performing cutover

Existing systems need to be migrated to the I.E. environment

  Box 20.2: Categorization of programs for migration

  Box 20.1: Steps in reverse engineering

  Box 16.1: Procedure for reverse engineering

BOX 1.3 *(Continued)*

Different types of systems need different lifecycle procedures.

| Box 21.2: Categories of lifecycle procedure |

For each of these types of lifecycle there are many variations.

SINGLE-ITERATION LIFECYCLE

| Box 21.3 |

MULTI-ITERATION LIFECYCLE

| Box 21.4 |

TIMEBOX LIFECYCLE

| Box 21.5 |

EVOLUTIONARY LIFECYCLE

EXPLORATORY LIFECYCLE

| Box 21.6 |

QUICK-RESULTS LIFECYCLE

| Box 21.7 |

DECISION-SUPPORT-SYSTEM LIFECYCLE

| Box 21.8 |

EXPERT-SYSTEM LIFECYCLE

2 SYSTEM DESIGN AND CONSTRUCTION

THE COMPETITIVE CORPORATION

The corporation of the future will be run with a vast mesh of interacting computers and database systems.

Computers in one corporation will interact on-line with computers in other corporations which are its customers, suppliers, agents, distributors, banks, service providers, and so on. We will have highly automated factories, distribution channels, and services with highly integrated networks of computers.

Innovative companies are perceiving how computers, networks, workstations, and other technology can enable them to launch preemptive marketplace attacks. We have entered the age when computing and information systems are strategic weapons, not a backroom overhead. As technology increases the competitive opportunities and threats, the time cycle for implementing computerized procedures shrinks. It is increasingly necessary to build new applications quickly and build them so that they can be quickly modified.

It will be impossible to manage and build the procedures for this complex environment without some form of information engineering, appropriately automated. It will be impossible to build and maintain computerized procedures quickly enough without automated tools.

Historians of the future will look back at the evolution of computing, destined to change so much in society, and will be amazed that the early attempts at data processing were done by hand. They will marvel that corporations survived the early incompatible mess that computing was before information engineering.

FAST DEVELOPMENT

A major objective of information engineering is to be able to develop systems *fast*. To compete in today's

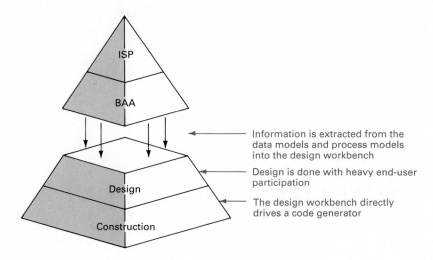

Figure 2.1   Design and construction.

increasingly fast-reacting world, a corporation must be able to implement computerized procedures *quickly*.

It takes time to develop the data models initially and process models of BAA (business area analysis). Once this has been done, the models can be kept up to date on an ongoing basis. Within this framework it is desirable that systems should be designed and constructed quickly. To achieve high-speed development, a CASE (computer-aided systems engineering) workbench for system design is needed which facilitates prototyping, and high-speed techniques such as *(JAD) joint application design* (Chapter 8) and *timebox methodology* (Chapter 9). The design workbench should be tightly coupled to a code generator. Database code, test data, job control code, and documentation should all be generated.

The term I-CASE, integrated CASE, is used for tool kits in which the planning and modeling tools are integrated with design tools and a code generator, all using the same encyclopedia. This is essential for high-speed development. The BAA information should be used directly to assist in design, and the design tools and code generator should be integrated (Fig. 2.1).

TOOLS NEEDED   The tools needed in the workbench for design and construction are as follows (Fig. 2.2).

- **Decomposition diagrammer.** Decomposition diagrams enable a higher-level overview statement about a design to be successively decomposed into finer and finer detail.

- **Action diagrammer.** Action diagrams facilitate the building of structured pro-

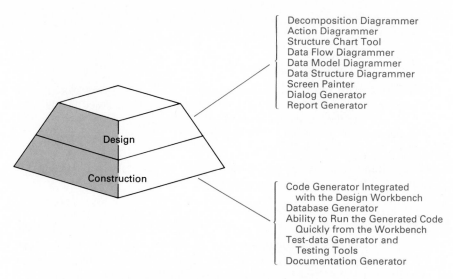

Decomposition Diagrammer
Action Diagrammer
Structure Chart Tool
Data Flow Diagrammer
Data Model Diagrammer
Data Structure Diagrammer
Screen Painter
Dialog Generator
Report Generator

Code Generator Integrated
  with the Design Workbench
Database Generator
Ability to Run the Generated Code
  Quickly from the Workbench
Test-data Generator and
  Testing Tools
Documentation Generator

Figure 2.2 Tools needed in the workbench for design and construction.

cedures and structured code and, again, the decomposition of a high-level overview into finer and finer detail.

- **Structure chart tool.** A structure chart is a form of decomposition diagram charting how program modules call submodules and what data and control information they pass to them.

- **Data flow diagrammer.** Data flow diagrams showing the flow of data among modules of procedures or programs.

- **Data model diagrammer.** The data modeling tool should allow portions of the overall data model developed in BAA to be extracted for use in the design stage.

- **Data structure diagrammer.** The data structure diagramming tool allows appropriate parts of the data model to be represented as the structures used by a particular database management system, for example, IMS (information management system) structures, IDMS (information database management system) structures, and relational structures.

- **Database code generator.** Database code, for example, IMS database descriptions, should be generated directly from the data structure diagrams.

- **Screen painter.** A screen painter should allow the screens of a computer-user dialog to be created quickly.

- **Dialog generator.** The screens may be linked together with a dialog generator. This may be done with an action diagrammer tool. The dialog generator may generate dialogs that conform to specified standards, for example, those of IBM's SAA (Systems Application Architecture).

- **Report generator.** A report generator should allow the structure and layout of a report to be created quickly, along with calculations of derived fields that are in the report.

- **Code generator.** A code generator should create executable code from the highest level specifications possible.

- **Ability to run the code.** If the code generator has an interpreter, it should be possible to run the code quickly after it has been generated. If the generator uses a compiler, it should generate the control language (such as JCL) and again provide the facilities for running the code quickly, controlling the run from the workstation.

- **Test data generator.** Program-testing aids are needed which generate test data and facilitate a sequence of testing steps.

We have stressed that the repository is the heart of a CASE tool. We distinguished between a dictionary and an encyclopedia, as summarized in Fig. 2.3. The encyclopedia "understands" the models and designs; the dictionary does not. In an I-CASE toolset the encyclopedia steadily accumulates information relating to the planning, analysis, design, construction, and, later, maintenance of systems.

Graphic representations are derived from the encyclopedia and are used to update it. The encyclopedia employs many rules relating to the knowledge it stores and employs rule processing, the artificial intelligence technique, to help achieve accuracy, integrity, and completeness of the plans, models, and designs.

Any one diagram on a CASE screen is a facet of a broader set of knowledge which may reside in the encyclopedia. The encyclopedia normally contains far more detail than is on the diagram. This detail can be displayed in windows.

In an I-CASE tool the encyclopedia drives a code generator. The goal of the design workbench is to collect sufficient information that code for the system can be generated. The generator should also generate database description code and job control language. It should generate a comprehensive set of documentation so that designers and maintenance staff can understand the system clearly.

Figure 2.4 shows the encyclopedia accumulating information from the planning, analysis, design, or construction tool kits and generating code, database descriptions and documentation. This diagram encapsulates the nature of an I-CASE toolset. The encyclopedia (drawn as a skull-like icon) is a facility that understands the planning models and designs and uses artificial intelligence rules to ensure their consistency and quality. In a complex enterprise using I-CASE development techniques, the encyclopedia will grow large, steadily accumulating information about the enterprise and its systems, its data models, data flows, rules, specifications, screen designs, and so on.

Systems design, then, starts by extracting relevant information which is already in the encyclopedia, established in the ISP (information strategy plan-

A **dictionary** contains names and descriptions of data items, processes, variables, and the like.

An **encyclopedia** contains complete coded representations of plans, models, and designs with tools for cross-checking, correlation analysis, and validation. Graphic representations are derived from the encyclopedia and are used to update it. The encyclopedia contains many rules relating to the knowledge it stores and employs rule processing, the artificial intelligence technique, to help achieve accuracy, integrity, and completeness of the plans, models, and designs. The encyclopedia is thus a *knowledge base* that not only stores development information but helps to control its accuracy and validity.

The encyclopedia should be designed to drive a code generator. The tool set helps the systems analyst to build up in the encyclopedia the information necessary for code generation.

The encyclopedia *understands* the modules and designs; a dictionary does not.

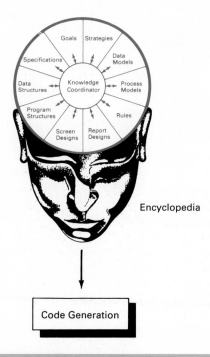

Figure 2.3   A dictionary as distinguished from an encyclopedia.

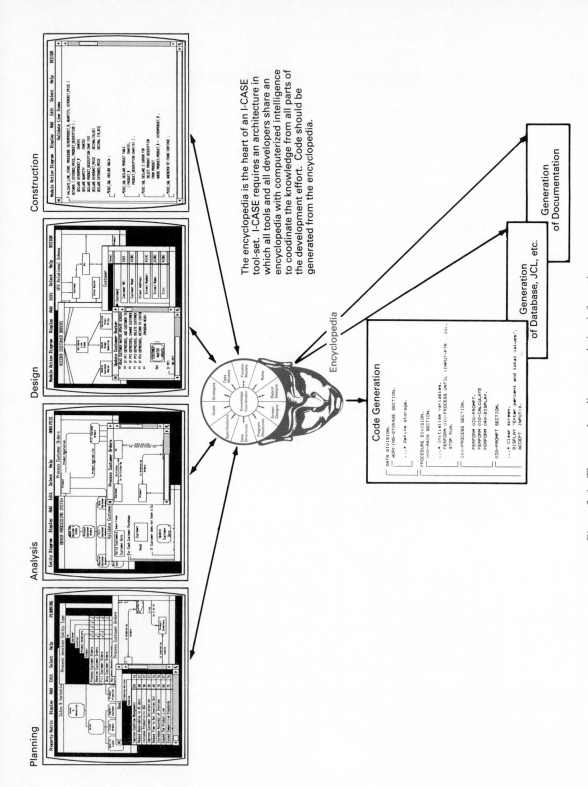

The encyclopedia is the heart of an I-CASE tool-set. I-CASE requires an architecture in which all tools and all developers share an encyclopedia with computerized intelligence to coordinate the knowledge from all parts of the development effort. Code should be generated from the encyclopedia.

Figure 2.4 The encyclopedia accumulating information.

ning) and BAA activities (and sometimes in other design activities). This information is taken into a design workbench with which initial designs, screens, reports, and prototypes can be created quickly. The functions that the system should perform are established in workshops with end users, and the initial design is done in an end-user workshop (Chapter 8). The design is refined, users give their reactions to prototypes, and code is generated from the design.

CENTRAL COORDINATION AND DISTRIBUTED DESIGN

Building and integrating the information systems needed in an enterprise is achieved by synthesizing the models and designs of many people scattered across the enterprise. CASE tools with a central encyclopedia make this possible. The amount and complexity of information in an enterprise is so great that synthesis is a practical impossibility unless computerized tools are used to achieve it.

Any one individual or design team is not familiar with the entire set of designs in the central encyclopedia. When the individual starts to create a design, he* will extract whatever information in the central encyclopedia relates to his design. For example, he may extract a portion of a data model. He may be

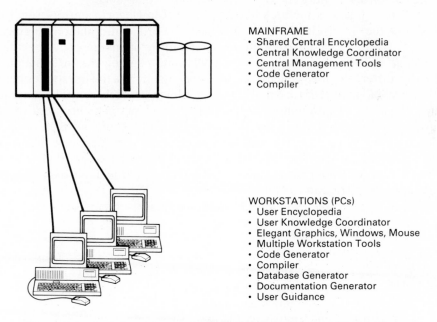

MAINFRAME
• Shared Central Encyclopedia
• Central Knowledge Coordinator
• Central Management Tools
• Code Generator
• Compiler

WORKSTATIONS (PCs)
• User Encyclopedia
• User Knowledge Coordinator
• Elegant Graphics, Windows, Mouse
• Multiple Workstation Tools
• Code Generator
• Compiler
• Database Generator
• Documentation Generator
• User Guidance

Figure 2.5 An information engineering tool set employs multiple tools on the personal computer and is usually linked to a mainframe for central maintenance of the shared encyclopedia, with a central knowledge coordinator and management tools.

*"He" and "his" are used to refer to either gender throughout the book.

designing the detail of a process which is already shown in a higher level representation. He then works on his design, largely independently of the central encyclopedia. When the design is ready for review it can be coordinated, with computerized help, with the knowledge already in the encyclopedia.

The designer thus extracts information from the central encyclopedia into the encyclopedia of his workbench, works on it in a local environment, and then coordinates it with the knowledge in the central encyclopedia. There may be many miniencyclopedias all being used in conjunction with the central encyclopedia.

Coordinating the knowledge across a large development or information engineering effort requires substantial computing and is likely to be done on the machine that controls the central encyclopedia. The analysts using CASE tools, however, need a fast response from their own workstation. It is desirable that there should be an encyclopedia and knowledge coordinator in that workstation. A distributed architecture is thus desirable.

The tools on the personal computer are linked to a mainframe as shown in Figure 2.5. The mainframe contains the central shared encyclopedia and its knowledge coordinator and management tools. The code generator and compiler may reside on the mainframe or on the personal computers.

Figure 2.6 shows the architecture of the KnowledgeWare tool set. Figure 2.7 shows the Texas Instruments tool set, the IEF (Information Engineering Facility^{TM}). The personal computer workstation contains an encyclopedia and knowledge coordinator which ensures consistency among the information provided by different tools which the developer uses. The mainframe contains a central encyclopedia with a knowledge coordinator which controls consistency among the work of different developers. The developer can check out from the central encyclopedia a *hyperview* or a set of objects which are then duplicated in his own encyclopedia. He can work with them, creating new information which is coordinated in her own workstation. When he is satisfied with it he checks it back into the central encyclopedia where coordination with the central information is carried out. Thus consistency is achieved across a large project or across multiple projects in an information engineering environment.

EVOLUTIONARY GROWTH OF SYSTEMS

The most impressive of complex systems are not created with a single design and implementation. They evolve, being improved in many steps at different times and places.

A system designer looks at the works of nature with awe. A cheetah watching for prey at dawn suddenly races through scrub at 70 miles per hour with astonishing grace to kill a leaping antelope. A hummingbird, which engineers once ''proved'' was an aerodynamic impossibility, flits from flower to flower and then migrates to South America. The human brain full of diabolical schemes and wonderful poetry has proven far beyond our most ambitious arti-

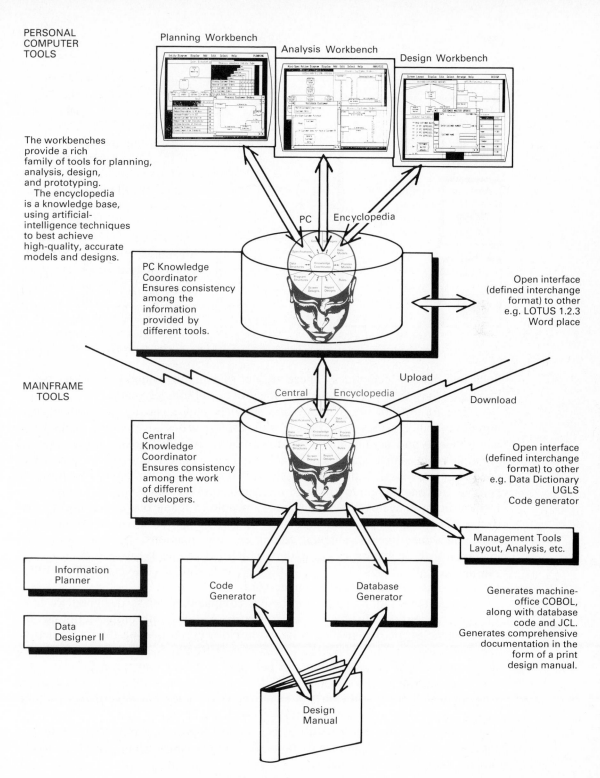

PERSONAL
COMPUTER
TOOLS

Planning Workbench

Analysis Workbench

Design Workbench

The workbenches
provide a rich
family of tools for planning,
analysis, design,
and prototyping.
   The encyclopedia
is a knowledge base,
using artificial-
intelligence techniques
to best achieve
high-quality, accurate
models and designs.

PC   Encyclopedia

PC Knowledge
Coordinator
Ensures consistency
among the
information
provided by
different tools.

Open interface
(defined interchange
format) to other
e.g. LOTUS 1.2.3
Word place

MAINFRAME
TOOLS

Central   Encyclopedia

Upload

Download

Central
Knowledge
Coordinator
Ensures consistency
among the work
of different
developers.

Open interface
(defined interchange
format) to other
e.g. Data Dictionary
UGLS
Code generator

Management Tools
Layout, Analysis, etc.

Information
Planner

Data
Designer II

Code
Generator

Database
Generator

Generates machine-
office COBOL,
along with database
code and JCL.
Generates comprehensive
documentation in the
form of a print
design manual.

Design
Manual

Figure 2.6   The KnowledgeWare tool set.

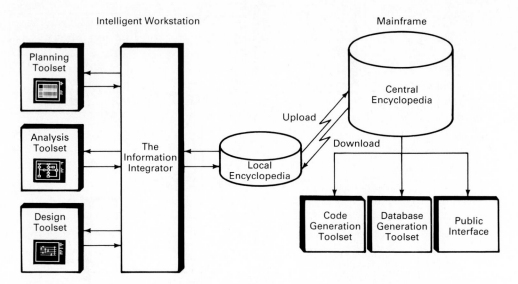

Figure 2.7   The Texas Instruments IEF tool set for information engineering.

ficial intelligence techniques. These are not systems for which God wrote specifications; they are systems which *evolved* over millions of years.

The future will bring impressive software and exceedingly complex corporate computer systems, and these will also be *grown* over many years with many people and organizations adding to them. It is difficult or impossible to grow software which is a mess. To achieve long-term evolution of software, we need structured models of data and structured models of processes. Designs too complex for one human to know all the details must be represented in an orderly fashion in an encyclopedia so that many people in many places can add to the design. The design need standards and reusable components and an architecture which facilitates the incremental adding of new functions. So that executives can control the behavior of computers which automatically place orders, select suppliers, make trades, and so on, the behavior should be expressible in rules and diagrams which executives understand.

Some corporations have impressive computer systems, designed to give them a competitive advantage, like American Airlines with online terminals in travel agencies, or Benetton with its worldwide system making the world activities ''transparent'' to the decision makers near Rome. Systems like these have demonstrated how a corporation can pull ahead of its competition by using information and automation better. Efficient corporations will evolve computing systems which are worldwide and exceedingly complex but nevertheless which enable procedures to be adapted quickly to changing needs.

To do this efficiently requires the methodologies of information engineering carried out with automated tools. It requires encyclopedia-based I-CASE tools.

CATEGORIES OF CASE TOOLS

It is desirable to have CASE tools for each of the four stages of IS development: *planning, analysis, design,* and *construction.* Some organizations sell separate workbenches for each of these sets of activities. It is desirable that such workbenches are fully integrated and employ a common encyclopedia. Work should evolve from the *planning* phase to *construction,* with the knowledge acquired in one phase being used in the next phase. There should be a seamless interface between the phases.

Some CASE tools are for system design and contain no planning and analysis components.

Some are code generators with planning, analysis, or design tools.

Some analysis and design tool kits have a process-oriented view of development with no data modeling capability.

Some provide data modeling tools without process analysis or design.

An I-CASE environment provides an integrated set of tools for all parts of the pyramid.

Some corporations have specialized in building code generators without front-end design and analysis tools. Other corporations have built planning, analysis, and design tools without a back-end code generator. Many attempts have been made to couple front-end analysis and design tools loosely to back-end code generators.

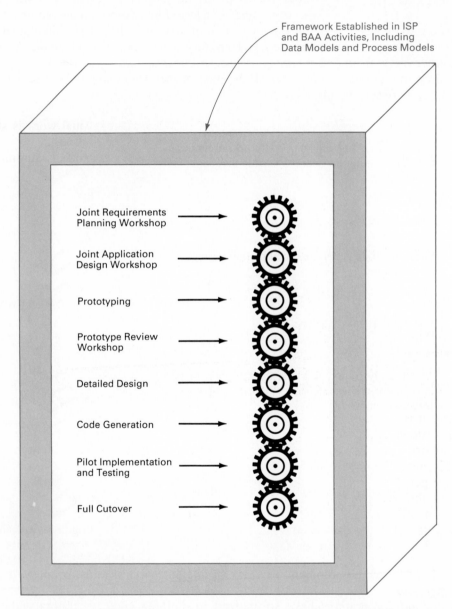

Figure 2.8 The development lifecycle for one project fits into the information engineering framework established in ISP and BAA.

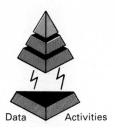

This is not a fully satisfactory solution because much manual work is still needed to make the code generator function. What is needed is full integration between the CASE front-end tools and the generator, so that code is automatically generated from the front-end tools.

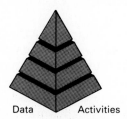

The term I-CASE should be used only to relate to products with this full integration. This implies that the front-end tools and the code generator use the same encyclopedia, and the encyclopedia is used to generate program code, database code, and documentation, as illustrated in Fig. 2.4.

The traditional technique of writing text specifications has four problems. First, it is slow. Second, users reading the text often have difficulty visualizing the systems and critiquing the design. Third, text specifications are usually full of errors, omissions, and ambiguities; a computer cannot understand them, so they cannot be checked by computer. Fourth, they cannot be used as input to a code generator. Text specifications need to be replaced by techniques which make the design visual and real to end users so that users can participate in the design process. The techniques should create specifications which a computer can analyze and cross-check, and which can be input to a code generator.

The most powerful of the techniques for involving end users directly are prototyping (Chapter 6), joint requirements planning (Chapter 7), and joint application design (Chapter 9). Designs should be created by end users and IS professionals working together using a structured procedure at a workshop. These techniques need automated tools.

I-CASE tools facilitate prototyping. At a low level of prototyping report designers and screen painters are used so that end users can look at the reports or sequence of screens that they will receive. At a somewhat higher level, portions of applications can be created quickly, without the ability to handle errors, exception conditions, recovery, security, high performance, and so on. The users work with the screens, reports, and applications and often suggest modifications and additions. Many changes may be made as prototypes evolve from an initial design concept to mature designs. Multiple design iterations, carried out quickly with strong user involvement, help to ensure that truly valuable systems are implemented.

THE LIFECYCLE

In traditional data processing each system has its own development lifecycle which progresses from paperwork specifications to program design and then to coding. In an information engineering environment the lifecycle of one project fits into the IE framework represented in the encyclopedia (Fig. 2.8). This framework was created in the ISP and BAA studies and may have been substantially enhanced when other systems were designed.

The lifecycle should be strongly end-user oriented. CASE tools and prototyping tools help to involve end users in the design process and are employed in workshop environments. The lifecycle in Fig. 2.8 has three end-user workshops, a joint requirement planning workshop, a joint application design workshop, and a prototype review workshop. Prototypes are built and used by end users after the joint application design workshop and before the prototype review workshop. The designers then enhance the design and generate code. The code is tested and possibly run for some time in a pilot implementation before it is polished and a full system cutover proceeds.

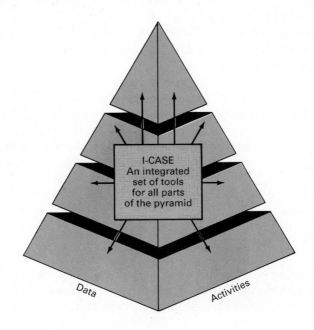

BOX 2.1　Basic characteristics of CASE tools

CASE software should perform the following functions:

- Enable the user to draw diagrams for planning, analysis, or design on a workstation screen.
- Solicit information about the objects in the diagram and relationships among the objects, so that a complete set of information is built up.
- Store the meaning of the diagram, rather than the diagram itself, in a repository.
- Check the diagram for accuracy, integrity, and completeness. The diagram types used should be chosen to facilitate this.
- Enable the user to employ multiple types of diagram representing different facets of an analysis or design.
- Represent specifications and programs with diagrams showing loops, conditions, CASE structures, and other constructs of structured programming.
- Enforce structured modeling and design of a type that enables accuracy and consistency checks to be as complete as possible.
- Coordinate the information on multiple diagrams, checking that they are consistent and *together* have accuracy, integrity, and completeness.
- Store the information built up at workstations in a central repository shared by all analysts and designers.
- Coordinate the information in the central repository, ensuring consistency among the work of all analysts and designers.

　　　These features are basic characteristics of CASE tools. A tool should not be referred to as "CASE" if it lacks any of these features.

SUMMARY OF TOOL CHARACTERISTICS　　Box 2.1 summarizes characteristics of CASE tools. Box 2.2 summarizes characteristics of I-CASE tools.

IS PRODUCTIVITY　　A major reason for needing CASE and I-CASE tools is to improve productivity in building computer applications. Many studies have been done of the effects of IS productivity tools, and these show major improvements in some organizations but low improvements in others which are using the same tools. To achieve high productivity it

BOX 2.2   Characteristics of I-CASE tools

- The activities of planning, analysis, design, and construction each have a software workbench with multiple tools. These workbenches are fully integrated so that one workbench directly employs the information from another.
- An encyclopedia stores the knowledge from the multiple workbenches in an integrated manner.
- A code generator is fully integrated with the design workbench (as opposed to having a bridge to a separate code generator with its own separate syntax).
- The generator employs the facilities of requisite operating systems and database management systems, including the data dictionary.
- The generator generates the requisite database statements and job control language.
- The tools support all phases of the project lifecycle in an integrated manner.
- In addition to supporting project lifecycles, an I-CASE tool kit supports enterprisewide planning, data modeling, and process modeling, to create a framework into which many project lifecycles fit. In other words, the tool kit is designed for information engineering rather than merely software engineering.
- System design employs entity-relationship models and data models with full normalization.
- The planning, analysis, and design workbenches can support user workshops such as JRP (joint requirements planning) and JAD (joint application design).
- The design workbench employs a screen designer, dialog designer, and report designer, integrated with the encyclopedia.
- Code structures are represented graphically (with action diagrams or similar diagrams).
- Thorough documentation is generated automatically.
- The tool kit enables highly complex systems to be subdivided into less complex systems which can be developed by separate small teams. The interface between the separate systems is defined with precision in the encyclopedia.
- The tool kit has the characteristics of CASE tools listed in Box 2.1.

is necessary to select the best tools and also to adapt IS organization and methods to take full advantage of these tools.

The simplest CASE tools are little more than diagramming aids. They might be thought of as being like word processors for diagrams. (They do not have all the characteristics listed in Box 2.1.) These tools enable diagrams to be drawn more quickly and enable them to be modified quickly and kept tidy. They have a productivity effort comparable to the introduction of word processors into a lawyer's office. Lawyers' word processors often result in far more text being created; diagramming tools often result in far more diagrams being created.

A more valuable effect of good CASE tools is the removal of errors and inconsistencies at the design stage. The designs are of higher quality, leading to fewer problems in subsequent time-consuming removal of errors from code.

Code generators enable implementors to produce a working program quickly, however if the generator is not employed with information engineering techniques, the programs generated may be incompatible fragments, ill-designed and not linking together.

To achieve high productivity the tools for design need to be tightly coupled to the code generator. The design tools should employ a data model and should enable the design to be represented in a powerful, visual, easy-to-modify form from which code is generated directly. The programs should be quickly executable so that the designer can observe what they do, adjust or add to the design, rerun the programs, enhance the design, and so on until a comprehensive system is created. The principle "What you see is what you get" should apply to the combination of visual design tool and code generator. The need for manual coding should be removed to the maximum extent.

The designer-generator tool should enable prototypes to be built and quickly modified. It should generate test data and provide testing tools. It should generate database code and job control code, so that programs can be quickly executed when design changes are made.

THE EFFECT OF LARGE TEAMS

System development productivity is strongly affected by the number of people in the system development team. Large teams tend to give low development productivity. The reason is that the number of interactions between team members increases rapidly as team size increases. If there are N people on a team, all interacting, the number of person-to-person interactions is $\dfrac{N(N-1)}{2}$.

When people interact, there are miscommunications. The attempt to lessen miscommunications by documenting the interactions is time consuming and often does not work well. The productivity-reducing effects are approximately proportional to the square of the number of interacting team members.

Statistics for conventional programming show much larger numbers of lines of code per person-day (averaged over the life of a project) for very small teams than for large teams. Application development projects with very large numbers of people are often disastrous. One-person projects exhibit the highest productivity.

An objective when using CASE tools should be to avoid having large teams. Big projects should be subdivided into small projects, each of which can be completed relatively quickly by one, two, or at most three implementors. The CASE tool should make it possible to define with computerized precision the interfaces between the components generated by separate teams. At the start of a large project an entity-relationship diagram should be created for the data that will be used, the data elements should be defined, and the data correctly normalized. The same data model should be used for all of the subprojects. The flow of data and control among the subprojects should be defined with the CASE tool.

Because of the power of an I-CASE tool, many projects or subprojects can be completed by one person. The brilliant, fast, or hard-working individual then has the capability to excel. Management should encourage the most capable implementors to learn the full power of an I-CASE tool set.

REUSABLE DESIGNS

Today's programmers constantly reinvent the wheel; they struggle to create something which has been created endless times before. Major productivity gains will result from employing reusable designs, data models, or code. Reusable components should be cataloged in a CASE encyclopedia so that they can be selected when needed, and modified as required.

A large enterprise should employ the same I-CASE tool set at all locations where systems are built so that common data models, designs, and program components can be used by multiple locations. Telecommunications access to mainframe encyclopedias facilitates the sharing of applications, document design, accounting procedures, and so on.

Reusable design and reusable code is discussed in Chapter 3.

MAINTENANCE

In systems developed by traditional manual techniques, maintenance is a major problem. Systems are often difficult and time consuming to change. After being modified multiple times they often become fragile and even minor changes result in bugs and breakdowns.

A goal of I-CASE tool sets is to produce systems which are quick and easy to change. Maintenance is not done by digging around in spaghetti code but by modification of the design screens, followed by regeneration of code. Changes can thus be made simply and quickly.

Traditional maintenance is often made more difficult by inadequate documentation. When maintenance programmers make changes, they often neglect to make corresponding changes to the documentation. The documentation then no longer reflects the program. With I-CASE tools the contents of the encyclopedia *are* the documentation. Paper documentation can be generated from the encyclopedia when required. When changes are made to the design, the encyclopedia is automatically updated.

While in some corporations the main thrust with I-CASE tools is to increase the productivity of application building, in others the thrust is to improve the quality of systems and achieve coordination across a complex enterprise by means of information engineering techniques. The use of I-CASE tools has prevented making the spaghettilike mess of the past and has produced cleanly structured design and code, with relatively fast and easy techniques for maintenance. The use of information engineering with I-CASE tools makes it possible to avoid the problems that arise from incompatible systems and incompatible data in an enterprise, and it enables IS expenditures to be more closely related to the needs of top management.

REVERSE ENGINEERING

There is a world of difference between maintenance of systems built fully with IE (information engineering) techniques and systems built with earlier methods. However large corporations have vast quantities of old systems built before the use of automated techniques and normalized data models. Eventually, these old systems have to be converted to the world of information engineering, relational databases, cooperative processing, improved forms of user dialog, IBM's Systems Application Architecture, and so on. The maintenance cost of the old systems is often very high, but it is too much work to convert them to the new form quickly.

Reverse engineering refers to a family of techniques for capturing the data structures and code of old systems and providing automated help in restructuring them so that they can be rebuilt with I-CASE tools. As they are rebuilt, they should employ the IE data models and reusable processes as much as is practical, and should be fully represented in the IE encyclopedia. They can then evolve in step with the other IE applications.

Chapter 20 discusses reverse engineering.

MEETING END-USER NEEDS BETTER

A critical need in system design is to meet the true needs of the end users better.

Traditional techniques for application development often resulted in systems mismatched to the needs of end users. In the worst cases multimillion-dollar systems were rejected or bypassed by end users. The tools and techniques discussed in Part II of this book make it possible to both meet user needs better and to speed up the delivery of systems. One factor of traditional development that prevents meeting user needs well is the slow delivery of systems and consequent multiyear backlog.

The joint requirement planning, joint application design, and prototype review stages should be intensive workshops which happen quickly in which the encyclopedia representation of the design is built and adjusted. The toolset should enable the conversion of this design into executable code as quickly as possible.

There are multiple variations of the lifecycle in Fig. 2.8. They should have the characteristics of being *faster* than the traditional paper-oriented lifecycle, *meeting the end-user needs better* because the end users see and discuss the design, screens, reports, and prototypes, and being *more rigorous* because computerized tools are used which check the design and link it to the data models. Documentation, most of which is in a computer-processable form, is built in the encyclopedia as the lifecycle proceeds.

TO ACHIEVE HIGH-SPEED DEVELOPMENT

In summary, the following are needed to achieve systems implementation that is of high speed as well as high quality:

- **Automated tools for design and construction.** The design workbench should provide the most powerful facilities possible and should directly drive a code generator that minimizes manual coding. The code generator must use the same encyclopedia as the design workbench. The design workbench and code generator should have been specifically created to enable the highest speed of development.

- **High-speed methodologies.** Productivity in building systems depends upon the methodology as well as the tool set. The methodologies used prior to CASE tools need to be fundamentally changed to take advantage of prototyping, interactive end-user workshops, design automation, reusable modules iterative development with code generation, and automated documentation.

- **Rapid prototyping.** The tool set used should allow prototypes to be built and modified quickly. The prototype should be capable of evolving into the final design.

- **Joint application design.** Requirements planning and design should be done in workshops with end users, using automated tools (Chapters 7 and 8). The workshops should be conducted so as to identify the true needs of the users and translate these quickly into formal designs that can drive a code generator. The designs of data, procedures, screens, reports, and prototypes done in the joint application design workshop should replace the slow, inadequate technique of writing text specifications.

- **Reusable design and code.** Methods which make possible the use of reusable design and reusable code should be employed wherever possible. Information engineering techniques which facilitate reusable models, design, and code should be employed wherever possible as described in Chapter 3.

- **Small teams.** In the I-CASE world, large projects should be broken into pieces that can each be done by one or two IS professionals working with end users. The pieces all use the same data model, and the process model defines the interfaces between the pieces.

- **Documentation generation.** Manual creation of documentation is time consuming and inadequate. The documentation should be the formally structured information in the encyclopedia. The code generator should print a development workbook.

- **Avoidance of bureaucracy.** Most methodologies of the 1970s were bureaucratic, spelling out many tasks with associated paperwork. It was impossible to develop systems quickly with these paper-intensive procedures. Today most manual paperwork is avoided when user requirements are captured directly into I-CASE tools and associated prototypes that link to formal data models, and documentation is generated from the encyclopedia.

- **Testing aids.** Test data should be generated, and the code generator should provide testing aids.

- **System evolution.** Most systems are going to evolve, often growing and becoming more complex. The successful corporation of the future will have very impressive software that has grown over many years. The software and the know-how it encapsulates will be so complex that no competitor could emulate it quickly. Systems should be designed so that they can grow in such a way that changes and additions can be done quickly and easily.

- **Attitude.** The attitude pervading the development and end-user organization ought to be that a modern enterprise must be able to change and grow its computerized procedures quickly. It cannot be fully competitive in today's fast-changing world if it cannot change its procedures when it needs to. A critical factor for the IS organization ought to be the ability to do high-speed development, and end-user organizations must be prepared to adapt to new procedures quickly when needed.

Lifecycles, methodology, and management of RAD (rapid application development) projects are discussed in more detail in the author's book *Rapid Application Development* [1]. The RAD lifecycle emphasizes *quality* of systems developed. It is possible to achieve much higher quality with the RAD lifecycle than with traditional lifecycles, partly by using tools that enforce quality, and partly by much stronger end-user involvement [1].

REFERENCE

1. James Martin, *Rapid Application Development*, Macmillan, New York, 1990.

3 REUSABLE DESIGN AND CODE

INTRODUCTION   One of the most powerful ways to improve the productivity of system building is to build from designs that have already been done, or to employ modules of reusable code. It is often much quicker to modify an existing design or use existing building blocks than it is to design and program from scratch. Perhaps the most revolutionary change in software development that workbench tools will bring is the enforcement of standards and the building of systems from reusable parts.

There is a direct analogy with CAD/CAM (computer-aided design/computer-aided manufacturing) systems used in engineering today. A design engineer creating a new product employs a graphics workstation which has access to a library of components and products. Wherever possible, he employs existing designs rather than creating new parts. He often modifies an existing design to adapt it to his new needs. He is not building from scratch; he is building from existing parts wherever possible.

The key to reusable design is having a workbench environment which makes relevant designs easy to find, easy to understand, easy to modify, and easy to link to other components. The diagramming and graphics tools we have discussed make designs easy to understand and modify. The reusable components need to be represented in the format used by the I-CASE tool. The ability to analyze, compare, and synthesize designs helps in fitting the components together. Where components are defined in terms of a fully normalized data model, this helps define the interfaces between components. The ability to compare data types and structures and highlight differences graphically enables designers to see and to express what data conversion is needed to link components. It would be useful to have a generator which automatically generates subroutines to convert fields and records from one format to another.

It seems likely that in the future a section of the software industry will grow up which sells reusable designs and programs built with a workbench tool

BOX 3.1   Benefits of reusability

- **Speed of development.** Systems can be made operational very quickly.

- **One-person teams.** Development can often be done by one person or by small teams. The problems of large teams are avoided.

- **Documentation.** Reusable design should be well documented with workbench tools.

- **Higher quality.** Reusable designs should be thoroughly thought out, tested, and comprehensive. The resulting product is less likely to have errors, instability, omissions, and misunderstandings.

- **Shared expertise.** The reusable design may have a high order of shared expertise built into it.

- **Facilitates learning of good design.** The reusable designs should employ the best techniques. Persons who work with them learn these techniques.

- **Complexity.** Algorithms, structures, or knowledge of great complexity may be built into the reusable modules, facilitating the use of powerful techniques.

- **Intercommunication.** The standards imposed by the reusable modules facilitate communication among different systems.

- **Ease of change.** The reusable modules should be designed and represented by workbench tools such that they are as easy to change as possible and as easy to link to other modules.

so that they can be easily found, understood, modified, and interlinked. A vast range of value-added components and services can be built on top of the automated information engineering tools.

Box 3.1 lists the benefits of reusability.

INFORMATION ENGINEERING FACILITATES REUSABILITY

Information engineering makes possible a high degree of reusable design and code because it identifies common data and common processes across an enterprise. The same entity type is used in many different applications across the enterprise. The same (normalized) data structure is associated with the entity type. The entity type represents a type of object which has a certain behavior, regardless of where it is used. This behavior can be represented in reusable process modules. Two entity types may have a certain relationship. This relationship is the same throughout the enterprise. Certain behavior is associated with the relationship, which is, again, represented in reusable process modules.

The terms *object-oriented design* and *object-oriented database* are sometimes used to imply that objects (entities) are identified across an organization and behavior is associated with the objects and translated into code which may be invoked whenever the objects are used.

Today's programmers constantly reinvent the wheel. They struggle to create something which has been created endless times before. Major productivity gains will result from employing reusable designs, data models, or code. Reusable components should be cataloged in a CASE (computer-aided systems engineering) encyclopedia so that they can be selected when needed and modified as required.

A large enterprise should employ the same I-CASE tool set at all locations where systems are built so that common data models, designs, and program components can be used by multiple locations. Telecommunications access to mainframe encyclopedias facilitates the sharing of applications, document design, accounting procedures, and so on.

An objective of IE (information engineering) is to identify commonality in both data and processes and consequently to minimize the redundant system development work. Data modeling makes it clear that the same entity types are used in numerous applications. Whenever they are used there may be certain routines that will be invoked, such as computing derived attributes, applying integrity checks, or creating summary data. A corporation may have many factories which to a large extent have the same entity types. Many of the data processing procedures can be the same from one factory to another. Some will be entirely different. The accounting and reporting should be the same in each factory so that higher-level management can make comparisons. When process decomposition is done and processes are mapped against entity types, commonality among processes can be discovered.

Westpac, one of the largest banks in the southern hemisphere, based in Sydney, used information engineering across the entire bank, with the support of its top management who recognized that better use of computer technology was critical for the growth and success of the bank. Westpac identified 1100 processes, and each of these would probably have been programmed independently if software engineering (as opposed to IE) had been used. In practice there was so much commonality that the 1100 processes were reduced to 50, and these were designed, represented in an IE encyclopedia, and constructed with a code generator [1]. This 22:1 reduction in code generated saved much development time and is likely to reduce the maintenance effort greatly. It also helped to provide consistency of information and reporting which is valuable to management and good for customers. I contrast this with the bank that I use which tells me that it is "impossible" to compute net return on assets because "the computers cannot handle it."

Certain steps should be taken to identify reusable processes. First, it should be determined what application packages are to be used. The IE data models and process models may contain data and processes from application packages. Reusable processes within a business area should be identified when business area analysis (BAA) is done. Then processes which are reusable between business areas should be identified. Both of these may be done by first building an entity-relationship model and a process decomposition diagram and then associating the processes with entity types as discussed in Book II. The processes which are fully, or partially, reusable should be marked in the encyclopedia.

In some cases reusable designs need to be made into IS standards for the enterprise. The establishment of standards lessens the amount of work needed, especially during maintenance. An IS organization should establish standard forms of user dialog, standard use of function keys, standard access for networks and relational databases, standards for document formats, and so on. It should adopt application standards such as IBM's Systems Application Architecture, ANSI X.12 standards for electronic documents, CCITT X.400 standards for document interchange, and so on. If these are reflected in the CASE tool and encyclopedia, that can help to enforce standards and make the use of them more automatic.

If application design is approached on a project-by-project basis, little reusability is achieved. It is the top-down approach of information engineering and data administration that makes reusability practical across an organization. Some corporations have achieved massive reusability by using IE, with consequent reductions in development and maintenance costs.

ALL LEVELS OF THE PYRAMID

Reusable design is valuable at all levels of the pyramid.

At the top level, strategic planning models may be used to show people doing an information strategy plan what are typical goals, critical success factors, functions, entities and relationships for that type of enterprise. Given a rich and well-thought-out example, the planners can think about their own corporation and modify the example. The example helps direct their thoughts and give them ideas. Using it, they will probably produce a better enterprise model.

REUSABLE DATA MODELS

At the second level of the pyramid, industry data models and process models could be the starting point. There is now a large amount of experience in creating data models. Consultants who have done data modeling in different corporations of the same type usually comment that data models for the same area are remarkably similar. If the rules of full normalization are followed, the data model for one airline is very similar to the data model for another airline; the data model for one electric utility is very similar to that of another electric utility. It *usually* takes the data modeling team months to create an overall entity model or to create a detailed model for a given business area. If instead of working from sc.atch, they started with a graphically displayed industry model which is easy to modify, the time taken to build the required model would be much less, and often there would be fewer items omitted or misunderstood. The quality of the resulting model would be likely to be higher.

A large corporation often has many factories or local operations. A data model created for one of them can be transferred to the others. At each site local variations may be made in the model. Starting from the same data model at each site gives a higher level of uniformity of data among the sites. This makes it easier later to transfer procedure designs and programs from one site to many others. In some corporations a policy exists for achieving standardization of data among sites. The ability of the encyclopedia to compare separate data models and display the differences with highlighting or color makes it easy to examine incompatibilies and see whether they can be corrected.

It is desirable where possible to have the same data formats in different companies for such items as invoices, payments, receipts, orders, and acknowledgments. If this compatibility exists, a computer generating these documents in one company can transmit them electronically to the computer of another company, thus avoiding the need for printing, mailing, and keypunching (with its attendant errors). The U.S. National Bureau of Standards has created recommendations for such data formats. Various industries such as banking, trucking, and airlines have their own standard formats for intercorporate computer communications. The U.S. Department of Defense has recommended certain standard formats to its suppliers. Standards exist for CAD descriptions of parts and these descriptions are sent from one company to another. All these standards need to be represented with the techniques of the information engineering workbenches and should reside in the libraries of such tools.

PROCESS MODELS   While data models are very similar among similar corporations, process models have more differences. It is often the differences in processes or procedures that give corporations their uniqueness, sales arguments, and competitive advantages. As we have stressed, whereas data models can be designed to be stable processes and procedures in a vigorous healthy corporation tend to be dynamic and changing.

Having said that, the similarities are still striking. There are several types of invoicing procedures, mail-order procedures, accounting procedures, and so on. Where one particular type is used it is similar in most enterprises. The easy way to design it is to start with a graphic representation of a system or subsystem that has already been built, used, and debugged and adjust it as appropriate.

PROCEDURES   At the second level of the pyramid a *data model* is a valuable reusable component in its own right. A *process model* may also be useful in its own right though it is more valuable when linked to a data model. As we drop down to the third level of the pyramid, we are concerned with representing procedures in sufficient detail that they can be programmed. Here the concept of the hyperdiagram is important. The hyperdiagram links multiple aspects of the procedure: its data flow diagram, its decomposition diagram, its data model, its action diagram, and possibly other more detailed or precise representations. These different views are linked together logically in a miniencyclopedia which applies as many validation rules as possible. The designer has multiple windows which can display the different types of detail. Hyperdiagrams are discussed in the following chapter.

Using a multiple-view perspective is useful at level 2; it is essential at level 3. At level 2 it can link the process model and data model, and should show a matrix of processes and entity types. At level 3 it should impose a formality on the representation of the procedure which enables a designer to link the module to other modules with precision and to modify the module if desired.

REUSABLE CODE   At the bottom level of the pyramid we are concerned with reusable code.

Since the beginnings of computing attempts have been made to employ reusable code. Long ago there were macroinstructions, subroutines, and application packages. Libraries of these were established. Control mechanisms were made standard and usable by most programs—input/output control systems, file and database management systems, teleprocessing control programs, operating system, and so on. Later, application generators of various types were used, first simple ones such as report generators and screen painters and then more complex ones for generating complete applications.

Subroutines were the first labor-saving device invented by programmers. A subroutine for computing Sin *x* was written in 1944 for the Mark I calculator [2]. Most installations have a large library of useful subroutines, and this facilitates the programming of standard applications. When a subroutine is written to handle a general case, it employs parameters—values which can be changed from one subroutine call to another.

The use of subroutines, and reusable code in general, is a good idea, and there has been a long-standing desire in computer science to build and use libraries of standard software components. Unfortunately there has been only limited success in doing this. Most programmers still hand code procedures that could, in principle, come from a library.

Although most programmers make limited use of reusable code, it is interesting to study how the very best professional programmers do their work. The best programmers produce more than ten times the work of average programmers. A few genius programmers who specialize in specific areas such as compiler writing achieve an astonishingly high productivity. They appear to do so by having their own private and often informal library of structures and code which they can quickly adapt to a new set of requirements. They can quickly find the designs or code they need from what to other people would seem to be a large and disorganized mass of knowledge. They use their own computerized library of structures and subroutines but also have in their head many professional heuristics which enable them to find what they need from their library, modify it, and use memorized structures and techniques for building together the components.

The challenge of reusable code is to find how these techniques of the one-person genius can be made usable with automated assistance by the mass of programmers.

PROBLEMS WITH REUSABLE CODE

Today's low usage of reusable code stem from a number of fundamental problems:

- Difficulty of agreeing on what constitutes a reusable component
- Difficulty of understanding what a component does and how to use it
- Difficulty of understanding how to interface reusable components to the rest of a design
- Difficulty of designing reusable components so that they are easy to modify
- Difficulty of organizing a library so that programmers can find and use what they need
- Difficulty of knowing what is in the library
- Programming language dependence
- Lack of application standards

To overcome these problems we need a formalism for representing reusable components. The formalism needs to make the components easy to understand and easy to modify. Particularly important, it needs to make the interfaces with the outside world rigorous. To make formalism practical and standardized among many reusable components, workbench tools are needed.

The big problem with today's subroutine libraries and application packages is that this formalism is absent or is not visible. It is often too difficult to modify packaged applications. To make them easy to modify and link to other applications, they should be represented with data models and diagrams of procedures—a *perspective* with its own miniencyclopedia, usable as discussed in the previous chapter. Probably, one day, many subroutines and packages will be designed (or converted) to be used with information engineering tools using data models, diagrams, and formalism. Subroutines and packages will be designed to link to generators of reports, screens, spreadsheets, expert systems, database facilities, and so on.

Box 3.2 represents desirable properties of reusable components.

Massive amounts of electronic devices are being designed today for all manner of uses. Some household gadgets contain a hundred thousand transistors. There is no way that such an array of hardware could be designed transistor

BOX 3.2   Desirable properties of reusable components

- **Formal semantic basis.** A formalism should be used which describes the component with precision.

- **Expressiveness.** The formalism should be capable of expressing as many different kinds of components as possible.

- **Easy to understand.**

- **Easy to modify.**

- **Easy to add to.**

- **Designed for a graphics workbench.** To satisfy the three foregoing properties, the design should be represented with a graphic *perspective* which may interlink multiple diagrammatic representations.

- **Use the best structured techniques.** Canonically structured data and procedures should be represented graphically.

- **Use application standards.** Applications standards should be used wherever practical. These include standard forms of user dialog, standard use of function keys, standards such as IBM's Systems Application Architecture, standards for formating electronic documents (ANSI X.12 EDI standards), and so on.

- **Clear, simple, precise interfaces.** The formalism should define the interfaces between components with precision.

- **Self-contained.** The components should be self-contained and have predictable behavior. There should be data passed between modules but, where possible, no control flow between modules.

- **Verifiable.** Where practical, techniques for verifying the behavior of components should be used (e.g., by means of rules implemented with artificial intelligence techniques in a workbench).

- **Programming language independent.** The formalism should not be a specific programming language. It should be representable in multiple programming languages.

by transistor. Instead the designers use off-the-shelf chips each containing many thousands of transistors. The chip has well-defined properties that are well documented and well understood. Its behavior may be variable over a wide range with parameterization, read-only memory, and random-access memory. The building of software systems in the future needs to be similar. There will be many off-the-shelf building blocks with well-defined properties. Some projects have called them *software chips* [3].

In hardware engineering the change from transistor-by-transistor design to chip-by-chip design gave orders of magnitude improvements in productivity. It also made design by a much wider range of people practical. The change from line-at-a-time programming to design using software chips will be similar.

SELF-CONTAINED MODULES

It is highly desirable that reusable modules should be self-contained. They might be thought of as black boxes. Certain data go into the black box; it takes certain actions and produces certain output data.

Some program modules are written to handle multiple transactions simultaneously. The module may, for example, be waiting for a database action on one transaction while it continues processing another transaction. Such programs must be designed so that the separate transactions do not interfere with one another. One transaction, for example, must not modify switches in such a way that when control passes to a second transaction that transaction can change the switches and invalidate the ongoing processing of the first transaction. Programs which can be entered by multiple transactions without interference are referred to as *reentrant programs*. Reusable code modules need these types of safety features.

Often diagrams are drawn of program modules showing data and control information passing among the modules. The data types in such a situation can be precisely defined and should employ data from a formally designed data model. The passing of control information causes more of a problem and can generally be avoided. The modules should communicate with one another using only the data in the data model. Each module is then self-contained with clearly defined inputs and outputs.

DIFFERENT APPROACHES

There are a variety of different approaches to the creation of complex systems from reusable designs.

The first major distinction is between starting with a whole design and adapting it in some way, and starting with building blocks that become linked together. We will refer to these approaches as *start-with-the-whole* and *start-with-the-parts*.

START-WITH-THE-WHOLE

The *start-with-the-whole* approach is found in a number of application generators. A generic application may be provided which is intended to be modified in some way so that it becomes a specific application.

There are a variety of techniques for adaptation of the generic solution:

1. **The skeleton approach.** The designer may be provided with the skeleton of an application and given techniques for filling in the skeleton so that it becomes a working application. For example, the skeleton may be that of an online system which accepts transactions, performs calculations, updates a database, and generates reports. This skeleton can be converted into a purchase order system, an inventory control system, or many other types of system. The designer specifies the records to be used in the database, specifies the screen designs to be used, specifies the calculations to be done, and specifies the report formats. All of this may directly employ a data dictionary or data model. Where necessary the designer may add to the skeleton using a programming language (perhaps a fourth-generation language).

2. **The kitchen sink approach.** Rather than being given a skeleton which he has to add to, the designer may be given a facility richly endowed with optional features. One might say the facility has everything but the kitchen sink. Instead of adding to a skeleton the designer prunes the features which are not wanted. It is easier, especially for an unskilled designer, to delete unwanted features than to add features.

3. **The parameter approach.** The reusable software may have a set of parameters for varying its behavior. The designer may select parameters or features from menus. He may have a mouse-driven facility on a workstation for adapting the behavior of the software.

4. **Stepwise refinement.** The designer may use the approach of refining the behavior of the software in a succession of small steps, testing at each step to ensure that he has not introduced erratic behavior. The software may provide the testing tools for this purpose and be linked to design automation tools which make the software easy to modify.

START-WITH-THE-PARTS

In the *start-with-the-parts* approach the designer is provided with building blocks. He may want to modify the building blocks and this could be done with any of the foregoing techniques:

- The skeleton approach
- The kitchen sink approach
- The parameter approach
- Stepwise refinement

The building blocks, or modifications of them, may be linked using different approaches:

1. **Ad hoc linking.** The designer may create linkages between the building blocks himself in any way that he wishes.

2. **Linking employing a data model.** The only linkage between the building blocks may be data items or records which are defined in a formally designed data model.

3. **Linking employing formal rules.** The building blocks may be objects represented in an encyclopedia which can be linked with the help of workbench tools, which rigidly enforce the rules of the encyclopedia. The building blocks in this approach should be represented as *perspectives* and the workbench should assist in the integration of perspectives as described in the previous chapter.

4. **Formal decomposition—the HOS technique.** The HOS technique [4,5] is a top-down approach. A tree-structured decomposition of functions is used. The block at the top of the tree represents the entire system. It is decomposed into functions, these are decomposed into subfunctions, and so on to the bottom of the tree. The items at the right of each block are the data types which are inputs to that function, and the items at the left are the data types which are outputs. The blocks at the bottom of the tree are reusable modules for which code can be generated or produced from a library. These reusable modules may themselves have been designed with the HOS technique.

In most functional decomposition a function can be decomposed into subfunctions in any way the designer chooses. By contract in the HOS technique each decomposition is of a formal type, defined with mathematical axioms. The data types which are passed from parent to child blocks in the decomposition are also formally defined. Each decomposition and hence the entire tree of decompositions is mathematically provable [4].

A complex application can thus be built in a highly rigorous fashion. It is decomposed in formal steps each of which is mathematically provable until functions are reached for which code can be generated.

5. **Formal decomposition with a formal data model.** Rigorous decomposition defines how data items are passed among the functional modules. This technique should be linked to a data model which itself is designed with rigorous techniques. The combination of these introduces a level of rigor into software building which is not generally found today.

COMBINATIONS OF THESE TWO APPROACHES

A mature workbench for building systems from predesigned parts might provide *start-with-the-whole components* and *building-block components*. It might, for example, provide a skeleton application and building blocks which can be linked into the skeleton. For given business areas it might provide reusable data models which can be pruned or added to as necessary.

A major disadvantage of the *start-with-the-whole approach* is that it is not highly generalized. The "whole" rates to a specific form or class of application. A major advantage is that the "whole" can be designed very thoroughly. It can include checkpoint/restart procedures, security procedures, facilities for auditing, and so on that an average systems analyst might leave out or do badly. It can also be designed to be machine efficient.

INCOMPATIBLE DATA

It is likely that more and more application packages will be used in corporations. The growth of the software package industry will be helped by workbench tools which make packages easier to change.

A new application package is likely to have data which is incompatible with the data models that already exist in a corporation. The package itself may have (certainly should have) a data model. The techniques described in the previous chapter for comparing data models and for enabling incompatible data models and their applications to exist together, become important. There may be automatic conversion of data items or normalized data records as data passes from one compatibility zone to another.

GROWING A SYSTEM

It is more appropriate to talk about *building* than *writing* a complex program. The construction of software has analogies with other building processes. We use scaffolding; we assemble components. However, *unlike* the design of buildings, it is often not practical to specify a complex design and build to the specification. The systems we create today tend to grow a piece at a time. They are more like the growth of a city than the construction of a building. We need the tools and formalism to fit separate pieces together, where many of the pieces are predesigned and/or precoded, and ensure that the interface between the pieces is correct. As systems grow more precoded pieces go into their library. Small units are linked into larger units. A designer can employ the work of previous designers.

We may contrast the living things built by nature with the dead things built by human beings. The complexity of the constructs of living things is awesome to a computer professional. The brain is so intricate that it cannot be mapped, imitated, or understood in detail; it is rich in diversity, and yet it is self-protecting and self-renewing. The things of nature are complex because they are grown, not specified and built. As we continue to grow the components of software and information systems, they will become complex (though not compared with brain). We need disciplines and tools which facilitate and enable us to manage such growth.

The designers of the future must stand on the shoulders of the designers of the present.

LEARNING
BY EXAMPLE

A major advantage of reusable designs is that designers can learn from the designs that are used. There is much to be said for learning by example. The reusable designs ought to employ the best design techniques. Working with them and modifying them is a good way to learn and gain experience with the technique.

Learning by example in this is particularly useful for naive or inexperienced designers. However it is also valuable for many seasoned professionals because often the techniques such as data modeling, action diagrams, critical success factor hierarchies, and so on are better than the methods they have been using.

Some systems analysts have many years of experience but do sloppy work with poor techniques.

The gap between the best software engineering practice and the average practice is very wide—probably wider than in any other engineering discipline. When workbench tools are introduced there should be a goal of upgrading the quality of work of all analysts and implementors.

SUMMARY

Box 3.3 gives detail about the IE procedure for identifying reusable processes.

REFERENCES

1. Peter Horbiatiuck, presentation to KnowledgeWare User's Conference, Atlanta, GA, February 1988.

2. Carma McClure, "Reusable Software Components," Working paper, January 1986.

3. R. C. Waters, "The Programmer's Apprentice: A Session with KBEmacs," *IEEE Trans. on Software Engineering,* November 1985.

4. M. Hamilton and S. Zeldin, "Higher-Order Software—A Methodology for Defining Software," *IEEE Trans. on Software Engineering,* Vol. SE.2. no. 1, March 1976, pp. 25–32.

5. James Martin, *System Design from Provably Correct Constructs,* Englewood Cliffs, N.J.: Prentice Hall, 1985.

BOX 3.3

Create a preliminary data model
    Extract the entity-relationship model for this business area
      from the encyclopedia
  Determine what events occur in this business area.
  Associate the events with entity types (A behavior model)
  Draw the lifecycle of each entity.
  Enter initial attributes of each entity.

Create a preliminary process model
    Extract the business-function decomposition model for this
      business area from the encyclopedia.
  Decompose the functions into processes.

Successively refine the information in the following stages
    until a complete representation of the data and processes is achieved.
  Create a detailed data model

    | See Book II, BOX 12.3 |

  Create a detailed process model

    | See Book II, BOX 14.2 |

    Create a process decomposition diagram
      Decompose processes eventually into elementary processes.
        An elementary process is one which cannot be decomposed
          further without stating HOW a procedure is carried out.

    Create a process dependency diagram
      Correlate this with the process decomposition diagram.
      Consider what information flows from one process to another.

  Build matrices
    Generate an entity-type/process matrix.
      Build a matrix mapping elementary processes and entity types
      Indicate what process CREATES each entity record.
      Indicate what processes UPDATE, READ, or DELETE each entity
        record.

    Associate entity types, processes, and events with organizational
      units and locations.
    Associate entity types, processes, and events with goals and
      problems.

Identify reusable processes wherever possible

  Determine where application packages will be used

    For each application package
      Create a process model of the package.
      Create a model of the data stored by the package. Determine
        whether this will cause equivalent entity types to be stored
        redundantly.

  Identify processes that can be reusable within the business area
    Associate processes with entity types (using the process/entity-
      type matrix).

BOX 3.3   *(Continued)*

Identify processes that are associated with an entity type and
which are used whenever an entity is created, read, updated, or
deleted, for example validity checks, editing, user dialogue,
security checks, backup, accuracy checks, audit trail, and so on.
Identify processes that are associated with a relationship between
entity types (on the entity-relationship diagram) and which are
invoked each time that relationship is used, for example updating
accounts whenever an order is associated with a customer. Again,
validity checks, editing, user dialogue, security checks, backup,
accuracy checks, audit trail, and so on may be identified.
Identify processes which are not identical, but are similar enough
that common design can be used.

Identify processes that may be reusable BETWEEN business areas
Examine processes marked in previous BAA studies as potentially
reusable across different business areas.
Establish the extent to which common design can be used.
Examine those entity types which are used in other business areas
as well as the one being analyzed. Determine what processes can be
associated with those entity types or their entity relationships.
Mark processes from this BAA study which are potentially reusable
across different business areas.

Mark, in the encyclopedia, all processes which are fully or partially
reusable.

Design bridges necessary to employ reusable packages and modules
Design interfaces to reusable systems from other locations, if
necessary.
Design interfaces to application packages, if necessary.
Design interfaces to old systems which will remain in existence.
Design tests to ensure that these bridge facilities work correctly.

Analyze and correlate (automatically) the above information.
Use a workbench tool which analyzes and correlates the above
information with a knowledge coordinator.
Use the knowledge coordinator of the design tool to ensure
that the BAA is internally consistent, and consistent with
other knowledge in the encyclopedia.

enced designers. However it is also valuable for many seasoned professionals because often the techniques such as data modeling, action diagrams, critical success factor hierarchies, and so on are better than the methods they have been using.

Some systems analysts have many years of experience but do sloppy work with poor techniques.

The gap between the best software engineering practice and the average practice is very wide—probably wider than in any other engineering discipline. When workbench tools are introduced there should be a goal of upgrading the quality of work of all analysts and implementors.

SUMMARY   Box 3.3 gives detail about the IE procedure for identifying reusable processes.

REFERENCES

1. Peter Horbiatiuck, presentation to KnowledgeWare User's Conference, Atlanta, GA, February 1988.

2. Carma McClure, "Reusable Software Components," Working paper, January 1986.

3. R. C. Waters, "The Programmer's Apprentice: A Session with KBEmacs," *IEEE Trans. on Software Engineering,* November 1985.

4. M. Hamilton and S. Zeldin, "Higher-Order Software—A Methodology for Defining Software," *IEEE Trans. on Software Engineering,* Vol. SE.2. no. 1, March 1976, pp. 25–32.

5. James Martin, *System Design from Provably Correct Constructs,* Englewood Cliffs, N.J.: Prentice Hall, 1985.

4 DIAGRAMS USED IN SYSTEM DESIGN

Today's system design and implementation should be done with I-CASE (integrated computer-aided systems engineering) tools, and these tools are graphically oriented; with them the *types* of diagrams used for representing systems are critical.

When analysts draw diagrams on paper, they are often casual diagrams that can be drawn any way which appeals to the analyst. With information engineering the diagrams become a language of high precision. The computer must understand *exactly* the meaning of the diagram, must link it to other diagrams, and must apply a large number of rules to it to provide integrity checks and coordination. The computer must extract information from the diagrams to drive a code generator.

To achieve this, precise diagramming standards are needed. The standards need to be understood by every user. They are a vehicle for person-to-person communication as well as for person-to-machine communication. The diagramming standards need to be sufficiently easy to understand so that non-IS (information systems) staff employ them without difficulty.

A corporation intending to do IE (information engineering), now or in the future, must make a commitment to its diagramming standards. The appendixes discuss the diagramming standards used. They are discussed more fully in the author's book *Recommended Diagramming Standards for Analysts and Programmers* [1].

SYMBOLS USED   To make the various types of diagrams as easy to teach as possible, the diagrams should contain a minimum number of symbol types. The same type of symbol appears on different types of diagrams. Figure 4.1 shows the family of symbols that appear on IE diagrams. Appendix I illustrates how these symbols are used.

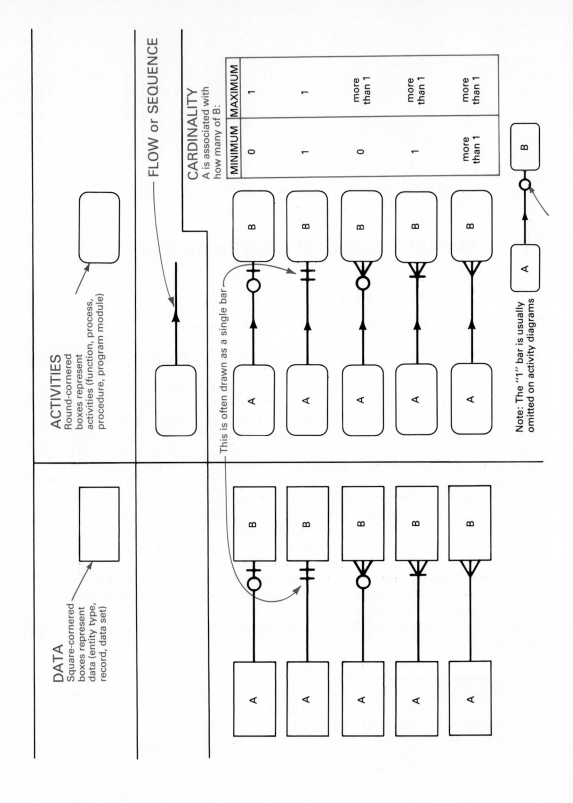

DATA
Square-cornered boxes represent data (entity type, record, data set)

ACTIVITIES
Round-cornered boxes represent activities (function, process, procedure, program module)

FLOW or SEQUENCE

CARDINALITY
A is associated with how many of B:

	MINIMUM	MAXIMUM
	0	1
	1	1
	0	more than 1
	1	more than 1
	more than 1	more than 1

This is often drawn as a single bar

Note: The "1" bar is usually omitted on activity diagrams

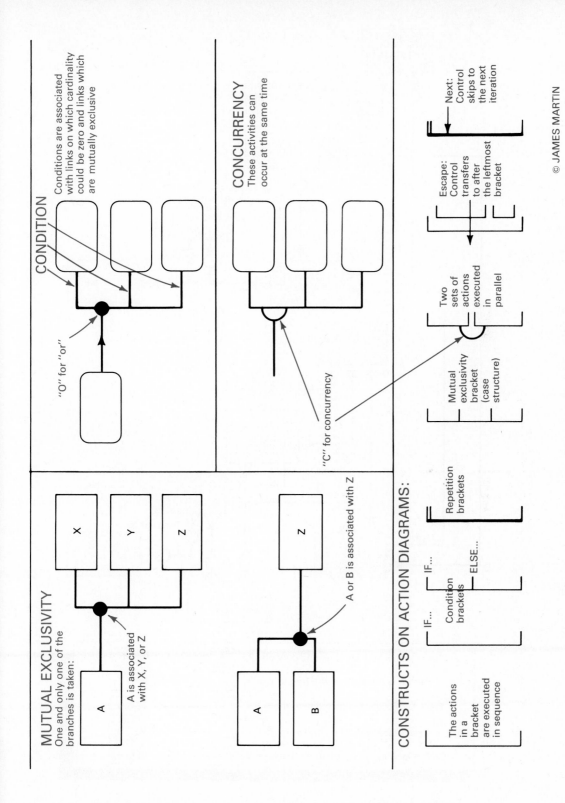

Figure 4.1 The symbols used on the various types of IE diagrams. (See Appendix I.)

© JAMES MARTIN

57

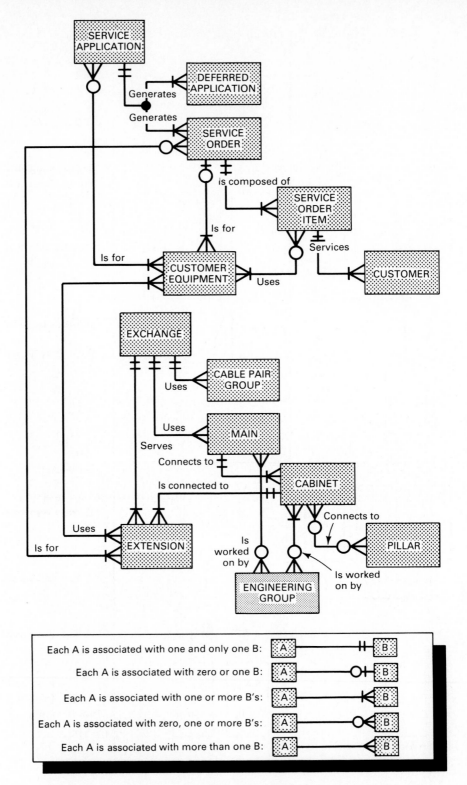

Figure 4.2 Part of an entity-relationship diagram for a telephone company, with the relationships labeled.

Figures 4.2, 4.3, and 4.4 show the main types of diagrams used in information engineering—and in non-IE software engineering with CASE (computer-aided systems engineering) tools.

ENTITY-RELATIONSHIP DIAGRAMS

Figure 4.2 shows an entity-relationship diagram. These were discussed in Book II. When a CASE tool is used to draw an entity-relationship diagram, windows are used to show details of an entity or details of a relationship. Figure 4.3 shows the screen of an I-CASE tool used for entity-relationship diagramming and shows a window with details of a relationship on the diagram.

DECOMPOSITION DIAGRAMS

Figure 4.4 shows a decomposition diagram. The function POLICY SERVING is divided into four processes: SELL TO CUSTOMER, SERVICE A POLICY, PROCESS A CLAIM, and TERMINATE A POLICY. SERVICE A POLICY is subdivided into five subprocesses.

These diagrams are used at the top level of the pyramid for describing the basic functions of the enterprise. They are used at the BAA (business area analysis) level for decomposing functions in processes and subprocesses (as described in Book II). They are used at the design level for decomposing procedures. They are sometimes referred to as *function decomposition, process decomposition,* and *procedure decomposition* diagrams.

A decomposition diagram can show cardinalities, conditions, and mutually exclusive decompositions. These are illustrated in Figs. 4.5 and 4.6. The decomposition diagram in Fig. 4.4 is drawn so that it spreads out horizontally; those of Figs. 4.5 and 4.6 are drawn so that they spread out vertically. Any decomposition can be drawn in either way. The vertical spread is more convenient if long titles or descriptions are used of each block. The user can scroll down vertical-spread diagrams like scrolling down text.

ACTION DIAGRAMS

Any decomposition can be represented as an action diagram. Figure 4.7 shows an action diagram equivalent to Fig. 4.6. A block diagram, like Fig. 4.4, may be more visually appealing than an action diagram, but an action diagram may contain more information as each item can be long and can be multiple lines where necessary. A decomposition diagram can be automatically converted into action diagram format, and the action diagram can be evolved into a program structure and then into executable code.

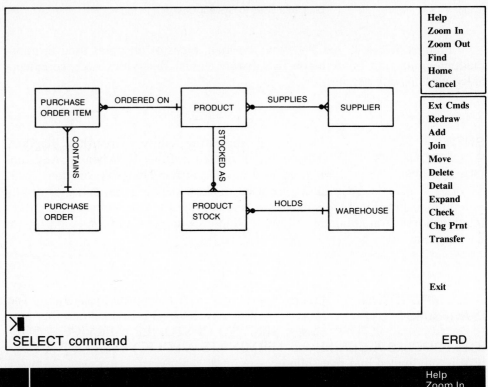

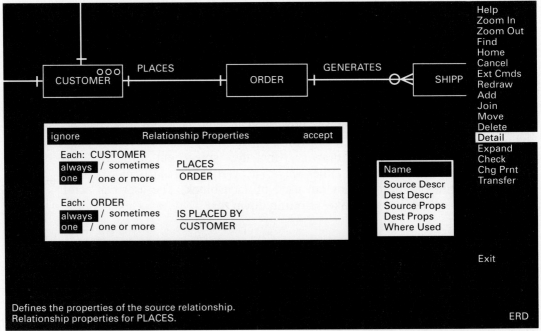

Figure 4.3 A screen of Texas Instruments' Information Engineering Facility™ showing an entity-relationship diagram and a window giving details of a relationship [2].

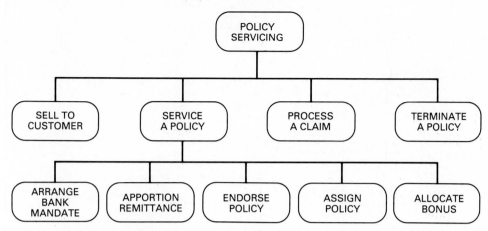

Figure 4.4 A decomposition diagram. The function POLICY SERVICING is decomposed into processes and subprocesses. This diagram is redrawn with cardinality symbols in Fig. 4.5 and is expanded into more detail in Figs. 4.6 and 4.7.

THREE DOTS

Three dots (an ellipsis) are used to indicate that more information exists than is shown on a diagram. The additional information can be displayed by pointing to the item in question and saying "EXPAND." Similarly by pointing to a high-level item and saying "CONTRACT," the items subordinate to that item can be hidden, and three dots will appear to show that they are hidden. Three dots appear in various places in Figs. 4.5 through 4.8.

This ability to expand and contract is extremely useful in working with complex information. The analyst or designer will often CONTRACT within CONTRACT or EXPAND within EXPAND.

DEPENDENCY DIAGRAM

A dependency diagram shows that certain processes or procedures are dependent on other processes or procedures. In other words, it is not possible to execute a process (or procedure) until one or more other processes (or procedures) have been completed. Figure 4.9 shows a simple dependency diagram. Here FILL ORDER cannot be performed until ACCEPT ORDER has been done. CREATE BILL and PREPARE DELIVERY are not done until FILL ORDER is performed.

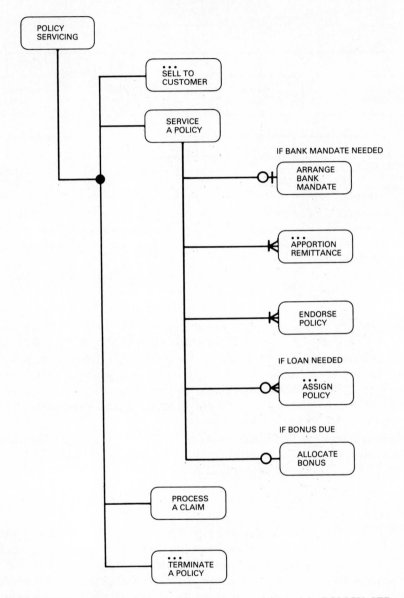

Figure 4.5 A decomposition of the processes performed in POLICY SER-
VICING. Three dots in several of the boxes indicate that parts of the diagram
have been contracted (on a workstation screen). Figure 4.6 shows the diagram
when these processes are reexpanded.

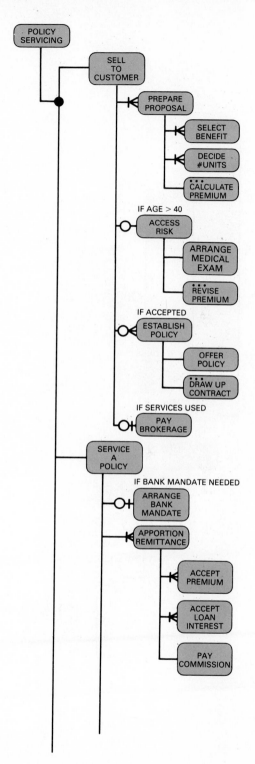

Figure 4.6 Three dots in some of the boxes in this decomposition indicate that the boxes can be further expanded on a workstation screen. The ability to use CONTRACT and EXPAND commands is very useful with large diagrams.

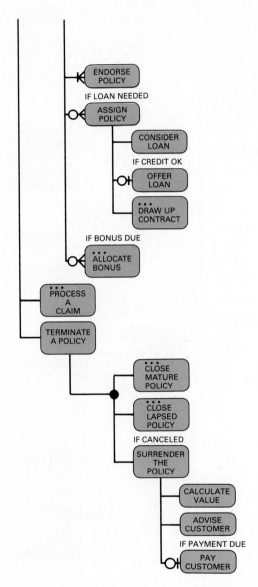

Figure 4.6   (Continued)

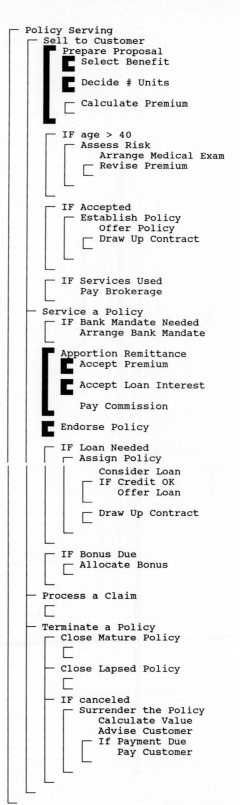

```
┌─ Policy Serving
  │  ┌─ Sell to Customer
  │  │  ┌─ Prepare Proposal
  │  │  ▐  Select Benefit
  │  │  ▐
  │  │  ▐  Decide # Units
  │  │  ▐
  │  │  │  ┌─ Calculate Premium
  │  │  ▐  └─
  │  │
  │  │  ┌─ IF age > 40
  │  │  │  ┌─ Assess Risk
  │  │  │  │     Arrange Medical Exam
  │  │  │  │  ┌─ Revise Premium
  │  │  │  └─
  │  │  └─
  │  │
  │  │  ┌─ IF Accepted
  │  │  │  ┌─ Establish Policy
  │  │  │  │     Offer Policy
  │  │  │  │  ┌─ Draw Up Contract
  │  │  │  └─
  │  │  └─
  │  │
  │  │  ┌─ IF Services Used
  │  │  │     Pay Brokerage
  │  │  └─
  │  ├─ Service a Policy
  │  │  ┌─ IF Bank Mandate Needed
  │  │  │     Arrange Bank Mandate
  │  │  └─
  │  │  ▐  Apportion Remittance
  │  │  ▐  Accept Premium
  │  │  ▐
  │  │  ▐  Accept Loan Interest
  │  │  ▐
  │  │  ▐     Pay Commission
  │  │  ▐
  │  │  ▐  Endorse Policy
  │  │
  │  │  ┌─ IF Loan Needed
  │  │  │  ┌─ Assign Policy
  │  │  │  │        Consider Loan
  │  │  │  │     ┌─ IF Credit OK
  │  │  │  │     │     Offer Loan
  │  │  │  │     └─
  │  │  │  │  ┌─ Draw Up Contract
  │  │  │  └─
  │  │  └─
  │  │  ┌─ IF Bonus Due
  │  │  │  ┌─ Allocate Bonus
  │  │  └─
  │  ├─ Process a Claim
  │  │  ┌─
  │  │  └─
  │  ├─ Terminate a Policy
  │  │  ┌─ Close Mature Policy
  │  │  │  ┌─
  │  │  │  └─
  │  │  ├─ Close Lapsed Policy
  │  │  │  ┌─
  │  │  │  └─
  │  │  ┌─ IF canceled
  │  │  │  ┌─ Surrender the Policy
  │  │  │  │     Calculate Value
  │  │  │  │     Advise Customer
  │  │  │  │  ┌─ If Payment Due
  │  │  │  │  │     Pay Customer
  │  │  │  └─
  │  │  └─
  └─
```

Figure 4.7 The same procedures as in Fig. 4.6 represented with an action diagram. The action diagram is somewhat easier to edit and add to than is the decomposition diagram.

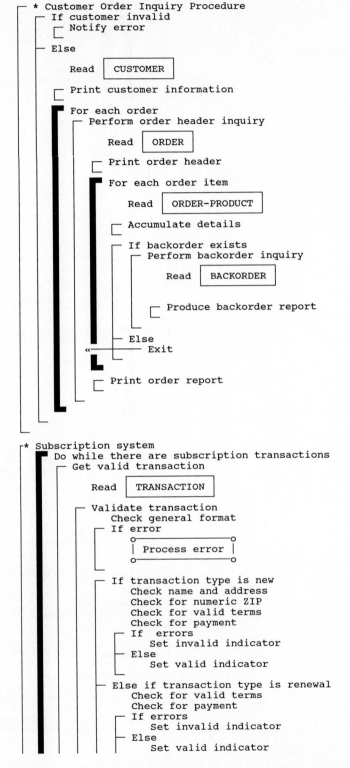

```
┌ * Customer Order Inquiry Procedure
│ ┌ If customer invalid
│ │  ┌ Notify error
│ │  └
│ ┌ Else
│ │
│ │     Read  ┌─────────────┐
│ │           │  CUSTOMER   │
│ │           └─────────────┘
│ │  ┌ Print customer information
│ │  └
│ │  ┌ For each order
│ │  ┃ ┌ Perform order header inquiry
│ │  ┃ │
│ │  ┃ │    Read  ┌─────────┐
│ │  ┃ │          │  ORDER  │
│ │  ┃ │          └─────────┘
│ │  ┃ │ ┌ Print order header
│ │  ┃ │ └
│ │  ┃ │ ┌ For each order item
│ │  ┃ │ ┃
│ │  ┃ │ ┃    Read  ┌────────────────┐
│ │  ┃ │ ┃          │  ORDER-PRODUCT │
│ │  ┃ │ ┃          └────────────────┘
│ │  ┃ │ ┃  ┌ Accumulate details
│ │  ┃ │ ┃  └
│ │  ┃ │ ┃  ┌ If backorder exists
│ │  ┃ │ ┃  │  ┌ Perform backorder inquiry
│ │  ┃ │ ┃  │  │
│ │  ┃ │ ┃  │  │   Read  ┌───────────┐
│ │  ┃ │ ┃  │  │         │ BACKORDER │
│ │  ┃ │ ┃  │  │         └───────────┘
│ │  ┃ │ ┃  │  │  ┌ Produce backorder report
│ │  ┃ │ ┃  │  │  └
│ │  ┃ │ ┃  ┌ Else
│ │  ┃ ╚══│──── Exit
│ │  ┃ │ ┗  └
│ │  ┃ │  ┌ Print order report
│ │  ┃ │  └
│ │  ┗
│ └
```

```
┌ * Subscription system
│ ┃ Do while there are subscription transactions
│ ┃ ┌ Get valid transaction
│ ┃ │
│ ┃ │    Read  ┌──────────────┐
│ ┃ │          │  TRANSACTION │
│ ┃ │          └──────────────┘
│ ┃ │ ┌ Validate transaction
│ ┃ │ │    Check general format
│ ┃ │ │ ┌ If error
│ ┃ │ │ │   o───────────o
│ ┃ │ │ │   │ Process error │
│ ┃ │ │ │   o───────────o
│ ┃ │ │ └
│ ┃ │ │ ┌ If transaction type is new
│ ┃ │ │ │    Check name and address
│ ┃ │ │ │    Check for numeric ZIP
│ ┃ │ │ │    Check for valid terms
│ ┃ │ │ │    Check for payment
│ ┃ │ │ │ ┌ If  errors
│ ┃ │ │ │ │    Set invalid indicator
│ ┃ │ │ │ ┌ Else
│ ┃ │ │ │ │    Set valid indicator
│ ┃ │ │ │ └
│ ┃ │ │ ┌ Else if transaction type is renewal
│ ┃ │ │ │    Check for valid terms
│ ┃ │ │ │    Check for payment
│ ┃ │ │ │ ┌ If errors
│ ┃ │ │ │ │    Set invalid indicator
│ ┃ │ │ │ ┌ Else
│ ┃ │ │ │ │    Set valid indicator
```

Figure 4.8   Two action diagrams used to represent specifications.

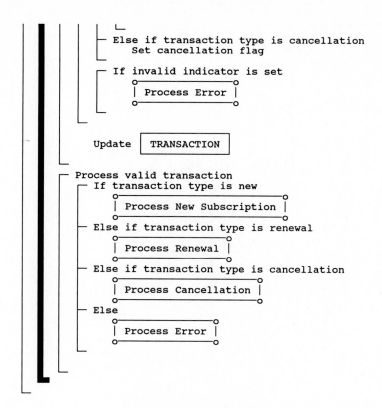

Figure 4.8   (Continued)

A decomposition diagram, such as the following, does not show this dependency:

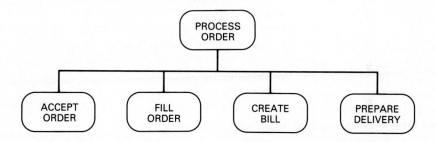

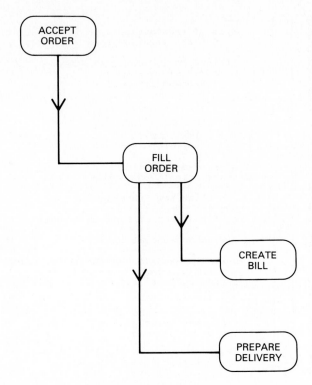

Figure 4.9 A process dependency diagram, sometimes called a process flow diagram. It shows how one process is dependent on another; that is, one process cannot be executed until a previous one has been executed. This diagram is expanded into a data flow diagram in Fig. 4.10, and further expanded in Fig. 4.11, and the analyst's thought process evolved further in Fig. 4.12 with action diagram.

DATA FLOW DIAGRAM

A data flow diagram is a special case of a dependency diagram. It is normally used with procedures (which show *how* something is done). In a data flow diagram one procedure is dependent on another procedure because data must pass between the procedures. A data flow diagram shows what data passes, and also shows the sources and destinations of data. Figure 4.10 shows a data flow diagram which is an extension of Fig. 4.9. A designer, using a CASE tool, may start by drawing a dependency diagram such as Fig. 4.9 and then extend it into a data flow diagram such as Fig. 4.10.

Data flow diagrams and dependency diagrams are usually *nested*. One block may be shown in more detail on another such diagram. For example, the block "ACCEPT ORDER" in Fig. 4.10 is expanded into another data flow diagram in Fig. 4.11. In Fig. 4.10 each of the procedure blocks has three dots,

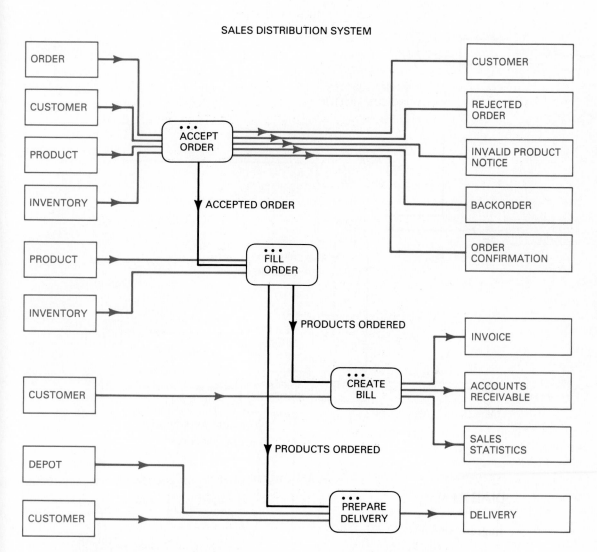

SALES DISTRIBUTION SYSTEM

Figure 4.10   A data flow diagram for a sales distribution system. The black
part shows procedures and data passing between procedures. The red part
shows the data stores used by the procedures. The three dots at the start of a
procedure label indicate that the procedure has been designed in more detail
and that an expanded version of the procedure may be displayed. Figure 4.11
shows the ACCEPT ORDER procedure in more detail.

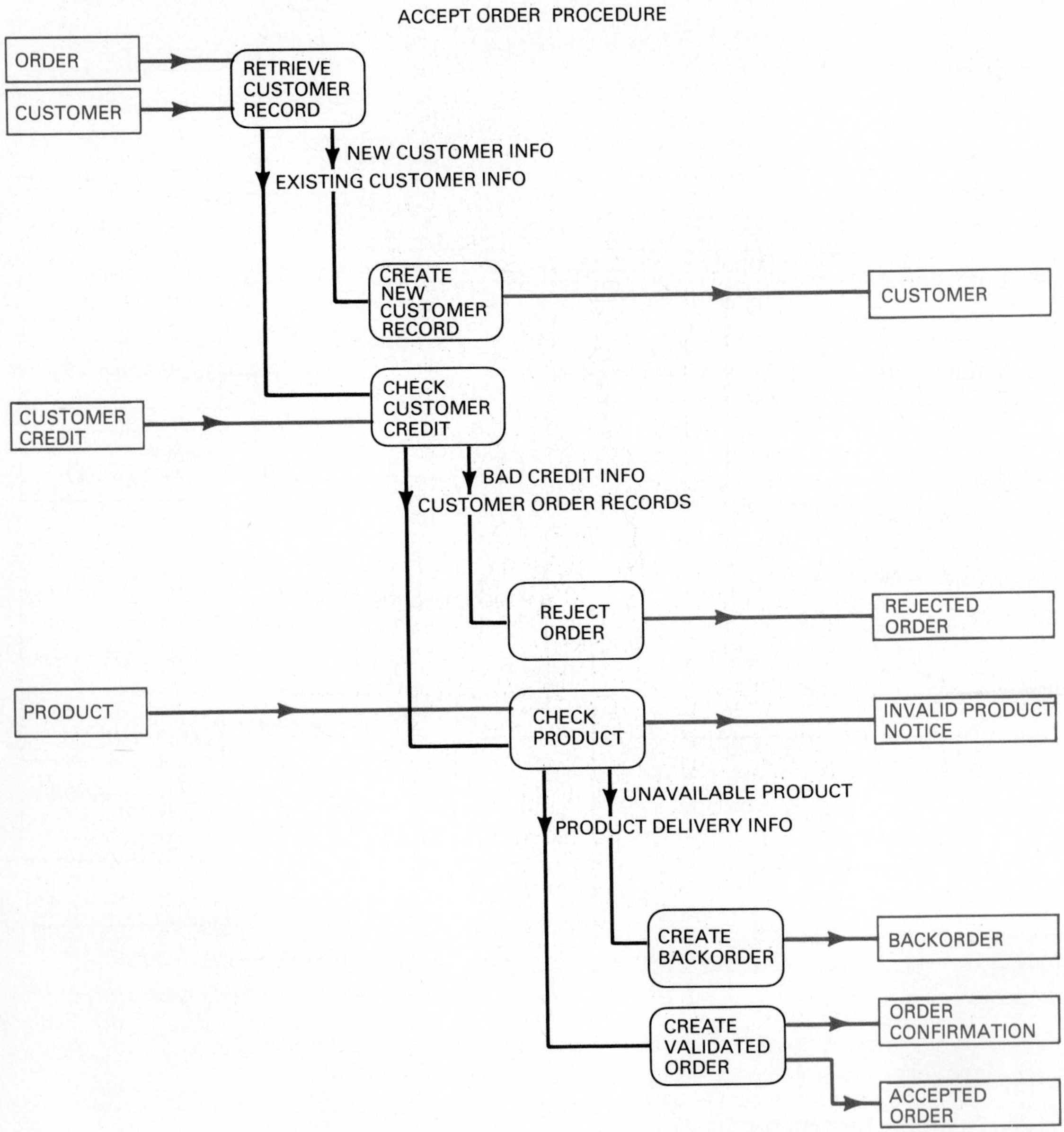

ACCEPT ORDER PROCEDURE

Figure 4.11 The top activity in Fig. 4.10 (ACCEPT ORDER) is expanded here into a more detailed data flow diagram.

showing that each of them can be expanded as a more detailed data flow diagram. The red parts of Figs. 4.10 and 4.11 show the sources and destinations of data—in this case records on the storage units.

SQUARE-CORNERED AND ROUND-CORNERED BOXES

The diagrams used for information engineering data are drawn as square-cornered boxes; activities are drawn as round-cornered boxes. The reader might glance back at Figs. 4.1 through 4.11 and observe the use of square-cornered and round-cornered boxes. Square-cornered boxes are used for entity types, records, data stores, files, and so on. Round-cornered boxes are used for the functions, processes, procedures, and program modules. In rough hand-drawn sketches, activities are sometimes sketched with ellipses because these are easier to draw freehand than most round-cornered boxes.

ADDING DETAIL TO DATA FLOW DIAGRAMS

The procedure blocks on a data flow diagram or dependency diagram need to be expanded into detail. The detail may be shown with an action diagram. The user of an appropriate CASE tool may point to a procedure block and say DISPLAY that block as an action diagram. The data flow diagram and corresponding action diagram may appear on the screen together as shown in Fig. 4.12.

The action diagram window on the right of Fig. 4.12 shows details of procedure VALIDATE CUSTOMER, which is the center block in the data flow diagram on the left on Fig. 4.12. Most action diagrams are much more complex than in this illustration and are scrolled up and down on the screen.

The boxes at the top and bottom of the action diagram contain the data input to and output from the action diagram. These must correspond exactly to the inputs to and outputs from the equivalent procedure on the data flow diagram (as they do in Fig. 4.12). The input and output boxes of the action diagram were probably generated from the data flow diagram. The action diagram may be expanded into substantial detail and code generated from it.

A dependency diagram or data flow diagram is useful to show high-level dependencies among processes or procedures. It is less useful for showing the detail of one procedure. Figure 4.13 shows the same procedure as Fig. 4.11 represented as an action diagram. The square-cornered boxes on the action diagram show data records read, updated, or created. Figure 4.13 has more detail than the data flow diagram of Fig. 4.11 and is an appropriate representation for code generation.

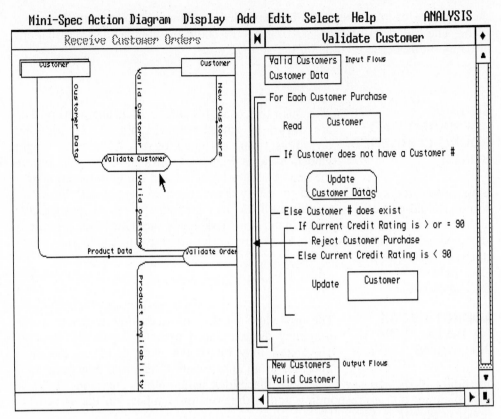

Figure 4.12   Action diagram window showing details of a block on a data flow diagram. The top and bottom of the action diagram indicate the input data and output data. These must correspond to the information on the data flow diagram (Courtesy of KnowledgeWare.)

DECISION TREES   Certain types of logic are best represented with decision trees or decision tables [1]. Figure 4.14 shows a decision tree for computing ORDER DISCOUNT PERCENTAGE. Decision trees or tables can be converted automatically to action diagrams or to code modules.

DIALOG STRUCTURES   Workstation dialogs often use hierarchical menus. Because action diagrams represent hierarchies, they are useful for designing such dialog structures, as shown in Fig. 4.15. Where dialogs are not hierarchical a different type of diagram can show the possible dialog interactions [1]. The diagram in Fig. 4.16

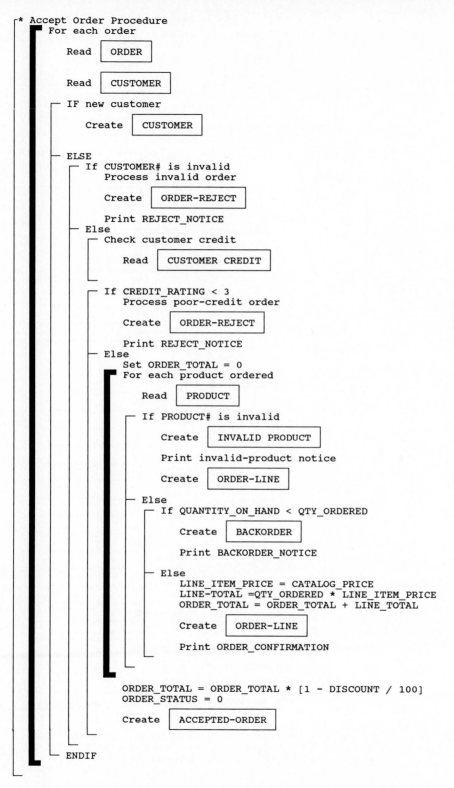

```
* Accept Order Procedure
    For each order

        Read    ┌─────────────┐
                │   ORDER     │
                └─────────────┘

        Read    ┌─────────────┐
                │  CUSTOMER   │
                └─────────────┘
    IF new customer

        Create  ┌─────────────┐
                │  CUSTOMER   │
                └─────────────┘

    ELSE
        If CUSTOMER# is invalid
           Process invalid order

            Create  ┌───────────────┐
                    │ ORDER-REJECT  │
                    └───────────────┘

            Print REJECT_NOTICE
        Else
            Check customer credit

                Read    ┌───────────────────┐
                        │ CUSTOMER CREDIT   │
                        └───────────────────┘


        If CREDIT_RATING < 3
           Process poor-credit order

            Create  ┌───────────────┐
                    │ ORDER-REJECT  │
                    └───────────────┘

            Print REJECT_NOTICE
        Else
            Set ORDER_TOTAL = 0
            For each product ordered

                Read    ┌─────────────┐
                        │  PRODUCT    │
                        └─────────────┘

                If PRODUCT# is invalid

                    Create  ┌───────────────────┐
                            │ INVALID PRODUCT   │
                            └───────────────────┘

                    Print invalid-product notice

                    Create  ┌───────────────┐
                            │  ORDER-LINE   │
                            └───────────────┘

                Else
                    If QUANTITY_ON_HAND < QTY_ORDERED

                        Create  ┌───────────────┐
                                │  BACKORDER    │
                                └───────────────┘

                        Print BACKORDER_NOTICE

                    Else
                        LINE_ITEM_PRICE = CATALOG_PRICE
                        LINE-TOTAL =QTY_ORDERED * LINE_ITEM_PRICE
                        ORDER_TOTAL = ORDER_TOTAL + LINE_TOTAL

                        Create  ┌───────────────┐
                                │  ORDER-LINE   │
                                └───────────────┘

                        Print ORDER_CONFIRMATION


            ORDER_TOTAL = ORDER_TOTAL * [1 - DISCOUNT / 100]
            ORDER_STATUS = 0

            Create  ┌─────────────────────┐
                    │  ACCEPTED-ORDER     │
                    └─────────────────────┘

    ENDIF
```

Figure 4.13 The designer who created the ACCEPT ORDER procedure in
Fig. 4.11 takes it into more detail here with an action diagram.

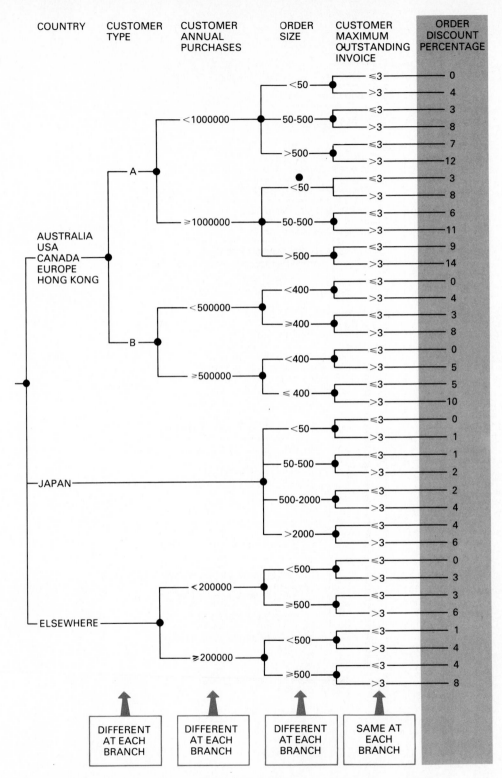

Figure 4.14 A decision tree in which branches are identical for some fields and different for others.

```
┌─ Opening menu
│   ┌─ 1. Customer Orders
│   │      1. Enter Customer Order
│   │      2. Get Next Customer
│   │      3. Get Customer by Name
│   └─     4. Get Customer by Number
│   ┌─ 2. Decorator Orders
│   │      1. Enter Decorator Order
│   │      2. Get Next Decorator
│   │      3. Get Decorator by Name
│   └─     4. Get Decorator by Number
│   ┌─ 3. Update Files
│   │   ┌─ 1. Update Master files
│   │   │      1. Update Customer Master File
│   │   └─     2. Update Decorator Master File
│   │
│   │      2. Initialize date
│   │      3. Correct Customer Invoice
│   └─     4. Correct Decorator Bill
│   ┌─ 4. Inquiry: Customers
│   │      1. Inquiry: Customer Status
│   │   ┌─ 2. Inquiry: Customer Order History
│   │   │      1. Last Three Months
│   │   │      2. Last Year
│   │   └─     3. Last Three Years
│   │
│   │      3. Inquiry: Specific Customer Orders
│   └─     4. Inquiry: Unpaid Invoices
│   ┌─ 5. Inquiry: Decorators
│   │      1. Inquiry: Decorator Status
│   │   ┌─ 2. Inquiry: Decorator History
│   │   │      1. Last Three Months
│   │   │      2. Last Year
│   │   └─     3. Last Three Years
│   │
│   │      3. Inquiry: Specific Decorator Orders
│   └─     4. Inquiry: Unpaid bills
│   ┌─ 6. Invoice Customers
│   │      1. Create Invoice
│   │      2. Send Invoice
│   │      3. Correct Customer Invoice
│   └─     4. Print Invoice Summary
│   ┌─ 7. Pay Decorators
│   │      1. Verify Decorator Bill
│   │      2. Correct Decorator Bill
│   │      3. Pay Decorator Bill
└── └─     4. Inquiry: Unpaid bills
```

Figure 4.15   A hierarchical dialog structure represented as an action diagram.

uses horizontal lines to represent screens and vertical lines to represent possible jumps between screens as the user interacts with the system. The designer might point to any of the horizontal lines and display the screen layout. A screen-painter tool should be connected to a dialog design tool.

DATA STRUCTURE DIAGRAM

During business area analysis, data are designed with entity-relationship diagrams and normalized data structures. In the system design phase an extract from this *data model* is represented with the structure of the chosen database management system, (that is, in an IMS (information management system) structure, IDMS (information database management system) structure, or relational structure, or possibly a file structure, for example, VSAM (virtual storage access method). A data structure diagram is used for this. Figure 4.17 illustrates one.

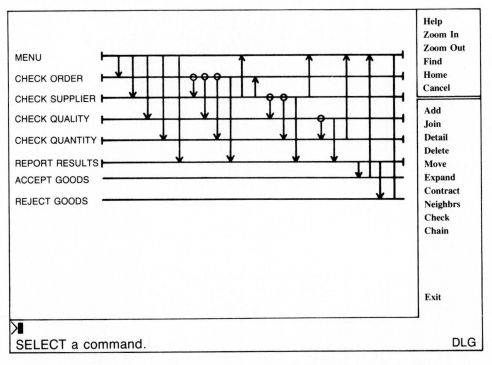

Figure 4.16 A dialog flow diagram from the Information Engineering Facility™ of Texas Instruments. The horizontal lines represent screen types; the vertical lines represent transitions among the screens [2].

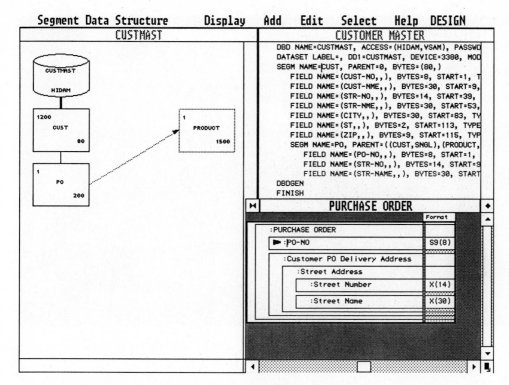

Figure 4.17 Data structure diagram for IMS. This is derived using the data model, and is used to generate the database description code. (From the KnowledgeWare tool set [3].)

The tool kit should be able to generate the database description directly from the diagrammatic representation, for example, generate the IMS, PSBs (program specification blocks), and DBDs (database description code).

PROGRAM STRUCTURE

A diagram showing program structure must be able to represent loops, conditions, multiway selection structures, escapes, database accesses, subroutine calls, and nested routines. Action diagram editors were designed for this purpose. The brackets and text of the action diagram can be set to executable code. This code may be produced by a generator.

Figure 4.18 shows COBOL in action diagram format on the screen of the IEF (Information Engineering Facility).

Boxes 4.1, 4.2, and 4.3 show executable code in action diagram format written in the languages C, PL/I, and the fourth-generation language IDEAL.

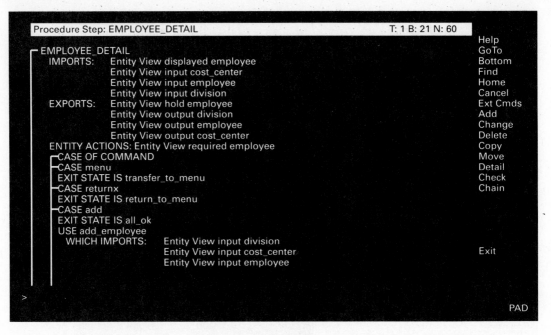

Figure 4.18   Action diagram of COBOL code from Texas Instruments [2].

Using an action diagram editor code ensures good structuring of code, makes the structure visible, and makes all structures appear like those in the programmers' training courses.

MATRICES

Matrices are used in information engineering to show the relationship among objects. They are used in planning, for example, to show which projects relate to goals, problems, critical success factors or strategic opportunities. They are used in business area analysis to show which entity types are used by which processes. Figure 4.19 shows a matrix, which is scrollable on the workbench screen, mapping entity types against business functions.

THE MEANING OF THE DIAGRAMS

As stressed earlier, a CASE tool should store the *meaning* of the diagrams and be able to process that meaning to detect errors, inconsistencies, and clues that something might be wrong. A good CASE tool does not store the pictures; it stores the meaning of the pictures. The tool should be an expert system which applies automated reasoning to the diagrammatic input, correlating the meaning

Key: (Enter highest classification only)

C = CREATE
D = DELETE
U = UPDATE
R = READ ONLY

ENTITY TYPES / BUSINESS FUNCTIONS

ENTITY TYPES	GOVERNMENT_CONTRACTS	PURHCASING	RECEIVING	WAREHOUSING	LEGAL_SERVICES	GENERAL_ACCOUNTING	COST_ACCOUNTING	ORDER_PROCESSING	SHIPPING	PACKING	MATERIAL_REQUIREMENTS	RELEASE_PLANNING	FINITE_CAPACITY_SCHEDU	FACTORY_MONITORING	METHODS_ENGINEERING	FACILITIES_MAINTENANC	BASIC_RESEARCH	PRODUCT_DESIGN	SCRAP_DISPOSAL	EMPLOYEE_RECORDS_MAIN	PAYROLL_AND_BENEFITS	EMPLOYEE_TRAINING	SECURITY	TRANSPORTATION_PLANNI	FLEET_MANAGEMENT	FLEET_ACQUISITION	FLEET_MAINTENANCE	VEHICLE_DISPOSAL
SALES ORDER						R	R	C	U	U	R	R	R				R							R	R			
CUSTOMER							U	R	R								R							R				
CONTRACT	C																R											
SHIPMENT			C																					R				
SUPPLIER	R	R	U		R	R											R							R				
PURCHASE ORDER						R	R				R	R	R				R						R					
PRODUCT		R	R			R		R	R	R	R	R	R				R	C	R					R				
RAW_MATERIAL		U	U								U						R											
CHEMICAL		U	U								U						R											
SHOP_SUPPLY		C									R	R																
WORK_ORDER											R	C	U	R														
WAREHOUSE			R	C																U								
BIN			U	C						R										U								
SUPPLIER_INVOICE	U	C			R	U																						
LEDGER_ENTRY						C	C																					
PRODUCT_INVENTORY		R	U	R				U		U	R	R								U								

Border menu: Files · Save · Print · Mode · Horiz · Vert · Cells · Edit · Add · Move · Delete · Edit · Screen · Home · End · Find · Utilities · Cluster · Stats · Sort · Erase · Tools · Quit

> **Business Function/Entity   Type Usage**

Select Mode from Border Menu

Figure 4.19   A matrix mapping entity-types and business functions [2].

of different types of diagrams. The meaning of the diagrams resides in an encyclopedia which applies automated reasoning to this knowledge (Fig. 4.20).

INTEGRATION OF THE DIAGRAMS

An information engineering tool kit should have a *knowledge coordinator* that can correlate the diagrammatic information across the entire area of information engineering. This coordination is not done in one large gulp but in small steps each time new knowledge is added to the encyclopedia.

A major advantage of computerized tools is that the machine can coordinate the information on multiple diagrams across the entire design span; the human brain cannot do that with accuracy.

Good system design starts by identifying the entity types, creating an entity-relationship diagram, and normalizing the data. The data model is used in designing the procedures with data flow diagrams, decision trees, screen and report designs, dialog flow diagrams, and action diagrams. Figure 4.21 indicates the progression of diagrams that are used for this.

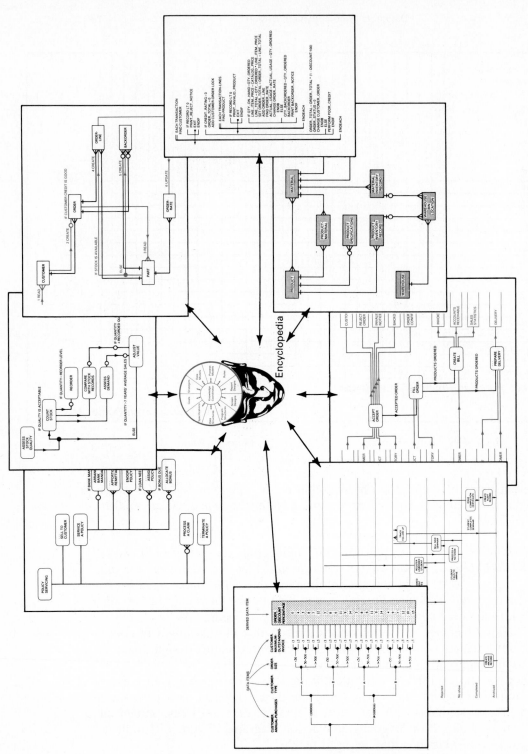

Figure 4.20 The meaning of the diagrams is stored in an encyclopedia. Using the encyclopedia, diagrams may be generated or one type of diagram may be converted into another. The encyclopedia often contains more detail than are displayed on a diagram. The additional detail may be displayed by pointing to an icon and requesting more detail.

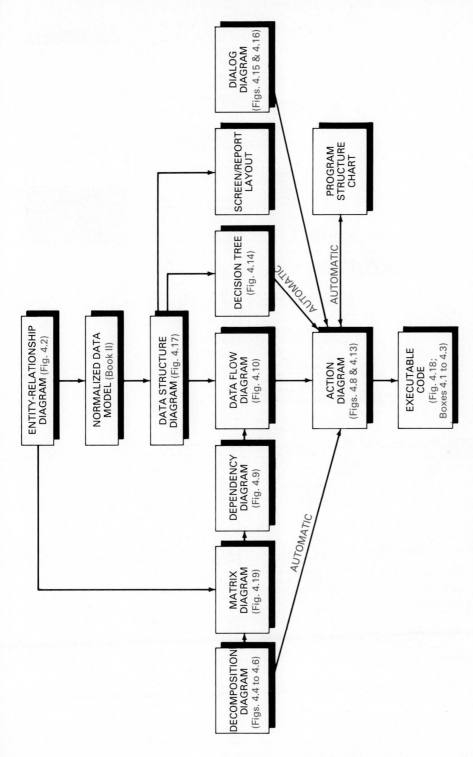

Figure 4.21 The progression of diagrams that are used for information engineering. The meaning represented by these diagrams needs to be fully integrated in the encyclopedia. Details are entered into windows. The progression leads to code generation.

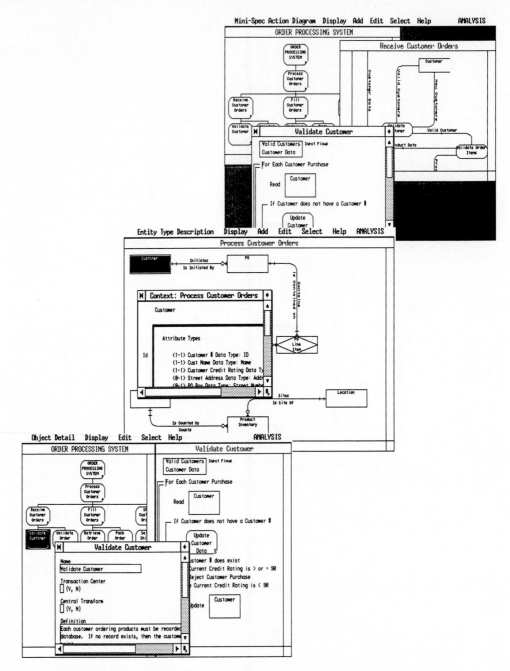

Figure 4.22 All of these diagrams are parts of one hyperdiagram. They are parts of a logically consistent whole. The analyst may examine more information about this hyperdiagram by selecting blocks (or links between blocks) and displaying them in detail windows. The windows can be scrolled or expanded to show more detail than here. The computer enforces consistency within the hyperdiagram and among hyperdiagrams.

HYPERDIAGRAM   As emphasized earlier, the diagrams are not isolated. There are many logical linkages among the diagrams. In combination the diagrams of an I-CASE form a *hyperdiagram* (Book I). When something is changed on one diagram, the change must be *automatically* reflected in other diagrams.

Each diagram is one of many manifestations of a more complex set of information. When that information is changed and diagrams are displayed, multiple different diagrams may reflect the change.

Figure 4.22 shows a set of diagrams, in windows of an IE tool set, which comprise one analyst's work—one hyperview. The separate diagrams are all logically interlinked and hence consistent.

GOOD   Because diagrams are the basis of analysis and design
DIAGRAMMING   in IE, it is essential that good diagramming tech-
TECHNIQUES   niques be used. Box 4.4 summarizes characteristics
                     that are desirable in diagramming techniques.

We have commented that an IS organization committed to IE should adopt diagramming standards. Box 4.5 states the principles of diagramming standards. The diagramming techniques should be a corporatewide standard, firmly adhered to.

REFERENCES

1. James Martin, *Recommended Diagramming Standards for Analysts and Programmers: A Basis for Automation* (Englewood Cliffs, NJ: Prentice Hall, 1987).

2. Information Engineering Facility™, copyright © 1988 Texas Instruments Incorporated, Plano, TX.

3. Knowledgeware, Inc., Atlanta, GA.

BOX 4.1   Action diagram of executable code written in C.

```
*   /* Executable Section */
    switch (adtab[curline].action){

    case ACT_JUNK:
    case ACT_CASE:
    case ACT_EXIT:
        itfrst = curline;
        itnext = curline +1;
        break;

    case ACT_BEGL:
    case ACT_BEGB:
        adlevel = 1;
        itfrst = curline;
        for (itnext = curline+1; itnext <= numadtab & adlevel >0; it6next++){

            switch (adtab[itnext].action) {
            case ACT_BEGL:
            case ACT_BEGB:
                adlevel++;
                break;
            case ACT_END:
                adlevel--;
                }
            }
        if (adlevel > 0)
            aborts ("ad: ? no matching end ??");

        break;

    default:
        itfirst = numadtab;
        itnext = numadtab;
        beep();
        }
    itdel = itnext - itfirst;
    for (itab = itfirst; itab < numadtab; itab++) {
        adtab[itab].action = adtab[itab+itdel].action;
        adtab[itab].count  = adtab[itab+itdel].count;
        adtab[itab].text   = adtab[itab+itdel].text;
        }
    numadtab -= itdel;
    if (curline > numadtab)
        curline = numadtab;

    showbuffer ();
```

BOX 4.2   Action diagram of executable code in the language PL/I.

```
SUBSCRIPTION_SYSTEM: PROCEDURE OPTIONS (MAIN);
* /*
    SUBSCRIPTION SYSTEM TRANSACTION PROCESSING
*/

* /* Variable Declarations */

    %DECLARE YES            CHARACTER;   %YES      = '''1''B';
    %DECLARE NO             CHARACTER;   %NO       = '''0''B';
    %DECLARE ERROR          CHARACTER;   %ERROR    = '''1''B';
    %DECLARE NO_ERROR       CHARACTER;   %NO_ERROR = '''0''B';

    DECLARE
        DATA_FILE               FILE SEQUENTIAL RECORD,
        EOF_DATA_FILE           BIT(1) INITIAL (NO),
        RC                      BIT(1),
        RC1                     BIT(1),
        RC2                     BIT(1),
        RC3                     BIT(1),
        RC4                     BIT(1),
        01 TRANSACTION,
            02 TYPE             CHARACTER(15),
            02 STATUS           BIT(1),
            02 CANCELLATION     BIT(1),
            02 CUSTOMER,
                03 NAME         CHARACTER(30),
                03 ADDRESS,
                    04 STREET   CHARACTER(30),
                    04 CITY     CHARACTER(30),
                    04 STATE    CHARACTER(30),
                    04 ZIP_CODE CHARACTER(9),


            02 TERMS (10)       CHARACTER(80),
            02 PAYMENT          CHARACTER(80);


ON ENDFILE (DATA_FILE)
    EOF_DATA_FILE = YES;

OPEN FILE (DATA_FILE);
DO WHILE (^EOF_DATA_FILE);

    /* GET TRANSACTION */
    READ FILE (DATA_FILE) INTO (TRANSACTION);

    /* VALIDATE TRANSACTION */
    CALL CHECK_FORMAT (TRANSACTION, RC);
    IF RC = ERROR THEN
        CALL PROCESS_ERROR (TRANSACTION, RC, NO, NO, NO, NO);
```

BOX 4.2   *(Continued)*

```
SELECT;
WHEN (TRANSACTION.TYPE = 'NEW') DO;
    CANCELLATION = NO;
    CALL CHECK_NAME_ADDRESS (CUSTOMER, RC1);
    CALL CHECK_ZIP_CODE (ZIP_CODE, RC2);
    CALL CHECK_TERMS (TERMS, RC3);
    CALL CHECK_PAYMENT (PAYMENT, RC4);
    IF (RC1 | RC2 | RC3 | RC4) = ERROR THEN
        STATUS = ERROR;
    ELSE
        STATUS = NO_ERROR;

    END;
WHEN (TRANSACTION.TYPE = 'RENEWAL') DO;
    CANCELLATION = NO;
    RC1 = NO_ERROR;
    RC2 = NO_ERROR;
    CALL CHECK_TERMS (TERMS,RC3);
    CALL CHECK_PAYMENT (PAYMENT, RC4);
    IF (RC3 | RC4) = ERROR THEN
        STATUS = ERROR;
    ELSE
        STATUS = NO_ERROR;

    END;
WHEN (TRANSACTION.TYPE = 'CANCELLATION') DO;
    STATUS = NO_ERROR;
    CANCELLATION = NO;
    END;
END;

/* PROCESS VALID TRANSACTION */
IF STATUS = NO_ERROR THEN
    SELECT;
    WHEN (TRANSACTION.TYPE = 'NEW')
        CALL NEW_SUBSCRIPTION (TRANSACTION);
    WHEN (TRANSACTION.TYPE = 'RENEWAL')
        CALL SUBSCRIPTION_RENEWAL (TRANSACTION);
    WHEN (TRANSACTION.TYPE = 'CANCELLATION')
        CALL SUBSCRIPTION_CANCELLATION (TRANSACTION);
    END;
ELSE
    IF STATUS = ERROR THEN
        CALL PROCESS_ERROR (TRANSACTION, NO, RC1, RC2, RC3, RC4);

/* GET NEXT TRANSACTION */
READ FILE (DATA_FILE) INTO (TRANSACTION);
END;

END SUBSCRIPTION_SYSTEM;
```

BOX 4.3   Action diagram of executable code written in the fourth-generation language IDEAL, from ADR.

```
┌─ <<ORDER PROCESSING>> PROC
│     EACH CUSTOMER
│  ┌─ IF CUSTOMER# INVALID
│  │     PRINT REJECT NOTICE
« ├──── END PROC
│  └─ END IF
│  ┌─ IF CREDIT_RATING > 3
│  │     WRITE CUSTOMER ORDER
│  │     SET ORDER_TOTAL = 0
│  │     LOOP WHILE EACH PRODUCT
│  │     ┌─ IF PRODUCT# INVALID
│  │     │     PRINT ERROR MESSAGE
« │     ├──── END PROC
│  │     └─ END IF
│  │     ┌─ IF QUANTITY_ON_HAND > 0
│  │     │     SET LINE_ITEM_PRICE = CATALOG_PRICE
│  │     │     SET LINE-TOTAL =QTY_ORDERED * LINE_ITEM_PRICE
│  │     │     SET ORDER_TOTAL = ORDER_TOTAL + LINE_TOTAL
│  │     │     WRITE ORDER_LINE
│  │     │     EACH ORDER_RATE
│  │     │     SET ACTUAL_USAGE = ACTUAL_USAGE + QTY_ORDERED
│  │     │     WRITE ORDER_RATE
│  │     ├─ ELSE
│  │     │     WRITE BACKORDER
│  │     │     PRINT BACKORDER_NOTICE
│  │     └─ END IF
│  │     END LOOP
│  │     SET ORDER_TOTAL = ORDER_TOTAL * [1 - DISCOUNT / 100]
│  │     SET ORDER_STATUS = 0
│  │     WRITE CUSTOMER_ORDER
│  ├─ ELSE
│  │     CALL POOR_CREDIT
│  └─ END IF
└─ END PROC
```

BOX 4.4   Summary of good diagramming techniques

Good diagramming techniques should be all of the following.

An Aid to Clear Thinking

Good diagrams help people to understand complex ideas. A diagramming notation should be designed to help thinking and communication and for computer-aided thinking. The diagrams should be an aid to teaching computer methods.

Easy to Understand

The diagrams should use constructs that are obvious in meaning and as familiar as possible. They should avoid mnemonics and symbols that are not explained on the diagram or with immediately available keys.

An Aid to End-User Communication

End users should be able to learn to read, critique, and draw the diagrams quickly, so that the diagrams form a good basis for communication between users and data processing professionals.

Meaningful

It is the meaning rather than the graphic image that is valuable. The meaning should be encoded in an encyclopedia from which one or more types of diagrams can be generated. The encyclopedia will often store more information than is visible on the screen. It may be displayed by pointing to an icon and saying SHOW.

A Basis for Program Code Generation

It should be possible to generate code from the diagrams along with tools such as dictionaries, report formatters, and screen pointers. To achieve this, the diagrams must be more complete and rigorous than the diagrams of the first generation of structured techniques.

(Continued)

BOX 4.4   *(Continued)*

Printable on Normal-Sized Paper

Wall charts of vast size are to be avoided because they inhibit change and portability. Diagrams should be subdividable into normal-sized pages. They may be designed to spread out vertically on fan-fold paper.

Subsettable

Complex diagrams should be subsettable so that they can be subdivided into easy-to-understand components. The user should be able to extract easy-to-use subsets at a computer screen.

Navigable

The user should be able to navigate easily around complex diagrams, changing their representation, if necessary, with the techniques, such as PAGE, SCROLL, ZOOM, ZOOC, NEST, EXPAND, and SHOW, listed in Box 3.1.

Designed for Minimum Searching

A user should be able to find information with as little searching as possible. Closely related information should be close together on the diagram to minimize page turning, interscreen navigation, and the following of lengthy lines.

Decomposable into Detail

A simple overview diagram should be decomposable into successively finer levels of detail. Where possible, the detail diagram should be of the same form as the higher-level diagram. The decomposition may proceed until appropriately diagrammed program code is reached.

Designed for Screen Manipulation

The diagrams should be designed to be manipulated easily and powerfully on a workstation screen (preferably a personal computer).

BOX 4.4 *(Continued)*

Designed for Computer-Aided Thinking

A computer can give a designer much help in stepping through the design, using data correctly, using library functions, using design verification, and so on. The computer-aided design technique should help the designer's thinking as much as possible.

Easy to Draw by Hand

Automation will not completely replace sheets of paper. The diagramming technique should facilitate quick sketching by hand with a template. Machine-drawn versions of the diagrams may improve on the hand-drawn versions by using color, shading, library techniques, motion, and computer manipulation.

Drawable on Cheap Printers

The diagrams should be drawable with desktop dot-matrix printers. A variant of the diagrams should be printable with the ASCII character set so that a mainframe line printer can print them. The ASCII variant may be relatively crude and may modify some of the conventions slightly. The need for ASCII printing should not prevent the use of well-human-factored icons and style on dot-matrix printers.

Designed with Minimum Types of Symbols

The number of graphic symbols a user must understand should be minimized. Each underlying idea should be represented by a single symbol, not by different symbols in different places. (There may have to be variations of a symbol to suit different printers or display devices.)

Assertive

The presence of a graphic symbol should denote the presence of some knowledge; the absence of the symbol should denote the lack of that knowledge. For example, the absence of a mark on a line should not

BOX 4.4 *(Continued)*

denote meaning about that line (such as a one-to-one association between the blocks linked by the line). Following this principle permits
a type of subsetting: producing a diagram in which some symbols are
omitted in order to highlight others or to avoid clutter or to produce
an overview diagram.

Based on Clear Visual Logic

There is a visual logic that makes some ways of depicting an idea
better than others. Diagrams should make abstract ideas concrete by
using images and spatial sense to capture ideas as logically as possible. For example, arrows should represent flow or sequence, as this
is intuitively clear, but a different symbol should represent cardinality.

Logical, Not Decorative

The use of decoration that does not enhance visual logic should be
avoided. The instinct to be artistic must be suppressed and replaced
with an urge to maximize clarity.

Readable Using English
(Human Language) Sentences

The symbols on a link or bracket should translate as directly as possible into a clear human language sentence, for example,

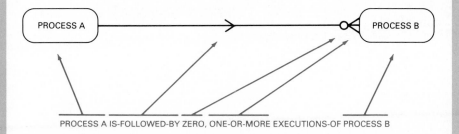

PROCESS A IS-FOLLOWED-BY ZERO, ONE-OR-MORE EXECUTIONS-OF PROCESS B

BOX 4.4 *(Continued)*

Able to Support Different Ways of Thinking with Consistent Symbols

Different styles of diagram are appropriate for different aspects of system design. Decision trees are appropriate for certain situations, data flow diagrams for others, decomposition diagrams for others, and so on. A common family of symbols should support the different ways of thinking about systems, data, and logic.

Automatically Convertible

It is sometimes useful to convert one style of representation (one view of the world) into another. For example, decision trees, dependency diagrams, or data navigation diagrams can be converted to action diagrams. The diagramming technique should be designed so that the conversion can be done by computer. The user may employ windows on a workstation screen showing the alternate representations. Different types of representations often need to be linked to represent an overall system design.

Methodologically Sound

Diagramming techniques are a visual representation of underlying methodologies. The methodologies need to be sound and to represent the most useful concepts of data analysis, structured techniques, and code generation.

BOX 4.5   Diagramming standards

1. Principals of diagramming standards

- IS professionals and end users should be provided with a set of diagramming techniques which are aids to clear thinking about different aspects of planning, analysis, design, and programming.
- The separate types of diagrams should use the minimum number of icons.
- They should be as easy to learn as possible.
- Conversion between diagrams should be automated whenever possible.
- The diagramming techniques should be a corporatewide standard, firmly adhered to.

2. Automation of diagramming

- The diagrams should be the basis of computer-aided planning, analysis, design, and construction, using I-CASE tools.
- Higher-level design diagrams should convert automatically to action diagrams where relevant. Action diagrams can be decomposed into executable code.
- The family of diagrams should be a basis for code generation.
- The diagrams should be easy to change and file at the computer screen.
- The diagrams should relate to data models.
- The diagrams convey *meaning* which is stored in a system encyclopedia. The encyclopedia often stores more detail than is shown on any one screen.
- The diagrams and associated text windows in the encyclopedia should be the system documentation.

PART **II** MEETING THE NEEDS OF THE END
USER MORE DIRECTLY

5 USER-ORIENTED DEVELOPMENT TECHNIQUES

INTRODUCTION　　　The traditional methods of data processing have often not met the needs of end users very effectively. They have been successful for building paper-processing applications such as payroll, order processing, billing, accounts receivable, and so on, but have *not* succeeded well with information systems for top management, decision-support systems, and systems with subtle end-user interactions. They work well with batch processing but often work poorly with the interactive mission-critical systems which are more vital to today's enterprise. Part II of this book is concerned with how complex and subtle end-user needs can be met better. This can only be done by harnessing the knowledge of creative end-users into the design process. A variety of techniques are used for this.

Given the vital importance of computing in today's enterprises and the swing from back-office paperwork applications to mission-critical applications which affect the efficiency of the basic processes of production and selling, it is urgent that the methods described in this section be made to work well.

MISREPRESENTATION OF USER NEEDS　　　Systems built with traditional techniques take a long time to develop and usually prove to be only partially satisfactory to end users. The costs of unsatisfactory design are very high. Studies by IBM, ITT, TRW, Mitre Corp., and other organizations show that more than half of the errors in applications delivered to users are there because of incorrect representation of the users' needs in specifications and design. Whereas errors in coding are not too expensive to correct, errors in specifications and design are very expensive because part of the system has to be rebuilt.

The expense of unsatisfactory design results from traditional systems analysis methodologies in which IS* analysts create thick binders of specifications which they ask end users to read. The users usually do not understand in detail the ramifications of the design. It is only when they see the resulting system that their minds go to work on ideas about what they would really have liked the system to do. The delivered system often does not link adequately to other systems and this causes large expenses for modification or "maintenance."

It is a common experience that when a system is cut over after years of development effort the users say it is not what they want. In the worst cases they try it for a time and then give up. A common reaction to this unfortunate situation has been to write the specifications in much greater detail before doing technical design and programming. This has often resulted in voluminous documentation but has not solved the problem.

PROBLEMS WITH THE SPECIFICATION PROCESS

When the traditional systems analyst and potential end users first come face to face they come from widely different cultures. It is rather like a Victorian missionary first entering an African village. However, they have to produce a very precise document—the specification of requirements.

The missionary is steeped in computer terminology and analysis methods. The villagers' culture is accounting, chemical engineering, or production control—cultures with a complex folklore. They use different languages. Somehow they are supposed to communicate with no ambiguities or misunderstandings. If the missionary is skillful at communicating and can offer the villagers a promise of better things, they can begin to learn each other's conceptual framework. However there is no way that either can understand the nuances and subtleties of the other's way of thinking.

In an attempt to clarify and formalize the process, specifications are written for the applications which must be programmed. This can take person-years to complete and results in a set of documents that are inches or even feet thick. For his own protection the missionary needs the villagers to sign this document.

The specification document is extremely important in the traditional system development lifecycle. It guides programmers and is supposed to answer numerous questions that arise about the system. In practice there are serious problems with it.

- It is often so long and boring that key managers do not read it. They read the summary.
- It lacks precision. It cannot be converted into computer code without many assumptions and interpretations.
- It is often ambiguous, inconsistent, and incomplete.

*The term IS is used throughout the book to refer to the Information Systems Department.

- It is often misinterpreted by both sides. Often its readers *think* they understand it but in fact do not.

- Sometimes much trivia and motherhood is added to the document. Both sides understand this. It increases the comfort level, but has zero value.

- The specification document is not designed for successive refinement as the problems become better understood. It is intended to be a complete document which users sign.

USER SIGN-OFF

The users are coerced to sign-off on the specification document. They know that until they do that the detailed design and programming will not begin. IS hopes that the need to sign-off will encourage the users to check the document very carefully and find any errors before programming starts.

The sign-off is invariably a moment of apprehension on both sides. The users are not sure whether it is really what they want. They often feel that their views on the system are changing as they learn and think more about it. Part way up a learning curve the specifications are *frozen*. It is important in the traditional development cycle to *freeze* the specifications when programming begins. IS is apprehensive because they are not sure that they understand all the users' needs. They are about to put much effort into the implementation and any imperfections in the specifications will prove expensive.

BUGS

Not surprisingly, the specification document contains errors.

In most installations there are more bugs in specifications than in program coding. In one typical case a large corporation found that 64 percent of its bugs were in requirements analysis and design—in spite of a formal sign-off by the user departments. Even worse, 45 percent of these bugs were discovered after the acceptance tests for the finished applications were completed.

This corporation had a formal development lifecycle and was following its installation standards meticulously. It was using a formal method of structured analysis in creating the specifications.

Figure 5.1 shows the distribution of bugs in a large bank: 56 percent were in the requirements document; 27 percent were in design and most of these were related to misinterpretation of the requirements document [1].

The bugs in the requirements specification are much more time consuming and expensive to correct than those in coding. Figure 5.1 illustrates this. Ninety-five percent of the cost of correcting bugs in this bank was for the bugs in requirements and design. The ratios in Fig. 5.1 are typical of many installations.

Distribution of Bugs

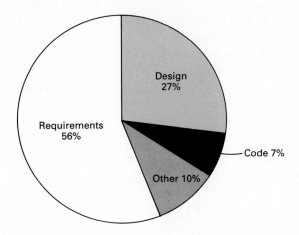

Distribution of Effort
to Fix Bugs

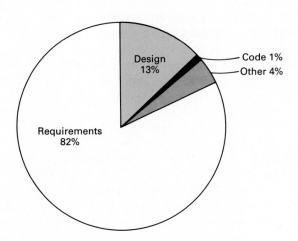

Figure 5.1 In a typical installation with a traditional development methodology more bugs occur in requirements specification and design than in coding. The bugs in requirements specification are much the most expensive ones to correct.

SOLUTIONS TO THE PROBLEM

The following chapters discuss various types of solutions to this problem:

- Prototyping (Chapter 6)
- Joint requirements planning (Chapter 7)
- Joint application design (Chapter 8)

- Timebox methodology (Chapter 9)
- Information Centers (Chapter 10)
- Decision-support systems (Chapters 11 and 12)
- Executive Information Centers (Chapter 13)

All these solutions use different ways to involve the users in the process of specifying their requirements and creating a system design. User-friendly tools and languages are important to this process. User languages are rapidly becoming more powerful and easier to use. This creates the danger that users build subsystems for their own purposes which do not link to the other systems in the enterprise. The situation can rapidly become a Tower of Babel with thousands of isolated noncommunicating systems. Many of these systems have been undocumented, unauditable, and unmaintainable. It is vital, then, to stress that the user-built or user-designed systems fit into the overall framework of information engineering.

Chapter 22 discusses IS organization structures for supporting user-oriented techniques.

USER COMPUTING

The corporation of the future will be highly dependent on knowledge workers being computer literate. Users will be able to extract the information they need from databases, generate reports, use spreadsheets to do better business calculations, and use highly sophisticated decision-support systems for analysis and modeling. They will be able to design their own procedures and create programs for them with tools that are increasingly user-friendly.

There are, however, things which users should not do with computers. Some activities need professional IS skills to do complex design, planning, integration, or optimization. Complex, heavy-duty systems should be built by IS professionals but with strong end-user involvement in requirements analysis and design. The right balance needs to be achieved between user activities and professional IS activities.

DIAGRAMS

We have stressed the importance of diagrams for representing and communicating complex designs. It is critical to select types of diagrams which users can learn to employ easily. These diagrams become a basis for users doing their own design and for users critiquing and adding to the designs of IS professionals.

Users should be taught to understand and use

- Action diagrams.
- Decomposition diagrams.

- Process flow diagrams.
- Entity-relationship diagrams.

Each of these diagram types can be taught easily to end users. The previous chapter gave illustrations of them.

When a graphics workbench is used, diagrams can be clear and uncluttered, but yet contain much detail because the detail can be shown in *windows* which are associated with each block and link on the diagram.

These four diagram types are a basis for clear thinking and can help users to structure their ideas about systems, and, where appropriate, build procedures which are free from spaghettilike entanglements. Experience has shown that end users can be taught how to read (but not necessarily create) these diagrams in a half-day training course, in preparation for a joint application design workshop.

REQUIREMENTS ANALYSIS   Various tools have helped achieve greater efficiency in the system development lifecycle. Coding is speeded up by the use of code generators and fourth-generation languages. Design is speeded up and improved in quality by the use of design automation tools. To achieve high productivity the design automation tool needs to be tightly coupled to a code generator. The design tool collects the information it needs to generate a fully working system. Debugging is drastically reduced when code generators are used. Maintenance is made easier and quicker by the ability to make changes with design workbenches and regenerate code. The absence of messy spaghettilike structures causes a major reduction in maintenance costs.

Figure 5.2 shows the effects of automated tools on the stages of the development lifecycle. Construction of systems with automated tools would still be unsatisfactory if the requirements analysis and specification of what is needed were not done well. Major changes to this aspect of system building have been made with joint requirement planning (Chapter 7), joint application design (Chapter 8), prototyping (Chapter 6), and where appropriate, users building their own systems (Chapters 10, 11, and 12). The construction of information systems for top executives is particularly important and extremely sensitive to analyzing top management information needs with the techniques discussed in Book II.

AUTOMATED COORDINATION   The user-oriented techniques described in the next eight chapters would be valuable with or without information engineering. Without information engineering, however, they are not part of the overall architecture of building a

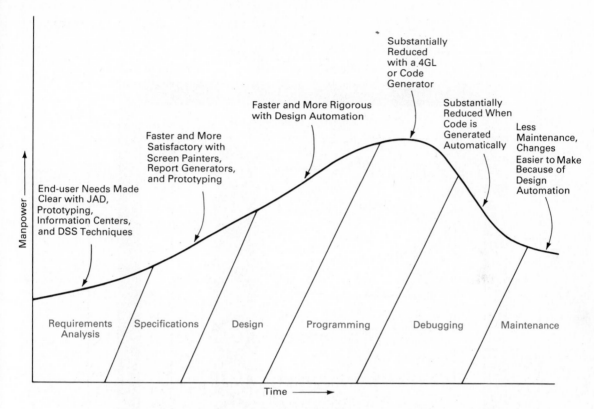

Figure 5.2   The productivity and quality of each stage of the development lifecycle can be improved with user-oriented techniques and automated tools. (From [1].)

computerized enterprise; they result in a mass of isolated user applications, usually with massive redundancy and chaotic data.

    The strategic part of information engineering helps to identify what are the most critical needs for information systems (some of which can be met relatively easily with the techniques discussed in Chapters 10 through 13). The BAA (business area analysis) part of information engineering builds models in an encyclopedia which form a framework into which user-oriented systems will fit. The data and process models speed up and clarify the design of systems. Automated tools linked to the encyclopedia enable systems to be built quickly, with reusable code and code generation. The knowledge coordinator of the encyclopedia ensures that the different parts of a system and different systems of an enterprise mesh together with precision like the separate parts of a clockwork mechanism.

    The development lifecycle should consist of user-oriented techniques meshing together as shown in Fig. 5.3, linked to the IE (information engineer-

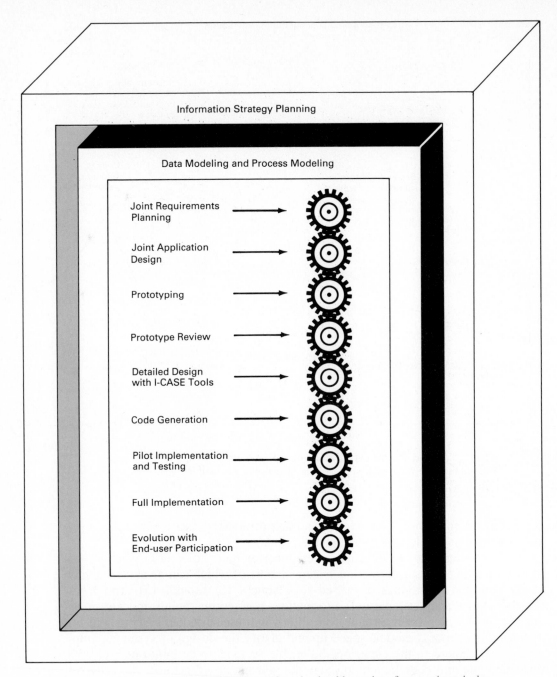

Figure 5.3 The development lifecycle should consist of user-oriented planning, prototyping, and design, fitting into the IE framework of strategic planning, and data and process modeling. The lifecycle for rapid application development (RAD) is discussed in reference [2].

ing) encyclopedia, and fitting within the framework of strategic planning and modeling described in Book II.

To build a computerized enterprise it is necessary to have the user-oriented techniques of the following chapters linked to the precision and coordination capabilities of information engineering.

REFERENCES

1. F. A. Comper, *Project Management for System Quality and Development Productivity,* Guide and Share Application Development Symposium, Proceedings, New York, 1979.

2. James Martin, *Rapid Application Development,* Macmillan, New York, 1990.

6 PROTOTYPING

INTRODUCTION   Prototyping is a technique for building a quick and rough version of a desired system or parts of that system. The prototype illustrates the system to users and designers. It allows them to see flaws and invent ways to improve the system. It serves as a communications vehicle for allowing persons who require the system to review the proposed design. For this purpose it is far more effective than reviewing paper specifications. It has been said that if a picture is worth a thousand words, a prototype is worth a hundred thousand words. But a prototype is fundamentally different from a paper description. It is real and manipulatable. It can be adjusted and modified. The would-be users get a *feel* for what their system will be like. Its flaws are visible and tangible rather than buried in difficult and boring text.

These advantages make a world of difference to system development, but in addition if the right tools are used *prototypes can be created much more quickly than written specifications*.

Prototyping ought to be used in the development of all interactive systems without exception. When a prototype is reviewed seriously by end users, they almost *always* change something. This suggests that if they had not reviewed, the prototype a system would have been built which was less than adequate.

Prototyping is one of the main techniques for user-oriented development. It should be made an integral part of the development lifecycle, as will be described. It does much to solve the problem discussed in the previous chapter of inadequate communication between designers and users, and the high proportion of system flaws that are in the requirements specification (Fig. 5.1). It links into the JAD (joint application design) techniques discussed in the following chapter.

The word "prototyping" suggests an analogy with engineering where prototypes are used extensively. There are, however, fundamental differences between the prototyping of software and the prototyping of machines. In engineering a machine prototype usually takes longer to build and is much more expensive than the ultimate product. The ultimate product may come from a mass-production line and the prototype is needed for testing the product before the production line is built. In software there is no manufacturing production line. Prototyping is only practical if the prototype can be built quickly and cheaply. Unlike production engineering a software prototype is not a full-scale version of the eventual system; it is usually a simplified version that has most of the functions of the working system but not the scale or performance. It lacks such features as security, auditability, recoverability, and ability to handle large volumes, large databases, or many users.

TOOLS FOR PROTOTYPING   Software prototyping became practical when fourth-generation languages and code generators emerged, with which a working model of a system could be built quickly. As these tools improved, it became possible to build and change aspects of systems very quickly so that a prototyping expert can react to users' suggestions and show them modifications in a day or so. Prototyping tools have screen painters, for example, with which a specimen screen can be created quickly. Screens can be linked to form dialogs. Reports can be generated on the fly. Database structures can be created and modified very quickly.

Fourth-generation languages and code generators are designed to create fully working systems rather than merely prototypes. Most of them, however, have facilities for creating prototypes quickly. When such tools are used, the prototype can evolve into the final working system.

The selection of tools is critical to the prototyping process. A decision that should precede all other decisions is whether the tool will be used to build the final system. It is highly advantageous for the prototype to evolve into the final working system. This avoids the work of having to recode and debug in a lower-level language such as COBOL or PL/I, and it greatly lowers the cost of future maintenance because facilities created with the prototyping tool can be changed much more easily than those in COBOL or PL/I.

Commitment to a fourth-generation language or code generator for full-scale development is a much broader decision than the choice of a prototyping language [1]. A major criterion is machine efficiency. Can the tool handle a large enough transaction volume, large enough databases, and a large enough number of simultaneous users? Ideally, the prototyping tool should be an integrated part of an IE CASE tool set which generates and optimizes the final code.

From the prototyping point of view the selection criteria relate mainly to how quick and easy the tool is to use, and how easy the prototype is to modify. The objective of prototyping is to adapt the prototype to the requirements of the users as quickly and flexibly as possible.

As discussed in the following chapter, prototypes should be used in joint application design workshops with end users. Some tools give the ability to generate screens and reports on the fly during the meeting and display them with a projector. This high-speed interaction is desirable. Some tools sold as prototyping tools are far from having such capability.

Box 6.1 lists selection criteria for prototyping tools.

USES OF PROTOTYPING

Prototyping is more valuable with some systems than with others. It is less valuable with batch processing than with interactive systems. Most batch systems, however, produce many reports and these can be prototyped quickly with a report generator. Online data entry may also be prototyped. Prototyping is of limited use in some logic-intensive systems although here partial prototypes may check the human interaction. Users may check portions of the logic to see whether it behaves as they expect.

Prototyping is particularly valuable in the following situations:

- Users are unsure of exactly what they want.
- The system changes a basic business operation.
- An end-user dialog should be tried out with the users to see if it can be improved.
- The functions are subtle, and the users understand them better than the analysts.
- Screen and reports should be checked with management to see if they can be made more useful or easy to use.
- There is scope for user creativity to improve the system. (There usually is.)
- The users do not understand all the impacts of the new system.
- The users have difficulty expressing all the system requirements.
- The prototype may act as a catalyst to elicit alternative ideas.
- The relative merits of alternative solutions need to be explored.

Prototyping is used mainly in the *specification* (or external design) stage of system building. It can also be used in the *project definition* (or requirements analysis) stage. It is part of the *construction stage* where an iterative or prototype-oriented lifecycle is used for construction (Chapters 9 and 21).

During *project definition* partial prototypes can help in checking the desirability of a system before committing funds. It can be used to stimulate user ideas or compare the attractiveness of alternative ideas. It can act as a catalyst to stimulate creative thinking about the system.

During *specification* it is used extensively in the design of screens, dialogs, and reports. It is used to check that the functions of a system are what the users really want. Often prototyping reveals the need to add or enhance functions. It

BOX 6.1   Criteria for selecting a prototyping tool

Characteristics of the Prototyping Tool

A primary decision in selecting a prototyping tool is whether the prototype will evolve into the final working system. If so, a tool is needed
which gives good enough machine performance, database access and network
access to the final system. Otherwise, these characteristics can be
lessened in favor of speed of building and ease of use.

The tool should:
o be interactive.
o be easy to use.
o facilitate quick building of prototypes or partial prototypes.
o make changes quick and easy.
o encourage stepwise refinement.
o support desirable dialog structures, such as scroll bars,
     mouse operation, an action bar, drop-down menus, etc.
o support appropriate database structures.
o support installation standards, such as IBM's SAA (Systems
     Application Architecture).

Ideally, the prototyping tool should be an integrated part of the
IE CASE toolset.

The tool should include the following:
o a versatile screen painter (which can be used very quickly
     in JAD sessions).
o ability to link screens and responses into a dialog.
o a versatile report generator (which can be used very quickly
     in JAD sessions).
o a fourth-generation language or code generator.
o a suitably flexible database management system.
o an integral dictionary.
o facilities for extracting data from files or dates, and
     loading them into the prototype database, OR on-line
     access to other files or databases.

If the prototype will become the final system
  The tool should have:
  o ability to achieve good machine performance (with an
       optimizing compiler).
  o ability to support the database structure of the final system.
  o appropriate networking access.
  o ability to handle a suitably large number of users.
  o ability to handle suitably large databases.
  o ability to handle suitably high traffic volumes.
  o possibly the ability to substitute segments of other languages
       languages (e.g. COBOL or Assembler) into the prototype to
       improve its performance.

  The system the tool generates should have:
  o features for recovery from failures.
  o features for fallback.
  o security features.
  o features for auditability.
  o features for ease of maintenance.

is used in joint application design sessions to help make the discussions more tangible.

During *construction* a tool may be used which permits the prototype to evolve into the final working system. Some construction methodologies, such as that in Chapter 9, are based on prototyping/code–generation tools. This approach to construction is powerful, highly recommended and will probably become the predominant means of building systems.

PARTIAL SYSTEM Some prototyping efforts create a version of a com-
PROTOTYPING plete application. Some tackle only one facet of an
application. Partial system prototyping has proven
particularly valuable on some systems. Often IS (information system) managers
have not considered this approach because they assume that a complete system
prototype is needed. Partial system prototyping can be easier and there may be
less excuse for not using it. Partial prototypes are of a variety of different forms:

- **Dialog prototype.** The prototype simulates the intended terminal interaction. This is probably the most common form of partial prototyping. It allows the end users to see what they will be receiving, play with it, suggest omissions, improve the ease of comprehension, generally react to the dialog, and finally sign off on its development. Various software products can be used as dialog simulators.

    The design of the terminal dialog greatly affects the usability and users' perception of the system. Many systems have been partial failures because of poor terminal dialogs. Amazingly, many systems analysts and programmers are not trained in what constitutes a psychologically effective dialog. They often create dialogs which are muddled, not clean, and which confuse some of the users. It helps to build a prototype dialog which can be tested, criticized, and improved before final implementation.

- **Data entry.** One group of users may perform data entry. The data-entry subsystem may be prototyped and adjusted independently and may be linked to an existing system. Data-entry prototyping may be done to check the speed and accuracy of the data entry. Validity and integrity checks may be tested.

    Some systems have been split into a *front end* and *back office*. The front end is interactive. The back office consists of multiple batch updating runs. The front end may be prototyped independently using software such as MAPPER, FOCUS, RAMIS, or NOMAD. The back office may remain in the form of COBOL programs.

- **Reporting system.** The reports provided to users may be tried out on them before full system implementation. They may be either batch or online. Often many adjustments are made in the reporting subsystem. Report generators may be used.

- **Data system.** A prototype database may be implemented with a small number of records. Users and analysts interact with it, generating reports or displaying information which might be useful to them. This interaction often results in requests for different types of data, new fields, or different ways of organizing the data.

With some prototyping tools, users or analysts have the ability to build their own files, manipulate them, and display information from them. Such tools are used to explore how the users will employ information, and what should be in the database.

- **Calculations and logic.** Sometimes the logic of an application, or the calculations, are complex. Actuaries, engineers, investment analysts, or other such users may use a language such as APL or JAVELIN to build examples of the computations they need. These may then be incorporated into larger systems, perhaps linked to other applications, to databases, or to many terminals. The users may employ their calculation prototypes to check the accuracy of the results.

- **Application package.** An application package may be tried out with a small group of uses to determine whether it is satisfactory. The need for various modifications may become clear. These are tried out before the package is linked to other applications or put into volume use.

- **Concept.** Sometimes the concept of an application is in question. It needs testing and refining before too much money is spent on building the system. The test may be done with a quick-to-implement data management system. Standard data-entry screens and standard report formats may be used so that the concepts may be tested and refined without too much work. Later, application-specific reports or screens may be built.

DIFFERENT HARDWARE

Sometimes prototyping is done on different hardware from that of the final system. This may be because the final hardware is not yet available. It may be because it is much easier to experiment on a minicomputer or personal computer than on the final complex system. Prototyping aids need to be selected which are easily adaptable to the final hardware.

REAL DATA

With some prototyping the analyst creates small files of made-up data to illustrate what the system will do. In other cases made-up data is not good enough. The users need to update real data or explore complex databases to experience what the proposed system will do for them.

If real data is required, the users may be given prototypes connected to a *live* data system or may be given data that have been *extracted* from a live data system. The latter is generally safer and more flexible.

If the users do not update the data, they may be given report generators or other facilities which use data in a live database but which cannot modify the data. Often, however, the users want to manipulate or update the data. They should then be given extracted data to do this with and be locked out of the live data.

In some prototyping efforts the users ask for information of various types. The analyst must find out where such data exist, capture them, and reconstruct them in the data management system of the prototyping tool. Sometimes they exist on batch files; sometimes in corporate databases; sometimes they can be obtained from external sources.

When real data is used the prototype sometimes grows into a system that the users do not want to give up; it becomes a real working system.

PROCEDURE FOR PROTOTYPING

The procedure for prototyping may include the following steps:

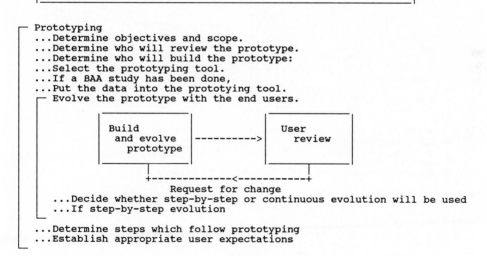

```
  The procedure given below may be modified with Action
  Diagrammer to meet the needs of the particular situation.
```

```
┌─ Prototyping
│   ...Determine objectives and scope.
│   ...Determine who will review the prototype.
│   ...Determine who will build the prototype:
│   ...Select the prototyping tool.
│   ...If a BAA study has been done,
│   ...Put the data into the prototying tool.
│   ┌─ Evolve the prototype with the end users.
│   │
│   │      ┌───────────────┐              ┌───────────────┐
│   │      │    Build       │              │    User       │
│   │      │  and evolve    │ ──────────>  │    review     │
│   │      │  prototype     │              │               │
│   │      └───────┬───────┘              └───────┬───────┘
│   │              ┝─────────────<───────────┥
│   │                    Request for change
│   │   ...Decide whether step-by-step or continuous evolution will be used
│   └─  ...If step-by-step evolution
│
│   ...Determine steps which follow prototyping
└─  ...Establish appropriate user expectations
```

Box 6.2 shows a more detailed action diagram of the procedure. Chapter 9 describes a particularly effective form of prototyping methodology.

BOX 6.2   A detailed procedure for prototyping

The procedure given below may be modified with Action
Diagrammer to meet the needs of the particular situation.

```
┌─ Prototyping
│  ┌─ Determine objectives and scope.
│  │     Establish the need for a system.
│  │  ┌─ Establish management's objectives for the project.
│  │  │     Interview appropriate end-user managers.
│  │  │     Write down the objectives.
│  │  └─    Obtain management agreement.
│  │
│  │  ┌─ Determine scope.
│  │  │     Determine which locations are involved.
│  │  │     Determine which departments are involved.
│  │  │  ┌─ If Business Area Analysis has been done
│  │  │  │     Extract relevant data and process models from the
│  │  │  │        encyclopedia.
│  │  │  ┌─ Else
│  │  │  │     Create relevant data and process models.
│  │  │  └─
│  │  │
│  │  │     Examine relevant goals, problems, and critical success factors
│  │  │        (from the encyclopedia).
│  │  │     Determine what business assumptions are to be made by the
│  │  └─       design group.
│  │
│  ┌─ Determine who will review the prototype.
│  │     The main reviewers are end users who need the system.
│  │     Ensure that sufficient commitment exists that a thorough review
│  │        job will be done.
│  │     In its final stages, the prototype may be reviewed by:
│  │     o  Technical staff who will build the system
│  │     o  Management
│  │     o  The executive sponsor
│  │     o  Possibly external reviewers such as customers
│  └─    o  Possibly an external consultant
│  ┌─ Determine who will build the prototype:
│  │     o  An I.S. professional
│  │     o  A small I.S. team
│  │     o  An end user
│  └─    o  An end user working with an I.S. professional
│  ┌─ Select the prototyping tool.
│  │     It is likely that the toolkit will be selected once and then applied
│  │        to many subsequent projects.
│  │
│  │  ┌─ If the prototype will become the final working system
│  │  │     Select a tool which will give adequate machine performance,
│  │  │        database access and network access.
│  │  ┌─ Else
│  │  │     Select a tool which is as easy to use as possible but which is not
│  └─ └─       fundamentally different from the final system.
```

BOX 6.2   *(Continued)*

```
Characteristics of the prototyping tool
   The tool should:
      o  be interactive
      o  be easy to use
      o  facilitate quick building of prototypes or partial prototypes
      o  make changes quick and easy
      o  encourage stepwise refinement
      o  support desirable dialog structures, such as scroll bars,
         mouse operation, an action bar, drop-down menus, etc.
      o  support appropriate database structures
      o  support installation standards, such as IBM's SAA (Systems
         Application Architecture).
   Ideally, the prototyping tool should be an integrated part of the
   IE CASE toolset.


   The tool should include the following:
      o  a versatile screen painter (which can be used very quickly
         in JAD sessions)
      o  ability to link screens and responses into a dialog
      o  a versatile report generator (which can be used very quickly
         in JAD sessions)
      o  a fourth-generation language or code generator
      o  a suitably flexible database management system
      o  an integral dictionary
      o  facilities for extracting data from files or dates, and
         loading them into the prototype database, OR online
         access to other files or databases

If the prototype will become the final system
   The tool should have:
      o  ability to achieve good machine performance (with an
         optimizing compiler)
      o  ability to support database structure of the final system
      o  appropriate networking access
      o  ability to handle a suitably large number of users
      o  ability to handle suitably large databases
      o  ability to handle suitably high traffic volumes
      o  possibly the ability to substitute segments of other
         languages (e.g. COBOL or Assembler) into the prototype
         to improve its performance.

   The system the tool generates should have:
      o  features for recovery from failures
      o  features for fallback
      o  security features
      o  features for auditability
      o  features for ease of maintenance
```

(Continued)

BOX 6.2 *(Continued)*

If a BAA study has been done,
   Extract the relevant information from the BAA study.
      Extract the relevant process decomposition diagram.
      Extract the relevant entity-relationship diagram.
      Extract the relevant data model.
      Extract or create the relevant process flow diagram,
         showing how the processes are dependent on one another.
      Add detailed comments to the above diagrams where necessary.
      Print relevant versions of the above diagrams from the
         encyclopedia for the participants to review.

Else
   Establish the data.
      Determine what data the system needs.
      Extract or establish a data model.
      Determine where the source data come from.

   Establish the design.
      Create a decomposition diagram.
      Create a process flow diagram showing how the processes are
        dependent on one another.
      Add detailed comments to the above diagrams where necessary.
      Print relevant versions of the above diagrams from the
        encyclopedia for the participants to review.

Put the data into the prototying tool.
      Obtain the source data.
      Determine whether the source data will need converting.
      Convert the source data if necessary.
      Extract the data into the prototyping tool.

Evolve the prototype with the end users.

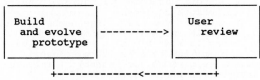

```
+----------------+           +----------------+
|                |           |                |
|  Build         |           |  User          |
|  and evolve    |---------->|  review        |
|  prototype     |           |                |
|                |           |                |
+----------------+           +----------------+
         |                            |
         +-------------<--------------+
              Request for change
```

Decide whether step-by-step or continuous evolution will be used
      STEP-BY-STEP EVOLUTION progresses from one planned prototype
      to another. Each prototype is reviewed until the final system
      is achieved.
      CONTINUOUS EVOLUTION progresses with a sequence of
      modifications continuously adjusting the prototype until
      the target is reached. This requires intelligent, understanding
      end user(s) working as a team with the developer(s) reviewing
      the evolution.

BOX 6.2 *(Continued)*

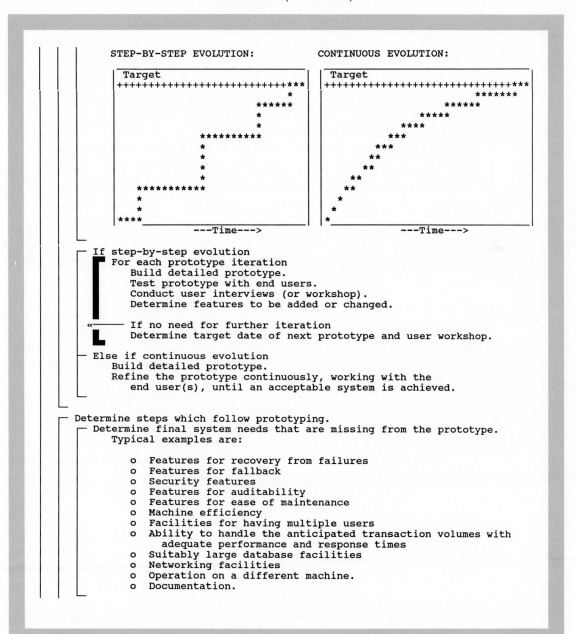

```
STEP-BY-STEP EVOLUTION:              CONTINUOUS EVOLUTION:
┌────────────────────────────┐   ┌────────────────────────────┐
│Target                      │   │Target                      │
│++++++++++++++++++++++++++***│   │+++++++++++++++++++++++++++***│
│                         *  │   │                      *******│
│                    ******  │   │                  ******    │
│                    *       │   │                *****        │
│                    *       │   │              ****          │
│          **********        │   │            ***             │
│          *                 │   │          ***               │
│          *                 │   │         **                 │
│          *                 │   │        **                  │
│          *                 │   │       **                   │
│**********                  │   │      **                    │
│*                           │   │     *                      │
│*                           │   │   *                        │
│****                        │   │ *                          │
└────────────────────────────┘   └────────────────────────────┘
        ---Time--->                      ---Time--->
```

If step-by-step evolution
  For each prototype iteration
    Build detailed prototype.
    Test prototype with end users.
    Conduct user interviews (or workshop).
    Determine features to be added or changed.

  «   If no need for further iteration
    Determine target date of next prototype and user workshop.

Else if continuous evolution
  Build detailed prototype.
  Refine the prototype continuously, working with the
    end user(s), until an acceptable system is achieved.

Determine steps which follow prototyping.
  Determine final system needs that are missing from the prototype.
    Typical examples are:

        o Features for recovery from failures
        o Features for fallback
        o Security features
        o Features for auditability
        o Features for ease of maintenance
        o Machine efficiency
        o Facilities for having multiple users
        o Ability to handle the anticipated transaction volumes with
           adequate performance and response times
        o Suitably large database facilities
        o Networking facilities
        o Operation on a different machine.
        o Documentation.

(Continued)

BOX 6.2   *(Continued)*

```
Establish the implementation plan.
    ○──────────────────────────────────────────○
    │  See Chapter 21: Lifecycle Procedures  │
    ○──────────────────────────────────────────○

Determine whether the prototype will be used for education and
  training purposes.
Establish appropriate user expectations.
    Ensure that the users know what has to be done before the system
      is cut over.
    Ensure that the users know when the system is to be cut over.
    Ensure that the users and management have realistic expectations
      about what the system will be like and when it will be available.
```

SCOPE AND OBJECTIVES

If BAA (business area analysis) has been done, the scope of the project may be defined with process blocks from the encyclopedia. A *perspective* is extracted which contains certain processes and entities.

The objectives of the system need to be established before design or prototyping begins. Relevant goals, problems, and critical success factors, from the ISP (information strategy planning) study, may be examined. It is determined what business assumptions should be made by the design group.

Which departments will use the eventual system should be determined, and what locations. This helps decide who will review the prototype.

WHO WILL REVIEW THE PROTOTYPE?

As part of the planning process the reviewers should be selected. The main reviewers are end users who will employ the eventual system. Some of the reviewers should be very knowledgeable about the application procedures.

A potential problem in prototyping occurs when reviewers do not spend the time or have the enthusiasm to do a thorough creative review. It is necessary to select reviewers with sufficient commitment who are determined that the system shall meet the needs of their area as effectively as possible.

When the prototype has evolved with the users to a fairly complete state it may be reviewed by other people including

- Management.
- The executive sponsor for the system.
- The technical staff who will build the system.
- In some cases external people such as customers, or agents are involved with the system, and may review a prototype.
- Sometimes an external consultant is used to give a professional viewpoint on the system.

WHO WILL BUILD THE PROTOTYPE?

Many prototypes are built by one person who is fast and competent with a fourth-generation language or generator. This person is often an IS professional, but could be an end user. In most situations IS professionals build the prototype and users review it; in some situations users build the prototype, and IS professionals review it.

The prototype may be built by a two-person team each with different knowledge, often a team with one end user and one IS professional. It is generally not appropriate to have large teams working on a prototype. Two people should be the maximum for most situations.

BUILDING THE PROTOTYPE

The prototype needs to be well designed. Prototyping should never be an excuse for casual work in which structured design is abandoned. Where this rule is not followed prototypes which grow complex, written in languages like FOCUS, RAMIS, NOMAD, and so on, can be a spaghettilike mess which becomes difficult to modify or convert to a working system. Good prototyping tools ought to *enforce* cleanly structured design, but many do not.

The prototypers should first build something simple. This starts a debate early in the evolution which may flush out misconceptions. The initial prototype is successively added to. With complex systems it is desirable to build the functionality first and then polish the human factoring.

Prototyping should be a way to introduce end-user creativity into the design process. To achieve this it is desirable to motivate the reviewers appropriately to make them excited about their role in evolving the system and encourage them to think inventively about how the system could improve their procedures. Brainstorming sessions may be used for discussing the potentials of the prototype.

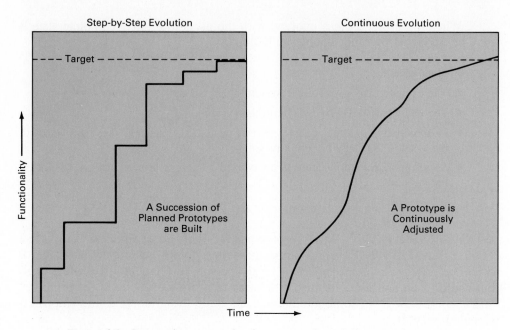

Figure 6.1   Prototyping can evolve in a succession of discrete releases, or continuous evolution can occur.

STEP-BY-STEP OR CONTINUOUS EVOLUTION

Prototypes can evolve either continuously or in a succession of discrete releases. The left of Fig. 6.1 shows discrete step-by-step evolution; the right shows continuous evolution.

With step-by-step prototyping, for each prototype a list of desirable enhancements is created and a target date is set for when the next version will be available for review. In one highly complex financial system, six prototypes were built over a period of six months. The prototypes steadily converged to the required system, and the last prototype became the working system.

With continuous evolution the reviewers work regularly with the prototype builders examining each enhancement when it is working. Continuous evolution tends to be used when there is a closer-knit relationship between the builders and users. Sometimes in continuous evolution it is necessary to suspend the interaction while the builders step back, rethink, and "rearchitect" their system.

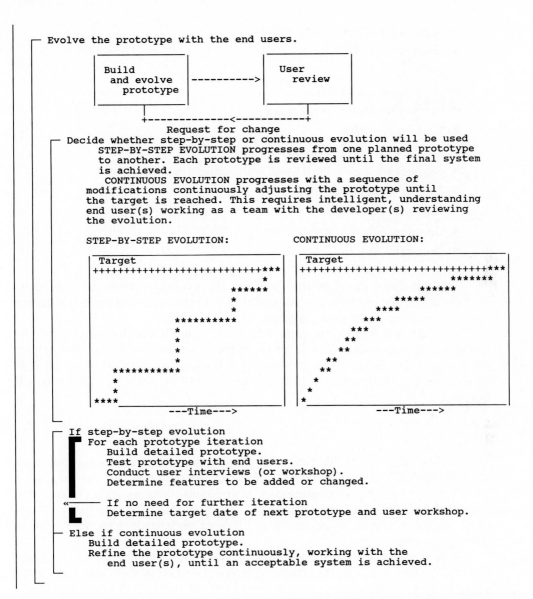

— Evolve the prototype with the end users.

```
  +----------------+          +----------------+
  |   Build        |          |   User         |
  | and evolve     |--------->|   review       |
  |  prototype     |          |                |
  +----------------+          +----------------+
          |                           |
          +------------<-----------+
              Request for change
```

— Decide whether step-by-step or continuous evolution will be used
      STEP-BY-STEP EVOLUTION progresses from one planned prototype
      to another. Each prototype is reviewed until the final system
      is achieved.
      CONTINUOUS EVOLUTION progresses with a sequence of
   modifications continuously adjusting the prototype until
   the target is reached. This requires intelligent, understanding
   end user(s) working as a team with the developer(s) reviewing
   the evolution.

STEP-BY-STEP EVOLUTION: CONTINUOUS EVOLUTION:

```
 ┌─────────────────────────────┐  ┌─────────────────────────────────┐
 │Target                       │  │Target                           │
 │+++++++++++++++++++++++++++***│  │+++++++++++++++++++++++++++++++***│
 │                          *   │  │                          *******│
 │                    ******    │  │                   ******        │
 │                    *         │  │                *****            │
 │                    *         │  │              ****               │
 │            *********         │  │            ***                  │
 │            *                 │  │          ***                    │
 │            *                 │  │          **                     │
 │            *                 │  │         **                      │
 │            *                 │  │        **                       │
 │   **********                 │  │      **                         │
 │   *                          │  │      **                         │
 │   *                          │  │      *                          │
 │****                          │  │   *                             │
 └─────────────────────────────┘  └─────────────────────────────────┘
      ---Time--->                         ---Time--->
```

— If step-by-step evolution
     For each prototype iteration
         Build detailed prototype.
         Test prototype with end users.
         Conduct user interviews (or workshop).
         Determine features to be added or changed.

     «——— If no need for further iteration
         Determine target date of next prototype and user workshop.

— Else if continuous evolution
     Build detailed prototype.
     Refine the prototype continuously, working with the
         end user(s), until an acceptable system is achieved.

FROM PROTOTYPE TO WORKING SYSTEM

When the prototype is regarded as complete, there may still be much work to do in building the operational system. A list should be created of the system features which are missing from the prototype. These may include:

- Features for recovery from failures.
- Features for fallback.
- Security features.
- Features for auditability.
- Features for ease of maintenance.
- Machine efficiency.
- Facilities for having multiple users.
- Facilities for high-volume usage with adequate response times.
- Larger database facilities.
- Networking facilities.
- Operation on a different machine.
- Documentation.

In some cases the prototype becomes the working system. In other cases it needs rearchitecting before it is usable. In yet other cases an entirely different system is built in a different language.

Sometimes a fourth-generation language is used to build a working system and this language is first used to create prototypes. The resulting programs may have somewhat inadequate performance, so portions of them are replaced with subroutines in a more efficient language (e.g., COBOL, PL/I, or ASSEMBLER language).

EXPECTATION MANAGEMENT

A danger of prototyping is that the users, motivated to be excited about the prototype so that they make constructive suggestions, acquire expectations that cannot be fulfilled. They may expect a working system similar to the prototype to be available almost immediately and cannot understand why they have to wait for so long.

It is necessary to manage the expectations of the users. They should know why the prototype has to be rebuilt (if it does) and what functions have to be added to it. They should be given the timetable for building the working system with an explanation of why it takes this amount of time.

PROTOTYPES AND TRAINING

The prototype may be a useful training vehicle. People who will eventually use the system can work with the prototype for training and practice so that they are ready for the system when it eventually arrives.

THE DEVELOPMENT Prototyping techniques should be built into the over-
LIFECYCLE all development lifecycle. Prototyping may be used
in conjunction with JAD sessions as discussed in the
following chapter, and JAD should be built into the development lifecycle.

Different types of development lifecycles are appropriate for different situations as is discussed in Chapter 21. Most of them can use prototyping.

PILOTS The term *pilot* is also used for a system not yet fully
operational. A *prototype* is used where the functions
and detailed design of a system are not yet fully understood. The prototype is
used to explore and solidify the functions and design.

A *pilot* is a preliminary system in which the functions and design are
thought to be understood but the system is cut over in a limited form so that

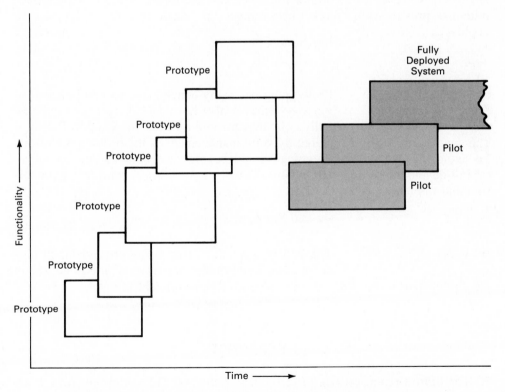

Figure 6.2 Some of the functionality of the final prototype may be cut back
when the first pilot is installed.

experience can be gained with it before the full system is cut over. For example, if the final system is to have five hundred terminals, it might be initially operated with five. If the system is to be installed in a thousand dealerships, it might first be operated in ten. As a result of this pilot operation, modifications are usually made before the system is fully deployed.

Sometimes a powerful prototyping tool enables its users to build much functionality into the prototypes as they progress through multiple iterations. The designers of the system may decide to cut down on some of the functions when the first pilot system is built. They may do this because some functions are deemed to be of limited value or may duplicate other functions, or because some functions would worsen machine performance or implementation difficulty. Enthusiastic prototyping sometimes results in overengineering. It is desirable to avoid this in the expensive implementation phase.

Figure 6.2 shows a typical progression of a complex system for which the functions were only partially understood at the beginning. There are six prototypes of growing functionality. After the sixth prototype the system is rearchitected and some functions are eliminated. The first pilot comes into use in a live environment. After a time minor improvements are made to it. After the second pilot has proven itself, more improvements are made and the full system is deployed.

**BENEFITS
AND DANGERS**   Prototyping has many benefits and should be used for most systems. It also has some dangers if used casually. The benefits and dangers are listed in Box 6.3. The dangers are easily countered by good management of the prototyping effort. To avoid the dangers, prototyping should be regarded as a component of an overall development lifecycle, where the rest of the lifecycle enforces good design and implementation.

ACTION DIAGRAM   The action diagram of Box 6.2 gives a detailed procedure for prototyping. This may be modified to suit the circumstances and to fit it into the overall development lifecycle.

REFERENCE

1. The Martin report on *High-Productivity Languages* (Marblehead, MA: Martin Report.

BOX 6.3 Benefits and dangers of prototyping

Benefits of Prototyping

- It introduces early reality testing into a project. The users can see what is being built for them and critique it.
- Without prototyping there is a substantial risk of building an inadequate system, wrong features, or at worst a system which users will reject.
- It encourages users to have creative input into the design process.
- Users understand and react to prototypes far better than paper specifications. Often they fail to understand, or miss important points, in paper specifications.
- With a good tool it is quicker to build a prototype than to build paper specifications.
- When using and reviewing a prototype users tend to be unbiased by existing systems.
- Prototyping enables errors and weaknesses to be caught before expensive design and programming is done.
- Prototypes, or partial prototypes, are of great help in joint application design (JAD, or IE/JAD) sessions.
- Prototypes can generate excitement and improve the morale of the users and developers.
- Prototypes are valuable for communicating what is required to programmers.
- Prototypes provide early work experience for users and may be used as a training tool.
- With appropriate software, prototypes may evolve into the final system.
- Used in the right way, prototyping can give faster development than the traditional lifecycle.

Dangers of Prototyping

- Quick-and-casual design may replace well-structured design.
- The users' expectation may become too high. They may think they can have the system immediately.
- There is a temptation to make the prototype the production system without adequate consideration of security, auditability, fallback, recovery, maintainability, performance, networking, or documentation.
- The user may take the prototype too literally when the implemented system will be different.
- The user may be too casual about the prototype and not take the time to identify its potential flaws.

The dangers are generally overcome with the timebox methodology described in Chapter 9.

7 JRP AND JAD: USER WORKSHOPS FOR PLANNING AND DESIGN

When systems are built by IS (information systems) professionals, it is important to harness the end users into the processes of requirements planning and design. This chapter and the next describe twin techniques for doing this: JRP (joint requirements planning) and JAD (joint application design). These techniques have been particularly successful and have spread in many corporations. They have speeded up the requirements analysis and design process and resulted in designs that meet the end users' needs much better.

The basic idea of JRP and JAD is to select key end users and conduct workshops which progress through a structured set of steps for planning and designing a system. At the start of the workshop the users are encouraged to do most of the talking. IS staff in the session translate what the users want into structured specifications and design, in such a way that the users can understand and discuss the results.

The success of JRP and JAD is highly dependent on the person who organizes and conducts the workshops. This is a skilled task. The same person usually conducts both JRP and JAD workshops. We will refer to this person as the JAD leader. This should be a full-time position so that the person can develop his or her skill in managing JRP and JAD to the full.

Sometimes joint requirement planning and joint application design are combined into one activity; sometimes they are separate. A JRP session is usually shorter than a JAD session, and without technical detail. It often involves higher-level managers and has sometimes been done at the top-management level. A JRP session establishes the requirements and justification for a system and the detailed functions the system will perform. It may be done before there is a go-ahead decision to build the system. The JAD session establishes the detailed design of the system. It establishes the data model and process model for the system, detailed specifications, the screen designs, report designs, and possibly rough prototypes:

The early uses of JAD were done without automation. JAD is far more effective when done with tools for graphic design automation, screen design, report generation, and prototyping. JAD needs to be part of information engineering. It needs to use the information in the encyclopedia, employ the IE (information engineering) design tools, and store its results in the encyclopedia.

JAD recognizes that users cannot design complex procedures without professional help. At the same time IS professionals have difficulty understanding the subtleties of the user requirements. The traditional methods of interviewing users and writing text specifications have been inadequate for this purpose. The answer is to have a joint design session in which the users are guided through a series of structured steps which causes them to think about and describe the procedures they require. A JAD session makes the user interact with easy-to-understand design diagrams, screen layouts, printed reports, and simple prototypes. When the users are made responsible for the design, they take a strong interest in it, often creating imaginative new procedures, and the results are much more valuable.

A well-managed JAD session, conducted with integrated CASE (computer-aided systems engineering) tools, produces a high-quality design much faster than do the techniques of traditional structured analysis.

BENEFITS OF JRP

A major benefit of JRP is making business executives think creatively about how information systems can help them. The workshop causes an examination of the goals, problems, critical success factors, and strategic opportunities which may have been analyzed in the ISP (information strategy planning) study (Book II) or may be examined for the first time in the JRP workshop. A JRP workshop may be the technique used during the ISP study.

Business executives and end users brainstorm the possible functions of the system, identify the most useful functions and climate, or defer those of questionable value.

Box 7.1 lists the benefits of joint requirements planning.

BENEFITS OF JAD

Well-conducted JAD sessions result in designs which meet the end users' needs better because the design largely *comes from the users*. In addition the design process can be much faster than the elapsed time with traditional IS analysis techniques. A corporation well organized to conduct JAD workshops can prepare for a workshop in about three weeks and complete the JAD in another two or three weeks. The total elapsed time is often a fifth of that for conventional design [2].

One large insurance company, CNA in Chicago, compared the productivity of JAD with conventional analysis and design, by using the function point productivity measurement technique [1].

BOX 7.1   Benefits of JRP and JAD

1. Benefits of JRP

- JRP harnesses top business executives into the system planning process. JRP links system planning to the ISP analysis of goals, problems, critical success factors, and strategic systems opportunities.

- JRP encourages brainstorming of what the most valuable systems functions are likely to be.

- JRP eliminates functions of questionable value.

- JRP encourages creative business executives to think about how they can use information systems to enhance business opportunities.

2. Benefits of JAD

- JAD harnesses the end users into the design process and helps to avoid dissatisfied users.

- JAD replaces voluminous paper specifications with live screen designs, report designs, prototypes, concise structures, and design diagrams which are easily edited. These, especially when created with rigorous design tools, give much more help to the programmers or system implementors.

- With JAD sessions the specification and design of systems take a much shorter elapsed time than with traditional systems analysis.

- JAD results in systems which often have higher quality and greater business value.

- JAD tends, along with the Information Center, to produce a user community with greater computer literacy. It often causes users to be imaginative and inventive about creating better procedures.

- JAD saves money by avoiding the need to preprogram or modify systems of inadequate design. Maintenance expenses are less.

- JAD substantially improves productivity of the development process.

- JAD removes the information systems analyst from the role of resolving conflicts between end users. The end users in potential conflict resolve their differences in the JAD workshop.

- If built with information engineering tools the design can be made rigorous and easy to maintain. JAD links into other systems and employs stable data structures.

Function points are a measure of application complexity used when comparing the productivity of different forms of system design and construction [1]. The technique counts certain elements of a program and classifies them by three levels of complexity. A weighting factor is then applied to the total of each element. This method has been used extensively in IBM and advocated by the *IBM Guide* user group. In the CNA comparison JAD achieved 2.5 person-hours per function point; the equivalent requirements analysis and external design took 8 person-hours per function point—a productivity improvement of more than 300 percent. More people are concurrently involved in a JAD session than during conventional systems analysis.

Box 7.1 also lists the benefits of joint application design.

With the traditional development lifecycle most of the work was programming and testing. If automated development tools are taken advantage of, the main body of work swings to the front of the lifecycle. Code generation is more automatic, but a better job needs to be done of requirements planning and design. The design work should be done in such a way that automated code generation can occur whenever possible (and hence debugging time is much less). Techniques such as JRP and JAD need to harness the knowledge of the users and business managers. There is thus more work for users at the front of the lifecycle, but the system is built more quickly. Figure 7.1 illustrates this.

THE JAD LEADER   The skills of the person who organizes and presides over the workshop are particularly critical to the success of JRP and JAD. As we commented, this person should be employed full-time conducting such workshops so that he or she can become highly proficient at the task. Usually one person conducts both JRP and JAD workshops. He or she is often referred to as *the JAD leader,* and we use that terminology here.

The JAD leader should be chosen mainly for his human communication skills. He could come from either the end-user or IS community. In practice most come from IS. Some JAD leaders are, or have been, Information Center staff. Some have a marketing background. In some cases they are an external consultant.

The JAD leader needs to be impartial, diplomatic, and not associated with any politics that affect the session. It is his job to prepare the session, orchestrate the session, make discussions occur within a structured framework, and make the session move reasonably quickly to the required conclusions. He acts as the focal point for tying together the views of management, the end users, and IS professionals (Fig. 7.2).

The JAD leader needs to be comfortable standing in front of a group of people. He needs to be confident in his task and have the ability to direct the discussion and fact finding. He needs to command the respect of all parties at the session. To do so he must be well prepared, knowledgeable about the busi-

Traditional Development:

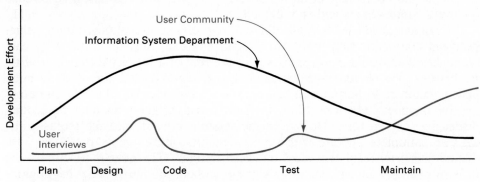

Development with JAD and Prototyping:

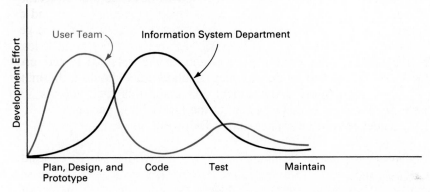

Figure 7.1 JAD harnesses the end users to achieve faster designs which meet the users' needs better. IE/JAD anchors this design into information engineering and provides tools for aiding the JAD sessions.

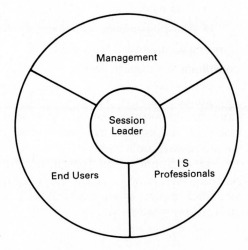

Figure 7.2 A JRP or JAD session needs the committment of management and the partnership of management, end users, and IS professionals. Their cooperation is facilitated and coordinated by an impartial session leader.

ness area, and competent in the techniques that are used. He needs to be able to control controversies and stay flexible.

A good session leader can eliminate the effects of politics, power struggles, and communication gaps. He puts IS and end users on equal terms and establishes them as partners. He assumes the role of a referee at times, arbitrating debates. He should constantly elicit questions. He should encourage the quieter members to participate, ask questions, and respond when the more aggressive members take a position. He knows that certain goals must be accomplished by a given time. He moves the session forward until the requisite designs are completed, along with screens, reports, and possibly prototypes. He obtains concurrence of the users on these designs. The goal is to discuss the ideas fully and reach agreement as a group without too much delay haggling.

It is important for the session leader to be enthusiastic about JRP or JAD and to convey his excitement about how well it can work to the participants.

SESSION LEADER TRAINING

An organization which incorporates JRP and JAD into its development methodology should train one or more JAD leaders and make this their job for two years or more. JAD leaders become skilled at the task with experience.

The JAD leader should be trained in the following areas:

- Communication skills
- Negotiating skills
- Group dynamics
- Information engineering
- Analysis and design
- Data modeling
- The diagramming techniques
- The automated tools used
- Project management

He should have had on-the-job training in other JRP and JAD sessions. A mock-up session can put him in a variety of problematical situations, and can videotape and critique his performance. He should have thorough practice with the automated tools used.

In addition to the foregoing, the JAD leader should have management skill, business savvy, and a good reputation, because credibility will make his job much easier when working with a variety of end users, executives, and information systems staff.

THE USER PARTICIPANTS

Selecting the best user participants is particularly important. The participants should have the right mix of knowledge about the business. They should have the authority to make decisions about the design. All should be people who communicate well. There is often one or more key person who is critical to creating the design and having it accepted. If the key players are not available, *the workshop should not be run.*

JRP and JAD are often most valuable for projects which span user organizations or for applications which affect multiple locations or disciplines. It is useful for resolving operational, organizational, or procedural differences. The end users or managers in question confront each other at the workshop under the guidance of a session leader trained in negotiating skills and must sign off on a design which both sides accept. The systems analyst is removed from the middle of such conflicts, and the conflicts are brought into the open in a constructive design session.

Often contentious political issues are known about before the workshop. They should be dealt with by appointing an executive sponsor at a suitably high level and having him meet with the parties in question seeking consensus on the issues or motivating the parties to achieve consensus during the workshop.

Increasingly today, systems are being built in one enterprise with different enterprises online. Corporations are placing workstations in the locations of agents, wholesalers, retailers, buyers, suppliers, or dealers. Online cooperation between organizations is important for minimizing inventory costs and improving service. It can be very valuable to have representatives of the external organization present at the JRP or JAD session when such systems are designed.

GROUP DYNAMICS

JRP and JAD sessions work because of the group dynamics. The session leader needs to know how to use group dynamics as constructively as possible. The participants are shut away in a workshop knowing that they have a given task to accomplish by a given time, with a given agenda. This task-oriented environment helps participants to concentrate on idea sharing and achieving the established goals. It helps to ensure that the information provided is complete. When appropriately motivated, such groups tend to police themselves and avoid politics. Bickering and pettiness are seen for what they are and tend to disappear.

The leader may follow the agenda by asking questions of the users at each stage:

"What functions do you perform here?"

"What information do you need to make better decisions here?"

"How can this step be done more effectively if information is available from the customer database?"

"Could this step be eliminated or done by machine?"

"Should not this decision be made in a different place?"

The answers and discussions should be made as tangible as possible by quickly generating and displaying screens or reports which future users could employ. This fast competent use of a generator is essential. As new flows or structures are designed, these should be printed by the design tool so that session members can study them and make notes on them.

The number of participants varies from one organization to another. The session should not be too big. Large groups tend to argue too much or to waste the time of participants. The most effective sessions often have fewer than eight people.

The group should follow a structure with agreed-upon stages, goals and deliverables. In this way time-wasting ad hoc debate is avoided.

JRP PROCEDURE

Box 7.1 has outlined the procedure for joint requirements planning. Information established previously in the ISP study (Book II) may be used in establishing the opportunities and scope of the proposed system:

```
┌─ Determine opportunities and scope
│      Examine strategic business opportunities which may be relevant
│        to this system.
│      Examine relevant goals, problems, and critical success factors
│        (from the encyclopedia).
│      Determine which locations are involved.
│      Determine which departments are involved.
│      Establish management's objectives for the project.
│      Determine what business assumptions are to be made by the
│        planning group.
└─     Determine which BAA processes are involved.
```

In preparing the material prior to the JRP workshop, information in the encyclopedia should be used. If an ISP has not been done for this area, then the goals, problems, critical success factors, and strategic opportunities relevant to the system may be established prior to or at the start of the JRP workshop:

```
If an ISP study or similar planning has been done
    Extract the relevant information
        List possible strategic opportunities.
        List relevant critical success factors.
        Print matrices from the encyclopedia mapping goals, problems,
          critical success factors, and so on with corporate functions,
          locations, executives, and so on (See Book II).
        Add detailed comments to the above matrices where necessary.
        Print relevant versions of the above matrices from the
          encyclopedia for the workshop participants to review.

Else
    Adjust the JRP agenda (below) so that information equivalent to that
      above is created at or before the start of the JRP session.

    Research similar systems that might offer guidance or ideas to
      the workshop participants.
    Prepare slides or foils illustrating the business activities.
```

If a BAA has not been done, then a process decomposition and dependency diagnosis may be sketched out prior to or at the start of the JRP session.

Similar systems elsewhere should be examined as part of the task of preparing for the JRP workshop. The workshop leader is responsible for ensuring that sufficient preparatory work has been done prior to the workshop. The participants are given materials to study before attending the workshop.

Box 7.2 gives a detailed JRP procedure. This should be adjusted to the situation in question and a detailed agenda prepared.

The documentation from the workshop may include the following:

- The scope of the system
- List of system objectives
- List of possible system functions
- Estimated return on investment of the functions
- List of intangible benefits of the functions
- Prioritization of the functions
- List of functions to be implemented on the first version of the system
- A process decomposition diagram of the system (in the encyclopedia)
- Relationships with other systems (from the encyclopedia)
- Listing of unresolved issues
- Implementation target dates
- What happens next?

At the end of the workshop it is desirable to give the participants realistic expectations of what happens next, and how long it might take to build the system.

BOX 7.2   Joint requirements planning.

Description
    Joint Requirements Planning, JRP, is a technique for harnessing
business executives and end users in the examination of requirements
of a proposed system. It is a highly successful technique when used
correctly, and should be employed for most systems.
    Key executives and users are selected to participate in workshops
in which a requirements document is created. The workshop progresses
through a planned set of steps under the guidance of a skilled JRP
leader, who is usually the JAD leader who will conduct a follow-on
Joint Application Design session. The JRP session is similar to the
JAD session.
    At the start of the workshop the users are encouraged to do most
of the talking. IE professionals relate the end users' statements
to the knowledge in the encyclopedia, and attempt to create a
pragmatic list of system requirements that will make the system as
valuable as possible.

> The procedure given below may be modified with Action
> Diagrammer to meet the needs of the particular situation.

JRP Procedure
  Initiate
      Establish the need for a system.
      Appoint the JRP session leader.
          It is desirable to have a full-time person, with appropriate
          skills, to conduct JRP and JAD sessions. A well-chosen JAD
          session leader becomes skilled with experience.
          He should be trained in the following:
              o   Communication skills
              o   Negotiation skills
              o   Group dynamics
              o   Information engineering
              o   Analysis and design
              o   Data modeling
              o   The diagramming techniques
              o   The automated tools used
              o   Project management
              o   He should have on-the-job training in other JAD sessions

      Determine opportunities and scope
          Examine strategic business opportunities which may be relevant
          to this system.
          Examine relevant goals, problems, and critical success factors
          (from the encyclopedia).
          Determine which locations are involved.
          Determine which departments are involved.
          Establish management's objectives for the project.
          Determine what business assumptions are to be made by the
          planning group.
          Determine which BAA processes are involved.

BOX 7.2   *(Continued)*

```
Determine the key user executives
     Determine which end users feel strongly about the need for the
     system.
     Determine which user executives will be involved with the system.
     Determine what end users are particularly knowledgable about the
     subject areas of the system.
     Determine who will participate in the JRP workshop.

Prepare
  Select the workshop participants.
     Select end-user workshop participants.
          The workshop should not be held until the key participants
          are available.
        Workshop participants:
        o  End users who want the system (the key players)
        o  User executives will be involved with the system.
        o  Outside users
             If the system serves individuals in other corporations
               such as suppliers, distributors, buyers, or customers,
               their attendance should be considered.

     Select other workshop participants
        Workshop participants:
        o  Session leader
        o  IE professional
        o  Visiting specialists
        o  Scribe

  Prepare the materials
     Prepare slides or foils illustrating the business activities.
     If an ISP study or similar planning has been done
        Extract the relevant information
           List possible strategic opportunities.
           List relevant critical success factors.
           Print matrices from the encyclopedia mapping goals, problems,
             critical success factors, and so on with corporate functions,
             locations, executives, and so on (See Book II).
           Add detailed comments to the above matrices where necessary.
           Print relevant versions of the above matrices from the
             encyclopedia for the workshop participants to review.

     Else
        Adjust the JRP agenda (below) so that information equivalent
          to that above is created at or before the start of the JRP
          session.
```

(Continued)

BOX 7.2 *(Continued)*

```
  If a BAA study has been done
      Extract the relevant information from the BAA study
          Extract the relevant process decomposition diagram.
          Extract the relevant entity-relationship diagram.
          Extract or create the relevant process flow diagram,
              showing how the processes are dependent on one another.
          Add detailed comments to the above diagrams where necessary.
          Print relevant versions of the above diagrams from the
              encyclopedia for the participants to review.
  Else
      Adjust the JRP agenda (below) so that a process decomposition
          and process flow diagram is created for the system at or
          before the start of the JRP session.

    Research similar systems that might offer guidance or ideas to
        the workshop participants.

  Customize the JRP agenda
      Duplicate and modify this action diagram to represent the
          agenda to be used.
      List the processes involved.
      Prepare an agenda, if necessary, for each process involved.

  Prepare the participants.
      Give participants literature on the JRP procedure (this chapter).
      Give them the JRP agenda.
      Give participants the preparatory material for them to study.
      Inform them that they must understand it well before the
          workshop.

Conduct the workshop
  Opening speech
      Have an appropriate executive make the opening speech.

  Initial review
      Review with participants the purpose and objectives.
      Review the agenda.
      Describe any strategic business opportunities from the system.
      Review relevant goals, problems, and critical success factors.
      Review the business assumptions that are to be made.

  For the system as a whole, determine its functions
      List the system objectives.
      Brainstorm the possible functions of the system
      Description
          Brainstorming means that a creative group of individuals
          attempt to produce a stream of ideas without inhibition.
          A rule of a brainstorming session is that there can be
          no implied criticism for making an impractical or stupid
          suggestion. The session is intended to generate as many
          ideas as possible. At the end of the session only certain
          of the ideas will be recorded for possible use.
```

BOX 7.2   *(Continued)*

List those functions which seem valuable.
Relate the functions to the goals, problems, critical success
  factors, and strategic business opportunities.
Evaluate return on investment of the functions.
List intangible benefits of the functions.
Prioritize the functions.
Determine what functions should be implemented in the next version
  of the system, eliminating those which are of questionable value
  or which are difficult to build at this stage.
Adjust the decomposition diagram to reflect the functions selected.

For each process
    List its objectives.
    Brainstorm ways to streamline the system, lessen overhead, and
      lessen human work.
    Describe how the process will operate.
    Adjust the function list if necessary.
    Specify audit and security requirements.
    Address unresolved issues
        List unresolved issues.
        Determine responsibility and deadline for unresolved issues.
        Details of issue
            o   Issue:
            o   Assigned to:
            o   Assign date:
            o   Date to be resolved by:
            o   Resolution:

    List questions and suggestions ready for the JAD workshop.

Create the documentation
    The documentation should include:
        o   The scope of the system.
        o   List of system objectives.
        o   List of possible system functions.
        o   Estimated return on investment of the functions.
        o   List of intangible benefits of the functions.
        o   Prioritization of the functions.
        o   List of functions to be implemented in the first version of
              the system.
        o   A process decomposition diagram of the system (in the
              encyclopedia).
        o   Relationships with other systems (from the encyclopedia).
        o   Listing of unresolved issues.
        o   Implementation target dates.
        o   What happens next.

Expectation management
    Give the users realistic expectations of when the completed
        system could become available.

Present the results to the executive who will sponsor the system.
Have an appropriate executive make the closing speech.

The JAD activity may follow directly from the JRP activity and is described in the next chapter.

**WORKSHOPS AT
ALL LEVELS OF
THE PYRAMID**

Workshops with users and executives, prepared and moderated by a JAD leader, are appropriate at all levels of the IE pyramid.

At the highest level, top management participation is needed in *information strategy planning*. At the second level data modeling and process modeling need to be done *jointly* with the users. At the third level *joint application design* can greatly improve the design process. At the bottom layer, end users may employ report generators or user-oriented fourth-generation languages. On the other hand, *construction* may be done entirely by IS professionals but in an iterative fashion in which the users interact with prototypes.

Sometimes a rough business area analysis has been done. The JAD session reveals its imprecision, and so the data models and process models are adjusted as the JAD progresses. This is more likely to happen to the process models than to a fully normalized data model. Often the flow of work among processes is redesigned during the JRP or JAD session. Sometimes the flow of work between departments should be changed. Today's networks make databases accessible from every desk, and this often changes the places where decisions ought to be made, sometimes causing middle-management functions to be bypassed, or whole business areas to be restructured. If redesign on this scale is needed, it is necessary that the managers who can put such changes into effect be present at the session.

Such workshops may thus cut across the organization from high-level managers to clerks. It can be very constructive to have this range of players present in a workshop, using precise design diagrams and having the goal of achieving consensus on new procedures.

Where high-level restructuring is under discussion the joint session may remain entirely at the business area analysis level and not drop down to design issues. Screen design and detailed data flow may be saved for a later JAD session. The diagrams representing the restructuring are stored back in the encyclopedia.

JAD-like sessions can thus take different forms and operate at different levels. Many such sessions have been used only for requirements definition and external design. Some companies, as illustrated in Fig. 7.3, have also used such workshops for strategic planning and some for internal design. With an encyclopedia-based tool, workshops at higher levels may feed workshops at lower levels.

JRP has also been used for application package selection and review, pack-

Company	JRP		JAD	
	Strategic Planning	Requirements Definition	External Design	Internal Design
Texas Instruments		X	X	
Travelers		X	X	
IBM-Sterling Forest		X	X	X
CNA	X	X	X	X
Transamerica Interway		X	X	
Ray Chem	X	X	X	
Liberty Mutual		X	X	
Continental		X	X	
Hartford		X	X	
Chase		X	X	
TWA	X	X	X	X

Figure 7.3 JRP sessions are used for strategic planning and requirements definition. JAD sessions are used for both external and internal design. This chart shows examples of how companies use JRP and JAD. (From *GUIDE* [3]).

age modification, and maintenance planning. With systems that cover many locations, the JRP or JAD documentation developed at one location has then been used at other locations. Distant locations may extract the information from the encyclopedia, via a network, for local use.

JAD sessions have also been used to review the ongoing progress of development. This may be particularly important where an iterative lifecycle is used (Chapter 21).

REFERENCES

1. A. J. Albrecht, *Measuring Application Development Productivity,* Proceedings of the Joint Share/Guide/IBM Application Development Symposium, October 1979.

2. Gary Rush, "The Fast Way to Define System Requirements, In Depth," *Computerworld,* October 7, 1985.

3. *Proceedings of GUIDE,* Session no. MP-7460, Los Angeles, March 1986.

8 IE/JAD: JOINT APPLICATION DESIGN

As commented on in the previous chapter, a JAD (joint application design) session goes into much more technical detail than does a JRP (joint requirements planning) session. The two activities may be done jointly or separately and should be an integral part of the overall development lifecycle. Figure 8.1 summarizes a development lifecycle which includes JRP, JAD, and prototype evolution. Chapter 21 shows a variety of lifecycles, in more detail, incorporating JRP and JAD. The RAD (rapid application development) lifecycle is a more refined version of these, which is generally more effective [1].

A JAD session uses a top-down approach to system design. The diagrams used and system representations must be as easy as possible for the end users to understand. The session is highly visual. Overhead projectors are used. Often a design is built up on white boards or on walls hung with flip charts. The system design evolves with cooperative discussion.

AUTOMATED TOOLS

Some primitive JAD workshops are conducted without automated tools. Experience has shown that JAD produces far better designs when CASE and prototype tools are used. The *scribe* should operate the tools, building up the design in a CASE encyclopedia as the workshop progresses. This gives more rigorous design, anchored into existing data models, from which code can be produced more quickly. The participants examine the screens that are painted, the sample reports generated, the screen dialog, and the structured design representation in decomposition diagrams, data flow diagrams, and action diagrams. Periodically parts of the design are printed for the users to review or take to their hotel rooms. Participants may examine or modify parts of the design on their own personal computers.

The JAD leader leads the participants through a preplanned set of steps.

```
┌─ Iterative development lifecycle
│
│  ...Initiate the project.
│  ...Scope the project.
│  ┌─ JRP procedure
│  │     The requirements planning is done in a JRP workshop.
│  │     o─────────────────────────────────────o
│  │     │  See Box 7.2:   JRP procedure        │
│  │     o─────────────────────────────────────o
│  └─
│  ┌─ JAD procedure
│  │     The specifications and initial design are produced in a JAD workshop.
│  │     o─────────────────────────────────────o
│  │     │  See Box 8.1:   JAD procedure        │
│  │     o─────────────────────────────────────o
│  └─
│  ...Evolve the prototype.
│  ...Create physical design.
│  ...Design for cutover.
│  ...Build pilot system.
│  ...Prepare for cutover.
│  ...Install and adjust pilot system.
└─ ...Expand pilot to full system.
```

Figure 8.1

The scribe records the results with a CASE tool and periodically interrupts because the tool detects inconsistencies or ambiguities. The tool helps to ensure
that the deliverables from the workshop are rigorous, consistent, and complete.

In some JAD sessions a projector is used which displays the contents of
the workstation screen on a large screen so that the workshop participants can
all view it. This can help in the discussion of designs and prototypes. Many
JAD sessions employ a CASE tool without this large-screen projection facility.
The scribe builds the design in the CASE tool as it evolves on the white boards
and periodically prints parts of it.

JAD sessions with a CASE tool are sometimes referred to as *interactive
JAD*.

IE/JAD

There is a major difference between JAD using conventional systems design techniques and JAD with
information engineering (IE/JAD).

With IE/JAD, information is taken from the encyclopedia to prepare for
the session. Before the session begins, its participants should study the relevant
data models and process models. Diagrams are created with the design automation tools, and when agreement is reached, the design is stored in the encyclopedia. The encyclopedia's knowledge coordinator is used to ensure consistency and integrity in the design.

The top-down design proceeds with the use of an action diagram editor for
system summaries and specifications and overview representations of the design
using decomposition diagrams, flow diagrams, and entity diagrams.

A screen generator, report generator, and prototype generator should be used by an IS expert who can obtain results with such tools quickly and competently, to present the most realistic view of the design to the end users and have it discussed in the session.

WHO ATTENDS A JAD SESSION?

The following types of personnel should be involved in a JAD session:

- **An executive sponsor who has made a commitment to have the system built.** He should kick off the session but may not stay long. He should visit periodically to lend support and examine the design as it evolves.

- **The key players are the end users who want a system to automate or streamline a given set of functions.** End users should be chosen who are easy to work with, who know the business area well, and who express their opinions easily.

- **The JAD leader.** This individual directs the session, encourages the players to participate, and moves the session along to meet its goals. A session leader, who like a good board chairman or TV moderator can direct the human dialog constructively and avoid squabbles, is essential.

- **IS professionals.** There should be one or more IS professionals who build the design and ensure that it is good technically. A part of this task is the building or extraction of the requisite normalized data model.

- **Scribe.** The scribe is responsible for the documentation. He makes notes during the session at the screen of a CASE tool and polishes them after the session. The final documentation is the CASE representation with attached commentary.

- **Tool specialist.** One person should be present who is skilled with the tools that are used to build and edit action diagrams, create the design, extract encyclopedia information, build screen designs and reports, and create prototypes. Sufficient competence should exist to do these things quickly. Usually, today, this person is the scribe. The scribe builds the design with the CASE tool.

- **Visiting specialists.** Specialists may attend the session part-time to give advice on specific areas.

- **The project manager.** The manager responsible for implementing the project may be present at a JAD session. He should not be the session leader because JAD depends upon having an objective impartial outsider as its leader to resolve differences between users and the project team.

DURATION OF THE SESSIONS

JAD sessions vary in their duration and pattern of involvement. Most common are sessions which last about a week. Sessions for very complex systems may last longer. The session may take place in a hotel to isolate the users from business distractions. There should be a firm goal of having a design in an IE-CASE tool and possibly rough prototypes by the end of the period. The time pressure encourages the participants to work hard and cooperate. Many JAD sessions go on until late at night. Often excellent creative designs come together in a pressure-cooker environment with a firm deadline.

Some designs have evolved in multiple sessions of a few days at a time. Some employ the users for half of each day, and the IS professionals build design models, screens, reports, and prototypes during the other half of each day. The most productive form of workshop is usually an unbroken session of a week or more, in a room with no telephones.

Very large applications need to be broken into subsystems with a design tool that ensures consistent data models and precise interfaces between the subsystems. Separate one-week JAD sessions may then be used for the separate subsystems.

The procedure which is perhaps the most effective for most systems is to have two workshops. At the first the initial design is done. After that workshop the design is solidified and cleaned up by IS professionals. Prototypes are built. The users examine the design documents and work with the prototypes. At the second workshop the experience with the prototypes is reviewed and enhancements to the design are discussed. Substantial design improvements or additions may be made. Before the first workshop, steps are taken to initiate the JAD procedure and a kickoff meeting is held. After the second workshop the design is further solidified and then finalized.

We will use this form of JAD in our more detailed discussion of the procedure:

```
┌─ JAD Procedure
│  ...Initiate.
│  ...Prepare.
│  ...Hold kickoff meeting.
│  ...Conduct the first design workshop.
│  ...Extend the prototypes and solidify the design.
│  ...Conduct the second design workshop.
└  ...Finalize.
```

JAD AND PROTOTYPING

JAD and PROTOTYPING are both powerful tools to use for the start of development lifecycle. They should be used in conjunction with one another. Many valuable prototypes emulate part of a system, not all of it. Some partial prototypes can be created very quickly. For example a person skilled with a screen painter can generate the screens used in dialogs quickly. These can be linked together to simulate a dialog. Reports can be designed and generated very quickly. If end users see a simulated dialog, menus, and reports, they begin to form a good idea of what the system will be like. This level of prototyping should be done during the workshops. More elaborate prototyping may require the time interval between workshops. The IS professional using the prototyping tool may work late at night during the session in order to build prototypes for the following day.

TYPES OF DIAGRAMS

The choice of diagram types is important to the success of JAD sessions. The diagrams must be very easy to understand because they are the primary form of communication with the end users. Some diagram types in use for systems analysis and design are complex, cluttered, or unclear.

End users can be taught to understand action diagrams, decomposition diagrams, process flow diagrams, and entity-relationship diagrams. These, in a simple form, should be the means of drawing the procedures and structures. If drawn with a computerized workbench, that tool should have the ability to remove or add detail such as labels on links and cardinality symbols so that users can see simple uncluttered structures and be able to understand and think about them. When the user understands the simple structure, the computer can add more detail. It can add windows showing text, properties of the blocks and links between blocks, data structures, comments, or diagrams showing finer detail.

The users should be given a brief training about the meaning of the diagrams prior to the JAD session. They should be given diagrams showing the external context of the new system. For example, they should be shown relevant data models and process models (from level 2 of the pyramid) before starting the design of level 3. They should be asked to study these diagrams as preparation for the new design work.

When users do not understand the meaning of system diagrams, they resort to text descriptions which are far from adequate.

Action diagrams are important for the structuring of specifications and their decomposition into structured code. An action diagram editor gives the capability to build action diagrams and to contract and summarize them. This ability to contract, expand, and navigate through diagrams is very valuable for conducting the JAD session.

The agenda of the JAD session itself should be printed as an action diagram, like that in Box 8.1, so that the attendees become used to this format. The attendees will sometimes adjust the agenda during the session, and this can be done immediately with the action diagram editor.

THE LANGUAGE OF BUSINESS

The language used throughout the session, and the language on the diagrams, should be the language of business, the language of the application, or the lan-

BOX 8.1   Procedure for IE/JAD, Joint Application Design.

Description
     Joint Application Design, JAD, is a technique for harnessing
end users into the requirements analysis, specification, and
design of systems. It is a highly successful technique when used
correctly, and should be employed for most systems.
     Key end users are selected to participate in workshops in
which the preliminary design of the system will be created. The
workshops progress through a planned set of steps as described
here.
     At the start of the workshop the users are encouraged to do
most of the talking. Data processing staff in the session
translate what the users want into structured specifications
and design, in such a way that the users can understand and
discuss the design. Along with the specifications are created
the relevant data model, the screen designs, report designs,
and possibly rough prototypes.

The procedure given below may be modified with Action
Diagrammer to meet the needs of the particular situation.

JAD Procedure
  Initiate.
     Establish the need for a system.
     If a JRP workshop has been conducted,
        o─────────────────────────────────o
        │ See Figure 7.2: JRP Procedure   │
        o─────────────────────────────────o
          edit the procedure below so that it is a natural follow-on from
          the JRP session.
  Else
     Proceed as below.

  Appoint the JAD session leader.
     If a JRP workshop has been conducted,
        the JRP leader may now become the JAD leader.
     Else
        Appoint a JAD leader.

     It is desirable to have a full-time person, with appropriate
     skills, to conduct JRP and JAD sessions. A well-chosen JAD
     session leader becomes skilled with experience.
     He should be trained in the following:
        o Communication skills
        o Negotiating skills
        o Group dynamics
        o Information engineering
        o Analysis and design
        o Data modeling
        o The diagramming techniques
        o The automated tools used
        o Project management
        o He should have on-the-job training in other JAD sessions

BOX 8.1　*(Continued)*

Determine scope.
　Conduct management interviews.
　Establish management's objectives for the project.
　Determine which locations are involved.
　Determine which departments are involved.
　Determine which BAA processes are involved.
　Examine relevant goals, problems, and critical success factors
　　(from the encyclopedia).
　Determine what business assumptions are to be made by the
　　design group.

Obtain commitment of executive sponsor.
　The JAD session should not proceed unless a suitably high-
　　level executive is fully committed to creating the system
　　and to using JAD for this purpose.

Prepare.
Select the participants.
　Select end-user workshop participants.
　　The workshop should not be held until the key participants
　　　are available.
　Select other workshop participants.
　　Workshop participants:
　　　o　Executive sponsor (occasional visits)
　　　o　Session leader
　　　o　End users who want the system (the key players)
　　　o　I.S. professionals (possibly one I.S. professional)
　　　o　Visiting specialists (possibly)
　　　o　Outside users (possibly)
　　　　　If the system serves individuals in other corporations
　　　　　　such as suppliers, distributors, buyers, or customers,
　　　　　　their attendance should be considered.
　　　o　Scribe (who uses an IE CASE tool during the session to
　　　　　document the design, remove inconsistencies, generate
　　　　　screen and report designs, and illustrate the design to
　　　　　the participants as it emerges)
　　　o　The project manager who will be responsible for the system
　　　　　(possibly)

Prepare the materials.
　Prepare slides or foils illustrating business activity.
　If a BAA study has been done
　　Extract the relevant information from the BAA study.

　　　Extract the relevant process decomposition diagram.
　　　Extract the relevant entity-relationship diagram.
　　　Extract or create the relevant process flow diagram,
　　　　showing how the processes are dependent on one another.
　　　Add detailed comments to the above diagrams where necessary.
　　　Print relevant versions of the above diagrams from the
　　　　encyclopedia for the participants to review.

　Else
　　Adjust the JAD agenda (below) so that the above information
　　　is created at the start of the JAD session.

(Continued)

BOX 8.1 *(Continued)*

Customize the JAD agenda.
    Determine number and duration of JAD sessions if different
        from that below.
    Duplicate and modify this action diagram to represent the
        agenda to be used.
    Prepare agenda for each process.

Prepare the participants.
    Give participants literature on the JAD procedure.
    Give them the JAD agenda.
    Train participants in the diagramming techniques, where necessary.

Obtain agreement of executive sponsor.
    Ensure that the executive sponsor is prepared to participate
        briefly in the meetings.

Hold kickoff meeting.
    Have the executive sponsor make the opening speech.
    Review with participants the purpose and objectives.
    Review the agenda.
    Give participants the preparatory material for them to study.
        Inform them that they must understand it well before the first
        workshop.
    Review the initial data models and process models with the
        participants.
    Review relevant goals, problems, and critical success factors.
    Review the business assumptions that are to be made.

Conduct the first design workshop.
    Executive sponsor should visit the workshop periodically to
        lend support.
    Review the system objectives.
    Design activities
        Examine and adjust the relevant information from the BAA study.

        Examine the process decomposition diagram, adjusting it as
            necessary.
        Examine the process flow diagram, adjusting it as
            necessary.
        Examine the entity-relationship diagram, adjusting it as
            necessary.
        Add detailed comments to the above diagrams where necessary.

    Clarify the scope of the design activity.

BOX 8.1 *(Continued)*

For each process block

  ─ Determine what are the steps in the procedure.
       The procedure steps may be examined with the following framework:

       1: PLANNING
          A planning process provides or creates information about work that will be received.

       2: RECEIVING
          Work is received.
          Resources to do the work may be received.
          A unique identification for each item of work or each resource received is entered into the system and validated.

       3: PROCESSING RECEIPTS
          The time of reporting the receipt is recorded.
          The receipt is validated.
          The receipt is processed.
          The relevant records are updated.
          Transactions may be generated to notify other locations of the receipt.

       4: MONITORING
          The receipts are monitored to see whether they are as planned.
          Management are notified of exceptions to the plan.
          Requirements for additional resources may be generated.

       5: ASSIGNING
          Work is assigned or scheduled.
          Work instructions, identification, and reporting documents are created.

       6: PROCESSING
          Work is performed.
          Work may be guided through multiple stages.
          The performance is monitored.
          Reports are generated for administrative feedback and planning.

       7: RECORDING
          The system processes data about the work.
          A date/time stamp is recorded for each step.
          The system may validate that the work is done correctly.
          Client-requested notifications may be produced.
          Completion of the work is recorded.

       8: SENDING
          Work is routed to other locations or customers.
          Documents or labels are produced to identify the work done.
          Work departures are recorded.
          Accounting is done.
          Billing is done.

(Continued)

BOX 8.1   *(Continued)*

9: EVALUATING
   Work measurements and summaries are provided.
   Trends may be assessed.
   Information on resource utilization may be created.
   Comparisons with goals and objectives may be created.

Build an initial data flow diagram showing the steps.
   Enter the procedure steps into the data flow diagram
      on the screen of a workbench tool.

   The initial diagram is an approximate diagram. If the
      workbench has a knowledge coordinator or comprehensive
      checking capabilities, these are switched off at this
      time. They will be used later to solidify the design.

Examine each procedure step in more detail.
   Describe its purpose.
   Determine its input data.
   Determine its output data.
   Determine what processing occurs. Represent this with an
      action diagram.
   Adjust the data flow diagram if necessary.
   Design and paint the screens.
   Design and create the reports.

For each procedure step create a partial prototype.
   Create prototype of the screens, dialog, and reports used.
   Develop and enhance more complete prototypes as appropriate.

Address security.
   Determine security requirements.
   Design authorization scheme.
   Determine how security will be handled.

Address unresolved issues.
   List unresolved issues.
   Determine responsibility and deadline for unresolved
      issues.
   Details of issue
      o   Issue:
      o   Assigned to:
      o   Assign date:
      o   Date to be resolved by:
      o   Resolution:

Establish date and time of the second workshop.

BOX 8.1 *(Continued)*

Extend the prototypes and solidify the design.
    Create or enhance the prototypes.
    Install prototypes for user review.
    Formally analyze the specifications and design, and improve
      them where necessary.
    Use the knowledge coordinator of the design tool to ensure
      that the design is internally consistent, and consistent with
      other knowledge in the encyclopedia.
    Create the documentation.
      The documentation should include:
        o   Management objectives.
        o   Business questions the system will answer.
        o   The scope of the system (from the encyclopedia).
        o   The process flow diagram (from the encyclopedia).
        o   Relationships with other systems (from the encyclopedia).
        o   Data model for the system (from the encyclopedia).
        o   Data item definitions (from the encyclopedia).
        o   Data flow diagrams (from the encyclopedia).
        o   Action diagrams of procedures (from the encyclopedia).
        o   Screen and report layouts (from the prototypes).
        o   Menu layouts (from the prototypes).
        o   Interfaces to other systems (from the encyclopedia).
        o   Listing of unresolved issues.
        o   Schedule for implementation.
        o   What happens next.

    Give the documentation to the end users for study prior
      to the second workshop.
    End users should list questions and suggestions ready for the
      second workshop.

Conduct the second design workshop.
    Review experience in using the prototypes.
    Review the end users' questions and suggestions.
    Discuss enhancements that are necessary.
    For each procedure step
      Review the inputs and outputs.
      Review the screens and dialog used.
      Review any reports generated.
      Review and enhance more complete prototypes as appropriate.
      Review the overall data flow diagram.
      Review the information in the database.

    Review the overall design and update as necessary.
    Specify security requirements.
    Estimate volumes.
    Address unresolved issues.
      List unresolved issues.
      Determine responsibility and deadline for unresolved
        issues.
      Details of issue
        o   Issue:
        o   Assigned to:
        o   Assign date:
        o   Date to be resolved by:
        o   Resolution:

(Continued)

BOX 8.1 *(Continued)*

```
    Determine whether a further JAD workshop is required.
  ┌ Expectation management
  │    Give the users realistic expectations of when the completed
  │       system will become available.
  │    Have executive sponsor attend the closing session and make
  │       the closing speech.
  └

┌ Finalize.
│    Further enhance the prototypes if necessary.
│    Formally analyze the specifications and design, and improve
│       them where necessary.
│    Use the knowledge coordinator of the design tool to ensure
│       that the design is internally consistent, and consistent with
│       other knowledge in the encyclopedia.
│  ┌ Create the documentation.
│  │    The documentation should include:
│  │       o    Management objectives.
│  │       o    Business questions the system will answer.
│  │       o    The scope of the system (from the encyclopedia).
│  │       o    The process flow diagram (from the encyclopedia).
│  │       o    Relationships with other systems (from the encyclopedia).
│  │       o    Data model for the system (from the encyclopedia).
│  │       o    Data item definitions (from the encyclopedia).
│  │       o    Data flow diagrams (from the encyclopedia).
│  │       o    Action diagrams of procedures (from the encyclopedia).
│  │       o    Screen and report layouts (from the prototypes).
│  │       o    Menu layouts (from the prototypes).
│  │       o    Interfaces to other systems (from the encyclopedia).
│  │       o    Listing of unresolved issues.
│  │       o    Schedule for implementation.
│  │       o    What happens next.
│  └
│    Present the results to the executive sponsor.
└
```

guage of the user, not technical language. The diagrams should be populated with business or application terms, not technical terms.

It is often necessary to define the application terms used. Group consensus should be achieved about the definitions, and they should be stored in the design tool.

TRAINING

The participants in a JAD workshop may need some training prior to the workshop. They need to be able to read and think constructively about the four types of diagrams which are used: decomposition diagrams, flow diagrams (data flow and dependency diagrams), entity-relationship diagrams, and action diagrams. These four types of diagrams can be taught to end users in a half-day training course. In some organizations two half-day training sessions are used to ensure that the diagrams are correctly understood.

Users who have not participated in JAD before need to be familiarized with what it is and what they are expected to contribute. The author made a set of four videotapes with Applied Learning International, Inc. (ALI) [2], to teach JAD. These tapes show a live JAD session, with the scribe using a CASE tool. In many corporations these tapes are viewed by the participants prior to the JAD session.

A JAD ROOM

Some corporations have a specially designed JAD room. A design workbench is connected to a large-screen projector so that the participants can observe the diagrams, screen designs, and so on. The projector may project on to a white board so that participants can scribble on the design that is projected. The workbench tool has a printer so that parts of the design, specifications, agenda, and so on, can be printed and distributed to the users.

Figure 8.2 shows typical layouts of JAD rooms. There should be large white boards to create sketches and lists which remain visible throughout the session. An overhead projector is used to make prepared presentations and sketch diagrams during the session. There may also be a slide projector. These projectors will be used when training sessions take place in the room. The session leader may arrange for slides to be available of the processes which need automating. A CASE workbench is available in the room. It may be able to access a mainframe encyclopedia. A printer and a copying machine are available.

Refreshments are available in the room, but *there is no telephone*. An important aspect of the workshop is the isolation from the interruptions of daily business.

The JAD room may be designed to serve other functions also, such as other meetings, training, demonstrations, and sales presentations. The upper layout in Fig 8.2 is typical of a JAD session taking place in a hotel.

INITIATING JAD

Before a JAD session is planned there needs to be a session leader who is well trained in JAD techniques. The first JAD sessions in an enterprise may use an external consultant as the session leader. One or more people selected to be in-house session leaders gain experience from these sessions.

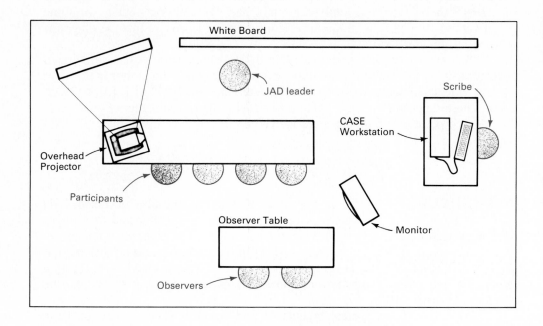

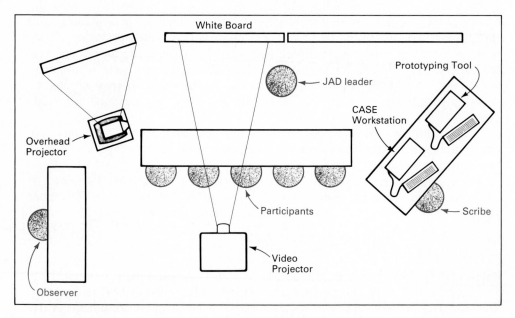

Figure 8.2 Examples of JAD room layouts.

When the need for a system is established the scope of the project is assessed, and the commitment of an executive sponsor is obtained.

```
┌─ Initiate
│      Establish the need for a system.
│   ...If a JRP workshop has been conducted,
│   ...Appoint the JAD session leader.
│   ┌─ Determine scope
│   │      Conduct management interviews.
│   │      Establish management's objectives for the project.
│   │      Determine which locations are involved.
│   │      Determine which departments are involved.
│   │      Determine which BAA processes are involved.
│   │      Examine relevant goals, problems, and critical success factors
│   │         (from the encyclopedia).
│   │      Determine what business assumptions are to be made by the
│   └─        design group.
│   ...Obtain commitment of executive sponsor.
└─
```

A suitably high-level executive sponsor is needed who is fully committed to building the system, employing the JAD technique, and helping to make the JAD technique work well. Without such commitment, JAD should not proceed.

PREPARATION FOR JAD

To prepare for a JAD session it is necessary to select the participants carefully, prepare the materials, create the agenda, and prepare the participants. The executive sponsor must agree to what is planned.

```
┌─ Prepare
│   ...Select the participants.
│   ...Prepare the materials
│   ...Customize the JAD agenda
│   ...Prepare the participants.
└─  ...Obtain agreement of executive sponsor.
```

As we have stressed, obtaining the right participants is critical. The session should not proceed until the key end users are available. The session leader prepares the materials for the session. He may arrange for slides to be taken showing the current procedures.

If a business area analysis study has been done, much relevant material already exists. This should be extracted from the encyclopedia and edited into a starting document for the participants. If a BAA has not been done, then equivalent information needs to be created as part of the JAD session.

```
┌─ Prepare the materials
│     Prepare slides or foils illustrating business activity.
│  ┌─ If a BAA study has been done
│  │  ┌─ Extract the relevant information from the BAA study
│  │  │
│  │  │   Extract the relevant process decomposition diagram.
│  │  │   Extract the relevant entity-relationship diagram.
│  │  │   Extract or create the relevant process flow diagram,
│  │  │      showing how the processes are dependent on one another.
│  │  │   Add detailed comments to the above diagrams where necessary.
│  │  │   Print relevant versions of the above diagrams from the
│  │  └      encyclopedia for the participants to review.
│  │
│  ├─ Else
│  │     Adjust the JAD agenda (below) so that the above information
│  │     is created at the start of the JAD session.
└  └
```

The session leader creates the JAD agenda, editing an action diagram of a JAD procedure such as that in this chapter. He ensures that the participants have the basic knowledge necessary to take part in the session.

```
┌  ...Customize the JAD agenda
│  ┌─ Prepare the participants.
│  │     Give participants literature on the JAD procedure.
│  │     Give them the JAD agenda.
│  └     Train participants in the diagramming techniques, where necessary.
│
└  ...Obtain agreement of executive sponsor.
```

```
...Hold kickoff meeting
```

THE KICKOFF MEETING

The kickoff meeting reviews with the participants what is going to happen. The participants are given materials to study prior to the first workshop. Considerable enthusiasm should be generated in this session. The executive sponsor should make the opening speech.

```
┌─ Hold kickoff meeting
│     Have the executive sponsor make the opening speech.
│     Review with participants the purpose and objectives.
│     Review the agenda.
│     Give participants the preparatory material for them to study.
│        Inform them that they must understand it well before the first
│        workshop.
│     Review the initial data models and process models with the
│        participants.
│     Review relevant goals, problems, and critical success factors.
└     Review the business assumptions that are to be made.
```

Figure 8.3 summarizes what takes place prior to the first design workshop.

```
┌ JAD Procedure
│  ┌ Initiate.
│  │     Establish the need for a system.
│  │  ┌ If a JRP workshop has been conducted,
│  │  │     o─────────────────────────────────────o
│  │  │     │  See Figure 7.2: JRP Procedure      │
│  │  │     o─────────────────────────────────────o
│  │  │        edit the procedure below so that it is a natural follow-on from
│  │  │        the JRP session.
│  │  ┌ Else
│  │  │     Proceed as below.
│  │  └
│  │
│  │     ...Appoint the JAD session leader.
│  │  ┌ Determine scope.
│  │  │     Conduct management interviews.
│  │  │     Establish management's objectives for the project.
│  │  │     Determine which locations are involved.
│  │  │     Determine which departments are involved.
│  │  │     Determine which BAA processes are involved.
│  │  │     Examine relevant goals, problems, and critical success factors
│  │  │       (from the encyclopedia).
│  │  │     Determine what business assumptions are to be made by the
│  │  │       design group.
│  │  └
│  └    ...Obtain commitment of executive sponsor.
│  ┌ Prepare.
│  │     ...Select the participants.
│  │  ┌ Prepare the materials.
│  │  │     Prepare slides or foils illustrating business activity.
│  │  │  ┌ If a BAA study has been done
│  │  │  │  ┌ Extract the relevant information from the BAA study.
│  │  │  │  │
│  │  │  │  │     Extract the relevant process decomposition diagram.
│  │  │  │  │     Extract the relevant entity-relationship diagram.
│  │  │  │  │     Extract or create the relevant process flow diagram,
│  │  │  │  │       showing how the processes are dependent on one another.
│  │  │  │  │     Add detailed comments to the above diagrams where necessary.
│  │  │  │  │     Print relevant versions of the above diagrams from the
│  │  │  │  │       encyclopedia for the participants to review.
│  │  │  │  └
│  │  │  ┌ Else
│  │  │  │     Adjust the JAD agenda (below) so that the above information
│  │  │  │       is created at the start of the JAD session.
│  │  │  └
│  │  └
│  │     ...Customize the JAD agenda.
│  │     ...Prepare the participants.
│  └    ...Obtain agreement of executive sponsor.
│  ┌ Hold kickoff meeting.
│  │     Have the executive sponsor make the opening speech.
│  │     Review with participants the purpose and objectives.
│  │     Review the agenda.
│  │     Give participants the preparatory material for them to study.
│  │       Inform them that they must understand it well before the first
│  │       workshop.
│  │     Review the initial data models and process models with the
│  │       participants.
│  │     Review relevant goals, problems, and critical success factors.
│  └    Review the business assumptions that are to be made.
└       ...Conduct the first design workshop.
```

Figure 8.3 The events that occur prior to the first design workshop.

THE DESIGN PROCEDURE

The initial design of the system is done in the first design workshop. To begin, the objectives of the system are reviewed with the participants. The relevant information from the BAA study is then examined. It may be projected on to the workshop screen live from the workbench tool. Adjustments may be made and comments added.

```
┌─ Examine and adjust the relevant information from the BAA study

     Examine the process decomposition diagram, adjusting it as
        necessary.
     Examine the process flow diagram, adjusting it as
        necessary.
     Examine the entity-relationship diagram, adjusting it as
        necessary.
     Add detailed comments to the above diagrams where necessary.
└─
```

The scope of the design activity is then clarified.

Each process, represented by a process block on the process flow diagram, is then examined in detail. This may be done in five stages:

```
┌ For each process block

  ...Determine what are the steps in the procedure
  ...Build an initial data flow diagram showing the steps
  ...Examine each procedure step in more detail.
  ...For each procedure step create a partial prototype
  ...Address security
  ...Address unresolved issues
└
```

The initial pass determines what steps are in the procedure. Many processes require steps which fall into the following categories:

```
...1: PLANNING
...2: RECEIVING
...3: PROCESSING RECEIPTS
...4: MONITORING
...5: ASSIGNING
...6: PROCESSING
...7: RECORDING
...8: SENDING
...9: EVALUATING
```

These steps form a valuable structure for examining the processes. They are shown in more detail in Fig. 8.4.

At the second pass the workbench operator enters the steps into a data flow diagram. The initial diagram is an approximate diagram which will become successively refined. If the workbench can do comprehensive checking of the diagram, this capability may be switched off for the time being. It will be used later to solidify the design.

The procedure steps may be examined with the following framework:

1: PLANNING
    A planning process provides or creates information about work that will be received.

2: RECEIVING
    Work is received.
    Resources to do the work may be received.
    A unique identification for each item of work or each resource received is entered into the system and validated.

3: PROCESSING RECEIPTS
    The time of reporting the receipt is recorded.
    The receipt is validated.
    The receipt is processed.
    The relevant records are updated.
    Transactions may be generated to notify other locations of the receipt.

4: MONITORING
    The receipts are monitored to see whether they are as planned
    Management are notified of exceptions to the plan.
    Requirements for additional resources may be generated.

5: ASSIGNING
    Work is assigned or scheduled.
    Work instructions, identification, and reporting documents are created.

6: PROCESSING
    Work is performed.
    Work may be guided through multiple stages.
    The performance is monitored.
    Reports are generated for administrative feedback and planning.

7: RECORDING
    The system processes data about the work.
    A date/time stamp is recorded for each step.
    The system may validate that the work is done correctly.
    Client-requested notifications may be produced.
    Completion of the work is recorded.

8: SENDING
    Work is routed to other locations or customers.
    Documents or labels are produced to identify the work done.
    Work departures are recorded.
    Accounting is done.
    Billing is done.

9: EVALUATING
    Work measurements and summaries are provided.
    Trends may be assessed.
    Information on resource utilization may be created.
    Comparisons with goals and objectives may be created.

Figure 8.4 A framework for examining each process.

At the next pass, the steps are examined in detail and information should be recorded for each step as follows:

```
Examine each procedure step in more detail.
    Describe its purpose.
    Determine its input data.
    Determine its output data.
    Determine what processing occurs. Represent this with an
        action diagram.
    Adjust the data flow diagram if necessary.
    Design and paint the screens.
    Design and create the reports.
```

The next pass creates prototypes of the screens and reports that are used. The screens may be linked to form a simulated dialog. More complete prototypes may be created of processes which need to be examined in more detail.

UNRESOLVED ISSUES AND CONSIDERATIONS
Sometimes an issue is not resolvable during the JAD workshop. The session leader writes down the issue and has the group appoint an individual to be responsible for its resolution. A date is assigned for completion of the resolution.

A form or computer screen may be used for the resolution of issues. It should contain the following information:

```
ISSUE:
ASSIGNED TO:
ASSIGN DATE:
DATE TO BE RESOLVED BY:
RESOLUTION:
```

An "issue" has a direct effect on the design and must be resolved. A "consideration" relates to other aspects of the business or other systems and may be written during a JAD session. For example, a note may be made that "The sales manual should eventually be online."

```
Address unresolved issues
    List unresolved issues.
    Determine responsibility and deadline for unresolved
        issues.

    Details of issue
        o    Issue:
        o    Assigned to:
        o    Assign date:
        o    Date to be resolved by:
        o    Resolution:
```

Figure 8.5 shows the procedure for the first JAD workshop.

Conduct the first design workshop.
    Executive sponsor should visit the workshop periodically to
       lend support.
    Review the system objectives.
    Design activities
       Examine and adjust the relevant information from the BAA study

          Examine the process decomposition diagram, adjusting it as
            necessary.
          Examine the process flow diagram, adjusting it as
            necessary.
          Examine the entity-relationship diagram, adjusting it as
            necessary.
          Add detailed comments to the above diagrams where necessary.

       Clarify the scope of the design activity.

       For each process block

          Determine what are the steps in the procedure.
            The procedure steps may be examined with the following
            framework:

          ...1: PLANNING
          ...2: RECEIVING
          ...3: PROCESSING RECEIPTS
          ...4: MONITORING
          ...5: ASSIGNING
          ...6: PROCESSING
          ...7: RECORDING
          ...8: SENDING
          ...9: EVALUATING

          Build an initial data flow diagram showing the steps.
            Enter the procedure steps into the data flow diagram
              on the screen of a workbench tool.

            The initial diagram is an approximate diagram. If the
              workbench has a knowledge coordinator or comprehensive
              checking capabilities, these are switched off at this
              time. They will be used later to solidify the design.

         Examine each procedure step in more detail.
           Describe its purpose.
           Determine its input data.
           Determine its output data.
           Determine what processing occurs. Represent this with an
             action diagram.
           Adjust the data flow diagram if necessary.
           Design and paint the screens.
           Design and create the reports.

         For each procedure step create a partial prototype.
           Create prototype of the screens, dialog, and reports used.
           Develop and enhance more complete prototypes as appropriate.

         Address security.
           Determine security requirements.
           Design authorization scheme.
           Determine how security will be handled.

Figure 8.5   The first design workshop.

(Continued)

```
┌ Address unresolved issues.
│    List unresolved issues.
│    Determine responsibility and deadline for unresolved
│       issues.
├ Details of issue
│    o   Issue:
│    o   Assigned to:
│    o   Assign date:
│    o   Date to be resolved by:
│    o   Resolution:

└ Establish date and time of the second workshop.
```

Figure 8.5   (Continued)

SOLIDIFICATION   When JAD participants use diagrams in creative arguments, they may draw the diagrams on a white board or flip chart. As agreements are reached, the diagram is entered into the design tools. A good design tool has a *knowledge coordinator* which cross-checks all aspects of the design. The designer must eventually resolve the issues which the knowledge coordinator reveals, but to do that during the JAD session may slow it down so the knowledge coordinator may be switched off during the session. Rough designs are produced during the session and in the solidification period after the session the knowledge coordinator is used to create a more thorough design.

Also in the solidification period the prototypes are improved and the end users work with them. The enhanced design diagrams are printed and the documentation is produced. Documentation and enhanced diagrams should be available to all session members within a week (or possibly two weeks) from the end of the session.

Figure 8.6 is an expansion of the JAD procedure showing the solidification and finalization activities after the workshop.

THE SECOND WORKSHOP   The second design workshop takes place after the end users have worked with the prototypes and studied the documentation. If they do this thoroughly, they will probably have many questions and suggestions. The second workshop addresses their questions, suggestions, and experience with the prototypes. The design is enhanced as necessary, and unresolved issues are again recorded.

The second workshop should address the issue of security. The volumes of transactions should be estimated in preparation for physical design and configuring the hardware.

The executive sponsor should address the closing session.

Figure 8.7 shows the procedure for the second workshop.

```
┌─ Extend the prototypes and solidify the design.
│     Create or enhance the prototypes.
│     Install prototypes for user review.
│     Formally analyze the specifications and design, and improve
│        them where necessary.
│     Use the knowledge coordinator of the design tool to ensure
│        that the design is internally consistent, and consistent with
│        other knowledge in the encyclopedia.
│  ┌─ Create the documentation.
│  │     The documentation should include:
│  │        o    Management objectives.
│  │        o    Business questions the system will answer.
│  │        o    The scope of the system (from the encyclopedia).
│  │        o    The process flow diagram (from the encyclopedia).
│  │        o    Relationships with other systems (from the encyclopedia).
│  │        o    Data model for the system (from the encyclopedia).
│  │        o    Data item definitions (from the encyclopedia).
│  │        o    Data flow diagrams (from the encyclopedia).
│  │        o    Action diagrams of procedures (from the encyclopedia).
│  │        o    Screen and report layouts (from the prototypes).
│  │        o    Menu layouts (from the prototypes).
│  │        o    Interfaces to other systems (from the encyclopedia).
│  │        o    Listing of unresolved issues.
│  │        o    Schedule for implementation.
│  └─       o    What happens next.
│
│     Give the documentation to the end users for study prior
│        to the second workshop.
│     End users should list questions and suggestions ready for the
└─       second workshop.
```

Figure 8.6   Solidification activities after the first workshop.

EXPECTATION MANAGEMENT

A good JAD session generates excitement about the forthcoming system. End users often want the system *immediately,* especially if they work with prototype versions of it. It is important to establish realistic expectations, explaining to them the nature of the development schedule. At the end of the final workshop the timetable for delivering a pilot system, and later a full system, should be given.

In general it is necessary to manage the expectations of a JAD session. The technique is powerful but does not automatically produce solutions to difficult business problems.

THE DEVELOPMENT LIFECYCLE

In some organizations the traditional development life-cycle is regarded as unchangeable. It is treated as though it was handed down by Moses. JAD sessions in such organizations will be used to create the documentation required by the traditional lifecycle.

Other organizations recognize that the traditional lifecycle ought to be substantially changed and improved by the use of prototyping, JAD, iterative development, timebox methodologies, design automation, code generators, and

```
┌─ Conduct the second design workshop.
│     Review experience in using the prototypes.
│     Review the end users' questions and suggestions.
│     Discuss enhancements that are necessary.
│   ┌ For each procedure step
│   █    Review the inputs and outputs.
│   █    Review the screens and dialog used.
│   █    Review any reports generated.
│   █    Review and enhance more complete prototypes as appropriate.
│   █    Review the overall data flow diagram.
│   █    Review the information in the database.
│
│     Review the overall design and update as necessary.
│     Specify security requirements.
│     Estimate volumes.
│   ┌ Address unresolved issues.
│   │    List unresolved issues.
│   │    Determine responsibility and deadline for unresolved
│   │        issues.
│   │  ┌ Details of issue
│   │  │    o   Issue:
│   │  │    o   Assigned to:
│   │  │    o   Assign date:
│   │  │    o   Date to be resolved by:
│   │  └    o   Resolution:
│   └
│
│     Determine whether a further JAD workshop is required.
│   ┌ Expectation management
│   │    Give the users realistic expectations of when the completed
│   │        system will become available.
│   │    Have executive sponsor attend the closing session and make
│   └        the closing speech.
└
```

Figure 8.7   The second workshop.

information engineering. Chapter 21 discusses this topic. Ideally a JAD session should relate to the third level of the pyramid (DESIGN), assuming that a relevant business area analysis has already been done. Sometimes, however, the business area analysis has not been done, and so the tasks of the JAD session include creating a *data model* and *process model* for the functions in question.

VARYING THE PROCEDURE

Box 8.1 gives a JAD procedure shown as an action diagram. The details of this are likely to vary from one JAD to another. The person planning the events may start with the action diagram in Box 8.1 and modify it to fit the specific situation.

The modified action diagram, or portions of it, can be printed to form an agenda for the workshop participants. The agenda may be displayed on the projector screen and modified in the meeting if necessary.

SUMMARY   In summary IE/JAD works and has been highly successful because

- It harnesses the know-how of the users.
- It cuts across organizational barriers.
- The group dynamics drive the design.
- It employs easy-to-understand diagrams.
- Screen generators, report generators, and rough prototypes make the design tangible.
- It is an organized, controlled, structured process.
- A session leader facilitates discussion and drives the session to complete its agenda.
- It includes management direction.
- It anchors into the higher levels of the pyramid.
- The IE tools enforce rigor.
- It utilizes IS advice and perspective.
- It creates designs which are implementable quickly and easy to maintain.

REFERENCES

1. James Martin, *Rapid Application Development*, Macmillan, New York, 1990.

2. *JAD, Joint Application Design*, four videotapes for training in JAD, Applied Learning, Naperville, IL, 1987.

9 TIMEBOX METHODOLOGY

INTRODUCTION   A major change in the design and implementation of systems is brought about by

- JAD (joint application design) with a CASE (computer-aided systems engineering) tool linked to the IE (information engineering) encyclopedia.
- Prototyping.
- Design automation tools.
- Code generators linked to design tools (integrated CASE).

In combination these are extremely powerful and bring about a revolutionary change in the development of systems.

Some authorities advocate JAD, some advocate prototyping, some design automation, and some code generation. In practice a combination of all four is needed so that all aspects of the development lifecycle are improved. Furthermore, this combination needs to fit into the umbrella discipline of information engineering; otherwise, uncoordinated redundant systems will proliferate.

This chapter takes the best aspects of these methodologies and links them into an overall methodology for system design and implementation.

One of the dangers of prototyping methodologies or iterative development is that the functions of a system can grow in an uncontrolled fashion. Users or developers often add functionality so that the design does not converge quickly into a usable system. This is sometimes referred to as *creeping functionality*. The more powerful the prototyping tools, the more the developers are encouraged to experiment, add functions, or overengineer the system. This can become expensive and can prevent a system from being delivered on time.

THE TIMEBOX

Perhaps the best way to combat creeping functionality is to place a rigid limit on the time permitted to produce a working system. The methodology we advocate creates a *timebox*. Within this timebox a working system must be built. Before the timebox, the functions and design framework of the system are defined. After the timebox, the system is evaluated and a quick decision is made whether to put it into production.

Figure 9.1 illustrates this process.

The timebox is not extendable. A system must be produced within the time allocated. The functionality of the system may be trimmed back in order to complete it within the timebox. The system produced by the end of the timebox must be a system which is intended to be implemented.

Within the timebox, *continuous* iterative development is done (the right-hand side of Fig. 9.1), by end users and IS developers working closely together. This team is under pressure to produce a working system by the end of the timebox.

The timebox methodology depends upon having a powerful, easy-to-use development tool which generates executable code. It should be easy to build and evolve prototypes with this tool. The tool should be capable of generating systems with good machine efficiency *so that the prototype becomes the final working system*. The development techniques employed by the tool should be sufficiently user-friendly that users can easily participate in the development process. It is desirable that the tools provide a design workbench to speed up the design process, check the design, and generate code from the design.

A typical length for the timebox is 60 days. The team working within this period should not be large. Often it is a two-person team. From two to six people are appropriate. Typical costs for the timebox activity vary from $20,000 to $60,000.

A general concept of the timebox methodology is that it is better to have a working system of limited functionality *quickly* than to wait two years for a more comprehensive system. Much experience will be gained from implementing the limited system, and the timebox can be reentered to produce subsequent versions of the system with greater functionality. The timebox methodology puts pressure on the participants to produce results quickly.

Creative people in many other walks of life have a deadline. A magazine writer, television producer, or seminar developer creates material for a certain date. Whatever else happens he must not fail to meet the deadline. He may allow the contents to slip. There may be items he wants to include, but cannot do so in time. Similarly, in timebox development the functionality of a system may slip, but the deadline is immovable. Under such time constraints the most important 90 percent of the material or functionality is completed; the other 10 percent might have taken as long again. The 90 percent is achieved with a relatively low development cost. The unfinished 10 percent would have had a much higher cost. The result is a relatively high return on investment.

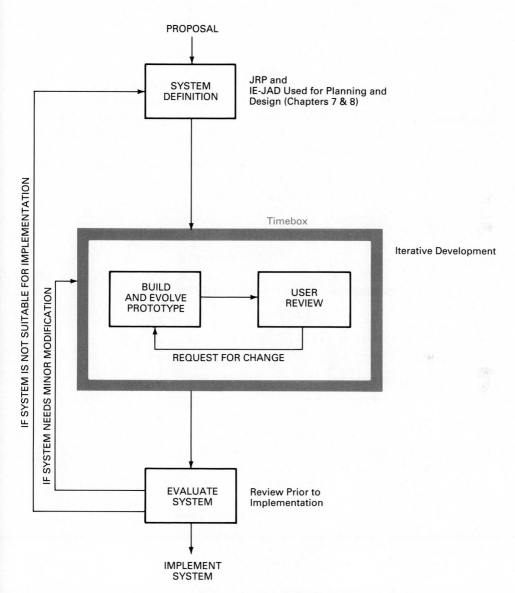

Figure 9.1 Use of a timebox in the system development procedure.

If the system is misconceived, it is better to find out after 60 days (and $20,000 to $60,000) than after the long time and high expense of traditional development. After working with the limited system, the requirements for subsequent versions are often different from what they would otherwise have been.

MULTIPLE TIMEBOXES

Some systems are too complex to finish in one timebox. These are split into subsystems, each of which performs a function in its own right which can be demonstrated, and which is small enough to be built in one timebox of 60 days by a small team. As experience builds up with the prototyping and code generation tools that makes the timebox methodology practical, it becomes easier to estimate what should be accomplishable in the 60 days. This estimate may relate

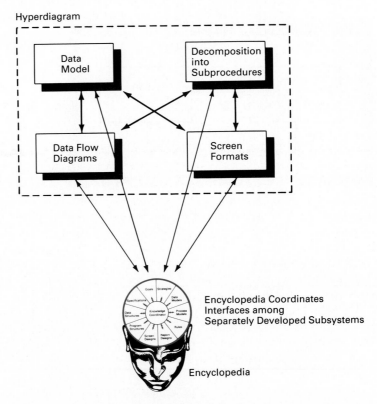

Figure 9.2 CASE tools allow a data model to be built and complex systems subdivided into pieces which use the data model, and which can each be built by a small team (or one person). The interfaces between the pieces is controlled online with computerized precision.

to function points (the most commonly used complexity metric) or to the numbers of screens, reports, and logical files used.

The separate subscriptions all use the same data model. The system should be split into subsystems using an IE-CASE tool. The encyclopedia coordinates the interfaces among the separately developed subsystems, as shown in Fig. 9.2.

Almost any data processing project can be subdivided in this way. Organizations that have used this approach comment that if you cannot subdivide a large data processing project you do not yet understand it well enough and that proceeding without such understanding is to ask for trouble.

Figure 9.3 shows experience with a project which would have been about 100,000 lines of code if developed by traditional methods. It was built in the Textile Fibers Division of DuPont, using the Cortex Application Factory. The project was split into ten timeboxes as shown, each staffed with one, two or three developers. The dictionary-controlled code generator made possible this use of small teams working quickly.

EXPERIENCE AT DUPONT   A timebox methodology has been used with great success at DuPont [1]. DuPont stress that the methodology works well for them and is highly practical. It has resulted in automation being introduced more rapidly and effectively. DuPont quotes large costs savings from the methodology, as illustrated in Fig. 9.4.

DuPont uses a 60-day timebox for most projects. Complex projects must be implemented in phases where each phase can be completed with a 60-day timebox. The tool used by DuPont is Application Factory from Cortex [2]. This produces efficiently coded systems which operate on VAX computers. The Cortex tool did not allow complete freedom of development. It constrained its uses to menu-driven systems with a certain style of easy-to-use dialog. This constraint, to a large extent, made possible the rapid system development. During the timebox about 70 percent of the development time used nonprocedural facilities of Application Factory and 30 percent used procedural facilities (fourth-generation program coding). The nonprocedural facilities gave a $20:1$ improvement in developer hours over FORTRAN (the language previously used for these applications in DuPont). The procedural coding gave a $2:1$ improvement. Overall this resulted in approximately a $15:1$ improvement. The methodology, however, gave more than these savings; it resulted in more satisfactory systems.

The overall time for completing a project with one timebox in DuPont was about 90 days. This included the system definition and approval prior to the timebox and the evaluation after the timebox. DuPont found that 90-day implementations produced systems as fast as the end users could adapt to them. The limiting factor was no longer design and programming but user training and change in human procedures. Partly because of the end-user cutover time,

APPLICATION	Number of Developers	DATES START	DATES END	COST($ Thousands) Actual	COST($ Thousands) Estimated	COST($ Thousands) Savings	APPLICATION STATISTICS Screens	APPLICATION STATISTICS Reports	APPLICATION STATISTICS Files
1 PASSIVE DATA	3	09/01/85	10/01/85	15.0	52.6	37.6	108	41	49
2 PRODUCTION ORDER	2	10/01/85	04/01/86	90.2	315.6	225.5	52	10	45
3 TIME CARD	2	12/01/85	02/01/86	30.1	105.2	75.2	14	3	16
4 STANDARD OPER'N COND' (SOC)	3	02/01/86	05/01/86	45.1	157.8	112.7	30	5	25
5 PRODUCT SEPARATION	3	11/01/85	04/01/86	75.2	263.0	187.9	23	2	32
6 PROCESS TEST	2	04/01/86	08/01/86	60.1	210.4	150.3	30	2	32
7 TRACKING	2	07/01/86	08/01/86	15.0	52.6	37.6	25	4	32
8 CREATE PRODUCT	1	01/01/86	05/01/86	60.1	210.4	150.3	31	3	55
9 SYSTEM IMPROVEMENT	1	07/01/86	08/01/86	15.0	52.6	37.6	10	4	8
10 JOB ASSIGNMENTS	1	07/01/86	08/01/86	15.0	52.6	37.6	12	2	16

Total Savings: 1053.3

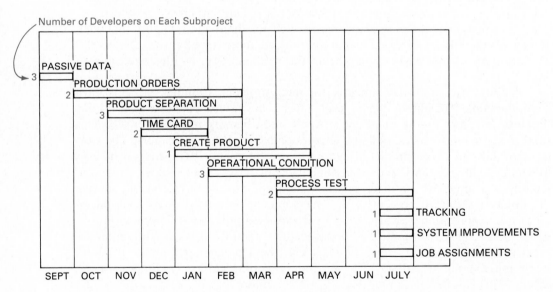

Figure 9.3 An example of an information engineering project in DuPont built with multiple timeboxes. With traditional techniques it would have taken about 20 person-years and an elapsed time of 2 years. It was subdivided into the ten pieces shown each of which was implemented by one to three developers using a code generator. It took 4½ person-years and 11 months. The saving from this approach exceeded $1 million. [1].

	Number of Screens	Number of Reports	Number of Files	Development Costs ($ Thousands)		
				Estimated	Actual	Savings
BCF (Bulk Continuous Filament) Stretch Wrap	3	5	11	168	30	138
BCF Inspection and Packing	250	27	65	1000	450	550
Suggestion	5	12	3	50	8	42
Spinning	16	4	12	50	25	25
Feedstock	12	4	11	45.1	7.5	37.6
Transfer	12	11	12	125	20	105
Kevlar Information System	313	119	76	1472.9	420.8	1052.1

Figure 9.4　Experience in the DuPont Fibers Division during the first year of using a timebox methodology. The estimated development costs are for their traditional methodology. The actual costs are their experience with the timebox methodology [1].

DuPont targeted 120 days rather than 90 days for systems built after the first year or so of using the methodology.

A typical use of timebox methodology in DuPont was in a highly automated plant making bulk continuous filament (something like nylon) at Waynesborough, Pa. This spotless factory has many robots and few people. Spinning machines produce large quantities of spun filament which are wound on to bobbins. The bobbins are automatically wrapped and packed. The filament and bobbins are continuously inspected for quality. Any quality defect must be tracked back to its cause, and other bobbins affected by the problem must be identified. Bobbins of different quality go to different customers. The inspection and packing system also includes calculation of tare weights, label generation, historical records, shipping documents, and so on. It was developed with the timebox methodology.

The system employed

250 screens.

27 reports.

12 subsystems.

65 logical files with 300 fields.

The system employed online equipment such as weighing machines and was made more complex by interfaces to other systems.

The original estimate called for 16 to 18 developers and development cost of over a million dollars. Using the timebox methodology with Application Factory the system was built by 4 developers at a cost of $550,000 less. The total time to develop the first version was 2½ months. The original definition of the system contained something that would not have worked in practice. The users would have spent far too much time entering screen data. This misconception was discovered and corrected early with the timebox methodology. With traditional implementation, it probably would not have been found until a $1.5 million system had been built, which would have been a disaster.

THE SYSTEM REVIEW BOARD

The development is controlled by a group called the Review Board. The Review Board signs off on the system definition prior to entering the timebox. When the system is complete at the end of the timebox, it is evaluated by the Review Board. The Review Board (or individual members of that group) examine the prototype periodically as it evolves in the timebox.

When evaluation is done after the timebox, it is hoped that the system can be approved for immediate implementation. In some cases there may be minor modifications needed. For unavoidable reasons, the requirements may have changed slightly. If the modifications can be made with another prototyping iteration, the Review Board permits the timebox to be reentered, setting a deadline for the change being completed.

If the system proves to be unsuitable for implementation, another system definition workshop is held to determine what the problem is and to modify the system definition. In the DuPont experience with their timebox methodology, this has never happened (at the time of writing).

The Review Board should be relatively small. An end-user leader and an IS leader should be represented on it. Both these individuals should be decision makers.

The Review Board should include

- The executive sponsor or his representative. He is an end-user manager responsible for project funding and allocating user resources. He has the final vote on resolving major end-user issues.

- An IS professional responsible for application quality.

- An IS professional responsible for information engineering control who will ensure that the system uses and conforms to the data and process models in the encyclopedia.

The Review Board *may* include or call upon

- A user who will be primarily responsible for the use of the system.
- A representative of the organization which supports production systems.
- An auditor, if the system is sensitive from the auditor's point of view. (Many are not.)

EXECUTIVE SPONSOR

The executive sponsor is the end-user executive who has made a commitment to have the system built. He participates in the initiation of the project and in the JAD session as described in Chapters 7 and 8. He may participate in the Review Board.

THE USER COORDINATOR

The user coordinator is the lead end user in the prototyping activity. He is a member of the timebox team which builds the system in the timebox. He also serves on the Review Board. He represents the end-user community and may involve other end users where appropriate to help review the prototypes.

He arranges for user documentation and training.

In some cases the user coordinator spends all of his time on the project. In other cases he has another job to do and commits to spend 10 to 20 percent of his time on the project.

THE TIMEBOX TEAM

We will refer to the team which builds the system in the timebox as the Timebox Team.

The Timebox Team should include end users and IS professionals. The team should be as small as possible. Often a two-person team is the most appropriate—one end user and one IS professional. Teams ranging from two people to six people have been used effectively.

The team should include

- The user coordinator.
- The lead IS developer.
- Other developers as required, on larger projects.

Either the user coordinator or the lead IS developer should be appointed project manager, with overall responsibility for development and product quality.

The team should be strongly motivated to succeed. Management should create an environment in which the Timebox Team can complete the system within the timebox. The team is told that success or failure is judged by whether they create, by the deadline, a system which is in fact implemented. They are told that most timebox efforts do indeed succeed and that they must not distinguish themselves by being one of the rare failures. They should be assured that success will be rewarded, and that their efforts are very visible to higher management. They should be told that if they succeed a major victory celebration will be held.

Prior to building the system, the Timebox Team will participate in defining it. They will be members of the JAD session that precedes the timebox.

After the timebox they will participate in implementing the system and either preparing the closing report or else participating in a new JAD to define a new phase of development that will be built with a new timebox.

A more refined and detailed version of timebox methodology and its management is given in reference [3].

TOOL CHARACTERISTICS

The timebox methodology is dependent on the prototyping tool. Some prototyping tools cannot generate code of sufficient machine efficiency for implementation. Some code generators are not user-friendly enough to be employable by typical end users. The combination of user-friendly design automation and efficient code generation is needed. The tool must be powerful in its functionality so that systems of realistic complexity can be built quickly.

It is desirable that the tool should have an efficient code generator which is an extension of a graphics design workbench. An encyclopedia-based workbench is desirable.

The tool should

- Be interactive.
- Be easy to use.
- Facilitate quick building of prototypes.
- Make changes quickly and easily.
- Encourage stepwise refinement.
- Support appropriate database structures.

The tool should include

- A versatile screen painter (which can be used very quickly in JAD sessions).
- Ability to link screens and responses into a dialog.

- Ability to support the fast creation of a standard form of dialog such as a menu dialog, or those defined in the Common User Access (CUA), IBM's Systems Application Architecture (SAA).
- A versatile report generator (which can be used very quickly in JAD sessions).
- A fourth-generation language or code generator.
- A suitably flexible database management system.
- An integral dictionary.
- Facilities for extracting data from files or databases, and loading them into the prototype database, or on-line access to other files or databases.

A tool which is merely a prototyping tool does not have to give good machine performance. For this methodology, the tool needs to be able to build the final working system which has characteristics not required in a prototype.

Because the prototype will evolve into the final system the tool should have

- Ability to achieve good machine performance (with an optimizing compiler).
- Ability to support the database structure of the final system.
- Appropriate networking access.
- Ability to handle a suitably large number of users.
- Ability to handle suitably large databases.
- Ability to handle suitably high-traffic volumes.

The system the tool generates should have

- Features for recovery from failures.
- Features for fallback.
- Security features.
- Features for auditability.
- Features for ease of maintenance.

Ability to build systems with good security, auditability, checkpoint/restart, fallback, and so on is missing in some prototyping tools, but is critical here.

STEPS IN THE PROCEDURE

Steps in the timebox development lifecycle are likely to be as follows:

```
┌  Timebox procedure
│  ┌  Establish the methodology.
│  │     This methodology is highly dependent on a toolset which enables
│  │     fast and easy design, and a rapid cycle of modify-generate-test.
│  │     The methodology is built around the toolset and adapted to it.
│  │     Selecting the right toolset is highly critical.
│  │
│  │  ...Select the tools
│  └  ...Adapt the methodology to the toolset
│  ┌  Timebox lifecycle methodology
│  │  ...Initiate the project.
│  │  ...Obtain commitment of executive sponsor.
│  │  ...Determine the scope and objectives.
│  │  ...Appoint the User Coordinator.
│  │  ...Establish the Review Board.
│  │  ...Estimate the required effort and cost.
│  │  ...Establish the Timebox Team(s).
│  │  ...Motivate the Timebox Team(s).
│  │  ...Prepare for cultural changes.
│  │  ...JAD procedure
│  │  ...Design for cutover.
│  │  ┌  Build the system.
│  │  │  ┌  Perform timebox development.
│  │  │  │  ...Build and evolve a prototype.
│  │  │  │  ...Evolve the prototype, with continuous user review,
│  │  │  │     into a fully operational system, within the 60 days
│  │  │  └     of the timebox.
│  │  │
│  │  │  ...Have the Review Board evaluate the results.
│  │  └     Adjust if necessary.
│  └
│  ...Create physical design.
│  ...Prepare for cutover.
│  ...Install and adjust pilot system.
└  ...Expand pilot to full system.
```

Box 9.1 shows this procedure in more detail.

Many variations are possible in the procedure and different organizations are likely to adjust the action diagram to their own requirements.

SCOPE AND OBJECTIVES

Before any substantial work is done an executive sponsor should be appointed. Following that, the scope and objectives of the system are established. The objectives should be determined from interviews with user managers and written down.

BOX 9.1 Timebox lifecycle

The timebox methodology is a highly successful form of lifecycle that emphasizes high-speed development. It constrains the functionality of the first release of a system in order to have a fully working system within a short time frame.

The lifecycle employs continuous-evolution prototyping with a tight deadline. It requires an I-CASE toolset designed to make design fast and easy and give a rapid cycle of modify-generate-test. End users are involved continuously throughout the lifecycle.

The costs and risks of new system development are minimized by emphasizing JRP, JAD, prototyping, and high-speed development, with continuous user involvement, within an IE framework.

```
The procedure given below may be modified with Action
Diagrammer to meet the needs of the particular situation.
```

```
┌─ Timebox procedure
│ ┌─ Establish the methodology.
│ │     This methodology is highly dependent on a toolset which enables
│ │       fast and easy design, and a rapid cycle of modify-generate-test.
│ │     The methodology is built around the toolset and adapted to it.
│ │     Selecting the right toolset is highly critical.
│ │
│ │ ┌─ Select the tools.
│ │ │ ┌─ Characteristics of the prototyping tool
│ │ │ │     The toolset should be an integrated-CASE tool which uses
│ │ │ │       the IE encyclopedia.
│ │ │ │     The toolset should:
│ │ │ │       o  be interactive
│ │ │ │       o  be easy to use
│ │ │ │       o  facilitate quick building of prototypes
│ │ │ │       o  give the most automated capability for design and code
│ │ │ │          generation
│ │ │ │       o  give the fastest possible cycle of modify-generate-test
│ │ │ │
│ │ │ │     The toolset should include the following:
│ │ │ │       o  a powerful design workbench tightly coupled to the
│ │ │ │          analysis (BAA) workbench
│ │ │ │       o  a code generator which is an extension of the design
│ │ │ │          workbench
│ │ │ │       o  a versatile screen painter (which can be used very quickly
│ │ │ │          in JAD sessions)
│ │ │ │       o  ability to link screens and responses into a dialog
│ │ │ │       o  a versatile report generator (which can be used very
│ │ │ │          quickly in JAD sessions)
│ │ │ │       o  use of a suitably flexible database management system
│ │ │ │       o  an integral dictionary
│ │ │ │       o  facilities for extracting data from files or databases,
│ │ │ │          and loading them into the prototype database
```

(Continued)

BOX 9.1   *(Continued)*

Because the prototype will become the final system the tool
  should have:
  o ability to achieve good machine performance (with an
       optimizing compiler)
  o ability to support the database structure of the final
       system
  o appropriate networking access
  o ability to handle a suitably large number of users
  o ability to handle suitably large databases
  o ability to handle suitably high-traffic volumes

The system the tool generates should have:
  o features for recovery from failures
  o features for fallback
  o security features
  o features for auditability
  o features for ease of maintenance

Adapt the methodology to the toolset.
  It is desirable to select one toolset and perfect its use. The
  methodology given below should be adapted to fit the toolset. The
  methodology should be applied to many projects and tuned on the
  basis of experience.

Timebox lifecycle procedure
Initiate the project
  Determine need for system.
  Obtain executive sponsor.

Obtain commitment of executive sponsor.
  The JAD session should not proceed unless a suitably high-
    level executive is fully committed to creating the system
    and to using JAD for this purpose.

Determine the scope and objectives.
  Establish management's objectives for the project.
    Interview appropriate end-user managers.
    Write down the objectives.
    Obtain management agreement.

JRP procedure
  o─────────────────────────────o
  │ See Box 7.2: JRP procedure │
  o─────────────────────────────o
  The requirements should be listed in a JRP workshop and the
    following activities performed.

BOX 9.1   *(Continued)*

Determine scope.
    Determine which locations are involved.
    Determine which departments are involved.
    If Business Area Analysis has been done
       Extract relevant data and process models from the
        encyclopedia.
    Else
       Create relevant data and process models.

    Examine relevant goals, problems, and critical success
       factors (from the encyclopedia).
    Determine what business assumptions are to be made by the
       design group.

Summarize the benefits and risks.
    Assess the benefits.
       o   Financial savings.
       o   Opportunity costs.
       o   Better quality.
       o   Improved competitive position.
       o   Other tangible benefits.
       o   Intangible benefits.

Determine how to maximize the benefits.
    Look for business ways to obtain leverage from the system.
    Determine which potential functions of the system have the
       most effect on profits or business objectives.

Assess the risks.
       o   There may be inadequate user motivation.
       o   Lack of user acceptance of changed way of working.
       o   User difficulties learning or adapting to the system.
       o   Possible misconceptions in the system concept.
       o   Possible development cost overruns.
       o   Possible technical problems.

Determine how to minimize the risks.
    The risks should be examined in detail.
    An executive sponsor at a suitably high level must be
       totally committed to the project. He should address his
       attention to user motivation.
    Use of JAD substantially reduces the risks of user non-
       acceptance and business misconceptions.
    A prototyping methodology substantially reduces the risks
       as misconceptions and technical difficulties are more
       likely to be discovered early.
    The development risks are likely to be much less if the
       project fits comfortably into the timebox methodology
       and can be developed with the tools in question.

Obtain a decision whether the project goes ahead.

(Continued)

BOX 9.1 *(Continued)*

Appoint the User Coordinator.
  The User Coordinator:
    o is the lead user developer on the timebox team(s).
    o involves other users where appropriate to help review the
       evolving prototypes.
    o arranges for user documentation and training.
    o serves on the Prototype Review Board.

Establish the Review Board.
  The Review Board reviews the requirements prior to the timebox,
  and reviews the results at the end of the timebox.
  The Review Board includes
    o Leading spokespeople of the end users who need the system.
    o The executive sponsor.
    o An IE executive.
    o Possibly external reviewers such as customers.
    o Possibly an external consultant.
  Ensure that sufficient commitment exists that a thorough review
     job will be done.

Estimate the required effort and cost.
  The estimating method must relate to experience with the
     prototyping/code-generator tool. Manpower statistics for
     COBOL/PLI/FORTRAN have almost no relevance.
  Obtain manpower statistics of experience with the prototyping/
     generator tool.
  Estimate the number of screens.
  Estimate the number of reports.
  Estimate the number of logical files.
  Estimate the proportion of the system that can be generated
     nonprocedurally, and the proportion that needs procedural
     (fourth-generation) coding.
  Estimate the number of lines of procedural code.
  Estimate the manpower effort for procedural code.
  Split the project into multiple timeboxes, if necessary.
    Estimate what application functions can be built during the
       60-day timebox with a small (2- or 3-person) team.
    If the project is too large for one timebox, divide it into
       multiple timeboxes which can proceed simultaneously.
    Use the workbench tools to do the subdivision into separate
       timebox efforts (process decomposition diagram and process
       dependency diagram or data-flow diagram).
    Ensure that the interfaces between the separate timebox efforts
       are defined with precision with the I-CASE tool.

Establish the Timebox Team(s).
  The team should be small. Two- or three-person teams are the
     most appropriate. Large projects should be subdivided so that
     more than one timebox is used simultaneously, each staffed by
     a small team

  The team should include:
    o The User Coordinator (who may work with more than one timebox
       simultaneously).
    o The lead I.S. developer.
    o Other I.S. or user developers as appropriate.

  Either the end user or the lead I.S. developer should be
     appointed project manager, with overall responsibility for
     development and product quality.

BOX 9.1 *(Continued)*

Motivate the Timebox Team(s).
  Ensure that the team knows that success or failure is determined
    by whether they build an implementable system by the end of the
    timebox. They cannot extend the timebox deadline.
  Ensure them that success will be rewarded.
  Tell them that a victory celebration will be held when the system
    is judged successful.
  Tell them that failures are rare and that they must not distinguish
    themselves by creating a failure.
  Ensure them that their activities are very visible to higher
    management.

JAD Procedure
  The specifications and initial design are produced by JAD in
    conjunction with prototyping.
  ...Appoint the JAD session leader.
  Prepare.
    ...Select the participants.
    ...Prepare the materials
    ...Customize the JAD agenda
    ...Prepare the participants.
    ...Obtain agreement of executive sponsor.

  Hold kickoff meeting.
    Have the executive sponsor make the opening speech.
    Review with participants the purpose and objectives.
    Review the agenda.
    Give participants the preparatory material for them to study.
      Inform them that they must understand it well before the
      first workshop.
    Review the initial data models and process models with the
      participants.
    Review relevant goals, problems, and critical success factors.
    Review the business assumptions that are to be made.

  Conduct the first design workshop.
    Executive sponsor should visit the workshop periodically to
      lend support.
    Review the system objectives.
    Design activities.
      Examine and adjust the relevant information from the BAA
          study.

      Examine the process decomposition diagram, adjusting it as
          necessary.
      Examine the process flow diagram, adjusting it as
          necessary.
      Examine the entity-relationship diagram, adjusting it as
          necessary.
      Add detailed comments to the above diagrams where
          necessary.

      Clarify the scope of the design activity.

(Continued)

BOX 9.1 *(Continued)*

For each process block

Determine what are the steps in the procedure.
The procedure steps may be examined with the following framework:

1: PLANNING
A planning process provides or creates information about work that will be received.

2: RECEIVING
Work is received.
Resources to do the work may be received.
A unique identification for each item of work or each resource received is entered into the system and validated.

3: PROCESSING RECEIPTS
The time of reporting the receipt is recorded.
The receipt is validated.
The receipt is processed.
The relevant records are updated.
Transactions may be generated to notify other locations of the receipt.

4: MONITORING
The receipts are monitored to see whether they are as planned.
Management are notified of exceptions to the plan.
Requirements for additional resources may be generated.

5: ASSIGNING
Work is assigned or scheduled.
Work instructions, identification, and reporting documents are created.

6: PROCESSING
Work is performed.
Work may be guided through multiple stages.
The performance is monitored.
Reports are generated for administrative feedback and planning.

7: RECORDING
The system processes data about the work.
A date/time stamp is recorded for each step.
The system may validate that the work is done correctly.
Client-requested notifications may be produced.
Completion of the work is recorded.

BOX 9.1　*(Continued)*

```
      ┌─ Do physical database design.
      │     o─────────────────────o
      │     │ See procedure in Box 15.1  │
      │     o─────────────────────o
      │
      │   Determine hardware requirements.
      │   Examine how to optimize performance.
      │   Complete documentation (in the encyclopedia) of the final design.
      └─

   ┌─ Prepare for cutover.
   │     o─────────────────o
   │     │ See details in Box 18.1 │
   │     o─────────────────o
   │   ...Develop the conversion system.
   │   ...Finalize the development product.
   │   ...Prepare for final testing.
   │   ...Carry out the final testing.
   └─  ...Plan and conduct the training program.

   Install and adjust pilot system.
    ┌─ Perform cutover.
    │     o─────────────────o
    │     │ See detail in Box 18.2  │
    │     o─────────────────o
    │   ...Set up the production procedures.
    │   ...Install the production system environment.
    │   ...Perform data conversion.
    │   ...Implement the new system in production.
    └─  ...Review the system installation.

    ┌─ If no modifications needed
    │
«───┼──── Exit
    ├─ Else
    │     Document adjustments needed.
    │     Determine date for installation of next version.
    └─    Make adjustments.


   ┌─ Expand pilot to full system.
   │     Measure the system performance.
   │   ┌─ Optimize the database design.
   │   │   o─────────────────────────o
   │   │   │ See data use analysis in Box 14.1   │
   │   │   o─────────────────────────o
   │   │   o─────────────────────────o
   │   │   │ See database design in Box 15.1   │
   │   └─  o─────────────────────────o
   │
   │     Determine what hardware is needed to handle the full load.
   │
   │   ┌ Expand the system a stage at a time.
   │   └     Monitor the system performance.
   └─
```

If the earlier stages of information engineering have been done, information in the encyclopedia will help in determining the scope of the system:

```
┌─ Determine scope.
│     Determine which locations are involved.
│     Determine which departments are involved.
│  ┌─ If Business Area Analysis has been done
│  │     Extract relevant data and process models from the
│  │       encyclopedia.
│  ├─ Else
│  │     Create relevant data and process models.
│  └─
│
│     Examine relevant goals, problems, and critical success
│       factors (from the encyclopedia).
│     Determine what business assumptions are to be made by the
│       design group.
└─
```

A JRP workshop may be used to determine the functions of the system.

Next it is necessary to estimate the effort and cost to build the system. The number of screens, number of reports, and number of files may be estimated. An estimate should be made of what proportion of the system can be generated nonprocedurally and what proportion needs procedural coding. Such numbers are used to estimate the personnel effort required, or the detail of functionality that can be achieved in the 60-day timebox.

```
┌─ Estimate the required effort and cost.
│     The estimating method must relate to experience with the
│       prototyping/code-generator tool. Manpower statistics for
│       COBOL/PLI/FORTRAN have almost no relevance.
│     Obtain manpower statistics of experience with the prototyping/
│       generator tool.
│     Estimate the number of screens.
│     Estimate the number of reports.
│     Estimate the number of logical files.
│     Estimate the proportion of the system that can be generated
│       nonprocedurally, and the proportion that needs procedural
│       (fourth-generation) coding.
│     Estimate the number of lines of procedural code.
│     Estimate the manpower effort for procedural code.
│  ┌─ Split the project into multiple timeboxes, if necessary.
│  │     Estimate what application functions can be built during the
│  │       60-day timebox with a small (2- or 3-person) team.
│  │     If the project is too large for one timebox, divide it into
│  │       multiple timeboxes which can proceed simultaneously.
│  │     Use the workbench tools to do the subdivision into separate
│  │       timebox efforts (process decomposition diagram and process
│  │       dependency diagram or data-flow diagram).
│  │     Ensure that the interfaces between the separate timebox efforts
│  └─    are defined with precision with the I-CASE tool.
└─
```

The risks and benefits of the system should be assessed:

```
Summarize the benefits and risks.
  Assess the benefits.
        o   Financial savings.
        o   Opportunity costs.
        o   Better quality.
        o   Improved competitive position.
        o   Other tangible benefits.
        o   Intangible benefits.

  Determine how to maximize the benefits.
     Look for business ways to obtain leverage from the system.
     Determine which potential functions of the system have the
        most effect on profits or business objectives.

  Assess the risks.
        o   There may be inadequate user motivation.
        o   Lack of user acceptance of changed way of working.
        o   User difficulties learning or adapting to the system.
        o   Possible misconceptions in the system concept.
        o   Possible development cost overruns.
        o   Possible technical problems.

  Determine how to minimize the risks.
     The risks should be examined in detail.
     An executive sponsor at a suitably high level must be totally
        committed to the project. He should address his attention
        to user motivation.
     Use of JAD substantially reduces the risks of user non-
        acceptance and business misconceptions.
     A prototyping methodology substantially reduces the risks as
        misconceptions and technical difficulties are more likely
        to be discovered early.
     The development risks are likely to be much less if the
        project fits comfortably into the timebox methodology and
        can be developed with the tools in question.
```

A decision should then be made by the executive sponsor whether to go ahead with the project.

DESIGN USING JAD

When the go-ahead is obtained, the functionality of the system must be defined and user needs understood in sufficient detail to go ahead with the timebox activity. This is done with a JAD workshop.

Prior to the workshop the user coordinator, Review Board, and Timebox Team are appointed. They will participate, as appropriate, in the JAD activity.

```
...Appoint the User Coordinator.
...Establish the Review Board.
...Estimate the required effort and cost.
...Establish the Timebox Team(s).
...Motivate the Timebox Team(s).
┌─ JAD Procedure
│      The specifications and initial design are produced by JAD in
│        conjunction with prototyping.
│   ...Appoint the JAD session leader.
│   ...Prepare.
│   ...Hold kickoff meeting.
└   ...Conduct the design workshop.
```

The JAD technique in Box 8.1 used two workshops, the second being to comment on the initial prototypes. The JAD technique recommended here uses one workshop. User comments on the evolving prototypes will be obtained during the timebox development. Box 9.1 shows the detailed procedure for this JAD activity. As with any JAD, the agenda action diagram is likely to be adjusted to the circumstances in question.

An objective of the timebox methodology is to create systems quickly, so the initiation and design steps must not take long. A 90-day or 120-day period for the total lifecycle should be used and this includes the 60-day timebox. The initiation, scoping and JAD activity should be completed in about three weeks or so.

TIMEBOX ACTIVITIES

Figures 9.5 and 9.6 illustrate the timebox activities. It is important that a fully working system is built rather than merely a prototype. A prototyping/generator tool is needed which makes this practical.

Members of the Review Board should monitor the progress during the 60 days to ensure that it is on track, and to make helpful suggestions wherever they can.

Appropriate documentation should be created during the 60 days.

AFTER THE TIMEBOX

After the timebox, implementation should proceed quickly of a full system if it is small, or a pilot system if it is large. New functions may be requested as implementation or usage proceeds. These may give rise to a further iteration of the entire lifecycle.

A brief summary report may be written after implementation, documenting experience which may help with subsequent implementations.

The Timebox Team has a specified time (maximum 60 days) in which to develop a fully working system. They are not permitted to slip the end date.

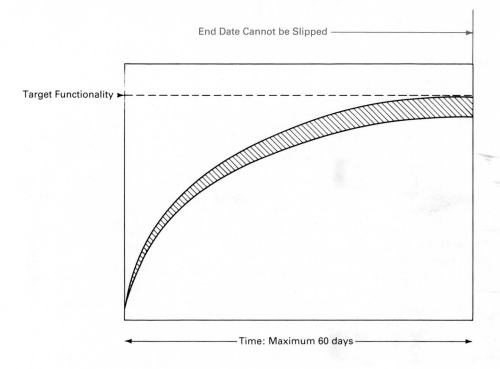

Continuous Evolution is used. Continuous evolution progresses with a sequence of modifications continuously adjusting the prototype until the target is reached. This requires an intelligent, understanding end user(s) working as a team with the developer(s) reviewing the evolution.

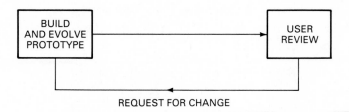

Figure 9.5 During the 60-day timebox continuous evolution is used. The team must produce a fully working system before the end of the timebox.

```
 ┌─ Perform timebox development.
 │  ...Build and evolve a prototype.
 │     The Review Board should review the evolving prototype at
 │       suitable intervals.
 │     Plan to use the prototype for education and training purposes
 │       at a suitably early stage.
 │     Plan for cutover at an early stage, as described below.
 │  ┌─ Evolve the prototype into a fully working system.
 │  │     Ensure that the final version covers the following needs
 │  │       adequately:
 │  │
 │  │       o   Features for recovery from failures
 │  │       o   Features for fallback
 │  │       o   Security features
 │  │       o   Features for auditability
 │  │       o   Features for ease of maintenance
 │  │       o   Machine efficiency
 │  │       o   Facilities for having multiple users
 │  │       o   Ability to handle the anticipated transaction volumes
 │  │             with adequate performance and response times
 │  │       o   Suitably large database facilities
 │  └       o   Networking facilities
 └
 ┌─ Evaluate the results.
 │     After the timebox the Review Board examines the results in
 │     detail and decides whether the system will be implemented.
 │  ┌─ If minor modifications are needed before implementation
 │  │     Specify the modifications.
 │  │     The Review Board establishes a deadline for
 │  │       making the modifications.
«├──────── Re-enter the timebox.
 │  ┌─ Else if the system is not suitable for implementation
 │  │     Specify the reasons for rejection.
 │  │     Reschedule a JAD session.
«├──────── Conduct a JAD session to determine what action to take.
 │  ┌─ Else
 │  └     Hold victory celebration.
 └
```

Figure 9.6   The activities that occur in the timebox.

REFERENCES

1. Information from Mr. Scott Shultz, manager, Information Engineering, E. I. du Pont de Nemours and Company, Inc., Palmerton, PA.

2. Application Factory manuals are available from Cortex Corp., 55 William St., Wellesley, MA 02181.

3. James Martin, *Rapid Application Development*, Macmillan, New York, 1990.

10 INFORMATION CENTERS

We are entering an era when all white-collar workers (and some blue-collar ones) use computers. Many of them create their own procedures with LOTUS 1-2-3, JAVELIN, FOCUS, and so on; some of them program with end-user languages. Some end users build very sophisticated financial models or decision-support models.

An Information Center is a facility designed to encourage and support end-user computing. In an early phase it is a catalyst to make end users employ computers; in a later phase it helps to manage and support user computing and direct it toward the most profitable applications. It may still play the role of catalyst for more advanced systems, for example, end users building expert systems.

THE MISSION OF THE INFORMATION CENTER

Box 10.1 gives the mission of the Information Center. The mission should emphasize better decision making, improved knowledge worker productivity, and better procedures rather than the spread of user computing or technology for its own sake.

Box 10.2 lists typical end-user activities supported by information centers.

Both the tools used and the types of applications differ greatly. Many end users employ personal computers; others use mainframe or departmental computers. Increasingly the personal computer will be tightly linked to mainframe tools with cooperative processing. Some users employ simple facilities such as query languages; others do highly sophisticated computing such as business modeling. Office automation facilities should be supported along with computational tools. Some users build only personal systems; others build departmental systems.

BOX 10.1 The mission of the Information Center

- Encourage better decision making through the use of computerized tools and information.
- Achieve strategic systems opportunities through well-planned end-user computing.
- Encourage end users to invent better procedures and cut administrative costs.
- Increase knowledge worker productivity.
- Bypass the development backlog of the IS department.
- Greatly speed up the development of most systems that end users require.
- Ensure that user-built systems are well designed and maintainable.

BOX 10.2 Typical end-user activities supported by Information Centers

- Querying databases
- Generating reports
- Using business graphics
- Word processing
- Electronic mail and message sending
- Desktop publishing
- Creating personal databases and tools
- Using spreadsheets
- Building spreadsheet applications
- Financial computations
- Business modeling
- Creating departmental applications
- Putting packaged applications to use
- Building and using decision-support systems
- Using analysis and modeling tools
- Using engineering or design software
- Creating simple expert systems
- Creating strategic business thrusts with end-user computing

The rise of the information center originally came because of the need to bypass the lengthy application backlog of the IS department. It was discovered that when knowledge workers are taught to build their own applications they build different ones from those in the IS backlog. The Information Center thus has resulted in many new and valuable types of applications.

One IS department was required to calculate the return on investment of all IS developed applications. The average was 37 percent with an average payback period of 30 months. This same IS department created an Information Center. This gave 100 percent return on investment [1]. A large firm in Chicago quoted a return on investment of 300 percent on its Information Center activities. A Nolan, Norton survey reports a tenfold return on investment for planned strategic thrusts based on personal computers [2]. Some end-user expert systems have achieved a 100 percent return on investment [3]. The reasons for the high figures are that the users are tackling problems which have a direct impact on cost or revenue, for example, making better financial decisions, optimal purchases of bulk chemicals, maximizing the goods that can be handled with given resources, or new strategic business thrusts.

Box 10.3 lists quotes from executives in large corporations about the effects of their Information Centers.

BOX 10.3   Quotations from executives at companies that employ Information Centers

Vice-President, McDonald's

"The information center is our single most important productivity tool."

C. L. Dunn, Vice-President, Bank of America

"We have an active library right now of 53,000 NOMAD procedures written by end users with only a little assistance from our technical staff. Those procedures contain almost four million lines of instructions that would have taken 2,120 man years to develop using traditional tools and approaches." [4]

R. Jackson, Senior Internal Consultant, Dow Chemical Co.

"By 1987, end users at Dow will be handling 50% of their computer application needs without help from the Data Processing staff." [4]

(Continued)

BOX 10.3 *(Continued)*

S. G. Abbey, Director, Morgan Stanley & Co., New York

"Several years ago we realized that Morgan Stanley's product is really information; our goal is to provide it in the most productive manner." [4]

Dick Wood, Manager, Harris Corporation

"The most important factor in our success is direct, active, involvement by end users. Our information center employs only one technician; the rest are MBA's who speak the same language as users do. You have to turn over information center services to the end users if you expect to achieve the benefits you seek." [4]

Operations Executive, Santa Fe Railroad

"The freight we carry has more than doubled. That increase has been handled without any increase in staff. We couldn't have possibly handled the increase in business with our existing staff without (systems built by end users employing the tool) MAPPER."

Production Coordinator, Oil Consortium

"By building an information center I was able to process selected key indicators quickly, interpret them and present an analysis of the situation by the time of the daily operations meeting held at 7:00 A.M. About 80% of the time nothing unusual was going on, and I was able to use the information center data to debottleneck production capacity. During the critical 20% of the time, I was in a position to work with operational managers on an hour-by-hour basis to balance the flow from the fields to the refinery and the export terminal.

The management system supported by information center concepts enabled us to export *an additional million barrels a month at no additional cost.*"

Norton Survey

"Companies advanced in the use of personal computing are reaping a 10-fold vs. 10 percent return on investment (ROI) [by focus on strategic uses of knowledge-worker computing])." [2]

WHAT SYSTEMS SHOULD BE BUILT BY END USERS?

A critical issue is what systems should end users build and what should be built by IS professionals.

In general, systems which are technically difficult, or where machine performance is critical, should be built by IS. Systems which span many departments should be built at least with IS cooperation. Systems within one department, which can be created with easy-to-use tools, may be built by end users. If practical, users with subtle problems should solve their own problems. Analysis of complex information for decision-making needs to be done by the decision-maker or decision analyst. Systems which improve knowledge worker productivity are often best invested and improved by the knowledge worker himself or herself.

Tools that are easy to use and do not require programming should usually be put to work by end users. These tools are rapidly becoming more numerous

BOX 10.4 What end users usually can and cannot do

End Users Can:	End Users Cannot:
• Specify their information needs.	• Analyze the impact on other information systems.
• Set priorities.	• Analyze dependencies on other information systems.
• Make surprisingly inventive use of end-user tools.	• Select the best implementation vehicle.
• Understand the subtleties of their decision making better than IS professionals.	• Prepare architectures for decision support.
• Exploit a good base of systems and data.	• Do good database design.
• Evolve the use of existing decision-support systems.	• Optimize machine performance.
• Be highly constructive in JAD sessions.	• Detect the flaws in classical specifications.
• Assist in the evolution of prototypes.	
• Build departmental systems.	• Build corporatewide systems.
• Build low-volume systems.	• Build high-volume systems.

and more powerful. Many end users do program in fourth-generation languages. Bank America has more than 100,000 procedures created by end users with the NOMAD 2 language. DuPont has about 3000 professional programmers and 15,000 LOTUS users. It is not desirable, however, to turn the accountants into programmers. The user should only employ a tool if it enables him to be more productive at his primary job.

Box 10.4 summarizes things which end users generally can and cannot do. For every project it is desirable to assess realistically whether end users *should* build it. In the enthusiasm for programming end users sometimes try to create systems which would be better built by IS. For many systems close teamwork between user developers and IS professionals is needed.

THE NEED FOR MANAGEMENT

End-user computing needs management. Without help, training, and controls, all manner of problems can develop. The Information Center is the management vehicle for user computing. The reasons we need such management are as follows:

- To help avoid the numerous types of mistakes that users can make.
- To spread the culture of user computing so that it reaches its full potential.
- To direct end-user computing toward strategic applications (which may need nationwide or worldwide computing).
- To ensure that data entered or maintained by the users are employed to their full potential rather than being in isolated personal electronic files.
- To assist the users so that they develop applications as efficiently as possible.
- To ensure that adequate accuracy controls on data are used.
- To avoid unnecessary redundancy in application creation.
- To avoid integrity problems caused by multiple updating of data.
- To ensure that the systems built are auditable and secure, where necessary.
- To link the end-user activities into the information engineering process.

The Information Center concept should support a natural division of labor between the end users and IS staff. Each group provides what it is best equipped for. The end users know what information, reports, and decision support they need to do their jobs well, and usually they need results quickly. The IS support group knows how these results can be obtained. The two groups work together in close partnership, balancing their resources for maximum productivity. To achieve this result the end users must be trained, encouraged, and motivated, and their competence developed to a point where they can generate and manipulate the reports that they need, and perform calculations, answer "what-if" questions, perform simulations, and so on. In some cases end users have created major computer procedures.

End-user development is a force which should be harnessed, encouraged and supported to the full. If it happens in an *uncontrolled* fashion it can store up trouble for the future because multiple versions of incompatible data come into existence and multiple machines cannot be interlinked. If it is a force harnessed by the designers of strategic systems, it can give a high return on investment.

USER IC SPECIALISTS

At the start of the 1980s most end-user computing was done with terminals connected to mainframes. By the mid-1980s most end-user computing was done with personal computers. As this rapid evolution occurred, the nature of the Information Center changed.

The personal computer, with easy-to-use filing and spreadsheet tools, caused a rapid spread of computer literacy. By the end of the 1980s most knowledge workers in efficient organizations had personal computers. There were far too many computer users for a central Information Center to help them personally or control their creation of data. Information Center guidance had to become distributed.

The most effective way to achieve widespread Information Center guidance was by appointing *user specialists* to interact with the Information Center consultants. This is like a teach-the-teachers program. The Information Center teaches end-user leaders who go back to their locations and give assistance to the other end users.

The user specialist is a computing expert in his own department. He is the person whom everyone in the department goes to to solve their computing problems. He helps other members of the department get started and guides their personal growth in effective use of software. He makes himself an authority on the tools used on the PC, minicomputer, and mainframe, as appropriate. He reports to the manager of the department but has a close link to the Information Center. He meets with the Information Center consultant when appropriate. He does his own job in the department as well as acting as the departmental link to the Information Center. When the Information Center adopts new software or new policies or implements new corporate thrusts, the user specialist communicates these to the members of his department. Where his department has overall computing problems, he communicates these to the Information Center, to see how they might be solved.

Figure 10.1 shows the growth of end-user computing in Texas Instruments. The red curve, the number of end users supported by the Information Center, is representative of the dramatic growth in other corporations also in the 1980s from near-zero to the majority of white-collar workers. Information Center staff are typically able to support about 50 end users each, on average. As

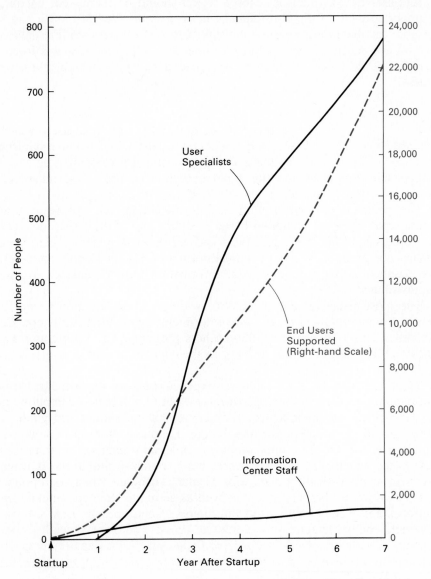

Figure 10.1 Growth in the number of IC user specialists, IC staff, and end users supported by the IC, at Texas Instruments.

the proportion of computer-using staff grows, the user specialists liaising with the Information Center become essential if central help and guidance is to be maintained.

COOPERATIVE PROCESSING

As end-user computing spread, many end users started to keep their own files and databases. They would enter data, extract data from mainframes, and update data on a personal basis, often not caring that these data should be used by other people. In many corporations, a concern spread that planning was being done and decisions being made on a parochial basis. Incompatible data proliferated. On the factory shop floor, for example, different planners with different concerns each used their own personal computers to keep their own data and make their own decisions. To minimize inventory, optimize the use of resources, and meet changing customer demands effectively, these different planners ought to be cooperating and making decisions with the shared data. The same concern was important in many other business areas.

The proliferation of end-user computing gave rise to a proliferation of separate uncoordinated collections of data. A strong need became felt to impose management on this data and achieve better integration of its use. Integration of the use of data translated directly into profits from lower work-in-progress, better job scheduling, higher utilization of resources, and better ability to meet changing customer demands. In other words, higher profits through better planning.

The era of isolated personal computers began to evolve into an era of networked personal computers which shared common databases. The term *cooperative processing* came into use to describe systems in which the best capabilities of the personal computer and the mainframe were combined. The personal computer can have excellent human factoring (with syntax that takes advantage of decisecond response times, color, bit-mapped graphics, icons, touch screens, a mouse, and so on.). The mainframe has high computer power and can maintain in one place a database being updated by many users simultaneously. Cooperative processing links the personal computer and mainframe to combine both sets of advantages. Sometimes complex cooperation is needed between the software which runs on the desktop.

IBM's SAA (Systems Application Architecture) is designed to provide standards for application development in an environment of cooperative processing. All applications have a similar look and feel in their user dialog and link to relational databases in multiple machines accessed by a common network.

A well-integrated network and applications with a common form of user access from personal computers make it possible for information to instigate the building of end-user databases. Texas Instruments (at the time of writing) has about 350 of these, accessible worldwide. Every end user has a catalog of the end-user databases.

The network of user IC specialists, equipped with such resources, makes it possible to direct end-user computing into channels which make it as profitable as possible.

The Information Center consultants work with the user specialists to find out what data they need and tell them what data can be made available. The user specialists show the staff in their department how to access and use the data which is available. The IC consultants help the user specialists and thence the end users to build decision-support systems, organizational support systems, possible expert systems, and so on.

RETURN ON INVESTMENT FROM PERSONAL COMPUTERS

The return on investment from personal computers varies greatly from one organization to another. In some cases personal computers generate no profit and represent a financial drain. In many cases individuals are employing personal computers for personal tasks; this improves their efficiency but often represents a return on investment of 10 percent or so. A much higher return on investment is achieved when personal computers are used fundamentally to change a business process. This sometimes happens at the departmental level, as when a department is reorganized to achieve a high level of efficiency in some operation with each member of the department having a personal computer application sharing the same database. The highest return on investment from personal computing is achieved when a strategic thrust is identified which achieves an order of magnitude improvement in efficiency or value of some business function by using computers. Often this requires a countrywide or worldwide organization to take advantage of computers and networks. It may involve links to customers or suppliers, electronic document interchange, or the use of an expert system. A list of potential opportunities of this type was given in the chapter on strategic systems vision in Book II of this trilogy.

A survey of corporate uses of personal computers by Nolan, Norton & Co. [2] finds it appropriate to divide them into four categories of evolution:

1. **Technical proficiency.** Early adapters are learning to be proficient with personal computers. No effort is made to measure benefits. Usually the benefits do not yet justify the expenditure of users' time, training, support, hardware, and software.

2. **Task automation.** The PC is used for automated individual tasks, usually personal tasks. A 10 to 20 percent return on investment may be obtained.

3. **Business process.** PCs have now penetrated a department. Investments are driven by a tactical vision, usually at the departmental level. The improve-

ment or automation of an entire process may be achieved. A threefold (i.e., 300 percent) return on investment may be attained.

4. **Business transformation.** PCs have now fully penetrated the business usually with corporatewide networking. The user community is now experienced with PCs and is capable of being creative. Investments are driven by strategic business vision (as described in Book II). There may be a major restructuring of business processes. A tenfold (1000 percent) return on investment may be achieved.

The most valuable use of an Information Center is to achieve the implementation of strategic thrusts. A planning team may develop strategic systems vision (Book II) and identify a strategic thrust which requires end-user computing. The design may require professional systems development as well as end-user computing. Information Center representatives should participate in a JAD session. The Information Center consultants help set up the end-user databases

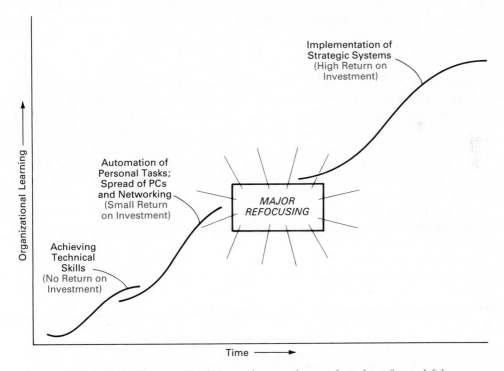

Figure 10.2 The growth of personal computing needs to be refocused following the systematic planning of strategic systems. Where this has occurred a tenfold return on investment has sometimes been achieved. A primary goal of the Information Center should be the achievement of strategic thrusts via end-user computing.

and train the user specialists; the user specialists lead implementation activities in their departments.

As in other new business thrusts, a period of investment is needed, and the results of the investment need continuous management attention, cultivating the new procedures and making adjustments until the results can be harvested.

A major refocusing of the Information Center and end-user computing may be needed to achieve the maximum value of end-user computing (Fig. 10.2). Once PCs are in widespread use and a corporatewide network provides connectivity at a suitable level, a technical infrastructure is in place that permits major strategic thrusts with end-user computing. The Information Center consultants and user specialists may be the staff who make it happen.

A new thrust using technology may give a corporation a strong competitive advantage for some years, but eventually the competitive edge is lost because most corporations use technology in the same way. What is a strategic systems opportunity at one point in time may be an operational imperative five years later. The corporations that pull ahead are the ones that seize the new opportunity first. There needs to be a constant reassessment of the new opportunities and threats that new technology is bringing.

CONNECTION TO INFORMATION ENGINEERING

Some Information Centers have been developed without any link to the information engineering process. This is clearly disadvantageous. It is better to regard the provision of an Information Center as an integral part of information engineering.

The Information Center needs access, potentially, to any of the information in an organization. It needs to comprehend fully the information resources and data models and have access to the data dictionaries. A well-run information center is in close contact with the information needs of users and management. Its knowledge of their requirements should be fed into the entity analysis and data modeling process.

Perhaps the biggest danger of information center operation, or of the spread of small computers and user-friendly software, is that multiple uncoordinated data structures will be used. The answer to this is well-controlled data administration. The data in the users' databases must be compatible, where necessary, with the data in the production databases.

Data are often extracted from production system databases and moved to separate end-user databases. Sometimes they are moved back in the opposite direction, with suitable accuracy controls. These operations require common data administration using the data and process models in the encyclopedia. Rather than having end users invent their own data structures, databases should be designed for end-user access. Many such databases may evolve.

DATA COORDINATOR

If end users are given the capability to create their own files with user-friendly software, data-item formats and definitions should be derived from a common dictionary. Sometimes in such installations a specially trained end user has the responsibility of ensuring consistency among the users' data. This *data coordinator* ought to report (at least for data administration purposes) to the official data administrator.

The data coordinator may have functions such as the following:

- Be aware of what data models exist and ensure that users' data is made consistent with such models.
- Make the dictionary definitions of data available to the users.
- Help set up extract databases for end-user access wherever this is valuable. Establish a catalog of such databases and ensure via the Information Center staff that end users know about them.
- Where the users' data is not yet represented in data models, coordinate with the data administrator to add the data to the models.
- Generally liaise with the data administrator about the users' data.
- Guide and encourage the users in employing encyclopedia facilities and automated tools.
- Move infrequently used reports or data offline (if this is not done automatically).
- Remove infrequently used "user views" of data.
- Contribute to a newsletter about end-user databases and available services.

CONFLICT IN SPEED OF RESULTS

There may be a conflict between the information engineering process and the objectives of the Information Center. The purpose of the Information Center is to obtain results as quickly as possible for end users. Business area analysis takes time and might delay the delivery of quick results.

Once the data models are completed and implemented, results may be obtained very quickly. Until that has been done a compromise is often necessary. Data for a given application may be captured, possibly normalized by the Information Center analysts and converted to the form needed by the user languages. Such data may have to be retrofitted later to the detailed models as they emerge. But the modeling process should not hold up the getting of valuable results to the users quickly.

The answer to this conflict is to get business area analysis done as soon as possible. The sooner the data models are in place, the sooner the enterprise can benefit fully from the Information Center methods.

To move rapidly into user-driven computing without information engineering is to risk a rapid spread of incompatible data as different users devise their own data. The mess in data will become rapidly worse.

Box 10.5 lists functions of the IC staff. A principle in most Information Centers is that the IC should not build or maintain applications. It helps end users to do that. The IC staff remains small compared to the number of end users it supports, as was illustrated in Fig. 10.1. The ratio of IC staff to end users supported at the right-hand side of Fig. 10.1 is about 1:500.

**BOX 10.5   Functions that should be carried out by
Information Center staff**

1. Central Planning

- Maintaining up-to-date knowledge of end-user tools. (The available tools change at a rapid rate.)
- Identifying the tools that will be supported. It is important to have a small number of well-chosen tools rather than a proliferation of many tools to support.
- Participating with planning groups to identify the most valuable end-user applications, particularly the identification of strategic thrusts.
- Identifying what central (or shared) end-user databases should be established.
- Establishing central (or shared) end-user databases and helping with the extraction of data into end-user facilities.
- Establishing catalogs to inform users what central (or shared) databases they can access.

2. By the IC Consultants (Whose Primary Skill is Communication with the Users), Working With the User Specialists Who Are the Departmental Interface With Information Center

- Training the users to employ the tools and create applications.
- Providing users with user encouragement, education, and selling.
- Assisting continually in improving the effectiveness of end-user computing.

BOX 10.5   *(Continued)*

- Introducing the technology necessary to achieve strategic thrusts with end-user computing.
- Introducing decision-support software and hardware to all users who are making decisions.
- Identifying all users who need decision-support tools.
- Ensuring that end-users know what databases are available to them.
- Consulting on user problems.
- Providing system setup and support.
- Dealing with technical and software problems.
- Assisting in choosing techniques or software for a given application.
- Providing debugging support when something goes wrong.
- Determining whether a proposed application is suitable for end-user or Information Center development, and selecting the software and methods.
- Demonstrating Information Center capabilities to users, including senior management.
- Engaging in general communication with senior management.
- Engaging in communication with traditional IS development.
- Ensuring that the data used conforms to the corporate data models.
- Forging close links to the data administrator(s) in defining and representing data, and evolution, if necessary, of the data models.
- Ensuring that end users employ good design techniques and that the system created will be maintainable.
- Ensuring that adequate documentation is produced for multiuser systems.
- Providing input to the various stages of information engineering.
- Providing coordination to prevent duplicate or redundant application development.
- Creating user databases and helping with the extraction of data into end-user facilities.
- Assisting the user in locating the data he or she needs. Arranging to have data converted where this is necessary.
- Assisting with maintenance changes.
- Assisting the user in obtaining authorization to access the required data.

(Continued)

BOX 10.5 *(Continued)*

- Conducting user-group meetings for users to interchange experience and workshops to develop proficiency in better techniques and user self-sufficiency.
- Providing administrative assistance to help users obtain an ID number, password, workspace, and so on.
- Acquiring information of the performance characteristics of user languages so that realistic decisions can be made about what they can handle.
- Advising in hardware selection. Ensuring the users have the workstation they need.
- Helping to establish appropriate local networks and access to corporate networks.
- Communicating with vendors.
- Monitoring system usage and planning future resources.
- Helping to tune or reorganize an application for better machine performance.
- Auditing system usage and application quality.
- Helping to provide backup, recovery, and archiving. End-user data on peripheral systems can be included in the overall backup and recovery plan.
- Implementing operation of schemes for motivating users.
- Tracking the benefits to the organization.
- Promoting the Information Center facilities and benefits at all levels in the organization.

3. Central Administrative Functions

- Assigning chargeback to users.
- Identifying major charges that can be cut.
- Identifying user applications which can be moved from the mainframe to a PC, to save money.
- Operating an Information Center display where users can see the hardware, software, and databases which the IC supports.
- Recruiting, budgeting, and general administration.
- Identifying user files or workspace which might be purged.
- Operating a discount scheme to encourage batch use of mainframes rather than interactive use.
- Identifying major interactive expenses which might be converted to batch usage.

Although the IC does not build applications, it is often desirable that IS professionals use the languages and tools advocated by the IC, to build certain types of systems quickly. The IC may assist IS professionals as well as end-users, with its skills and support for such tools.

Sometimes the IS organization has a Development Center to select tools and methodologies and give guidance to IS developers. The Development Center does for IS developers what the Information Center does for end-user developers. There is some overlap between these functions; occasionally the same tools will be used for IS development and for end-user development. The two organizations should have knowledge of fourth-generation languages and tools, and possibly have a common person for assessing such software.

A reason for the Information Center staff to *not* build systems is that it needs to avoid the possibility of becoming bogged down in development and having an application backlog. A major objective is to *bypass* the IS department's backlog so that quick results can be obtained.

The Information Center should avoid the trap of having a large number of programs to maintain.

If the Information Center charter says that it does not *build* applications but merely helps users to build them, it should be understood that this will not be of value to some of the most important users. Top management and often top-level staff do not build their own applications. There may therefore be a separate group which builds information systems for top-level management and staff. This may be called an *Executive Information Center*. There are certain tools and techniques appropriate for building *executive information systems*. These are discussed in Chapter 13.

COMMUNICATION SKILLS

A particularly important skill of the information center staff is communicating with the end users. Often the center is staffed by people trained as systems analysts. Their job changes fundamentally. They no longer write program specifications, draw data flow diagrams, and so on. They act more as consultants, listening to the end users' problems, solving them, determining the users' needs for information, encouraging, training, and selling ideas to the end users.

It is evidently important to train the Information Center staff in the new languages and software. However, sometimes the necessary communication skills come less naturally. A particularly valuable training for some Information Center staff has been courses on how to communicate well. Such courses should be followed by careful monitoring and guidance of their activities to help them acquire the style and techniques of a good consultant.

The success of the Information Center depends on the degree to which the businesspeople accept it as a means of directly solving their problems. This is not too likely to happen if technicians are in control. People with a business background need to be in control and greatly helped with the right technical support. They need to select the most useful tools and demonstrate their value throughout the organization.

Information Center professionals should be selected for their communication skills.

SPREADING THE SUCCESS

When IS staff are confident of their success and are capable of giving good support, the concept of information center operation needs to be *sold* throughout the organization.

A demonstration center should be set up and demonstrations given to all classes of users who should be employing the information center services. Demonstrations to senior management are particularly important. These should use *real* corporate data and be designed to show *interesting* results.

The objective of the demonstrations should be to show something of direct basic value to each area manager—something that affects how well his or her job is done. The demonstration content should be oriented to business results, not technical wizardry. The results-oriented data should be displayed as attractively as possible, for example, on color graphics terminals.

The author attended a demonstration in an insurance company before senior executives. Throughout almost the entire two-hour session the discussion was about business results and finances, not about computing technology. Data had been captured relating to the current concerns of the executives in question and had been converted to the relational structures which the software could manipulate. Breakdowns of expenses were analyzed, cash flows were shown in color graphics, and the comparative performance of competing insurance companies was analyzed. It was essential to use *real* data to generate the interest that was shown. A substantial amount of work had gone into developing the demonstrations. The persons who created the demonstrations operated the terminals and could quickly modify their nonprocedural code to answer the executives' questions. These top executives were fascinated to see how their business concerns could be explored: "What if the prime rate goes to 13%?" "What is the effect of holding down this budget to $600,000?" "Why did the Travelers Insurance Company do so well in this area?" and so on.

Such demonstrations can constitute a powerful form of selling. They can help to improve communication between IS and top management.

AUDITORS

Some types of user computing can be a problem for the auditors. It could increase the possibility that users could commit fraud. The auditors certainly need to know what is going on in this area.

One bank finds that the following arrangement for auditors works well. Every end-user–developed application is formally authorized. The chief auditor (who is a very powerful person in the bank) receives a copy of the authorization and a copy of any documentation which the end users produce. The end users are responsible for their own application documentation and standards are established for this. If the auditor wants to investigate the use system further, that is a matter between him and the users. The Information Center keeps out of it.

The chief auditor and his department became, themselves, major users of the Information Center. This mode of operation pleased them because it enabled them to make investigations and write checking programs without the IS organization or programmers knowing in detail what the auditors were doing or looking for. Previously they went to each branch periodically and went through the books manually looking for irregularities. Now they write programs which go through each branch's computer files in the head office. The IS manager states that the auditors created these programs *far faster* than the IS department could have. The auditors can modify the programs whenever they wish, maintaining secrecy over the modifications, and this improves the thoroughness with which they can search for irregularities.

In other organizations also, the auditors ought to employ user software to improve the thoroughness of their inspections. Auditors should be one of the first customers of the Information Center.

COSTS

The proportion of expenses that are for end-user computing has risen rapidly. In some corporations more than half the mainframe cycles are for end-user computing. The cost of personal computers (including hardware, software, training, and support) is often more than one-third of a corporation's total computer budget. It is important to control these costs.

The first golden rule is that the Information Center should be a profit center, not a cost center. The users should be charged for the facilities they employ. This has several advantages:

- It helps to ensure that the Information Center is operating as a justifiable part of the business.
- It causes the user departments to justify their use of computing or access to information.
- It increases the incentive of the Information Center to *sell* and to provide a level of service worth paying for.
- It is easy for users to take actions which use excessive computer time. Making them pay for the time they use seems the best way to control this.
- Sudden excessive upswings in usage are less likely to occur and so it is easier to plan and control growth.

How should the users be charged? Many information centers charge an hourly fee for the help they give and publish a billing rate. The charging for user machine time may be done by a separate organization. Some organizations have charged for connect time, CPU (central processing unit) hours, and disk space. When users ask for certain information to be made available on an existing information retrieval system, the main extra cost is the disk space, and the charge may relate to that.

It is almost impossible to find a completely fair and rational charging formula for machine resources. Attempts to do so with complex formulas have generally bewildered the users. It is better to have a simple, clear set of charges so that the users know how to budget and do not receive unpleasant surprises.

There should be an ongoing drive to reduce the costs of end-user computing by means such as

- Purging files and workspaces periodically.
- Examining all large user charges in the Information Center to determine how they can be reduced.
- Moving applications from mainframes to personal computers.
- Encouraging batch operation rather than interactive operation where practical.
- Avoiding peak-period mainframe operation where possible.

VALUE   Box 10.6 summarizes factors that help to make an Information Center as valuable as possible.

BOX 10.6   Factors that make an Information Center as valuable as possible

- Strong support and understanding by top management.
- Determination to change the use of computers throughout an entire organization.
- Focus on strategic systems opportunities.
- Affiliation with top-management planning of strategic thrusts.
- Emphasis on measured financial benefits.
- Quality-seasoned IC manager and professionals.
- Information Center staffed with businesspeople as well as appropriate technical support.
- Start-up staff have sufficient product expertise to ensure the first projects go flawlessly.

BOX 10.6 *(Continued)*

- Information Center employs new graduates who accept and spread new ideas.
- Information Center staff consists primarily of individuals with good inter-personal and communication skills, who can understand and react to users' problems.
- Establishment of IC user specialists in *all* departments to help computer users in the department and to interface with the Information Center.
- Good selection and training of IC user specialists.
- Skilled psychological motivation of all potential users.
- Identification of early adaptors.
- The existence of a corporatewide single-image network so that end-users everywhere can access mainframe databases and resources.
- Wide acceptance of application standards such as IBM's SAA.
- Good selection of user software.
- Support of a small number of well-chosen tools rather than a proliferation of tools.
- Selection of software which is intuitive, self-teaching, and as easy as possible.
- Constant evaluation of new software.
- Aggressive organizationwide selling of the IC capabilities once they are proven and powerful.
- Aggressive IC executive (once the initial building of expertise is done) who is determined to change the entire culture of computer usage.
- IC executive strongly oriented to business problems.
- Thorough linkage to the information engineering design stages.
- Ability to provide users with subsets of the data models.
- Good understanding and use of data analysis.
- Traditional IS organization is made to cooperate, providing data from production systems.
- Ability to access internal and external data stores; good data extraction facilities. The IC should act as a clearinghouse for data.
- Establishment of many valuable end-user databases.
- Catalog for all end users (online) of the databases they can access.

(Continued)

BOX 10.6 *(Continued)*

- Good online HELP facilities and documentation.
- User access to video and computer-based training.
- Excellent training of the IC consultants.
- Thorough training of the user specialists in the items of value to their department.
- An IC demonstrating center (by the cafeteria) where potential users can see the hardware, software, and databases which the IC supports.
- Demonstrations carefully constructed to address vital business needs. Demonstrations given to key executives.
- IC walk-in facilities which provide help to users and specialized services (such as slide making).
- Chargeback to user departments for all resources used. A clear, simple chargeback formula.
- An ongoing program to minimize costs. Examination of all large charges to see how they can be reduced.
- A large discount for batch as opposed to interactive mainframe usage.
- A discount for off-peak mainframe usage.
- Regular purging of user workspace and old files.
- An ongoing drive to move applications to the cheapest computing resource (usually the PC rather than a mainframe).
- Ability to tune applications which are frequently run, to lower their cost.
- Integration of the corporate library with the Information Center. (The library may report to the IC.)
- Regular user-group meeting to exchange experience and spread understanding.
- Seminars for users on strategic system possibilities.
- Operation as a profit center. The IC should operate as a business within a business.

REFERENCES

1. R. B. Rosenberger, *The Information Center, SHARE 56 Proceedings* (New York: Share, 1981).

2. *Managing Personal Computers in the Large Organization,* a report from Nolan, Norton Co., One Cranberry Hill, Lexington, MA, 1988.

3. E. Feigenbaum, P. McCorduck, and H. P. Nii, *The Rise of the Expert Company* (New York: Time Books, 1989).

4. Conferences on Information Centers, DDI and the University of Michigan, Ann Arbor, 1983.

11 SYSTEMS FOR IMPROVED DECISION MAKING

TWO TYPES OF SYSTEMS

A particularly valuable use of computers and networks is to improve the decision making in an enterprise. Systems which do this are commonly divided into two categories:

- Executive information systems (EIS)
- Decision support systems (DSS)

Executive information systems are targeted at executives or high-level managers who will not do detailed computational analysis of a decision. They are concerned with knowing *what* is happening, determining *when* human intervention is needed, having the *right information* to aid executive decision making, and *monitoring* the effects of their actions. The users of such systems often do not type except possibly reluctant one-finger pecking at a keyboard; they do not program; they do not learn mnemonics, coded commands, or special punctuation. An executive information system must be immediately valuable to the executive and very easy to use.

Decision-support systems are targeted at the manager, or staff person, who does substantial analysis of facts in order to make better decisions. The computational techniques vary from commonsense business calculations to highly sophisticated operations research techniques such as trend analysis, linear programming, goal seeking, and optimization techniques. A wide variety of software is available for decision-support systems. It varies from simplistic spreadsheet tools to elaborate analytical tools. Most decision-support computation can be done without conventional programming. Some is done using programs written in user-oriented fourth-generation languages. Most decision-support packages have software for generating a variety of chart types so that the results of the computations can be displayed or printed for executives to use. Graphics can be very valuable for exploring complex data and understanding the subtle causes of business phenomena. The purpose of much decision-support computation is to extract the truth from complex data.

The results of decision-support analysis should be made available to executives, and this may be done via executive information systems. It is desirable to integrate these two types of software.

Box 11.1 contrasts the facilities in executive information systems and decision-support systems. Chapter 12 discusses decision-support systems, and Chapter 13 discusses executive information systems.

BOX 11.1   Contrast between an executive information system and a decision-support system

EIS

- Brings together the data most valuable for an executive, from internal and external sources.
- Avoids irrelevant data.
- Summarizes, filters, and compresses the data.
- Makes the data very easy to access without typing.
- Presents the data with powerful graphics.
- Highlights, with color, information to which the executive's attention should be drawn.
- Enables the executive to track critical data to provide monitoring and feedback capabilities.

DSS

- Provides a database of data which has multiple dimensions, structured so that two-dimensional slices through this data can be analyzed.
- Provides a way to summarize, interrelate, and correlate data.
- Provides a variety of analysis tools (see Box 12.2).
- Provides modeling tools.
- Provides "what-if" analysis and modeling.
- Provides graphical presentation tools.

THE NEED FOR DECISION-SUPPORT COMPUTING

Everywhere in an enterprise there are needs for decision-support systems. Most decisions are made without adequate analysis, understanding, and information. The ISP (information strategy planning) techniques discussed in Book II reveal urgent needs for getting better information to management. Often these needs can be satisfied quickly, without programming, by use of executive information system or decision-support system software. It is often important to do this quickly, without being very elaborate at first, bypassing for the time being BAA (business area analysis), to get valuable information to executives.

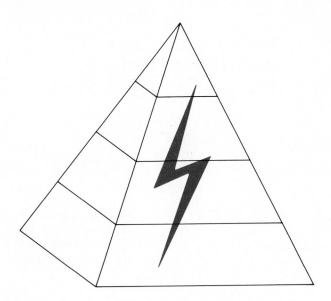

Box 11.2 lists the types of effects obtained from ISP techniques linked to effective DSS and EIS.

THE NATURE OF DECISION MAKING

There are five elements to decision making:

- Gathering the facts
- Gathering intelligence
- Analysis
- Modeling
- Choice

BOX 11.2   The types of objectives of effective use of EIS and DSS

- Obtaining market advantage
- Better sales planning
- Better choice of products
- More profitable market coverage
- Elimination of low-profit items
- Better choice of vendors
- Improvements in productivity
- Better ability to raise capital
- Design improvements
- Better production planning
- Consideration of new business opportunities
- Moving in new business directions

1. **Gathering the facts.** To gather the facts, appropriate databases need to be established. In most cases the facts already exist somewhere in the files or databases of the enterprise computers. They need to be extracted and restructured into a database designed to be as effective as possible with the decision-support software that is used.

    As a decision-support system becomes institutionalized, the extraction of data from other systems into the decision-support database should be made automatic.

2. **Gathering intelligence.** We use the word "intelligence" here as in the term "military intelligence"—the gathering of news and clues about a situation where full and open knowledge does not exist.

    Such information does not normally reside in the production databases of the enterprise but may be extremely important for decision making at the higher levels. It is often pieced together semi-intuitively by intelligent staff or executives who are strongly involved with the situation. Such information should be made accessible, where appropriate, on an executive information system.

    Examples include information about competing firms and products, indications of the strategic direction of competing firms, possible breakthroughs in technology, early warnings of customer needs or large contracts, intelligence about world oil prices or mineral prices, impending regulatory changes, competitive successes in advertising, and so on.

3. **Analysis.** A mass of complex facts can hide the truth. A purpose of decision-support tools is to extract the truth from complex data. Data processing often tries to serve

the needs of management with summaries of data. The higher the level of management, the greater the degree of aggregation or summary. In fact, high-level managers
often have questions more subtle or complex than those which can be answered by
the preplanned summaries. Computer-compiled summaries can be misleading. Facts
presented by standard accounting techniques, for example, are often deceptive because they aggregate the data in such a way that exceptional individual contributors
to high expenses, revenue, losses, or meeting goals, may be hidden.

The multidimensional database of a decision-support system should give its
users the ability to examine facts from different angles, looking for exceptional contributors. Sales information, for example, may be broken down by market, by city,
by product, by customer type, by customer corporation, by salesperson, and so on.
It may be correlated with advertising expenditure, with price changes, with new
announcements, with competitive moves, with economic trends, or with more specific events like outbreaks of flu affecting the sales of a pharmaceutical. Production
costs, inventory costs, sales costs, and revenue may be broken down by product to
establish the effective return on investment of different products. This often reveals
that some products are low contributors and might be dropped or changed, whereas
other products are high contributors and should be expanded or given more advertising.

In addition to being able to examine and summarize the data from multiple
viewpoints, a variety of techniques are needed for analyzing data. Trend analysis
shows how data changes with time. The trends may be seasonally adjusted, adjusted
for other factors, or smoothed, or moving averages may be plotted. Many trends
exhibit cyclical patterns. Tools exist for identifying these patterns and plotting the
trend so as to clarify or compensate for the cyclical pattern. Trends of different
variables are often plotted together for comparison purposes. Different variables may
be correlated in a variety of ways. The correlation can be charted with different types
of charts. The analyst is often trying to find the effect of one variable on another.
He may test multiple hypotheses by using correlation techniques. Visual inspection
of well-drawn graphs is often more informative than are statistics in enabling an
analyst to understand the numbers. He needs a tool which can instantly draw a
variety of types of chart. When he thinks he understands the reasons behind the
numbers he is analyzing, he needs to create charts which will make these reasons as
clear as possible to decision makers.

Sometimes a decision analysis tree is built showing all the alternative courses
that events may take. A probability may be associated with each branch, and an
indicator shows at which branching points there can be influence made on the course
of events. The cost, risk, or profit associated with the alternative courses may be
computed.

4. **Modeling.** Modeling is used to simulate situations or to encapsulate aspects of the
behavior of a marketplace, a production line, or other complex system. The analyst
asks many different "what-if" questions. What if the return on the mailing is only
0.2 percent? What factors would lead to a higher return? What would be the effect
on sales volume of a 5 percent increase in price? How would that affect overall
profit? How do items differ in their price elasticity? How would shop floor throughput change if a different machine tool layout was used?

Modeling techniques range from simple commonsense calculations to highly sophisticated operations research computations. The tools used range from basic spreadsheet tools to tools which use linear programming, critical path analysis, Monte Carlo simulation, and so on. Much decision making depends on business models in which a large number of equations representing the different components of revenue and expense are used to calculate profit or loss, and cash flow. Simulated profit-and-loss and balance sheet statements may be created. The user of the model can vary the assumptions made about sales, effectiveness of advertising, production costs, and so on.

Some models employ optimization techniques to minimize cost, maximize production throughput, or optimize a design. Some employ goal-seeking techniques, adjusting parameters of a model until a specified goal is met.

5. **Choice.** Given the calculations, analysis, and modeling, a choice must be made about alternatives. Sometimes the models make the choice clear. In other cases it requires human judgment. A decision analyst may present the facts, analysis, and models to an executive so that the executive makes an informed choice. The executive may use his intuitive feel for the situation in conjunction with the computed charts and tables.

STRUCTURED AND UNSTRUCTURED DECISIONS

H. A. Simon classified decisions as *programmed* and *nonprogrammed* [1]. Programmed decisions are those for which there is a firm procedure which could, at least in principle, be done by a computer. Nonprogrammed decisions are those for which there is no specific procedure but which require a general capacity for intelligent, adaptive judgment. Scott Morton and Gorry use the terms *structured* and *unstructured* decisions to have the same meaning, preferring these terms because they have no software connotation.

Fully programmed, or *structured, decisions* may be fully automated with a *closed-loop* system. With many decisions we do not close the loop; human judgment is thought to be necessary. Most closed-loop systems today are ones where the decision is fairly simple or where the decision must be made too quickly for human intervention.

There is not a clear distinction between programmable and nonprogrammable decisions. As time goes by, a steadily greater proportion of decisions become fully automated. This is because we improve our understanding of the decisions, and programming techniques become more sophisticated. Computers become cheaper and more powerful. Also computers become less prone to failure and so can be trusted with a higher proportion of closed-loop systems.

In previous years, for example, the reordering of stock was done by a well-paid member of middle management. This was thought to be a decision needing a high level of human skill. Today, in many firms, inventory reordering is done by computer. Using a formula for computing the economic order quantity, the machine can do a better job than most humans. The spread of artificial intelligence techniques will have a major effect on decision making in the future. The behavior of an expert decision maker can be captured in rules—sometimes a large number of rules. The rules can be tuned and added to until the machine performs as well as the expert decision maker. In some cases its greater precision enables it to perform *better* than human decision makers, as in the case of DEC's systems for configuring computers (XCON) and helping salespersons make pricing decisions (XSEL).

Fully unstructured decisions are ones where computers are of no value. A computer may be of no use for deciding which actress to select from a group of auditions, for example. Only a small proportion of decisions in an enterprise are ones for which a computer is of *no* value. A computer could, in principle, give *some* information or *some* assistance in most decision making. Most decisions are semistructured—a computer can be useful in certain ways, but it should not make the decision unaided. Innumerable decisions are made today without the aid of a computer when, in fact, the decision could be made better if computerized information, analysis, or modeling were used to help.

Some semistructured decisions require extensive computer modeling. Computing can be of great help in achieving a near-optimal decision. This would be true, for example, in making decisions about the routing of a tanker fleet or deciding where concentrators should be placed in a complex data network. These are classical operations research problems.

At the other extreme, modeling or calculation is of little use, but obtaining good information from a computer is of value. This would be true of a publisher deciding which of several books to publish—a decision depending more on the publisher's intuition and judgment than on computational techniques.

We thus have a spectrum of decisions ranging from fully structured to fully unstructured.

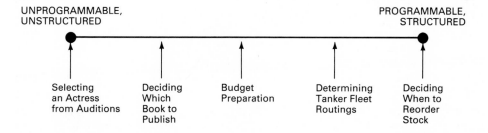

LEVEL OF DECISION　　　Junior management decisions are very different from top management decisions. It is common to categorize managerial activity in three levels:

- Strategic planning (top management)
- Managerial control (middle management)
- Operational control (junior management)

Robert Anthony [2] describes these as follows:

Strategic planning is "the process of deciding on objectives of the organization, on changes in these objectives, on the resources used to attain these objectives, and on the policies that govern the acquisition, use, and disposition of these resources" [3].

Management control is "the process by which managers assure that resources are obtained and used effectively and efficiently in the accomplishment of the organization's objectives" [4].

Operational control is "the process of assuring that specific tasks are carried out effectively and efficiently" [5].

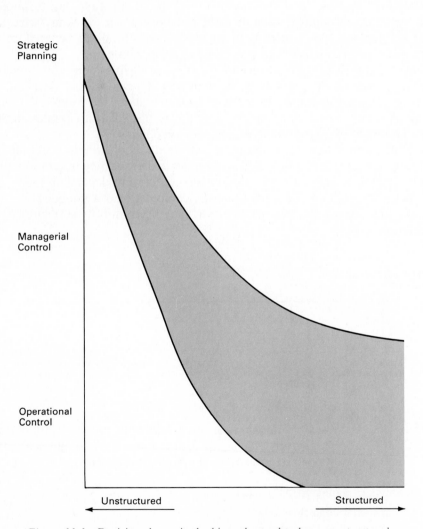

Figure 11.1 Decisions lower in the hierarchy tend to be more structured.

Virtually no tasks in strategic planning are fully programmable although computerized information, analysis, and modeling are very valuable. Some decisions in management control are fully programmable, such as the inventory reordering decision. Many decisions in operational control are fully programmable. In general, decisions lower in the control hierarchy tend to be more structured (Fig. 11.1). The higher the decision in this hierarchy the more likely the need for human judgment and wisdom. Before the 1980s there was very little use of computers by top management. However top management decisions are the most important and the payoff from using computers to improve these decisions is great. Executive information systems (Chapter 13) have, in some corporations, improved the information for top management decision making and helped executives to focus on items most needing their action.

Figure 11.2 contrasts characteristics of decisions at a low level and at a

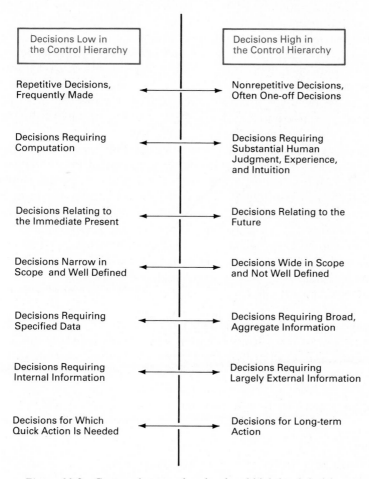

Decisions Low in the Control Hierarchy	Decisions High in the Control Hierarchy
Repetitive Decisions, Frequently Made	Nonrepetitive Decisions, Often One-off Decisions
Decisions Requiring Computation	Decisions Requiring Substantial Human Judgment, Experience, and Intuition
Decisions Relating to the Immediate Present	Decisions Relating to the Future
Decisions Narrow in Scope and Well Defined	Decisions Wide in Scope and Not Well Defined
Decisions Requiring Specified Data	Decisions Requiring Broad, Aggregate Information
Decisions Requiring Internal Information	Decisions Requiring Largely External Information
Decisions for Which Quick Action Is Needed	Decisions for Long-term Action

Figure 11.2   Contrast between low-level and high-level decisions.

high level in the control hierarchy. The techniques for building a system to help in top management decision making can be completely different from techniques for operational control decisions.

In the 1950s and 1960s, computers were used only for low-level operational decisions. In the 1970s they were increasingly used for managerial control systems. In the 1980s top-executive information systems became valuable.

FROM DATA TO JUDGMENT

When computers were first used, they merely processed data. Later it became common to distinguish between *data* and *information*. Data is a mass of undigested facts; information consists of summaries and analyses distilled from the facts so as to be useful for decision making.

When knowledge-base technology became understood, we distinguished among computerized *data, information,* and *knowledge.* Knowledge, in a computer, is data associated with rules which allow inferences to be drawn automatically so that the data can be employed for useful purposes. The data, for example, may be facts about components; knowledge may be these facts combined with rules to ensure that systems are correctly configured from those components.

To make decisions we need *understanding.* This means that we can identify the significance of, interpretation of, or explanation for certain data or information. The causes underlying the facts are perceived. To aid human understanding of data we have models which lead us to expect the data to fit certain patterns. These are often models in our head. Computers can help in the understanding of complex data by providing computational models. Models which aid understanding can be very valuable for management control and strategic planning. A variety of different types of models are used, for example, forecasting models which represent cyclical trends, models representing complex feedback and control mechanisms, and models consisting of large numbers of business equations.

To make high-level business decisions, *judgment* is needed. Judgment refers to human assessment, discrimination, and choice, requiring good sense and the discernment and wisdom that come from experience. Although judgment is a human capability it may be performed better if it is based on understanding which may be enhanced with computerized models.

Computers can thus help to provide the following:

- Data
- Information
- Knowledge

- Understanding
- Judgment

In the beginning computers were used almost exclusively for data, then for information. We need substantial improvement in the application of computers to better enhance knowledge, understanding, and judgment. The higher the level of the decision, the greater the need for human understanding and judgment.

The relative meaning of these terms is summarized in Box 11.3.

It will be seen that good decision making in an enterprise involves the skills of analysts and executives. Analysts need the best analytical tools and the right data. Executives need easy access to critical information and to the results of analyses. In combination this requires DSS and EIS. The data in an EIS or DSS is *not* a simple subset of the data in production systems or existing applications. However, some of the data in an EIS or DSS is *extracted* from existing systems (Fig. 11.3) and reformatted to provide the EIS or DSS database. Much of the data in an EIS and possibly some of the data in a DSS comes from external sources, as shown in Fig. 11.3.

The following chapters discuss the building of executive information systems and decision-support systems.

BOX 11.3   The relative meaning of the terms data, information, knowledge, understanding, and judgment

Data	A mass of undigested facts.
Information	Facts which are digested, analyzed, and summarized so as to be useful to decision makers.
Knowledge	Information associated with rules which allow inferences to be drawn automatically so that the information can be employed for useful purposes.
Understanding	Identification of the significance, interpretation, or explanation for certain data or information.
	Information and knowledge associated with models, computational or mental, which enable the causes underlying the facts to be perceived.
Judgment	Assessment, discrimination, and choice.
	The selection of an appropriate or optimal course of action, based on knowledge and understanding.

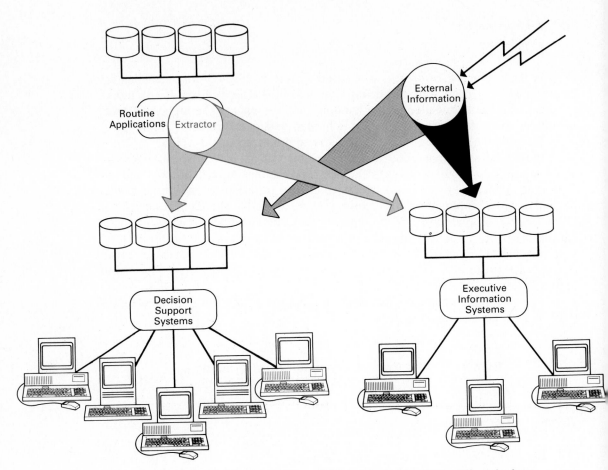

Figure 11.3   Data in an EIS or DSS is structured entirely differently from that in routine applications. Some of it is extracted from routine applications. Some of the data, especially in an EIS, comes from external sources.

REFERENCES

1. H. A. Simon, *The New Science of Management Decision* (New York: Harper & Row, 1960).

2. R. N. Anthony, *Planning and Control Systems: A Framework for Analysis* (Boston: Division of Research, Harvard Business School, 1965).

3. Ibid., p. 24.

4. Ibid., p. 27.

5. Ibid., p. 69.

12 BUILDING DECISION-SUPPORT SYSTEMS

INTRODUCTION   DSS (decision-support systems) provide help in accessing data for decision making, doing analysis and modeling of decisions, and making an optimum choice. They help to provide understanding of the decision environment and aid human judgment.

Much decision-support software exists. DSS packages help their users analyze data, answer "what-if" questions, create financial and other models, and generally extract the truth from complex data. They range from simple two-dimensional spreadsheet tools, such as LOTUS 1-2-3, to tools which can be used to manipulate data of many dimensions. The higher-level tools incorporate elaborate analysis techniques.

The simplest decision-support tools—the two-dimensional spreadsheet packages—are now familiar to many people who have used them on personal computers. At the opposite end of range are highly sophisticated tools such as EXPRESS [1] which incorporate many of the techniques of operations research. In the past financial or business models were created in programming languages. Today they can be created merely by writing business equations and manipulating curves with tools such as JAVELIN [2]. Easy-to-use DSS software brings analysis and modeling techniques to a much broader range of users.

BUILT BY THE USER   Decision-support systems ought to be built largely by their users. The managers and decision analysts, who work with the decisions in question, understand those decisions more completely than IS professionals.

IS professionals ought to help in selecting and establishing the best software, extracting the necessary data, and building the DSS database. IS professionals may be skilled with decision-making techniques such as forecasting, time-series analysis, or use of operations research tools. In many cases IS professionals work with the users to build the first version of the decision-support system, and then the users expand it to meet their needs and to do subtle investigations of the data in question. Users can be highly creative in their use of DSS tools. They often build highly complex models which evolve over time.

Decision-support systems vary from being very simple like spreadsheets to highly elaborate systems. While spreadsheet decision making can be done with little or no help from IS, elaborate DSS systems need careful planning and professional design. The simplest use of decision-support tools is little more than an extension of the calculations the user would have done with a pocket calculator. Elaborate DSS systems need careful database design and control of development.

Major DSS systems are usually built in stages as shown in Fig. 12.1. During the initiation stage the objectives of the system are determined and the software is selected. A prototype should be put to work as early as possible. The prototype may evolve substantially before a fully working system is built. The fully working system (pilot) may be employed by only one user or department and may be enhanced for many months before it is thought appropriate to institutionalize the system. Institutionalizing the system may mean that it has many users, and so needs a data network and a different database facility. A staging database may be used, as discussed later. When the system is institutionalized, it needs documentation and training and controlled maintenance.

The first working version of a decision-support system should be *simple* and easy to implement. Much is learned from the first working version that may affect the design of the eventual system, so the sooner it is in prototype use, the better. The software selected should permit rapid evolution of the prototype.

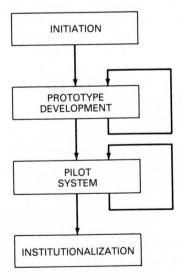

Figure 12.1 Major decision-support systems are usually built in stages, starting with prototype evolution.

MULTIDIMENSIONAL DATA Decision-support systems such as EXPRESS [1] and SYSTEM W [3] represent data in a multidimensional fashion. They provide, in effect, a multidimensional matrix of data that we are able to examine two dimensions at a time.

For example, suppose that certain variables are mapped against time. The sales revenue of each project an organization sells, for example, might be mapped against months. To help with market planning, we might like to project past sales into the future in different ways, with different "what-if" propositions. This gives a three-dimensional array of data, as illustrated in Fig. 12.2.

Most DSS languages allow us to explore one two-dimensional slice through the data at a time, as indicated by the shaded slice in Fig. 12.2. We might perform calculations, obtain statistics, or plot charts from this slice. We might do anything that we can do with two-dimensional spreadsheet software, such as LOTUS 1-2-3.

On the other hand, we might want to examine a slice relating to one time period, going through several "what-if" propositions, as shown in Fig. 12.3.

Product revenue is only one variable that is of interest about products. We might also want to see units sold, price, average order size, average cost of sales, average profit, type of product, age, and so on. We might want these variables mapped against time periods, as shown in Fig. 12.4.

We may not be content with average order size, average cost of sale, and average profit on sale. We might want these broken down by type of product and by customer. We might then like to see a histogram of these variables. Now we need more than three dimensions in our representation of data.

It is difficult to draw diagrams with more than three dimensions (even if the reader wears special glasses!). To view multidimensional data easily, we need a computer. Imagine the shaded slice in Fig. 12.4 moving from one time period to another at the press of a key: click, click, click. A computer enables us to deal with data in multiple dimensions easily.

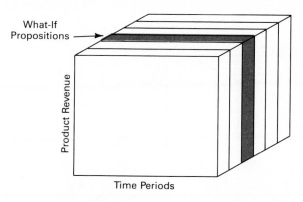

Figure 12.2   Three-dimensional array.

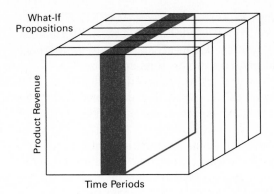

Figure 12.3   Examining one time period.

SYSTEM W supports the analysis of data of up to nine dimensions. Each two-dimensional slice through these data is called a *viewpoint*. The data of a viewpoint can be analyzed or plotted as with a good spreadsheet tool.

For each slice through multidimensional data, different types of reports may be useful. A decision-support system needs a flexible report generator and business graphics generator with which to display the information. A variety of calculations may be done using the data.

EXPRESS allows its users to state what slice through the data they want to see by using LIMIT statements. This is illustrated in Fig. 12.5.

In the top illustration of Fig. 12.5, the user says LIMIT PRODUCT TO PENICILLIN. This gives a two-dimensional slice through the data. The user then says DISPLAY SALES, and a sales report is displayed.

In the second illustration, the user employs two limit statements:

LIMIT YEAR TO 1981
LIMIT CUSTOMER TO DISTRICT NEWYORK

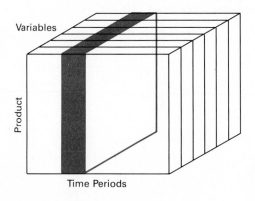

Figure 12.4   Mapping variables against time periods.

In the third illustration, the user displays two slices so that he can compare this month's sales with those of a year ago.

The data can be aggregated in various ways. In the third illustration of Fig. 12.5, the user says LIMIT PRODUCT TO DIVISION OTC. The products of this division are then displayed.

A diversity of computations need to be done to aid in decision making. Sometimes fairly elaborate nested conditions are needed to express the rules that govern the calculations.

Many of the calculations that help in decision making need standard types of analysis that can be preprogrammed, such as regression analysis, different types of forecasting, sensitivity analysis, and a variety of statistical functions. The user needs help in employing standard types of computation.

A decision-support software, then, needs the types of facilities listed in Box 12.1.

BUILDING A MODEL IN SYSTEM W

A SYSTEM W model can consist of *periods* and *variables*. To build a model, the user first specifies the periods. They can be expressed in any desired time units: days, weeks, months, years, or any other unit of time. In SYSTEM W, there are two types of periods, *history* and *forecast,* each of which can have up to 250 entries.

A *history period* contains actual data values in elapsed time periods. To build this part of the model, the user issues the SPECIFY HISTORY command:

SPECIFY HISTORY 12

This statement defines 12 history periods that can be used in the model.

A *forecast period* contains data values for the future. The SPECIFY FORECAST command is used to create forecast periods. For example,

SPECIFY FORECAST 10

This statement defines ten forecast periods that can be used in the model.

Period names are automatically assigned by SYSTEM W as the model is built. History periods begin with H1, H2, H3, up to a maximum of H250. Forecast periods begin with P1, P2, P3, up to a maximum of P250.

Figure 12.6 illustrates the conventions that are used by SYSTEM W in creating history and forecast period names. Figure 12.7 shows period descriptions that are associated with the periods.

The product manager can look at the sales totals for that product.
-> LIMIT PRODUCT TO PENICILLIN
-> DISPLAY SALES

PRODUCT PENICILLIN SALES
DOLLAR SALES

MONTH	WEST	EAST	SOUTH	CENTRAL	TOTAL
JAN81	980,957	1,004,613	515,221	467,683	2,968,474
FEB81	539,558	579,040	419,527	446,851	1,984,976
MAR81	527,900	639,302	339,811	401,464	1,908,477
APR81	478,699	498,513	351,408	369,857	1,698,477
MAY81	510,750	573,416	334,904	273,907	1,692,977
JUN81	517,737	501,260	283,531	243,446	1,545,974
JUL81	484,558	529,114	249,100	227,206	1,489,978
AUG81	435,095	585,827	189,950	226,606	1,437,478
SEP81	647,541	590,895	267,950	288,589	1,794,975
OCT81	652,618	692,888	319,242	279,805	1,944,545
NOV81	540,578	595,727	357,235	333,405	1,826,945
DEC81	997,931	968,584	429,208	475,781	2,871,504
	7,313,914	7,759,179	4,057,087	4,034,600	23,164,780

The New York district manager can look at sales data for the whole
year for each customer in the district.
-> LIMIT YEAR TO 1981
-> LIMIT CUSTOMER TO DISTRICT NEWYORK
-> DISPLAY SALES

NEW YORK DISTRICT SALES
DOLLAR SALES

CUSTOMER	VITA-PLUS	COUGH-OFF	KEN-TRANQ	PENICILLIN	TOTAL
DAVID	21,950	54,297	608,485	922,520	1,607,252
ACE	18,988	100,825	131,642	331,601	583,056
WILSON	64,423	230,586	832,903	1,079,243	2,207,155
LELISTER	119,967	5,197	112,740	86,493	324,397
MAJOR	23,001	20,949	5,281	1,684	50,915
CLASS	113,595	319,333	245,663	579,442	1,258,033
GLUSCO	5,195	22,972	84,422	59,334	171,923
	367,119	754,159	2,021,136	3,060,317	6,202,731

PRODUCT

REGION

TIME PERIOD

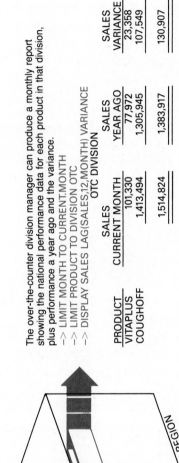

The over-the-counter division manager can produce a monthly report showing the national performance data for each product in that division, plus performance a year ago and the variance.

-> LIMIT MONTH TO CURRENT.MONTH
-> LIMIT PRODUCT TO DIVISION OTC
-> DISPLAY SALES LAG(SALES,12,MONTH) VARIANCE

OTC DIVISION

PRODUCT	SALES CURRENT MONTH	SALES YEAR AGO	SALES VARIANCE
VITAPLUS	101,330	77,972	23,358
COUGHOFF	1,413,494	1,305,945	107,549
	1,514,824	1,383,917	130,907

REGION

PRODUCT

TIME PERIOD

Figure 12.5 LIMIT statements in EXPRESS are used to display slices through multidimensional data. (Courtesy of Information Resources, Inc. [1]).

BOX 12.1   Facilities needed in decision-support software

- A *database* that structures data for multidimensional analysis (as in Fig. 12.5 but with more than three dimensions).
- A *query language* for querying the multidimensional data.
- A *report generator* with which the user can create reports showing different slices through the data.
- A *spreadsheet manipulator* for manipulating different two-dimensional slices through the data.
- A *graphics generator* that can create charts showing different views of the data.
- A *language* for performing calculations on the data, sometimes with complex nested conditions. A nonprocedural language may be used with which equations or search parameters can be expressed in any sequence.
- *Tools* for the following:
  - Statistical analysis
  - Trend analysis
  - Financial analysis
  - Forecasting
  - Goal seeking
  - Business modeling
  - Other *operations research* tools
- *What-if exploration:* the ability to change data or assumptions and rerun calculations or analyses to explore the effects of changes.
- *The ability to build models* and store the effects of alternate strategies.
- *Expert system tools* which encapsulate the decision-making techniques of experts by the use of *rules*.
- *User-friendly means* of employing the facilities discussed in such a way that any difficult syntax can be avoided.
- *Communication facilities* for communicating results to other people. People at distant locations should be able to see the same display on their screens and discuss it.

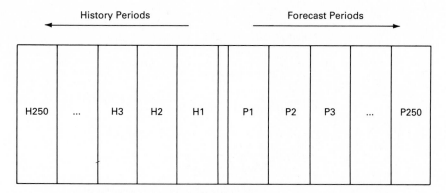

Figure 12.6   Illustration of the history and forecast periods of SYSTEM W.

Defining Variables

Variables are used to contain data values that change with the passage of time. The user can assign names to the variables and can optionally associate a description with a variable to clarify or explain further how the variables are used. SYSTEM W allows two types of variables: *input variables* and *calculated variables*.

Input variables contain values that are entered directly into the model. The following are examples of input variables:

- UNITS-SOLD
- PRICE
- QUANTITY

Calculated variables contain values that are calculated using constants and values contained in other variables. The following are examples of calculated variables:

- REVENUE = UNITS-SOLD * PRICE
- ROYALTY = 10% * REVENUE

H1	P1	P2	P3
Last Year	This Year	1991	1992

Figure 12.7   Period descriptions.

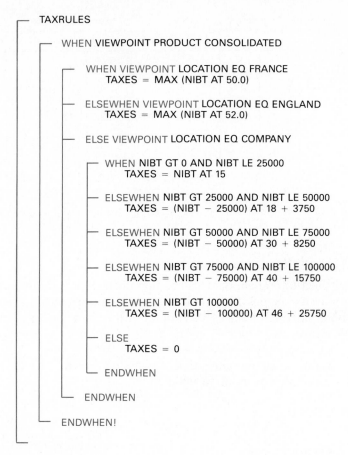

Figure 12.8   Statements in SYSTEM W used to calculate taxes. (NIBT is net income before taxes; NIBT AT 15 means 15 percent of NIBT.)

Figure 12.8 illustrates the calculation of taxes on income in a financial model. In practice, tax calculations can be much more complex than in Fig. 12.8. Action diagrams as in Fig. 12.8 help to clarify the logic of compound nested rules.

Statements such as the WHEN blocks shown enable the model to be built. The model will then be filled with data, either by entering the data directly or, more often, by extracting them from existing files or data bases. The commands and facilities that enable data to be extracted from production databases are particularly important.

When the model contains data, the user will examine different slices through the data and needs a good-quality report generator and graphics generator.

ANALYTICAL TOOLS   Decision-support systems vary greatly in the analytical tools they provide. Some have little other than the ability to take averages and totals. Others provide a rich and complex set of forecasting, time series, correlation, and other tools. Many of the tools of operational research are built into decision-support software.

Box 12.2 shows the tools provided by EXPRESS software. This is much more comprehensive than many such products.

BOX 12.2   Tools provided in the EXPRESS decision-support system for analyzing data [1]

Exploratory Data Analysis

- Mean
- Median
- Standard deviation
- Variance
- Other standard statistical functions
- Scatter plots
- Stem-and-leaf plots
- Box plots
- Normal probability plots

Time-Series Analysis and Forecasting

- Moving averages
- Moving totals
- Exponential smoothing
- Linear extrapolation
- Compound growth extrapolation
- Linear and compound growth triangles
- Trend curve fitting (including linear exponentials, power functions, multiple hyperbolic functions, and S-curves)
- X-11 deseasonalization and forecasting techniques (monthly and quarterly)

(Continued)

BOX 12.2 *(Continued)*

- Autocorrelation correction
- Polynomial distributed lags
- Multiple linear regression
- ARIMA (Box-Jenkins analysis)
- ACCUFOR
- Forecast accuracy measurement testing (actual versus forecast)

Causal Models and Survey Analysis (Cross-sectional Analysis)

- Autocorrelation correction
- Polynomial distributed lags
- Multiple linear regression
- Two-stage least squares
- Leapwise regression (which tests and determines best of all possible models)
- Crosstabs
- Correlation matrices
- Cluster analysis
- Factor analysis
- MONANOVA
- Automatic interaction detector (AID)

Advanced Analytical Tools

- Linear programming
- Critical path analysis
- Risk analysis
- Monte Carlo simulation

PAST AND FUTURE

Many decision-support models relate to time periods, as in Figs. 12.2 through 12.5. It is often desirable to use forecasting techniques to extend sales, profits, or other variables into the future. Figure 12.9 illustrates this. The future forecasts may be used to generate tentative financials, examine cash flows, plan equipment purchases, plan recruiting, and so on.

There is a diversity of techniques with which to examine past figures, adjust them for seasonal variations and other variations, combine them with growth targets or tentative assumptions about the future, and produce forecasts. Often the intuition of a skilled decision maker responds better to graphic representation of trends and forecasts than to tables of figures.

Some forecasting tools produce figures showing the percentage confidence of the forecast. This information, like the forecast itself, is often best displayed graphically. Figure 12.10 shows a line for actual and forecast sales data. The red line superimposed on this is a smoothed trend line. A band showing 90 percent confidence levels in the forecast surrounds the forecast itself.

The user of this system may have different techniques available to him for

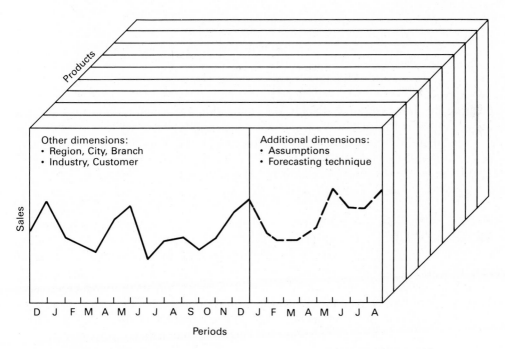

Figure 12.9 Figures from the past can be extended into the future with a variety of forecasting techniques. Future forecasts are then used to examine cash flows and help in making decisions such as capacity planning and labor planning.

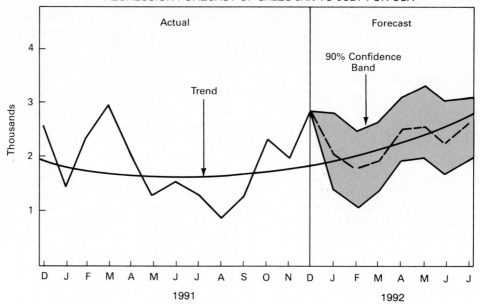

Figure 12.10   Past and future. The forecast line is surrounded by a confidence band, which can be set to different confidence levels. The red curve is a smoothed trend line.

creating the forecast, may display different confidence bands, and may keep a file of different forecasts relating to different assumptions.

Financial executives map the forecasts made into tentative cash-flow analyses, profit-and-loss statements, and other forms of financial analysis. Figure 12.11 shows a cash-flow forecast for a new division.

EFFECTIVE USE OF GRAPHICS   Figures 12.10 through 12.14 show effective uses of graphics. Almost all the tools in Box 12.1 can be made easier to use and to understand with good graphics.

Appropriate computer graphics can be a major aid to thinking creatively. They help to extract meaning from a complex morass of data and can help to explore the effects of different decisions and actions. A challenge of decision-support systems is to find the types of diagrams that will be most effective in helping to make decisions.

All the standard reports of accountants can be represented graphically. Figure 12.12 shows a graphics representation of a balance sheet. This helps to see, at a glance, the ratios between different items on the balance sheet. It helps to

ACTUAL AND FORECAST CASH POSITION, AI DIVISION

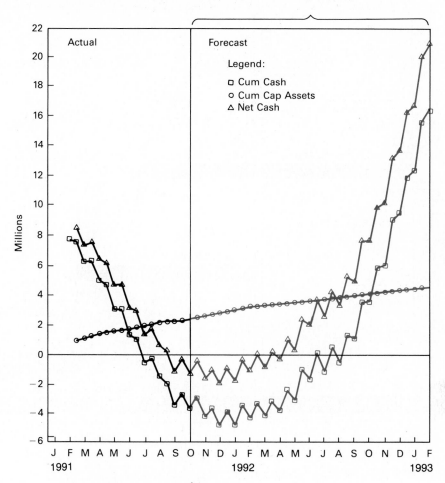

Figure 12.11   Cash-flow forecast for a new division.

visualize the effect of proposed changes (the barred tone part of Fig. 12.12). Similarly, one year's balance sheet can be compared with another graphically.

It is often useful to put two curves or bar charts onto one diagram. The sales of a product over time can be compared with the sales of a similar product. The sales of a product can be compared with the average sales to see whether it is rising or falling more than the average and to help separate the effects of product excellence from cyclical changes or general market movements.

Often a product that is really unprofitable is manufactured year after year because its detailed performance is hidden in aggregates. Sometimes a product

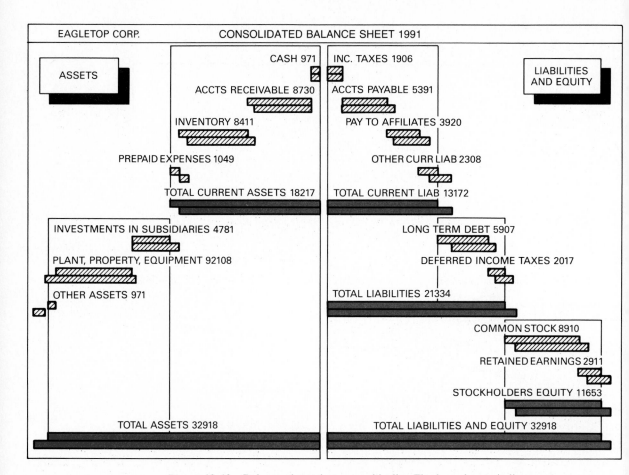

Figure 12.12   Balance sheet shown graphically. The barred tone indicates a possible variation in the balance sheet resulting from a ''what-if'' computation.

looks good because it has high unit sales but is, in fact, making insufficient profit. A good DSS should isolate the poor performers from the good ones.

Figure 12.13 shows a scatter diagram relating the sales of a pharmaceutical product to outbreaks of influenza. The marketing analyst may generate a similar diagram for other factors, attempting to find out what affects sales. In particular, he will be interested in the effects of advertising campaigns and mailings. He will want to isolate a variety of factors to attempt to find the most effective ways to spend the promotion budget. Should advertising be intensified quickly during outbreaks of flu, for example?

Figure 12.14 shows graphics used to explore the effects of establishing better air pollution controls on gasoline-powered vehicles. Carbon monoxide

⟶ PLOT SCATTER FLU-INC SALES

RELATIONSHIP BETWEEN FLU-INCIDENCE AND SALES (PRODUCT 248)

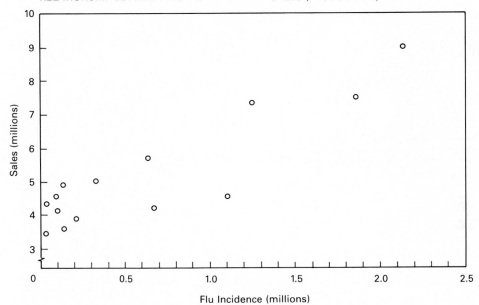

Figure 12.13 Scatter plot correlating the incidence of flu with the sales of a given pharmaceutical.

emissions, during high-traffic densities, can stress persons with cardiovascular conditions because carbon monoxide combines with oxygen-carrying hemoglobin in the blood, forming carboxyhemoglobin. This lessens the oxygen transport to the heart muscles. The black lines in Fig. 12.14 show the number of carbon monoxide-related angina attacks in the city of Denver. The top diagram is a historical diagram for 1975; the bottom diagram is a "what-if" forecast for 1985 [4]. Many such diagrams were produced to study the effects of alternate pollution control measures.

HELP TO USERS

Given a useful set of decision-support tools, it is important that a DSS language give users as much help as possible in employing them. Most persons who *should* use the tools have no training in operations research or computer science. They are accountants, market analysts, executives, and corporate staff. They need guidance from the software. The better the quality of this guidance, the greater the value likely to be obtained from the product.

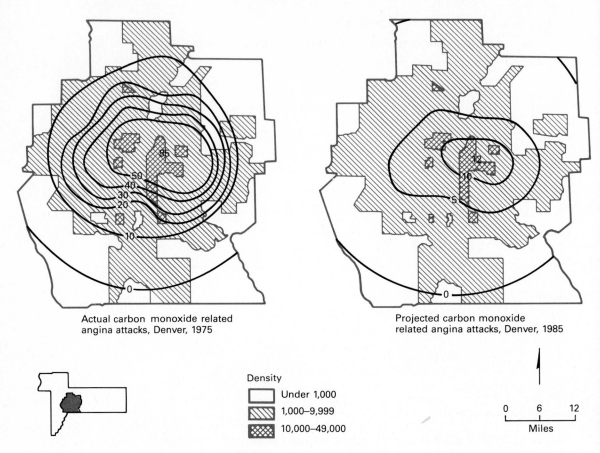

Actual carbon monoxide related
angina attacks, Denver, 1975

Projected carbon monoxide
related angina attacks, Denver, 1985

Density

☐ Under 1,000

▨ 1,000–9,999

▩ 10,000–49,000

0   6   12

Miles

Figure 12.14   What-if study of the effects of reducing auto emissions of carbon monoxide in Denver.

The following shows EXPRESS prompting a user in the fitting of a curve to a series of data:

```
─────────────►TRENDFIT
TIME SERIES TO BE ANALYZED: >ACTUALS
DESEASONALIZE BEFORE FITTING TREND? > NO
FOR WHICH MONTH(S): > JAN86 TO DEC90
FOR WHICH DIVISION(S): > CHEMICAL
FOR WHICH LINEITEM(S): > NETSALES
FOR WHICH CURVES?
1-UN,2-EXP,3-PWR,4-HYP1,5-HYP2,6-HYP3 >1 2 3

(TSRGMIN) BEST-FITTING CURVE: LINEAR
```

(TSRGRSQ)   COEFFICIENT OF DETERMINATION
(TSC1)   COEFFICIENT 1
(TSC2)   COEFFICIENT 2

TSTYPE	TSRGRSQ	TSC1	TSC
LINEAR	.909165	5,782.18	72.13123
EXPONENTIAL	.898473	5,922.45	.0093221
PWR FUNCTION	.823134	4,568.72	.1729885

The software can instantly produce graphics showing the trend fit and its extrapolation into the future. The user may need immediate help in understanding some of the items in the dialog, and this help should be available on the screen for all tools.

In the example, the user had to enter the word TRENDFIT. It would be better, in a fast-response environment, to give the user a menu of techniques he can use. The menu may appear at the top or bottom of a screen, the items on it being quickly selectable with a mouse, with arrow keys, or by entering letters. When the menu cursor is moved to any item, a sentence appears giving a simple explanation of that item; for example,

ARIMA, CLUSTER, FORECAST, REGRESSION, SENSITIVITY ,
TRENDFIT, WHAT IF?
SENSITIVITY ANALYSIS ALLOWS YOU TO CHANGE CERTAIN ITEMS
AND SEE THE EFFECTS OF THIS

On a PC workstation, the sentences change in deciseconds as the menu cursor is slid along the menu. The user may read the sentence before selecting an item. If the user selects the item by pressing the mouse button or ENTER key, a more detailed menu may appear:

ARIMA, CLUSTER, FORECAST, REGRESSION, SENSITIVITY,
TRENDFIT , WHAT IF
COMPUTES THE BEST-FITTING CURVE FOR A SET OF VALUES.

The user presses the mouse button, then moves the cursor to POWER on the following second-level menu:

LINEAR, EXPONENTIAL, POWER , HYP1, HYP2, HYP3, MULTIPLE,
HELP
COMPUTES THE BEST-FITTING POWER FUNCTION CURVE

The user moves the cursor to MULTIPLE:

LINEAR, EXPONENTIAL, POWER, HYP1, HYP2, HYP3, MULTIPLE ,
HELP
SELECTS THE BEST FIT OF SEVERAL CHOSEN CURVE TYPES.

The user presses the mouse button:

LINEAR, EXPONENTIAL, POWER, HYP1, HYP2, HYP3, ALL

CLICK THE MOUSE BUTTON ON THE ABOVE ITEMS OF YOUR CHOICE

The user selects several of these.

This type of menu system encourages the user to explore. He does not need to learn and memorize a software syntax. When beginning, users tend to slide the menu cursor to each menu item in turn and read its explanatory sentence. They can find out what the software does, asking for a more detailed explanation when they want it, by clicking on the HELP menu item.

AVOIDANCE OF AN ALIEN SYNTAX

Decision-support languages ought to be human factored so that they are extremely easy to use without an alien syntax. The excellent analytical tools and decision-support databases that exist today would probably have much greater usefulness if they did not present a syntax barrier to the most important decision makers. Advertisements for DSS products often extol the extreme ease of use of their ''English-like'' language when in fact their syntax provides a serious barrier to use by overworked managers and analysts.

PERSONAL COMPUTERS

It is very appealing to use personal computers for decision-support work because of their decisecond response times, mouse, and fast graphics. The relatively long response times of mainframe terminals greatly impede the dialog mechanisms that can be used, as discussed earlier. So it is appealing to employ personal computers with decisecond response times and better human factoring to work with data stored on the mainframe. The main decision-support database may be on a mainframe; portions of the data are downloaded to personal computers for manipulation (Fig. 12.15). The users may sometimes create or revise models on a personal computer and return these to the mainframe.

Many users keep their own decision-support data on a PC, often in the form of spreadsheet files. Many other powerful analytical tools are becoming available on the PC, and some of the mainframe DSS systems allow a PC to extract data for use with PC tools.

The central DSS databases need to be repositories of data that many deci-

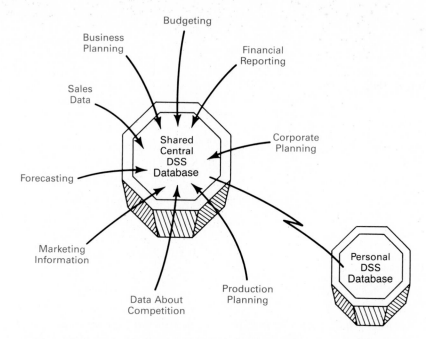

Figure 12.15   It is often very valuable for users to extract a portion of a DSS database for manipulation in their own personal computer.

sion-makers share and that may be updated continually. Software that facilitates distributed use of data while preserving the integrity and security of the data is needed.

WIDE SPECTRUM OF DSS PRODUCTS   There is a wide spectrum of decision-support software, ranging from simple products to highly complex products. A wide diversity of techniques can help in making decisions. Some of the simple software packages, such as the stand-alone spreadsheet tools, are extremely useful, but when users are familiar with them, it becomes desirable that they be able to extend their capability.

Figure 12.16 illustrates the range of functionality in DSS software. The capability to use spreadsheet tools can be extended in many ways—to the use of graphics, to analyzing slices through multidimensional data, to doing computations with 4GL languages, to analyzing data with operations research tools.

The personal computer is becoming steadily more powerful, and most of the tools mentioned in this chapter can operate on personal computers. It is attractive to knowledge workers to have their own decision-making environment of a personal computer. However, many decisions need data that are on a mainframe, centrally maintained and available to many end users. It is desirable to

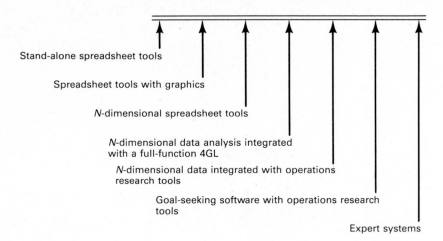

Stand-alone spreadsheet tools

Spreadsheet tools with graphics

N-dimensional spreadsheet tools

N-dimensional data analysis integrated
with a full-function 4GL

N-dimensional data integrated with operations
research tools

Goal-seeking software with operations research
tools

Expert systems

Figure 12.16   There is a wide spectrum of functionality in decision-support
software.

make the micro-mainframe connection as *transparent* as possible, so that the
user can employ his or her personal computer *either* with data stored on its
Winchester *or* with data stored on a mainframe.

When several users access data, integrity controls that are more complex
than for single-user access are needed. A great deal of decision-support data
needs to be shared (and sometimes updated) by many users.

Figure 12.17 adds a new dimension to Fig. 12.16, showing environments
for DSS ranging from personal computers to networked environments where the
user can access several multiuser systems.

Figure 12.18 adds a third dimension relating to data. The data may be
single-user data, shared central data, or fully distributed data. It may be kept in
the form of files, a decision-support database, an intelligent database, or a
knowledge base.

The industry needs to evolve from stand-alone products of limited functionality to products that integrate most of what is in Fig. 12.18 (see Fig.
12.19).

DECISION-SUPPORT   The access requirements of a decision-support data-
DATABASE   base are very different from those of a database for
routine computing. Databases for routine computing
are designed to be efficient with high-volume access and updating. Decision-
support databases are needed to handle multidimensional data efficiently and

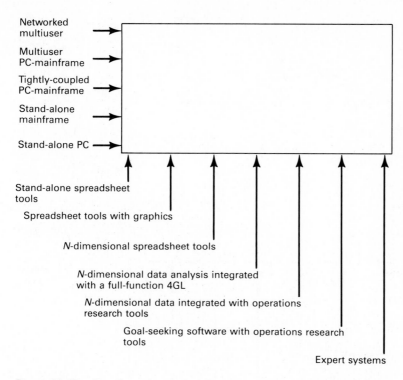

Networked
multiuser

Multiuser
PC-mainframe

Tightly-coupled
PC-mainframe

Stand-alone
mainframe

Stand-alone PC

Stand-alone spreadsheet
tools

Spreadsheet tools with graphics

N-dimensional spreadsheet tools

N-dimensional data analysis integrated
with a full-function 4GL

N-dimensional data integrated with operations
research tools

Goal-seeking software with operations research
tools

Expert systems

Figure 12.17 One dimension added to Fig. 12.16 showing the types of delivery mechanisms.

permit fully flexible relational operations such as searching, projecting, and joining relations.

A variety of mechanisms can be used to facilitate searching and joining of data—secondary indices, inverted files, ring structures, inverted list bit maps, and others. All such mechanisms tend to increase the complexity of updating the data. When the data is changed, the secondary indices, ring bit maps, or whatever have to be changed. These mechanisms degrade the performance of heavy-duty updating.

Data structures needed to support multidimensional data are different from those that support routine data processing. Data structures for routine data processing have a key such as PRODUCT# and a collection of attributes associated with the key:

PRODUCT#	NAME	DESCRIPTION	SOURCE	RELEASE DATE	PRICE	UNITS SOLD	REVENUE

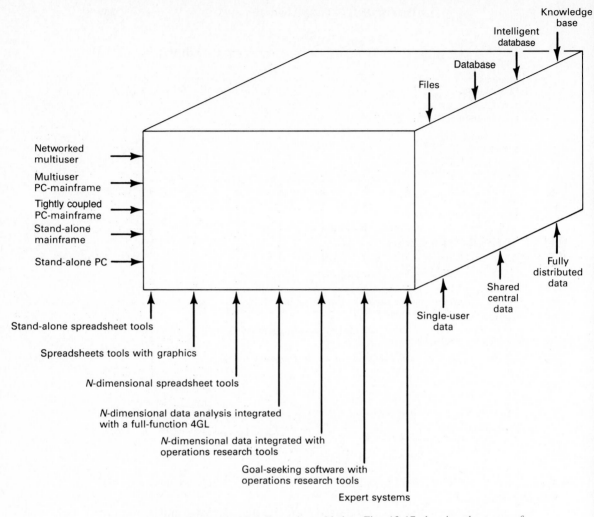

Networked
multiuser

Multiuser
PC-mainframe

Tightly coupled
PC-mainframe

Stand-alone
mainframe

Stand-alone PC

Files

Database

Intelligent
database

Knowledge
base

Single-user
data

Shared
central
data

Fully
distributed
data

Stand-alone spreadsheet tools

Spreadsheets tools with graphics

N-dimensional spreadsheet tools

N-dimensional data analysis integrated
with a full-function 4GL

N-dimensional data integrated with
operations research tools

Goal-seeking software with
operations research tools

Expert systems

Figure 12.18 A third dimension added to Fig. 12.17 showing the types of data facilities.

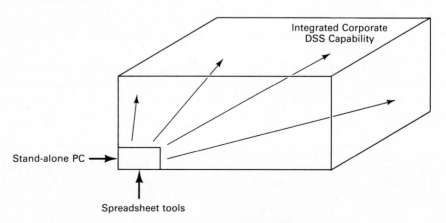

Integrated Corporate
DSS Capability

Stand-alone PC

Spreadsheet tools

Figure 12.19 It is desirable to extend DSS facilities in a corporation from stand-alone tools to an integrated DSS environment.

A record often has child (offspring) records associated with it:

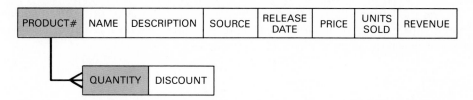

The data are designed with normalization techniques so that the attributes are each associated with a key that fully identifies them.

One of the attributes of the PRODUCT record is revenue. A decision-support database is likely to be concerned with where the revenue comes from. It can regard revenue as a variable with multiple subscripts:

$$\text{REVENUE}_{\text{PRODUCT}_{\text{MONTH}_{\text{REGION}}}}$$

Three subscripts give a three-dimensional array of data:

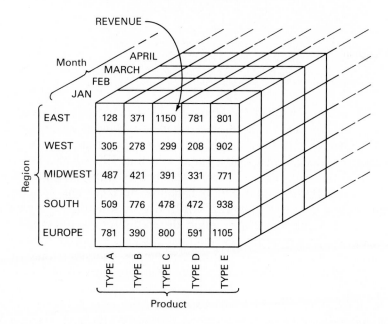

In the production database, REVENUE was an attribute of PRODUCT. Here, PRODUCT is a subscript of REVENUE.

There are often more than three dimensions. The revenues may be broken down further by type of sale, for example (mail order, direct, advertising, retail), or by type of customer, type of advertising, and so on.

The marketing staff might want to explore the effect of different discount structures or explore how different pricing structures would have affected revenues, on the basis of price-elasticity curves:

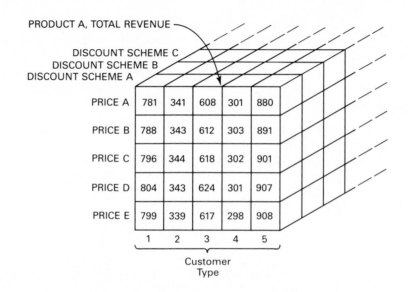

The figures for "what-if" revenue in this database are derived from the figures for actual revenue in the previous database. One decision-support array often needs to derive data from another decision-support array.

The efficient decision-support systems, such as EXPRESS, use data structures quite different from those in databases such as IMS (information management systems) or IDMS (information database management systems), which support production data processing. EXPRESS uses structures designed to store variables with multiple subscripts, quite different from a relational database. Some decision-support systems use relational databases, but the relations would be different from those stored for routine computing. Structures that are efficient for decision support with multidimensional data are inefficient for heavy-duty computing.

Because of this, data are often extracted from a corporation's production databases into a disjoint data structure that is designed for decision support (Fig. 12.20). This separate DSS database may be on the same computer as the production database or on a separate computer.

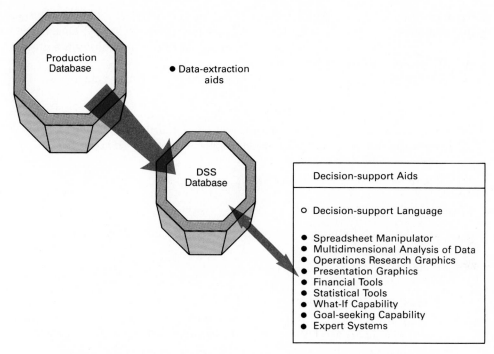

Figure 12.20   Decision-support tools often work on data structured especially for spreadsheet or multidimensional analysis. These data may be extracted from a production database and restructured.

A STAGING DATABASE

Data are often extracted from files or from production databases into a separate data structure that is designed for decision support. Sometimes this DSS database is on a personal computer. Sometimes it is on a departmental computer or on a mainframe.

In some cases data for decision support is extracted directly into the decision maker's software. In other cases a *staging* database is set up. This is a database designed for many decision-support users. It may be structured for a particular DSS software package, for example, with a relational or multidimensional data structure. It may reside on a central mainframe or on a departmental computer. Decision makers, each with their own personal computer or decision-support models, may access this shared database. Data may be moved from production files or databases into a DSS database on a regular basis.

One of the steps in designing a DSS is to determine whether a staging database is needed. A DSS at the prototype or early pilot stage may not have a staging database. The decision to set up a staging database may be made later when the DSS is institutionalized.

CHOICE OF SOFTWARE

The choice of software is particularly important in the building of decision-support systems. Disappointing results have occurred through employing software which is ill-suited to the users in question.

Software for decision-making can be divided into several categories:

- **Executive information systems**

  Systems which provide information but not analysis tools for executives. These are discussed in the following chapter. (They may be combined with the analytical tools lists that follow.)

  Example: COMMAND CENTER

- **Spreadsheet tools**

  Software for doing spreadsheet calculations and plotting information from spreadsheets.

  Example: LOTUS 1-2-3

- **Business modeling tools**

  Software for expressing business models with equations without programming. The inputs and results can be shown graphically or with spreadsheets.

  Example: JAVELIN

- **Financial analysis tools**

  Software for doing financial computations. In addition to creating conventional accounting reports these tools encourage financial analysts to do more sophisticated computations such as net present value, (which takes into consideration the time value of money), net return on investment, analysis of mergers and takeovers, and so on.

  Example: IFPS

- **High-level programming languages**

  The programming language APL has been used extensively for decision analysis and modeling. In wider uses are *fourth-generation languages* designed for end users, such as FOCUS, RAMIS, NOMAD, SAS, and so on.

- **Systems for generalized analysis of multidimensional data**

  Systems that employ a multidimensional database permit analysts to take slices through the data in many ways and use a variety of tools for analyzing the data, such as trend analysis, regression analysis, cluster analysis, and so on, and programming.

  Example: EXPRESS

These tools may be used by different categories of people as follows:

	President, Senior Executives	Controller, Financial Executives	Financial Analyst, Business Manager, Budget Manager.	Decision Analyst, Business Analyst	Product Manager, Brand Manager, Marketing Manager
Executive Information Systems	O	O			
Spreadsheets		O	O	O	
Business Modeling Tools		O	O	O	
Financial Analysis Tools		O	O	O	
High-level programming Languages				O	
Generalized Analysis of Multidimensional Data				O	O

There is substantial overlap among these different types of tools and the needs of different people, so there are many deviations from the preceding chart. The point that is important is that senior executives are not likely to use programminglike tools or detailed analysis tools, whereas business analysts or decision analysts need tools more powerful than spreadsheets. Marketing analysts need a detailed multidimensional database of sales. There are various specialized tools such as tools for production planning, critical path analysis, decision analysis trees, and so on.

DEVELOPMENT LIFECYCLE FOR DSS

The development lifecycle for building a decision-support system is different from the traditional development lifecycle. Box 12.3 gives a typical version of it.

REFERENCES

1. EXPRESS, Information Resources, Inc., 200 Fifth Avenue, Waltham, MA.

2. JAVELIN, Javelin Software Corporation, 1 Kendall Square, Building 200, Cambridge, MA.

3. SYSTEM W, from Comshare, Inc., P.O. Box 1588, 3001 South State Street, Ann Arbor, MI.

4. E. Teicholz and B. J. L. Berry, *Computer Graphics and Environmental Planning* (Englewood Cliffs, NJ: Prentice-Hall, 1983).

BOX 12.3   Development lifecycle for building a DSS

Description

   A decision-support system is designed to help make
better business decisions in a specific area. It requires
an appropriately structured database and a set of tools for
doing decision-support computations.
   Decision-support computations should generally be done by
end users because they understand the business problem they
are trying to solve. They may do this in an innovative, ad hoc
fashion without specifications. Often creative investigation
of numerical data is required. Highly complex business models
may result. Evolution through prototyping should occur before
the system is institutionalized.
   I.S. professionals should usually design the database and
the means of keeping it up to date. They may select or build
the tools which the end users employ, and guide the end users
in their use. The choice of decision-support software is critical.

Decision-support system procedure

   The procedure given below may be modified with Action
   Diagrammer to meet the needs of the particular situation.

Initiate the activity.
   Establish criteria and controls.
      Establish the long-term objectives of the development activity.
      Establish the objectives of the first working version.
      Comment
         The first working version should be SIMPLE and relatively
         easy to implement. Once a working version is fielded the
         system will tend to grow naturally if it is useful, with
         end users extending its functionality. The long-term
         potential should be understood and planned for from the
         beginning.

      Determine how results will be measured or judged.
      Establish a budget.
      Establish a target date for the first working system.
      Establish dates at which progress will be reviewed.
      Determine who will assess the progress and with what criteria.
   Determine who will build the system.
      Select the DP professional developer(s).
      Select the end-user developer(s).
      Determine what information center help is needed.
      Determine who, if anyone, will review the results.

Establish the software.
   Select decision-support software.
      Determine what categories of users the system is intended
      for:

BOX 12.3   *(Continued)*

```
                    *  Top management
                    *  Lower management, staff, or spreadsheet users
                    *  Financial analysts
                    *  General decision analysts

          Select a software category suitable for the above
             user category:
                    *  Executive information system
                    *  Spreadsheet tool
                    *  Business modeling tool
                    *  Financial analysis tool
                    *  Fourth-generation programming language
                    *  General decision-support tool

          Identify the most appropriate tool within this category.

       Ensure that the developers are fully trained in the use of
          the tools.

  Establish the data
       Determine what data the system needs.
       Establish a data model, or extract one from the encyclopedia.
       Determine where the source data comes from. (It is often extracted
          from mainframe production systems.)
       Determine how the source data will be converted or restructured.
       Determine whether a staging database will be used
             A staging database is a central repository of data in the DSS
                format that will be used independently by multiple users.
             Data is extracted from files or transaction databases into
             the staging database.  Individual users may extract data
             from the staging database into their own facilities.

       Extract the data into the tool that is used.
       Determine how the data in the decision-support system will be
          kept up to date.

  Prototype evolution
     Description
             The first prototype should be put to work as early as
          possible. This can usually be done very quickly with good
          decision-support software, once the requisite data is
          established, by a data-processing professional and end user
          working together. The end user may then evolve the system
          to do more sophisticated analysis. Eventually end users should
          take over the system, adapting it to help make the most
          effective decisions.

          ┌─────────────────────────────────────────────────┐
          │  Step-by-step or continuous evolution ?         │
          └─────────────────────────────────────────────────┘

             STEP-BY-STEP EVOLUTION progresses from one planned prototype
          to another until the target system is achieved.
             CONTINUOUS EVOLUTION progresses with a sequence of modifications
          continuously adjusting the prototype.
```

(Continued)

BOX 12.3   *(Continued)*

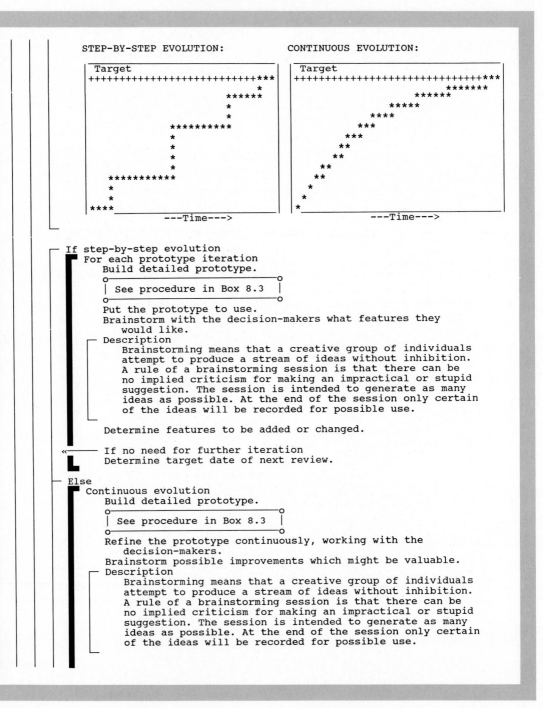

STEP-BY-STEP EVOLUTION:

```
Target
++++++++++++++++++++++++++++***
                              *
                         ******
                         *
                         *
                *********
                *
                *
                *
                *
      ***********
      *
      *
****
           ---Time--->
```

CONTINUOUS EVOLUTION:

```
Target
+++++++++++++++++++++++++++++***
                          *******
                       ******
                  *****
                ****
             ***
           ***
         **
        **
      **
     **
    *
   *
 *
              ---Time--->
```

If step-by-step evolution
For each prototype iteration
    Build detailed prototype.
    | See procedure in Box 8.3 |
    Put the prototype to use.
    Brainstorm with the decision-makers what features they
       would like.
    Description
       Brainstorming means that a creative group of individuals
       attempt to produce a stream of ideas without inhibition.
       A rule of a brainstorming session is that there can be
       no implied criticism for making an impractical or stupid
       suggestion. The session is intended to generate as many
       ideas as possible. At the end of the session only certain
       of the ideas will be recorded for possible use.

    Determine features to be added or changed.

    If no need for further iteration
    Determine target date of next review.

Else
Continuous evolution
    Build detailed prototype.
    | See procedure in Box 8.3 |
    Refine the prototype continuously, working with the
       decision-makers.
    Brainstorm possible improvements which might be valuable.
    Description
       Brainstorming means that a creative group of individuals
       attempt to produce a stream of ideas without inhibition.
       A rule of a brainstorming session is that there can be
       no implied criticism for making an impractical or stupid
       suggestion. The session is intended to generate as many
       ideas as possible. At the end of the session only certain
       of the ideas will be recorded for possible use.

BOX 12.3 *(Continued)*

« —— If an acceptable final result is achieved

Solidify
Review to ensure that the system is easy to use by other
    people if necessary.
Review to ensure that the business calculations
    can be easily checked by management.
Review to ensure that the system can be easily maintained.
Create the necessary documentation.

Build pilot system
A pilot system is a fully working system deployed at first
with only a small number of users, small number of terminals
or a small database. When it is found to be satisfactory the
number of users may be increased and the database expanded.

Determine what functions of the prototype will be included
    in the first pilot system.
Determine how decision-support information will be communicated
    among separate decision-makers.
Determine how decision-support information will be communicated
    with higher management.
Determine what networking facilities are needed. Will the
    decision-support facility link to an electronic mail or
    in-basket facility, for example.
Determine the nature of the ongoing connection to production
    databases.
Determine whether the system should be redesigned or
    rearchitected in order to produce a working pilot.
Make the necessary design changes.
Build and debug the pilot.

Install and adjust pilot system
Phase in system.
Conduct review meeting.

If no modifications needed

« —— Exit
Else
Document adjustments needed.
Determine date for installation of next version.
Make adjustments.

Institutionalize the system.
Determine what locations should use the system.
Determine whether a staging database should be established.
    A staging database is a central repository of data in the DSS
        format that will be used independently by multiple users.
        Data are extracted from files or transaction databases into
        the staging database. Individual users may extract data
        from the staging database into their own facilities.
If so
    Select the staging database software.
    Establish the staging database.
    Cut over the existing system to run with the staging database.

Establish the requisite training.
Establish an internal marketing program to make decision-
    makers aware of the system.

BOX 12.3 *(Continued)*

        With some decision-support systems this step has been
        particularly important. It may use:
          o   Memos
          o   Giving the system a memorable name and image
          o   Brochures
          o   Articles in the house magazine
          o   Presentations
          o   Film or video

    Expand the system a stage at a time.
      Monitor the system performance.
      Determine what hardware is needed to handle the full load.

13 EXECUTIVE INFORMATION CENTERS

INTRODUCTION The Information Center, as commonly operated, has the goal of helping end users to employ computerized tools (Chapter 10). It trains and supports them in the use of spreadsheet tools, fourth-generation languages, decision-support software, and so on. It often has the rule that the Information Center does not build applications itself, but enables end users to build them. It sets up procedures for enabling end users to help other end users, like teach-the-teachers programs. However, while business analysts, decision analysts, engineers, and junior management can be expected to put end-user languages to good use, most top management will not use them. Most high executives will never program, even in the most friendly languages, and, worse, will often not touch a typewriterlike keyboard.

Nevertheless a workstation on the desk can be of great value to top management. It can provide them with vital information, draw their attention to situations which need their intervention, and enable them to monitor situations most critical to them. Such systems are referred to as EIS (executive information systems).

Executive information systems are not programmed by the user. They provide the user with valuable information in the most attractive, easy-to-access form. EIS software is designed for this purpose. It provides access to facts, text, and charts without the need to type or remember mnemonics. Executive information systems are built by staff who are very sensitive to the executive's needs. Much of the information which is provided to executives may be that determined in the top-level information engineering methodologies such as critical success factor analysis (Book II).

Many information centers do not build executive information systems. Often this is because of their rule that the user must build his or her own systems and the Information Center can only provide support. In this case another organizational unit (or person) should build executive information systems. We will refer to this unit as an *Executive Information Center*.

THE CHARTER OF THE EXECUTIVE INFORMATION CENTER

The Executive Information Center selects the best EIS software and builds an executive information system. It identifies the information requirements of executives, captures the information needed, and identifies the best way to summarize and present it. Executive workstations should be selected which are as easy to use and uninhibiting as possible. They should employ touch screens or a mouse for selecting items for display. Much of the art of building executive information systems lies in designing displays which are the most appealing and informative to top management. The displays should enable them to track situations they are concerned with. It is necessary to select the most important information, filter it, summarize it concisely, highlighting that which is relevant and hiding detail which is not relevant. Attractive color charts should be used where appropriate. The system should give the executive the capability to drill down into more detail at the touch of a screen button. EIS systems should provide a feedback mechanism for senior executives enabling them to monitor the effectiveness of executive actions.

Box 13.1 gives the charter of an Executive Information Center.

BOX 13.1   Charter for the Executive Information Center

- Identify the information needs of all members of top management.
- Participate in critical success factor analysis to determine information needs.
- Become familiar with external sources of information relevant to top management needs.
- Select and install the best EIS software and facilities.
- Determine the best ways to summarize, structure, and display executive information.
- Encourage top management to use EIS workstations and monitor their reaction to the information provided.
- Keep the executive information up to date and constantly improve it.

RETURN ON EFFORT

Executive information systems are much easier to build than are traditional data processing systems or complex decision-support systems. Given today's software, no programming is required. The value of an EIS that is *really* used by executives can be great. It is especially great if CSF (critical success factor) analysis has been done so that the most important types of information are emphasized by the system.

That which is *measured* tends to be *managed*. It is desirable to find what information *should* be measured and bring it to desks of executives who can do the management.

One executive with an EIS comments that it both gives him more feeling of control and gives his managers more feeling of responsibility:

> We have all the information on the projects we manage in the organization. Managers at the first level use that information to do their job; they use it as a guide on how to manage. At the same time I can look at it any time I choose. I'm not hounding them, asking them for special reports. Those reports are generated for me. If I look at it today and find everything is within the parameters I'm comfortable with, I go about my business. They are operating as if they were independent entities; I rarely need to bug them at the operational level, and yet I have more control.

An EIS should enable an executive to spot potential troubles more quickly. It enables them to participate in key decisions when needed and keep out when things are going well. It can provide executive distance from day-to-day operations but alert the executive when his or her attention is needed.

Because executive information systems are relatively easy to build and particularly valuable, they should be emphasized by all IS executives. They can change the view that top management has of the IS department. IS becomes perceived as being truly helpful to top management rather than being a bunch of expensive, mysterious technicians. Prior to the growth of executive information systems, most top management had little use for IS people on a direct basis. Now the builders of executive information systems become *personally* useful to senior management. This new relationship has affected the careers of some IS staff.

The return on investment from developing an EIS may be great if it enables top management to spot and act on an emerging trend or problem earlier than they otherwise would.

THE CARIBBEAN QUESTION

In one case a chief executive officer was asked the question "If you spent a month in the Caribbean without telephones, when you came back what would

be the ten things you would most urgently want to know about your business?''
The executive thought about, and answered that question. A means was created
very quickly of extracting the ten pieces of information, presenting them attractively, reviewing them with the executive, and making them available in his
office on a workstation screen with color graphics and tables of numbers. He
was provided with ten ''buttons'' which he could touch, using a mouse, for the
ten sequences of charts and figures. He did not need to touch a keyboard. This
facility was built with COMMAND CENTER software [1] in a few weeks. A
staff person had the task of keeping the information up to date. The executive
found it valuable and became a convert. He started to ask for other information
and soon had a refined control mechanism enabling him to monitor important
activities and make executive interventions when needed. The system quickly
spread to other managers.

In addition to asking the Caribbean question, the techniques in Book II
should be used to identify formally the information most valuable to executives.

Given the cost of today's technology, no major executive should be without a system like this. A major reason for the low penetration of executive
information systems is that the IS organization in many enterprises is bogged
down building difficult systems and struggling to maintain badly designed systems, and is not building simple information systems which have a direct effect
on management. To have the direct effect on management, management itself
has to be converted. They will not be converted by merely giving them a personal computer; this can be disastrous because they may conclude that it is not
useful. They *can* be converted by asking the Caribbean question and following
through as quickly as in the foregoing example with a system free from any
need to use mnemonics, commands, or other forms of alien syntax. (The system
should *never* say ''BAD COMMAND OR FILE NAME.'') Such action should
be followed (or preceded) by a critical success factor study. The return on investment from such actions is often very high.

EIS VERSUS DSS   Figure 13.1 contrasts decision-support systems and
                       executive information systems. Decision-support sys-
tems are designed for the person who analyzes and models information. Executive information systems are designed for the person who works primarily with
people and who needs information to monitor situations, achieve management
measurements and controls, identify trends, and be given earlier warning of
problems which need executive action.

The user of the decision-support systems may create programs or build
elaborate business models. The user of executive information systems merely
wants the relevant facts. The EIS may have a touch screen or mouse designed
for maximum ease of use. The DSS is designed with a language that permits
flexible use of analytical tools. A powerful DSS may have the types of tools
listed in Fig. 12.2. The users of an EIS access the information in a sequence of

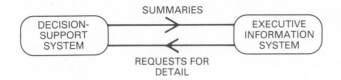

DECISION-SUPPORT SYSTEM	EXECUTIVE INFORMATION SYSTEM
• System Designed for Analyzing and Modeling Information	• System Designed for Displaying Information and Monitoring Situations
• Programmable	• Not Programmable
• Ad Hoc Access to Data	• Predesigned Access to Data
• Designed for Flexible Use of Analytical Tools	• Designed for Maximum Ease of Use (e.g., with Touch Screens)

Figure 13.1　Contrasts between decision-support systems and executive information systems.

steps that is predesigned for them. The users of a DSS need flexible ad hoc access to a multidimensional database.

At the time of writing, much EIS software such as COMMAND CENTER [1] is separate from much DSS software such as EXPRESS [2]. Some software, such as METAPHOR [3], is designed to bridge these two worlds. This is desirable because the analyst who uses a DSS should be able to create displays which are intended to make complex facts clear to executives. A DSS should send information summaries to an EIS. Some decision-support software, such as SYSTEM W, links an executive information system from the same organization (COMMANDER) [4]. An executive using an EIS may send requests for detail to a DSS. He should be encouraged to ask ''what-if'' questions that can be answered with a DSS.

TYPES OF INFORMATION IN AN EIS　　　Figure 13.2 lists some of the types of information that may be used in an EIS.

This includes external as well as internal data. Some companies use an opening touch screen with a list of internal data on the left and external data on the right, as in Fig. 13.3. If the executive touches ''CRITICAL SUCCESS FACTORS,'' a screen appears

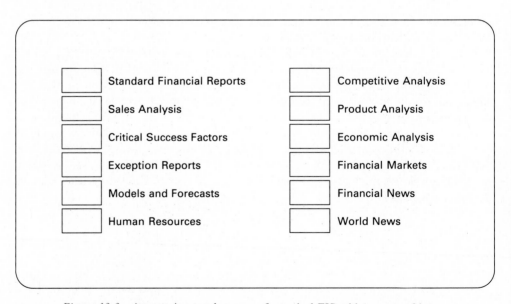

INTERNAL DATA

Basic Corporate Data   **Models**   **Soft Data**

Sales   Budgets   Customer satisfaction
Profits   Forecasts   Employee attitudes
Customers   Scenarios   Perception of trends
Finance
Productivity

EXTERNAL DATA

From Public Data Sources   **Compiled Internally**

Economic trends   Information about competitors
Currency movements   Information about products
Market surveys   Forecasts
General news   Industry analysis
Industry news

ELECTRONIC MAIL

Figure 13.2 Types of information that may be accessible at the screen of an executive information system.

	Standard Financial Reports		Competitive Analysis
	Sales Analysis		Product Analysis
	Critical Success Factors		Economic Analysis
	Exception Reports		Financial Markets
	Models and Forecasts		Financial News
	Human Resources		World News

Figure 13.3 An opening touch screen of a typical EIS with a menu of internal data on the left and external data on the right. Touching any item gives a more detailed menu.

listing the critical success factors. If he touches any one of these, he sees a chart of measurements showing the degree of success in achieving the critical success factor. Touching the screen again may show more detailed numbers or analysis.

Touching "ECONOMIC ANALYSIS" on the external menu gives a list of leading economic indicators. Touching one of these gives a chart showing the trend of that indicator. Touching "WORLD NEWS" results in a list of today's headlines; touching one of the headlines results in the detailed story being displayed. External data can be purchased from a variety of sources such as Compustat and Data Resources, Inc. There are special sources of data for specific industries. For example, the oil industry has computerized information available of the prices of crude oil and other products, which vary continuously. These external data sources can be fed automatically into the EIS database. Software exists for this purpose.

Much market analysis information is sold. This may be digested, filtered, and made available via an EIS. The corporation's performance may be charted against competitive performance. In some corporations, many competing corporations are tracked in this way. If the executive selects two or many corporations a chart is generated comparing their performance. Various different measures of their performance may be charted.

Most corporate executives are interested in sales and revenue. Touching the "SALES ANALYSIS" button on Figure 13.3 may result in a summary of current sales and a touch menu which invites the executive to examine a breakdown by product, by region, by customer, and so on.

At the highest level, one enterprise comprised of multiple corporations displays financial statements for these corporations:

	Profit and Loss	Balance Sheet	Cash Flow
Consolidated results	☐	☐	☐
Company A	☐	☐	☐
Company B	☐	☐	☐
Company C	☐	☐	☐

Touching any of these buttons results in a display of the report in question. Touching highlighted numbers on the reports results in a more detailed breakdown of those numbers. Where analysis of sales, profits, or other items has been done with a decision-support system, the analyst may have come to conclusions about why items are particularly high or low. The EIS may indicate that these conclusions are available to the executive. The executive pushes the screen button indicated and sees the analyst's narrative possibly with charts to illustrate his conclusions. The display may give the phone number of the analyst.

Figures 13.4 to 13.11 give illustrations of screens used in executive information systems using the software COMMAND CENTER [1].

There is thus a strong link between DSS and EIS. The same multidimensional database may be used by both. However, providing useful information from an EIS can be done immediately before a detailed DSS and models have been established.

DRAWING THE EXECUTIVE'S ATTENTION

Color should be used on EIS displays to draw executives' attention to items they need to be interested in. Items that are on target may be uncolored. Items significantly below target may be colored red, and items significantly above target may be green. An executive may browse through the information examining the red parts in detail.

One organization does this with a set of *key indicators* broken down by area. Touching any one indicator shows a detailed chart of the information. Both the key indicators and the detailed numbers are colored red or green if

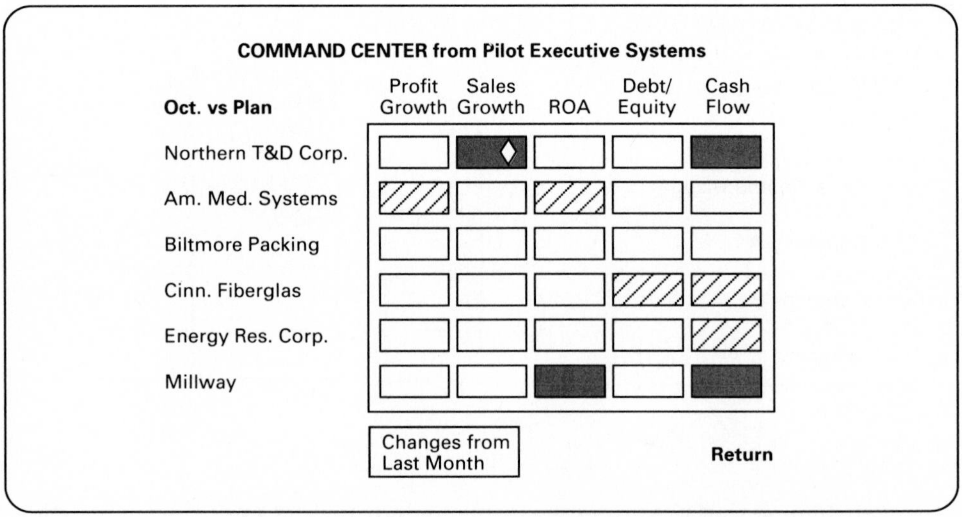

Figure 13.4   A COMMAND CENTER display.

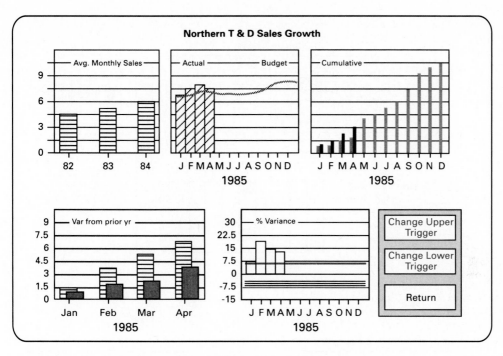

Figure 13.5   A COMMAND CENTER display.

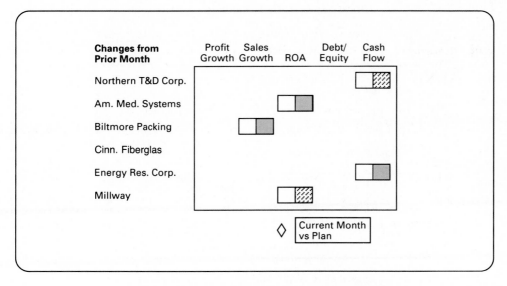

Figure 13.6   A COMMAND CENTER display.

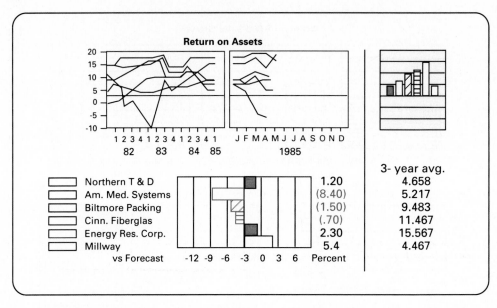

Figure 13.7 A COMMAND CENTER display.

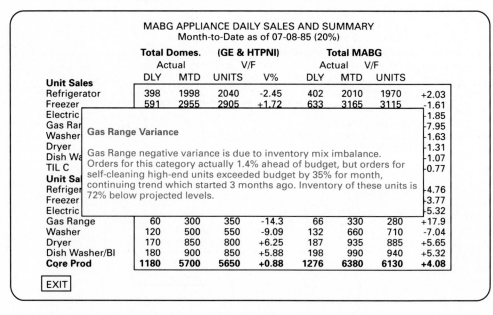

Figure 13.8 A COMMAND CENTER display.

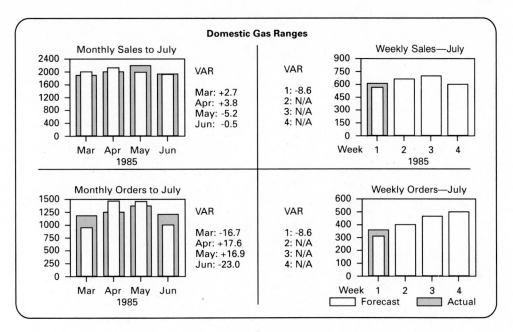

Figure 13.9 A COMMAND CENTER display.

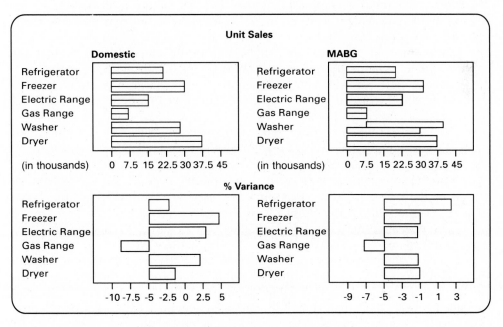

Figure 13.10 A COMMAND CENTER display.

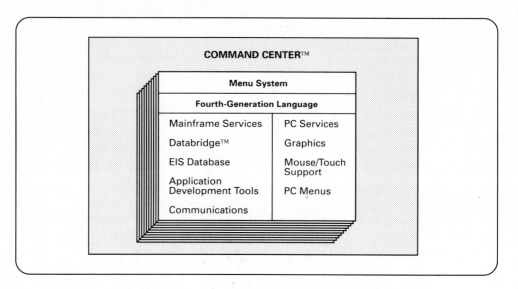

Figure 13.11   A COMMAND CENTER display.

necessary. A similar scheme with critical success factors is desirable, so that the executive can put pressure on those areas where better performance is necessary.

Colors may also be used to show significant differences from the previous month. Some systems allow the executive to set his own levels such that if performance falls below that level he is alerted. This can provide a powerful type of feedback, directing the executive's attention to where his energies are most needed.

Most executives are concerned with forecasts—forecasts of sales, revenues, project completion, and so on. When the curves showing forecasts come from an analyst, the analyst may put touch buttons on the curve which take the user to a screen giving details of the assumptions made or the reasons for the shape of the curve. Special colors may be used to show which comments or details it is particularly important for the executive to take note of.

The executive may be given a display which compares this month's forecast with last month's and the month's before, so that he can see whether the forecasts are getting better or worse. If they are worsening, executive attention is needed. Figure 13.12 shows the effects on profit and loss of forecasts made at three different times. This chart shows that the corporation is assuming greater financial risks than originally anticipated, with greater short-term losses and greater eventual profits. The time taken to break into profitability is about the same as originally forecast.

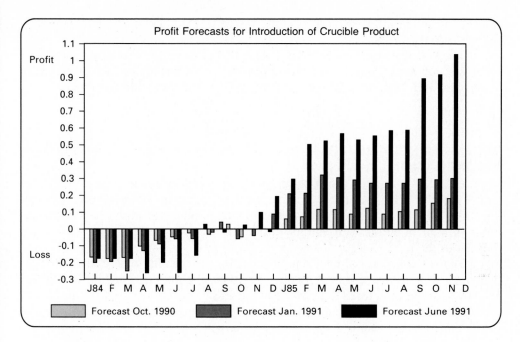

Figure 13.12 Plot showing how forecasts made at different times vary in their profit predictions.

Imaginative use of color graphics is particularly valuable in executive information systems.

START SIMPLE

When an EIS is first set up, it should be simple. It should concentrate on those few types of information most valuable to the executive in question. The Caribbean question may be asked to determine what those are. The executive should find the first version of the workstation on his desk directly useful to him. He is then likely to ask for more detail or for other types of information. It is important that an EIS should be highly focused on the true needs of the executive or on the critical success factors.

The system may start by serving one executive or a small group of executives. If successful it will expand to serve other executives and other types of information. For this reason, EIS access tends to proliferate. This is useful because it helps and encourages managers to hit the targets identified. There may eventually be hundreds of users, geographically spread. A system with PC access to a central database is necessary so that integrity can be assumed and all users see that same information. The system should not be allowed to become full of too much information that is expensive to maintain. It must remain easy to use and highly focused.

Some of the information in an EIS is highly sensitive. Software should be selected with good security features so that access to valuable data is carefully controlled and theft or malignant modification of the data will not occur.

MICRO-MAINFRAME COOPERATION

Good EIS software operates both on the executive workstation and on a central computer. The workstation should be a personal computer; the central machine may be a mainframe or a departmental computer. Workstations in many locations may be linked to the central computer. Some executives have workstations in their home as well as their office for accessing information that is important to them.

The software on the workstation provides the opening dialog and automatically signs on to the central computer. The central computer contains a database established and structured specially for the EIS. The information in the central database must be kept up-to-date and accessible by multiple executives and staff. Parts of the central database may be downloaded to the workstation.

The workstation provides the easy-to-use, mnemonics-free dialog which employs screen "push buttons" operated with a touch screen or mouse. It provides fast responses when the user pushes the buttons and occasionally indicates that a longer response will occur while it retrieves the requested data. The workstation has elegant graphics software. A stream of numbers may be transmitted from the central machine, and the workstation creates color charts from these numbers.

The central computer contains application development tools which make it easy to search and join data and do computations. The central computer may have telecommunications links to other computers with other databases. Data from external sources (such as Compustat or Data Resources, Inc.) may be transmitted to the central computer and stored in its database ready for access.

The division of work between the central computer and workstation may thus be as follows:

CENTRAL COMPUTER	WORKSTATION
EIS database	Elegant user-friendly interface
Application development tools	Automatic sign-on to the central computer
Links to other databases	Mouse or touch-screen control
Links to external data sources	Powerful graphics software

The software on the workstation needs to cooperate with the software on the central computer in a seamless fashion.

GOAL-ORIENTED INFORMATION

Two types of reports can be given to top management: reports that give information in the form of traditional accounting and reports that provide measures of the achievement of corporate goals and critical success factors. The latter are generally more useful to executives. The EIS should be tightly coupled to studies of goals, problems, and critical success factors (Book II).

A survey of installed executive information systems, done by Pilot Executive Software [1], concluded that only 20 percent of EIS were specifically designed to help management hit the goals and CSF measures. People two or three levels from the top in most corporations surveyed did not know what the corporate goals were. This is a severe waste of opportunity. Goals and critical success factors should be made the basis of EIS. Managers below the top level should know what is being measured and monitored. If they know that certain ratios are being monitored by higher management, they will try to improve those ratios. *That which is monitored tends to improve.* EIS is a useful tool to help achieve critical success factors and goals.

STAFF REQUIREMENTS

The building of executive information systems needs a small amount of technical skill and a large amount of business savvy. The technical skill comes mostly at the beginning in selecting the software, making it work, and establishing the network connections. There is an ongoing need to communicate with the executives, understand their information needs, keep track of data sources, and translate the data into attractive, informative displays. The EIS screens are in constant evolution. There should be continuous prototyping and discovery of how to make the system more valuable to executives. The executive appetite for detail can never be satisfied. The number of screens accessible steadily grows.

The Executive Information Center may be staffed primarily by people who understand the business information needs and sources. They may "contract out" the technical work to the IS department. The staff in the center may include decision-support analysts who own business models and can use them to answer "what-if" questions and display the results.

The Executive Information Center may be involved in preparing for board meetings, shareholder meetings, or top management planning sessions. The staff create the charts used in such meetings and may generate charts during a planning session.

The center may initiate or keep track of critical success factor analysis or technology impact analysis (Book II) and make sure that information relevant to these is in the EIS.

The Executive Information Center, or its equivalent, is part of the IS Department in some enterprises and external to it in others. This relates to the extent to which the top IS executive perceives himself as being responsible for the strategy of business information planning. The Executive Information Center relates more to the top level of the information engineering pyramid than to the bottom levels.

However it is organized, it is a vital function in today's corporations. Many senior executives still do not have a workstation on their desk. Some have tried to employ one and abandoned it because it is not useful enough to warrant their effort. However, many senior executives who have experienced the best designed EIS systems have concluded that they could no longer manage effectively without one.

REFERENCES

1. Figures 13.4-13.11 courtesy of COMMAND CENTER, Pilot Executive Software, 40 Broad Street, Boston, MA.

2. EXPRESS, Information Resources, Inc., 200 Fifth Avenue, Waltham, MA.

3. METAPHOR, Inc., Mountain View, CA.

4. SYSTEM W and COMMANDER, Comshare, Inc., P.O. Box 1588, 3001 South State Street, Ann Arbor, MI.

PART  TECHNICAL DESIGN AND CUTOVER

14 DATA USE ANALYSIS

Many computer applications have low transaction volumes and there is little concern with machine performance. Some applications have high transaction volumes and performance calculations must be done carefully. Machine performance considerations sometimes cause designers to split a database into multiple disjoint databases, or possibly to distribute the data. To make such decisions it is necessary to analyze the use of data. This chapter is about data use analysis. This analysis is employed in physical database design as discussed in the following chapter.

ADDING ACCESS DATA TO ACTION DIAGRAMS

The starting point for data use analysis is a collection of action diagrams showing data accesses. The action diagrams can range from an overview design showing navigation through a data model, to complete programs.

Figure 14.1 shows a portion of a data model, and Figs. 14.2 and 14.3 show two procedures which use it. There may be many such procedures which can use the data simultaneously.

The data model should contain the average cardinality of relationships between entities. For example, one relationship is

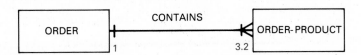

The red figures by the cardinality symbols indicate the average cardinality. An ORDER contains, on average 3.2 ORDER-PRODUCTS. An ORDER-PRODUCT relates to one and only one ORDER.

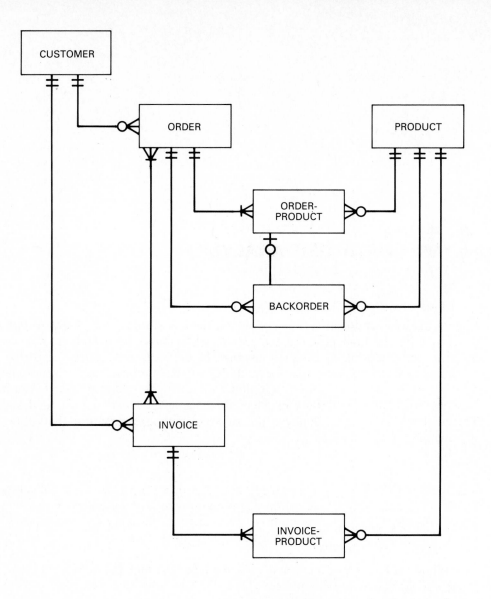

KEY	CARDINALITY	
	MINIMUM	MAXIMUM
	0	1
	0	MANY
	1	1
	1	MANY
	MANY	MANY

Figure 14.1 Data model used throughout this chapter to illustrate data use analysis.

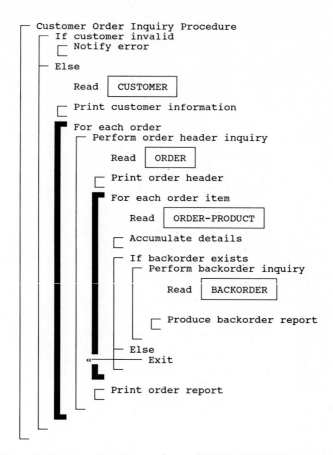

Figure 14.2   An action diagram for an ORDER INQUIRY procedure.

Figure 14.4 is the data model annotated to show the average cardinalities of the relationships.

To analyze the use of data, we annotate the action diagrams with information about data accesses and volumes. The first step in this procedure is shown in Fig. 14.5. Under each data access block the path through the data model is printed. If the action diagram was built with an encyclopedia-based workbench, this information may already exist in the encyclopedia and can be printed automatically. The designer checks that the access paths appear to be correct. This step provides a validation of the data model and its use.

Figure 14.6 shows the next step. The computer prints the average cardinalities of the access paths on the diagram.

```
* Order processing procedure

      Read  | CUSTOMER |

   If CUSTOMER# is invalid
       Process invalid order
       Print REJECT_NOTICE
   Else
      If CREDIT_RATING < 3
          Process poor-credit order

          Create  | ORDER-REJECT |

          Print REJECT_NOTICE
      Else
          Set ORDER_TOTAL = 0

          Create  | ORDER |

         If not subscription customer
           Prepare invoice header

             Print INVOICE-HEADER

             Create  | INVOICE |


         For each product ordered

            Read  | PRODUCT |

            If PRODUCT# is invalid
                Print error message
            Else
               If QTY_ON_HAND < QTY_ORDERED

                   Create  | BACKORDER |

                   Print BACKORDER_NOTICE
               Else
                   LINE_ITEM_PRICE = CATALOG_PRICE
                   LINE-TOTAL =QTY_ORDERED * LINE_ITEM_PRICE
                   ORDER_TOTAL = ORDER_TOTAL + LINE_TOTAL

                   Create  | ORDER-PRODUCT |

                  If not subscription customer

                      Create  | INVOICE-PRODUCT |

                      Print INVOICE-LINE


         ORDER_TOTAL = ORDER_TOTAL * [1 - DISCOUNT / 100]
         ORDER_STATUS = 0

         Update  | ORDER |

        If not subscription customer

            Update  | INVOICE |

            Print INVOICE-TOTAL
```

Figure 14.3 An action diagram for an ORDER PROCESSING procedure.

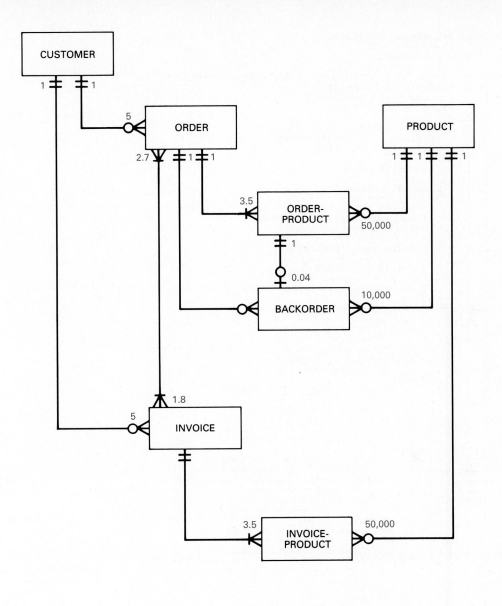

KEY	CARDINALITY	
	MINIMUM	MAXIMUM
——O⊦[	0	1
——O≺	0	MANY
——⊦⊦[	1	1
——≺[	1	MANY
——≺	MANY	MANY

Figure 14.4 The data model used in this chapter, annotated to show the average cardinalities of the relationships.

```
┌─* Order processing procedure
│
│      Read  ┌──────────────┐
│           │  CUSTOMER    │
│           └──────────────┘
│      ***Access path from Entry to CUSTOMER ***********************************
├─ If CUSTOMER# is invalid
│      Process invalid order
│      Print REJECT_NOTICE
├─ Else
│   ┌─ If CREDIT_RATING < 3
│   │      Process poor-credit order
│   │      Print REJECT_NOTICE
│   ├─ Else
│          Set ORDER_TOTAL = 0
│
│          Create  ┌──────────────┐
│                 │   ORDER      │
│                 └──────────────┘
│          ***Access path from CUSTOMER to ORDER ****************************
│       ┌─ If not subscription customer
│       │ ┌─ Prepare invoice header
│       │ │
│       │ │    Print INVOICE-HEADER
│       │ │
│       │ │    Create  ┌──────────────┐
│       │ │           │  INVOICE     │
│       │ │           └──────────────┘
│       │ │    ***Access path from CUSTOMER to INVOICE *******************
│       │
│       ┃  For each product ordered
│       ┃
│       ┃      Read  ┌──────────────┐
│       ┃           │  PRODUCT     │
│       ┃           └──────────────┘
│       ┃      ***Access path from Entry to PRODUCT **********************
│       ┃ ┌─ If PRODUCT# is invalid
│       ┃ │      Print error message
│       ┃ ├─ Else
│       ┃ │   ┌─ If QTY_ON_HAND < QTY_ORDERED
│       ┃ │   │
│       ┃ │   │      Create  ┌──────────────┐
│       ┃ │   │             │  BACKORDER   │
│       ┃ │   │             └──────────────┘
│       ┃ │   │      ***Access path from ORDER to BACKORDER ****************
│       ┃ │   │      Print BACKORDER_NOTICE
│       ┃ │   ├─ Else
│       ┃ │   │      LINE_ITEM_PRICE = CATALOG_PRICE
│       ┃ │   │      LINE-TOTAL =QTY_ORDERED * LINE_ITEM_PRICE
│       ┃ │   │      ORDER_TOTAL = ORDER_TOTAL + LINE_TOTAL
│       ┃ │   │
│       ┃ │   │      Create  ┌──────────────────┐
│       ┃ │   │             │  ORDER-PRODUCT   │
│       ┃ │   │             └──────────────────┘
│       ┃ │   │      ***Access path from ORDER to ORDER-PRODUCT*************
│       ┃ │   │   ┌─ If not subscription customer
│       ┃ │   │   │
│       ┃ │   │   │    Create  ┌────────────────────┐
│       ┃ │   │   │           │  INVOICE-PRODUCT   │
│       ┃ │   │   │           └────────────────────┘
│       ┃ │   │   │    ***Access path from INVOICE to INVOICE-PRODUCT*******
│       ┃ │   │   └    Print INVOICE-LINE
│       ┃ │   └
│       ┃ └
│       ┃
│       │      ORDER_TOTAL = ORDER_TOTAL * [1 - DISCOUNT / 100]
│       │      ORDER_STATUS = 0
│       │
│       │      Update  ┌──────────────┐
│       │             │   ORDER      │
│       │             └──────────────┘
│       │      ***Access path from CUSTOMER to ORDER ****************************
│       │   ┌─ If not subscription customer
│       │   │
│       │   │    Update  ┌──────────────┐
│       │   │           │  INVOICE     │
│       │   │           └──────────────┘
│       │   │    ***Access path from CUSTOMER to INVOICE *******************
│       │   └    Print INVOICE-TOTAL
└
```

Figure 14.5 The action diagram of Fig. 14.3 annotated to show the paths through the data model.

```
┌─* Order processing procedure
│
│      Read   ┌─────────────┐
│             │  CUSTOMER   │
│             └─────────────┘
│      ***Access path from Entry to CUSTOMER **********************************
│      ***Average path cardinality: NA ********************************************
┌─  If CUSTOMER# is invalid
│        Process invalid order
│        Print REJECT_NOTICE
├─  Else
│    ┌─  If CREDIT_RATING < 3
│    │        Process poor-credit order
│    │        Print REJECT_NOTICE
│    ├─  Else
│    │        Set ORDER_TOTAL = 0
│    │
│    │        Create  ┌─────────┐
│    │                │  ORDER  │
│    │                └─────────┘
│    │        ***Access path from CUSTOMER to ORDER *****************************
│    │        ***Average path cardinality: 5 ***********************************
│    │    ┌─  If not subscription customer
│    │    │ ┌─ Prepare invoice header
│    │    │ │
│    │    │ │    Print INVOICE-HEADER
│    │    │ │
│    │    │ │    Create  ┌───────────┐
│    │    │ │            │  INVOICE  │
│    │    │ │            └───────────┘
│    │    │ │    ***Access path from CUSTOMER to INVOICE ************************
│    │    │ │    ***Average path cardinality: 5 ********************************
│    │    │
│    │    │    For each product ordered
│    │    │
│    │    │        Read  ┌───────────┐
│    │    │              │  PRODUCT  │
│    │    │              └───────────┘
│    │    │        ***Access path from Entry to PRODUCT *************************
│    │    │        ***Average path cardinality: NA *****************************
│    │    │    ┌─  If PRODUCT# is invalid
│    │    │    │        Print error message
│    │    │    ├─  Else
│    │    │    │    ┌─  If QTY_ON_HAND < QTY_ORDERED
│    │    │    │    │
│    │    │    │    │        Create  ┌─────────────┐
│    │    │    │    │                │  BACKORDER  │
│    │    │    │    │                └─────────────┘
│    │    │    │    │        ***Access path from ORDER to BACKORDER *************
│    │    │    │    │        ***Average path cardinality: 0.04*****************
│    │    │    │    │        Print BACKORDER_NOTICE
│    │    │    │    ├─  Else
│    │    │    │    │        LINE_ITEM_PRICE = CATALOG_PRICE
│    │    │    │    │        LINE-TOTAL =QTY_ORDERED * LINE_ITEM_PRICE
│    │    │    │    │        ORDER_TOTAL = ORDER_TOTAL + LINE_TOTAL
│    │    │    │    │
│    │    │    │    │        Create  ┌─────────────────┐
│    │    │    │    │                │  ORDER-PRODUCT  │
│    │    │    │    │                └─────────────────┘
│    │    │    │    │        ***Access path from ORDER to ORDER-PRODUCT*********
│    │    │    │    │        ***Average path cardinality: 3.5 *****************
│    │    │    │    │    ┌─  If not subscription customer
│    │    │    │    │    │
│    │    │    │    │    │    Create  ┌───────────────────┐
│    │    │    │    │    │            │  INVOICE-PRODUCT  │
│    │    │    │    │    │            └───────────────────┘
│    │    │    │    │    │    ***Access path from INVOICE to INVOICE-PRODUCT****
│    │    │    │    │    │    ***Average path cardinality: 3.5 ****************
│    │    │    │    │    └─   Print INVOICE-LINE
```

Figure 14.6 Average path cardinality figures added to Fig. 14.5. These should be added by computer from the data model. The designer should check them.

(Continued)

```
ORDER_TOTAL = ORDER_TOTAL * [1 - DISCOUNT / 100]
ORDER_STATUS = 0

Update   ORDER

***Access path from CUSTOMER to ORDER ****************************
***Average path cardinality: 5 **********************************
If not subscription customer

   Update    INVOICE

   ***Access path from CUSTOMER to INVOICE ***********************
   ***Average path cardinality: 5 *******************************
   Print INVOICE-TOTAL
```

Figure 14.6   (Continued)

PROBABILITIES ON ACTION DIAGRAMS

Action diagrams have conditions or case structures which represent alternate paths through a procedure. The action diagram can be annotated with the probability of taking each path. The design tool can add panels to the action diagram asking for probability numbers.

In some cases these probabilities are related to the cardinality numbers on the data model. For example an ORDER-PRODUCT on Fig. 14.4 is associated with 0.04 BACKORDERS.

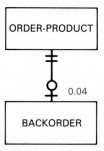

The action diagram may have a conditional bracket saying IF BACKORDER, or IF QUANTITY-ON-HAND < QUANTITY-ORDERED. This condition may be annotated with the probability statement:

****PROBABILITY OF THIS BRANCH: 0.04 ****

REPETITIONS ON ACTION DIAGRAMS

Action diagrams have repetition brackets. The action diagram can similarly be annotated with the average number of executions of a repetition bracket. The tool can ask the designer for these numbers.

Again the repetition numbers may be associated with cardinalities in the data model. For example, Fig. 14.4 shows that ORDER is associated with 3.5 ORDER-PRODUCTS on average.

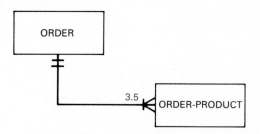

The action diagram may have a repetition bracket saying FOR EACH OR-DER-PRODUCT. This can be annotated with the following statement.

****Average no. of iterations per bracket: 3.5 ****

Figure 14.7 shows the action diagram of Fig. 14.6 annotated with probability and repetition statements. Using these numbers the average numbers of executions of each bracket are computed and printed on Fig. 14.7. The designer should manually check the reasonableness of these numbers.

NUMBER OF DATA ACCESSES   The probability and repetition figures are used to compute the numbers of data accesses in a given period.

It is generally appropriate to examine a period of one hour. We use a one-hour period throughout this chapter. Normally the peak traffic hour would be examined. There may be more than one peak hour with different traffic types.

It is necessary to estimate the number of transactions in the peak hour. From this the average number of accesses per hour can be computed for each access on the action diagram.

It is assumed that 200 orders per hour are processed. The peak-hour number is used to compute the numbers of data accesses. These are printed on the action diagram of Fig. 14.8. Figure 14.8 shows only the control flow, data access, and volumes of data accesses.

Figure 14.9 summarizes the data accesses. Some data references do not require a physical input/output operation. They access data items which are in a buffer. In Fig. 14.9, for example, an INVOICE record is created, then updated. This does not require two input/output operations. The record is created in a buffer, later updated, and then written on the disks. The same applies to the ORDER record. The rightmost column of Fig. 14.9 indicates which accesses

```
* Order processing procedure
    ***Average no. of executions per transaction: 1 ***************************

    Read │ CUSTOMER │

    ***Access path from Entry to CUSTOMER *********************************
    ***Average path cardinality: NA **************************************
─ If CUSTOMER# is invalid
    *******Probability of this branch: 0.007 *****************************
    ***Average no. of executions per transaction: 0.007*******************
    Process invalid order
    Print REJECT_NOTICE
─ Else
    *******Probability of this branch: 0.993 *****************************
    ***Average no. of executions per transaction: 0.993*******************
  ─ If CREDIT_RATING < 3
      *******Probability of this branch: 0.024 ***************************
      ***Average no. of executions per transaction: 0.023832*************
      Process poor-credit order
      Print REJECT_NOTICE
  ─ Else
      *******Probability of this branch: 0.976 ***************************
      ***Average no. of executions per transaction: 0.969168*************
      Set ORDER_TOTAL = 0

      Create │ ORDER │

      ***Access path from CUSTOMER to ORDER ******************************
      ***Average path cardinality: 5 ************************************
    ─ If not subscription customer
        *******Probability of this branch: 0.3 *************************
        ***Average no. of executions per transaction: 0.2907504**********
      ─ Prepare invoice header

        Print INVOICE-HEADER

        Create │ INVOICE │

        ***Access path from CUSTOMER to INVOICE ***********************
        ***Average path cardinality: 5 *******************************

      For each product ordered
        ***Average no. of iterations per bracket: 3.5 *****************
        ***Average no. of executions per transaction: 3.392088***********

        Read │ PRODUCT │

        ***Access path from Entry to PRODUCT *************************
        ***Average path cardinality: NA ******************************
      ─ If PRODUCT# is invalid
          *******Probability of this branch: 0.005 *******************
          ***Average no. of executions per transaction: 0.01696044******
          Print error message
      ─ Else
          *******Probability of this branch: 0.995 *******************
          ***Average no. of executions per transaction: 3.2224836*******
```

Figure 14.7 The action diagram annotated to show probabilities of branches and numbers of repetitions. Some of these numbers relate to the data model cardinalities. The number of executions per transaction are computed for each bracket.

```
        ─ If QTY_ON_HAND < QTY-ORDERED
              ******Probability of this branch: 0.04 ******************
              ***Average no. of executions per transaction: 0.12889934***

              Create  [ BACKORDER ]

              ***Access path from ORDER to BACKORDER ******************
              ***Average path cardinality: 0.04**************************
              Print BACKORDER_NOTICE
        ─ Else
              *******Probability of this branch: 0.96 ******************
              ***Average no. of executions per transaction: 3.0935842****
              LINE_ITEM_PRICE = CATALOG_PRICE
              LINE-TOTAL =QTY_ORDERED * LINE_ITEM_PRICE
              ORDER_TOTAL = ORDER_TOTAL + LINE_TOTAL

              Create  [ ORDER-PRODUCT ]

              ***Access path from ORDER to ORDER-PRODUCT****************
              ***Average path cardinality: 3.5 ************************
          ─ If not subscription customer
                *******Probability of this branch: 0.3 ************* ***
                ***Average no. of executions per transaction: .92807526*

                Create  [ INVOICE-PRODUCT ]

                ***Access path from INVOICE to INVOICE-PRODUCT**********
                ***Average path cardinality: 3.5 **********************
              Print INVOICE-LINE


    ORDER_TOTAL = ORDER_TOTAL * [1 - DISCOUNT / 100]
    ORDER_STATUS = 0

    Update  [ ORDER ]

    ***Access path from CUSTOMER to ORDER ****************************
    ***Average path cardinality: 5 **********************************
  ─ If not subscription customer
        ******Probability of this branch: 0.3 *************************
        ***Average no. of executions per transaction: 0.2907504**********

        Update  [ INVOICE ]

        ***Access path from CUSTOMER to INVOICE ************************
        ***Average path cardinality: 5 ********************************
      Print INVOICE-TOTAL
```

Figure 14.7   (Continued)

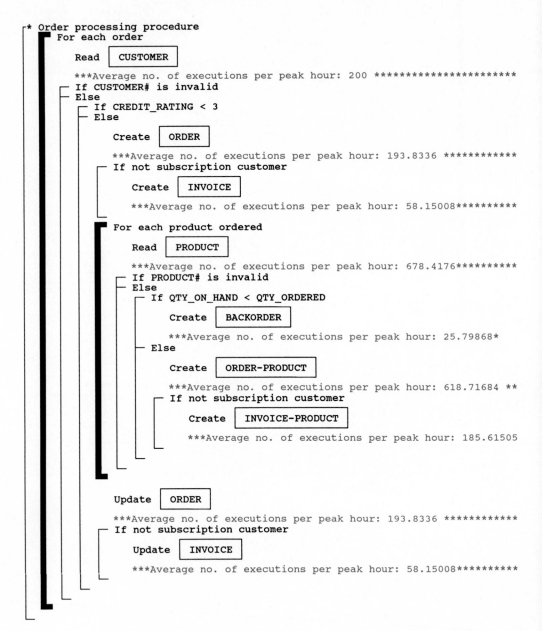

```
* Order processing procedure
  For each order

      Read    CUSTOMER

      ***Average no. of executions per peak hour: 200 **********************
   If CUSTOMER# is invalid
   Else
      If CREDIT_RATING < 3
      Else

          Create    ORDER

          ***Average no. of executions per peak hour: 193.8336 ***********
      If not subscription customer

          Create    INVOICE

          ***Average no. of executions per peak hour: 58.15008**********

      For each product ordered

          Read    PRODUCT

          ***Average no. of executions per peak hour: 678.4176**********
       If PRODUCT# is invalid
       Else
          If QTY_ON_HAND < QTY_ORDERED

              Create    BACKORDER

              ***Average no. of executions per peak hour: 25.79868*
          Else

              Create    ORDER-PRODUCT

              ***Average no. of executions per peak hour: 618.71684 **
           If not subscription customer

              Create    INVOICE-PRODUCT

              ***Average no. of executions per peak hour: 185.61505

      Update    ORDER

      ***Average no. of executions per peak hour: 193.8336 ***********
   If not subscription customer

      Update    INVOICE

      ***Average no. of executions per peak hour: 58.15008**********
```

Figure 14.8 The action diagram annotated to show the numbers of accesses in the peak hour (computed from the information in Fig. 14.7 and the number of transactions per peak hour).

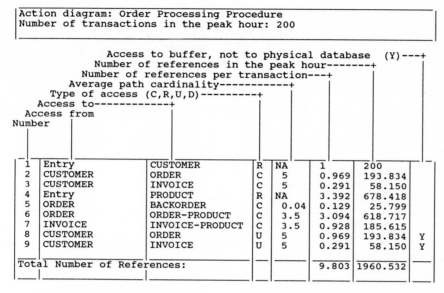

Figure 14.9 A summary of the data accesses for the ORDER PROCESSING procedure (from Fig. 14.8).

are to a buffer rather than secondary storage. These accesses are not included in the list of accesses for physical database design and are not added into the total number of accesses shown at the bottom of Fig. 14.9.

MULTIPLE CONCURRENT PROCEDURES

The data in a shared system are used by several applications simultaneously. Each application causes a number of data accesses. To do physical database design, the accesses of many applications must be aggregated.

A computerized tool can take multiple action diagrams, do the computations represented by Figs. 14.5 to 14.9 and then aggregate them into a single table of accesses.

Figure 14.10 shows the action diagram of Fig. 14.2 annotated with information for data use analysis.

CONSOLIDATED ACCESS TABLE

Figure 14.11 shows a *consolidated access table* for a system which has three procedures running at one

```
Customer Order Inquiry Procedure
      ***Average no. of executions per peak hour: 30 ****************************
  If customer invalid
      ****Probability of this branch: 0.01 **********************************
      Notify error
  Else
      ****Probability of this branch: 0.99 **********************************

      Read    CUSTOMER

      ***Access path from Entry to CUSTOMER ******************************
      ***Average path cardinality: NA ***********************************
      ***Average no. of executions per peak hour: 27.9 ********************
      Print customer information

      For each order
          ***Average no. of iterations per bracket: 5 ***********************
          Perform order header inquiry

              Read    ORDER

              ***Access path from CUSTOMER to ORDER ************************
              ***Average path cardinality: 5 ******************************
              ***Average no. of executions per peak hour: 148.5 ***************
              Print order header

              For each order item
                  ***Average no. of iterations per bracket: 3.5 ***************

                  Read    ORDER-PRODUCT

                  ***Access path from ORDER to ORDER-PRODUCT *******************
                  ***Average path cardinality: 3.5 ****************************
                  ***Average no. of executions per peak hour: 519.75 ***********
                  Accumulate details

                  If backorder exists
                      *******Probability of this branch: 0.04 ******************
                      Perform backorder inquiry

                          Read    BACKORDER

                          ***Access path from ORDER-PRODUCT to BACKORDER *********
                          ***Average path cardinality: 0.04 *********************
                          ***Average no. of executions per peak hour: 20.79 ******

                          Produce backorder report

                  Else
              «       Exit

          Print order report
```

Figure 14.10 The CUSTOMER ORDER INQUIRY procedure (Fig. 14.2)
annotated for data use analysis.

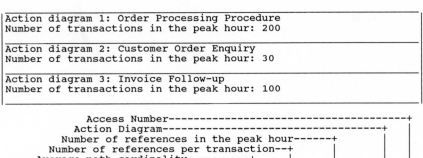

Action diagram 1: Order Processing Procedure
Number of transactions in the peak hour: 200

Action diagram 2: Customer Order Enquiry
Number of transactions in the peak hour: 30

Action diagram 3: Invoice Follow-up
Number of transactions in the peak hour: 100

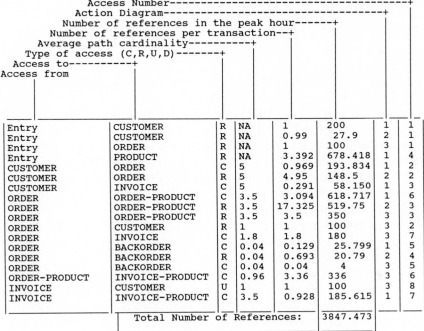

```
                    Access Number---------------------------------------+
              Action Diagram---------------------------------+          |
          Number of references in the peak hour------+       |          |
        Number of references per transaction--+      |       |          |
      Average path cardinality----------+     |      |       |          |
    Type of access (C,R,U,D)-------+     |     |      |       |          |
  Access to----------+             |     |     |      |       |          |
Access from          |             |     |     |      |       |          |
```

Access from	Access to	Type	Avg path card	Refs per trans	Refs peak hour	Action Diagram	Access Number
Entry	CUSTOMER	R	NA	1	200	1	1
Entry	CUSTOMER	R	NA	0.99	27.9	2	1
Entry	ORDER	R	NA	1	100	3	1
Entry	PRODUCT	R	NA	3.392	678.418	1	4
CUSTOMER	ORDER	C	5	0.969	193.834	1	2
CUSTOMER	ORDER	R	5	4.95	148.5	2	2
CUSTOMER	INVOICE	C	5	0.291	58.150	1	3
ORDER	ORDER-PRODUCT	C	3.5	3.094	618.717	1	6
ORDER	ORDER-PRODUCT	R	3.5	17.325	519.75	2	3
ORDER	ORDER-PRODUCT	R	3.5	3.5	350	3	3
ORDER	CUSTOMER	R	1	1	100	3	2
ORDER	INVOICE	C	1.8	1.8	180	3	7
ORDER	BACKORDER	C	0.04	0.129	25.799	1	5
ORDER	BACKORDER	R	0.04	0.693	20.79	2	4
ORDER	BACKORDER	C	0.04	0.04	4	3	5
ORDER-PRODUCT	INVOICE-PRODUCT	C	0.96	3.36	336	3	6
INVOICE	CUSTOMER	U	1	1	100	3	8
INVOICE	INVOICE-PRODUCT	C	3.5	0.928	185.615	1	7
	Total Number of References:				3847.473		

Figure 14.11   The accesses from three action diagrams consolidated into one table.

time. The procedures are represented by three action diagrams:

1. **ORDER PROCESSING procedure** (Fig. 14.3); 200 transactions per hour.
2. **Customer order inquiry** (Fig. 14.2); 30 transactions per hour.
3. **Invoice follow-up;** 100 transactions per hour.

The table shows all the data accesses for these three procedures, along with the numbers of references per transaction and references per peak hour. The total number of references in the peak are added up. The contribution of each transaction type to the total load is seen in the table.

TOTAL ACCESS TABLE

Figure 14.11 shows several transaction usage paths moving in the same direction between the same records. These can be added to show the total load over that path.

For example the following numbers of accesses occur in the peak hour from ORDER to ORDER-PRODUCT:

ORDER PROCESSING procedure	618.717
Customer order inquiry	519.75
Invoice follow-up	350

The references per peak hour for this path can be added (1488.467) references per peak hour).

Figure 14.12 shows the total number of accesses over each path in the data model. It is illustrated in Fig. 14.13. From such a report or diagram the database designer can determine the total processing load along each usage path and the relative contribution made to that load by each type of transaction. The processing of response-critical transactions can be optimized by considering various physical file or data base design techniques. Performance for the physical representation of the data model as a whole can be optimized.

It is desirable for physical design to distinguish between batch accesses and interactive accesses. These two types of accesses may be separated in the total access table (Fig. 14.12).

The information in Fig. 14.12 (or 14.13) shows which of the paths between records are heavily used. The path from ORDER to ORDER-PRODUCT, for example, is heavily used. The path from ORDER to BACKORDER is lightly used. This information strongly affects the physical layout and design of the records.

Access from	Access to	Number of accesses in the peak hour
Entry	CUSTOMER	227.9
Entry	ORDER	100
Entry	PRODUCT	678.418
CUSTOMER	ORDER	342.334
CUSTOMER	INVOICE	58.15
ORDER	ORDER-PRODUCT	1488.467
ORDER	CUSTOMER	100
ORDER	INVOICE	180
ORDER	BACKORDER	50.589
ORDER-PRODUCT	INVOICE-PRODUCT	336
INVOICE	CUSTOMER	100
INVOICE	INVOICE-PRODUCT	185.615
Total Number of References:		3847.473

Figure 14.12 The table of Fig. 14.12 showing the total peak-hour accesses over each path in the data model.

300

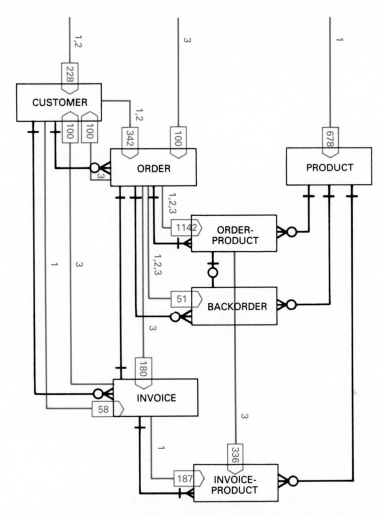

Figure 14.13　A map showing the usage of the paths through the data model in the peak hour (the information in Fig. 14.12). The figures for relative utilization of the paths help to optimize the physical database design. Action Diagram 1: Order Processing Procedure; Action Diagram 2: Customer Order Inquiry; Action Diagram 3: Invoice Follow-up.

A variety of techniques can be used to improve physical database performance for heavily used paths. These include

- Laying out records so that those used together are physically close.
- Laying out records so that a disk access arm need not be moved in traversing the path.

- Combining records to minimize the number of physical input/output references. Main storage references to data are executed at CPU (central processor unit) speed; secondary storage references are executed at much slower speeds.
- Using "physical" rather than "logical" access paths in a DBMS (database management system) such as IMS (information management system).
- Adjusting the use of indices, pointers, or hashing.

RESPONSE TIMES

Access tables for one action diagram, such as Fig. 14.9, are useful in estimating response times. The relative numbers of accesses for different transactions can be compared. A rough calculation of response times may indicate that certain transactions are critical. For certain transactions it may be difficult to meet the response time requirements of end users. The physical design may be adjusted to optimize the performance of response-critical transactions.

SEARCHING, JOINING, ETC.

Some database operations cause data to be searched or cause other compound relational operations such as a *join*. These operations strongly affect the physical performance and optimization, as is discussed in the next chapter. They may be recorded separately from the single-record types of access paths discussed earlier.

PROCEDURE FOR DATA USE ANALYSIS

Box 14.1 gives a procedure for data use analysis.

BOX 14.1   An action diagram showing the procedure for data use analysis.

```
┌─ Procedure for data use analysis
│
│     Determine what transaction types the database will support.
│     Establish or extract a data model containing the data for all these
│        transactions.
│     Add average cardinality to all relationships in the data model.
│  ┌─ Determine what is the peak hour.
│  │     There may be more than one peak hour with different types of
│  │        transactions. For example a peak for interactive transactions
│  │        may occur at a different time from the peak for batch
│  └─     operations.
```

BOX 14.1   *(Continued)*

```
For each transaction type
    Determine the number of transactions in the peak hour.
    Obtain an action diagram for the transaction.

    * Fig 14.3 shows an example: Order processing procedure

        Read   | CUSTOMER |

        If CUSTOMER# is invalid
            Process invalid order
            Print REJECT_NOTICE
        Else
            If CREDIT_RATING < 3
                Process poor-credit order

                Create   | ORDER-REJECT |

                Print REJECT_NOTICE
            Else
                Set ORDER_TOTAL = 0

                Create   | ORDER |

                If not subscription customer
                    Prepare invoice header

                    Print INVOICE-HEADER

                    Create   | INVOICE |


                For each product ordered

                    Read   | PRODUCT |

                    If PRODUCT# is invalid
                        Print error message
                    Else
                        If QTY_ON_HAND < QTY_ORDERED

                            Create   | BACKORDER |

                            Print BACKORDER_NOTICE
                        Else
                            LINE_ITEM_PRICE = CATALOG_PRICE
                            LINE-TOTAL =QTY_ORDERED * LINE_ITEM_PRICE
                            ORDER_TOTAL = ORDER_TOTAL + LINE_TOTAL

                            Create   | ORDER-PRODUCT |

                            If not subscription customer

                                Create   | INVOICE-PRODUCT |

                                Print INVOICE-LINE
```

(Continued)

BOX 14.1   *(Continued)*

```
            ORDER_TOTAL = ORDER_TOTAL * [1 - DISCOUNT / 100]
            ORDER_STATUS = 0

        Update   | ORDER |

      ┌ If not subscription customer

            Update   | INVOICE |

            Print INVOICE-TOTAL
```

Ensure that the action diagram contains all the data accesses.
Ensure that the data model supports all the accesses.
┌ Print details of access paths on the action diagram

  ┌* Fig 14.5 shows an example: Order processing procedure

```
        Read   | CUSTOMER |

        ***Access path from Entry to CUSTOMER ***************************
      ┌ If CUSTOMER# is invalid
            Process invalid order
            Print REJECT_NOTICE
      ┌ Else
        ┌ If CREDIT_RATING < 3
            Process poor-credit order
            Print REJECT_NOTICE
        ┌ Else
            Set ORDER_TOTAL = 0

            Create   | ORDER |

            ***Access path from CUSTOMER to ORDER ******************
          ┌ If not subscription customer
            ┌ Prepare invoice header

                Print INVOICE-HEADER

                Create   | INVOICE |

                ***Access path from CUSTOMER to INVOICE ****************
```

BOX 14.1 *(Continued)*

```
For each product ordered
    Read   PRODUCT

    ***Access path from Entry to PRODUCT *******************
    If PRODUCT# is invalid
        Print error message
    Else
        If QTY_ON_HAND < QUANTITY_ORDERED

            Create   BACKORDER

            ***Access path from ORDER to BACKORDER **********
            Print BACKORDER_NOTICE
        Else
            LINE_ITEM_PRICE = CATALOG_PRICE
            LINE-TOTAL =QTY_ORDERED * LINE_ITEM_PRICE
            ORDER_TOTAL = ORDER_TOTAL + LINE_TOTAL

            Create   ORDER-PRODUCT

            ***Access path from ORDER to ORDER-PRODUCT********
            If not subscription customer

                Create   INVOICE-PRODUCT

                **Access path from INVOICE to INVOICE-PRODUCT**
                Print INVOICE-LINE


ORDER_TOTAL = ORDER_TOTAL * [1 - DISCOUNT / 100]
ORDER_STATUS = 0

Update   ORDER

***Access path from CUSTOMER to ORDER ****************
If not subscription customer

    Update   INVOICE

    ***Access path from CUSTOMER to INVOICE ****************
    Print INVOICE-TOTAL
```

(Continued)

BOX 14.1 *(Continued)*

```
Add mean cardinality of access paths to the diagram (automatically)

* Fig 14.6 shows an example: Order processing procedure

    Read    CUSTOMER

    ***Access path from Entry to CUSTOMER **************************
    ***Average path cardinality: NA ********************************
If CUSTOMER# is invalid
    Process invalid order
    Print REJECT_NOTICE
Else
    If CREDIT_RATING < 3
        Process poor-credit order
        Print REJECT_NOTICE
    Else
        Set ORDER_TOTAL = 0

        Create    ORDER

        ***Access path from CUSTOMER to ORDER *****************
        ***Average path cardinality: 5 ****************************
        If not subscription customer
            Prepare invoice header

            Print INVOICE-HEADER

            Create    INVOICE

            ***Access path from CUSTOMER to INVOICE ****************
            ***Average path cardinality: 5 *************************

    For each product ordered

        Read    PRODUCT

        ***Access path from Entry to PRODUCT *******************
        ***Average path cardinality: NA ***********************
        If PRODUCT# is invalid
            Print error message
        Else
            If QTY_ON_HAND < QUANTITY_ORDERED

                Create    BACKORDER

                ***Access path from ORDER to BACKORDER **********'***
                ***Average path cardinality: 0.04*****************
                Print BACKORDER_NOTICE
            Else
                LINE_ITEM_PRICE = CATALOG_PRICE
                LINE-TOTAL =QTY_ORDERED * LINE_ITEM_PRICE
                ORDER_TOTAL = ORDER_TOTAL + LINE_TOTAL

                Create    ORDER-PRODUCT

                ***Access path from ORDER to ORDER-PRODUCT********
                ***Average path cardinality: 3.5 ****************
                If not subscription customer

                    Create    INVOICE-PRODUCT

                    ***Access path from INVOICE to INVOICE-PRODUCT*
                    ***Average path cardinality: 3.5 *************
                    Print INVOICE-LINE
```

BOX 14.1   *(Continued)*

```
        ORDER_TOTAL = ORDER_TOTAL * [1 - DISCOUNT / 100]
        ORDER_STATUS = 0

        Update  │ ORDER │

        ***Access path from CUSTOMER to ORDER ****************
        ***Average path cardinality: 5 *****************************
      ┌ If not subscription customer

          Update  │ INVOICE │

          ***Access path from CUSTOMER to INVOICE ****************
          ***Average path cardinality: 5 *************************
      └   Print INVOICE-TOTAL
```

```
  Assign probabilities to the branches on the action diagram.
┌ Perform a manual reasonableness check on the access information
    Does the sequence of accesses appear correct?
    Do the cardinality figures appear correct?
    Do the condition probabilities appear correct?
    Do the bracket volumes appear correct?
  ┌ If any of the above appear incorrect, backtrack
  └   to a point at which suitable corrections can be made.
└
```

```
┌ Compute volumes for each bracket and condition (automatically)
    Mark probabilities under each condition on the action diagram.
    Mark number of iterations on each repetition bracket.
    Print number of executions per transaction by each condition
      and repetition bracket.

┌* Fig 14.7 shows an example: Order processing procedure
    ***Average no. of executions per transaction: 1 ****************

      Read  │ CUSTOMER │

    ***Access path from Entry to CUSTOMER **************************
    ***Average path cardinality: NA ********************************
  ┌ If CUSTOMER# is invalid
        *******Probability of this branch: 0.007 *******************
        ***Average no. of executions per transaction: 0.007**********
        Process invalid order
        Print REJECT_NOTICE
  ┌ Else
        *******Probability of this branch: 0.993 *******************
        ***Average no. of executions per transaction: 0.993**********
```

(Continued)

BOX 14.1   *(Continued)*

```
  If CREDIT_RATING < 3
      *******Probability of this branch: 0.024 *****************
      ***Average no. of executions per transaction: 0.023832*****
      Process poor-credit order
      Print REJECT_NOTICE
  Else
      *******Probability of this branch: 0.976 *****************
      ***Average no. of executions per transaction: 0.969168*****
      Set ORDER_TOTAL = 0

      Create  | ORDER |

      ***Access path from CUSTOMER to ORDER *****************
      ***Average path cardinality: 5 ***************************
  If not subscription customer
      *******Probability of this branch: 0.3 ****************
      ***Average no. of executions per transaction: 0.2907504*
    Prepare invoice header

      Print INVOICE-HEADER

      Create  | INVOICE |

      ***Access path from CUSTOMER to INVOICE ***************
      ***Average path cardinality: 5 ************************

  For each product ordered
      ***Average no. of iterations per bracket: 3.5 *********
      ***Average no. of executions per transaction: 3.392088**

      Read  | PRODUCT |

      ***Access path from Entry to PRODUCT ******************
      ***Average path cardinality: NA **********************
  If PRODUCT# is invalid
      *******Probability of this branch: 0.005 ***********
      ***Average no. of executions per transaction: 0.01696
      Print error message
  Else
      *******Probability of this branch: 0.995 ***********
      ***Average no. of executions per transaction: 3.22248
    If QTY_ON_HAND < QTY-ORDERED
        *******Probability of this branch: 0.04 *********
        ***Average no. of executions per transaction: 0.12

        Create  | BACKORDER |

        ***Access path from ORDER to BACKORDER **********
        ***Average path cardinality: 0.04*****************
        Print BACKORDER_NOTICE
    Else
        *******Probability of this branch: 0.96 *********
        ***Average no. of executions per transaction: 3.09
        LINE_ITEM_PRICE = CATALOG_PRICE
        LINE-TOTAL =QTY_ORDERED * LINE_ITEM_PRICE
        ORDER_TOTAL = ORDER_TOTAL + LINE_TOTAL

        Create  | ORDER-PRODUCT |

        ***Access path from ORDER to ORDER-PRODUCT********
        ***Average path cardinality: 3.5 ****************
```

BOX 14.1 *(Continued)*

```
                        If not subscription customer
                            *******Probability of this branch: 0.3 ********
                            ***Average no. of executions per transaction: .

                        Create │ INVOICE-PRODUCT │

                            ***Access path from INVOICE to INVOICE-PRODUCT*
                            ***Average path cardinality: 3.5 *************
                            Print INVOICE-LINE


            ORDER_TOTAL = ORDER_TOTAL * [1 - DISCOUNT / 100]
            ORDER_STATUS = 0

            Update │ ORDER │

            ***Access path from CUSTOMER to ORDER ****************
            ***Average path cardinality: 5 ***************************
            If not subscription customer
                *******Probability of this branch: 0.3 ****************
                ***Average no. of executions per transaction: 0.2907504*

                Update │ INVOICE │

                ***Access path from CUSTOMER to INVOICE ****************
                ***Average path cardinality: 5 **********************
                Print INVOICE-TOTAL


Perform a manual reasonableness check on the volumes.
    Do the figures for "Average no. of executions per transaction"
        appear correct?

Compute peak hour volumes for each data access (automatically)

* Fig 14.8 shows an example: Order processing procedure
    For each order

        Read │ CUSTOMER │

        ***Average # executions/peak hour: 200 **********************
        If CUSTOMER# is invalid
        Else
            If CREDIT_RATING < 3
            Else

                Create │ ORDER │

                ***Avg. # executions/peak hour: 193.8336 **************
                If not subscription customer

                    Create │ INVOICE │

                    ***Avg. # executions/peak hour: 58.15008************
```

(Continued)

BOX 14.1   *(Continued)*

```
For each product ordered

    Read    PRODUCT

    ***Avg. # executions/peak hour: 678.4176*************
    If PRODUCT# is invalid
    Else
        If QTY_ON_HAND < QTY_ORDERED

            Create    BACKORDER

            ***Avg. # executions/peak hour: 25.79868*
        Else

            Create    ORDER-PRODUCT

            ***Avg. # executions/peak hour: 618.71684******
            If not subscription customer

                Create    INVOICE-PRODUCT

                ***Avg. # executions/peak hour: 185.61505***


    Update    ORDER

    ***Avg. # executions/peak hour: 193.8336 **************
    If not subscription customer

        Update    INVOICE

        **Avg. # executions/peak hour: 58.15008**************
```

BOX 14.1 *(Continued)*

Produce a table (automatically) showing the total accesses

Fig 14.9 shows an example of a Transaction Access Table

Action diagram: Order Processing Procedure
Number of transactions in the peak hour: 200

```
                         Access to buffer, not to physical database  (Y)---
                  Number of references in the peak hour-------+
               Number of references per transaction---+
            Average path cardinality-----------+
         Type of access (C,R,U,D)---------+
       Access to-----------+
      Access from
   Number
```

Number	Access from	Access to	Type	Avg path card.	Refs/trans	Refs peak hour
1	Entry	CUSTOMER	R	NA	1	200
2	CUSTOMER	ORDER	C	5	0.969	193.834
3	CUSTOMER	INVOICE	C	5	0.291	58.150
4	Entry	PRODUCT	R	NA	3.392	678.418
5	ORDER	BACKORDER	C	0.04	0.129	25.799
6	ORDER	ORDER-PRODUCT	C	3.5	3.094	618.717
7	INVOICE	INVOICE-PRODUCT	C	3.5	0.928	185.615
8	CUSTOMER	ORDER	U	5	0.969	193.834
9	CUSTOMER	INVOICE	U	5	0.291	58.150
Total Number of References:					9.803	1960.532

Determine whether the transaction is response critical
   Make a rough estimate of the transaction response time.
   Assess user response-time need for the transaction.
   Determine whether the database needs to be optimized physically
      to achieve this response time.

Produce (automatically) a table aggregating the transaction accesses

Fig 14.11 shows a table consolidating the accesses of 3 procedures
   The following is an example of a Consolidated Access Table:

Action diagram 1: Order Processing Procedure
Number of transactions in the peak hour: 200

Action diagram 2: Customer Order Enquiry
Number of transactions in the peak hour: 30

Action diagram 3: Invoice Follow-up
Number of transactions in the peak hour: 100

(Continued)

BOX 14.1 *(Continued)*

```
              Access Number----------------------------------------+
              Action Diagram----------------------------------+    |
              Number of references in the peak hour------+     |    |
              Number of references per transaction--+    |     |    |
              Average path cardinality----------+   |    |     |    |
              Type of access (C,R,U,D)-------+  |   |    |     |    |
              Access to----------+          |  |   |    |     |    |
              Access from        |          |  |   |    |     |    |
```

Access from	Access to	Type	Avg card	Refs/txn	Refs peak hr	Action Diag	Access No
Entry	CUSTOMER	R	NA	1	200	1	1
Entry	CUSTOMER	R	NA	0.99	27.9	2	1
Entry	ORDER	R	NA	1	100	3	1
Entry	PRODUCT	R	NA	3.392	678.418	1	4
CUSTOMER	ORDER	C	5	0.969	193.834	1	2
CUSTOMER	ORDER	R	5	4.95	148.5	2	2
CUSTOMER	INVOICE	C	5	0.291	58.150	1	3
ORDER	ORDER-PRODUCT	C	3.5	3.094	618.717	1	6
ORDER	ORDER-PRODUCT	R	3.5	17.325	519.75	2	3
ORDER	ORDER-PRODUCT	R	3.5	3.5	350	3	3
ORDER	CUSTOMER	R	1	1	100	3	2
ORDER	INVOICE	C	1.8	1.8	180	3	7
ORDER	BACKORDER	C	0.04	0.129	25.799	1	5
ORDER	BACKORDER	R	0.04	0.693	20.79	2	4
ORDER	BACKORDER	C	0.04	0.04	4	3	5
ORDER-PRODUCT	INVOICE-PRODUCT	C	0.96	3.36	336	3	6
INVOICE	CUSTOMER	U	1	1	100	3	8
INVOICE	INVOICE-PRODUCT	C	3.5	0.928	185.615	1	7

```
                    Total Number of References:   3847.473
```

— Produce (automatically) a table totaling the transaction accesses

  — Fig 14.12 shows a table consolidating total peak hour accesses
    The following is an example of the Total Access Table:

Access from	Access to	Number of accesses in the peak hour
Entry	CUSTOMER	227.9
Entry	ORDER	100
Entry	PRODUCT	678.418
CUSTOMER	ORDER	342.334
CUSTOMER	INVOICE	58.15
ORDER	ORDER-PRODUCT	1488.467
ORDER	CUSTOMER	100
ORDER	INVOICE	180
ORDER	BACKORDER	50.589
ORDER-PRODUCT	INVOICE-PRODUCT	336
INVOICE	CUSTOMER	100
INVOICE	INVOICE-PRODUCT	185.615

```
        Total Number of References:   3847.473
```

BOX 14.1 *(Continued)*

```
     Note which are the heavily loaded paths in the data model.
     Determine what can be done to minimize the physical access time
          in the DBMS for the most heavily used paths through the data
          model.
     FOR example:
          o  Lay out records so that those together are physically
             close.
          o  Lay out records so that a disk access arm does not have to
             be moved to follow the heavily used path.
          o  Combine records to minimize physical input/output references
             for heavily used paths.
          o  Use physical rather than logical access paths in a DBMS
             such as IMS.
          o  Appropriately adjust the use of indices, pointers, or hashing.
```

15 PHYSICAL DATABASE DESIGN

INTRODUCTION   An enterprise is likely to have many databases. Although they may be derived from a common data model, they are physically separate. In some cases the same data reside in more than one database in order to improve machine performance or increase the usability of the data. Controlled redundancy is introduced for system design reasons.

The separate databases may be implemented with the same database management system, or they may be fundamentally different types of databases implemented with different types of software.

The physical organization of the data and access methods has a major effect on the cost, performance, and response times of a database system.

Some of the worst database horror stories relate to systems for which the physical design was done inadequately (or not done at all). One of the world's most prestigious banks had a large computer delivered for database operation and later discovered that there was no conceivable way it could do the intended work. Only a token attempt had been made at calculating the system performance. There was no easy way out of the dilemma because the machine was purchased, not rented.

In many less dramatic cases the runs take much longer than they should because inappropriate access methods or disk layouts have been selected; the response times are sometimes much longer than expected and inadequate for the needs of the end users. An attempt to reorganize the physical design of a database sometimes results in major performance improvements.

The database design process seeks to optimize the performance according to criteria which often conflict somewhat; as with most complex system design a careful choice among compromises is needed.

**IMPLEMENTING
THE DATA MODEL**
The database designer creates the software schemas and physical designs for the databases which are implemented. In doing this he should work from the *data model* (such as that in the previous chapter).

In a CODASYL database he will design the *set* structures which are implemented, the physical layout of the sets on the storage media and the access methods for retrieving, updating, deleting, and inserting data. In a DL/I database she will design and code the *physical database description* and *logical database description*. Similarly in other types of databases the specific database descriptions must be created.

The designer should take into consideration the means of preserving data security and integrity, and recovering and restarting after failures have occurred, without damaging the data, and possibly operating in a fallback mode during a period of disk failure.

**STAGES IN
DATABASE
DESIGN**
Physical database design may include the following stages:

```
┌─ Procedure for physical database design
│  ...Determine whether the data will be distributed.
│  ...List and categorize the database procedures that will occur.
│  ...List and categorize the database queries that will occur.
│  ...Determine whether more than one type of DBMS will be needed.
│  ...Determine whether the data will be split into separate databases.
│  ...Select the DBMS(s).
│  ┃ For each specific database, do the detailed design.
│  ┃ ...Obtain data usage information required for the design.
│  ┃ ...Perform data-use analysis.
│  ┃ ...Determine what are the performance-critical aspects of the design.
│  ┃ ...Consider security, auditability, restart, recovery, and fallback.
│  ┃ ...Evaluate the design techniques.
│  ┃ ┌─ Design the database.
│  ┃ │ ┃ Design is likely to proceed iteratively through the following
│  ┃ │ ┃    steps to converge on an appropriate design:
│  ┃ │ ┃
│  ┃ │ ┃ ...Consider the alternate structures available for the DBMS.
│  ┃ │ ┃ ...Design the stored record formats.
│  ┃ │ ┃ ...Design the record clustering into storage media areas.
│  ┃ │ ┃ ...Lay out the data on the storage media.
│  ┃ │ ┃ ...Design the access methods.
│  ┃ │ ┃ ...Adapt the programs to the design where necessary.
│  ┃ └─
│  ┃
│  ┃ ...Design the operations facilities.
│  ┃ ...Design the implementation facilities.
└─
```

Box 15.1 shows this procedure in more detail. Like most such procedures, it is likely to be modified to fit the situation in question, and often proceeds iteratively, converging on an appropriate design.

DISTRIBUTION OF DATA

The first step in the foregoing procedure is to consider distribution of the data. As computers proliferate, data is increasingly likely to be distributed. Data distribution analysis is discussed in the following chapter.

CATEGORIZATION OF PROCEDURES

The second step is to determine what procedures are being considered. These may be already represented in the encyclopedia. The procedures may be categorized according to what database techniques they require. For example, as we stressed in Chapter 12, decision-support systems are likely to need very different database structures from routine production systems.

The types of data management may be categorized as follows:

1. **File systems.** These are relatively simple data structures, often designed for one application, as opposed to the multiapplication environment of database systems. They can give good machine efficiency for their one application.

2. **Application databases.** These are database structures designed to support a narrow group of applications with fairly good machine efficiency.

3. Subject databases. These are more generalized databases where all the data about specific data subjects are stored together. For example, all the data relating to parts are stored together, all the data relating to customers are together, and so on. Subject databases help give a database environment consistency because one copy rather than multiple copies are kept. When a change is made, it is automatically reflected in all of the applications which use that data.

4. **Information retrieval systems.** These store information that may be retrieved with multiple different search parameters. Extensive search indices or inverted files are used. This makes updating of the data relatively expensive. Storage management systems for information retrieval are generally inefficient with high-volume production computing.

5. **Decision-support systems.** These support multidimensional data structures, as described in Chapter 34, optimized for highly flexible decision-support activities. They are generally inefficient or inadequate for high-volume production computing.

Different types of systems need different choices of data management system from the preceding list. The same data model may be represented (redundantly) in different systems for example, an application database and a decision-support database.

Sometimes the data model is implemented on multiple machines in a distributed environment.

PROGRAM INDEPENDENCE

A commonly stated principle of database systems is that they provide physical data independence. The programmer does not need to know about the detailed physical structuring of the database. The physical database can be reorganized to improve its performance with any change to the programs which use it.

This principle is important. Many databases are reorganized without changing the programs, and many programs (especially with fourth-generation languages) are written without any knowledge of the physical data structures. Nevertheless optimal performance of a system with heavy database usage needs program design and database design to be coupled. Modification of a navigational access method such as that in a CODASYL or IMS (information management system) system requires modification of programs. The change from a navigational access method to an entry-point access method would need program changes. In a heavy-duty system data structures are sometimes denormalized (i.e., the records are not in third normal form) to achieve performance improvements.

A major decision in the design process is whether the program design *will* be independent of the physical database design. Physical data independence should not be given up unless there are major machine performance implications, because it complicates program design and increases the difficulties of maintenance. The majority of programs in an installation should be written using the logical data model structure. Certain systems with high-traffic volumes or very large databases may have the program design and physical database design adjusted together for performance reasons. In some cases the simple resequencing of the database accesses in a program can have a major effect on performance.

Programs may be categorized into three groups:

- **Programs written without consideration of physical database design.** This is appropriate for systems with low-traffic volumes that do not search large bodies of data—the majority of programs in most installations.

- **Programs in which the data accesses are adjusted to fit the physical database design.** A technician who understands the physical database design may advise how the data accesses in the programs should be written.

- **Heavy-duty programs for which the data structures are changed to achieve optimal performance.** The data may be denormalized. Record layouts are optimized for a particular application or group of applications. This is done to achieve a high throughput (transactions per second) or to handle a heavy daily load with lower machine costs. In some cases data are denormalized in order to search large bodies of data. Some hardware can achieve fast searches but slow joins so joins are avoided by denormalizing the data.

DATABASE QUERIES

Database queries can be classified into four types.

1. Primary-key queries. A record is accessed by means of its primary key. This can be done quickly and uses few machine cycles.

An example of a primary-key query would be "PRINT DETAILS OF THE SHIP ACHILLES". SHIP-NAME is a primary key for accessing a naval database. A single record is looked up, and its contents are printed.

2. Single-secondary-key queries. This type of query may be represented on a data model diagram as a secondary-key path. If it is anticipated a secondary index or other mechanism may be used. It requires far more machine cycles than a primary-key query.

An example of a single-secondary-key query would be "PRINT DETAILS OF ALL SHIPS WITH A READINESS-RATING = C1." If the question was anticipated by the system designer there may be a secondary-key index showing what ships have a given readiness rating.

3. Multiple-secondary-key queries. This requires more than one secondary-key access. It can be substantially more complex and expensive in machine cycles than a single-secondary-key access.

An example of such a query might be "PRINT DETAILS OF ALL RUSSIAN SHIPS WITHIN 900 MILES OF THE STRAITS OF HORMUZ CARRYING TORPEDOES WITH A RANGE GREATER THAN 20 MILES". A secondary index to the weapons database may be used to find which weapons are torpedoes with a range greater than 20 miles. There may be a secondary-key index showing which ships are Russian. It may be necessary to examine their records to find whether they carry those weapons. This produces a list of ships. The area around the Straits of Hormuz is then examined to find which ships are within 900 miles of that location. These ships are compared with the previous list. This requires a considerable amount of machine activity, especially if there are many ships.

4. Unanticipated search queries. Secondary-key queries may take place relatively quickly if there is a suitable secondary index. If there is not then it may be necessary to search the records in question a record at a time. This is very expensive in machine time.

DEDICATED MACHINES

If a computer did nothing other than process one query at a time, a relatively inexpensive machine might be used. Even if it processed multiple similar queries at once, machine time need not be a serious problem.

Unfortunately many systems are designed to do conventional high-volume data processing, with queries fitting in as required. An IS (information system) manager has to decide which activities have priority. Queries about Russian ships near the Straits of Hormuz may have very high priority, but ordinary commercial use of an end-user query language may not.

The end user with a language like query-by-example can very quickly enter a query like

EMPLOYEE	EMPLOYEE#	NAME	LOCATION	SALARY	YEAR-OF-HIRE
	_A	P.	P.	<55000	>1975

SKILLS	SKILL-TYPE	GRADE	EMPLOYEE#
	ACCOUNTANT	>6	_A

The user may have no concept of how much is involved in processing this query. The response time might be quite long. If this type of query is given a low priority the response time might become degraded to a level which seems unacceptable to end users. If the necessary secondary indices do not exist and the EMPLOYEE or SKILLS records have to be searched, the time taken may be excessive.

EXPENSE

When a query initiates the searching of a database on a large system, it may be more expensive than the end user realizes. Often there is no indication of the cost involved when a database facility is used. The user may not know the wide difference in cost between a primary-key query and one which triggers searching operations. It would be useful if computers would tell the user the cost before they process the query, but most do not.

Sometimes user management is surprised by the charges and unable to comprehend them.

CATEGORIES OF DATA SYSTEM

Figure 15.1 shows seven categories of data system. In its early years database usage employed predominantly primary-key access paths. The high-volume activity of most computers is category 1 in Fig. 15.1: production data processing. Primary-key queries are used with the production systems with no problem (category 2).

Offline secondary-key queries can be saved and processed in a scheduled batch fashion (category 3 in Fig. 15.1). This does not disrupt the production system.

	Is the information produced on a scheduled basis by the system?	
Type of Access	Yes: Scheduled	No: On-Demand
Primary key	① Routine production data processing	② Simple queries
Anticipated single secondary key and multiple secondary key	③ Complex offline queries	④ Complex online queries
Unanticipated access to normalized records	⑤ Slow reaction information system	⑥ Generalized information systems
Unanticipated access to multidimensional data structures	—	⑦ Decision-support systems

Figure 15.1   Categories of data systems. Categories 4, 6, and 7 may need to be in a different computer to category 1.

Category 4 is much more disruptive of the production system. A database designed to be efficient for high-volume production is not usually efficient for complex secondary-key queries, and vice versa. Categories 6 and 7 are worse. The queries are not planned and may require parts of the database to be searched.

It is often desirable that categories 4, 6, and 7 be in a separate computer system to the category 1 high-volume production systems. End-user departments might have their own computer—either a decision-support system or a production system. This may make sense both for performance and other reasons.

Category 5 in Fig. 15.1 is less useful. Nonpredefined information requests might be satisfied by visual inspections of listings produced on a scheduled basis. Although this has been common with some computer systems, it is generally a rather unsatisfactory way of answering spontaneous requests for information.

SCHEDULING AND RESPONSE-TIME PROBLEMS

Some database systems have severe scheduling and response-time problems. This is especially so when secondary-key paths have high-volume usage. IS operations are tending to swing from mainly primary-key usage of data to a substantial amount of secondary-key usage. This will be increasingly so in the future as good end-user database inquiry languages become popular. A large traffic figure associated with a secondary-key path is an indication of potential scheduling problems.

Given the falling cost of minicomputer information systems, it often makes sense to create functional information systems *separate* from the high-volume production systems. The one-to-many access paths in the data model may indicate a need for this.

Scheduling problems are generally caused by having conflicting types of activity combined on the same machine. Sometimes different forms of database activity conflict from the machine performance point of view. Sometimes a high-volume nondatabase activity such as sorting interferes badly with the response times of the database.

A database designer is sometimes not aware of how database jobs are run in the data center in terms of machine allocations and scheduling. Once jobs are accepted into the data center for scheduling, the data center manager may make his own decisions. If he runs the wrong mix of jobs then he impacts the performance of any online operation. Sometimes he has to run big compiles or sorts alongside the online jobs and response time goes to pieces. Sometimes he is forced to do this because of job pressures. Sometimes because another machine is down.

The degradation in response time that results from such scheduling problems is sometimes severe. In bad cases a 2-second response time has changed to 30 seconds or more. This is insufferably frustrating for the end users.

EXCESSIVE GROWTH IN UTILIZATION

A critical form of performance problem occurs when a database becomes perceived by end users as giving a particularly valuable interactive service. The good news spreads and the utilization can expand too rapidly for the system to handle. This has happened to many database systems, particularly when powerful end-user languages have been employed which enable the users, often unwittingly, to trigger database searches.

Primary-key linkages are often predictable in their usage, but secondary-key usage may grow suddenly and unpredictably. The data administrator can predict the forms of secondary-key usage with an appropriate modeling tool, but it is often not able to predict surges in volume of their use.

Figure 15.2 shows a common pattern of growth for useful interactive systems. The value of the system is perceived slowly at first, or there is a reluctance to use it because it is strange. Users do not want to appear foolish by

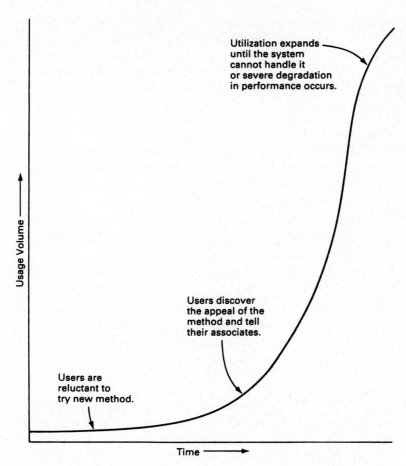

Figure 15.2 "If a service is created which is sufficiently useful, utilization expands until it knocks out the system!" Many end-user services have had a growth pattern similar to this diagram.

employing the terminal incorrectly. It represents a change in office culture and cultural changes come slowly. The system instigators are sometimes disappointed by the slow acceptance, but gradually the users find out that it does give a valuable service. They tell their associates. Leading users are seen to employ the terminals and the others want to follow suit. There is positive feedback and the utilization grows rapidly, often explosively, until the system cannot handle it.

The caption of Fig. 15.2 quotes a somewhat cynical law: "If a service is created which is sufficiently useful, utilization expands until it knocks out the system!"

The answer is often to give the users their own system. They can do what they want in their own system and pay for it. They can expand or duplicate the system if they wish. The data is organized for the activity in question, and so the activity is much more efficient than if it were carried out with data organized differently, for heavy-duty production runs.

SEPARATE DBMSs   The foregoing considerations cause separate database management systems to be used. The following are reasons why there may be more than one DBMS:

- Production systems and decision-support systems use different DBMSs.
- A fourth-generation language used has its own DBMS, different from those used for earlier systems.
- High-productivity tools and heavy-duty systems have different DBMSs.

In some cases the separate DBMSs are designed to function cooperatively. For example, the software may enable data to be spun off from a production system into a spreadsheet tool or decision-support system.

SEPARATE   Often separate databases are implemented with the
DATABASES   same DBMS. For example, a high-volume production system may use a stand-alone group of applications tuned for high machine performance; other applications of the same data, which could degrade the performance, are run separately.

Some applications need data to be searched or joined. The software facilitates the establishment of indices to achieve this. However such indices must be updated whenever the data change. The indices substantially increase the amount of machine time required to update the data.

If machine performance is of concern on a heavy-duty updating application, the data should not have search indices. Instead, data should be spun off into a separate database where it is rebuilt with a structure optimized for searching, joining, decision-support computing, or flexible manipulation. This separate structure will not contain the latest updates. The updates will be added to it periodically, for example, once a night or once a week.

This is practical because information systems or decision-support systems do not, in general, need up-to-the-second data. Last week's data is good enough. The knowledge worker making decisions with such data may occasionally need to access records which are up-to-date, for example, the record of a customer account. But this access does not involve searching or *compound* relational operations. The knowledge worker may thus use two types of data, up-to-the-second data which is not searched and older data which is used in complex decision-support activities.

DETAILED DATABASE DESIGN

For each database, detailed design needs to be done. The first step in detailed design is the activity described in the previous chapter (Box 14.1). It is determining what transactions the database will handle, what access paths through the data model will be used, and what the volumes of usage will be.

The designer should identify what are the critical aspects of the design. What are the most heavily used paths through the data model? What transactions are particularly critical in achieving adequate response times? What applications or runs most stress the design? The designer will focus on the heavily used paths and response-critical transactions in selecting the physical structures and access methods.

```
Design is likely to procede iteratively through the following
    steps to converge on an appropriate design:

...Consider the alternate structures available for the DBMS
...Design the stored record formats
...Design the record clustering into storage media areas
...Lay out the data on the storage media
...Design the access methods
...Adapt the programs to the design where necessary
```

For each database access method, there are many variations on how exactly the data (and indices) can be organized. How are new records inserted and old records deleted? How much free space should be left for new records? How often should the database be reorganized? What storage devices should be chosen? Where should the data be placed on the devices? Should the indices be on a different device from the data?

These factors affect the performance in subtle, complex ways, and there are so many factors and conflicting objectives that no single algorithm can be used for optimizing the database. Algorithms can be used for optimizing certain aspects of the design, but the overall design remains a heuristic process.

The penalty for bad design is higher in a database system than in a file system. In one well-known corporation a database application was programmed and, when it was eventually run, to everybody's horror it took about 60 hours. A hue and cry ensued, and a manufacturer's specialist redesigned the database to achieve a runtime of 12 hours. The system operated like this for some months while a more fundamental redesign was done which eventually brought the runtime down to 3 hours.

The database designer needs to understand the choices which are open to him with the DBMS in question. He needs to be able to estimate the number of accesses, the length of accesses, and the queueing delays that occur, for different data organizations.

ALTERNATE STRUCTURES

If it is decided to implement a certain data model, often a portion of an overall model, there are multiple ways to represent it either as a hierarchical or a CODASYL database structure. (There is only one *direct* translation of a third-normal-form model into a relational database.)

Figures 15.3 and 15.4 illustrate this. The simple five-record model at the top of these figures can be represented as four possible hierarchical database structures (e.g., DL/I, IMS, TOTAL, IMAGE 3000) or four possible CODASYL database structures (IDMS, IDS, DMS 1100, etc.). In either case machine performance considerations will usually determine which is the preferred structure.

In the hierarchical structures (Fig. 15.3), following paths *within* a hierarchy takes less machine time than following paths which span hierarchies (the red links). The database designer will take the paths through the model which have a high usage, first, and ensure that those are within a hierarchy. The low-usage paths can be paths which stretch between hierarchies. The paths often require a machine *seek,* whereas the paths within a hierarchy usually do not.

The record labeled ORDER + PART is the individual item on an order. The path from ORDER to ORDER + PART may be more frequently used than any other path. Therefore the bottom two versions are ruled out. The path from PART to SUPPLIER + RULE may be much more frequently used than the path from SUPPLIER to SUPPLIER + PART. Therefore the second of the four versions is chosen.

Given a set of usage path weights on a complex model, the best combination of hierarchies to represent that model can be selected *automatically*.

In the CODASYL versions in Fig. 15.4, the path from PART to ORDER + PART may be followed frequently. Use of this path should be in a *separate set* from the path from PART to SUPPLIER + PART. One of the bottom two versions is therefore selected. The paths from SUPPLIER to ORDER or SUPPLIER + PART are followed infrequently. These may therefore be in the same set, and the third of the four CODASYL versions is selected.

Whereas a normalized data model is not concerned with machine performance, the selection of hierarchical or CODASYL structure needs to take this into consideration.

LAYOUT AND ACCESS METHODS

Having determined what set structures or hierarchies are to be implemented, the database designer must choose the access methods to be used.

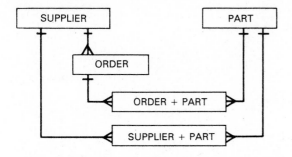

This plex structure can be represented as two hierarchical structures with links between them. There are four possible ways to accomplish this, shown below. The red lines show the links between hierarchies.

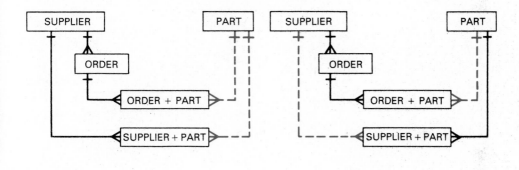

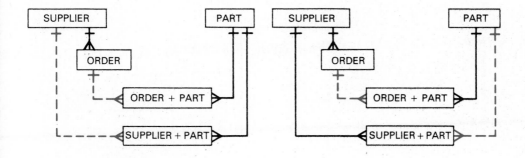

The database designer using a hierarchical approach must select which of these four gives the best machine performance.

Figure 15.3

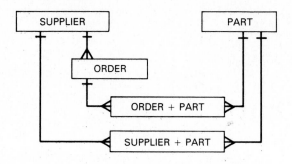

This plex structure can be represented with four possible combinations of CODASYL sets. The red lines show the sets:

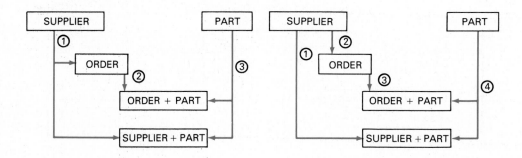

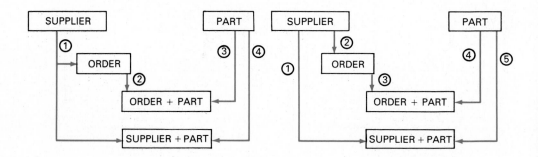

The database designer using a CODASYL approach must select which of these four gives the best machine performance.

Figure 15.4

If the records are always used one at a time in no particular sequence, a *random-access method* would be selected. The computer needs to go directly to the record in question and the term *direct-access method* is used, DAM. The most common direct-access method uses *hashing*.

Hashing or other direct-access methods, results in data being laid out on the disks in no particular sequence. This is not efficient for a high-volume batch operation. In a large-batch operation, it is desirable that the data should be laid out in the sequence of their primary keys. The run then progresses through the data in the same sequence as that in which they are laid out on the disks, and consequently the number of seeks are reduced. The data may be read into main memory a track (or part of a track) at a time. With direct-access methods a separate *seek* is needed for almost every record accessed.

If data is used *only* for batch processing in one particular sequence a *sequential-access method (SAM)* can be used. Almost always, however, there is need to access individual records, one at a time. Therefore, a means of finding records quickly in the middle of a sequential file is needed. For this an index is employed. We have an *indexed sequential access method (ISAM)*.

Data can be laid out in the sequence of its primary keys but then not in the sequence of any other data item. It cannot in general be in the sequence of its secondary keys. If it is required to access the data by a secondary key, another index may be used—a *secondary index*. A secondary index is usually much bulkier than a primary index because if the records are not in sequence by the indexed data item then most techniques for compacting the index are not applicable.

Just as records laid out in sequence may be scanned, so records not in sequence may be searched. Similar values of certain data items may be strung together with pointers forming *chain* or *ring* structures. Following chains or rings through a mechanical storage unit is very time consuming, so other means of searching are also employed.

We thus have five main types of access methods:

- **Sequential-access method (SAM),** useful only for sorted batch operations with no random access.

- **Indexed sequential-access method (ISAM),** in which the data are in sequence by primary key but an index is used for accessing them randomly.

- **Direct-access method (DAM),** usually hashing. The data are directly accessible without an index but are not in sequence for fast batch processing.

- **Secondary indices,** for finding records with particular values of a secondary key.

- **Searching techniques,** for searching data to answer unanticipated queries. Various different searching techniques are used.

Some database systems are used for processing a mass of routine transactions, for example, the processing of orders in a mail-order house or the processing of claims in a large insurance company. With such systems the designer knows the predominant uses of the machine. He will select the physical database structure, the disk layouts, and access methods which give the best machine efficiency.

Such systems are very different from database systems which are predominantly used for inquiry processing or for nonroutine low-volume transactions. They need different access methods and data layouts. Although the two can be combined, it often pays to separate the heavy-duty database from the nonroutine database or information system, even though their data is partially the same and their structures are derived from the same data model. Sometimes the same DBMS is used for the heavy-duty and nonroutine databases although these are separate. They may be disjoint databases residing in the same machine.

It is desirable to distinguish between different types of queries, as indicated. Simple queries can be efficiently handled by a heavy-duty database system. Complex queries often cannot. Unanticipated compound queries can present severe performance problems unless appropriate data structures are used.

COMPROMISES

In general a logical data model provides guidance for the physical database design, but is not necessarily mapped directly into a physical design. Often the database designer finds that compromises are desirable. He may split the data model or implement separate file systems, for performance reasons.

The designer might decide to deviate from *third-normal form* for performance reasons. He might group a nonthird-normal-form collection of data items into a record because that record is used in a very-high-volume run. (This does not usually improve performance, but it can do so in certain cases.) When deviation from third-normal form is suggested, the data administrator should evaluate the extent to which it will increase future maintenance costs. It is often the case that the increase in future maintenance costs is greater than the saving in machine costs. Both sides of the situation need to be evaluated.

DESIGN TOOLS

The designer of the physical database needs to design the stored records (How are multiple logical records grouped into one physical record?), design the record clustering into storage areas, lay out the data on the storage media, and determine the access methods and design the indices or access mechanisms.

These steps involve some intricate calculations. It is desirable to employ software which does these calculations. Some database management systems have tools for database design. Some tools exist independent of the DBMS software. Before the detailed design is done the appropriate tools should be acquired.

Design often requires multiple iterations of the design steps to converge on a solution.

```
Consider security, auditability, restart, recovery, and fallback
  Determine requirements for security.
      How is invalid access to the data prevented?
      How is unauthorized tampering with the data prevented?
      What controls against hackers are needed?
      What records should be stored offsite as protection in case
         of catastrophy, such as fire?
      How often should off-site data be renewed?

  Determine requirements for auditability.
      How are unauthorized uses of the database detected?
      How are invalid uses of the data prevented?
      What batch or on-line audit programs are needed?
       Auditors' requirements are more complex than most systems
         analysts realize, so auditors should be involved where
         appropriate in reviewing the design.

  Determine what accuracy controls are needed.
      What accuracy controls does the DBMS software provide?
      What additional accuracy controls are needed?
      Will hash totals or other totals be used to validate data
         entry?

  Determine requirements for restart after failure.
      How does the system restart after a hardware, transmission,
         or software failure?
      What controls prevent data being invalidated during a
         failure and subsequent restart?
      How are partially processed transactions backed out?
      Does the DBMS provide automatic backout under all
         circumstances?
      Must additional support be developed?

  Determine requirements for recovery and rebuilding damaged data.
      How are single records reconstructed if accidentally damaged?
      How are entire files restored or rebuilt if damaged?
      What back-up or archival data should be kept for recovery
         purposes?

  Determine requirements for fallback operation.
      When a disk has crashed or a storage unit is inaccessible
         does the system continue to operate in a mode of lower
         functionality?
      What different fallback modes are there?
```

INTEGRITY DESIGN

An important aspect of physical database design is the design of integrity.

```
 ┌─ Determine what are the performance-critical aspects of the design
 │     Determine which transactions are response-critical.
 │     Note which applications or runs most stress the design.
 │  ┌─ Produce (automatically) a table totaling the transaction accesses
 │  │  o─────────o
 │  │  │  See Fig 14.12.  │
 │  └─ o─────────o
 │
 │     Note which are the heavily loaded paths in the data model.
 └─    Note which is batch and which is interactive use.
```

We are concerned with both physical and logical integrity.

Physical integrity takes into account data base hardware failure and program failure, through recovery and restart:

Recovery relates to the ability of the DBMS product—following hardware failure (such as a disk head crash)—to rebuild a damaged database to some designated prior status. This recovery may involve restoring the database from a copy, and then updating that restored database with all processing activity applied since the copy was taken.

Restart applies to the ability of the DBMS product to reestablish the database system operating environment after interruption due to either hardware or software failure. Such interruption may not have permitted normal completion of processing; partially processed transactions or programs may be outstanding against the database. Restart generally involves backing out (removing) any partially processed transaction or program activity from the point of failure, to some prior known valid database status.

Logical integrity relates to invalid access to data and invalid use of data (audit).

Security relates to the ability of the DBMS product to protect the database from unauthorized access.

Audit relates to the ability of the DBMS product to detect, report and correct invalid, unauthorized or incorrect use of the database, as well as the ability to verify its correctness.

AUDIT REQUIREMENTS   The audit controls to be enforced by the database system need to be identified. These audit controls may have been defined during previous security and audit examination. Procedures designed to detect, report, and correct invalid, unauthorized or incorrect use of the database are specifically defined. Such audit procedures may be established through the development of separate batch or online audit programs. The audit strategy to be adopted is established.

Alternatively, some DBMS products permit audit routines to be incorporated in the database schema, as database procedures. (These procedures are invoked by the CHECK clause, in the case of CODASYL database products).

DATABASE CORRUPTION RECOVERY

Procedures to be adopted for recovery in the event of physical damage or corruption are defined. These procedures may utilize recovery utilities provided with the DBMS product; the DBMS recovery support may need to be extended to satisfy particular recovery requirements.

BATCH/ONLINE RESTART

On unanticipated interruption of database processing (where programs or transactions may have been unable to complete due to a hardware or software failure), that incomplete processing may need to be backed out (removed) to reestablish the database to its status at some prior (known) state. This backout processing is essential in the event of a hardware failure or a power failure which abnormally terminates the complete database system processing. Alternatively, backout processing may be necessary following a program failure. The program failure may not have caused abnormal termination of the entire database processing environment, only that failed transaction or program may need to be backed out.

Some DBMS products provide dynamic transaction backout, to remove the uncompleted processing of individual programs. To do this, the DBMS may reference a disk copy of the database system log, which records all database changes carried out by programs currently being executed. This transaction processing log activity is maintained only for the duration of execution of each program; on normal program completion, this disk log activity is no longer required, and the relevant disk space is released for reuse.

On abnormal termination of the entire database processing environment, all batch programs and online transactions which were concurrently processing against the database—and unable to complete their processing at the time of failure—must be backed out. Most DMBS products provide specific database restart utilities to achieve this purpose. Some products permit selective reprocessing of transactions following backout, to reestablish the database as close to the point of abnormal termination as possible.

The effectiveness of the DBMS recovery and restart support is assessed. Additional support is defined and developed as necessary to address deficiencies (if any) in the provided support, to ensure that the full needs of the database system are addressed.

SECURITY DURING RECOVERY/RESTART

The need to maintain security control over the processing carried out by specific transactions, and their access to the database, is well accepted. What is not so obvious is the need to maintain this security control not only during normal operation, but also during recovery and restart. During this period a database system may be vulnerable to unauthorized access to data. Security controls must be enforced.

ARCHIVE DESIGN

Archive design considers the retirement of data from the database to other storage media, based on the future required accessibility of that data. Access to data required in seconds (in an online environment) might demand that data be maintained always in an online database. However, over a period of time the need to reference specific data online may be less frequent. An example can be seen in online order entry. Once the orders have been satisfied, reference to those orders may be less frequent—until a point is reached where little reference is made at all. This data may then have value only for historical or statistical processing; it may be migrated from the online database to a batch database, or perhaps magnetic tape. This migration is called archiving.

Figure 15.5 illustrates the trade-off between the degree of accessibility

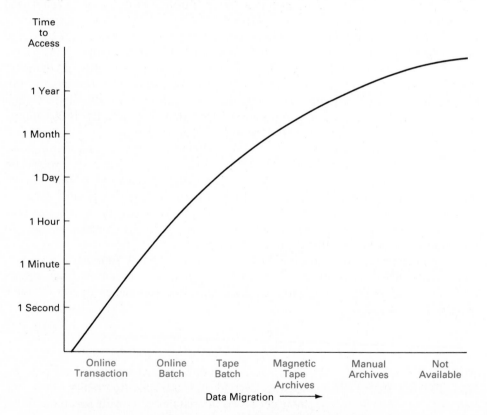

Figure 15.5 Degree of accessibility versus data archiving.

(ranging from access in seconds to access in years) and the degree of archiving. Data may be archived to less accessible (and less expensive) storage media. Alternatively, data may not be stored but may be transferred to paper (by printing) or to microfilm (through COM computer output microfilm, processing).

Equally as important as the archive medium is also the optimum time for archiving. Figure 15.5 illustrates the archiving profiles of different types of data. This shows the access requirements in the vertical axis ranging from slow-access to fast-access requirement, plotted against time on the horizontal axis ranging from days through weeks, months, and quarters to years.

Three typical data types are illustrated in Fig. 15.6: a customer record, an airline flight record, and an order and associated invoice set of records.

- The CUSTOMER record indicates an initial requirement for fast access when the customer record is first added. This customer addition may have been brought about because of the need to process an order, say, placed by that customer. If the customer remains active and orders regularly, then we may continue to provide fast access. However, as the customer's activity drops away, we may reach a point (indicated by an asterisk on the curve in Fig. 15.6) where the customer record is so inactive that we may consider archiving it and removing it completely from the database.

- The AIRLINE FLIGHT record, on the other hand, shows a gradual increase in activity over time. Reservations may be received for that flight several months prior to its scheduled date. As the date of the flight approaches, activity builds up until the time immediately following the flight, when access activity dramatically drops away. Such a drop in activity suggests that an ideal time for archiving is as asterisked on the curve.

- The ORDER AND ASSOCIATED INVOICE SET record exhibits rather different access activity from that of the previous two. This shows a period of initial activity when the order is first placed, followed by a trough of inactivity until the invoice becomes due for payment and is eventually paid. Activity then drops away again over time. Two possible archive points are suggested (and asterisked): if the period between completion of the order and payment of the invoice is sufficiently long—as indicated by a wide trough—the order information might reasonably be archived during this period. (Alternatively, it may be required to be accessible for resolution of inquiries.) The second archive point is after complete processing and payment of the invoice.

- In some cases, such as in handling a backorder, there may be two troughs and three peaks of activity. The first activity peak is in handling the initial order, the second peak is in satisfying the backorder, the third peak is in processing the paid invoice. This situation suggests additional possible archive points.

The optimum time to archive, and storage medium to be used, therefore can only be determined by examining the access activity of specific data over time, and also the degree of accessibility required.

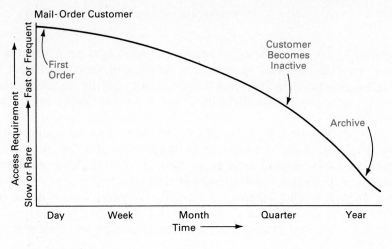

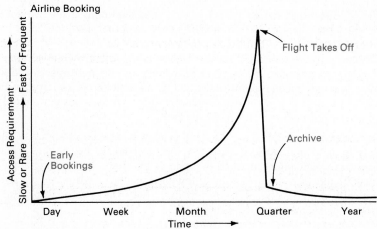

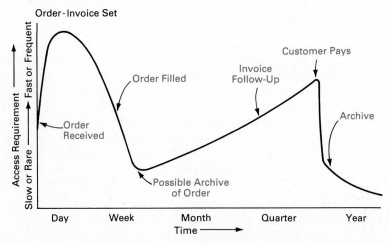

Figure 15.6 Variation in number of accesses with time.

REORGANIZATION AND RESTRUCTURING

A database will grow, over time, reflecting operational (day-to-day) processing and accumulation of transaction data. Data may be removed and new data incorporated in the database. Archiving, deletion, and addition of data should be carried out by the DBMS. Due to unavailability of disk space, it may not be possible always to store newly added records physically close to existing records in the database with which they are related. Similarly, gaps may be present in the database (representing records which have been deleted). Many DBMS products reuse the disk space released by deleted records. To maintain optimum placement of related records (and hence optimum performance), it may be necessary periodically to reorganize and restructure the database.

PERFORMANCE MONITORING

We have seen in the previous chapter how the frequency of occurrence of related records participating in relationships, and transaction volumes, are used to estimate transaction performance. These estimates are made during initial design. Once the database system goes into production, these statistics can be directly drawn from the live data base processing environment—for performance monitoring.

This performance monitoring ensures that procedures are incorporated that will permit *measurement* of frequencies of occurrence and *actual* transaction volumes. These statistics provide input to system performance evaluation stages. They enable a more accurate assessment to be made of performance. Performance can also be tracked over time. The performance impact of new data or transactions added to the database can be more accurately evaluated. The physical structuring of the database may need adjusting over time as different transaction patterns evolve.

SUMMARY

Box 15.1 shows the overall procedure for physical database design.

BOX 15.1   Physical database design

> The procedure given below may be modified
> to meet the needs of the particular situation.

Procedure for physical database design
  Determine whether the data will be distributed

  See Chapter 16.

  List and categorize the database procedures that will occur
      Extract a list of the relevant procedures from the encyclopedia.
      Categorize the procedures by types of data management system
          needed
          The types of data management software may be categorized as
          follows:
          1. File systems.
              o Simple data structures.
              o Often designed for one application as opposed to
                 multi-application databases.
              o Good machine efficiency.
          2. Application databases.
              o Database structures designed to support a narrow group
                 of applications.
              o Fairly good machine efficiency.
          3. Subject databases.
              o All the data about specific data subjects are stored
                 together.
              o One copy, rather than redundant copies, are kept of all
                 data, which makes updating and consistency control
                 straightforward.
          4. Information retrieval systems.
              o Information is stored for retrieval with multiple
                 different search parameters.
              o Extensive search indices or inverted files are used.
              o Not appropriate for data which are frequently updated.
          5. Decision-support systems.
              o Support multi-dimensional data structures, optimized for
                 highly flexible decision-support activities.
              o Inefficient or inadequate for high-volume data
                 processing.

      Categorize the procedures by physical data independence criteria
          Categorize the programs into one of the following three
              groups:
          1. Programs written without consideration of physical data-
             base design.
              o Systems with low traffic volumes.
              o Systems which do not search large bodies of data.
              o The majority of systems in most installations.
          2. Programs in which the data accesses are adjusted to fit
             the physical database design.
              o Programs which are used frequently enough to be worth
                 tuning.
          Such programs are tuned by a technician who understands the
              effects of physical database design.

(Continued)

BOX 15.1   *(Continued)*

3. Heavy-duty systems for which the data structures are
   changed to achieve optimal performance.
   o Systems with a high throughput (transactions per second)
   o Systems with a high daily load which makes it desirable
      to reduce machine costs.
   o Systems which search large bodies of data.
Data structures are optimized for a particular application or
   group of applications.
Data may be denormalized to achieve better performance.

List and categorize the database queries that will occur
   List what database queries are likely to be made.
   Categorize the queries
      into one of the following types:

   o Single-record primary-key queries.
      A single record is accessed by means of its primary key.
   o Multi-record primary-key queries.
      A simple program may be written for handling this type
         of query.
   o Anticipated single-record searches.
      Queries requiring a search of a single logical file.
      Because they are anticipated, an efficient search index
         or other search mechanism can be set up.
   o Anticipated multiple-record queries.
      Queries which need a relational JOIN or the equivalent.
      Because they are anticipated, an efficient mechanism for
         handling the query can be set up.
   o Unanticipated search or JOIN queries.
      These queries are more expensive in machine time. They
         can be extremely expensive with large databases.

   Estimate the query volumes.

Determine whether more than one type of DBMS will be needed

Determine whether the data will be split into separate databases

Select the DBMS(s)

For each specific database do the detailed design
   Obtain data usage information required for the design
      Determine what transaction types the database will support.
      Establish or extract a data model containing the data for all
         these transactions.
      Determine average cardinality for all relationships in the
         data model.
   Determine what is the peak hour.
      There may be more than one peak hour with different types
         of transactions. For example a peak for interactive
         transactions may occur at a different time from the
         peak for batch operations.

   Perform data-use analysis

      ┌─────────────────────────────────o
      │ See procedure in Box 14.1   │
      o─────────────────────────────────┘

BOX 15.1   *(Continued)*

Determine what are the performance-critical aspects of the design
    Determine which transactions are response-critical.
    Note which applications or runs most stress the design.
    Produce (automatically) a table totaling the transaction accesses

        | See Fig 14.12. |

    Note which are the heavily loaded paths in the data model.
    Note which is batch and which is interactive use.

Consider security, auditability, restart, recovery, and fallback
    Determine requirements for security.
        How is invalid access to the data prevented?
        How is unauthorized tampering with the data prevented?
        What controls against hackers are needed?
        What records should be stored offsite as protection in case
            of catastrophy, such as fire?
        How often should off-site data be renewed?

    Determine requirements for auditability.
        How are unauthorized uses of the database detected?
        How are invalid uses of the data prevented?
        What batch or on-line audit programs are needed?
            Auditors' requirements are more complex than most systems
            analysts realize, so auditors should be involved where
            appropriate in reviewing the design.

    Determine what accuracy controls are needed.
        What accuracy controls does the DBMS software provide?
        What additional accuracy controls are needed?
        Will hash totals or other totals be used to validate data
            entry?

    Determine requirements for restart after failure.
        How does the system restart after a hardware, transmission,
            or software failure?
        What controls prevent data being invalidated during a
            failure and subsequent restart?
        How are partially processed transactions backed out?
        Does the DBMS provide automatic backout under all
            circumstances?
        Must additional support be developed?

    Determine requirements for recovery and rebuilding damaged data.
        How are single records reconstructed if accidentally damaged?
        How are entire files restored or rebuilt if damaged?
        What back-up or archival data should be kept for recovery
            purposes?

    Determine requirements for fallback operation.
        When a disk has crashed or a storage unit is inaccessible
            does the system continue to operate in a mode of lower
            functionality?
        What different fallback modes are there?

(Continued)

BOX 15.1 *(Continued)*

Evaluate the design techniques.
   Determine what design tools are available for the DBMS selected.
   Determine what can be done to minimize the physical access time
        in the DBMS for the most heavily used paths through the data
        model.
     For example:
        o Lay out records so that those together are physically
             close.
        o Lay out records so that a disk access arm does not have to
             be moved to follow the heavily used paths.
        o Combine records to minimize physical input/output
             reference for heavily used paths.
        o Use physical rather than logical access paths in a DBMS
             such as IMS.
        o Optimize the set structures in a CODASYL database.
        o Appropriately adjust the use of indices, pointers or
             hashing.

Design the database.
   Design is likely to proceed iteratively through the following
        steps to converge on an appropriate design:

     Consider the alternate structures available for the DBMS.

     Design the stored record formats.

     Design the record clustering into storage media areas.

     Lay out the data on the storage media.

     Design the access methods.

     Adapt the programs to the design where necessary.

Design the operations facilities.
   Design the facilities needed for archiving.
   Design facilities for reorganization and restructuring.
   Design facilities for performance monitoring and tuning.
   Design the operational interfaces.

Design the implementation facilities.
   Generate the database definitions for implementing the
        database.
   Design the database test facilities.
   Generate the data needed for testing.

16 DISTRIBUTION ANALYSIS

INTRODUCTION As computers and storage drop in cost, distributed processing becomes increasingly widespread, and with it distributed data. When data are stored in multiple locations on relatively cheap machines, the need for top-down design and control is even greater than with centralized database systems. If top-down design does not exist or is not enforced by management every systems analyst or user group is likely to create its own design for the data at its own location. In some corporations distributed processing and the spread of small computers has been a formula for chaos in data representation. Many others are plunging down the same path.

The advantages of small computers and distributed data are many, quite apart from the low cost of the hardware. It is desirable to reap those advantages without the harm caused by data incompatibilities. This needs distribution of the data administration function and firm management control in the execution of a top-down plan for data.

In some cases user management become extremely determined to have their own computer with systems designed as *they* want them.

To prevent the chaotic spread of incompatible data, it is necessary to ensure that the data in distributed machines conform to the data models described earlier. Subsets of these models can be generated to represent the data in each distributed computer.

DISTRIBUTION CONFIGURATIONS During the early stages of information engineering, the question of how the data is distributed need not be considered. The data model can be implemented in many different distributed configurations. These configurations will almost certainly change as technology and procedures change, but the data model should not change except for minor additions and enhancements.

The question of how data should be distributed is a complex one. No algorithm can completely determine how data should be distributed. There are many and varied subjective reasons for distribution.

PERSONAL DATA   It is necessary to distinguish between two types of data: *purely personal data* and *shared data*. Purely personal data is often created by one person for his own use. They are not employed for other uses by other persons in the enterprise. Shared data are those which may be used in a personal fashion, for example, in a decision-support system, but which are derived from or transmitted to databases (or files) which have other uses.

Much of the data used in personal computing is *not* purely personal data. It is used somewhere else for some other purpose.

Purely personal data need not conform to the enterprise data models; all other data must.

REASONS FOR   If the technology cost permits, it often makes sense
DISTRIBUTING   to store the data where it is used.
DATA   It has been shown repeatedly that when user departments regard files of data as "our data" and have full responsibility for data entry and accuracy, they are more careful about data accuracy. In many installations data entry and storage have reverted from being a central IS (information system) function to a function under full control of the using department and the accuracy of the data has improved greatly.

There are properties inherent in certain data which lead naturally to distribution and properties in other data which lead naturally to centralization. Boxes 16.1 and 16.2 list these.

On many systems data exist which are of both types: naturally centralized and naturally kept locally. Much of the information in a department is of use only in that department. However, other departmental information is needed in centralized information or control systems, or centralized applications such as purchasing or production control.

The main property for distribution is that the data is used at one peripheral location and is rarely used at other locations. Much of the information in a branch office, for example, client addresses, is of no use anywhere but that branch office. However, other information generated in a branch office is needed elsewhere, for example, customer orders which are needed in manufacturing plants, sales figures which are needed for central purchasing, or insurance company policy figures which are needed for actuarial calculations in the head office.

An important reason for distribution is that separate decision-support systems are created. Users employ fourth-generation languages, and these require

BOX 16.1 Properties inherent in certain data which lead naturally to distribution

1. The data is used at one peripheral location; it is rarely or never used at other locations. To transmit such data for storage may be unnecessarily complex and expensive.

2. The accuracy, privacy, and security of the data are a local responsibility.

3. The files are simple and are used by one or a few applications. Hence there would be little or no advantage in employing complex centralized software.

4. The update rate is too high for a single centralized storage system.

5. Peripheral files are searched or manipulated with an end-user language which implicitly results in inverted list or secondary key operations. Too many end-user operations of this type can play havoc with the performance of a central system. They may be better located in a peripheral system with end users responsible for their usage and costs.

6. Fourth-generation languages are used which employ a relational (or other) database, different from the database of production systems.

7. A localized decision-support system is used.

data structures different from those of production systems. Decision-support packages running on departmental computers are often powerful and effective.

The spread of departmental computers increasingly encourages the use of departmental data.

REASONS FOR CENTRALIZING DATA

Box 16.2 lists properties of data which lead naturally to centralization.

A property of data which argues strongly for centralization is that the data is being constantly updated and referred to by multiple users in different geographical locations. The users need to have an up-to-the-minute picture of the data as a whole, and the data is being modified by users in different locations. One copy of the data is therefore kept in one place. This is done on reservation systems for airlines, hotels, and rented cars. It is also done on inventory control systems, military early-warning systems, credit-checking systems, and so on.

Data to which many inquiries are made could be distributed if the data are updated only infrequently, if the data given to the inquirers can be a few hours old rather than up-to-the-second or, possibly, if the updates come from only one

BOX 16.2 Properties inherent in certain data which lead naturally to centralization

1. Data is used by centralized applications such as a corporatewide payroll, purchasing, or general accounting.

2. Users in all areas need access to the same data and need the current up-to-the-minute version. The data is frequently updated. Data may be centralized to avoid the problems of real time synchronization of multiple copies with a high update level.

3. Users of the data travel among many separate locations, and it is cheaper to centralize their data than it is to provide a switched data network.

4. The data as a whole will be searched. They are part of an information system which will provide answers to spontaneous queries from users, many of which can only be answered by examining many records. Searching data which is geographically scattered is extremely time consuming. The software and hardware for efficient searching require the data to be in one location. Secondary indices may be used and the indexing software refers only to data in one storage system.

5. Mainframe database software is needed.

6. A high level of security is to be maintained over the data. The protection procedures may be expensive, possibly involving a well-guarded, secure vault and tight control of authorized users. The data are better guarded if they are in one location, with external backup copies, than if they are scattered.
   Catastrophe protection is often an argument for bicentral systems rather than for single centralized storage.

7. The data is too bulky to be stored on inexpensive peripheral storage units. The economies of scale of centralized bulk storage is desirable.

8. To make systems auditable, details are sometimes kept of what transactions updated certain data. It may be cheaper, and more secure, to dump these in a large centralized archival storage unit.

source. In an information service in which a wide variety of information is made available at terminals, the data can be replicated in many locations. If there are a large number of references to it, this will save transmission costs. The data is updated infrequently from a central source. A stock market system giving the current stock prices and other information could employ multiple replicated copies of the same data. The updates are frequent but come from a single source.

If a user always employs terminals at the same location, it might be possible to store the data of interest to him at that location. If users move geographically, then either the data must be centralized, or else a means of switching must be employed to connect a user to the system which contains data relevant to him. In a bank with many branches, customer records might be stored at the branch which holds their account. A major advantage of banking automation, however, is that customers can use *any* branch. Many banking systems with distributed intelligence therefore have centralized customer record storage. Customer transactions may be stored locally and transmitted to the center at appropriate intervals. Possibly only balances and account restrictions will be stored centrally as this would be enough to serve most of a customer's demands when he is in a branch other than his own. It is likely that only a small fraction of all customer visits are to branches other than their home branch, so a switching mechanism might route nonhome-branch transactions to the home-branch computer when necessary.

Different patterns of use often exist in the same system. Because of this, some data in the same system may be centralized and some decentralized.

In an airline reservation system, the majority (often 90 percent) of the messages are for information about flights and seat availability. This is a small fraction of the total data and could easily be stored at the terminal location. Other data, particularly passenger booking records, occupy much more space. Bookings for a specific flight would all go to one location where that flight is controlled. This location might be a central computer, but not necessarily; different flights might be controlled by distributed computers close to where the most bookings for the flights originate (especially on worldwide airlines). The computer which controls the flight would send messages to the terminal computers when the booking level on the flight became critical. It would keep the seat availability records of the terminal computers up to date. This form of operation would have various advantages over a fully centralized system: low telecommunications costs, low response times, better reliability. It is interesting to note that it is closer to the way airlines operated before the introduction of today's centralized reservation systems.

Other properties of data that favor centralization are listed in Box 16.2.

One is bulk. The data occupy a sufficiently large volume that the economies of scale of large storage units are desirable.

The other is security. Highly professional security is needed for certain data. These are usually a small proportion of all the data in a corporation. Their protection procedures may involve a fireproof, bombproof, intruderproof vault, possibly with the storage unit inside it accessible via coaxial cable. Guards are used at the secure location and a security officer who is responsible for tight programmed controls on access to the data [1]. A corporation may have more than one secure storage location. Catastrophe protection is often an argument for bicentral systems.

A strong argument for data being in one machine is that the data have to be searched as whole. Secondary-key operations may have to be performed in order to answer certain types of user questions. The data organization may be part of an information system which will provide answers to spontaneous queries from users, many of which can only be answered by examining many records. Excellent software is available for these types of operations, but it requires the data in question to be in one machine. Searching or secondary-key operations on geographically scattered data would be very time consuming and inefficient. To improve the performance of information systems, hardware is likely to become available to assist in associative or secondary-key operations. Again this will require the data to be in one machine. The one machine could be centralized or peripheral as with small functional information systems.

MULTIPLE COPIES OF DATA

The cost of small storage units is dropping much faster than is the cost of transmission. This swings the argument in favor of distribution of data. When machines are cheap, multiple replicated copies become economic even if the data is fairly frequently updated, provided that appropriate software mechanisms and controls exist.

In the early days of database management, a major argument for databases was the avoidance of redundant copies of data. Some authorities (but not the author) defined a database as a nonredundant collection of data. There are economic advantages in redundancy in certain circumstances provided that software controls exist for updating the redundant copies and ensuring their integrity. When redundant copies exist their structure should be derived from the same nonredundant logical model of the data.

Box 16.3 lists reasons for having multiple distributed copies of the same data.

Multiple copies of data can cause integrity and data synchronization problems unless good distributed database software exists. In some installations deficiencies in such software have been overcome by implementation of customer-produced control mechanisms.

Other problems with distributed data are listed in Box 16.4. These need to be taken into consideration in the planning of distributed systems.

SIX FORMS OF DISTRIBUTED DATA

Distributed data can exist in six fundamentally different forms:

1. Duplicated data
2. Subset data
3. Reorganized data

4. Partitioned data

5. Separate-schema data

6. Incompatible data

Duplicated Data

Duplicated data refers to the keeping of identical copies of the same data at different locations. The main reason for doing this is that duplicate storage avoids the need for transmission of data between systems and is cheaper. Such an organization makes sense only when the frequency of references to the data is much lower than the frequency of updates. Much replicated data is unchanging data (or rarely changing data because almost no data is completely static).

An example would be a public data service such as *videotex* systems). These make data available on home television sets or personal computers. Mul-

BOX 16.3   Reasons for multiple distributed copies of data

A system may be designed with more than one copy of the same data in different locations for any of the following reasons:

1. **Transmission costs.** It may be cheaper to have replicated copies than to transmit data over long distances.

2. **Response time.** Access to local, rather than remote, data may significantly improve the response time.

3. **Availability.** Access to local data, or to alternate copies of data, may significantly increase the availability of the data.

4. **Security.** Two or more copies of data may be used in case one copy is destroyed. (The term ''survivability'' is used in the military to imply that data are still accessible after multiple copies of them have been destroyed.)

5. **Data organization.** The same data may be organized differently in different machines, for example, in a production system and information system.

6. **Conversion expense.** Old existing files may be preserved after databases or distributed systems are implemented because of the cost and time of converting their programs to work with the new data structures.

Problems arise in controlling the integrity of multiple copies when the data falls into certain classes.

BOX 16.4   Problems with distributed data

Distributed data can have a number of problems associated with them. These problems have solutions but are such that it is often desirable not to have unconstrained distribution and replication of data.

The problems are as follows:

1. **Interference between updating transactions.** Two transactions may be updating the same data item on a remote storage unit and can interfere with one another, giving incorrect data. This can be prevented by appropriate locks or protocols.

2. **Inconsistent reads.** With more than one copy of data, and sometimes with only one copy of distributed data, inconsistent information can be obtained when reading the data. Sometimes, due to timing problems, the data read can be invalid. This can also be prevented with appropriate locks or protocols.

3. **Deadly embrace.** The locking of distributed data to prevent update interference could cause deadlocks unless appropriate (fairly complex) protocols are used.

4. **Protocol overhead.** Unless carefully thought out, the protocols to prevent invalid updates, inconsistent reads, and deadly embrace situations can incur excessive overhead, especially when multiple replicated copies of data are used.

5. **Recovery.** Recovery after failure needs to be controlled so that updates are not accidentally lost or double processed.

6. **Recovery of multiple copies.** When multiple copies of data exist they may be different states of update after a period of failure. They have to be brought back to the same state—resynchronized—but it may be complex to do this while real-time transactions are being processed.

7. **Different data representation.** Because of lack of data administration or firm management control, the same data are represented differently in different locations.

8. **Auditing.** It is difficult on some distributed systems to find out who did what to the data. Appropriate design for auditability is needed.

9. **Security and privacy protection.** Security controls and privacy protection are sometimes poor on distributed systems and need to be built into the basic design.

tiple copies of the same data are stored on relatively small distributed systems. This data will be updated from a central system. Another example is a multinational corporation using data to which inquiries are made in many countries. It is cheaper to store replicated copies in different countries than to handle the inquiries with an international data network.

Replication of data is becoming increasingly attractive economically because the cost of small storage units is dropping much faster than the cost of telecommunications. This trend is likely to continue.

Subset Data

Data is often stored in peripheral computers which are a subset of data in a larger computer. There are two main reasons for doing this. First, the data is used frequently at the peripheral location. Second, the data is created at that location. In a data-entry operation, data is often keyed into a local computer. They are checked there, accuracy controls and auditing controls are applied to a batch of data, and the batch is then transmitted to a distant database.

Subset data is a form of replicated data. We distinguish it because it does not usually have the complete schema or the complete key set of the parent data.

Usually a master copy of the data is kept in the higher-level machine. When a change is made to the data in the lower-level machine, this change must be passed up to the higher-level machine—sometimes immediately, sometimes later in an updating cycle.

In other systems the lower machines may store some of the data that is in the higher machine and also have some which is its own and which is never passed upward. The lower machines, for example, might keep addresses of and general information about customers. This bulky data is never needed by the higher-level system. The higher-level system might, however, store customer numbers, names, credit information, and details of orders. These are also stored by the lower machines, and any modification to them must be passed upward.

Too often, because of lack of coordinated planning, the data in a lower-level machine is incompatible with that in a higher-level machine. This inhibits the interchange of data between the machines.

Reorganized Data

We have stressed that a decision-support database needs data organized differently from a production database. An information system or decision-support system usually contains some of the same data as a routine production system, but it is reorganized with inverted lists, secondary indices, or relational mechanisms which facilitate searching, extracting, and joining data.

All the data in a decision-support system may be culled from databases (or files) in other machines (or even in the same machine), but the data is summarized, edited, and reorganized. To make this work satisfactorily, both types of database should have the same data item representation; they should be derived from the same data model and dictionary representation.

Partitioned Data

Partitioned data implies that the same schema is used in two or more machines, but that each machine stores different data. Each machine has different records (different primary keys), but they are identically structured.

This is a common and valuable form of distribution. The system in district A keeps district A data. That in B keeps B data, and so on. There may be a separate computer in each branch office, of an organization, each retail store, each warehouse, or other such business location. They all use the same programs. Most of the transactions originate and are processed where their data are. A few may require data elsewhere, and these are either transmitted to the data location or the data are transmitted to them.

Separate-Schema Data

With separate-schema data, the different computers contain different data and different programs and are usually installed by different teams. For example, one system may handle *production* data, another *purchasing* data, another *general accounting,* and so on.

Although their schemas are different these separate data systems should be part of a common top-down plan; otherwise, harmful redundancies and inconsistencies will develop. One of the computers often needs to send transactions to or request data from another computer. The production system, which might be in a factory, creates purchasing requisitions, and these are transmitted to the purchasing system. Both the purchasing and the production systems generate data which must be passed to the general accounting system.

Incompatible Data

Sometimes the data in separate systems have no commonality of design or planning. A user is sometimes able to access multiple separately developed systems from one terminal via a computer network. He must learn about each computer's data separately, and how to access and use these data.

Sometimes such systems are set up by different authorities for different purposes, like the multitude of systems accessible via some computer networks. Sometimes they exist within one corporation and are incompatible because there was no top-down planning.

SYNCHRONOUS AND NONSYNCHRONOUS DATA

In the first three types of data distribution—*duplicated, subset,* and *reorganized* data—the same data may exist on two or more machines. In that case an important design question is: "Are the multiple copies of data synchronized?" In other words when the value of an attribute is changed in one copy, is it immediately changed in the other copies?

The control mechanisms for keeping two or more copies of data in synchronization are complex because hardware or transmission failures can occur at any time. One copy falls out of synchronization perhaps by several hours. During the attempt to recover synchronization, updates are still being made to the data, and other hardware or transmission failures may occur. Some database software does handle the synchronization of multiple copies of data in a failsafe fashion, but most does not.

In most cases there is no need to maintain up-to-the-minute synchronization between remote copies of data. One copy can be an hour or a day out of synch. Only one copy is updated interactively. These updates are transmitted in a batch to the other copies and controls are used to ensure that the batch is transmitted and applied without loss of updates or accidental double updating.

This distinction between synchronous and nonsynchronous copies of data gives, in effect, nine types of data distribution:

- Duplicated data (synchronous)
- Duplicated data (nonsynchronous)
- Subset data (synchronous)
- Subset data (nonsynchronous)
- Reorganized data (synchronous)
- Reorganized data (nonsynchronous)
- Partitioned data
- Separate-schema data
- Incompatible data

Figure 16.1 summarizes these.

At some point the planning of distributed systems needs to distinguish between these categories of data. There is, of course, one further category. The data may *not* be distributed. Scattered terminals or computers may access one single centralized database.

LOGICAL, NOT GEOGRAPHICAL, PLANNING

The top-down charts of the previous chapters have not shown where the data exists geographically. *It is usually desirable to create a strategic plan for data*

1. Duplicated Data

Multiple copies of the same data are stored at different locations because this is cheaper than transmission. Updates to the multiple copies are carefully controlled.

2. Subset Data

Subset of data, compatible with a parent database, are stored separately, for data entry, retrieval, or local processing.

3. Reorganized Data

Data in an information or decision support system is derived from data in a routine production system.

4. Partitioned Data

The same data structure is used in different locations, but not the same data.

5. Separate-schema Data

Different data structures are used in different locations forming an integrated system.

6. Incompatible Data

Independent computer systems set up by different authorities, or departmental data designed without coordination.

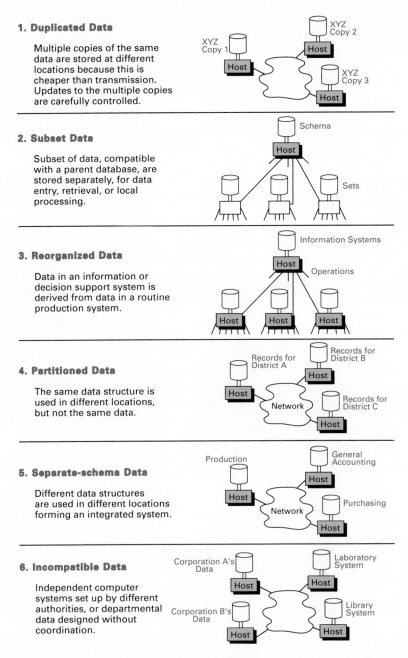

Figure 16.1 Distributed data can exist in six fundamentally different forms.

which does not take into account its distribution, at least at first. A reason for this is that the factors to be considered in deciding whether to distribute, or how to distribute, are complex, and some of them change with time, for example, network availability, costs of small computers and storage, costs of transmission, distributed database software, and location of offices. A strategic plan for data takes a long time to implement, and during this time the distribution parameters can change substantially. The strategic planning should initially create *logical,* not *geographical,* maps of data.

On the other hand an early, and clear, decision might be that one given factory or division has its own computer. Strategic planning of data might be done for that area because that is a more tractable problem than attempting to grapple with the entire corporation. The disadvantage of doing top-down planning for discrete pieces of an organization is that, although that is easier, the planning will not reveal the *corporatewide* redundancies, commonalities, and anomalies. Often the same database schemas and programs can be used by multiple branch offices or other corporate locations, each of which has its own computer. A decision about the span of control of a top-down strategy is a very important one to make at the beginning. Within this span, all the entity types should be charted, initially *without* charting the distribution. It is, however, convenient to collect information about distribution while the other information is being collected.

DISTRIBUTION MATRICES

Many locations in an enterprise carry out identical processes. For example, every branch office has the same tasks to perform. Factories will often be somewhat different because their management control is usually different. Their processes and required databases differ in detail. There may be a *production* database in each factory but each of these is differently structured.

The business processes can be mapped against the geographical locations where they take place. Figure 16.2 illustrates this. Such a chart may show major responsibility for a business process, major involvement with it and also minor involvement with it.

It is a good idea to verify the charting of processes by interviewing executives who are responsible for them. A matrix can be drawn showing what *locations* various executives are involved with, in order to assist in finding out how locations use the various processes.

Similarly, as entity clusters are developed, these can be mapped against the locations where they are used, as in Fig. 16-3. Figure 16.3 is not concerned with whether the data is distributed, or how. This is a complex decision. When that decision is made the matrix can be filled in as in Fig. 16.4 to show the types of data distribution: subset, replication, partition, and so on.

PROCESS	Factory A	Factory B	Factory C	Branch Office	District Office	Warehouse	Head Office
Market Analysis					X		X
Product Range Review					X		X
Sales Forecasting					X		X
Financial Planning							X
Capital Acquisition							X
Funds Management							X
Product Design	\	\	\	\			X
Product Pricing							X
Product Spec. Maint.	\	\	\				X
Materials Requirements	X	X	X				
Purchasing	X	X	X				
Receiving	X	X	X			\	
Inventory Control	X	X	X			\	
Quality Control	X	X	X				
Capacity Planning	X	X	X				\
Plant Scheduling	X	X	X				
Workflow Layout	X	X	X				
Materials Control	X	X	X				
Sizing and Cutting	X	X	X				
Machine Operations	X	X	X				
Territory Management				X	X		
Selling				X	X		
Sales Administration				X	X		
Customer Relations				X	X		
Finished Stock Control						X	
Order Serving				X		X	
Packing						X	
Shipping						X	
Creditors & Debtors	X	X	X				X
Cash Flow	X	X	X	\	\	\	X
Payroll	X	X	X	\	\	\	X
Cost Accounting	X	X	X				X
Budget Planning	X	X	X				X
Profitability Analysis	X	X	X				X
Personnel Planning	X	X	X				X
Recruiting	\	\	\	\	\	\	X
Compensation Policy	\	\	\				X

KEY:
X = Major Involvement
\ = Minor Involvement

Figure 16.2   The locations involved with each process.

DATA STRUCTURE	Head Office	Warehouse	District Office	Branch Office	Factory A	Factory B	Factory C
Planning	C		U				
Budget	C		U		U	U	U
Financial	C		U		U	U	U
Product	C				U	U	U
Product Design	C				U	U	U
Parts Master					C	C	C
Bill of Materials					C	C	C
Open Requirements					C	C	C
Vendor	C				C	C	C
Procurements					C	C	C
Materials Inventory					C	C	C
Machine Load					C	C	C
Work in Progress					C	C	C
Facilities	C				C	C	C
Shop Floor Routings					C	C	C
Customer	U		U	C	U	U	U
Sales	U		U	C			
Sales Territory	U		U	C			
Fin. Goods Inventory		C			U	U	U
Orders	U	U		C	U	U	U
Payments	C		U	U			
Costs	C				C	C	C
Employee	C	C	C	C	C	C	C
Salaries	C	C	C	C	C	C	C

KEY

U = Use
C = Create and Use

The above chart shows which locations use which data structures. It does not yet say how the data is to be distributed. Later, when the parameters affecting distribution have been analyzed, it can indicate whether data is distributed and, if so, what kind of distribution as follows in Fig. 16.4.

Figure 16.3   The entity clusters at each location showing the types of data distribution.

With replicated, subset, or reorganized data, a *master copy* of the data is usually kept. This is shown with an "M" on Fig. 16.4.

FINER RESOLUTION

Figures 16.2, 16.3, and 16.4 are overview charts with course resolution. If appropriate information engineering dictionaries exist, a finer resolution approach can be taken.

DATA STRUCTURE	Head Office	Warehouse	District Office	Branch Office	Factory A	Factory B	Factory C
Planning	M		T				
Budget	M		T		T	T	T
Financial	M		T		T	T	T
Product	M				S	S	S
Product Design	M				S	S	S
Parts Master					P	P	P
Bill of Materials					V	V	V
Open Requirements					V	V	V
Vendor	M				S	S	S
Procurements					P	P	P
Materials Inventory					P	P	P
Machine Load					V	V	V
Work in Progress					V	V	V
Facilities	V				V	V	V
Shop Floor Routings					V	V	V
Customer	M		R	P	R	R	R
Sales	T		M	P			
Sales Territory	T		M	P			
Fin. Goods Inventory		M			T	T	T
Orders	M	R		R	T	T	T
Payments	M		T	T			
Costs	M				V	V	V
Employee	P	P	P	P	P	P	P
Salaries	P	P	P	P	P	P	P

KEY

M = Master data: unique in one location.
V = Variant: different schema version on different locations.
P = Partitioned data: same schema, different values.
D = Replicated data: identical data in different locations.
S = Subset data.
R = Reorganized data.
T = Teleprocessing: data not stored on this location.

Figure 16.4   The data structures at each location showing the types of data distribution.

Figure 16.2 lists processes in an enterprise. We commented earlier that some practitioners of strategic data planning break processes into activities and map actions against the entities they employ. This approach has been very useful in the planning of database systems. It is described in James Martin's *Strategic Data Planning Methodologies* [3].

The locations at which an activity takes place can be recorded in a dictionarylike system.

A procedure like PREPARE PURCHASE ORDER may take place at many locations. It is highly desirable that it should be programmed once not, as in the past, but many times. If it is slightly different at different locations, the differences should be represented in data controlling the procedure so that reusable code can be employed.

Physical records do not necessarily reside at the same location as the procedure which uses them. Programs at multiple locations may use common records at a central location.

When procedures are designed, the IE repository should show what entity types they use, at what location(s) the procedure takes place, and how many times per period (e.g., per week) they are used.

The repository-based tools can generate reports that are used in the planning of data distribution.

INTERNODAL TRAFFIC

A good distribution arranges data and programs into clusters such that each cluster has a high level of autonomy and there is a low level of interdependence between clusters.

If machines were very inexpensive it would seem advantageous, at first sight, to place the data and programs at the same location as the user activity. Unfortunately, much data is shared by activities at multiple locations. If this data were replicated so that it could be stored at the user locations, then changes to the data would have to be distributed to each location.

If data is *updated* by activities in multiple locations *and the updates must be current,* it is easier to have one copy of the data. To keep multiple copies current is complex, increases the amount of messages transmitted, and requires intricate recovery procedures for the many types of failures that can occur. Having one copy achieves the objective of lowering the interdependence between data clusters.

We could judge the different forms of distribution by calculating the amount of internodal traffic they generate.

Let us consider a system with terminals in N locations. Users at these locations generate some transactions which *use* data and some which *change* the data.

Suppose that

$$A_u = \text{actions per hour taking place which } use \text{ the data}$$

and

$$A_c = \text{actions per hour taking place which } change \text{ the data}$$

Suppose that these actions are evenly distributed over the N locations.

We will define a *traffic unit* as a message which is transmitted to the data node and a response to that message which is sent back. Let

$$T = \text{the number of traffic units per hour}$$

Let us suppose that that data are *centralized, at one of the user nodes.* Then the total traffic units per hour is

$$T_{\text{centralized}} = (A_u + A_c)\frac{N - 1}{N}$$

If the data is decentralized (i.e., stored at all user locations), the actions which *use* the data do not generate traffic; the actions which *change* the data each generate $N - 1$ traffic units.

$$T_{\text{decentralized}} = A_c(N - 1)$$

Distribution of data creates less traffic than does centralization of data if

$$(A_u + A_c)\frac{N - 1}{N} > A_c(N - 1)$$

that is, if

$$\frac{A_u}{A_c} > N - 1$$

If there are two user locations, it is better to distribute the data, that is, if

$$\frac{A_u}{A_c} > 1$$

If there are 100 user locations, it is better to distribute the data, that is, if

$$\frac{A_u}{A_c} > 99$$

Let us suppose that there is *one change* made for every *ten uses* of the data, that is,

$$\frac{A_u}{A_c} = 10$$

Then the breakeven point between centralization and decentralization would be when there are 11 user locations, that is, centralize if there are more than 11 user locations.

The situation is different if the changes to data can be applied after some delay.

Let us suppose that a change can be applied to the data up to D hours after it originates. Every D hours a message could be sent to every data location giving the changes that have occurred since the last update or, for control purposes, indicating that there have been no changes. With data centralized at one of the user nodes this needs $(N - 1)/D$ traffic units per hour. With decentralized data but the updates being relayed by a centralized location, this needs $2(N - 1)/D$ traffic units per hour.

$$T_{\text{centralized}} = A_u \frac{(N - 1)}{N} + \frac{N - 1}{D}$$

$$T_{\text{decentralized}} = \frac{2(N - 1)}{D}$$

The breakeven point occurs when $A_u = N/D$.

If $D = 2$ hours and the users generate 500 references to the data per hour, in total, then it pays to distribute if there are less than $2 \times 500 = 1000$ locations.

The breakeven point has swung greatly in favor of distributed, duplicated data.

OTHER COMPLICATIONS

Unfortunately, systems design is not that simple. There are many other conflicting considerations. What is the operating cost of the user installations? Will other types of transactions need to search the entire collection of data or draw summarized information from it? What are the software problems when many copies of the same data are maintained? Failures of all different types may occur: How is recovery accomplished after a failure? What if another failure occurs during the recovery operation? What type of network structure is needed?

Nevertheless, the foregoing calculations are an impressive indication that as machines continue to drop in cost there should be a major use of highly distributed, replicated data. In its early years database technology was thought of as handling nonredundant data. It is clear from calculations such as those just presented that substantial redundancy of data makes sense in distributed systems when the hardware becomes cheap. It is necessary that database control software evolves to permit the easy handling of distributed, duplicated data without integrity problems.

The factor which makes practical a high degree of distributed, duplicated data is that the data is updated periodically rather than constantly. The designer should determine whether this can apply to the data in question. Data with this characteristic is likely to be highly distributed in future systems.

Traffic calculations cannot, by themselves, answer the question: Should a distributed configuration be used or not? They can, however, provide insight into how data should be distributed between computers which will exist anyway.

Take a relatively simple case. A factory and a head office both have a computer system. Between them they will carry out a certain set of *procedures*. Data structures have been planned. Some of the data is needed by procedures *both* in the factory and in the head office. Where should the data be placed?

One solution is to place the data such that it minimizes the traffic. If a database is more frequently accessed from the factory, it is placed there. If not, it is placed in head office.

Figure 16.5 shows a matrix of locations and data structures. The numbers in the matrix indicate the traffic units for each database from each location.

For each data structure the traffic from each location can be added. That data structure can be placed in the location with the highest traffic, as is shown in the second part of Fig. 16.5. The traffic shown as numbers outside of the red boxes is internodal traffic. This can be lessened by suitable duplication of the data (duplication, subset, or reorganized data). The primary candidates for duplication are the ones for which the numbers in the columns add to the largest total. The third part of Fig. 16.5 shows databases D_1 and D_5 duplicated. It is necessary to calculate the number of traffic units needed to keep the duplicated data updated. This depends upon the required currency of the data.

PROGRAMS AND DATA TOGETHER

It is generally desirable that programs and the data they use should be in the same location. It requires considerable overhead for a program in one location to access data in a different location.

Unfortunately, a program often needs data in more than one data structure, and one data structure is accessed by multiple programs. It is desirable to *cluster* the programs and data so as to minimize the internodal traffic.

Figure 16.6 illustrates this. The first part of Fig. 16.6 shows a collection of programs and the data structures they access. Again, the numbers in the matrix are traffic figures. Computer algorithms can cluster the programs and data structures into clusters of 2×2, 3×3 or any other size. Figure 16.6 illustrates this. The numbers outside the rectangles represent the traffic between clusters. The total traffic between clusters generally becomes smaller as the clusters become larger. The minimum intercluster traffic is achieved when there is only one cluster.

Subject databases mapped against locations and processes. The figures are the traffic volumes in hundreds of transactions per day.

	Subject Databases				
	D_1	D_2	D_3	D_4	D_5
LOCATION 1					
Process P_1	501				
Process P_2		17			301
Process P_3				42	210
LOCATION 2					
Process P_1	319		1		
Process P_4				105	
LOCATION 3					
Process P_1	217				
Process P_5				110	
Process P_6			38		
Process P_7				405	
LOCATION 4					
Process P_1	63				
Process P_2		219			609
Process P_8			72		36

The above databases located where their traffic is highest. The figures outside of the red rectangles are volumes of traffic transmitted.

	Subject Databases				
	D_1	D_4	D_2	D_3	D_5
LOCATION 1					
Process P_1	501				
Process P_2			17		301
Process P_3		42			210
LOCATION 2					
Process P_1	319			1	
Process P_4		105			
LOCATION 3					
Process P_1	217				
Process P_5		110			
Process P_6				38	
Process P_7		405			
LOCATION 4					
Process P_1	63				
Process P_2			219		609
Process P_8				72	36

The above databases, with replication of databases D_1 and D_5 to lessen the traffic transmitted.

	Subject Databases				
	D_1	D_4	D_2	D_3	D_5
LOCATION 1					
Process P_1	501				
Process P_2			17		301
Process P_3		42			210
LOCATION 2					
Process P_1	319			1	
Process P_4		105			
LOCATION 3					
Process P_1	217				
Process P_5		110			
Process P_6				38	
Process P_7		405			
LOCATION 4					
Process P_1	63				
Process P_2			219		609
Process P_8				72	36

Figure 16.5

1. Applications mapped against the data structures they use. Some clustering of applications and data structures is needed.

Applications

Subject Databases

	1	2	3	4	5	6	7	8
A	1	6						
B					17	5		1
C			20					
D					30		6	
E			12		22		17	
F			2					
G	14	16					1	
H				3	1			

2. Applications and data structures clustered into 2 x 2 matrices so as to minimize the traffic between clusters.

Applications

Subject Databases

	5	7	1	2	3	8	6	4
D	30	6						
E	22	17			12			
G		1	14	18				
A			1	6				
C					20			
F					2			
B	17					1	5	
H								3

3. Applications and data structures clustered into 3 x 3 matrices so as to minimize the traffic between clusters.

Applications

Subject Databases

	5	7	6	3	2	1	4	8
D	30	6						
E	22	17		12				
B	17		5					1
C				20				
G		1			18	14		
A					1	6		
F				2				
H	1						3	

Figure 16.6

An activity can be further broken into procedures which we represent with procedure maps (the event diagrams of Chapter 11). One procedure consists of multiple events. Thus we have

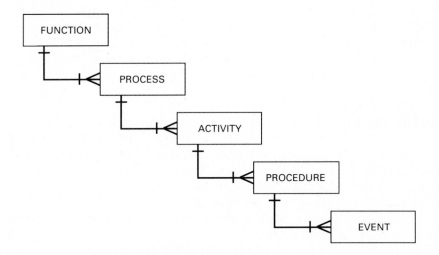

A process, like CUSTOMER RELATIONS, may take place at multiple locations and be different at each location. An activity, like PREPARE PUR-CHASE ORDER, is the same at each location where it occurs. If it is different it should be referred to with a different activity name. An activity, then, uses the same procedures, procedure maps, and events at different locations.

It also uses the same normalized records. One event employs one normalized record. This record is part of an entity cluster or grouping of records which reside together. A procedure employs one entity cluster which is usually not split geographically. Thus,

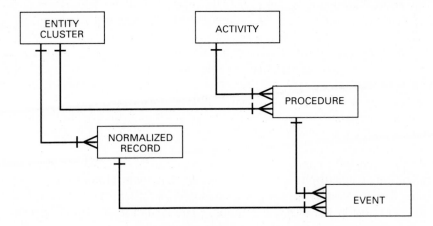

Designs that minimize traffic between programs and the data they use tend to lead to centralization. Designs that minimize traffic between user locations and data locations tend to lead to distribution.

SUBJECTIVE FACTORS

Quantitative analysis and clustering is useful with some systems. Often, however, subjective factors are more important than quantitative factors in deciding how data or systems should be distributed.

FACTOR TABLES

Multiple factors are involved in the decision whether to centralize or distribute the application programs for a process. A design technique first used at the Sloan School, M.I.T. [2], employs a table for each process listing the pros and cons. The arguments for centralized or decentralized *development* are different from those for *operations* and those for *management*. The columns of Fig. 16.7 relate to different aspects of these. The rows of Fig. 16.7 relate to factors to consider in the choice of centralization and decentralization.

For any process there are likely to be conflicting factors. The *factor table* gives the capability to see these at a glance.

Different organizations may choose the factors which they think are relevant in different ways. Figures 16.8 and 16.9 show two examples.

Figure 16.9 is for a bank with many branches. The factor table relates to the decision on how to automate the handling of customer checking accounts. The letters in red indicate the factors which were considered to be dominant. One of the most important was that a customer should be able to walk into a branch in any location and obtain the service he requires. This factor is a strong argument for a centralized database with information about the customer's account. The importance of control and auditability was also an argument for centralization, though a lesser one. The other factors in Fig. 16.9 argue for decentralized data and decentralized processing. Particularly important were the need for high availability and high protection from catastrophes such as fire or bombs. Making the system available at all times argues for storage at user locations, avoiding the dependence on telephone lines, but with telephone line backup to a central system in case of a local failure. Catastrophe protection argues for *not* having *one* centralized facility.

High accuracy needed on input argues for peripheral input editing and checking. The large network with fast responses argues for peripheral intelligence for data communications.

In practice the bank designed a system with mixed centralization and decentralization. Catastrophe protection argued that there should be two centers, not one. Transaction processing was handled peripherally, but could also be handled centrally in the event of a failure. The design team would have liked to

KEY
C: Strong Reason for Centralization
c: Weak Reason for Centralization
D: Strong Reason for Decentralization
d: Weak Reason for Decentralization
DC: Cooperation Between Central & Local Groups

	System Development				System Operations						
	Application Selection	Application Development	Design of Data	Hardware/Software Selection	Input & Editing	Processing	Function Distribution	File	Database	Management Control	Strategic Planning
Needs data which are stored centrally.			DC					C	C		
Most data can be stored locally.				d	D	D		D			
Needs database (as opposed to file) management.			DC						C		
Data are integrated with those of other locations.			DC						C	DC	C
Generates data needed by central management.			DC							DC	C
Application is simple.	d	d			d	d	d			d	
Application requires much computer expertise.	C		c								
Application requires much local knowledge.	D		d	d							
Application rarely changes.	c	c									
Application changes frequently due to local factors.	D	D	D								
Application changes frequently due to nonlocal factors.	C	C	C				C				
Application is unique to one location.	D	D	D	D							
Application is replicated in many locations.	C	C	C	C							
Application affects central corporate management.	c	DC	DC							c	C
Local subunits are highly similar.	c	c	c								
Local subunits are diverse in structure.	d	d	d	d							
Application location is a long distance from DP center.		d	d	d	d	d	d	d		d	c
Application location is in a different country from DP center.	D	D	D	D	D	D	D	D	D	D	
Fast response time is important.					D	D	D	D			
High availability is important.				d	D	D	D	D			
There is a large application backlog.	D	d	d		d	d		d			
Application is already implemented centrally.	C					C		C	C		
Application is entrepreneurial in nature.	D	D	D	d	d	d	d			d	
Application is highly sensitive and critical for the subunit.	D	D	D	D	D	D		D			
High subunit management involvement.	D	D	D	D							
Need to make subunit management responsible for the application.	D	D	D	D	D	D		D		D	
Application security is vital to the entire corporation.							C	C	C		
Large memory or large CPU facilities needed intermittently.							C	C	C		
Local staff skilled and intelligent in general.	d	d	d							d	
Local staff skilled with computers.	D	D	D	D	d	d				d	
Local staff unskilled.	C	C	C	C						C	c
Central group reliable and responsive.	C	C	C	c							
Central group overworked or unresponsive.	D	D	D	d							

Figure 16.7 A factor table for distribution design. [2].

	System Development				System Operations					Management Control	Strategic Planning
	Application Selection	Application Development	Design of Data	Hardware/Software Selection	Input & Editing	Processing	Function Distribution	File	Database		
Customer account data may be needed by any branch.								C	c	c	c
Application identical at many bank branches.	c	C	C	C							
Branches are highly similar.	c	C	C	C							
Application does not require much local knowledge.	c	c	c	c							
Application rarely changes.											
Some branches are far apart.							D				
Fairly quick response time needed.					d	d	d	d			
System should be available at all times.					D	D	d	D			
Offline terminal operations are desirable.					d	d	d				
Many operators must be trained using the terminal.					d	d	d				
Auditability is very important.		c	c				c		c	c	
High catastrophe protection is vital.							D		D	d	
High accuracy is needed (input validation).					D	d					c
Local groups have no DP skills.	c	c	c	c							c
Central DP group is reliable and responsive.	c	c	c	c							

Figure 16.8 A factor table applied to customer transactions in a bank with many branches. The items marked in red were considered dominant in the choice.

have stored enough information about *every* customer to handle his or her essential requirements at any branch. The storage at the peripheral machines was not large enough, so the team stored critical information about every customer in a geographical region at each branch of that region. When a customer strays into a branch outside his region he has to be served by the central system. When in his own region, his inquiries can be handled when the central system is inaccessible. Also a small number of inquiries are from foreign regions.

The factors in Fig. 16.8 all argued for application development by the central IS (information system) group, and this was done.

Figure 16.9 shows a factor table used in another organization for the development of a customer credit scoring system [2]. The factors considered to be dominant are shown in the table in *red:*

- Critical application for the user groups requesting it
- Integration with other files and application groups
- Large memory required intermittently
- Reliable and responsive control IS group

The first of these factors was a reason for decentralization because of the investment the subunits had in the success of the system. The other three were reasons for centralization. The application relied heavily on an existing customer database and involved a complex scoring algorithm. It would have been expensive to duplicate the database in decentralized minicomputers.

A centralized system was eventually used, with centralized development. The dominant reason was the excellent reputation of the central IS group. The subunits had confidence that their previous experience with this group would hold true again.

Where user groups have succeeded in wrenching control away from a central IS group, the dominant factor has sometimes been IS unresponsiveness, poor service, congested scheduling or time, or low availability of the central facilities.

	SYSTEMS DEVELOPMENT	SYSTEMS OPERATIONS
APPLICATION GROUP		
Critical application for subunit	d	D
Operation control application needing high availability		d
High degree of DP expertise required	c	
Sophisticated processing	c	
Adaptability to rapid change is needed	d	
Integration with other files and application groups	C	C
Large memory required, intermittently		C
SUBUNIT		
Specialized task		d
Rapid change environment		d
Good management talent available	d	
Resident DP expertise in subunit	d	d
ENVIRONMENT		
Organization currently centralized	c	c
DP currently centralized	c	c
DP group are reliable and responsive	C	C

Figure 16.9 Factor table for a consumer credit scoring application [2]. The items in red were considered dominant.

The system configuration that is finally chosen often depends not on one process, but many. The decision may be made with a set of factor tables like Figs. 16.8 or 16.9. In some cases the set of tables indicates that certain processes ought to be run on separate computers, sometimes network-connected computers and sometimes stand-alone machines. The banking system of Fig. 16.8, for example, chose to run several applications, such as the processing of traveler's checks on small free-standing computers.

Often, as we have stressed, a dominant reason for distribution is that user groups should have their own computer with which they can file and manipulate their own data, generate reports, explore "what-if" questions, or build their own decision-support facility with fourth-generation languages. The reasons which make this the best approach are predominantly human ones which are nonquantifiable.

PROCEDURE FOR DISTRIBUTION DESIGN

The designer examining how programs and data should be distributed may proceed in the following steps:

```
...Determine the procedures and data involved in the design
...Determine the locations involved in the design
...Cluster the procedures into procedure-groups
...Cluster the entity-types into data-structures
...Generate a matrix mapping procedure-groups and data-structures.
  Fill in the data-structure/location matrix
    ...Examine the arguments for multiple distributed copies of data
    For each data-structure
      Decide whether multiple copies of the same data structure can exist.
        ...Determine whether updates can be delayed and batched

      Mark the possible locations of the data structure on the location/
        data-structure matrix.
    ...Create a factor table for distribution of programs
    ...Create a factor table for distribution of data
    Categorize the data according to type of distribution:
    ...Enter codes into the matrix for type of data distribution.
    Categorize the data according to whether multiple copies must
      have synchronous (up-to-the-second) updates or whether updates
      can be deferred (for example, made at night)
    ...Enter codes into the matrix for this.
```

He groups the data into data structures which will remain together throughout the distribution. He groups the procedures into procedure groups which will remain together. He generates (automatically from the encyclopedia, given the right tools) a matrix of procedure groups and data structures. He checks the validity of the CREATE, READ, UPDATE, and DELETE codes in this matrix.

He generates (automatically) a matrix mapping procedures against the locations at which the work of that procedure is done. The data for each procedure might reside at the location of the procedure, and that may be the starting point for developing a matrix mapping data structures against locations. He examines the arguments for having one copy of a data structure versus multiple distributed copies. For each data structure he decides whether multiple copies can exist and marks the possible locations of the copies on the matrix. Particularly important is the question of whether the updates to distributed copies of data will be up-to-the-second or whether they can be deferred and batched (or whether a new copy of the data structure will be extracted periodically from a central system).

The designer should examine and edit a list of arguments for centralization versus decentralization of programs and centralization versus decentralization of data. In factor tables he should mark the arguments which are most significant. Out of a mass of arguments certain ones emerge as being the critical ones which determine that data should be distributed or otherwise. The type of distribution is marked on the matrix, and also whether the updated or distributed copies can be deferred:

```
      Categorize the data according to type of distribution:
    ┌ Enter codes into the matrix for type of data distribution.
    │ ...Categories of data distribution
    │
    │     Codes for indicating types of data distribution:
    │     ***********************************************
    │     M:   Mastercopy
    │     V:   Variant (different-schema version at different locations)
    │     D:   Duplicated data (identical data at different locations)
    │     S:   Subset (an extracted subset of a larger database)
    │     R:   Reorganized data
    │               (e.g., reorganized into a decision-support database)
    │     P:   Partitioned data (same schema, different values)
    │     I:   Incompatible data
    └     T:   Teleprocessing access to data not stored at this location

      Categorize the data according to whether multiple copies must
        have synchronous (up-to-the-second) updates or whether updates
        can be deferred (for example, made at night)
    ┌ Enter codes into the matrix for this.
    │
    │     Codes for indicating synchronous or deferred updates:
    │     ********************************************************
    │     DD:  Duplicated data with deferred updates
    │     SD:  Subset data with deferred updates
    │     RD:  Reorganized data with deferred updates
    │     DS:  Duplicated data with synchronous updates
    │     SS:  Subset with synchronous updates
    └     RS:  Reorganized data with synchronous updates
```

Many designs for distribution suffer from the design team having failed to consider all the pros and cons for different types of distribution. Using factor tables in this way helps to encourage a thorough examination of the alternatives.

Box 16.5 shows the procedure in more detail.

BOX 16.5   Distributed data design

> The procedure given below may be modified with Action
> Diagrammer to meet the needs of the particular situation.

The steps listed below assume that when the higher levels of analysis
where done the locations of functions, processes and procedures
where recorded in the encyclopedia.

A good distribution design arranges data and programs into clusters
such that each cluster has a high level of autonomy and there is a
low level of interdependence between clusters.

```
Determine the procedures and data involved in the design
    Extract the procedures and entity-types from the encyclopedia.
    Generate a matrix mapping procedures and entity-types.
    Validate the matrix to ensure that it is correct and complete.

Determine the locations involved in the design
    Extract from the encyclopedia the locations where the work
        associated with each procedure is carried out.
    Generate a matrix mapping procedures and locations.
    Validate the matrix to ensure that no locations are missing.

Cluster the procedures into procedure-groups
    Cluster the procedures into groups which are likely to be carried
        out at the same location.
        (We will refer to these as procedure-groups.)
        Use the procedure/location matrix for this.
    Generate (automatically) a matrix showing procedure-groups and
        locations.
        The matrix with the locations where the procedure-group is
        physically performed.
    Mark the matrix with the locations where the procedure PROGRAM
        may be executed.

Cluster the entity-types into data-structures
    Cluster the entity-types into entity-relationship structures
        containing entities which are likely to reside at the same location.
        (We will refer to these as data-structures.)
        Use the entity/location matrix for this.
    Generate a matrix showing data-structures and locations
        (unfilled at this point).

Generate a matrix mapping procedure-groups and data-structures.
    This matrix shows which data structures are accessed by each
        procedure-group.
    Use this matrix to validate the clustering of entities into data-
        structures and procedures into procedure-groups.
    Mark the matrix with data accesses
        Use CREATE, READ, UPDATE, and DELETE codes at the matrix intersections.
```

BOX 16.5 *(Continued)*

Fill in the data-structure/location matrix.
Examine the arguments for multiple distributed copies of data.

For each data-structure
Decide whether multiple copies of the same data structure can exist.
Determine whether updates can be delayed and batched.
Determine whether the data in the data structure must be kept up
to date to the second or whether updates can be delayed and
batched.
(If updates can be delayed and batched this makes it much
easier to have multiple replicated copies of the data.)

Mark the possible locations of the data structure on the location/
data-structure matrix.
Create a factor table for distribution of programs.
List the reasons for centralizing data or decentralizing data.
Add to or edit the following list of reasons:
The data should be where the program resides.
Identical procedures used at many locations.
High availability is important.
The software cannot maintain multiple synchronous copies.
The data are used at one location only.
The data are updated by one location only.
Local users create and own the data.
Local management is responsible for the data.
Local inventiveness in the use of the data.
Data are highly sensitive to the subunit.
There can be multiple copies of the data.
Data transmission is expensive or undesirable.
Very fast response time is needed.
A departmental decision-support system is used.
Data are used by centralized applications.
Users in distant areas need the current
up-to-the-second version of the data.
Users who travel among many locations need an
up-to-the-second version of the data.
Large searches or joins are required.
Data security is vital.
Auditability is a major concern.
Application is maintained centrally.
The power of a large computer is needed.
The database is very large.
Catastrophe protection is vital.
The data are updated by multiple people in a department.
There should be one single copy of the data.

List the strength of the reason applied to centralized computing,
departmental computing, or personal computing:

```
                                Programs should execute on:
                                ***************************
                                                 Remote computer
                              Local (shared) computer    |
                           Personal computer(s)      |   |
                                               |     |   |
Reason:                                        |     |   |
*******                                      __|___|___|___|__

Identical procedures used at many locations:   |   |   |   |
High availability is important:                |   |   |   |
  Etc...                                        |   |   |   |
```

BOX 16.5 *(Continued)*

```
Create a factor table for distribution of data.
   List the reasons for centralizing data or decentralizing data.
      Add to or edit the following list of reasons:
          The data should be where the program resides.
          Identical procedures used at many locations.
          High availability is important.
          The software cannot maintain multiple synchronous copies.
          The data are used at one location only.
          The data are updated by one location only.
          Local users create and own the data.
          Local management is responsible for the data.
          Local inventiveness in the use of the data.
          Data are highly sensitive to the subunit.
          There can be multiple copies of the data.
          Data transmission is expensive or undesirable.
          Very fast response time is needed.
          A departmental decision-support system is used.
          Data are used by centralized applications.
          Users in distant areas need the current
                up-to-the-second version of the data.
          Users who travel among many locations need an
                up-to-the-second version of the data.
          Large searches or joins are required.
          Data security is vital.
          Auditability is a major concern.
          Application is maintained centrally.
          The power of a large computer is needed.
          The database is very large.
          Catastrophe protection is vital.
          The data are updated by multiple people in a department.
          There should be one single copy of the data.


Create a factor table for distribution of data.
...List the reasons for centralizing data or decentralizing data.
   List the strength of the reason applied to centralized data,
       departmental data, or data on a personal computer:

                        Data structure should reside on:
                        *********************************
                                              Central computer
                                    Local (shared) computer
                              Personal computer(s)
        Reason:
        *******

        The data should be where the program resides:
        Identical procedures used at many locations:
        High availability is important:
        The data are used at one location only:              XXXXX
        The data are updated by one location only:           XXXXX
        Local users create and own the data:                 XXXXX
        Local management is responsible for the data:        XXXXX
        Local inventiveness in the use of the data:          XXXXX
        Data are highly sensitive to the subunit:            XXXXX
        There can be multiple copies of the data:            XXXXX
        Data transmission is expensive or undesirable:       XXXXX
        Very fast response time is needed:                   XXXXX
        A departmental decision-support system is used       XXXXX
```

BOX 16.5 *(Continued)*

```
      Data are used by centralized applications:   XXXXX XXXXX
      Users in distant areas need the current
            up-to-the-second version of the data:  XXXXX XXXXX
      Users who travel among many locations need an
            up-to-the-second version of the data:  XXXXX XXXXX
      Large searches or joins are required:        XXXXX XXXXX
      Data security is vital:                      XXXXX XXXXX
      Auditability is a major concern:             XXXXX XXXXX
      Application is maintained centrally:         XXXXX XXXXX
      The power of a large computer is needed:     XXXXX XXXXX
      The database is very large:                  XXXXX XXXXX
      Catastrophe protection is vital:             XXXXX XXXXX
      The data are updated by multiple people in a
            department:                            XXXXX
      There should be one single copy of the data: XXXXX

      Sum the weights in each category.
      Decide which of the above reasons should dominate the decision
        about where the data is placed.
 Categorize the data according to type of distribution:
 Enter codes into the matrix for type of data distribution.
    Categories of data distribution
        (See chapter text)
      Duplicated data

      Subset data

      Reorganized data

      Partitioned data

      Separate-schema data

      Incompatible data



      Codes for indicating types of data distribution:
      ***********************************************
      M:  Mastercopy
      V:  Variant (different-schema version at different locations)
      D:  Duplicated data (identical data at different locations)
      S:  Subset (an extracted subset of a larger database)
      R:  Reorganized data
             (e.g., reorganized into a decision-support database)
      P:  Partitioned data (same schema, different values)
      I:  Incompatible data
      T:  Teleprocessing access to data not stored at this location
 Categorize the data according to whether multiple copies must
    have synchronous (up-to-the-second) updates or whether updates
    can be deferred (for example, made at night).
 Enter codes into the matrix for this.

      Codes for indicating synchronous or deferred updates:
      *****************************************************
      DD:  Duplicated data with deferred updates
```

BOX 16.5   *(Continued)*

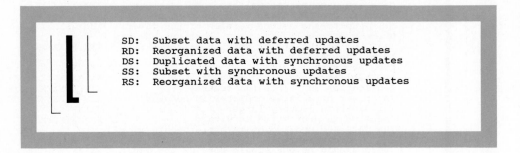

SD:	Subset data with deferred updates
RD:	Reorganized data with deferred updates
DS:	Duplicated data with synchronous updates
SS:	Subset with synchronous updates
RS:	Reorganized data with synchronous updates

REFERENCES

1. James Martin, *Privacy, Accuracy, and Security in Computer Systems* (Englewood Cliffs, N.J.; Prentice-Hall, 1974).

2. J. F. Rockart, C. V. Bullen, and J. L. Levantor, *Centralization v. Decentralization of Information Systems: A Preliminary Model for Decision Making* (Cambridge, MA: Center for Information Systems Research, Sloan School, M.I.T.).

17 PLANNING FOR CUTOVER

In an information engineering environment the construction phase may occur in a much shorter time than in a noninformation engineering environment because of the use of a code generator and reusable modules. In most systems in the past, construction has taken a long time and has been the main cause of delay in putting a new system to work. However, in some installations skilled in automated design and code generation, the software is now constructed quickly, and cutover phase has been the main cause of delay. It takes time to train the users, modify their procedures, and make the system operate smoothly. Because of this, preparation for cutover needs to be done in parallel with the construction phase and needs to be well planned so that it does not delay the cutover.

With this exception, cutover in an information engineering environment is essentially the same as in a noninformation-engineering environment.

This chapter and the next describe four phases of cutover:

- Prepare for cultural changes.
- Design for cutover.
- Prepare for cutover.
- Perform cutover.

New systems can cause severe cultural changes in an organization. A major reorganization may be desirable in order to take maximum advantage of the new system. Jobs may be displaced, or new types of talent may be necessary. The staffing levels often need to change. There may be changes in business policies as well as procedures. It is desirable to ask: Where is the optimum place that each business decision should be made, given flexible databases, a ubiquitous network, and much computing power on any individual's desk?

These cultural factors need to be addressed as early as possible in the development lifecycle. It may take substantial time to accomplish the necessary changes, and if not addressed well they could cause the system to fail. Where possible they should be addressed in the BAA (business area analysis) phase. They should be examined carefully when a specific system is being planned.

Design for cutover should be done when the system is being designed, and the design workbench should be employed. Preparation for cutover should begin as soon as the construction phase begins, so that the actual cutover can be performed smoothly as soon as the system has been tested.

PREPARE FOR CULTURAL CHANGES

Preparation for cultural changes can be broken into the following activities:

- Identify any cultural changes.
- Design the organizational changes.
- Identify responsibilities for organizational changes.
- Schedule the organizational changes.

Box 17.1 shows these activities in more detail.
Cultural changes include the following:

- Changes in organizational structure
- Changes in policies
- Changes in business procedures
- Changes in staffing levels
- Changes in job content
- Changes in skill requirements

The first step of planning for cultural changes should be to list all changes of the foregoing types which the new system may bring about. The organizational units which are affected should be listed. Some organizational units may be affected in a minor way. In others the change may be drastic—a department might be eliminated for example. It is desirable to make those changes which maximize the benefits from the new system. The list of such changes should be reviewed with top management.

In some cases new organizational units or new job positions are created. A mission statement should be written for the new units and a job description written for the new jobs. These should be reviewed with high-level end-user management. It is often the case that some end-user managers are opposed to the desirable changes. The benefits from the changes must be understood by a level of management high enough to affect the changes.

BOX 17.1　**Preparing for Cultural Changes.**

Prepare for cultural changes.
　　Identify any cultural changes.
　　　　List the following types of cultural changes which the new system
　　　　might bring about:
　　　　o　Changes in organizational structure
　　　　o　Changes in policies
　　　　o　Changes in business procedures
　　　　o　Changes in staffing levels
　　　　o　Changes in job content
　　　　o　Changes in skill requirements

　　　　Review this list with top management.

　　Design the organizational changes.
　　　　Determine what change in existing organizational units is necessary
　　　　　to gain optimal benefits from the new system.
　　　　Determine organizational units that will no longer be needed.
　　　　Determine organizational units whose functions will change.
　　　　Design an organizational structure that provides the appropriate
　　　　　skills and appropriate numbers of people at the required locations.
　　　　Create a mission statement for any new or changed organizational
　　　　　units.
　　　　Where required, create new position descriptions or revise existing
　　　　　ones.
　　　　Review the user dislocation and organizational disruption with top
　　　　　management.

　　Identify responsibilities for organizational changes.
　　　　Ensure that top management understand the cultural changes implied
　　　　　by the system.
　　　　Identify which high-level end-user management should be responsible
　　　　　for preparing for the cultural changes.
　　　　Determine whether human resource specialists or organizational
　　　　　design specialists are needed to assist in making the changes.
　　　　Determine the role of the information systems staff in making
　　　　　the changes.

　　Schedule the organizational changes.
　　　　Create a plan for an orderly transition to the new organization.
　　　　List the actions required to accomplish this transition.
　　　　Determine the individual responsible for each item on the list.
　　　　List what resources must be acquired, replaced, or eliminated.
　　　　Chart the sequence and timing of the necessary actions.
　　　　Mesh the transition schedule with the development and cutover
　　　　　schedule.
　　　　Obtain approval and sign-offs from appropriate levels of manage-
　　　　　ment for the transition schedule. (It is vital to obtain these
　　　　　sign-offs early enough, otherwise timely cutover to the new system
　　　　　could be jeopardized).

It is necessary at an early stage to assign the responsibility for bringing about the organizational changes. It should be decided whether any specialized help is needed from human resource consultants or specialists in organizational change. The role of the information systems staff in bringing about the changes should be clarified.

A plan should be created for an orderly transition to the new organization. The actions required to accomplish the transition should be listed, along with the individual who is responsible for each one. The necessary resources should be listed. The sequence and timing of the actions should be charted. This set of actions should be meshed with overall development and cutover schedule.

Approval should be obtained from the managers who are affected by the changes. It is necessary to obtain sign-offs on these approvals early in the development cycle; otherwise, a timely cutover might be jeopardized.

DESIGN FOR CUTOVER

Design for cutover can be broken into the following activities:

- Establish the implementation standards.
- Design the conversion procedure.
- Design the production procedures.
- Plan the hardware installation.
- Determine the testing strategy.
- Plan the testing environment.
- Create the technical documentation.
- Create the user documentation.
- Create the training program.

Box 17.2 shows these activities in more detail.

Most organizations have standards which they use when planning the implementation of a system. There are installation standards, standards for setting up code libraries, job control and documentation libraries, testing procedures, documentation standards, and so on. The standards may need to be changed when new software approaches are introduced. Naming conventions and dictionary use may be changed when a code generator comes into use. Standards may be changed to take better advantage of IBM's SAA (Systems Application Architecture) and the facilities associated with it. When the system is being planned the standards for implementation should be reviewed and adjusted if necessary.

An important part of planning for cutover is the creation of end-user documentation. Documentation used to consist of paperwork manuals. Today it is desirable to avoid paperwork manuals where possible and put user documenta-

BOX 17.2　Design for Cutover

Design for cutover.
- Establish the implementation standards.
  - Review existing implementation standards and determine whether any modifications are needed.
  - Determine what software-related standards are to be used, for example IBM's SAA, built-in HELP functions, or documentation produced by an application generator.
  - Establish the HELP interfaces and conventions.
  - Establish library standards for migration controls.

- Design the conversion procedures.
  - Design bridges to/from application packages and reusable modules.
    - Design interfaces to application packages, if necessary.
    - Design interfaces to reusable systems from other locations, if necessary.
    - Design interfaces to old systems which will remain in existence.
    - Design tests to ensure that these bridge facilities work correctly.

  - Plan for conversion.
    - Determine the sequence of steps required for conversion.
    - Define the sequence of steps that will be used to load the database and verify that it is correct.
    - Review the conversion procedure with end-user management.
    - Determine the resources required for conversion.
    - Determine when these resources will be required.
    - Assign individuals to steps for which end users are responsible.
    - Document the conversion sequence and responsibilities.
    - Develop a schedule for the cutover to the new system in production mode.

  - Examine each data element.
    - For each data element in the new system determine the source in the existing system, if any.
    - Divide the data elements into those which can be obtained automatically and those which require manual work.
    - Design the steps necessary to convert current data into the future format.
    - Review the data conversion steps with user management, and revise the conversion steps, if necessary.

  - Design the manual data conversion procedures.
    - Collect samples of the documents that will be used for manual data entry.
    - Determine how the manually entered data will be checked for accuracy and completeness.
    - Design the software to load manually prepared data into the new system.
    - Prototype the screens for manual entry of new data and review the prototypes with the end users who will employ them.
    - Carry out dry runs of the manual data entry and review the results.
    - Estimate how long manual data entry will take.

  - Design the automated data conversion procedures.
    - Design the software for automated data conversion.
    - Create the software for data conversion quickly with an automated tool, and test it.
    - Design conversion procedures for unrecoverable data errors and missing data. Determine how such situations will be handled.
    - Determine how automatically converted data will be checked for accuracy and completeness (e.g., batch balancing of control totals)
    - Estimate the resources needed for the data conversion task.

(Continued)

BOX 17.2 *(Continued)*

Design the conversion tests.
 Design the sequence of tests and acceptance criteria that will be
 used to verify a successful conversion.
 Review the acceptance test criteria with end-user management.
 Modify the procedures for data conversion, if necessary, to meet
 the test requirements.
 Document the acceptance test criteria.

Design the production procedures.
 Design the procedures for normal system operation.
 Design any manual or paperwork procedures that must accompany
 the new installation.
 Design the procedures for restart and recovery.
 Design the fallback procedures.
 Design the procedures for security.
 Design the audit procedures.

Plan the hardware installation.
 Determine whether the hardware will be phased in a stage at a time,
 e.g., one location at a time. If so, plan the staged installation
 of the hardware.
 Coordinate with vendors to arrange for the installation to meet
 the project schedule.

Determine the testing strategy.
 Develop the detailed test plan.
 For each type of activity
 Create detailed test script.
 List the groups of test cases and their sequence.
 For each group
 List the transaction types.
 List the characteristics of each test case.

 Review the testing plan with user management.
 Refine the test scripts as needed.

Determine what types of tests are needed for the system.
 Program test
 For each transaction type in the above list
 Plan how to test that the program handles the transaction
 in all cases without crashing.

 Integration test
 Plan the integration tests needed to verify that the system
 accepts input from and provides output to other systems with
 which it interfaces.
 Plan how to test that the systems work together fully.

 Volume test
 Plan how large volumes of transactions are to be tested
 (simulation or actual data tests).

BOX 17.2 *(Continued)*

Regression test for maintenance changes
    Plan the procedures for verifying that the system still works
    as maintenance changes are made.

Acceptance test
    Plan how verification will be obtained from end users that the
    system is acceptable for production.

Sequence the testing stages.
    If the system is to be phased in one subsystem at a time, plan
    the test sequences reflect this.
    Ensure that systems which produce data for other systems are
    tested first.
    Verify that the construction sequence matches the testing
    sequence so that modules will be ready when needed.

Plan the testing environment.
    Determine what software will be used for testing.
        If a test generator is to be used
            Select the test generator
                (e.g., the CA-DATAMACS Test Data Generator).
        Else
            Determine how test data will be generated.

        Determine whether testing tools not already available need
            to be purchased.
        If custom software is needed for testing
            Design testing software.
            Determine the schedule for building testing software.
            Build testing software.

    Determine what testing libraries are needed for programs
        (source and object) and for data (execution/job control).
    Establish the testing library conventions.

Create the technical documentation.
    Create documentation for ease of maintenance.
    Documentation for maintenance should be in the encyclopedia.
    Comments may be added to the diagrams in the encyclopedia.
    Preferably a code generator should be used which automatically
        prints a workbook with complete technical documentation.
    Where possible code changes should be made by REGENERATING,
        rather than modifying low-level code.

Create the user documentation.
    Determine what user documentation should be on the system, and what
        should be external paper documentation. (Minimize the external
        documentation.)
    Design the on-line documentation.
        o   HELP screens.
        o   Literature.
        o   Computer-based training.
    Test the on-line HELP and teaching aids with end users to ensure
        that it works well, with a usability-lab environment employing
        a low-cost video camera to record the users' reactions for later
        study.
    Design the paper documentation.
        o   Literature
        o   A "Getting Started" manual
    Review the documentation with end users.

(Continued)

BOX 17.2   *(Continued)*

Create the training program.
  Determine the training objectives and audience.
      Identify the skills and methods that will change.
      Determine the objectives of the training.
      Determine who needs to be trained.
      Review the above with end-user management.

  Outline the curriculum.
      Develop a subject matter outline.
      Determine who will conduct the training.
      Determine the techniques that will be used for training.
        Lectures with slides.
        Classroom training with overhead projector foils.
        Personal assistance in the user's department.
        Use of prototypes.
        Use of extended HELP screens.
        Computer-based training.
        Videotape.

      Determine what training sessions will be needed.

  Plan the development of training materials.
      Determine what training materials will be used:
          o Slides
          o Foils
          o Course materials
          o HELP screens
          o Prototypes of the software
          o Computer-based training
          o Video training
      Determine which of these already exist.
      Determine whether purchased training courses can be used (for
        example, for training users to use SQL or windows).
      Determine whether prototypes will be used for training purposes
        before the final system is available. (When a code generator is
        used the system may be built quickly so that training has to
        proceed in parallel with development.)
      Determine what HELP screens are needed for training.
      Allocate responsibility for making the prototypes and HELP
        screens good enough.
      Allocate responsibility for making the training materials.

  Develop the training schedule.
      Determine the schedule for developing training materials.
      Determine the schedule for training the trainers.
      Determine the schedule for delivering training.
      Mesh the training sequence with the development sequence.

  Produce the training materials.
      Test the prototypes that will be used for training.
      Design, write, and implement the HELP screens.
      Design the structure of lectures or courses.
      Design the projection foils and other materials.
      Review the training materials with users.
      Adjust the training materials based on user feedback.
      Package the training materials with an overall training curriculum
        and plan.
      If necessary, develop an instructor's guide.

tion into the product itself, accessible on the user workstation. Users, like computer professionals, usually do not read the paper documentation.

Standards, if they do not already exist, should be established for online documentation. IBM's Common User Access provides software and guidelines for creating multiple levels of HELP screens which can guide the end user and replace much paperwork. Standards should be adopted for the building of HELP screens, and it is necessary to decide early in the implementation cycle who builds them.

CONVERSION PROCEDURES

A major part of the planning for cutover is the design of the conversion procedures. The sequence of steps should be determined that are necessary for conversion. Some may be concerned with conversion from manual procedures, others with conversion of computer systems. Particularly important are the steps needed to convert or capture the data, load the database, and verify that it is correct.

When the steps necessary for conversion have been listed, they should be reviewed with end-user management and refined as necessary. The resources required for conversion should be determined and a plan drawn up for obtaining the resources at the appropriate time. Individuals should be assigned to steps for which end users are responsible.

The sequence of steps necessary for conversion should be charted and meshed with the overall development schedule.

The design of the data conversion procedures should begin by examining the data structures used in the new system. Every data element should be examined and a determination made of whether it will be entered manually or obtained automatically from an existing system. Both the manual data-entry procedures and automatic conversion procedures need to be designed. Before designing them in detail the list of data elements and their proposed conversion procedures should be reviewed with appropriate end users to determine whether anything has been overlooked.

To design the manual procedures, the documents which contain the data should be examined. Data-entry screens must be built for the manual entry. These screens, created quickly with a screen painter, should be prototyped with the end users who will do the data entry. Dry runs of the manual data entry should be done to ensure that it will go well when cutover occurs, and an estimate should be made of how long it will take.

The software for automated data conversion should be designed, built quickly with an automated tool, and tested to ensure that it works well. There should be a determination of how data errors and missing data will be dealt with.

It should be decided how both the manual and automatic data conversion will be checked for accuracy. Batch runs for balancing control totals may be used, along with other means for checking accuracy. The sequence of tests and acceptance criteria that will be used to verify a successful conversion should be designed, and reviewed with end-user management. End users sometimes have much subtle knowledge about sources of errors, and how to avoid errors, in data. The procedures for data conversion may be modified to meet the test criteria. The test criteria should be documented.

PRODUCTION PROCEDURES

The procedures for operation of the system need to be designed. These include computer center operations, end-user computer operations, and the manual and paperwork procedures that must accompany the new system. The procedures should be planned and reviewed with end-user management at an early stage in the development lifecycle. Substantial preparation may have to be done by user departments, and this may delay cutover when a high-speed lifecycle is used if it is not planned well in advance.

As well as planning for normal system operation, it is vital to plan what will be done when things go wrong. Fallback procedures must be designed describing how to function when the system fails. Procedures must be designed for restart and recovery. These procedures need to be reviewed with end-user management.

Security procedures should be carefully thought out, along with how the system will be audited. If the system is sensitive from the security point of view, a decision should be made whether to employ a security specialist.

The installation of the hardware needs to be planned. It should be decided whether the hardware will be phased in a stage at a time, for example, one location at a time. If so, a staged installation plan should be designed. Vendors should be contacted to arrange for the installation to meet the project schedule.

PLANNING FOR TESTING

A thorough plan must be drawn up for how the system will be tested. For each type of activity, a detailed test plan should be created.

All the cases that need testing should be listed, and a detailed test script created. The tests may be performed in groups. For each group the transaction types should be listed, and the characteristics of each test case. This testing plan should be reviewed with end-user management to ensure that nothing has been forgotten.

The following types of tests need to be planned:

- **Transaction test.** For each transaction type, plan how to test that the program handles the transaction correctly in all cases.

- **Integration test.** Plan the integration tests needed to verify that the system accepts input from and provides output to other systems with which it interfaces. Plan how to test that the systems work together fully.

- **Volume test.** Plan how large volumes of transactions are to be tested (simulation or actual data tests).

- **Regression test for maintenance changes.** Plan the procedures for verifying that the system still works as maintenance changes are made.

- **Acceptance test.** Plan how verification will be obtained from end users that the system is acceptable for production.

The sequence of testing should be planned. If the system is to be phased in one subsystem at a time, the test sequence should reflect this. Ensure that systems which produce data for other systems are tested first. The construction sequence and the testing sequence should be meshed.

A test generator should be used to generate the test cases (for example, the DATAMACS test data generator from Computer Associates). Where such a product cannot generate the test cases completely, it should be planned how the test data will be created.

There may be other types of software needed for testing. It should be determined whether testing tools not already available need to be purchased. Some custom software may be needed for testing. If so, this should be determined and the software designed and built in plenty of time.

The libraries necessary for testing need to be planned—libraries of source code and object code, job control code, and data. The library software and conventions need to be planned if they are not already an installation standard.

DOCUMENTATION

Documentation is necessary both for cutover and for subsequent operation and maintenance. Two categories of documentation are needed: technical documentation and documentation for end users. Both of these have changed since the traditional development lifecycle was used.

Technical documentation should reside in the encyclopedia. Much of it is now formal and computable and is created as part of the analysis and design process. A code generator should be used which automatically generates complete technical documentation in the form of a development workbook. Comments, which are intended for humans rather than computers, are added to the formal models and design representations and appear in the printed workbook. A major purpose of the comments is to help the maintenance task. Building this type of documentation as analysis and design are being done is part of good management practice in an information engineering environment.

User documentation has changed with modern tools because, as far as possible, it should be online. There should be little or no external paperwork documentation. Most users do not read the user manuals. They need help at the screen when they get into trouble.

IBM's SAA defines six categories of HELP that can be created for each application:

- **HELP.** This provides help about the field the cursor is positioned on.
- **Extended HELP.** This tells users about the task they are performing in the application panel.
- **Keys HELP.** This produces a list of each key this application uses and its function.
- **HELP index.** This produces an alphabetical index of all the HELP information for the application.
- **HELP contents.** This produces a table of contents of HELP information, organized by topic.
- **Tutorial HELP.** This provides access to a tutorial related to the panel that the user is working on.

To employ these six levels of help, HELP menus and text need to be written. The type of skill needed to write these well is different from the skill of the average programmer. It needs a sense of literacy and teaching skills. The time needed must be estimated, and the person to do it assigned. The HELP screens should be tested with end users, and adjusted to make them as effective as possible. It is often a good idea to set up a usability laboratory in which the reactions of users can be videotaped for later study, with an inexpensive camera.

The design of user documentation should include the following steps:

- Determine what user documentation should be on the system and what should be external paper documentation. (Minimize the external documentation.)
- Determine whether other online documentation is to be used.
- Design the HELP screens.
- Test the online HELP and teaching aids with end users to ensure that they work well, with a usability lab environment employing a low-cost video camera to record the user reactions for later study.
- Design the paper documentation.
- Review the documentation with end users.

USER TRAINING

Good user training is essential to achieving success with a new system. The training needs careful preparation and the time available for this is much less when development is done with a high-speed automated lifecycle. Development of the training should proceed in parallel with the development of the system.

Development of the training should progress through the following stages:

- Determine who needs training and what the objectives are.
- Outline the curriculum.
- Plan the development of training materials.
- Develop the training schedule.
- Produce the training materials.

These stages are outlined in more detail in the action diagram of Box 17.2. The first step is to identify what skills and methods will change and consequently cause a need for training. The objectives of the training should be written down, and then a determination should be made of who has to be trained. This should all be reviewed with end-user management.

An outline of the curriculum must then be created. The author does this with an action diagram editor because this makes it easy to build and continuously change the hierarchical structures which represent the curriculum.

It should then be decided who will conduct the training and what media will be used. It may be necessary to develop a teach-the-teachers program if a large number of users have to be trained. Often a most appropriate form of training is to make a selected user in each department a specialist who will train and help the other users in his department. The question of who will do the training relates to the question of what media will be used. The following types of teaching should be considered.

- Lectures with slides
- Classroom training with overhead projector foils
- Personal assistance in the user's department
- Use of prototypes
- Use of extended HELP screens
- Computer-based training
- Videotape

It is desirable to make the system self-teaching to the extent that this is practical and economic. Good use of HELP screens and online documentation is desirable for this. Sometimes computer-based training may be appropriate, though often this is too expensive. For some systems it is appropriate to make a videotape for mass introduction to the system. It should also be determined whether training purchased from an outside source would be available.

To help in creating the training, and also be a training aid itself, prototypes of the system should be used early in the development lifecycle.

A schedule should be drawn up for creating the training materials, preparing the trainers, and delivering the training. The schedule should indicate when prototypes will be available. The training schedule should be meshed with the system development schedule.

The process of creating the training should include the following steps:

- Test the prototypes that will be used for training.
- Design, write, and implement the HELP screens.
- Design the structure of lectures or courses.
- Design the projection foils and other materials.
- Review the training materials with users.
- Adjust the training materials based on user feedback.
- Package the training materials with an overall training curriculum and plan.
- If necessary, develop an instructor's guide.

18 CUTOVER

This chapter describes the process of cutover. It assumes that design for cutover has been done, as was described in Chapter 17.

Prior to cutting over the system, the following activities need to be done.

- Develop the conversion system.
- Finalize the development product.
- Prepare for final testing.
- Carry out the final testing.
- Plan and conduct the training program.

Box 18.1 shows these activities in more detail.

In some installations using application generators and fast development methodologies, a goal is to get a version of the system into operation quickly, learn from the experience of this system, and then if necessary, produce a modified version of the system. A succession of improved versions may be built so that the business procedures become as streamlined and strategic as possible.

CONVERSION　　　As described earlier, systems are needed for automatic conversion of data and for manual entry of those data which cannot be converted automatically. These systems should be built as quickly as possible, with automated tools. They should be carefully tested and reviewed with end-user management. Tests need to be designed to ensure that the converted data works well with the new application programs.

The new system may have to work in conjunction with old systems. Data has to be converted so that it can pass from the old systems to the new one, and possibly from the new system to the old ones so that the old ones can

BOX 18.1   Preparation for Cutover

```
┌ Prepare for cutover
│ ┌ Develop the conversion system
│ │    Determine what is needed for conversion.
│ │    Generate subsystems needed to convert existing data.
│ │    Generate systems needed for the entry of new data.
│ │    Develop an interface to old systems which will remain in existence.
│ │    Develop an interface to application packages, if necessary.
│ └    Design tests to ensure that conversion facilities work correctly.
│
│ ┌ Finalize the development product
│ │ ┌ Perform quality audit
│ │ │ ┌ If a code generator is used
│ │ │ │    Ensure that it has been used in an approved manner.
│ │ │ │    Review any manually created code.
│ │ │ │    Ensure that adequate documentation is generated.
│ │ │ ├ Else
│ │ │ │    Review the development product to ensure that it is correctly
│ │ │ │       structured.
│ │ │ │    Ensure that it conforms to the development and operational
│ │ │ │       standards.
│ │ │ └    Ensure that the technical documentation is good enough.
│ │ │
│ │ ┌ Refine the development product
│ │ │    Correct any poorly written code.
│ │ │    Identify and repair any code inefficiencies.
│ │ │    If necessary use a code optimizer to improve code performance (for
│ │ │       example, the COBOL optimizer from Computer Associates).
│ │ │    Identify any differences between the development environment and
│ │ │       the production environment that may require modification to the
│ │ │       development product (for example, the Job Control Language may
│ │ └       require changes). Make the necessary changes.
│ │
│ ┌ Prepare for final testing
│ │ ┌ Install the software to be used for final testing
│ │ │    Install test data generator.
│ │ │    Install test utilities.
│ │ └    Install network debugging utilities.
│ │
│ │    Build the test libraries.
│ │    Coordinate the testing with the development team
│
│ ┌ Carry out the final testing.
│ │ ┌ Program test
│ │ █ For each transaction type
│ │ █    Verify that the program handles all its transactions
│ │ █       correctly.
│ │ █    Perform transaction crash test.
│ │ █    Verify that the program handles the transaction in all
│ │ █       cases without crashing.
│ │ └
│ │ ┌ Integration test
│ │ │    Verify that the system accepts input from and provides
│ │ │       output to other systems with which it interfaces.
│ │ └    Verify that the systems work together fully.
```

BOX 8.1 *(Continued)*

```
    ┌─  Volume test
    │      Verify that the system can process the volume of transactions
    │         expected
    │   ┌─  Regression test for maintenance changes
    │   │      Verify that the system still works as maintenance changes are
    │   │         made
    │   ┌─  Acceptance test
    │   │      Obtain verification from the users that the system is
    │   │         acceptable for production
    │      Collect statistics for project management
    └      Document the test results.
  ┌─  Plan and conduct the training program
  │   ┌─  Develop the training plan
  │   │      Determine who will create the training materials.
  │   │      Determine who will conduct the training.
  │   │      Determine which users will be trained initially.
  │   │      Determine the time and location of training.
  │   ┌─  Conduct training
  │   │      Conduct the first training session.
  │   │      Evaluate the success of the training to determine if the user
  │   │         understanding of the system meets the requirements.
  │   │      Refine the training materials and HELP screens on the basis of
  │   │         experience.
  │   [   Conduct further training courses.
  │   │      Refine training materials and HELP screens as appropriate.
  └   └
```

remain in use. This interface between the old and the new systems needs to be designed well in advance, and built and tested.

It may be necessary to develop an interface to application packages. This also requires data conversion which should be designed, built, and tested well in advance.

Prior to cutover, all the necessary files should be converted and the necessary data entered.

FINALIZE THE DEVELOPMENT PRODUCT

There should be a quality audit of the development product prior to cutover, to ensure that it has good code, is well structured, and well documented, and conforms to the installation standards. This audit may examine the machine performance of the system and recommend areas where improvement is necessary. The quality audit will be quicker and easier if a good application generator is used.

Any defects or inefficiencies revealed by the quality audit should be corrected. It may be necessary to use a code optimizer to improve code performance. Most generators generate fully structured code, and this does not run quite as efficiently as code which has been carefully optimized. To correct this an automatic code optimizer may be used, such as the COBOL optimizer from Computer Associates.

There may be differences between the development environment and the production environment that may require modification to the development product (e.g., the job control language may require changes). The necessary changes should be identified and made.

FINAL TESTING

To prepare for final testing, the software must be installed, the test libraries built, and the test data generated. If possible test data generator software should be used. The testing must be coordinated with the development team and may progress through the following stages:

```
Program test
    For each transaction type in the above list
        Plan how to test that the program handles the transaction
            in all cases without crashing.

Integration test
    Plan the integration tests needed to verify that the system
     accepts input from and provides output to other systems with
     which it interfaces.
    Plan how to test that the systems work together fully.

Volume test
    Plan how large volumes of transactions are to be tested
     (simulation or actual data tests).

Regression test for maintenance changes
    Plan the procedures for verifying that the system still works
     as maintenance changes are made.

Acceptance test
    Plan how verification will be obtained from end users that the
     system is acceptable for production.
```

Statistics should be collected on these tests for project management purposes, and the test results should be documented.

CONDUCT TRAINING

Training of the users must take place prior to cutover. Where possible, cutover should be a phased operation, with experience from the initial installation being used to make the subsequent installation operate as smoothly as possible.

It should be determined which end users will be trained initially. This training should be done, and its success evaluated. The training materials and technique should be improved on the basis of this experience. This may require changes in the software HELP screens and error messages.

A plan should exist for the spread of training, corresponding to the deployment of the system.

PERFORM CUTOVER

The actual cutover process can be broken into the following activities:

- Set up the production procedures.
- Install the production system environment.
- Perform data conversion.
- Implement the new system in production.
- Review the system installation.

Box 18.2 shows these activities in more detail.

THE PRODUCTION PROCEDURES

A variety of procedures is needed to operate the system. Manual and administrative procedures have to accompany the computerized procedures. These should have been designed, documented, and verified well before cutover. The procedures are often designed so that the new system can operate in parallel with the old system until confidence is built up in the new system.

The production procedures need to be set up as follows:

- Set up the procedures for normal system operation.
- Set up any manual or paperwork procedures that must accompany the new installation.
- Set up the procedures for restart and recovery.
- Set up the fallback procedures.
- Set up the procedures for security.
- Set up the audit procedures.
- Set up the procedures for phasing out the old system when the new system is running satisfactorily.
- Review the foregoing procedures with the data center personnel to ensure their understanding.
- Review the foregoing procedures with the end users to ensure their understanding.

BOX 18.2   Procedure for performing cutover.

```
Perform cutover.
  Set up the production procedures.
      Set up the procedures for normal system operation.
      Set up any manual or paperwork procedures that must accompany
        the new installation.
      Set up the procedures for restart and recovery.
      Set up the fallback procedures.
      Set up the procedures for security.
      Set up the audit procedures.
      Set up the procedures for phasing out the old system when the new
        system is running satisfactorily.
      Review the above procedures with the data center personnel to
        ensure their understanding.
      Review the above procedures with the end users to ensure their
        understanding.

  Install the production system environment.
      Install the initial production hardware.
      Confirm that a complete test of the hardware has been successfully
        completed.
      Coordinate with systems programming administration to schedule
        the installation.
      Install the software on the production system.
      Test that the software is correctly installed.
      Coordinate with vendors for the ongoing hardware installation at
        other sites.

  Perform data conversion.
      Execute the data conversion programs.
      Load existing data into the system's database.
      Load manually-prepared data, if needed.
      Test the data loading and conversion to verify data quality.
      Review the results to ensure that acceptance test criteria are met.

  Implement the new system in production.
      Move the new system to production mode, following the migration
        plan, possibly running in parallel with the old system.
      Lock the new software components into the development and test
        library.
      Phase out the old system as confidence is developed in the new
        system.

  Review the system installation.
      Evaluate the system performance.
      Determine what system tuning is needed.
      Evaluate user acceptance of the system.
      Determine what improvements are needed in user training.
      Schedule the improvements in training.
      Determine what system modifications are needed.
      Schedule the system modifications.
```

The new system may be installed in one location, adjusted until it is working smoothly, and then fanned out to many locations. A timetable for this fan-out is necessary so that the procedures can be set up appropriately in all locations.

The hardware needs to be installed with a schedule which relates to the planned fan-out. The ongoing installation of the hardware at other sites needs to be coordinated with the vendors. There needs to be a complete test of the hardware and its software. The systems programming administration must schedule the time needed to install and test the software.

INSTALLATION

When the software is installed, the data is loaded into the system's database. The data conversion programs are executed and the manually prepared data is entered. The resulting database is tested to verify the data quality, and the results are reviewed to ensure that the acceptance test criteria are met.

The new system is moved into production mode, following the migration plan, possibly running in parallel with the old system. The new software components are locked into the development and test library. The old system is phased out as confidence is developed in the new system.

INSTALLATION REVIEW

When experience is gained with the new system, the system should be reviewed, with the intent of improving its performance where necessary, ensuring the best user acceptance, and optimizing the system functionality.

The following steps are taken:

- Evaluate the system performance.
- Determine what system tuning is needed.
- Evaluate user acceptance of the system.
- Determine what improvements are needed in user training.
- Schedule the improvements in training.
- Determine what system modifications are needed.
- Schedule the system modifications.

REFERENCE

1. James Martin and Carma McClure, *Action Diagrams: Clearly Structured Specifications, Programs, and Procedures,* 2nd edition (Englewood Cliffs, N.J.: Prentice Hall, 1989).

PART **IV** MANAGEMENT AND MIGRATION

19 PERSPECTIVES, VERSIONS, AND COORDINATION

INTRODUCTION   Information engineering (IE) is achieved by synthesizing the knowledge and design work of many people who may be scattered across a large enterprise. The encyclopedia provides the repository of this knowledge and the tools for helping to synthesize it. It is from this synthesis that many of the advantages of IE derive, including the ability to achieve reusability on a large scale. Synthesis is essential because no one person has more than a fraction of the knowledge that corporate computing requires. The amount and complexity of information is so great that synthesis is a practical possibility only if computerized tools are used to achieve it.

As discussed earlier, the objective is to achieve as much internal consistency as possible in the knowledge in the encyclopedia. In a large organization complete consistency is unlikely to be achieved, especially early in the evolution of information engineering. The methodology and tools need to be designed to enable an enterprise to work toward consistency, but also to operate with different versions of designs, different versions of objects, zones of internal consistency, and possibly interfaces between zones which are agreed to be inconsistent. Some of the zones may be those built around application packages which have data inconsistent with the overall data model.

VIEWS AND HYPERVIEWS   A common term in database technology is "view." A *view* of a database is a representation of data that is perceived by one person or program. The structure of the database may be far more complex than the structure of the view. The view shows only those fields in which the user is interested at this time. The view is a subset of the overall database structure.

A CASE (computer-aided systems engineering) repository (encyclopedia) contains many objects and associations among objects. A workbench normally displays some of those objects and associations at one time. It displays a view from the encyclopedia contents. An analyst or designer creates a view when he works at the screen. When this view is checked into the central encyclopedia, it becomes part of a much larger representation.

The view may have a name and may be referred to in the encyclopedia index so that that view can be quickly retrieved. Many views may be logically linked to form a *hyperview,* just as many diagrams are logically linked to form a hyperdiagram. A hyperview is represented with multiple logically related CASE screens.

Some of these screens show diagrams such as data flow diagrams, decomposition diagrams, and action diagrams; some are windows which the tool uses like forms to gather information; some are dialog screens or report designs; some are textual comments. The displays are logically interlinked as in Fig. 19.1, they contain objects and associations in common, and these objects and associations in stored and indexed in the encyclopedia.

CONSISTENCY AMONG DIAGRAMS

Different types of diagrams show different manifestations of the same information. These diagrams are linked together into hyperviews. Data may be entered in one type of diagram and displayed with a different type of diagram. The encyclopedia ensures that the different diagrams reflect a consistent meaning. If a procedure block is added to a data flow diagram that procedure must appear on the equivalent decomposition diagram, and vice versa. If the analyst has two windows on the screen with different diagram types of the same information, when he changes one diagram the change needed on the other diagram to ensure consistency should appear automatically. He may add a process block to a decomposition diagram, for example, and the equivalent block appears on a data flow diagram. Because the software does not know how to link it to the other blocks on the data flow diagram, it asks for that information.

In this way one type of diagram can be converted into another or used as a component of another diagram. For example, knowledge "X" may be best entered into the encyclopedia by Mr. Jones via a data flow diagram. Ms. Smith then requests the same information from the encyclopedia, reinterpreted automatically, as an entity-relationship diagram. This logically interconnected family of diagrams constitute a *hyperdiagram* with which the implementor can explore and add to an integrated set of knowledge.

PERSPECTIVES

Each analyst or designer creates a view of a part of the enterprise. We refer to these views as *perspectives.* A perspective, then, involves multiple types of diagrams which are logi-

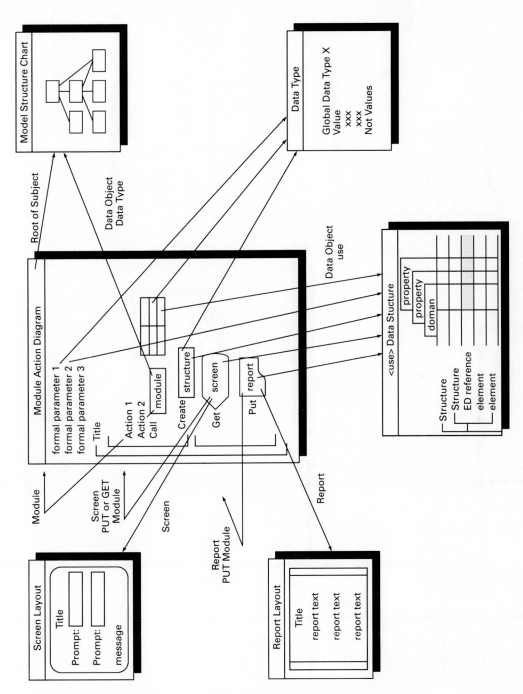

Figure 19.1(a) Displays logically interlinked in a hyperdiagram.

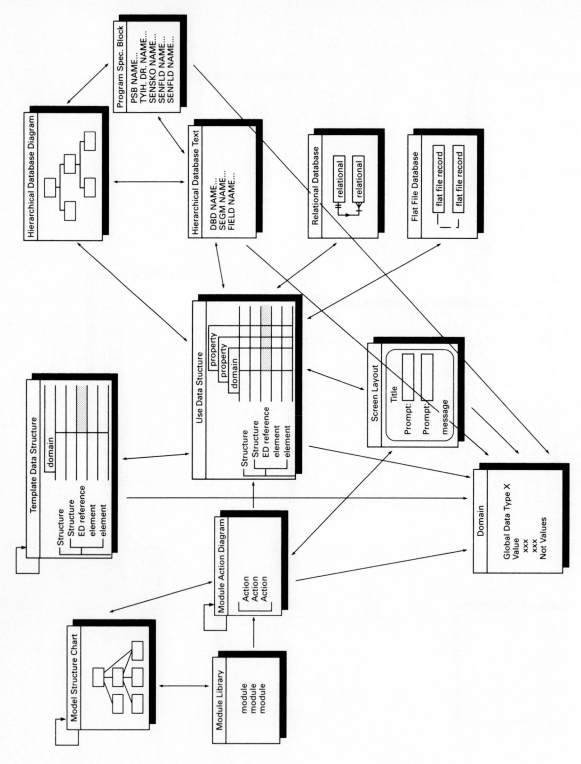

Figure 19.1(b) Displays logically interlinked in a hyperdiagram.

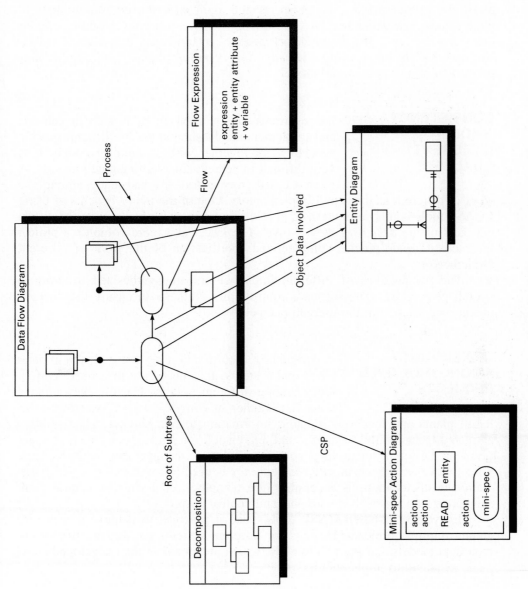

Figure 19.1(c) Displays logically interlinked in a hyperdiagram.

cally related. A perspective is a collection of knowledge about a given activity or group of activities, and the data which these activities use. The perspective has an identification number and is one of the formal objects that are kept track of by the encyclopedia. The perspective is built with the diagramming techniques and tools which we have described. The central encyclopedia contains many perspectives. The different perspectives overlap, just as views of a database overlap. In other words they may use common objects, and employ data derived from a common data model.

CONSISTENCY AMONG DIFFERENT ANALYSTS

Large projects are worked on by a team of analysts and implementors. Designs done by different people need to work together with absolute precision. It is very difficult to achieve this with manual methods. A good I-CASE tool enforces consistency among the work of different analysts and implementors. One of the major benefits of using I-CASE tools is this computerized enforcement of consistency among the different parts of the design as they evolve. The larger and more complex a project the more it needs precise computerized coordination of the work of different implementors.

The perspectives of different implementors are synthesized to form an overall perspective. The software controls this synthesis to ensure that there is precise consistency in the merged perspective.

CONSISTENCY AMONG MULTIPLE PROJECTS

A computerized corporation has many different databases and systems. It is necessary to achieve consistency among different systems because they interact with one another in complex ways. Systems in different plants and locations transmit information to one another. Data is often extracted from multiple systems and aggregated for purposes of business management. Different locations need commonality of management measurements. Sometimes the term *corporate transparency* is used to mean that detailed information in all locations is accessible in a computerized form to a central management group for decision-support and control purposes.

Encyclopedia-based CASE tools make it practical to achieve consistency among multiple projects. Designs for different systems are derived from common data models and process models, which are stored in the encyclopedia and made available to implementors.

THE KNOWLEDGE COORDINATOR

An integral part of encyclopedia-based systems is software which coordinates the knowledge of different perspectives and ensures that it is consistent. The *knowledge coordinator* automatically ensures consistency among the different pieces of knowledge that reside in the encyclopedia. It applies artificial intelligence rules to the information that is checked into the encyclopedia. When a person using a workstation enters new information into that workstation the knowledge coordinator checks that it obeys the rules and is consistent with what is already in the encyclopedia.

A person using a CASE workstation builds his own model or design. This is represented in a local perspective. The knowledge coordinator enforces consistency within that perspective. The local perspective is built with objects which are extracted from a central encyclopedia and use the detail that is centrally stored. There is thus consistency between the local perspective and the central representation.

The person at the workbench may create new objects, new associations, or new detail. This will eventually be entered into the central encyclopedia. The knowledge coordinator then has the task of ensuring that the local perspective is consistent with the central information. It will indicate any inconsistencies, and these must be corrected. The local workbench user will normally correct the inconsistencies arising from his work. Sometimes a central (human) administrator has to resolve conflicts about how objects are designed or described.

Two implementors may create two separate perspectives. The knowledge coordinator has the task of examining them in combination to ensure complete consistency between them. In this way consistency is achieved in a multiperson project or in a multiproject environment.

It is difficult or impossible to achieve consistency among the work of many analysts or implementors with manual techniques. A computer with CASE representations can enforce absolute consistency. Achieving consistency becomes a human problem of resolving different opinions, rather than a technical problem of detecting inconsistencies. The computerized corporation of the future could not be built without computerized enforcement of consistency among its many information systems.

PEOPLE INVOLVED WITH A PERSPECTIVE   A particular analyst or team works on one perspective at a time. This work takes place with an integrated-CASE workbench. The workbench contains a miniencyclopedia with descriptions of the objects, relationships, notes, and so on that constitute the perspective. These can be manipulated with diagrams and windows. The knowledge of the perspective is loaded into the workbench from the central encyclopedia when it is needed. In some cases the easiest way for a team to create a perspective is to load a similar perspective and modify it.

The work of developing a perspective is called *drafting* the perspective. One person is responsible for drafting the perspective—usually a systems analyst or designer. He is called the perspective's *owner*. Many people may look at the perspective but not modify it. These are called *users* of the perspective.

The perspective may also have a *manager*. The manager establishes a *charter* for the perspective. The charter gives the management framework for the perspective. It gives information such as target completion date, who may modify the perspective, the scope of the perspective, and so on.

The perspective represents knowledge from a *knowledge source*. The knowledge source may be an end user, a group of end users, a JAD (joint application design) session, a BAA (business area analysis) team, a document or policy statement, or possibly an application package or reusable module.

There are thus four types of people involved with a perspective:

- The owner
- The manager
- Users
- The knowledge source

The owner and the knowledge source may be the same person where information engineering is done by true "user analysts." This is unlikely to be true at the strategy and analysis levels. The knowledge sources are experts on some aspect of the business and the owner is a consultant who is evoking and translating the knowledge of the source.

At the analysis and design levels, some end users learn how to use workbench tools and create their own designs. Often it is desirable to have a professional designer and prototype implementor who harnesses the knowledge of the end users and adjusts the design and prototype to fit their needs.

An implementor often owns multiple perspectives. His influence on the systems and their integration steadily grows. It is generally bad practice for a perspective to have more than one owner. There should be one individual who is responsible for the perspective and who knows how to elicit the requisite knowledge from others and build it into the workbench representation. End users at various levels should be fully encouraged by the owner to check the perspective. This needs to be done at each level of the pyramid.

THE SCOPE OF A PERSPECTIVE

Each participant has investment and expertise in some subset of the encyclopedia but not in all of it. It is desirable to have a clear definition of the area of interest of each owner and knowledge source. The perspectives of each owner and knowledge source should be stored, along with the scope of each perspective.

The *scope* expresses the area of interest that is in the perspective. This may be defined in terms of the diagrams and windows in the perspective, or it may be defined in terms of objects, properties and associations among objects. A workbench tool can automatically define and index the scope that a manager has built into a perspective. A participant should then be consulted about proposals that may change the objects in his perspective, thus protecting his investment in this information.

The intent of scoping is to give each participant a piece of the encyclopedia which he can develop more or less independently of the rest of the encyclopedia. Each participant may be allowed to see objects not in his scope but can change only his version of objects within the scope. Where the scope of different owners overlaps care is needed in synthesizing the knowledge.

Some objects may be excluded from general read access. Most corporations, for example, do not allow free access by technical staff to corporate goals, problems, and other planning data.

SYNTHESIS OF PERSPECTIVES

Different perspectives are often drafted simultaneously by independent teams. Because of this independent development, perspectives may contain conflicting information. They may contain incompatible descriptions of the same objects. A goal of information engineering is to remove such incompatibility.

Incompatibility is minimized by employing the descriptions of data and other objects which are in the central encyclopedia wherever possible. Selected contents of one perspective may be copied into another. This use of already-defined objects and copying of perspectives speeds up the development process.

When a perspective has been drafted it should then be *synthesized* with the information in the encyclopedia. Synthesis should be carried out with the help of IE tools, which display any inconsistencies which have to be resolved.

When two perspectives are incompatible, their owners have to agree on what they change to achieve compatibility. This process of forming agreements begins with perspectives in the same business area. *Local problems should be resolved locally*. The synthesis expands until there is concentration on more global integration.

The perspectives which individual designers work on are called *source perspectives*. Two closely related source perspectives may be synthesized to form a higher-level *integrated perspective*. Integrated perspectives may *themselves* be combined to form higher-level integrated perspectives. In a perfect world this could continue until a single overall perspective was reached with no inconsistencies. The overall perspective is called the *base perspective* (see Fig. 19.2).

Bottom-up synthesis is performed in a hierarchical fashion starting at the bottom of the hierarchy in Fig. 19.2. In the synthesis hierarchy an integrated perspective supports two or more lower-level perspectives. A block with a double frame is the icon used for a *perspective:*

The following rule defines the support relationship in the synthesis hierarchy:

If perspective *P* supports perspective *Q,* then the synthesis is complete only when *P* contains the same version of every object, property, and association that appears in *Q,* in other words, when *Q* is a subset of *P.*

VERSIONS　　　　　　　　In practice it is unlikely that complete consistency will ever be achieved across a large organization. Suppose that the perspectives in Fig. 19.2 have been fully synthesized. A new business requirement then arises which causes source perspective *A* to be modified in a manner that causes it to be inconsistent with *B, C,* and *F. B,* perhaps,

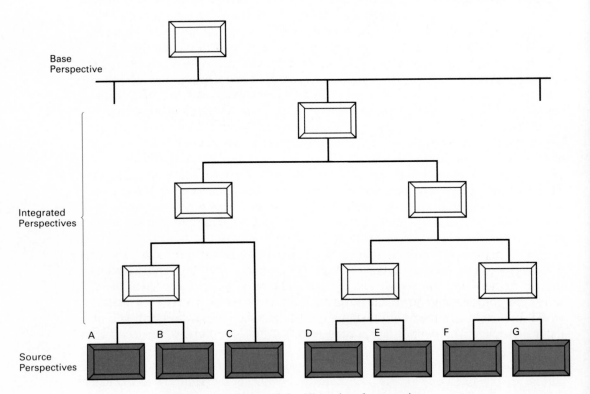

Figure 19.2　Hierarchy of perspectives.

can be modified to achieve consistency with the new version of *A*. *C* and *F*, however, are now working programs and cannot be modified without substantial expense. It is not an optimum use of resources to modify *C* or *F* at this time. Because of this the encyclopedia must be able to store inconsistent objects. To do so it has *multiple versions* of objects, groupings of objects, and perspectives.

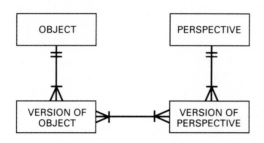

SIX STATES

When a perspective is being created it is in *draft* form. After the drafting is done, the perspective is submitted for synthesis and is in a *proposed* state. After synthesis it is *published* and then it is made accessible to all analysts and designers. One and only one version of a published perspective is the *approved* version. In some cases old versions are now considered wrong and harmful. They may still exist because systems which use them have not yet been modified. These old and harmful versions are referred to as *deviant*. A perspective may be deleted from active use but archived because it may be worth examining in the future.

Box 19.1 summarizes these six states that a perspective version can be in.

DRAFTING

Drafting is usually an activity carried out by one individual. It could be done on a personal computer without involving the central encyclopedia. However use of the central encyclopedia is desirable to ensure that when objects and data are needed that have already been defined the drafter uses them. He should not reinvent the wheel. He should employ reusable modules to the maximum extent.

He should use the existing encyclopedia to ensure compatibility to the greatest extent. Particularly important, he should ensure compatibility with the data model.

He may begin his drafting activity by copying the objects he needs from the central encyclopedia. He may then work without much use of the central encyclopedia until a tentative draft is finished. Then he requests the coordination services of the central encyclopedia to check that his draft conforms to the data

BOX 19.1 A perspective can be in one of six possible states

- **Draft:** A person or team is working on the perspective, but has not yet finished.
- **Proposed:** The draft design is finished and is submitted for central automated analysis and approval by the knowledge administrator.
- **Published:** When the perspective meets the desirable consistency requirements it is "published." All other analysts and designers can then see and use this perspective.
- **Approved:** There may be multiple versions of a perspective, but only one is the approved version.
- **Deviant:** An old version of a perspective may now be considered wrong and harmful. This version remains active in the encyclopedia because certain systems still use it. When these systems come up for maintenance, they will be modified to use the approved version.
- **Archived:** A perspective may be deleted from active use but is archived because designers may want to examine it in the future.

Perspectives which are in the *published, approved,* or *deviant* states are accessible for analysts and designers to examine and copy. Normally, they would copy only the *approved* version.

model or can be synthesized with other perspectives. The tool should be able to compare two perspectives and report on

- Where they agree.
- Where they conflict.
- Where they differ but do not conflict.

The draftsperson will adjust his or her draft to remove all conflicts before involving other people by putting the draft into the proposed state.

Only one perspective is active at the workstation at one time. This perspective may include many different diagrams and detail windows. The drafter can modify only the active perspective. He may need to look at and copy items from other perspectives. He may need to analyze and coordinate his own perspective with other perspectives or other versions of his own perspective.

A developer may check out a perspective from a central encyclopedia, and possibly copy other items that he will use. He can then work largely independently of the central computer and, indeed, may work on a portable personal computer. When a perspective is checked out, the checkout dialog should ask who is checking it out and whether he intends to modify it. It can then keep track of any modifications in progress. When, or before, the owner submits *proposed* changes, a synthesis dialog takes place. The central encyclopedia highlights any conflicts and asks for appropriate modifications. This checkout/ checkin procedure avoids the need to have locking or freezing mechanisms such that when one group is modifying an object, others cannot work with it.

The workbench should impose validation checks on a perspective when it is checked in. It should not allow a perspective to be published until it passes at least some of the tests. The same tests and their associated analyses will often be run voluntarily before checkin. The tests are of two types: tests for internal consistency, such as those discussed earlier in the report, and tests for external consistency determining that this perspective is consistent with other perspectives. Of the external consistency tests, some may *have* to be passed before publication, and some may be optional. An example of a mandatory external test may be that no nonunique identifiers would result from synthesizing this perspective into the one that supports it.

POWER DRAFTING

In normal application development there is much redundant effort. A good workbench should enable its users to employ data already modeled, objects which have defined behavior, perspectives already built, and subroutines already written. There should be as much use of reusable code and reusable design as possible.

Capturing already existing segments of design, programs, and knowledge is referred to as *power drafting*. It can save much work, and it greatly lessens the problems with incompatibility. Reusable design should be the way of life in information engineering wherever practical.

A drafter will often begin by copying an entire perspective which he sets out to modify. In this environment it is often easier to build by copying and modifying than by entering details of the objects from scratch. A designer may start on a draft by copying the parts of the integrated perspective which supports it.

Power drafting helps to eliminate the mass of avoidable conflicts, redundancies, and misunderstandings that happen when people work in mutual isolation, not realizing that they are all inventing the same wheel. When it works as intended, power drafting achieves much of the work of synthesis informally. It weeds out the problems that are just misunderstandings, leaving only the real problems—the disagreements among people about how the enterprise and its procedures and systems ought to work.

Power drafting requires a set of commands that make it easy to integrate all or part of some other perspective into the work taking place on a new perspective. This can be done graphically with highlighting or color on existing diagrams and windows. A designer may ask for selected objects, for a whole diagram, for all the objects in a given perspective that are not in his own perspective, or for all the objects on which two perspective versions disagree.

When this copying results in incompatible objects within the draft, a *synthesis dialog* may ensue to enable the drafter to resolve the conflicts and merge the different objects, details or associations.

PRECISE MAPPING OF CONFLICTS   To enable a drafter to explore potential conflicts the workbench should allow him to ask: "What other versions of this diagram or object exist?" "Exactly how do they differ?" "Who believes in these versions?" "How would my perspective have to change if I accepted all the proposals from perspective *X*?" "Conversely how would perspective *X* have to change if its owner accepted my current perspective?"

The results of such comparisons may be displayed on diagrams using highlighting, reverse video, or color.

Many conflicts are resolved quickly and the requisite change to the perspective made easily by copying objects and their detail from one perspective to another. A good information engineering workbench should make it easy to see conflicts visually and easy to eliminate them by copying.

No tool can prevent this process from getting stuck because of human disagreements. People become locked into stubborn arguments, endlessly pingponging proposals back and forth. Political battles of many sorts—and the same ones that were conducted manually—are now fought via the workbench and its perspectives. Software cannot stop these but it can clarify them, showing who is in disagreement and what objects the disagreements relate to. It may show the history of the conflict by analyzing earlier versions. Time-stamping may help show what persons are stalling. When political battles rage at least you have a map of the battlefield.

THE KNOWLEDGE ADMINISTRATOR   The owner of an integrated perspective may have the job of resolving the arguments. His is a different job from that of the owner of the source perspective. He is not concerned with capturing and translating raw knowledge from the enterprise, but with integrating already captured knowledge into a consistent picture. This job needs overall understanding of the business or system and the ability to negotiate with perspective owners.

A project manager or his assistant may be the owner of integrated perspectives which relate to his project.

At a higher level an individual must be made responsible for the overall coordination of the knowledge built into the encyclopedia. As discussed earlier this job is similar to the task of a data administrator and may be thought of as an extension of the data administration function. We refer to this person as the *knowledge administrator*. Sometimes the term "encyclopedia administrator" has been used.

Like the data administrator, the knowledge administrator needs computerized tools to help him analyze and coordinate the knowledge. He will examine many perspectives, helping to synthesize them into as consistent a whole as possible.

Many corporations now have a decade of experience of data administration and have well-established techniques for doing it as effectively as possible [1]. This important task of data administration is a subset of the task of administering the overall contents of the encyclopedia. The knowledge administrator may have a data administrator working for him, or the data administrator may have been promoted to the larger task of being the knowledge administrator.

CONTROL OF COMPLEXITY

A complex organization is likely to have many of its systems being worked on concurrently. These systems are small parts of something that must eventually be integrated. The programs and designs of diverse teams must interconnect and work together like a complex piece of machinery.

The work of one designer or programmer considerably affects the work of others. The circles in Fig. 19.3 represent segments of design or programs. The dark circles and connecting line are the series of programs that handle the progress of one piece of work in the corporation.

The lines and arrows of Fig. 19.4 represent logical interactions among the separate programs. The figure shows a small number of circles, but there might be many hundreds, and the pattern of interactions among them could be very complex. The complexity of the interactions represent a severe problem for program development and maintenance. It is necessary to structure the interactions so as to minimize the complexity.

Programmers and designers constantly make changes, both during the design of a system and, later, during maintenance. Programs tend to grow and

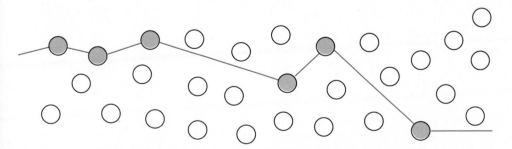

Figure 19.3   A collection of items in an organization.

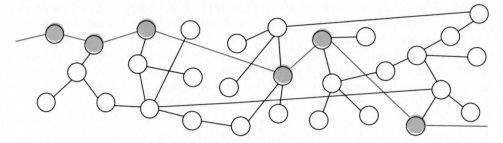

Figure 19.4 The lines show logical interactions among the items. A change in one circle is likely to affect the work on any of the items linked to it. In reality many changes occur, and communicating these changes is a severe problem in an organization with hundreds of items.

develop, rather like the growth of a city. If a change to one circle in Fig. 19.4 affects the others linked to it by an arrow, control is complex and difficult.

An essential part of the solution to this problem is to divide the programs or subsystems into self-contained groups. This is illustrated in Fig. 19.5. It is rather like making subassemblies in mechanical engineering. The behavior of each subassembly is clearly defined, and the way it fits into the rest of the machinery is specified in detail. This done, the subassembly can be defined and constructed independently of the remainder.

Figure 19.5 shows the circles of Fig. 19.4 divided into groups. The clustering of the procedures into systems may be done with the affinity analysis techniques discussed in Book II. The red lines in Fig. 19.6 show the interfaces between the groups.

Each circle in Fig. 19.6 may be a design in its own right with its own source perspective. The boxes of Fig. 19.6 show integrated perspectives. A

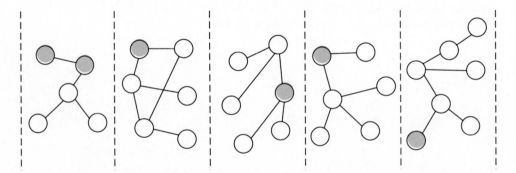

Figure 19.5 Part of the solution to the problem illustrated in Fig. 19.4 is to divide the organization or system into largely self-contained units. Within each unit, changes are manageable. Interfaces between units need to be held constant as far as possible.

Integrated Perspectives:

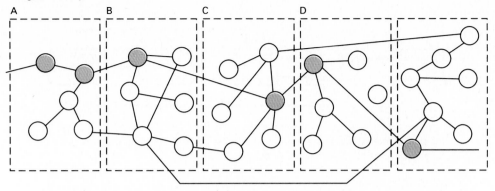

Figure 19.6 The clusters are represented in integrated perspectives. The lines here show interfaces between perspectives. Version control is applied to the integrated perspectives.

separate diagram on the workbench screen may show the integrated perspectives and interactions among them, as in Fig. 19.7. A perspective may go through multiple versions without affecting the work on other perspectives provided that its interface with other perspectives remains unchanged. The interfaces represented by the lines between boxes in Fig. 19.7 must be precisely defined and held constant. Each integrated perspective is insulated as completely as possible from the work on other perspectives. However much modification occurs within one of the perspectives in Fig. 19.7, every attempt will be made to avoid modifying its interface to other perspectives. The rules enforced by the encyclopedia will help to avoid interface changes which will cause problems. Should an interface change become unavoidable, the encyclopedia will send messages to the owners of the perspectives involved and ensure that changes are made which enable the pieces to work together correctly. The designers or programmers will have a relatively small number of changes to keep up with compared with the deluge that would have resulted from the amorphous structure of Fig. 19.4.

PERSPECTIVES THAT CANNOT BE CHANGED

Sometimes a perspective can be changed relatively easily because it is at the design stage. Sometimes a perspective cannot be changed, at least not quickly, because an operational set of programs exists based on it. Often a design is frozen while the programming of that system is done. The encyclopedia should have knowledge about what can and cannot be modified. Often as one system changes a *bridge* is needed to connect it to other systems which do not change.

A list of required changes may be kept for a perspective (or a new draft may be created) to await the time when maintenance is done on a system. The changes may be made in the diagrams and detail windows and may constitute a new version of the perspective which is not yet implemented.

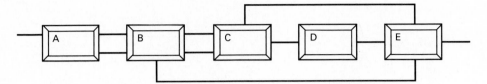

Figure 19.7   The integrated perspectives of Fig. 19.6. The red lines show
the interfaces between perspectives that must be held constant as far as possible and controlled via the encyclopedia.

The pressure to change and improve systems is constantly present. It is
rare that a good programmer reaches the end of a piece of coding without want-
ing to rewrite it. He sees ways of cleaning up the logic, speeding up the program, making it perform better. In a large system with many designers and
coders, this is much more true. There will be many deficiencies in the early
versions which can be improved upon. Saving all the possible changes for a
new version enables one version to be implemented fairly quickly so that experience can be gained from using it. The encyclopedia, then, should be designed
to help manage version-by-version buildup.

Perspective versions allow an implementor to tinker harmlessly with a
draft of a perspective, including running analyses and integration checks on it,
and it only needs to see the light of day when or if it turns out useful and the
project management is ready for it.

Most systems today ought to be built with prototyping. Design feedback
from a prototype is used to improve the final system. There may be a succession
of prototypes designed to evolve with an iterative lifecycle. Subunits may be
prototyped independent of the rest of the system. The encyclopedia is used to
design the prototypes, ensure that they employ correct data models, and control
their interface to other subsystems.

**PROPOSED
FEATURES**   A management problem that can become difficult
with an inventive programming team is deciding
which of the many features they devise should be in-
corporated. There is often not time or money to add them all. It can be difficult
to decide whether programming or feature proposal is worthwhile when it is
considered on its own. However, when all the various ideas are discussed together in deciding on the features of a new version or model, their relative
merits can be compared. The desirable goals of the new system should be clear.
The proposed features may be mapped against the goals with indicators showing
the extent to which they help meet the goals. This may be done with workbench
matrix manipulation.

Features are commonly proposed because they are elegant or attractive to a programmer or designer. Often an individual wants them because he is intoxicated with the originality of his own ideas. Mapping the features against the project goals helps to avoid overengineering. If such decisions are left to technicians, most systems tend to be overengineered.

STABLE DATA MODEL   In our discussion of perspectives and versions, it is important to state that the data model is treated separately from the design of activities.

It is one of the principles of information engineering that data used in a corporation can and should be modeled separately from the design of specific procedures. Entities and relationships are independent of specific procedures. Data can be fully normalized and stability analysis applied to it as described in Book II. Computerized techniques should be used to synthesize the data model and make it available for subsequent analysis and design.

When a designer is creating procedures she should use the data model and avoid changing it unless absolutely necessary. The data model links to all the procedures as shown in Fig. 19.8. It helps enforce the use of compatible data among the procedures. Most of the interaction between one procedure and another will be via a database or by passing records directly, where the data in question is defined in the data model. There will often be a succession of version changes for the activities, but these versions will not change the data model.

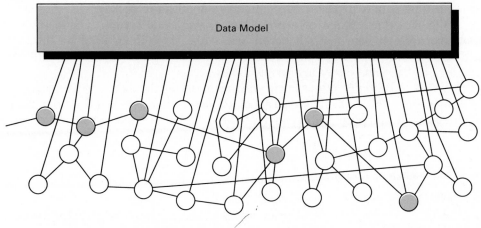

Figure 19.8 The design of activities is linked to a fully normalized data model designed to be as stable as possible. (See Book II.)

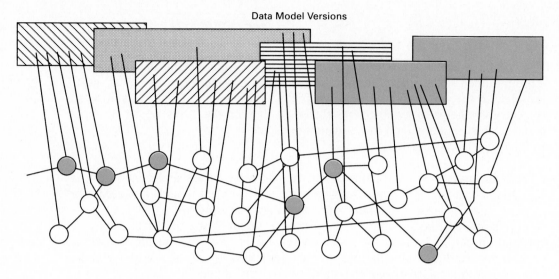

Data Model Versions

Figure 19.9   Although the data model is designed to be as stable as possible, multiple incompatible versions of certain data may have to exist.

DATA MODEL VERSIONS

Let us suppose that many procedures have been programmed and use a mature data model as shown in Fig. 19.8. Suddenly a new procedure requires some of the data to be changed. This can happen because of changes in government regulations, changes in the scope of the business, and so on. The encyclopedia will indicate what reprogramming or design would be needed to accommodate the change. Usually this reprogramming cannot be done quickly, so a decision may have to be made to live with incompatible versions of some of the data. Incompatible data exist also to accommodate application packages.

Whereas one version of a procedure *replaces* the earlier version, two or more versions of data may all be current at the same time, used by different activities as shown in Fig. 19.9. The encyclopedia needs to equate the different versions of the same entity and its attributes.

Where differently represented versions exist of the same entity, software may be needed to convert the data when it passes from one activity to another. The conversion program will be one of the modules indexed by the encyclopedia.

COMMUNICATIONS AMONG DEVELOPERS

Communications among members of a large design and programming team have traditionally been a problem. In some organizations, the designers or programmers are inundated with memos describing changes. They often have neither the time nor inclination to digest all these memos.

The encyclopedia should be designed to simplify this communication problem. Announcements of newly published perspectives can be made automatically to owners or managers who are directly affected by those perspectives. Hierarchical communication as in Fig. 19.9 helps to avoid overload. Local synthesis may take place before persons in more remote areas become involved.

A person drafting a perspective may be notified automatically when a new publication affects him. The notification is rather like an electronic mail system saying ''There is mail for you.'' The announcement may be made only if the new publication causes a conflict.

A person may be able to tell the coordinating software what types of publication announcements he wants to see. In this way he can build his own announcement filter based on criteria such as the following:

- A list of perspectives for which he wants announcements.
- Any changes to objects in the perspective he is working on.
- Any changes to perspectives which are supported by a given perspective (i.e., beneath it in the perspective hierarchy).

THE ACHIEVEMENT OF CONSISTENCY

Achieving consistency in complex systems requires both top-down and bottom-up design. Both are used in information engineering.

Top-down design is achieved by phasing the stages of building the encyclopedia—first, information strategy planning; then, business area analysis; then, design and construction. The lower levels of design and construction are constrained to make use of the data models and process models established at the higher level. The work at level 2 (business area analysis) helps to refine the models of level 1 (information strategy planning). As the details of design are worked out at level 3, the level 2 model might be adjusted.

Bottom-up design is essentially a synthesis process. Separate views of data at level 2 are synthesized into the overall data model with full normalization of the data being performed. At level 3 separate design perspectives are built by separate teams and synthesized a stage at a time as in Fig. 19.2.

Box 19.2 summarizes the techniques that should be used to achieve consistency.

REFERENCE

1. James Martin, *Managing the Data-Base Environment* (Englewood Cliffs, NJ: Prentice-Hall, 1983).

BOX 19.2 To achieve consistency several techniques are needed

- **Top-down design.** Level 1 of the pyramid produces an overview model of the enterprise. Level 2 builds data models and process models which expand on the overview model. Consistency at level 1 is fairly easy to achieve. Consistency, in an ideal world, should be achieved at level 2 before level 3 designs are built.

- **Online access to the central encyclopedia.** When an individual or a local team are working on a design, the definitions of objects used should be retrieved from the central encyclopedia wherever possible.

- **Data consistency should be achieved first.** As we have stressed, a fully normalized data model can be relatively stable even though the procedures which use it change constantly. Data stability techniques need to be emphasized. Data models should be synthesized by a computerized tool which achieves full normalization. Deviations from the data model should be avoided. Where this rule cannot be upheld a discussion of the data representation should take place with the data administrator.

- **Automated consistency checking.** When a local design has been done, it should be analyzed by the central tools to determine consistency with the central encyclopedia. Inconsistencies should be resolved before the design is published.

- **Hierarchical synthesis.** Synthesis of local designs takes place a stage at a time. A design is synthesized with closely related designs first. Progressively higher levels of integration are achieved as illustrated in Fig. 19.2.

- **Power drafting.** New perspectives should be derived where possible by modifying perspectives already validated in the encyclopedia. These include perspectives from a higher level in the pyramid and perspectives from the same level. It is often easier to modify an existing correct perspective than to create a new perspective.

- **Visual comparisons.** Graphics techniques should be used for highlighting items of inconsistency between perspectives. Highlighting or coloring the diagrams and windows can make the areas of disagreement very visual.

- **Precise modularization.** Complex organizations of systems are divided into modules with precisely defined interfaces between modules. Except for the interfaces, consistency control is not needed between two modules. The encyclopedia should control the interfaces.

- **Knowledge administrator.** A high-level individual should be responsible for coordination of the knowledge in the encyclopedia. The now-conventional work of a data administrator is a subset of this task.

20 MIGRATION AND REVERSE ENGINEERING

INTRODUCTION   The eventual goal of information engineering is that all systems are built with an IE tool set and so have the following properties:

- All data are represented in normalized data models in the encyclopedia.
- All procedures are mapped in the encyclopedia.
- Reusable procedures are identified.
- All programs are generated or built in a fully structured fashion using the encyclopedia contents.
- Procedures and programs are easy to modify using the encyclopedia-based design workbench and code generator.

The enterprise then has clean engineering of its computer applications and can evolve its procedures rapidly to meet changing needs.

Some information engineers lie awake at night dreaming of working in a new corporation that does not yet have any data processing. Its data and procedures could be modeled correctly and cleanly from the start. Top-down plans could be implemented without problems caused by existing systems. Unfortunately, most information engineers have to live with the sins and systems of the past.

The existing systems in most enterprises have large quantities of old code, most of which was hand-built in an unstructured fashion. Their data has usually not been modeled, and little or no attempt has been made to achieve data compatibility between different systems. As well as *file* systems there are often old database systems designed before today's principles of good database design were understood. The data is unnormalized and unrelated to the data administration process. Many of these old systems are fragile and expensive to maintain.

Traditional maintenance of programs is an unsatisfactory and expensive process. It has been likened to attempting to repair a wooden boat while it is at sea. New planks can be replaced only by using existing planks for support. The process must be done in small steps; otherwise, the boat will sink. After much maintenance of this type has been done the boat becomes fragile. Attempts to change its design at sea are frustrated because no plans accurately reflect its current design. Sooner or later the boat must be brought to a shipyard and rebuilt.

Old systems need to be rebuilt using CASE (computer-aided system engineering) tools, the encyclopedia and information engineering principles. They cannot all be rebuilt quickly because this would be too much work. The best that can be hoped for is a steady one-at-a-time *migration* of the old systems into the cleanly engineered form.

In corporations which have successfully implemented I-CASE (integrated computer-aided software engineering) methodologies there are two development worlds. The I-CASE world has the ability to evolve systems, constantly improving their design and regenerating code. They may evolve within an IE framework with stable data models. The systems are cleanly engineered and easy to change. However, there is also an underworld of old systems, badly structured with manual code and manual design and no data models (Fig 20.1). In many corporations more programmers work in this underworld, maintaining bad-quality code, than work in the upper half of Fig. 20.1.

The problem is rather like the slum clearance problem in a city. A city might have a new center, elegant architecture, a well-thought-out street plan with pedestrian malls and parks, but still has large abominable areas of slums and old decrepit buildings. There is no easy solution to the slum clearance problem. The best that can be hoped for is a steady migration from the slums and their replacement with well-planned facilities.

Many corporations have attempted a major conversion of a file system to a database system and have failed. They have abandoned the attempt before it was completed. Often the reason for this is that it takes much more manpower than was anticipated; so much has to be reprogrammed. Often the attempt to convert is killed by the persons who control the IS finances. The conversion process itself creates no new applications. User management perceives a large amount of effort and expense with nothing to show for it. There is a long and serious application backlog. Management says: ''Why are you spending all of this time on conversion when we desperately need you to be creating new application systems? Get on with something more useful!'' In one organization after another the attempt to make a major conversion has failed. This has been true in some of the most prestigious data processing organizations.

The costs of maintenance in the non–I-CASE world gets ever higher. One of America's best telephone switches ran into so many software maintenance difficulties that its cost of maintenance exceeds $1 million per day. The switch would never have been built if that figure could have been forecast. A study by

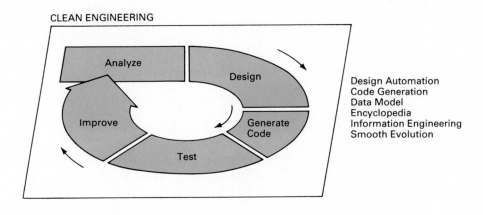

CLEAN ENGINEERING

Analyze

Design

Improve

Generate
Code

Test

Design Automation
Code Generation
Data Model
Encyclopedia
Information Engineering
Smooth Evolution

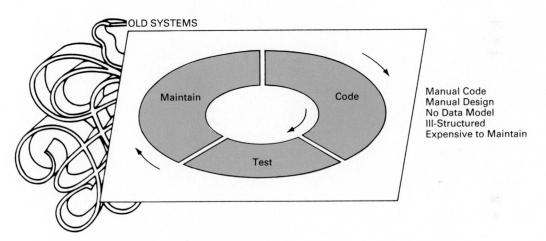

OLD SYSTEMS

Maintain

Code

Test

Manual Code
Manual Design
No Data Model
Ill-Structured
Expensive to Maintain

Figure 20.1 New information-engineered systems have to coexist with poor-quality systems built in the past.

the U.S. Air Force estimated that if maintenance productivity cannot be changed, it will require a quarter of the draft age population of the United States by 2000 A.D. to maintain its software [1]!

Fortunately, new tool sets are becoming available which facilitate the complex process of rebuilding systems. The old system is *reverse engineered* into a cleanly structured form using tools which automate the tedious parts of this process. The new structure is adapted so that it uses the IE data models. The programs are captured and represented in a CASE format so that they can then be modified as required using CASE tools.

Figure 20.2 shows a reverse-engineering step. The code of the old system is restructured with an automated tool and entered into an I-CASE tool so that

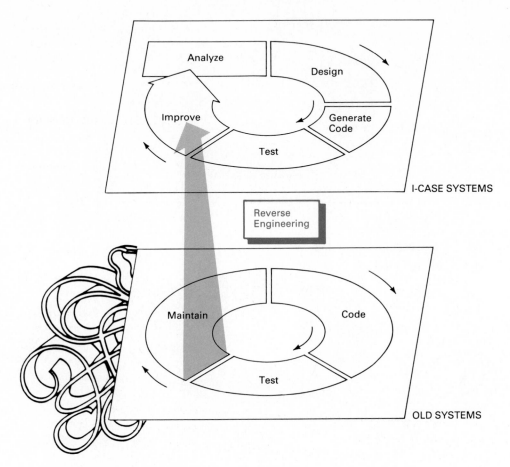

Figure 20.2 Data and code structures from the old systems should be captured and entered into the IE toolset.

it can be analyzed and redesigned and become part of the I-CASE evolutionary lifecycle.

Three terms are used in connection with this which are defined as follows:

Restructuring: Conversion (with an automated tool) of unstructured code into fully structured code.

Reverse engineering: Conversion of unstructured code into structured code and entry (automatically) of this into an I-CASE tool with which it can be improved or redesigned.

Reengineering: Modification of the design of a system, adding functionality where required, and (automated) production of code for the improved system.

If reverse engineering is done as shown in Fig. 20.2, the old systems can be rebuilt as evolutionary systems in the upper part of the diagram. Eventually, the messy underworld of Fig. 20.2 should disappear.

**THREE
APPROACHES**

There are basically three approaches to the IS slum clearance problem:

1. Do not convert. Allow applications to continue their existence unconverted, but *build a bridge* when necessary to the systems which use the IE data models and process models.

2. Restructure. Restructure the messy applications quickly (preferably with automated tools) but do not rebuild them to conform to the IE world. The slum areas are improved but not rebuilt to be part of the new planning. It is necessary to build a bridge in many cases to the IE world.

3. Rebuild. Reverse engineer the old applications to conform to the IE data models and process models. This is like redesigning and rebuilding access of the city.

In large installations using IE a mix of these three approaches will probably be used.

An old system exists. How should you decide whether to convert it? There are two questions that should be asked: First, does it work? If it works well then there is a strong argument for letting it alone. If it works inadequately, then it should be revamped anyway and may be cutover to the IE environment.

Second, does it incur high maintenance costs? If so then it is a candidate for restructuring or rebuilding with automated tools.

It may be deemed appropriate to restructure and modify it automatically by programming rather than to rebuild it with reverse engineering and I-CASE tools. If an application system works adequately and needs little maintenance, then its conversion should probably be postponed. Spend the effort on something else; there are so many other applications needed. If the decision is made that an old application should live on without being rebuilt, then it is often necessary to build a bridge between it and the IE environment.

In planning data resources it is often unwise to assume that old systems will be converted easily to the IE form. A realistic appraisal is needed of the costs and difficulties of conversion. The dismal history of uncompleted conversions should be weighed. Often system designers in the initial enthusiasm for information engineering assume that the old systems will be converted. It is discovered too late that they will not. It is safer instead to assume that many old systems will survive and plan a bridge that links them to the new world.

STEPS IN REENGINEERING

The term reverse engineering usually implies that automated tools will be used. Today no tool will convert old programs automatically so that they conform to IE models. Several tools help in doing this task, and it should be regarded as a computer-assisted human task.

Several tasks need to be done to reengineer an application.

1. Structuring the code. The application may be written with spaghetti code. It needs to be converted to structured programming. Several tools exists for automatically restructuring COBOL programs. The product RECODER from Language Technology, Inc., for example, converts COBOL programs that are messy, unstructured, and badly coded into fully structured COBOL. It prints diagrams of the structured program.

It is completely automatic, leaving no part of the structuring task to be done manually. Its vendor claims that it can structure any COBOL program, no matter how patched or complex [2]. The resulting program is functionally identical to the original.

Any logic errors in the original program will be transferred automatically to the restructured program, but they will probably be easier to identify and correct. The restructuring tools automatically identify dead branches in the code and produce reports on these. The restructured code is usually more bulky than the original, and may execute somewhat more slowly. After the following reengineering stages, the new code may be fed through a code optimizer to automatically make it more efficient.

The restructured code may be tested, perhaps with the original test data, to ensure that it is functionally equivalent to the original.

2. Entering the restructured code into a CASE tool. To work further on the program it should be entered into a CASE tool. After the program has been converted to a fully structured form it should be converted into an action diagram in a CASE tool which can display this diagram in other forms (decomposition diagram, structure chart) and link it to data models, screen designs, and so on.

3. Capturing the data description of the old system. The data description represented in the COBOL data division, dictionary, and so on, should be captured automatically.

4. Converting the data elements. The data elements (fields) in the old program are probably incompatible with the data elements in the IE data dictionary. Each data element from the old program should be associated with a data element in the IE dictionary. If no corresponding data element can be found, a new one should be entered into the IE data model. The data elements in the old program should then be converted automatically.

When the data elements have been converted the restructured programs may again be tested to ensure that they work well, before more complex redesign is started.

Some data dictionaries collect data definitions (with varying degrees of automation) from existing files, COBOL data divisions, and directories of database management systems. This variety of definitions can be gathered into a data dictionary. Definitions and data element formats which are more uniform can be substituted a step at a time.

If data definitions from many applications are loaded into the dictionary, the mess revealed may be so great as to discourage starting to clean it up. It is generally desirable to tackle a small area at a time.

5. Normalizing the data structures to conform to the IE models. The data in the old program is likely to be unnormalized. Even when the data elements are made the same as those in the IE data model, they are not necessarily grouped into records which conform to the data model. The data structures need to be converted. Converting the record structures may proceed in stages. First, the data structures from the existing programs are captured automatically and displayed. Second, the data elements are converted as done earlier. Third, the data is normalized and the normalized structure is made to conform to the IE data model. Normalization should be done at the screen of a CASE tool, with automated assistance.

6. Conversion of the file management or database management system. The application may be modified to use a different database management system. It may be converted from file management to database management. It may be converted from an hierarchical DBMS (like IMS), or a CODASYL DBMS (like IDMS), to a relational DBMS (like DB2, ORACLE, INGRES, etc.). Database design tools and a database generator may be used to help accomplish this.

7. Modifying the application to conform to new process models. The basic procedure is often redesigned when applications are modified. New process models which are part of IE design may be used. New modules may be linked into the old.

8. Adoption of new standards. The installation strategy may be to adopt standards when applications are rebuilt, for example, IBM's SAA (Systems Application Architecture) or the Department of Defense 2167 Standard. A CASE tool set may be used which relates to these standards.

9. Converting system interfaces. The application may be modified to use a different telecommunications monitor or operating system. Again, it may be adapted to IBM's Systems Application Architecture, for example. A code generator may be used to help in this conversion.

10. Generating modified data structures. From the data model new data structures will be created for the database management system in question. This work is essentially the same as the design stage of creating a new application and needs the same CASE tools which help to convert data model diagrams in data structure diagrams.

Creating the new data structures often needs modification of the way the programs access the data. It therefore needs to be done in conjunction with program design as it would be when a new application is being built. It needs the hyperdiagrams which link data design and program design.

11. Generating data description code. From the new data structure diagrams, data description code for the programs should be generated automatically (which, again, the CASE tools do).

Conversion of data is thus done at three levels as shown in Fig. 20.3: the physical data level represented in the program, the schema description, and the data model (or conceptual schema). These are the three levels of the classic ANSI SPARC description of database technology.

12. Converting or enhancing reports. It is usually desirable to improve the reports produced by the old program. New reports may be designed with the CASE report generator.

13. Redesigning the human interface. The user screen dialog of the old program may need improving. It may be the strategy of the IS organization to adopt IBM's Systems Application Architecture, for example, to achieve uniformity of style for all user interactions so that systems become familiar to users and easy to use. The CASE screen painter may be employed to redesign the screens.

14. Generate new program code and documentation. The program may be rebuilt using a code generator in order to make future modification quick and easy to accomplish. The decision to use a code generator affects steps 3 to 13.

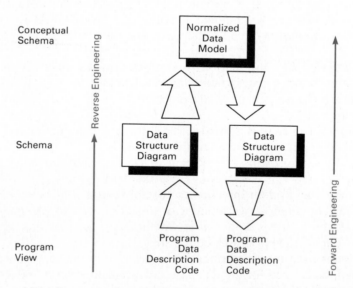

Figure 20.3 Reverse engineering captures the data description code, creates a data structure diagram, and modifies this to conform to (and possibly add to) the normalized data model (conceptual schema). Design of the data in new systems progresses with CASE tools from the data model to the data structure diagram to database code (the right of this diagram).

The CASE tools or code generator should generate documentation to help with subsequent maintenance. This documentation should conform to the installation's standards.

15. Use of a code optimizer. Because structured code is sometimes less machine efficient than nonstructured code, a code optimizer may be used to improve its efficiency.

Box 20.1 summarizes the 15 steps of reverse engineering. Steps 5 to 15 are done with I-CASE tools which were intended for the design of new systems rather than for reverse engineering. Tools also exist which restructure code automatically and aid in the conversion of data elements. These tools need to be integrated with the I-CASE tools to give a complete toolset for reverse engineering.

BOX 20.1   Reverse engineering

```
Reverse engineering may proceed in 15 possible steps.
  Structure the code (automatically).
     Use software for automatically converting the old program
        into a fully structured program, if possible, (for example,
        RECODER from Language Technology, Inc.).

  Enter the restructured code into the IE CASE tool.
     The restructured code should be in action diagram format so that
        it can be displayed and manipulated on the screen of the CASE
        tool. It is desirable that conversion to action diagram format
        should be done automatically. If the tools do not do this it
        must be done manually.

  Capture the data of the old system (automatically).
     The data division of COBOL, or its equivalent in other languages,
        should be read automatically into the CASE tool.
     The CASE tool should display the data structures graphically.

  Convert the data elements.
     Data elements should be converted one at a time to conform to
        the data element representation in the IE dictionary.
     This should be done with computer assistance so that no instances
        of the data element are omitted.
     Any data elements that do not have equivalents in the IE
        dictionary should be added to it.

  Normalize the data to conform to the IE model.
     The old data structures and the IE data structures should be
        shown graphically on the screen so that they can be compared.
     With the aid of the CASE tool the old data structures should
        be converted into normalized structures.
     It should be determined what conversion must be to take the old
        data structures into the IE environment.
```

(Continued)

BOX 20.1   *(Continued)*

Consider adoption of a new DBMS.
  If the old system used file management, as opposed to database
  management, or used a non-relational DBMS, it may be converted
  to use a relational database.
  The system may be redesigned to use a distributed database (See
  Chapter 16).

Adapt the application to the IE process model.
  Determine what changes are needed in the programs to make them
  conform to the IE process model.
  Adapt the design to make maximum use of reusable modules.
  Adapt the design to make use of object-oriented (entity-
  oriented) procedures where desirable.

Adapt the application design to new standards if necessary.
  The application may be redesigned to conform to IBM's SAA, or
  equivalent.
  The application may be redesigned to conform to application
  standards of the installation.

Adapt the application design to new system interfaces if necessary.
  The application may be redesigned to use new networking
  standards.
  The application may be redesigned to use cooperative processing
  or personal computers.
  The application may be redesigned as a distributed system.
  The application may be adapted to new hardware.

Generate modified data structures from the IE model.
  The normalized IE model is adjusted so that it can encompass
  the old system.
  Data structures for the DBMS in question are created with the
  CASE tool, as they would be for a new system.

Generate the data description code.
  The code generator of the IE tool should be used to generate the
  data description code.

Redesign the reports.
  Create the reports needed quickly, using a report generator,
  which is preferably part of the IE CASE toolset.
  Review the reports with the end users.
  The new reports may be designed and reviewed in a JAD session.
  Adjust the reports as required.

Redesign the human interface.
  The human interface should conform to modern standards such
  as IBM's CUA (The Common User Access of SAA, Systems
  Application Architecture).
  Create the new screens quickly, using a screen painter, which
  is preferably part of the IE CASE toolset.
  Link the screens into a dialog.
  Review the screens and dialog with the end users.
  The new dialog may be designed and reviewed in a JAD session.
  Adjust the dialog as required.
  Create online HELP facilities.

BOX 20.1 *(Continued)*

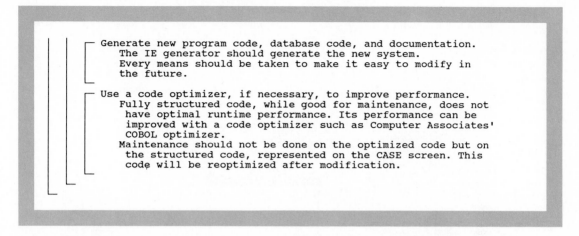

Generate new program code, database code, and documentation.
The IE generator should generate the new system.
Every means should be taken to make it easy to modify in
the future.

Use a code optimizer, if necessary, to improve performance.
Fully structured code, while good for maintenance, does not
have optimal runtime performance. Its performance can be
improved with a code optimizer such as Computer Associates'
COBOL optimizer.
Maintenance should not be done on the optimized code but on
the structured code, represented on the CASE screen. This
code will be reoptimized after modification.

TOOLS FOR REVERSE ENGINEERING THE DATA

Figure 20.4 illustrates the tools needed for reverse engineering the data.

At the bottom left is a tool which captures the physical descriptions of data from the programs. A CASE data structure diagramming tool may be used. The data captured may be in file form or in the form of a database structure such as IMS or IDMS. The diagramming tool may represent this structure. An analyst may clean up the data at this stage, removing redundancies and adjusting data types and definitions to make them conform to those in a data administrator's dictionary.

The data descriptions are then taken into a data analysis tool with which they can be represented as an entity-relationship model and the data fully normalized. The central encyclopedia of data models is used so that maximum conformity can be achieved with the data models for that business area.

The data in the normalized data models is then redesigned as a data structure diagram for the database management system in question (as they would be when new systems are being designed). At the bottom right of Fig. 20.4 the redesigned data structures are converted into database code that will be used by the redesigned program.

Human intelligence is likely to be needed at both the data modeling and the data structure stages of Fig. 20.4. The analyst needs a CASE tool which allows him to adjust the models and structures on the screen. He may be given guidance in both the data modeling and data structuring stages by an expert system. As in other tools using the encyclopedia, rule-based processing should ensure that full consistency and correct design is achieved.

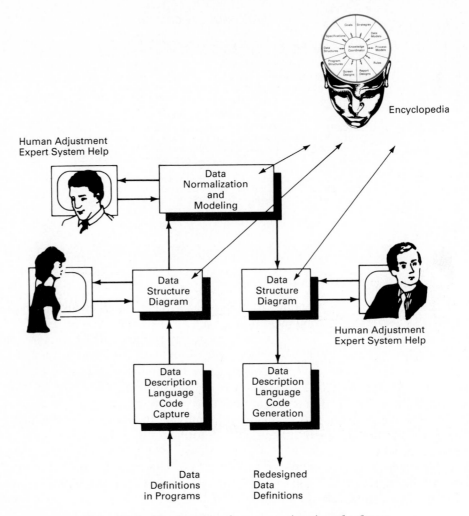

Figure 20.4   The data side of reverse engineering of software.

TOOLS FOR REVERSE ENGINEERING THE CODE

Figure 20.5 illustrates the tools needed for reverse engineering the program code.

At the bottom left, spaghetti code is taken into a restructuring engine. The restructured code is represented with diagrams that can be displayed and manipulated on the screen of a CASE tool. The best way of representing and manipulating structured code is with an action diagram. The screens, dialog, and reports produced by the programs will usually be redesigned. The CASE design tool needs a powerful screen painter and report generator. The new screens, dialog, and reports will be built into the action diagram structure.

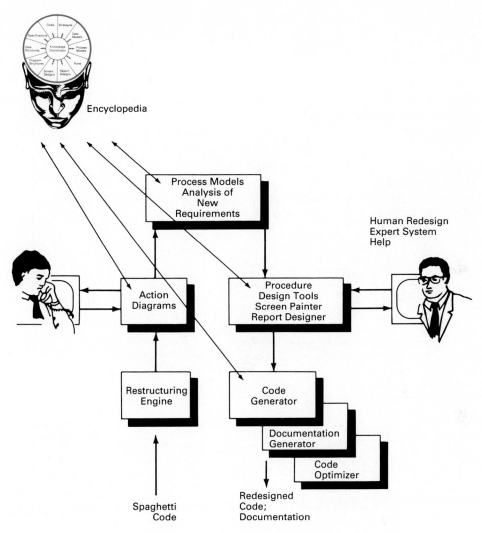

Figure 20.5   The process side of reverse engineering of software.

At the top of Fig. 20.5 are CASE tool representations of process models and new requirements. These may be used to aid the redesign of the programs. Again an expert system may be used to guide the designer and rule-based processing in conjunction with the encyclopedia should ensure complete consistency and good design.

When the program is redesigned, the design tool should drive a code generator which produces machine-efficient code. The design tools and code generator may conform to standards for application design. These may be standards of the installation in question or they may be industry or vendor standards such as IBM's SAA. They may employ reusable designs or building blocks that reside in the corporation's encyclopedia.

INTEGRATING CODE AND DATA REDESIGN   The reverse engineering of data (in Fig. 20.4) and program design (in Fig. 20.5) need to be combined. Fig. 20.6 is an overall diagram showing how the tools of Fig. 20.4 and Fig. 20.5 need to be integrated. The data models, data structure diagrams, action diagrams, procedure design diagrams, screen designs, and report designs are all logically interrelated and need to be linked into hyperdiagrams using a common encyclopedia with integrated knowledge coordination, as described earlier.

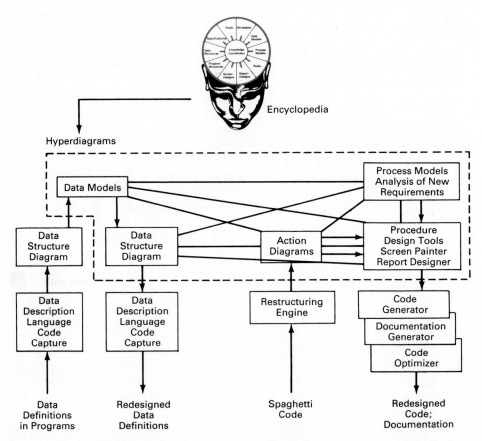

Figure 20.6   The procedures in Figs. 20.4 and 20.5 need to be integrated with the hyperdiagrams of an I-CASE tool set.

SIX CATEGORIES OF PROGRAM

Migrationwise, all programs should be classified into one of six categories, summarized in Box 20.2:

- Those that are static.
- Those requiring minor maintenance.
- Those requiring restructuring but not reengineering.
- Those requiring reengineering, but not to the IE environment.
- Those requiring reengineering to the IE environment.
- Those for which complete redevelopment is needed.

A study of maintenance costs done in IBM showed that if 12 percent or more of the code is to be changed, it is cheaper to scrap the program and redevelop it. This breakeven percentage is likely to be lower when I-CASE tools are used to generate the program.

There is often a strong argument for reengineering or redeveloping programs so that they conform to the IE models and then fit into an evolutionary lifecycle in which they can be constantly improved with I-CASE tools. In other words there is a strong argument for moving them from the underworld of Fig. 20.1 to the upper cleanly engineered world.

BOX 20.2   For migration purposes all programs should be categorized into one of the following categories

1. **Static.** No change required.
2. **Minor maintenance.** The most economic solution is to maintain the program in its present form.
3. **Restructure but do not reengineer.** The most economic solution is to restructure the program (automatically) and maintain it in that form without reengineering it.
4. **Reengineer, but not to the IE environment.** The most economic solution is to reverse engineer the program into a CASE tool and use that to maintain it, but not to convert it fully to the IE environment.
5. **Reengineer to the IE environment.** The most economic solution (for the long term) is to reverse engineer the program into the IE environment, designing it for low-cost maintenance in that environment.
6. **Scrap and rebuild.** The most economic solution is to scrap the program and create a new one.

The decision of which the foregoing five categories of program falls into is largely a financial decision. Reengineering or reconstructing with a code generator may be less expensive than maintaining the old code for several years. Often there is a major intangible benefit associated with the system being on the upper plane of Fig. 20.1, because this enables the enterprise to improve its procedures when it needs to. It is expensive to be locked into the straightjacket associated with the traditional DP backlog, because business procedures are not improved when they should be.

As the windows of opportunity shorten in our increasingly computerized world, it will be highly undesirable to be trapped on the lower plane of Fig. 20.1.

BUILDING A BRIDGE

With categories 1, 2, and 3, the old programs continue to exist, with their old structures of data which are probably incompatible with the IE data models. It will therefore be necessary to build a bridge such that whenever data is passed from the old systems to the new ones, or vice versa, the data is converted.

Figure 20.7 shows a typical bridge. At the center of Fig. 20.7 is the IE environment with well-modeled data. At the top is the output file from an existing application program. The data in it must update the IE databases, and a simple utility program is written for this. The old file records become a ''user view'' or subschema which must be represented in the databases. To accomplish this, some of the field formats may have to be adjusted by the utility program. There may be items in the file which would not have appeared in the databases if they had been designed by themselves, but they must now be there for compatibility reasons.

The databases are updated by new programs, and from the updated version the old files are derived. The bottom of Fig. 20.7 shows this being done by another utility program. This conversion program is needed every time the old application programs are used. It may be in effect a high-speed dump which creates batch files to be run once a week or so. It may create online files for terminal usage. This bridge must be one of the first database programs to be tested to ensure that the old application programs continue to run.

In many cases an input to a database system must also be used to create input to a separate file system, possibly on a different machine. Such input should be entered into the system only once, and a necessary function of the database system is to create the required input for other operations.

A similar bridge may be used for creating files that end users manipulate in their own way. This use of separate *extract files* keeps end users out of production databases. Disjoint end-user databases are created for report generation or decision-support purposes.

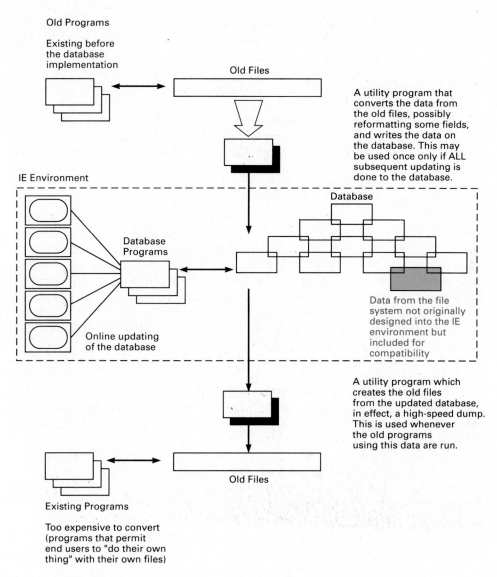

Old Programs

Existing before
the database
implementation

Old Files

A utility program that
converts the data from
the old files, possibly
reformatting some fields,
and writes the data on
the database. This may
be used once only if ALL
subsequent updating is
done to the database.

IE Environment

Database

Database
Programs

Data from the file
system not originally
designed into the IE
environment but
included for
compatibility

Online updating
of the database

A utility program which
creates the old files
from the updated database,
in effect, a high-speed dump.
This is used whenever
the old programs
using this data are run.

Old Files

Existing Programs

Too expensive to convert
(programs that permit
end users to "do their own
thing" with their own files)

Figure 20.7   A bridge between old applications and the information engineering environment.

**CONVERSION
MODELING**

Whether old systems are converted or a bridge is
built, the process needs to be taken into consideration
in the data modeling operation.

If conversion is done, the user views employed by the old systems should
be an input to the data modeling process. If a bridge is used, again the design

of the bridge should be an input to the data modeling and procedure modeling. The resulting data model will often contain data items that would not have been included had the bridge to the old world been unneccessary. They are put into the new databases to permit coexistence with old systems. This is a messy but necessary compromise which the data administrator must plan.

Such planning and modeling is an essential part of evolving from the old systems to an information engineering environment. The conversion programs—one might think of them as utility programs—are not difficult to write, but they have to be planned well ahead. They should be almost the first database programs to be tested, because the old systems must keep going.

GRADUAL CONVERSION

In long-established installations, conversion to an IE environment usually has to be a gradual process. There are too many files and programs for quick conversion, and the investment in them is high. It becomes a long-term strategic goal eventually to have all applications use the data and process models and be built with the encyclopedia-based tools. Once rebuilt, especially if rebuilt with an application generator, applications become much cheaper to maintain. In a typical corporation's portfolio of applications, *most* will be rebuilt at some time in the next eight years. The portfolio is slowly adapted to conform to the IE environment, and then the information resource of the corporation is under control.

What types of systems be converted first? The applications that fall into categories 4 and 5 should be rebuilt with information engineering. In general applications where there is the largest financial payoff are likely to be tackled first.

In some installations different areas of activities have been tackled one at a time. Insurance companies refer to their different types of insurance as ''lines of business.'' One insurance company approached the conversion problem by bringing one line of business at a time into database operation with integrated data models.

Some installations have implemented all the online applications of a given database with an integrated data model and have left the offline (batch) systems in an unconverted form for the time being, with bridges like that in Fig. 20.7. All online systems or end-user systems have conformed to the IE environment.

MAKING FUTURE CONVERSION EASY

It is desirable to build systems which will be easy to change in the future. A major objective of clean engineering is to make systems easy to change.

The slum clearance problem is difficult and expensive to cope with. A major goal in enterprises today should be to stop building slums. Applications being built today should be fully structured and based on normalized data models in a CASE encyclopedia. It is irresponsible to build applications today without clean engineering.

A major reason for moving to database is to make application conversion easier. Different reports and query processing can be generated quickly. The ease of modifying major applications depends on whether the database management system has field sensitivity and other features which aid maintenance. It also depends on whether the data is correctly normalized. Good database installations have achieved much greater conversion flexibility.

There are, however, ways in which database systems have made conver-

BOX 20.3   Design systems for ease of migration in the future

- Use CASE tools for planning, analysis, design, and construction.
- Use a code generator driven by the CASE design tools.
- Establish diagramming standards for all analysis and design diagrams.
- Adhere to the principles and practice of information engineering.
- Create BAA (business area analyses) data and process models which are independent of specific procedures.
- Create procedure designs which are independent of technology which is likely to change.
- Employ a code generator which can translate the designs into implementations with different technology (e.g., a generator which can generate code and data descriptions for different database environments).
- Use fully normalized data models (not less than third-normal form).
- Use fully structured code built with an action diagram editor which is part of a CASE environment.
- Use of relational database where possible.
- Use application standards such as IBM's Systems Application Architecture.
- Use a database management system with field independence and features which enable changes to be made without rewriting existing programs.
- Avoid unusual hardware, operating systems, or facilities which could make future migration difficult.
- Plan to do future maintenance by regeneration.
- Make high management fully aware of the business reasons for achieving clean engineering and automation in application development.

sion more difficult. The attempt to change to a different DBMS can be difficult, and extremely difficult if that DBMS is differently structured, for example, the change from a CODASYL to hierarchical database. Using a code generator can make the conversion much easier if the generator can generate code for both types of databases. The generator which generates database code for multiple database management systems can insulate the program from DBMS conversion problems.

To achieve ease of conversion in the future, applications should be developed with the characteristics listed in Box 20.3.

Box 20.4 summarizes a procedure for reverse engineering.

BOX 20.4   Procedure for reverse engineering

```
Schedule the system-building projects.
    Decide what new systems will be built.
    Obtain approval for specific system projects.
    Determine the resources needed.
    Present the results to the executive sponsor.
    Schedule the development activity.

Develop a reverse engineering strategy.

    Reverse engineering may proceed in 15 possible steps.
        Structure the code (automatically).
            Use software for automatically converting the old program
            into a fully structured program, if possible, (for example,
            RECODER from Language Technology, Inc.).

        Enter the restructured code into the IE CASE tool.
            The restructured code should be in action diagram format so that
            it can be displayed and manipulated on the screen of the CASE
            tool. It is desirable that conversion to action diagram format
            should be done automatically. If the tools do not do this, it
            must be done manually.

        Capture the data of the old system (automatically).
            The data division of COBOL, or its equivalent in other languages,
            should be read automatically into the CASE tool.
            The CASE tool should display the data structures graphically.

        Convert the data elements one at a time to those in the IE encyclopedia.
            Data elements should be converted one at a time to conform to
            the data element representation in the IE dictionary.
            This should be done with computer assistance so that no instances
            of the data element are omitted.
            Any data elements that do not have equivalents in the IE
            dictionary should be added to it.

        The following steps are done with I-CASE tools for building new systems:
            Normalize the data to conform to the IE model.
                The old data structures and the IE data structures should be
                shown graphically on the screen so that they can be compared.
                With the aid of the CASE tool the old data structures should
                be converted into normalized structures.
```

BOX 20.4 *(Continued)*

It should be determined what conversion must be to take the old data structures into the IE environment.

Consider adoption of a new DBMS.
If the old system used file management, as opposed to database management, or used a non-relational DBMS, it may be converted to use a relational database.
The system may be redesigned to use a distributed database (See Chapter 16.

Adapt the application to the IE process model.
Determine what changes are needed in the programs to make them conform to the IE process model.
Adapt the design to make maximum use of reusable modules.
Adapt the design to make use of object-oriented (entity-oriented) procedures where desirable.

Adapt the application design to new standards if necessary.
The application may be redesigned to conform to IBM's SAA, or equivalent.
The application may be redesigned to conform to application standards of the installation.

Adapt the application design to new system interfaces, if necessary.
The application may be redesigned to use new networking standards.
The application may be redesigned to use cooperative processing or personal computers.
The application may be redesigned as a distributed system.
The application may be adapted to new hardware.

Generate modified data structures from the IE model.
The normalized IE model is adjusted so that it can encompass the old system.
Data structures for the DBMS in question are created with the CASE tool, as they would be for a new system.

Generate the data description code.
The code generator of the IE tool should be used to generate the data description code.

Redesign the reports.
Create the reports needed quickly, using a report generator, which is preferably part of the IE CASE toolset.
Review the reports with the end users.
The new reports may be designed and reviewed in a JAD session.
Adjust the reports as required.

Redesign the human interface.
The human interface should conform to modern standards such as IBM's CUA (The Common User Access of SAA, Systems Application Architecture).
Create the new screens quickly, using a screen painter, which is preferably part of the IE CASE toolset.
Link the screens into a dialog.
Review the screens and dialog with the end users.
The new dialog may be designed and reviewed in a JAD session.
Adjust the dialog as required.
Create online HELP facilities.

Generate new program code, database code, and documentation.
The IE generator should generate the new system.

(Continued)

BOX 20.4 *(Continued)*

Every means should be taken to make it easy to modify in the future.

Use a code optimizer, if necessary, to improve performance.
Fully structured code, while good for maintenance, does not have optimal runtime performance. Its performance can be improved with a code optimizer such as Computer Associates' COBOL optimizer.
Maintenance should not be done on the optimized code but on the structured code, represented on the CASE screen. This code will be reoptimized after modification.

Categorize applications by migration requirement.
Use the list of all application programs. Record an estimate of the cost of maintaining the program in its current form for each of the next five years.
Categorize all applications into the following six migration categories:

1. STATIC

No change required.

2. MINOR MAINTENANCE

The most economic solution is to maintain the program in its present form.

3. RESTRUCTURE BUT DO NOT RE-ENGINEER

The most economic solution is to restructure the program (automatically) and maintain it in that form without re-engineering it.

4. RE-ENGINEER, BUT NOT TO THE IE ENVIRONMENT

The most economic solution is to reverse engineer the program into a CASE tool and use that to maintain it, but not to convert it fully to the IE environment.

5. RE-ENGINEER TO THE IE ENVIRONMENT

The most economic solution (for the long term) is to reverse engineer the program into the IE environment, designing it for low-cost maintenance in that environment.

6. SCRAP AND REBUILD

The most economic solution is to scrap the program and create a new one.

Design a data conversion bridge for non-IE programs.
When data from non-IE programs pass to programs in the IE environment, or vice versa, the data will have to be converted. This is the case when application packages are used, as well as with in-house non-IE programs.
Determine what data conversions are necessary.
Chart the links needing data conversion on a data-flow diagram.
Design the data conversion.
Determine whether the data conversion program can be created automatically.
Schedule the building and testing of the data conversion bridge.

REFERENCES

1. From a paper by Eric Bush, ''A CASE for Existing Systems,'' Language Technology, Inc., Salem, MA, 1988.

2. Literature on RECODER from Language Technology, Inc., Salem, MA, 1988.

21 NEW DEVELOPMENT LIFECYCLES

INTRODUCTION   Prior to the mid-1980s most systems were developed with a development lifecycle which is now referred to as the *traditional lifecycle*. It is illustrated in Fig. 21.1. Different variations of this lifecycle are in the standards manuals for data processing of most organizations. They are sold as *methodologies* by consulting companies, accounting firms, and methodology companies. Figure 21.2 shows the U.S. Department of Defense variant, and Fig. 21.3 shows that in a large aerospace corporation. Standard forms and documentation were created to assist or formalize the traditional lifecycle.

The world of information engineering and fourth-generation methodologies has brought new types of lifecycle. New and better lifecycles are possible because of new tools and techniques. The tools and techniques listed in Box 21.1 did not exist when the traditional lifecycle grew to prominence.

As experience has grown with I-CASE tools this has been distilled into a new lifecycle for achieving high-quality systems at high speed. This RAD (rapid application development) lifecycle, which has evolved since the present book was written, is described in the author's book, *Rapid Application Development* [1]. A computerized methodology is available for the RAD lifecycle which attempts to gather together the best experience with I-CASE toolsets [2].

It is desirable to employ new forms of development lifecycle because

- The traditional lifecycle is very slow. Some systems must be built more quickly.

- The traditional lifecycle often fails to meet the needs of the end users. New techniques can meet their needs much better.

- The traditional lifecycle tends to result in severe maintenance costs. Other techniques can help avoid the maintenance burden.

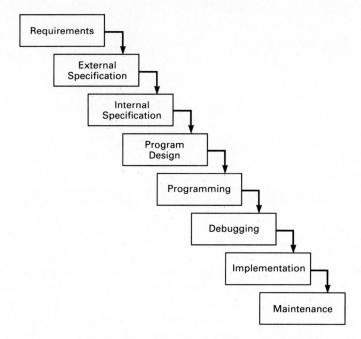

Figure 21.1   The traditional lifecycle.

- Higher IS productivity is needed than is possible with the traditional lifecycle.
- The traditional lifecycle prevents exploratory design and programming which is necessary in creative areas.
- The traditional lifecycle often fails to provide the rigor needed for complex integration.
- It is often possible to achieve much lower development costs than with the traditional lifecycle.
- The end users should perform much of the development work for applications such as business modeling and decision support.
- Evolutionary development is needed in which systems continually grow, being added to by different people in different places, at different times.

We will represent the procedures for development lifecycles with action diagrams. It is often desirable to modify the procedure for a specific project. An action diagram editor enables the procedure to be adjusted for the project in question.

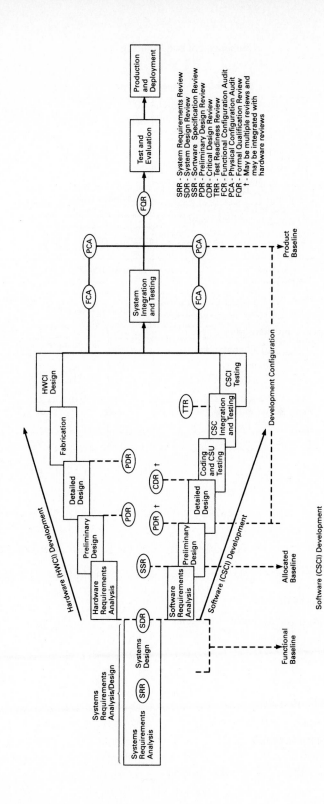

Figure 21.2 The standard lifecycle of the U.S. Department of Defense.

449

System Development Lifecycle

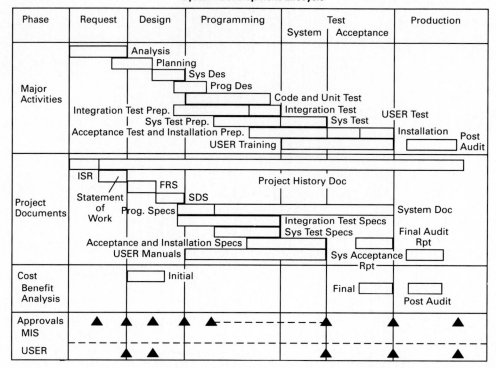

Figure 21.3 The lifecycle standard of a large aerospace corporation.

TYPES OF LIFECYCLES

Project lifecycles can be divided into several categories:

- Single-iteration lifecycle
- Multi-iteration (or iterative) lifecycle
- Evolutionary lifecycle
- Timebox lifecycle
- Exploratory lifecycle
- Quick-results lifecycle
- Decision-support-system lifecycle
- Expert-system lifecycle

Box 21.2 describes these lifecycles, briefly.

BOX 21.1　The historical lifecycle grew up before the following tools and techniques existed

- Nonprocedural languages
- Languages for rapid prototyping
- Languages for end users
- Code generators
- Computable specification languages
- Rigorous verification techniques
- PC workstations with mouse-driven graphics
- Online graphics tools for design
- Formal data modeling tools
- Strategic data planning techniques
- Information engineering
- The encyclopedia concept
- Techniques for reusability
- Distributed processing, distributed database
- Cooperative processing
- Standards for applications such as IBM's SAA (Systems Application Architecture)
- Macintoshlike user interface
- The information center concept
- Expert systems
- Rule-based processing
- Artificial intelligence techniques

PREEXISTING MODELS

An important aspect of lifecycles in an information engineering environment is that data models and process models exist *before the projects for building systems begin.* In other words, BAA (business area analysis) has been done. A piece of the lifecycle, then, is the extraction of the relevant portion of these models for incorporation in the design. This speeds up the design process, and helps to give understanding and precision to a JAD (joint application design) session. As the data models become implemented in database systems, this fa-

BOX 21.2 Lifecycle categories

For each of these types of lifecycle there are many variations.

SINGLE-ITERATION LIFECYCLE
A single-iteration lifecycle creates a specification for a system. The specification is converted into a program design, coded, tested, and installed. The classical lifecycle of the 1970s is one form of single-iteration lifecycle.
Prototyping tools, design automation, code generators and information engineering change the nature of the single-iteration lifecycle. Such tools should be used to involve the end users in the design of systems, to make the design more rigorous, to speed up code production and debugging, to speed up maintenance, and to integrate the system into the corporate facilities with information engineering.

MULTI-ITERATION LIFECYCLE
A multi-iteration lifecycle creates a succession of prototypes of the target system. The prototypes are improved a stage at a time until they converge to what the end users agree is a valuable system. The final prototype may become the final system, or may be rebuilt.
While simple systems can be designed in one step, complex or subtle systems become understood only by attempting to build a prototype, learning from it, and rebuilding the prototype until it represents a valuable design.
The iterative lifecycle first establishes a clear set of objectives for the system. There must be a clearly defined target towards which the iterative design and prototyping progresses. The iterative lifecycle is made practical by tools which enable us to build prototypes quickly and change them easily. Sometimes the final prototype needs rebuilding or rearchitecting to achieve clean design and good machine performance.

TIMEBOX LIFECYCLE
The timebox methodology is a highly successful form of lifecycle which emphasizes high-speed development. It constrains the functionality of the first release of a system is order to have a fully working system within a short timeframe.
The lifecycle employs continuous-evolution prototyping with a tight deadline. It requires an I-CASE toolset designed to make design fast and easy, and give a rapid cycle of modify-generate-test. End users are involved continuously throughout the lifecycle.
The costs and risks of new system development are minimized by emphasizing JRP, JAD, prototyping, and high-speed development, with continuous user involvement, within an IE framework.

EVOLUTIONARY LIFECYCLE
Many future business systems will grow continuously over many years within an information-engineering framework, eventually becoming very complex systems that are a uniquely valuable corporate resource. They will be added to by different developers, at different times, in different places. They should be planned and built so that this long-term evolution is accomplished as smoothly and easily as possible.
The lifecycle for a major addition to a system designed for evolution starts with a detailed description of the system, in the encyclopedia, and an analysis of what changes in its functions are needed. The changes may be built with a multi-iteration or timebox lifecycle, using JAD, prototyping, I-CASE tools, and information engineering. The same code generator and application standards should be used as in the existing version of the system.

452

BOX 21.2 *(Continued)*

EXPLORATORY LIFECYCLE

Whereas conventional lifecycles start with a clearly defined target, an exploratory lifecycle is one in which the target could not be defined in detail at the beginning.

An exploratory lifecycle is more in the nature of research and needs to be managed like research. It explores what is possible by building a system with ad-hoc creativity. The resulting prototypes usually have to be discarded and rearchitected to achieve a working system.

Whereas an evolutionary lifecycle promises a deliverable system at the end of the procedure, an exploratory lifecycle should not. The exploratory lifecycle finds out what it may be practical to deliver.

QUICK-RESULTS LIFECYCLE

A quick-results lifecycle applies to simple applications such as report generation and business calculations. It is used in information-center environments, either by end users or data-processing professionals. The application is simple enough to avoid formal specification and design. It may require formal documentation.

Quick-results computing is an extremely important part of data processing capable of having a vital effect on the running of the enterprise. It is made much more valuable and generally applicable by the building of appropriate databases. Information engineering should create facilities so that quick-results computing can be as useful as possible.

DECISION-SUPPORT-SYSTEM LIFECYCLE

A decision-support system is designed to help make better business decisions in a specific area. It requires an appropriately structured database and a set of tools for doing decision-support computations.

Decision-support computations should generally be done by end users because they understand the business problem they are trying to solve. They may do this in an innovative, ad-hoc fashion without specifications. Often creative investigation of numerical data is required. Highly complex business models may result. Evolution through prototyping should occur before the system is institutionalized.

Data-processing professionals should usually design the database and the means of keeping it up to date. They may select or build the tools which the end users employ, and guide the end users in their use. The choice of decision-support software is critical.

EXPERT-SYSTEM LIFECYCLE

An expert system is designed to capture human expertise in a specific area so that other people can use that expertise to make better decisions or to perform their activities faster.

An expert-system shell must be chosen and populated with knowledge. This knowledge consists primarily of data and rules which apply to that data. The data may be already described in the IE data models. An A.I. or I.S. professional should usually select the tools and initiate the knowledge acquisition process, interacting with the experts on the subject matter. The experts or end users may themselves learn to participate in the process of adding to and tuning the rules that comprise the system.

Where possible, the evolution of the knowledgebase should be done by end users because the evolution may be continual and the end users understand the business problems they are trying to solve and have direct experience with the system in operation.

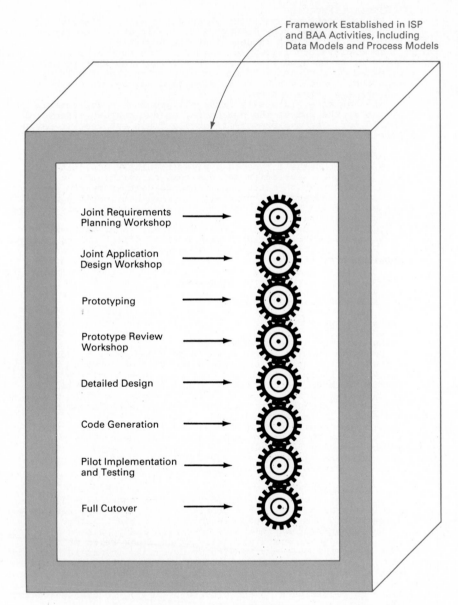

Joint Requirements Planning Workshop

Joint Application Design Workshop

Prototyping

Prototype Review Workshop

Detailed Design

Code Generation

Pilot Implementation and Testing

Full Cutover

Figure 21.4 The development lifecycle for one project fits into the information engineering framework established in ISP (information strategy planning) and BAA (business area analysis).

cilitates the fast building of prototypes. It aids and helps to control information center activities. Reusable processes have been identified and in some cases designed. The development lifecycle should be thought of as something which fits into the framework of BAA, as shown in Fig. 21.4.

In the traditional lifecycle, all the work is done as part of the lifecycle. In the new lifecycles, much work has been done before the lifecycle begins and is available in an encyclopedia.

Systems are still sometimes designed before business area analysis has been done or the requisite models built. In this case the data modeling and process modeling should be an early part of the project lifecycle.

BETTER UNDERSTANDING THE NEEDS OF THE END USERS

As we have stressed, a particularly inadequate aspect of the traditional lifecycle is the requirements analysis and specification. Often the true end-user needs and what users would do with the system were poorly understood. It was very expensive to have a programming team build a system and then discover inadequacies that required a redesign.

In advanced methodologies this problem is solved in ways such as the following:

- Joint requirement planning (Chapter 7)
- Joint application design (Chapter 8)
- Prototyping (Chapter 6)
- Evolutionary development
- Timebox methodology (Chapter 9)
- Information Center techniques (Chapter 10)
- Executive Information Centers (Chapter 13)

Joint application design makes users participate in establishing the system requirements and creates a design in sufficient detail that data processing professionals can build prototypes and extend the design into what is needed for implementation.

Prototyping enables end users to work with prototypes of the system. The prototypes are adjusted to meet the users' needs as fully as possible. There is a world of difference between users critiquing a prototype and critiquing a three-ring binder of text specifications.

Iterative development is used to progress toward a complex system in stages, ensuring that the subtleties of the system are fully understood. Evolution is used to enable systems to be added to by different teams at different times.

Information Center techniques may be built into the design so that users can create their own reports, extract data into spreadsheets, or manipulate information from the system's database. The system is made adaptable by end users, as far as is possible.

SINGLE-ITERATION LIFECYCLE

The single-iteration lifecycle should involve joint application design, prototyping, design automation, and code generation where possible. The stages of the cycle may be as follows:

```
┌ Single-iteration procedure
│  ...Initiate the project
│  ...Select tools
│  ...Scope the project
│  ...Prepare for cultural changes
│  ...JRP procedure
│  ...JAD procedure
│  ...Create physical design
│  ...Design for cutover
│  ...Build pilot system
│  ...Prepare for cutover
│  ...Install and adjust pilot system
└  ...Expand pilot to full system
```

The JRP and JAD procedure, here, dominates the front end of the lifecycle. As discussed in Chapters 7 and 8, the system requirements are analyzed and agreed on. Between the first and second JAD workshops, data processing professionals solidify the design and build prototypes which the users work with. The prototypes are reviewed and the design enhanced in the second design workshop.

During the JAD session, information is extracted from the encyclopedia and designs built with the graphics tools. The designs which are created during the JAD workshop may be approximate designs. Where the tool has a *knowledge coordinator,* for example, this may be switched off during the JAD session so that rough designs can be built quickly. After both the first and second JAD workshops, the design is improved and analyzed with the knowledge coordinator, and the prototypes are enhanced.

The JAD session is not concerned with detailed physical design, physical database design, performance optimization, or those aspects of design which are in the province of the data professional and not the end user. The lifecycle stage of creating the final design addresses those issues:

```
┌─ Single-iteration procedure

  ...Initiate the project
  ...Select tools
  ...Scope the project
  ...Prepare for cultural changes
  ...JRP procedure
  ...JAD procedure
  ┌─ Create physical design
  │  ┌─ Determine whether data will be distributed
  │  │  o───────────────────────────o
  │  │  │ See procedure in Box 16.1  │
  │  │  o───────────────────────────o
  │
  │     Determine traffic volumes.
  │  ┌─ Perform data use analysis
  │  │  o───────────────────────────o
  │  │  │ See procedure in Box 14.1  │
  │  │  o───────────────────────────o
  │
  │  ┌─ Do physical database design
  │  │  o───────────────────────────o
  │  │  │ See procedure in Box 15.1  │
  │  │  o───────────────────────────o
  │
  │     Determine hardware requirements
  │     Examine how to optimize performance.
  │     Complete documentation (in the encyclopedia) of the final
  │        design.
  └─
  ...Design for cutover
  ...Build pilot system
  ...Prepare for cutover
  ...Install and adjust pilot system
  ...Expand pilot to full system
└─
```

When large systems are installed it is good practice to install a pilot system, ensure that it works well, and extend it a step at a time until it becomes the final system. The pilot is a fully working system but may, at first, have only a small number of terminals, a small number of users or a small number of transactions. It may possibly run on a smaller computer than the final system. When it is found to be satisfactory, the volumes of transactions are increased and it is deployed on a larger scale.

When the prototypes are extended into a pilot system an important question is: "Should the same language or code generator be used?" The fourth-generation language used for prototyping may give poor machine performance. This may not matter if the transaction volume and system usage are low. It is advantageous for the prototyping language to be the final language, but this may not be practical. This is an issue which should be addressed during the selection of the tools used.

Where possible the language or code generator should be an extension of, or should be tightly coupled to, the design workbench.

If the prototype has to be recoded to achieve the performance necessary for the final system, the recoding should employ the same action diagram, and, if possible, the same action diagram editor. This lessens the chance of introducing bugs while recoding.

Building and extending the pilot system is an important part of the lifecycle.

```
┌─ Single-iteration procedure
│
│  ...Initiate the project
│  ...Select tools
│  ...Scope the project
│  ...Prepare for cultural changes
│  ...JRP procedure
│  ...JAD procedure
│  ...Create physical design
│  ...Design for cutover
│  ┌─ Build pilot system
│  │
│  │  ┌─ If the prototype can have good enough performance to
│  │  │    become the working system
│  │  │
│  │  │    Improve the prototype so that it becomes a pilot system.
│  │  ┌─ Else
│  │  │  ┌─ If the whole system must be built in a different language
│  │  │  │    Recode using the same action diagram as far as possible.
│  │  │  │
│  │  │  ┌─ Else if only portions of the code need be changed
│  │  │  │
│  │  │  │    Replace code where needed (possibly with a more efficient
│  │  │  │    language) using the same action diagram where possible.
│  │  │  └
│  │  │    Debug the system so that it is stable enough to use as a
│  │  │    pilot doing actual work.
│  │  └
│  └
│  ...Prepare for cutover
│  ▐ Install and adjust pilot system
│  ▐ ┌─ Perform cutover
│  ▐ │  o─────────────────────────────o
│  ▐ │  │  See detail in Box 18.2     │
│  ▐ │  o─────────────────────────────o
│  ▐ │  ...Set up the production procedures
│  ▐ │  ...Install the production system environment
│  ▐ │  ...Perform data conversion
│  ▐ │  ...Implement the new system in production
│  ▐ └  ...Review the system installation
│  ▐ ┌─ If no modifications needed
│  ▐ │
│ «──┼──── Exit
│  ▐ ┌─ Else
│  ▐ │    Document adjustments needed.
│  ▐ │    Determine date for installation of next version.
│  ▐ └    Make adjustments.
│
│  ...Expand pilot to full system
└
```

Box 21.3 gives the single-iteration lifecycle procedure in more detail.

MULTI-ITERATION LIFECYCLE

The multi-iteration lifecycle differs from the single-iteration lifecycle mainly in its use of prototyping. A complete prototype system is built, and this may

BOX 21.3　Single-iteration lifecycle

Description
　　A single-iteration lifecycle creates a specification for
　　a system. The specification is converted into a program
　　design, coded, tested, and installed. The classical lifecycle
　　of the 1970s is one form of single-iteration lifecycle.
　　　　Prototyping tools, design automation, code generators and
　　information engineering, change the nature of the single-
　　iteration lifecycle. Such tools should be used to involve
　　the end users in the design of systems, to make the design
　　more rigorous, to speed up code production and debugging, to
　　speed up maintenance, and to integrate the system into the
　　corporate facilities with information engineering.

Has Business Area Analysis been done ?

　　| See BAA Action Diagram in Book II |

　　If BUSINESS AREA ANALYSIS has been done then much of the information
　　for design already exists in the encyclopedia.

Single-iteration procedure

　　　　The procedure given below may be modified with Action
　　　　Diagrammer to meet the needs of the particular situation.

　　Initiate the project.
　　　　Determine need for system.
　　　　Obtain executive sponsor.

　　Select tools.
　　　　Select design tools.
　　　　　　(An encyclopedia-based workbench is desirable.)
　　　　Select prototyping tools.
　　　　　　(The question of whether the prototyping language can
　　　　　　become the final language should be addressed.)
　　　　Select programming language / generator.
　　　　　　(It is desirable to have a code generator which is tightly
　　　　　　　coupled to, or is an extension of, the design workbench.)

　　Scope the project.
　　　　If Business Area Analysis has been done
　　　　　　Extract relevant data and process models from the
　　　　　　encyclopedia.
　　　　Else
　　　　　　Create relevant data and process models.

　　Prepare for cultural changes.
　　　　| See detail in Box 17.1 |

(Continued)

BOX 21.3 *(Continued)*

    Identify any cultural changes.
     List the following types of cultural changes which the new system
     might bring about:
     o Changes in organizational structure
     o Changes in policies
     o Changes in business procedures
     o Changes in staffing levels
     o Changes in job content
     o Changes in skill requirements

     Review this list with top management.

  ...Design the organizational changes.
  ...Identify responsibilities for organizational changes.
  ...Schedule the organizational changes.

JRP procedure
  The requirements planning is done in a JRP workshop.

   | See Box 7.2: JRP procedure |

JAD procedure
  The specifications and initial design are produced by JAD in
  conjunction with prototyping.

   | See Box 8.1: JAD procedure |

Create physical design.
  Determine whether data will be distributed.

    | See procedure in Box 16.1 |

  Determine traffic volumes.
  Perform data use analysis.

    | See procedure in Box 14.1 |

  Do physical database design.

    | See procedure in Box 15.1 |

  Determine hardware requirements.
  Examine how to optimize performance.
  Complete documentation (in the encyclopedia) of the final design.

Design for cutover.

   | See detail in Box 17.2 |

...Establish the implementation standards.
...Design the conversion procedures.
...Design the production procedures.
...Plan the hardware installation.
...Determine the testing strategy.
...Plan the testing environment.
...Create the technical documentation.
...Create the user documentation.
...Create the training program.

BOX 21.3 *(Continued)*

Build pilot system.
  Description
      A pilot system is a fully working system deployed at first
      with only a small number of users, small number of terminals
      or small number of transactions. When it is found to be
      satisfactory the volumes of transactions are increased and
      it is deployed on a larger scale.

  If the prototype can have good enough performance to
      become the working system

      Improve the prototype so that it becomes a pilot system.
  Else
      If the whole system must be built in a different language
          Recode using the same action diagram as far as possible.

      Else if only portions of the code need be changed

          Replace code where needed (possibly with a more efficient
          language) using the same action diagram where possible.

      Debug the system so that it is stable enough to use as a
      pilot doing actual work.

Prepare for cutover.
  ┌─o────────────────────────────o─┐
  │ See details in Box 18.1 │
  └─o────────────────────────────o─┘
  ...Develop the conversion system.
  Finalize the development product.
      ...Perform quality audit.
      ...Refine the development product.

  Prepare for final testing.
      ...Install the software to be used for final testing.
      Build the test libraries.
      Coordinate the testing with the development team.

  Carry out the final testing.
      ...Program test
      ...Integration test
      ...Volume test
      ...Regression test for maintenance changes
      ...Acceptance test
      Collect statistics for project management
      Document the test results.

  Plan and conduct the training program.
      Develop the training plan.
          Determine who will create the training materials.
          Determine who will conduct the training.
          Determine which users will be trained initially.
          Determine the time and location of training.

      ...Conduct training.

(Continued)

BOX 21.3   *(Continued)*

```
┌  Install and adjust pilot system.
│  ┌ Perform cutover.
│  │     o───────────────────────o
│  │     │  See detail in Box 18.2  │
│  │     o───────────────────────o
│  │     ...Set up the production procedures.
│  │     ...Install the production system environment.
│  │     ...Perform data conversion.
│  │     ...Implement the new system in production.
│  └     ...Review the system installation.
│
│  ┌ If no modifications needed
«─┼────── Exit
│  ┌ Else
│  │     Document adjustments needed.
│  │     Determine date for installation of next version.
│  └     Make adjustments.
│
┌  Expand pilot to full system.
│        Measure the system performance.
│  ┌ Optimize the database design.
│  │     o───────────────────────────o
│  │     │  See data use analysis in Box 14.1   │
│  │     o───────────────────────────o
│  │     o───────────────────────────o
│  │     │  See database design in Box 15.1    │
│  └     o───────────────────────────o
│
│        Determine what hardware is needed to handle the full load.
│
┌  Expand the system a stage at a time.
└        Monitor the system performance.
```

evolve over an extended period of time through multiple version as the system becomes better understood.

Evolution can be of two types, discrete or continuous. *Discrete,* or step-by-step, *evolution* progresses as a set of discrete prototyping projects. Each prototype is employed by end users and reviewed with the designers. A list of defects and required enhancements is created, and a target date is established for the next prototype. Continuous evolution progresses as a sequence of modifications continuously adjusting the prototype until the target is reached. Figure 21.5 illustrates the difference between step-by-step and continuous evolution.

Step-by-step evolution is the normal form of evolutionary development. It can be controlled more formally.

Continuous evolution is appropriate where the controlling end user or users

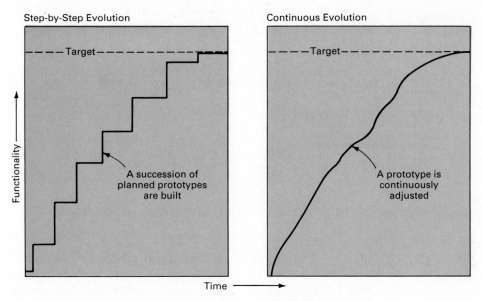

Figure 21.5   Step-by-step versus continuous evolution.

understand and want more involvement in the creative process. Continuous evolution is sometimes more creative but is more difficult to manage in a formal way. It requires intelligent, innovative end users. It is sometimes conducted like a two-person team with an end user being a part-time team member. Sometimes larger teams are used, but it tends to work well only with small tightly knit teams.

Many systems in the future are likely to be built with an iterative procedure:

```
┌─ Multi-iteration procedure
│
│   ...Initiate the project.
│   ...Select tools.
│   ...Scope the project.
│   ...Prepare for cultural changes.
│   ...JRP procedure
│   ...JAD procedure
│   ┌─ Prototype evolution
│   │   ┌─ If step-by-step evolution
│   │   █   For each prototype iteration
│   │   █     Build detailed prototype.
│   │   █       o─────────────────────o
│   │   █       │ See procedure in Box 6.3 │
│   │   █       o─────────────────────o
│   │   █   Test prototype with end users.
│   │   █   Conduct user workshop, or interviews.
│   │   █   Determine features to be added or changed.
│   │   █
│   │   «───── If no need for further iteration
│   │   █      Determine target date of next prototype and user workshop.
│   │   ██
│   │   L█
```

```
  ┌  ┌  ┌─ Else if continuous evolution
  │  │  │     Build detailed prototype.
  │  │  │     o────────────────────────────o
  │  │  │     │ See procedure in Box 6.3   │
  │  │  │     o────────────────────────────o
  │  │  │     Refine the prototype continuously, working with the
  │  │  │         end user(s), until an acceptable system is achieved.
  │  └  └
  │  ...Create physical design.
  │  ...Design for cutover.
  │  ...Build pilot system.
  │  ...Prepare for cutover.
  │  ...Install and adjust pilot system.
  └  ...Expand pilot to full system.
```

Box 21.4 shows the multi-iteration lifecycle procedure in more detail.

TIMEBOX LIFECYCLE

A particularly valuable form of iterative lifecycle is the timebox lifecycle, in which the goal is to implement systems much more quickly than with the traditional lifecycle. It constrains the functionality of the first release of the system in order to have a fully working system within a short time.

BOX 21.4   Multi-iteration lifecycle.

```
┌─ Description
│     A multi-iteration lifecycle creates a succession of
│  prototypes of the target system. The prototypes are improved
│  a stage at a time until they converge to what the end users
│  agree is a valuable system. The final prototype may become
│  the final system, or may be rebuilt.
│     While simple systems can be designed in one step, complex
│  or subtle systems become understood only by attempting to
│  build a prototype, learning from it, and rebuilding the
│  prototype until it represents a valuable design.
│     The multi-iteration lifecycle first establishes a clear set of
│  objectives for the system. There must be a clearly defined
│  target towards which the iterative design and prototyping
│  progresses. The iterative lifecycle is made practical by tools
│  which enable us to build prototypes quickly and change them
│  easily. Sometimes the final prototype needs rebuilding or
└  rearchitecting to achieve clean design and good machine performance.

┌─ Multi-iteration procedure
│     ┌──────────────────────────────────────────────────────┐
│     │ The procedure given below may be modified with Action │
│     │ Diagrammer to meet the needs of the particular situation. │
│     └──────────────────────────────────────────────────────┘
│
└
```

BOX 21.4 *(Continued)*

```
┌─ Initiate the project.
│     Determine need for system.
└     Obtain executive sponsor.

┌─ Select tools.
│     Select design tools.
│       (An encyclopedia-based workbench is desirable.)
│     Select prototyping tools.
│       (The question of whether the prototyping language can
│       become the final language should be addressed.)
│     Select programming language / generator.
│       (It is desirable to have a code generator which is tightly
└         coupled to, or is an extension of, the design workbench.)

┌─ Scope the project.
│  ┌─ If Business Area Analysis has been done
│  │     Extract relevant data and process models from the
│  │       encyclopedia.
│  ├─ Else
│  │     Create relevant data and process models.
│  └
└

┌─ Prepare for cultural changes.
│     o─────────────────────────o
│     │ See detail in Box 17.1  │
│     o─────────────────────────o
│  ┌─ Identify any cultural changes.
│  │     List the following types of cultural changes which the new system
│  │       might bring about:
│  │     o  Changes in organizational structure
│  │     o  Changes in policies
│  │     o  Changes in business procedures
│  │     o  Changes in staffing levels
│  │     o  Changes in job content
│  │     o  Changes in skill requirements
│  │
│  └     Review this list with top management.
│  ...Design the organizational changes.
│  ...Identify responsibilities for organizational changes.
└  ...Schedule the organizational changes.

┌─ JRP procedure
│     The requirements planning is done in a JRP workshop.
│     o─────────────────────────────────o
│     │ See Box 7.2:  JRP procedure      │
└     o─────────────────────────────────o

┌─ JAD procedure
│     The specifications and initial design are produced by JAD in
│       conjunction with prototyping.
│     o─────────────────────────────────o
│     │ See Box 8.1:  JAD procedure      │
└     o─────────────────────────────────o
```

(Continued)

BOX 21.4 *(Continued)*

```
┌─ Prototype evolution
│  ┌─ Description
│  │
│  │      ┌─────────────────────────────────────────┐
│  │      │  Step-by-step or continuous evolution?  │
│  │      └─────────────────────────────────────────┘
│  │
│  │         STEP-BY-STEP EVOLUTION progresses from one planned prototype
│  │      to another until the target system is achieved. This the usual
│  │      form of evolutionary development.
│  │         CONTINUOUS EVOLUTION progresses with a sequence of
│  │      modifications continuously adjusting the prototype until
│  │      the target is reached. This requires an intelligent,
│  │      understanding end user working as a team with the
│  │      developer(s) reviewing the evolution.
│  │
│  │      STEP-BY-STEP EVOLUTION:              CONTINUOUS EVOLUTION:
```

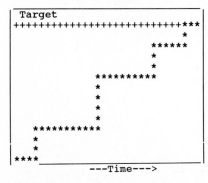 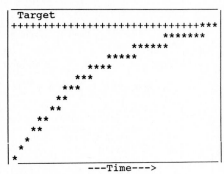

```
│  ┌─ If step-by-step evolution
│  │  █ For each prototype iteration
│  │  █     Build detailed prototype.
│  │  █     o─────────────────────────o
│  │  █     │ See procedure in Box 6.3 │
│  │  █     o─────────────────────────o
│  │  █  Test prototype with end users.
│  │  █  Conduct user workshop, or interviews.
│  │  █  Determine features to be added or changed.
│  │  █
│  │  «─────── If no need for further iteration
│  │  █        Determine target date of next prototype and user workshop.
│  │
│  ┌─ Else if continuous evolution
│  │     Build detailed prototype.
│  │     o─────────────────────────o
│  │     │ See procedure in Box 6.3 │
│  │     o─────────────────────────o
│  │     Refine the prototype continuously, working with the
│  │        end user(s), until an acceptable system is achieved.
```

BOX 21.4 *(Continued)*

Create physical design.
  Determine whether data will be distributed.

| See procedure in Box 16.1 |

  Determine traffic volumes.
  Perform data use analysis.

| See procedure in Box 14.1 |

  Do physical database design.

| See procedure in Box 15.1 |

  Determine hardware requirements.
  Examine how to optimize performance.
  Complete documentation (in the encyclopedia) of the final design.

Design for cutover.

| See detail in Box 17.2 |

...Establish the implementation standards.
...Design the conversion procedures.
...Design the production procedures.
...Plan the hardware installation.
...Determine the testing strategy.
...Plan the testing environment.
...Create the technical documentation.
...Create the user documentation.
...Create the training program.

Build pilot system.
  Description
      A pilot system is a fully working system deployed at first
      with only a small number of users, small number of terminals
      or small number of transactions. When it is found to be
      satisfactory the volumes of transactions are increased and
      it is deployed on a larger scale.

  If the prototype can have good enough performance to
      become the working system

      Improve the prototype so that it becomes a pilot system.
  Else
      If the whole system must be built in a different language
          Recode using the same action diagram as far as possible.

      Else if only portions of the code need be changed

          Replace code where needed (possibly with a more efficient
          language) using the same action diagram where possible.

      Debug the system so that it is stable enough to use as a
      pilot doing actual work.

(Continued)

BOX 21.4 *(Continued)*

```
  ┌ Prepare for cutover.
  │     o─────────────────────────o
  │     │ See details in Box 18.1 │
  │     o─────────────────────────o
  │  ...Develop the conversion system.
  │  ┌ Finalize the development product.
  │  │  ...Perform quality audit.
  │  └  ...Refine the development product.
  │
  │  ┌ Prepare for final testing.
  │  │  ...Install the software to be used for final testing.
  │  │     Build the test libraries.
  │  │     Coordinate the testing with the development team.
  │  └
  │
  │  ┌ Carry out the final testing.
  │  │  ...Program test
  │  │  ...Integration test
  │  │  ...Volume test
  │  │  ...Regression test for maintenance changes
  │  │  ...Acceptance test
  │  │     Collect statistics for project management
  │  └     Document the test results.
  │
  │  ┌ Pla1 and conduct the training program.
  │  │  ┌ Develop the training plan.
  │  │  │     Determine who will create the training materials.
  │  │  │     Determine who will conduct the training.
  │  │  │     Determine which users will be trained initially.
  │  │  └     Determine the time and location of training.
  │  │
  │  └  ...Conduct training.

  ┌ Install and adjust pilot system.
  │  ┌ Perform cutover.
  │  │     o─────────────────────────o
  │  │     │ See detail in Box 18.2  │
  │  │     o─────────────────────────o
  │  │  ...Set up the production procedures.
  │  │  ...Install the production system environment.
  │  │  ...Perform data conversion.
  │  │  ...Implement the new system in production.
  │  └  ...Review the system installation.
  │
  │  ┌ If no modifications needed
  │  │
«─┼──┼── Exit
  │  ┌ Else
  │  │     Document adjustments needed.
  │  │     Determine date for installation of next version.
  └  └     Make adjustments.
```

BOX 21.4 *(Continued)*

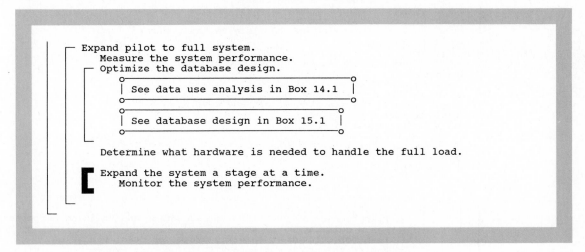

```
    ┌─ Expand pilot to full system.
    │    Measure the system performance.
    │  ┌─ Optimize the database design.
    │  │   ○───────────────────────────────────────○
    │  │   │  See data use analysis in Box 14.1   │
    │  │   ○───────────────────────────────────────○
    │  │   ○───────────────────────────────────────○
    │  │   │  See database design in Box 15.1     │
    │  └─  ○───────────────────────────────────────○
    │
    │     Determine what hardware is needed to handle the full load.
    │  ┌─ Expand the system a stage at a time.
    │  └    Monitor the system performance.
    └─
```

This lifecycle is very dependent on its tool set. It requires an integrated-CASE tool set designed to make design fast and easy and give a rapid cycle of modifying the system, generating code for the modification, and testing it. The methodology is adapted to fit the capabilities of the tool set:

```
┌─ Timebox procedure
│  ...Establish the methodology.
│  ┌─ Timebox lifecycle methodology
│  │  ...Initiate the project.
│  │  ...Obtain commitment of executive sponsor.
│  │  ┌─ Determine the scope and objectives.
│  │  │  ...Establish management's objectives for the project.
│  │  │  ┌─ JRP procedure
│  │  │  │   ○───────────────────────────────────────○
│  │  │  │   │  See Box 7.2:  JRP procedure         │
│  │  │  │   ○───────────────────────────────────────○
│  │  │  │   The requirements should be listed in a JRP workshop and the
│  │  │  │     following activities performed.
│  │  │  │
│  │  │  ┌─ Determine scope.
│  │  │  │     Determine which locations are involved.
│  │  │  │     Determine which departments are involved.
│  │  │  │  ┌─ If Business Area Analysis has been done
│  │  │  │  │     Extract relevant data and process models from the
│  │  │  │  │       encyclopedia.
│  │  │  │  ┌─ Else
│  │  │  │  │     Create relevant data and process models.
│  │  │  │  │
│  │  │  │  │   Examine relevant goals, problems, and critical success factors
│  │  │  │  │     (from the encyclopedia).
│  │  │  │  │   Determine what business assumptions are to be made by the
│  │  │  └─ └─    design group.
```

(Continued)

```
        ┌─ Summarize the benefits and risks.
        │  ...Assess the benefits.
        │  ...Determine how to maximize the benefits.
        │  ...Assess the risks.
        └─ ...Determine how to minimize the risks.

        Obtain a decision whether the project goes ahead.

 ...Appoint the User Coordinator.
 ...Establish the Review Board.
 ...Estimate the required effort and cost.
 ...Establish the Timebox Team(s).
 ...Motivate the Timebox Team(s).
 ...JAD Procedure
 ...Prepare for cultural changes.
 ...Design for cutover.
┌─ Build the system.
   ┌─ Perform timebox development.
   │   ...Build and evolve a prototype.
   │   The Review Board should review the evolving prototype at
   │     suitable intervals.
   │   Plan to use the prototype for education and training purposes
   │     at a suitably early stage.
   │   Plan for cutover at an early stage, as described below.
   └─ ...Evolve the prototype into a fully working system.

   ┌─ Evaluate the results.
   │   After the timebox, the Review Board examines the results in
   │     detail and decides whether the system will be implemented.
   └─ ...If minor modifications are needed before implementation
```

```
┌─ Create physical design.
   ...Determine whether data will be distributed.
   Determine traffic volumes.
   ...Perform data use analysis.
   ...Do physical database design.
   Determine hardware requirements.
   Examine how to optimize performance.
   Complete documentation (in the encyclopedia) of the final design.

...Prepare for cutover.
Install and adjust pilot system.
...Perform cutover.
┌─ If no modifications needed

«──────── Exit
┌─ Else
      Document adjustments needed.
      Determine date for installation of next version.
      Make adjustments.
```

```
┌─ Expand pilot to full system.
   Measure the system performance.
   ...Optimize the database design.
   Determine what hardware is needed to handle the full load.

   ┌─ Expand the system a stage at a time.
       Monitor the system performance.
```

The timebox lifecycle is described in Chapter 9 and is illustrated in detail in Box 21.5.

EXPLORATORY LIFECYCLE

Certain types of systems need to be built with techniques which are more like those used in research than in formal development. This is often true in the building of expert systems, for example. There are important types of system for which specifications could not be written at the start of the lifecycle. The

BOX 21.5 Timebox lifecycle

> The timebox methodology is a highly successful form of lifecycle which emphasizes high-speed development. It constrains the functionality of the first release of a system is order to have a fully working system within a short timeframe.
>
> The lifecycle employs continuous-evolution prototyping with a tight deadline. It requires an I-CASE toolset designed to make design fast and easy, and give a rapid cycle of modify-generate-test. End users are involved continuously throughout the lifecycle.
>
> The costs and risks of new system development are minimized by emphasizing JRP, JAD, prototyping, and high-speed development, with continuous user involvement, within an IE framework.

> The procedure given below may be modified with Action Diagrammer to meet the needs of the particular situation.

```
┌─ Timebox procedure
│  ┌─ Establish the methodology.
│  │    This methodology is highly dependent on a toolset which enables
│  │    fast and easy design, and a rapid cycle of modify-generate-test.
│  │    The methodology is built around the toolset and adapted to it.
│  │    Selecting the right toolset is highly critical.
│  │
│  ┌─ Select the tools.
│  │  ┌─ Characteristics of the prototyping tool
│  │  │    The toolset should be an integrated-CASE tool which uses
│  │  │       the IE encyclopedia.
│  │  │    The toolset should:
│  │  │       o  be interactive
│  │  │       o  be easy to use
│  │  │       o  facilitate quick building of prototypes
│  │  │       o  give the most automated capability for design and code
│  │  │             generation
│  │  │       o  give the fastest possible cycle of modify-generate-test
```

(Continued)

BOX 21.5 *(Continued)*

The toolset should include the following:
- o a powerful design workbench tightly coupled to the analysis (BAA) workbench
- o a code generator which is an extension of the design workbench
- o a versatile screen painter (which can be used very quickly in JAD sessions)
- o ability to link screens and responses into a dialog
- o a versatile report generator (which can be used very quickly in JAD sessions)
- o use of a suitably flexible database management system
- o an integral dictionary
- o facilities for extracting data from files or databases, and loading them into the prototype database

Because the prototype will become the final system the tool should have:
- o ability to achieve good machine performance (with an optimizing compiler)
- o ability to support the database structure of the final system
- o appropriate networking access
- o ability to handle a suitably large number of users
- o ability to handle suitably large databases
- o ability to handle suitably high-traffic volumes

The system the tool generates should have:
- o features for recovery from failures
- o features for fallback
- o security features
- o features for auditability
- o features for ease of maintenance

Adapt the methodology to the toolset.
It is desirable to select one toolset and perfect its use. The methodology given below should be adapted to fit the toolset. The methodology should be applied to many projects and tuned on the basis of experience.

Timebox lifecycle procedure
Initiate the project
Determine need for system.
Obtain executive sponsor.

Obtain commitment of executive sponsor.
The JAD session should not proceed unless a suitably high-level executive is fully committed to creating the system and to using JAD for this purpose.

Determine the scope and objectives.
Establish management's objectives for the project.
Interview appropriate end-user managers.
Write down the objectives.
Obtain management agreement.

BOX 21.5 *(Continued)*

JRP procedure

> See Box 7.2:   JRP procedure

The requirements should be listed in a JRP workshop and the
following activities performed.

Determine scope.
    Determine which locations are involved.
    Determine which departments are involved.
    If Business Area Analysis has been done
        Extract relevant data and process models from the
          encyclopedia.
    Else
        Create relevant data and process models.

    Examine relevant goals, problems, and critical success
        factors (from the encyclopedia).
    Determine what business assumptions are to be made by the
        design group.

Summarize the benefits and risks.
    Assess the benefits.
        o   Financial savings.
        o   Opportunity costs.
        o   Better quality.
        o   Improved competitive position.
        o   Other tangible benefits.
        o   Intangible benefits.

    Determine how to maximize the benefits.
        Look for business ways to obtain leverage from the system.
        Determine which potential functions of the system have the
          most effect on profits or business objectives.

    Assess the risks.
        o   There may be inadequate user motivation.
        o   Lack of user acceptance of changed way of working.
        o   User difficulties learning or adapting to the system.
        o   Possible misconceptions in the system concept.
        o   Possible development cost overruns.
        o   Possible technical problems.

    Determine how to minimize the risks.
        The risks should be examined in detail.
        An executive sponsor at a suitably high level must be
          totally committed to the project. He should address his
          attention to user motivation.
        Use of JAD substantially reduces the risks of user non-
          acceptance and business misconceptions.
        A prototyping methodology substantially reduces the risks
          as misconceptions and technical difficulties are more
          likely to be discovered early.
        The development risks are likely to be much less if the
          project fits comfortably into the timebox methodology
          and can be developed with the tools in question.

Obtain a decision whether the project goes ahead.

(Continued)

BOX 21.5   *(Continued)*

Appoint the User Coordinator.
   The User Coordinator:
      o is the lead user developer on the timebox team(s).
      o involves other users where appropriate to help review the
           evolving prototypes.
      o arranges for user documentation and training.
      o serves on the Prototype Review Board.

Establish the Review Board.
   The Review Board reviews the requirements prior to the timebox,
     and reviews the results at the end of the timebox.
   The Review Board includes
      o Leading spokespeople of the end users who need the system.
      o The executive sponsor.
      o An IE executive.
      o Possibly external reviewers such as customers.
      o Possibly an external consultant.
   Ensure that sufficient commitment exists that a thorough review
     job will be done.

Estimate the required effort and cost.
   The estimating method must relate to experience with the
     prototyping/code-generator tool. Manpower statistics for
     COBOL/PLI/FORTRAN have almost no relevance.
   Obtain manpower statistics of experience with the prototyping/
     generator tool.
   Estimate the number of screens.
   Estimate the number of reports.
   Estimate the number of logical files.
   Estimate the proportion of the system that can be generated
     nonprocedurally, and the proportion that needs procedural
     (fourth-generation) coding.
   Estimate the number of lines of procedural code.
   Estimate the manpower effort for procedural code.
   Split the project into multiple timeboxes, if necessary.
      Estimate what application functions can be built during the
        60-day timebox with a small (2- or 3-person) team.
      If the project is too large for one timebox, divide it into
        multiple timeboxes which can proceed simultaneously.
      Use the workbench tools to do the subdivision into separate
        timebox efforts (process decomposition diagram and process
        dependency diagram or data-flow diagram).
      Ensure that the interfaces between the separate timebox efforts
        are defined with precision with the I-CASE tool.

Establish the Timebox Team(s).
   The team should be small. Two- or three-person teams are the
     most appropriate. Large projects should be subdivided so that
     more than one timebox is used simultaneously, each staffed by
     a small team

   The team should include:
      o The User Coordinator (who may work with more than one timebox
           simultaneously).
      o The lead I.S. developer.
      o Other I.S. or user developers as appropriate.

   Either the end user or the lead I.S. developer should be
     appointed project manager, with overall responsibility for
     development and product quality.

BOX 21.5 *(Continued)*

Motivate the Timebox Team(s).
  Ensure that the team knows that success or failure is determined
    by whether they build an implementable system by the end of the
    timebox. They cannot extend the timebox deadline.
  Ensure them that success will be rewarded.
  Tell them that a victory celebration will be held when the system
    is judged successful.
  Tell them that failures are rare and that they must not distinguish
    themselves by creating a failure.
  Ensure them that their activities are very visible to higher
    management.

JAD Procedure
  The specifications and initial design are produced by JAD in
    conjunction with prototyping.
...Appoint the JAD session leader.
  Prepare.
  ...Select the participants.
  ...Prepare the materials
  ...Customize the JAD agenda
  ...Prepare the participants.
  ...Obtain agreement of executive sponsor.

  Hold kickoff meeting.
    Have the executive sponsor make the opening speech.
    Review with participants the purpose and objectives.
    Review the agenda.
    Give participants the preparatory material for them to study.
      Inform them that they must understand it well before the
      first workshop.
    Review the initial data models and process models with the
      participants.
    Review relevant goals, problems, and critical success factors.
    Review the business assumptions that are to be made.

  Conduct the first design workshop.
    Executive sponsor should visit the workshop periodically to
      lend support.
    Review the system objectives.
    Design activities.
      Examine and adjust the relevant information from the BAA
        study.

        Examine the process decomposition diagram, adjusting it as
          necessary.
        Examine the process flow diagram, adjusting it as
          necessary.
        Examine the entity-relationship diagram, adjusting it as
          necessary.
        Add detailed comments to the above diagrams where
          necessary.

      Clarify the scope of the design activity.

(Continued)

BOX 21.5 *(Continued)*

For each process block

  Determine what are the steps in the procedure.
      The procedure steps may be examined with the following
      framework:

     1: PLANNING
        A planning process provides or creates information
          about work that will be received.

     2: RECEIVING
        Work is received.
        Resources to do the work may be received.
        A unique identification for each item of work or
          each resource received is entered into the system
          and validated.

     3: PROCESSING RECEIPTS
        The time of reporting the receipt is recorded.
        The receipt is validated.
        The receipt is processed.
        The relevant records are updated.
        Transactions may be generated to notify other
          locations of the receipt.

     4: MONITORING
        The receipts are monitored to see whether they are
          as planned.
        Management are notified of exceptions to the plan.
        Requirements for additional resources may be
          generated.

     5: ASSIGNING
        Work is assigned or scheduled.
        Work instructions, identification, and reporting
          documents are created.

     6: PROCESSING
        Work is performed.
        Work may be guided through multiple stages.
        The performance is monitored.
        Reports are generated for administrative feedback
          and planning.

     7: RECORDING
        The system processes data about the work.
        A date/time stamp is recorded for each step.
        The system may validate that the work is done
          correctly.
        Client-requested notifications may be produced.
        Completion of the work is recorded.

     8: SENDING
        Work is routed to other locations or customers.
        Documents or labels are produced to identify the
          work done.
        Work departures are recorded.
        Accounting is done.
        Billing is done.

BOX 21.5　*(Continued)*

```
9: EVALUATING
   Work measurements and summaries are provided.
   Trends may be assessed.
   Information on resource utilization may be created.
   Comparisons with goals and objectives may be created.

Build an initial data flow diagram showing the steps.
   Enter the procedure steps into the data flow diagram
      on the screen of a workbench tool.

   The initial diagram is an approximate diagram. If the
      workbench has a knowledge coordinator or comprehen-
      sive checking capabilities, these are switched off
      at this time. They will be used later to solidify
      the design.

Examine each procedure step in more detail.
   Describe its purpose.
   Determine its input data.
   Determine its output data.
   Determine what processing occurs. Represent this with
      an action diagram.
   Adjust the data flow diagram if necessary.
   Design and paint the screens.
   Design and create the reports.

For each procedure step create a partial prototype.
   Create prototype of the screens, dialog, and reports
      used.
   Develop and enhance more complete prototypes as
      appropriate.

Address security.
   Determine security requirements.
   Design authorization scheme.
   Determine how security will be handled.

Address unresolved issues.
   List unresolved issues.
   Determine responsibility and deadline for unresolved
      issues.
   Details of issue
      o   Issue:
      o   Assigned to:
      o   Assign date:
      o   Date to be resolved by:
      o   Resolution:

...Create the documentation.
   Present the results to the executive sponsor.
```

(Continued)

BOX 21.5   *(Continued)*

Prepare for cultural changes.

| See detail in Box 17.1 |

Identify any cultural changes.
  List the following types of cultural changes which the new system
  might bring about:
  o Changes in organizational structure
  o Changes in policies
  o Changes in business procedures
  o Changes in staffing levels
  o Changes in job content
  o Changes in skill requirements

  Review this list with top management.

...Design the organizational changes.
...Identify responsibilities for organizational changes.
...Schedule the organizational changes.

Design for cutover.
  This should be done while the system is being built (in parallel
  with the following bracket) because the time available for cutover
  is short.

| See detail in Box 17.2 |

...Establish the implementation standards.
...Design the conversion procedures.
...Design the production procedures.
...Plan the hardware installation.
...Determine the testing strategy.
...Plan the testing environment.
...Create the technical documentation.
...Create the user documentation.
...Create the training program.

Build the system.
  Perform timebox development.
    Build and evolve a prototype.
      End users and I.S. developers work closely together in doing
      this.
        They have a specified time (maximum 60 days) in which to
      develop a fully working system. They are not permitted to
      slip the end date.

BOX 21.5 *(Continued)*

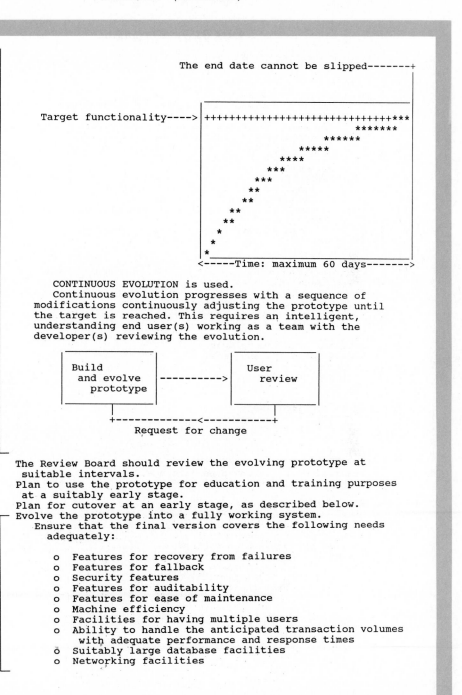

```
                              The end date cannot be slipped-------+
                                                                   |
                              _____
Target functionality---->  +++++++++++++++++++++++++++++++++++***
                                                          ******
                                                      ******
                                                  *****
                                               ****
                                            ***
                                         ***
                                       **
                                      **
                                  **
                                 **
                              *
                             *
                           *
                           <-----Time: maximum 60 days------->
```

CONTINUOUS EVOLUTION is used.
   Continuous evolution progresses with a sequence of
modifications continuously adjusting the prototype until
the target is reached. This requires an intelligent,
understanding end user(s) working as a team with the
developer(s) reviewing the evolution.

```
   _____                    _____
  | Build          |                  |                |
  | and evolve     |---------->       | User           |
  | prototype      |                  | review         |
  |_____|_____|                  |_____|_____|
           |                                   |
           +-------------<-----------+
              Request for change
```

The Review Board should review the evolving prototype at
  suitable intervals.
Plan to use the prototype for education and training purposes
  at a suitably early stage.
Plan for cutover at an early stage, as described below.
Evolve the prototype into a fully working system.
   Ensure that the final version covers the following needs
     adequately:

       o Features for recovery from failures
       o Features for fallback
       o Security features
       o Features for auditability
       o Features for ease of maintenance
       o Machine efficiency
       o Facilities for having multiple users
       o Ability to handle the anticipated transaction volumes
            with adequate performance and response times
       o Suitably large database facilities
       o Networking facilities
```

*(Continued)*
```

BOX 21.5   *(Continued)*

```
      Evaluate the results.
          After the timebox the Review Board examines the results in
          detail and decides whether the system will be implemented.
        If minor modifications are needed before implementation
          Specify the modifications.
          The Review Board establishes a deadline for
            making the modifications.
«          Re-enter the timebox
        Else if the system is not suitable for implementation
          Specify the reasons for rejection.
          Reschedule a JAD session.
«          Conduct a JAD session to determine what action to take.
        Else
          Hold victory celebration.


  Create physical design.
    Determine whether data will be distributed.
         ┌───────────────────────────┐
         │ See procedure in Box 16.1  │
         └───────────────────────────┘

    Determine traffic volumes.
    Perform data use analysis.
         ┌───────────────────────────┐
         │ See procedure in Box 14.1  │
         └───────────────────────────┘

    Do physical database design.
         ┌───────────────────────────┐
         │ See procedure in Box 15.1  │
         └───────────────────────────┘

    Determine hardware requirements.
    Examine how to optimize performance.
    Complete documentation (in the encyclopedia) of the final design.

  Prepare for cutover.
         ┌───────────────────────────┐
         │ See details in Box 18.1 │
         └───────────────────────────┘
  ...Develop the conversion system.
  ...Finalize the development product.
  ...Prepare for final testing.
  ...Carry out the final testing.
  ...Plan and conduct the training program.
```

BOX 21.5 *(Continued)*

```
      ┌─ Install and adjust pilot system.
      │    ┌─ Perform cutover.
      │    │      o─────────────────────────o
      │    │      │  See detail in Box 18.2  │
      │    │      o─────────────────────────o
      │    │   ...Set up the production procedures.
      │    │   ...Install the production system environment.
      │    │   ...Perform data conversion.
      │    │   ...Implement the new system in production.
      │    └   ...Review the system installation.
      │
      │    ┌─ If no modifications needed
      │    │
   «──┼────┼─── Exit
      │    ┌─ Else
      │    │      Document adjustments needed.
      │    │      Determine date for installation of next version.
      │    └      Make adjustments.
      │
      │
    ┌─ Expand pilot to full system.
    │        Measure the system performance.
    │      ┌─ Optimize the database design.
    │      │    o──────────────────────────────────o
    │      │    │  See data use analysis in Box 14.1  │
    │      │    o──────────────────────────────────o
    │      │    o──────────────────────────────────o
    │      │    │  See database design in Box 15.1   │
    │      └    o──────────────────────────────────o
    │
    │        Determine what hardware is needed to handle the full load.
    │
    │      ┌ Expand the system a stage at a time.
    │      └   Monitor the system performance.
    └
```

system can only come into existence with creative innovation. Such systems may be built with an exploratory lifecycle.

Although the exploratory lifecycle does not promise a deliverable system at the end of the procedure, it should have firm objectives. It is desirable to establish goals, criteria, and controls:

```
  ┌─ Establish criteria and controls.
  │      Establish the objectives of the development activity.
  │      Determine how results will be measured or judged.
  │      Establish a budget.
  │      Establish a target end date.
  │      Establish dates at which progress will be reviewed.
  └      Determine who will assess the progress and with what criteria.
```

At the start of the project, tools should be selected that are powerful for exploratory development. Some of the tool kits from companies like Intellicorp and Neuron Data specializing in artificial intelligence techniques, enable their users to build exploratory systems of substantial complexity in a short time.

Languages such as PROLOG, LISP, and SMALLTALK are powerful in the hands of skilled, creative practitioners.

It is particularly important at the start of exploratory development to ask how the system will be deployed in the field if it turns out to be valuable. Exploratory development often results in prototypes which cannot be fielded without being completely rearchitected. Addressing the subject of how the system might eventually be deployed can affect the choice of tools. For example, the team may select tools which will lead to deployment on a personal computer, or tools which will be able to access existing databases over existing networks.

At the start of an exploratory project, thorough research should be conducted on existing systems of a similar nature. Creative programmers tend to reinvent existing facilities much more than their counterparts in other branches of engineering. Examining existing systems or products can provide many ideas about how the new system should function.

Exploratory projects should employ brainstorming both at the start of the project and as it progresses. Brainstorming means that a creative group of individuals attempt to produce a stream of ideas without inhibition. A rule of a brainstorming is that there can be no implied criticism for making an impractical or stupid suggestion. The session is intended to generate as many ideas as possible. At the end of the session, only certain of the ideas will be recorded for possible use.

After exploratory prototyping is completed the lifecycle may proceed to the building and deployment of pilot systems:

```
┌─ Exploratory procedure

  ...Establish criteria and controls.
  ...Initiate the activity.
  ┌─ Determine possible functions and techniques.
  │     Research similar systems that might offer guidance or
  │        ideas to the developers.
  └─ Brainstorm the possible functions of the system.

  ┌─ Prototype evolution

  │  ┌─ If step-by-step evolution
  │  │  ▌ For each prototype iteration
  │  │  ▌     Build detailed prototype.
  │  │  ▌     Review the prototype with creative end-user or manager.
  │  │  ▌     Determine features to be added or changed.
  │  │  ▌     Brainstorm possible improvements which might be valuable.
  │  │  ▌
  │  │  «──── If no need for further iteration
  │  └─ ▙     Determine target date of next review.
```

```
    ┌─ Else
    │   ┌ Continuous evolution
    │   █      Build detailed prototype.
    │   █      Refine the prototype continuously, working with a
    │   █          creative end-user or manager.
    │   █      Brainstorm possible improvements which might be valuable.
    │   █
    │  «──── If an acceptable final result is acheived
    └─
   ...Design for cutover.
   ...Prepare for cutover.
   ...Build pilot system.
   ...Install and adjust pilot system.
   ...Expand pilot to full system.
```

Box 21.6 shows the exploratory lifecycle in more detail.

**QUICK-RESULTS
LIFECYCLE**   A problem with the traditional lifecycle is that it takes a long time to build anything. The objective of information center computing is that results should be obtained quickly. With some IS professionals computing this is also an important goal. It is usually done by employing fourth-generation languages and avoiding formal specification and review. This can be an extremely valuable

BOX 21.6   Exploratory lifecycle

┌ Description
│   Whereas an evolutionary lifecycle starts with a
│ clearly defined target, an exploratory lifecycle is one in
│ which the target could not be defined in detail at the beginning.
│ An exploratory lifecycle is more in the nature of research and
│ needs to be managed like research. It explores what is possible
│ by building a system with ad-hoc creativity. The resulting
│ prototypes usually have to be discarded and rearchitected to
│ achieve a working system.
│   Whereas an evolutionary lifecycle promises a deliverable
│ system at the end of the procedure, an exploratory lifecycle
│ should not. The exploratory lifecycle finds out what it may be
│ practical to deliver.

┌ Exploratory procedure

    ┌───┐
    │ The procedure given below may be modified with Action   │
    │ Diagrammer to meet the needs of the particular situation.│
    └───┘

(Continued)

BOX 21.6 *(Continued)*

Establish criteria and controls.
    Establish the objectives of the development activity.
    Determine how results will be measured or judged.
    Establish a budget.
    Establish a target end date.
    Establish dates at which progress will be reviewed.
    Determine who will assess the progress and with what criteria.

Initiate the activity.
    Select the developer(s).
    Select tools which are powerful for exploratory development.
    Determine how the system will be fielded if the exploratory
      development is successful. (This step is often omitted,
      resulting in unfieldable prototypes.) The need to eventually
      field the system may affect the choice of tools.
    Ensure that the developers are fully trained in the use of
      the tools.

Determine possible functions and techniques.
    Research similar systems that might offer guidance or
      ideas to the developers.
    Brainstorm the possible functions of the system.
    Description
        Brainstorming means that a creative group of individuals
        attempts to produce a stream of ideas without inhibition.
        A rule of a brainstorming session is that there can be
        no implied criticism for making an impractical or stupid
        suggestion. The session is intended to generate as many
        ideas as possible. At the end of the session only certain
        of the ideas will be recorded for possible use.

Prototype evolution
    Description

        Step-by-step or continuous evolution?

        STEP-BY-STEP EVOLUTION progresses from one planned prototype
    to another until the target system is achieved.
        CONTINUOUS EVOLUTION progresses with a sequence of modifications
    continuously adjusting the prototype until the target is reached.
    A manager or creative end user may review the progress on an
    ongoing basis as it evolves

STEP-BY-STEP EVOLUTION: CONTINUOUS EVOLUTION:

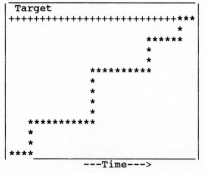
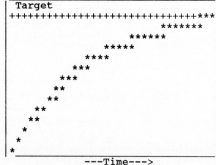

BOX 21.6   *(Continued)*

```
  If step-by-step evolution
    For each prototype iteration
        Build detailed prototype.
        Review the prototype with creative end user or manager.
        Determine features to be added or changed.
        Brainstorm possible improvements which might be valuable.
        Description
            Brainstorming means that a creative group of individuals
            attempt to produce a stream of ideas without inhibition.
            A rule of a brainstorming session is that there can be
            no implied criticism for making an impractical or stupid
            suggestion. The session is intended to generate as many
            ideas as possible. At the end of the session only certain
            of the ideas will be recorded for possible use.


  «        If no need for further iteration
           Determine target date of next review.
  Else
    Continuous evolution
        Build detailed prototype.
        Refine the prototype continuously, working with a
            creative end user or manager.
        Brainstorm possible improvements which might be valuable.
        Description
            Brainstorming means that a creative group of individuals
            attempt to produce a stream of ideas without inhibition.
            A rule of a brainstorming session is that there can be
            no implied criticism for making an impractical or stupid
            suggestion. The session is intended to generate as many
            ideas as possible. At the end of the session only certain
            of the ideas will be recorded for possible use.


  «        If an acceptable final result is achieved


  Design for cutover
    This should be done while the system is being built (in parallel
        with the following bracket) because the time available for cutover
        is short.

        o──────────────────────────o
        |  See detail in Box 17.2  |
        o──────────────────────────o
    ...Establish the implementation standards
    ...Design the conversion procedures
    ...Design the production procedures
    ...Plan the hardware installation
    ...Determine the testing strategy
    ...Plan the testing environment
    ...Create the technical documentation
    ...Create the user documentation
    ...Create the training program
```

(Continued)

BOX 21.6 *(Continued)*

Prepare for cutover
```
o─────────────────────────o
│ See details in Box 18.1 │
o─────────────────────────o
```
...Develop the conversion system
...Finalize the development product
...Prepare for final testing
...Carry out the final testing.
...Plan and conduct the training program

Build pilot system
A pilot system is a fully working system deployed at first
with only a small number of users, small number of terminals
or small number of transactions. When it is found to be
satisfactory the volumes of transactions are increased and
it is deployed on a larger scale.

Determine what functions of the prototype will be included
in the first pilot system.
Determine whether the system should be redesigned or
rearchitected in order to produce a working pilot.
Build and debug the pilot.

Install and adjust pilot system
Perform cutover
```
o─────────────────────────o
│ See detail in Box 18.2  │
o─────────────────────────o
```
...Set up the production procedures
...Install the production system environment
...Perform data conversion
...Implement the new system in production
...Review the system installation

If no modifications needed

«──────── Exit
Else
Document adjustments needed.
Determine date for installation of next version.
Make adjustments.

Expand pilot to full system
Measure the system performance.
Optimize the database design
```
o─────────────────────────────────o
│ See data use analysis in Box 14.1 │
o─────────────────────────────────o
o─────────────────────────────────o
│ See database design in Box 15.1 │
o─────────────────────────────────o
```

Determine what hardware is needed to handle the full load.

Expand the system a stage at a time.
Monitor the system performance.

form of computing, but it can also result in an unmanageable mass of unmaintainable programs if no controls are employed.

The following types of control are particularly important:

- Use existing data models and data definitions.
- Build links to existing databases, where appropriate.
- Use design tools, where appropriate, to create maintainable code.
- Build systems which are easily auditable by management.
- Create documentation or "HELP" facilities if other end users will employ the programs.

PURELY PERSONAL COMPUTING?

It is desirable to distinguish between purely personal computing and computing which involves more than one person. If it is *purely* personal computing, the individual in question may be left alone to build his own system. It is desirable that he should not be slowed down by bureaucratic or unnecessary controls. Controls *are* needed if other people

- Are involved in building the system.
- Will use the system.
- Will maintain the system.
- Will use data from the system.

```
┌─ Is this PURELY personal computing?
│  ┌─ If more than one person is involved in building the system
│  │     Use design-automation techniques that aid multi-person
│  │        development.
│  ├─ Else
│  │  ┌─ If other people will use the system
│  │  │     Ensure that the human interface is well designed.
│  │  │     Ensure that the system is auditable if necessary (e.g.,
│  │  │        management can easily assess and check how business
│  │  │        computations are done).
│  │  │     Create documentation for end users.
│  │  │     Determine how end users will be trained.
│  │  ├─ Else
│  │  │  ┌─ If other people will maintain the system
│  │  │  │     Use design-automation techniques which will ensure that
│  │  │  │        other people will be able to maintain the system
│  │  │  │        easily.
```

```
          ┌  Else
          │    ┌  If the system creates data which are used elsewhere
          │    │     Establish controls on data accuracy, integrity, and
          │    │        security.
          │    ┌  Else
          │    │   ┌─────────────────────────────────┐
          │    │   │                                 │
          │    │   │  PURELY PERSONAL COMPUTING       │
          │    │   │                                 │
          │    │   └─────────────────────────────────┘
          │    │
          │    │     The individual may be left alone to build his own
          │    │        system in his own way.
          │    └
          │  └
          └
```

When quick-results computing is initiated it is necessary to assess the objectives, select appropriate tools, determine what help is needed, and determine who will review the results:

```
┌  Initiate the activity.
│     Establish the objectives of the system.
│  ...Determine who will build the system.
│     Determine what tools will be used.
│     Determine what information-center help is needed.
└     Determine who, if anyone, will review the results.
```

Quick-results computing may then proceed as follows:

```
┌  Establish the data.
│     Determine what data the system needs.
│     Extract or establish a data model.
│     Determine where the source data comes from.
│     Determine whether the source data will need converting.
└     Extract the data into the tool that is used.

┌  Evolve the application.
│     Build detailed application.
│     Refine the application continuously, working with a
│        creative end-user or manager if necessary.
└     Brainstorm possible improvements which might be valuable.

┌  Solidify.
│     Review to ensure that the system is easy to use by other
│        people if necessary.
│     Review to ensure that the business calculations
│        can be easily checked by management.
│     Review to ensure that the system can be easily maintained.
└     Create the necessary documentation.
```

Box 21.7 shows the quick-results lifecycle.

BOX 21.7 Quick-results lifecycle

Description

A quick-results lifecycle applies to simple applications
such as report generation and business calculations. It is
used in information-center environments, either by end users
or data-processing professionals. The application is simple
enough to avoid formal specification and design. It may require
formal documentation.

Quick-results computing is an extremely important part of
data processing capable of having a vital effect on the running
of the enterprise. It is made much more valuable and generally
applicable by the building of appropriate databases. Information engineering should create facilities so that quick-results
computing can be as useful as possible.

Types of quick-results lifecycle

PURELY PERSONAL COMPUTING

Personal computing implies, here, that a system is being
built by one person for his sole use. No one else will
use or maintain it, and it does not create data used elsewhere.
Short cuts may then be taken in design and documentation, in
order to obtain quick results.

SHARED COMPUTING

Shared computing implies that other persons will use or maintain
the application. The system must have design and documentation
suitable for this.

The following types of controls are particularly important:

o   Use existing data models and data definitions.
o   Build links to existing databases where appropriate.
o   Use design tools, where appropriate, to create
        maintainable code.
o   Build systems which are easily auditable by management.
o   Create documentation or "HELP" facilities if other
        end users will employ the programs.

Quick-results procedure

> The procedure given below may be modified with Action
> Diagrammer to meet the needs of the particular situation.

Initiate the activity.
    Establish the objectives of the system.
    Determine who will build the system.
        Quick-results computing is usually done by one person.
            In some cases it is a two-person team, a data-processing
            professional working with an end user.

            An end user.

            A data-processing professional.

            A data-processing professional and end user working
                together

    Determine what tools will be used.
    Determine what information-center help is needed.
    Determine who, if anyone, will review the results.

(Continued)

BOX 21.7 *(Continued)*

```
┌─ Is this PURELY personal computing?
│   ┌─ If more than one person is involved in building the system
│   │     Use design-automation techniques that aid multi-person
│   │        development.
│   ├─ Else
│   │   ┌─ If other people will use the system
│   │   │     Ensure that the human interface is well designed.
│   │   │     Ensure that the system is auditable if necessary (e.g.,
│   │   │        management can easily assess and check how business
│   │   │        computations are done.)
│   │   │     Create documentation for end users.
│   │   │     Determine how end users will be trained.
│   │   ├─ Else
│   │   │   ┌─ If other people will maintain the system
│   │   │   │     Use design-automation techniques which will ensure that
│   │   │   │        other people will be able to maintain the system
│   │   │   │        easily.
│   │   │   ├─ Else
│   │   │   │   ┌─ If the system creates data which is used elsewhere
│   │   │   │   │     Establish controls on data accuracy, integrity, and
│   │   │   │   │        security.
│   │   │   │   ├─ Else
│   │   │   │   │
│   │   │   │   │     ┌──────────────────────────────┐
│   │   │   │   │     │                              │
│   │   │   │   │     │  PURELY PERSONAL COMPUTING   │
│   │   │   │   │     │                              │
│   │   │   │   │     └──────────────────────────────┘
│   │   │   │   │
│   │   │   │   │     The individual may be left alone to build his own
│   │   │   │   └─      system in his own way.
│   │   │   └─
│   │   └─
│   └─
└─
```

```
┌─ Establish the data.
│     Determine what data the system needs.
│     Extract or establish a data model.
│     Determine where the source data comes from.
│     Determine whether the source data will need converting.
└─    Extract the data into the tool that is used.

┌─ Evolve the application.
│     Build detailed application.
│     Refine the application continuously, working with a
│        creative end user or manager if necessary.
│     Brainstorm possible improvements which might be valuable.
│   ┌─ Description
│   │     Brainstorming means that a creative group of individuals
│   │     attempt to produce a stream of ideas without inhibition.
│   │     A rule of a brainstorming session is that there can be
│   │     no implied criticism for making an impractical or stupid
│   │     suggestion. The session is intended to generate as many
│   │     ideas as possible. At the end of the session only certain
│   └─    of the ideas will be recorded for possible use.

┌─ Solidify.
│     Review to ensure that the system is easy to use by other
│        people if necessary.
│     Review to ensure that the business calculations
│        can be easily checked by management.
│     Review to ensure that the system can be easily maintained.
└─    Create the necessary documentation.
```

DECISION-SUPPORT LIFECYCLE

As discussed in Chapters 11 and 12, decision-support systems vary from being simple like spreadsheets to highly elaborate decision-making models. Simple decision-support applications are built with a quick-results lifecycle. Elaborate decision-support systems can be extremely valuable and need careful planning.

A decision-support system is designed to help make better business decisions in a specific area. It requires an appropriately structured database and a set of tools for doing decision-support computations.

Decision-support computations should generally be done by end users because they understand the business problem they are trying to solve. They may do this in an innovative, ad hoc fashion without specifications. Often creative investigation of numerical data is required. Highly complex business models may result. Evaluation through prototyping should occur before the system is institutionalized. Data processing professionals should usually design the database and the means of keeping it up to date. They may select or build the tools which the end users employ, and guide the end users in their use. The choice of decision-support software is critical.

Excellent decision-support software exists and an important part of the process of building decision-support systems is to select the best software for the task. As discussed in Chapter 12 the type of software depends on who will use the system. A major mistake is to employ software which is ill suited to the users in question. A part of the lifecycle, then, is establishing the DSS software:

```
┌ Establish the software.
│  ┌ Select decision-support software.
│  │    Determine what categories of users the system is intended
│  │       for:
│  │             *  Top management
│  │             *  Lower management, staff or spreadsheet users
│  │             *  Financial analysts
│  │             *  General decision analysts
│  │
│  │    Select a software category suitable for the above
│  │       user category:
│  │             *  Executive information system
│  │             *  Spreadsheet tool
│  │             *  Business modeling tool
│  │             *  Financial analysis tool
│  │             *  Fourth-generation programming language
│  │             *  General decision support tool
│  │
│  └    Identify the most appropriate tool within this category.
│
└    Ensure that the developers are fully trained in the use of
        the tools.
```

When a decision-support system project is initiated, it is desirable to establish the objectives and establish a budget and target date for the first working version. The long-term objectives are often very different from those of the first working version. The first working version should be *simple* and relatively easy to implement. When the first working system is implemented it will tend to grow naturally, if it is useful, with end users extending its functionality. The sooner the first working system is installed the better, but the long-term potential should be planned for from the beginning.

Initiating the development may include the following steps:

```
┌─ Establish criteria and controls.
│     Establish the long-term objectives of the development activity.
│     Establish the objectives of the first working version.
│     Determine how results will be measured or judged.
│     Establish a budget.
│     Establish a target date for the first working system.
│     Establish dates at which progress will be reviewed.
│     Determine who will assess the progress and with what criteria.
└─

┌─ Determine who will build the system.
│     Select the DP professional developer(s).
│     Select the end-user developer(s).
│     Determine what information-center help is needed.
│     Determine who, if anyone, will review the results.
└─
```

Particularly critical in a decision-support system is the database. It is necessary to determine what data is needed, where it comes from, whether it can be extracted from mainframe databases or other sources, and how it will be kept up-to-date. The data in a decision-support system is usually structured completely differently from the data in a production system. A data structure appropriate for multidimensional analysis is required. The necessary extraction and conversion facilities must be established.

```
┌─ Establish the data.
│     Determine what data the system needs.
│     Establish a data model, or extract one from the encyclopedia.
│     Determine where the source data comes from. (It is often extracted
│        from mainframe production systems.)
│     Determine how the source data will be converted or restructured.
│   ┌─ Determine whether a staging database will be used.
│   │     A staging database is a central repository of data in the DSS
│   │        format that will be used independently by multiple users.
│   │     Data are extracted from files or transaction databases into
│   │        the staging database.  Individual users may extract data
│   │        from the staging database into their own facilities.
│   └─
│
│     Extract the data into the tool that is used.
│     Determine how the data in the decision-support system will be
│        kept up-to-date.
└─
```

The first prototype should be put to work as early as possible. This can usually be done very quickly with good decision-support software, once the requisite data is established, by a data processing professional and end user working together. The end user may then evolve the system to do more sophisticated analysis. Eventually end users should take over the system, adapting it to help make the most effective decisions.

It should be decided whether the system will evolve with a formal set of planned releases, or whether evolution should be continuous.

DEPLOYING THE SYSTEM

A pilot system is a fully working version of the system which is intended to be deployed. The prototype version may need restructuring or reprogramming to create the pilot version. The pilot needs ongoing links to production databases. It may need electronic mail or in-basket facilities to provide communication among different persons who are involved in the decision making. The question of intercommunication among diverse decision makers or executives needs to be addressed. In some cases the system will be installed in separate locations around the world. It can provide a precise vehicle for communication which can help restructure the decision-making processes of an enterprise.

The following procedure relates to building a pilot system and institutionalizing the system.

```
┌─ Build pilot system.
│     A pilot system is a fully working system deployed at first
│     with only a small number of users, small number of terminals
│     or a small database. When it is found to be satisfactory, the
│     number of users may be increased and the database expanded.
│
│     Determine what functions of the prototype will be included
│        in the first pilot system.
│     Determine how decision-support information will be communicated
│        among separate decision-makers.
│     Determine how decision-support information will be communicated
│        with higher management.
│     Determine what networking facilities are needed. Will the
│        decision-support facility link to an electronic mail or
│        in-basket facility, for example.
│     Determine the nature of the ongoing connection to production
│        databases.
│     Determine whether the system should be redesigned or
│        rearchitected in order to produce a working pilot.
│     Make the necessary design changes.
└─    Build and debug the pilot.

   Install and adjust pilot system.
      Phase in system.
      Conduct review meeting.

      ┌─ If no modifications needed
«─────┤     Exit
      ├─ Else
      │     Document adjustments needed.
      │     Determine date for installation of next version.
      └─    Make adjustments.
```

(Continued)

```
┌─ Institutionalize the system.
│       Determine what locations should use the system.
│  ...Determine whether a staging database should be established.
│       Establish the requisite training.
│  ┌─ Establish an internal marketing program to make decision-
│  │       makers aware of the system.
│  │       With some decision support systems, this step has been
│  │       particularly important. It may use:
│  │          o   Memos
│  │          o   Giving the system a memorable name and image
│  │          o   Brochures
│  │          o   Articles in the house magazine
│  │          o   Presentations
│  └─         o   Film or video
│
│┌─ Expand the system a stage at a time.
││      Monitor the system performance.
││      Determine what hardware is needed to handle the full load.
└┘
```

Box 21.8 shows the decision-support lifecycle.

BOX 21.8   Decision-support system development

```
┌─ Description

        A decision-support system is designed to help make
   better business decisions in a specific area. It requires
   an appropriately structured database and a set of tools for
   doing decision-support computations.
        Decision-support computations should generally be done by
   end users because they understand the business problem they
   are trying to solve. They may do this in an innovative, ad-hoc
   fashion without specifications. Often creative investigation
   of numerical data is required. Highly complex business models
   may result. Evolution through prototyping should occur before
   the system is institutionalized.
        I.S. professionals should usually design the database and
   the means of keeping it up to date. They may select or build
   the tools which the end users employ, and guide the end users
   in their use. The choice of decision-support software is critical.

┌─ Decision-support system procedure

   ┌─────────────────────────────────────────────────────────┐
   │ The procedure given below may be modified with Action   │
   │ Diagrammer to meet the needs of the particular situation.│
   └─────────────────────────────────────────────────────────┘

┌─ Initiate the activity.
│  ┌─ Establish criteria and controls.
│  │       Establish the long-term objectives of the development activity.
│  │       Establish the objectives of the first working version.
```

BOX 21.8 *(Continued)*

Comment
  The first working version should be SIMPLE and relatively
  easy to implement. Once a working version is fielded the
  system will tend to grow naturally if it useful, with
  end users extending its functionality. The long-term
  potential should be understood and planned for from the
  beginning.

  Determine how results will be measured or judged.
  Establish a budget.
  Establish a target date for the first working system.
  Establish dates at which progress will be reviewed.
  Determine who will assess the progress and with what criteria.
Determine who will build the system.
  Select the DP professional developer(s).
  Select the end-user developer(s).
  Determine what information-center help is needed.
  Determine who, if anyone, will review the results.

Establish the software.
  Select decision-support software.
    Determine what categories of users the system is intended
      for:
            o Top management
            o Lower management, staff or spreadsheet users
            o Financial analysts
            o General decision analysts

    Select a software category suitable for the above
      user category:
            o Executive information system
            o Spreadsheet tool
            o Business modeling tool
            o Financial analysis tool
            o Fourth-generation programming language
            o General decision-support tool

    Identify the most appropriate tool within this category.

  Ensure that the developers are fully trained in the use of
    the tools.

Establish the data.
  Determine what data the system needs.
  Establish a data model, or extract one from the encyclopedia.
  Determine where the source data comes from. (It is often extracted
    from mainframe production systems.)
  Determine how the source data will be converted or restructured.
  Determine whether a staging database will be used.
    A staging database is a central repository of data in the DSS
      format that will be used independently by multiple users.
      Data are extracted from files or transaction databases into
      the staging database. Individual users may extract data
      from the staging database into their own facilities.

  Extract the data into the tool that is used.
  Determine how the data in the decision-support system will be
    kept up-to-date.

(Continued)

BOX 21.8   *(Continued)*

Prototype evolution
  Description

┌───┐
│   Step-by-step or continuous evolution?   │
└───┘

   STEP-BY-STEP EVOLUTION progresses from one planned prototype
to another until the target system is achieved.
   CONTINUOUS EVOLUTION progresses with a sequence of modifications
continuously adjusting the prototype until the target is reached.
A manager or creative end user may review the progress on an
ongoing basis as it evolves

STEP-BY-STEP EVOLUTION: CONTINUOUS EVOLUTION:

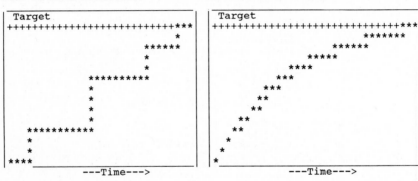

If step-by-step evolution
For each prototype iteration
     Build detailed prototype.
     ┌─────────────────────────────┐
     │ See procedure in Box 6.3   │
     └─────────────────────────────┘
     Put the prototype to use.
     Brainstorm with the decision makers what features they
          would like.
       Description
          Brainstorming means that a creative group of individuals
          attempt to produce a stream of ideas without inhibition.
          A rule of a brainstorming session is that there can be
          no implied criticism for making an impractical or stupid
          suggestion. The session is intended to generate as many
          ideas as possible. At the end of the session only certain
          of the ideas will be recorded for possible use.

     Determine features to be added or changed.

«────── If no need for further iteration
        Determine target date of next review.

BOX 21.8 *(Continued)*

```
 ├─ Else
 █  Continuous evolution
 █     Build detailed prototype.
 █     o─────────────────────────o
 █     │ See procedure in Box 6.3 │
 █     o─────────────────────────o
 █     Refine the prototype continuously, working with the
 █        decision makers.
 █     Brainstorm possible improvements which might be valuable.
 █   ┌─ Description
 █   │    Brainstorming means that a creative group of individuals
 █   │    attempt to produce a stream of ideas without inhibition.
 █   │    A rule of a brainstorming session is that there can be
 █   │    no implied criticism for making an impractical or stupid
 █   │    suggestion. The session is intended to generate as many
 █   │    ideas as possible. At the end of the session only certain
 █   │    of the ideas will be recorded for possible use.
 █   └─
 █
 «██──── If an acceptable final result is achieved
```

```
┌─ Solidify.
│     Review to ensure that the system is easy to use by other
│        people if necessary.
│     Review to ensure that the business calculations
│        can be easily checked by management.
│     Review to ensure that the system can be easily maintained.
│     Create the necessary documentation.
└─

┌─ Build pilot system.
│     A pilot system is a fully working system deployed at first
│     with only a small number of users, small number of terminals
│     or a small database. When it is found to be satisfactory the
│     number of users may be increased and the database expanded.
│
│     Determine what functions of the prototype will be included
│        in the first pilot system.
│     Determine how decision-support information will be communicated
│        among separate decision makers.
│     Determine how decision-support information will be communicated
│        with higher management.
│     Determine what networking facilities are needed. Will the
│        decision-support facility link to an electronic mail or
│        in-basket facility, for example.
│     Determine the nature of the ongoing connection to production
│        databases.
│     Determine whether the system should be redesigned or
│        rearchitected in order to produce a working pilot.
│     Make the necessary design changes.
│     Build and debug the pilot.
```

```
█ Install and adjust pilot system.
█     Phase in system.
█     Conduct review meeting.
█
█   ┌─ If no modifications needed
█   │
«█──┤     Exit
█   ├─ Else
█   │     Document adjustments needed.
█   │     Determine date for installation of next version.
█   │     Make adjustments.
█   └─
```

BOX 21.8 *(Continued)*

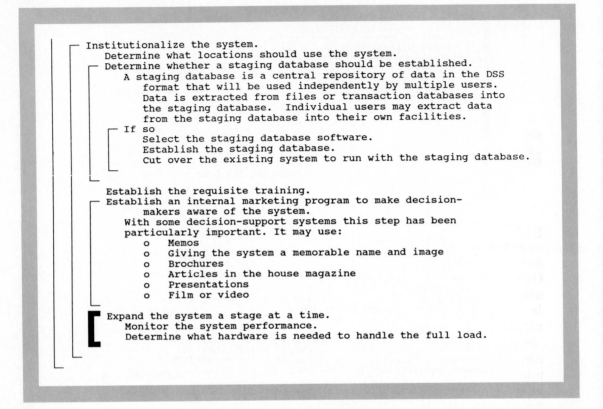

```
Institutionalize the system.
   Determine what locations should use the system.
   Determine whether a staging database should be established.
      A staging database is a central repository of data in the DSS
         format that will be used independently by multiple users.
      Data is extracted from files or transaction databases into
         the staging database.  Individual users may extract data
         from the staging database into their own facilities.
   If so
      Select the staging database software.
      Establish the staging database.
      Cut over the existing system to run with the staging database.


   Establish the requisite training.
   Establish an internal marketing program to make decision-
         makers aware of the system.
      With some decision-support systems this step has been
      particularly important. It may use:
         o   Memos
         o   Giving the system a memorable name and image
         o   Brochures
         o   Articles in the house magazine
         o   Presentations
         o   Film or video

Expand the system a stage at a time.
   Monitor the system performance.
   Determine what hardware is needed to handle the full load.
```

REFERENCES

1. James Martin, *Rapid Application Development* Macmillan, New York, 1990.

2. Methodologies for RAD (rapid application development) and IEM (information engineering methodology), are available from James Martin Associates, Reston, VA.

22 ORGANIZATION CHARTS

INTRODUCTION   This chapter comments on aspects of the IS (information systems) organization needed for IE (information engineering).

The highest executive concerned with computing ought to report to the corporate president or CEO (chief executive officer). He or she sometimes has the title CIO (chief information officer). The CIO is primarily concerned with how information technology can improve the business, enable it to pull ahead of its competition, or enable an enterprise to meet its goals better. The CIO must combine a deep understanding of the business and how to improve it with a deep understanding of technology and what new systems are achievable. A gut feeling for technology and a gut feeling for the business must reside in the same person, and that person must be an excellent communicator. The CIO may be the primary instigator of information engineering so that the systems of the enterprise can meet its needs as effectively as possible and so that computerized procedures can be built or changed quickly.

There needs to be an executive specifically in charge of implementing IE (information engineering). This person may report to the chief information officer. He or she may have the title CIE (chief information engineer).

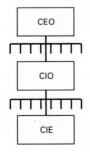

The chief information engineer is an important title in a computerized corporation. He or she is responsible for introducing IE, ensuring that appropriate tools are adopted, supervising the building of encyclopedias, and ensuring that the disciplines inherent in IE are followed. He converts the organization from messy data processing to clean engineering.

Although it is desirable that the top computing executive reports to the CEO, in many corporations this is not yet the case. In some corporations, information engineering is carried out at a lower level and has little or no communication with top management. Sometimes IE starts with data modeling and process modeling in one area of the enterprise, but no top-level planning is done. It gives strong advantages in providing compatible systems which link together, and computerized procedures which can be built and changed quickly. But it may miss the most important business potential of devising new competitive thrusts using technology.

In many corporations information engineering, and advanced development in general, is only a small portion of the overall IS (information systems) activity. A large number of developers still work on building and maintaining traditional systems. Some IS executives have created an advanced development organization that coexists with a traditional development organization.

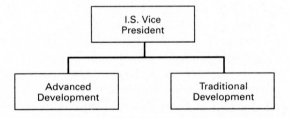

An objective should be to wind down steadily traditional development and replace it with the techniques described in this report. The traditional development organization eventually does no new development, only maintenance, and the systems being maintained are steadily converted to the information engineering environment. The advanced development organization should be set up so that it is a model of what eventually the whole development organization should be.

DEVELOPMENT SUPPORT

Some corporations employ a *development support organization* for supporting development by IS professionals. This organization does not build systems, but guides project managers in the building of systems. The chief information engineer may be part of the development support organization. He may be the person who heads it. He then has support staff reporting to him but not project managers or executives in charge of systems building. He needs to have enough clout to ensure that the encyclopedia is built, coordinated, and used to achieve the coordination that is essential to IE.

The term *Developmental Center* is used by IBM and other corporations to refer to a group that researches development tools and methodologies, encourages implementors to use them, and trains and guides them in obtaining the best results. The Development Center does not build systems; it attempts to improve the way other teams build them by achieving the maximum automation of development and the best practices for understanding user needs. The Development Center measures productivity of IS development and attempts to improve it.

JAD SUPPORT

We described in Chapters 7 and 8 how successful JRP (job requirements planning) and interactive JAD (job analysis design) has been and emphasized how dependent it is on the quality of the JAD leader. The JAD leader should be a full-time appointment, as such a person tends to become more skilled with ongoing experience.

The development support organization should include one person, and possibly a team, that provide JAD support. It should include one person, and possibly a team that have expertise on productivity tools—code generators, CASE (computer-aided systems engineering) tools, and fourth-generation languages. It should also include expertise on information engineering.

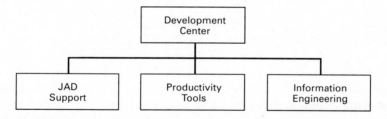

A meeting room with workstations and projectors, such as that described in Chapter 8 for IE/JAD sessions may be used for information center demonstrations and workshops, and for executive meetings, as well as for JAD sessions and prototype review.

ADVANCED DEVELOPMENT GROUP

In some IS organizations instead of having a Development Center which tells other professionals how to succeed, a group is established which identifies best tools and techniques and also uses them on projects. The view is sometimes held that an organization truly understands the new methodologies only if it uses them.

This has been given names such as Advanced Development Group or Advanced Technology Center. We will call it Advanced Development Group. The Advanced Development Group, when it starts to be successful, should be made highly visible, prestigious, and well paid. Some IS professionals are reluctant to change to better methodologies, and they should be given every motivation to do so. It is desirable to have the most productive analysts and developers clamoring to join the Advanced Development Group.

Some IS executives introduce automated tools into an otherwise traditional IS organization by setting up *high-productivity cells* to tackle selected projects. The best developers who are eager to use the new tools are put on to these projects and are given the most automated environment. The high-productivity cells steadily grow and multiply, their productivity being measured, until they eliminate most of the traditional development.

The Advanced Development Group and Development Center are not incompatible ideas. Some corporations have a small Development Center which keeps up-to-date with tools and methodologies and an Advanced Development Group which builds systems. The Development Center tries to ensure that the Advanced Development Group uses the most powerful tools and techniques. The JAD leader should be a skilled JAD professional, independent of any one project, and so may be part of a service group that supports multiple projects all of which use advanced tools and methodologies. The JAD leader may be part of the Development Center.

END-USER SUPPORT

Knowledge workers of all types are increasingly using personal computers and end-user mainframe facilities and are being involved in systems design and prototyping. To support end users, Information Center organizations have evolved as described in Chapter 10. An Information Center, like a Development Center, does not build systems (in most cases) but shows users how to use their own resources. An Executive Information Center, however, may build executive information systems as described in Chapter 13. Both of these may be part of end-user support:

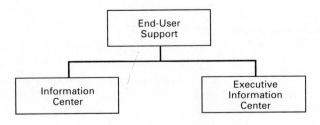

An Information Center may support four different types of systems, giving somewhat different types of support for each:

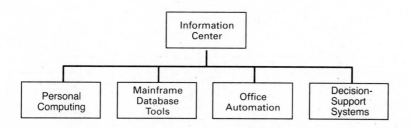

In some corporations the Information Center is responsible for the corporate libraries. In some corporations office automation, and in some decision-support systems, are handled separately from the Information Center. The argument for handling them together is that they all involve introducing tools to end users and guiding the users in employing the tools successfully. Supporting a decision-support package, like SYSTEM W, for example, is regarded as an extension of supporting spreadsheet tools. Office tools needed to be integrated with decision-support tools.

A major decision-support system or office automation system is designed for use by *many* end users. The structure of the system needs to be designed by IS professionals. It is deployed a stage at a time by IS professionals. Putting the system to good use, however, involves substantial creativity on the part of the users and may require them to do something equivalent to programming.

Some Information Centers support only single-user tools rather than the building of complex multiuser systems. A complex multiuser decision-support system is a hybrid of IS professional development and end-user development. It may require JAD sessions and prototyping. The building of such systems may be combined with the building of executive information systems. End-user support, then, may be divided into complex systems and single-user systems:

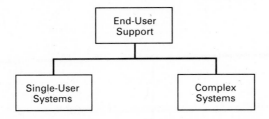

The *single-user systems* part of this organization supports end users building their own systems. The *complex systems* part supports hybrid efforts requiring IS professional development combined with end-user development.

There may be three parts to end-user support, the third being executive information systems:

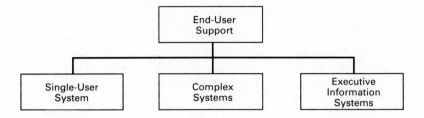

In some corporations the Development Center and Information Center are regarded as parallel activities, one supporting development by IS professionals and the other supporting development by end users. Both are part of an overall development support organization:

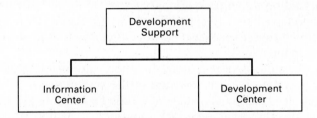

Some organizations have combined the support of end users and support of professional development. Other organizations have them entirely separate.

There is some commonality in the tools and software for end users and the tools and software useful for IS professionals. There may therefore be a group of specialists on tools and fourth-generation languages which helps both the Information Center and the Development Center.

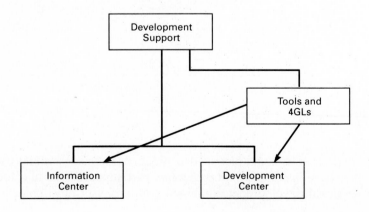

THE KNOWLEDGE Much experience of data administration exists in
ADMINISTRATOR many corporations. The data administrator has the
task of coordinating the logical representations of the
corporation's data. An extension of this task is the coordination of IE perspectives (Chapter 19) and the general coordination of what is in the encyclopedia.
We will refer to the person responsible for this task as the *knowledge administrator*. Sometimes the term "encyclopedia administrator" has been used.

Data administration, an important task, is a subset of the task of administering the overall contents of the encyclopedia. The knowledge administrator may have a data administrator working for him, or the data administrator may have been promoted to the larger task of being the knowledge administrator.

Even more than the data administrator, the knowledge administrator needs computerized tools to help her analyze and coordinate the knowledge. She will examine many perspectives, helping to synthesize them into as consistent a whole as possible.

Like the data administrator, the knowledge administrator ought to report at a suitably high level. Figure 22.1 shows the knowledge administrator reporting to the vice-president of IS. She has a dashed-line link to the Information Center, Development Center, and to project managers and is responsible for ensuring

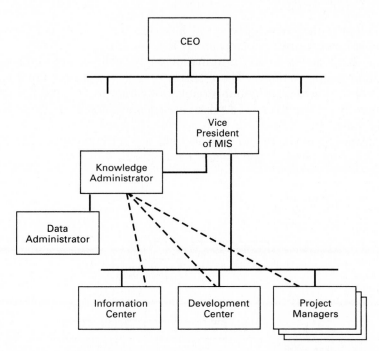

Figure 22.1 The keeper of the encyclopedia may be called the knowledge administrator. He needs to report at a suitably high level.

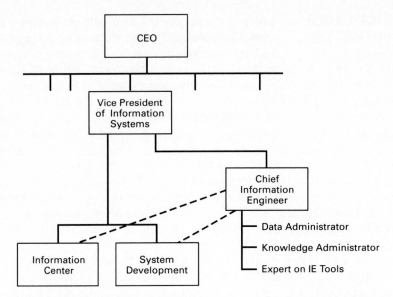

Figure 22.2 The chief information engineer may employ a data administrator and knowledge administrator who coordinate the data models and perspectives in the encyclopedia.

that they employ the encyclopedia and link into the data model, and that the best possible coordination of perspectives is achieved.

Figure 22.2 shows a chief information engineer reporting to the vice-president of information systems. The chief information engineer employs a data administrator, a knowledge administrator, who tries to achieve the maximum coordination of perspectives, and possibly specialists such as an expert on development tools.

An advanced development organization should encompass end-user support, development support, and system development projects:

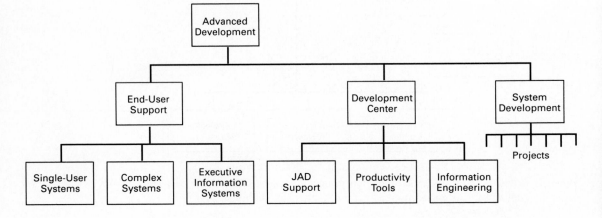

The advanced development organization may report to an IS vice-president who is also responsible for planning and strategy, network management, and information engineering. The planning and design of corporatewide networks needs to be done at a high level. IS planning and strategy, and information engineering also needs to be done at a high level:

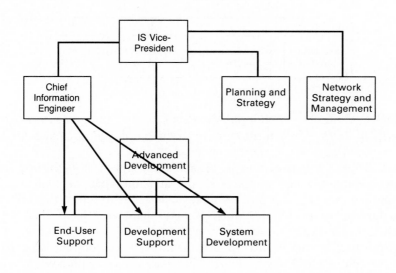

End-user support, development support, and individual projects need to link into information engineering, using the data models and process models. Control of these linkages should be managed with the aid of the encyclopedia and its knowledge coordinator coordinating, where appropriate, the separate development efforts. The chief information engineer needs to report at a high enough level to be able to ensure that the encyclopedia is used as it should be by the many development groups.

ARTIFICIAL INTELLIGENCE

The practical application of artificial intelligence should be understood by all IS executives. There are numerous potential applications of expert systems in every corporation, some of them highly valuable. Some of the major strategic systems opportunities relate to rule-based inference processing.

Because the tools and techniques used in building expert systems (and other types of AI systems) are different from those for building traditional systems (at the time of writing), it makes sense to have a group of professionals skilled in this technology. This may be part of the Development Center or Advanced Technology Group, but more often it is a separate group which helps to identify and build AI systems. An overall advanced development organization may have departments for end-user support, development support, system development with advanced techniques, and artificial intelligence systems:

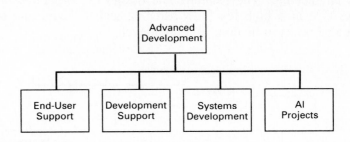

AN EMBRYO IE ORGANIZATION

Multiple variations on the foregoing forms of organization have been employed to make information engineering succeed.

One difference between an IE organization and an organization for traditional development is that IE spans all the divisions that can realistically have integration data models and process models. It needs to report at a high enough level to be able to accomplish this. It may span what have been separately managed IS organizations, each reporting to local executives.

Large parts of the earlier IS organizations may continue to exist. They have to maintain the existing systems. They may coexist with new groups which are part of an integrated IE organization.

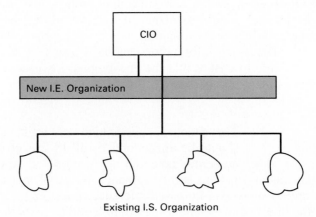

Figure 22.3   The IE organization spans the enterprise and is designed to be an embryo of what all IS development will eventually become. Existing IS organizations using older methodologies will be absorbed over time into the new organization as old systems are rebuilt or reverse engineered to become IE systems.

Some corporations have established a new IS organization having the structure which they believe will work best for information engineering. This new organization coexists with the old organizations which are continuing to maintain and enhance current systems (Fig. 22.3). The new organization may be small initially compared to the masses of people working on existing systems, but it is the embryo of what the whole IE organization will eventually become. Over time the old systems are rebuilt or reverse engineered to become IE systems, and the old IS organization is steadily absorbed into the new IE organization.

PART **V** APPENDICES

I DIAGRAMMING STANDARDS

INTRODUCTION

Information engineering depends heavily on its use of diagramming. Diagrams showing facets of highly complex designs need to be as easy to understand as possible. Diagrams, and their associated windows for displaying details, need to have precision so that a computer can use them as a basis for design automation and code generation. A complex design is often represented by multiple diagram types in such a way that the computer can interrelate the diagrams (a hyperdiagram). This subject is examined in more detail in the author's book *Recommended Diagramming Standards for Analysts and Programmers* [1]. The standards in that book have been the basis for most of the computer industry's leading CASE (computer-aided systems engineering) tools for information engineering.

To gain control of its computing, an enterprise must establish a set of standards for IS diagrams. The standards should be the basis of the training given to both data processing professionals and end users. Enterprisewide standards are essential for communication among all persons involved with computers, for establishing corporate or interdepartmental data models and procedures, and for managing the move into CASE tools.

Many corporations have adopted diagramming conventions from methodologies of the past which today are inadequate because they are narrowly focused, ill-structured, unaware of database techniques, unaware of fourth-generation languages, too difficult to teach to end users, clumsy and time consuming, inadequate for automation, or as is usually the case, tackle only part of problems that should be tackled.

This appendix summarizes the constructs that we need to be able to draw. Similar symbols are needed on many different types of diagrams. A consistently drawn set of symbols can be used on the following basic tools:

- Decomposition diagrams
- Dependency diagrams
- Data flow diagrams
- Action diagrams
- Program structure diagrams, for which we employ action diagrams
- Data analysis diagrams
- Entity-relationship diagrams
- Data structure diagrams
- Data navigation diagrams
- Decision trees and tables
- State transition diagrams and tables
- Dialog diagrams

All of these types of diagrams should be drawn from the same small set of blocks and symbols. These blocks and symbols are described in this appendix.

CHANGING METHODS

Diagramming techniques in computing are still evolving. This is necessary because when we examine techniques in common use today, many of them have *serious* deficiencies. Flowcharts are falling out of use because they do not give a structured view of a program. Some of the early structured diagramming techniques need replacing because they fail to represent some important ideas. *Indeed, one of the remarkable deficiencies of the early structured techniques is their use of diagrams that cannot represent many of the important constructs.* We are inventing more rigorous methods for creating better specifications. Vast improvements are needed and are clearly possible in the specification process. These improvements bring new diagramming methods.

One of the problems with computing is that it is so easy to make a mess. Very tidy thinking is needed about the complex logic, or the result is a rat's nest. Today's structured techniques are an improvement over earlier techniques. However, we can still make a mess with them. Most specifications for complex systems are full of ambiguities, inconsistencies, and omissions. More precise mathematically based techniques are evolving so that we can use the computer to help create specifications without these problems. As better, more automated techniques evolve, they need appropriate diagramming methods.

Sometimes the advocates or owners of a particular diagramming technique defend it more like pagan priests defending a religion than like computer scientists seeking to advance their methods. It is very necessary to look objectively at the changes needed for full *automation* and *integration* of diagramming techniques, and to speak openly about the defects of earlier techniques.

Many of the diagramming techniques in common use are old and obsolete. The IBM diagramming template, which most analysts use, is two decades old. It contains symbols for ''magnetic drum,'' ''punched tape,'' and ''transmitted tape.'' It was created before database systems, display terminals, or structured techniques were in use.

BOX I.1 Principles of diagramming standards

Principles of Diagramming Standards

- Analysts, programmers, and end users should be provided with a set of diagramming techniques which are aids to clear thinking about different aspects of analysis, design, and programming.
- The multiple diagramming tools should use the minimum number of icons.
- They should be as easy to learn as possible.
- Conversion between diagrams should be automatic whenever possible.
- The diagramming techniques should be a corporatewide standard, firmly adhered to.

Automation of Diagramming

- The diagrams should be the basis of computer-aided analysis and design—the basis of CASE tools.
- Higher-level design diagrams should convert automatically to action diagrams where relevant.
- The family of diagrams should be a basis for code generation.
- The diagrams should be easy to change and file at the computer screen.
- The diagrams should relate to data models.
- The diagrams convey *meaning* which is stored in a system encyclopedia. The encyclopedia often stores more detail than is shown on any one screen.
- The diagrams and associated encyclopedia should *be* the system documentation.

We need an integrated set of diagramming standards with which we can express all of the constructs that are necessary for the automation of system design and programming. The old techniques *must* give way to techniques that can draw all the concepts we need in an integrated fashion appropriate for computer-aided design and code generation. Box I.1 lists principles that should apply to diagramming standards.

STRUCTURED PROGRAM DESIGN

Structured programs are organized hierarchically. There is only one root module. Execution must begin with this root module. Any module can pass control to a module at the next lower level in the hierarchy—a parent module passes control to a child module. Program control enters a module at its entry point and must leave at its exit point. Control returns to the invoking (parent) module when the invoked (child) module completes execution.

A tree-structured diagram is used to draw the program modules that obey this orderly set of rules. Tree structures can be drawn in various ways. It is common to draw them as a set of blocks with the root block at the top, and each parent above its children. A neater way to show the flow of control is to draw them with brackets. Children are within, and to the right of, their parent bracket:

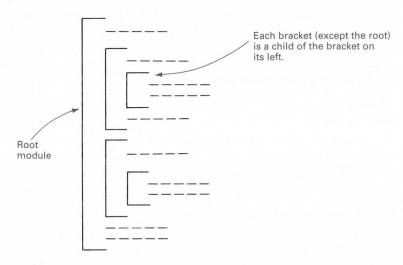

In creating structured programs, four basic constructs are used.

- SEQUENCE   Items are executed in the stated sequence.
- CONDITION   A set of operations are executed only if a stated condition applies.
- CASE   One of several alternative sets of operations are executed.

- REPETITION   A set of operations is repeated, the repetition being terminated on the basis of a stated test. There are two types of
repetition control, one (DO WHILE) where the termination
test is applied *before* the set of operations is executed, the
other (DO UNTIL) where the terminated test is applied *after*
the set of operations is executed.

Amazingly, some of the diagramming techniques used for representing
structured programs cannot show these four basic constructs. The four constructs can be shown very simply with brackets:

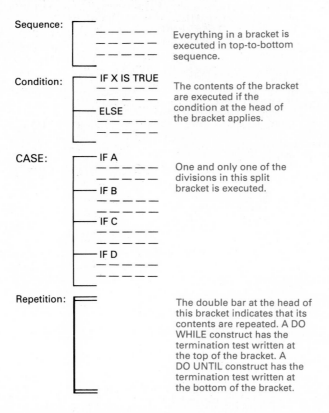

Sequence: Everything in a bracket is executed in top-to-bottom sequence.

Condition: IF X IS TRUE / ELSE The contents of the bracket are executed if the condition at the head of the bracket applies.

CASE: IF A / IF B / IF C / IF D One and only one of the divisions in this split bracket is executed.

Repetition: The double bar at the head of this bracket indicates that its contents are repeated. A DO WHILE construct has the termination test written at the top of the bracket. A DO UNTIL construct has the termination test written at the bottom of the bracket.

The words used in fourth-generation languages can be appended to the
brackets. The diagram is thus edited until it becomes an executable program.
Figure I.1 shows an executable program drawn in this way. This type of diagram is called an action diagram. At its initial stage it can be a tree structure
representing a high-level overview or decomposition. It is successively extended
until it becomes an executable program. This can be done in a computer-aided
fashion, with software ending the words of a particular computer language. Action diagrams can be generated automatically from decomposition diagrams, de-

```
┌─── TO PRODUCE A DIARY REPORT */
│   ┌── PROCEDURE DIARRE =
│   │      BEGIN
│   │        INCLUDE:S DIARY;
│   │        PROGRAM DIARREP = <OUTPUT DIARY;
│   │                            DIARRENT GET 1;
│   │                            OUTPUT T;
│   │                            >;
│   └──    END;
│
│   ┌── SPECIFY DIARRENT () =
│   │      BEGIN
│   │        STADATE: = PROMPT("Enter start date for report (YYYYMMDD) ",STRING);
│   │        FINDATE: = PROMPT("Enter end date for report (YYYYMMDD) ",STRING);
│   │        ST1DAT: = SUBSTR(STADATE,3,6); PICTURE (ST1DAT,"99/99/99");
│   │        FI1DAT: = SUBSTR(FINDATE,3,6); PICTURE (FI1DAT,"99/99/99");
│   │        CHECK GET E.WHO,E.WHEN,E.WHERE,E.WHAT
│   │          WHERE E.WHEN GE ST1DAT
│   └──         AND E.WHEN LE FI1DAT;
│          END;
│
│   ┌── SPECIFY CHECK (WHO,WHEN,WHERE,WHAT) =
│   │      BEGIN
│   │  ┌─ INIT
│   │  │    BEGIN
│   │  │      PICTURE(WHEN,"99/99/99");
│   │  └─   END;
│   │
│   │  ┌─ CHANGE WHO:
│   │  │    BEGIN
│   │  │    ISOSTA : = DATETOINT(STADATE);
│   │  │
│   │  │  ┌─ IF WHO EQ "ARH" THEN
│   │  │  │      BEGIN
│   │  │  │        NAME: = "Instructor 1";
│   │  │  │      END
│   │  │  ├─ ELSE
│   │  │  │      BEGIN
│   │  │  │        NAME: = "Instructor 2";
│   │  │  └─   END;
│   │  │
│   │  │      ┌──────────────────────────────────────────────────┐
│   │  │      │   Name : ";NAME;                        51;"      │
│   │  │      │   Period Starts : ";ST1DAT;"Ends : ";FI1DAT; 51;" │
│   │  │      │   Date     Location     Activity                  │
│   │  │      └──────────────────────────────────────────────────┘
│   │  │
│   │  └─   END;
│   │       WHEN1: = DATETOINT(CONCAT("19",WHEN));
│   │  ┌─ WHILE WHEN1 GET ISOSTA DO
│   │  │    BEGIN
│   │  │      TODAY: = SUBSTR(INTTODATE(ISOSTA),3,6);
│   │  │      PICTURE(TODAY,"99/99/99");
│   │  │      "1";TODAY;"1 ";      25;"1 ";          51;"1";
│   │  │      ISOSTA: = ISOSTA + 1;
│   │  └─   END;
│   │
│   │       "1";WHEN ; "1 ";WHERE; 25;"1 ";WHAT;           51;"1";/;
│   │       ISOSTA: = WHEN1 + 1;
│   └──     END;
└───
```

Figure 1.1   A complete MIMER PG program in action diagram format.

pendency diagrams, data flow diagrams, data navigation diagrams, decision trees, state transition diagrams, and dialog diagrams. Action diagrams are discussed in Appendix II.

BOXES

The foregoing family of diagramming tools use blocks to represent activities or data. To distinguish between activities and data, activities are drawn as round-cornered blocks, data are drawn as square-cornered boxes:

ARROWS

Many types of diagrams have lines connecting boxes. An arrow on a line is used to mean *flow* or *sequence*. Flow implies that activities are performed in sequence:

Arrows are drawn in the middle of a line connecting boxes rather than at the end, because the ends of the line are used for cardinality symbols.

High-level decomposition diagrams are usually unconcerned with sequence. They use a tree structure to show how a function is composed of lower-level functions. Lower-level decomposition diagrams may need to show sequence. They may show how an activity is composed of subactivities which are executed in a given sequence. To show this, an arrow is used pointing in the direction of the sequence. This direction should be drawn top to bottom on a *vertical tree* or left to right on a *horizontal tree*.

It is usually better to show sequence on a dependency diagram than on a decomposition diagram:

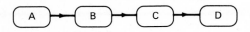

CROW'S FOOT

The term *cardinality* refers to how many of one item is associated with another. There can be one-with-one and one-with-many cardinality. Sometimes numbers may be used to place upper or lower limits on cardinality.

A crow's-foot connector from a line to a box is drawn like this:

It means that one or more than one instances of *B* can be associated with one instance of *A*. It is referred to as a *one-with-many association*.

ONE-WITH-ONE CARDINALITY

On a diagram of data, one-with-one cardinality is drawn with a small bar like a "1" across the line:

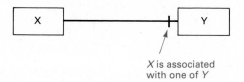

X is associated with one of *Y*

ZERO CARDINALITY

A zero as part of the cardinality symbol means that there may be zero of that block in the association:

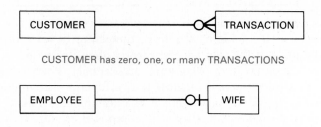

CUSTOMER has zero, one, or many TRANSACTIONS

EMPLOYEE has zero or one WIFE

A line may have cardinality indicators in both directions:

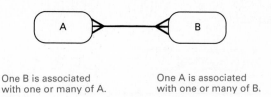

One B is associated with one or many of A.

One A is associated with one or many of B.

On data diagrams it is recommended that a line representing a relationship between data entities should *always* have the cardinality symbols drawn at both ends. It is sloppy diagramming to draw a line connecting to a data box with no cardinality symbol. On activity diagrams the cardinality is usually one-with-one;

because of this the one-with-one symbol is often omitted. A line with no cardinality symbol implies one-with-one (as on a typical data flow diagram, for example).

MAXIMUM AND MINIMUM

The cardinality indicators express a maximum and a minimum:

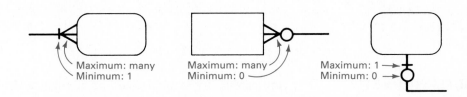

Maximum: many
Minimum: 1

Maximum: many
Minimum: 0

Maximum: 1
Minimum: 0

The maximum is always placed next to the box it refers to.

There may be more detailed information about cardinality stored in the encyclopedia associated with the diagram. It might say, for example that the maximum is 25, or that the maximum and minimum are both 3.

Where the minimum and maximum are both 1, two bars may be placed on the line:

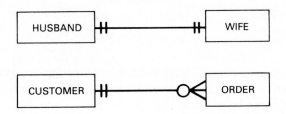

This may be read as meaning "one and only one." Often, a single bar is used to mean "one and only one."

CONDITIONS

Zero cardinality has a special role to play. It means that something may or may not exist. With activities it means that an activity may or may not be performed. On activity diagrams a *condition* is associated with zero cardinality. The condition may be shown on the link. In some cases a complex network of conditions is required between two blocks. These may be shown on a different diagram.

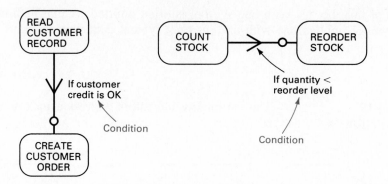

ALTERNATIVE PATHS

The zero cardinality symbol could be at either end of a line with an arrow on it:

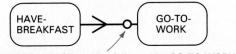

HAVE-BREAKFAST may be followed by GO-TO-WORK

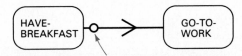

GO-TO-WORK may occur without HAVE-BREAKFAST

In each case the zero is placed against the box that may not exist.

When an activity may be triggered by many different activities, a zero may be placed on the paths from these activities:

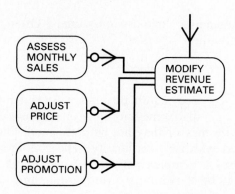

The diagram above says that neither ASSESS MONTHLY SALES, nor ADJUST PRICE, nor ADJUST PROMOTION has to exist for MODIFY REVENUE ESTIMATE to occur.

The case structure of action diagrams is similar in shape to the branching mutual-exclusivity line:

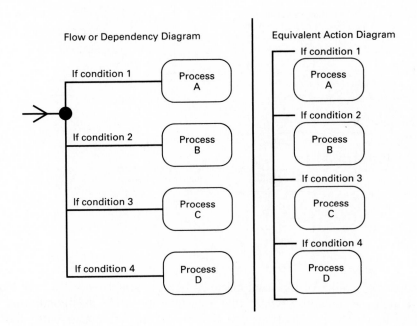

MUTUAL EXCLUSIVITY

Sometimes a block is associated with *one* of a group of blocks. This is indicated with a branching line with a filled-in circle at the branch:

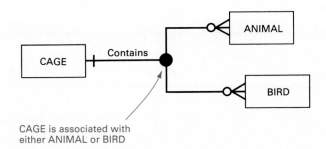

CAGE is associated with either ANIMAL or BIRD

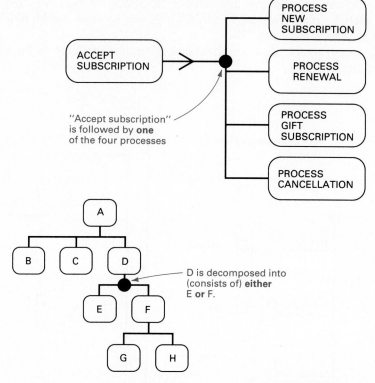

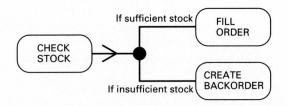

The reader may think of the solid circle as being a small letter "o" for "or".

A mutual-exclusivity circle, like a cardinality circle, has conditions associated with it. These conditions are written on, or associated with, the lines leaving the circle:

When we convert dependency diagrams, data navigation diagrams, or other diagrams into action diagrams ready for creating executable code, the condition statement will appear on the action diagrams. Figure I.2 shows the possible combinations of two activities and their translation to action diagrams.

LABELING OF LINES

One some types of diagrams the lines connecting boxes should be labeled. Lines between *activity*

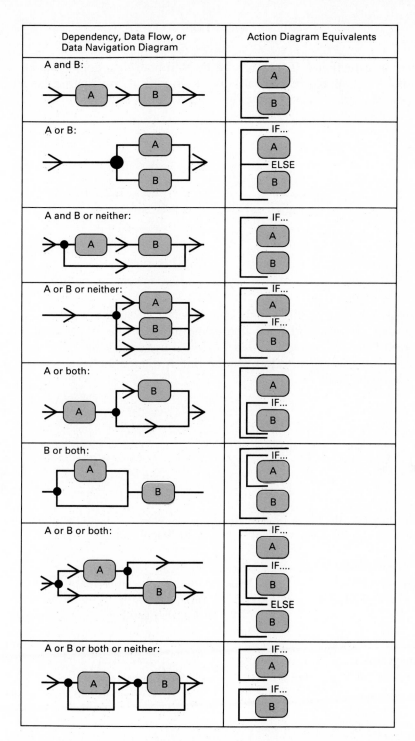

Figure I.2 Diagrams showing activities, such as dependency diagrams, data flow diagrams, or data navigation diagrams.

boxes are unidirectional. There may be lines in both directions between activity boxes, but these should be separate lines each with its own particular meaning. Lines between *data* boxes, on the other hand, are bidirectional. The line could be read in either direction:

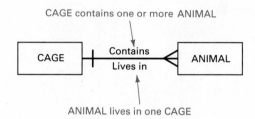

It is usually necessary to label only one direction of such a line.

A label *above* a horizontal line is the name of the relationship when the line is read from left to right. A label *below* a horizontal line is the name when the line is read from right to left. As the line is rotated the label remains on the same side of the line:

Thus the label to the right of a vertical line is read when going *down* the line. The label on the left of a vertical line is read when going *up* the line.

READING LINKS LIKE SENTENCES   Lines between boxes give information about the relationship between the boxes. This information ought to read like an English sentence. For example:

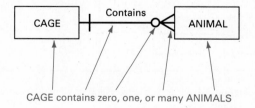

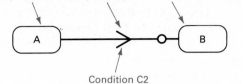

Activity A is followed by activity B if condition C2 is satisfied

Condition C2

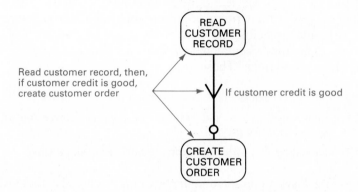

Read customer record, then, if customer credit is good, create customer order

If customer credit is good

LARGE ARROWS

A large arrow on a diagram is used to show that an event occurs:

This may be used on a dependency diagram, data flow diagram, or state transition diagram:

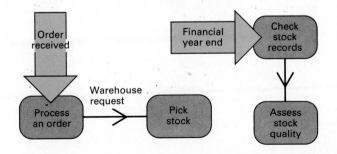

CONCURRENCY   For the first four decades of computing, almost all computers performed their operations sequentially. A major difference between the fourth and fifth generations of computers is likely to be that a fifth-generation machine will have multiple processors and will execute operations in parallel where this is possible. Where parallel processing is possible we need a construct on our diagrams which indicates that specified activities can happen concurrently.

The language OCCAM* is a tight programming language that can express concurrency. It is used for writing programs for multi-microprocessor configurations, or transputer systems. To control the order of execution of processes, OCCAM uses three fundamental mechanisms in addition to the conventional WHILE and IF constructions. These are:

- SEQ   indicating that operations are carried out in *sequence*.
- ALT   indicating that one and only one operation is carried out of several *alternate* operations.
- PAR   indicating that operations can be carried out in *parallel*.

SEQ and ALT are represented in the brackets discussed earlier, ALT being a *case* structure. PAR requires a new diagramming construct. We will indicate that brackets can be executed concurrently by linking them with a semicircular arc:

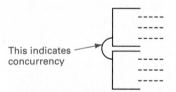

The reader might think of the arc as being a "C" for concurrency.

The basic constructs SEQ, ALT, and PAR are then drawn as follows:

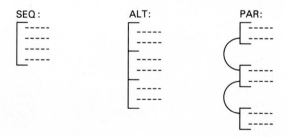

---

*OCCAM manuals are available from INMOS at: INMOS Ltd., Whitefriars, Lewins Mead, Bristol, England BS1 2NP.   Tel: (0272) 290861; or INMOS Corp., P.O. Box 16000, Colorado Springs, CO 80935, U.S.A.   Tel: 303-630-4000.

Whereas OCCAM is designed for machine programming at a low level, the HOS specification language is designed for systems analysts who begin with a high-level overview of the systems they are designing [2]. This specification language has three forms of decomposition: JOIN, OR, and INCLUDE. These again express *sequence, alternates,* and *concurrency.* Where they are binary decompositions, they can be drawn as follows:

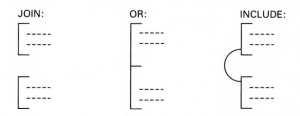

A decomposition can be drawn with diagram symbols rather than with the words JOIN, INCLUDE, and OR:

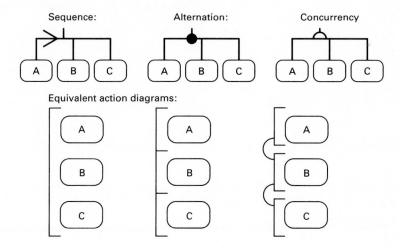

In some cases the concurrency symbol is on one bracket or block only, indicating that this bracket or block relates to parallel activities. This one subroutine may initialize and use a parallel array of processors. In OCCAM, for example, we may have the following:

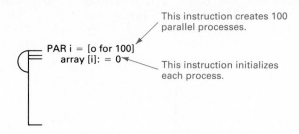

While the other types of constructs in the book have been used extensively in practice, the concurrency indicator has not as yet because of the essentially serial nature of today's programming. Concurrency will be vitally important in future system design.

DIAGRAM CONNECTORS

A pentagon arrow is used as a connector to connect lines to a distant part of a diagram:

The connector symbol may be used to connect to other pages. This is often unnecessary with computerized graphics because the user scrolls across large complete diagrams.

THREE DOTS

Three dots in front of a name on a box or a line of an action diagram indicate that that item can be expanded with the EXPAND command.

When a large diagram is contracted, the three dots are inserted automati-

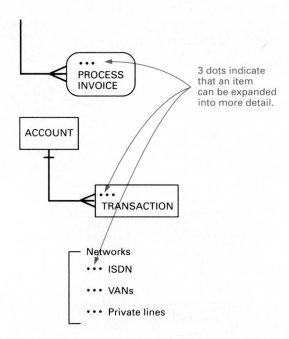

3 dots indicate that an item can be expanded into more detail.

cally to show the view that it may be expanded to its original form. Expansion and contraction are illustrated in Fig. I.3.

ENTITY-RELATIONSHIP DIAGRAM

An entity-relationship diagram shows entity types as square-cornered boxes. (An entity is any person or thing about which data is stored.) The entity types are associated with one another; for example, a PRODUCT entity *is purchased by* a CUSTOMER entity. Lines linking the boxes show these associations. The lines have cardinality indicators. Figure I.4 shows an example of an entity-relationship diagram.

CONVERSION OF DIAGRAMS TO EXECUTABLE CODE

There is a correspondence among the differing diagramming types. They need to be associated in order to automate as fully as possible the tasks of the analyst and programmer. It is this drive toward computer-aided design that makes it so important to have consistent notation among the different types of diagrams.

A data navigation diagram is drawn using an entity-relationship diagram. A data navigation diagram can be converted automatically into an action diagram. Similarly, decomposition diagrams, dependency diagrams, data flow diagrams, decision trees, state transition diagrams, and dialog diagrams can be

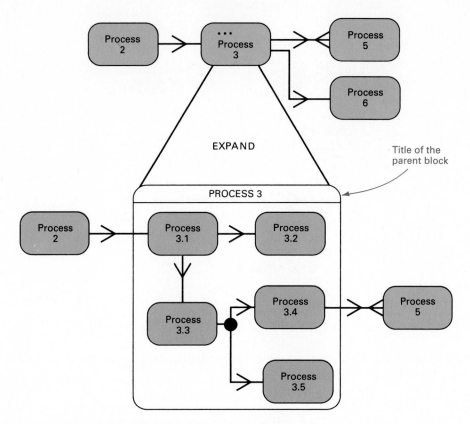

Figure I.3 The command "EXPAND" explodes a box into a diagram *of the same type*. The converse command is "CONTRACT."

automatically converted to action diagrams if drawn rigorously (see the author's *Recommended Diagramming Standards for Analysts and Programmers* [1]). An action diagram is edited in computer-aided fashion until it becomes executable code. This computer-aided progression from high-level overview diagrams or data administrator's data models to executable code makes it possible to increase the productivity of the systems analyst by a large amount.

Figure I.5 shows the relationship between diagramming techniques and the forms of conversion to action diagrams. Code generation can occur from action diagrams and representations of data, screens, and reports.

HAND-DRAWN DIAGRAMS

The diagrams of this report are intended to be created with a modern workstation or a dot-matrix printer. When they are drawn by hand, a template like that in Fig. I.6 should be used.

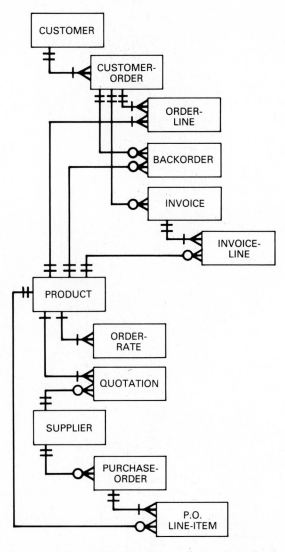

Figure I.4 An entity-relationship diagram for a wholesale distributor.

ASCII CHARACTER DIAGRAMS

Sometimes diagrams have to be drawn on a line printer or printer with an ASCII character set. In this case the crow's foot has only two toes and is represented with $<$, $>$, $\vee$, or $\wedge$:

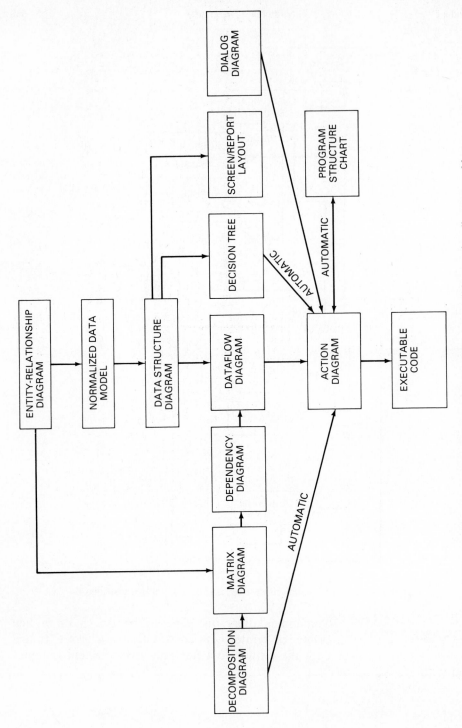

Figure 1.5 Various types of diagrams are automatically convertible to action diagrams and hence to executable code.

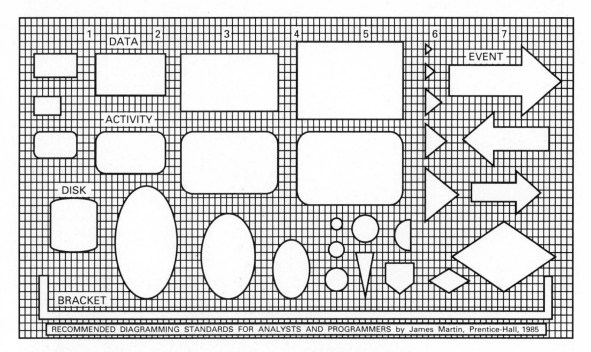

Figure I.6 A template for drawing the diagrams in this book.

Square-cornered and round-cornered boxes can be represented as boxes with a + or o, respectively, at their corners:

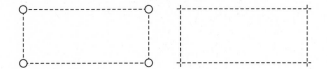

ASCII diagrams are not likely to be as elegant as drawings done with a graphics screen and dot-matrix printer.

REFERENCES

1. James Martin, *Recommended Diagramming Standards for Analysts and Programmers: A Basis for Automation.* Englewood Cliffs, N.J.: Prentice-Hall, 1987.

2. James Martin, *System Design from Provably Correct Constructs.* Englewood Cliffs, N.J.: Prentice-Hall, 1985.

Appendix

 ACTION DIAGRAMS

OVERVIEW VERSUS DETAILED LOGIC DIAGRAMMING

Of the diagramming techniques that evolved in the 1970s and earlier, some are usable for the *overview* of program structure and some are usable for the *detailed* program logic. Structure charts, HIPO diagrams, Warnier-Orr diagrams, and Michael Jackson charts draw overall program structures, but not the detailed tests, conditions, and logic. Their advocates usually resort to structured English or pseudocode to represent the detail. Flowcharts and Nassi-Shneiderman charts show the detailed logic of a program, but not the structural overview.

There is no reason why the diagramming of the *overview* should be incompatible with the diagramming of the *detail*. Indeed, it is highly desirable that these two aspects of program design should employ the same type of diagram because complex systems are created by successively filling in detail (top-down design) and linking together blocks of low-level detail (bottom-up design). The design needs to move naturally between the high levels and low levels of design. The low level should be a natural extension of the high level. *Action diagrams* achieve this. They give a natural way to draw program overviews such as structure charts, HIPO or Warnier-Orr diagrams, *and* detailed logic such as flowcharts or Nassi-Shneiderman charts. They were originally designed to be as easy to teach to end users as possible and to assist end users in applying fourth-generation languages. Most of the leading CASE tools use action diagrams.

Glancing ahead, Figs. II.2 and II.3 show simple examples of action diagrams. Figure II.8 shows an extension of Fig. II.2. They are useful for showing, and modifying, human agendas and procedures, and are used in the procedure boxes throughout this trilogy. They are particularly useful because of the ease with which they can be expanded, contracted, and edited on the screen of a personal computer.

537

BRACKETS

A program module is drawn as a bracket:

Brackets are the basic building blocks of action diagrams. The bracket can be of any length, so there is space in it for as much text or detail as is needed.

Inside the bracket is a sequence of operations. A simple control rule applies to the bracket. You enter it at the top, do the things in it in a top-to-bottom sequence, and exit at the bottom.

Inside the bracket there may be other brackets. Many brackets may be nested. The nesting shows the hierarchical structure of a program. Figure II.1 shows the representation of a hierarchical structure with brackets.

Some brackets are *repetition* brackets. The items in the bracket are executed many times. The repetition bracket has a double line at its top:

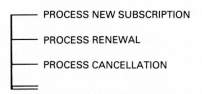

When one of several processes is to be used (mutually exclusive selection), a bracket with multiple divisions is used:

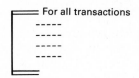

This is the programmer's multiple-option structures, called a "case structure." One, and only one, of the divisions in the bracket above is executed.

ULTIMATE DECOMPOSITION

Figure II.2 illustrates an action diagram overview of a program structure. It can be extended to show conditions, case structures, and loops of different types—it can show detailed program logic. Figure II.3 expands the process in Fig. II.2 called VALIDATE SUB ITEM. Figures II.2 and II.3 could be merged into one chart.

Glancing ahead, Fig. II.7 shows *executable* program code written in a

Decomposition Diagram, Structure Chart, HIPO Chart, etc.

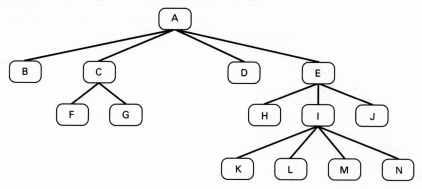

Action Diagram

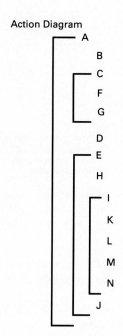

Figure II.1   A hierarchical block structure and the equivalent action diagram.

fourth-generation language. This diagramming technique can thus be extended all the way from the highest-level overview to working code in a fourth-generation language. When it is used on a computer screen the developers can edit and adjust the diagram and successively fill in detail until they have working code that can be tested interpretively. We refer to this as *ultimate decomposition*.

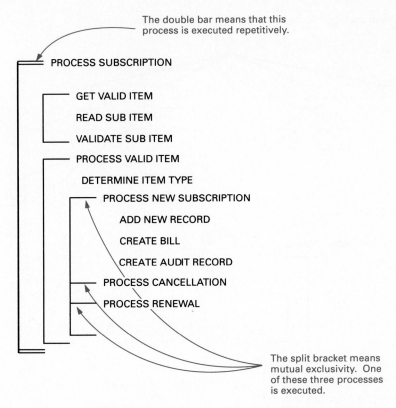

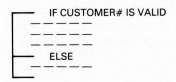

Figure II.2 A high-level action diagram. This action diagram can now be expanded into a chart showing the detailed program logic. VALIDATE SUB-ITEM from this chart is expanded into detailed logic in Fig. II.3.

CONDITIONS

Often a program module or subroutine is executed only IF a certain condition applies. In this case the condition is written at the head of a bracket:

```
┌── IF CUSTOMER# IS VALID
│   — — — — —
│   — — — — —
│   — — — — —
└
```

A condition bracket should normally have an "ELSE" partition:

```
┌── IF CUSTOMER# IS VALID
│   — — — — —
│   — — — — —
├── ELSE
│   — — — — —
└
```

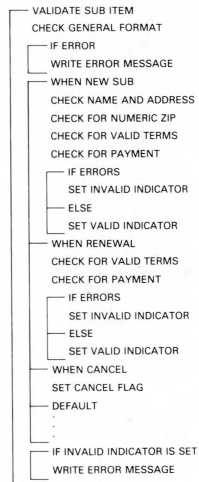

Figure II.3 An action diagram showing the detailed logic inside the process VALIDATE SUBITEM. This diagram showing detailed logic is an extension of the overview diagram of Fig. II.2.

This has only two mutually exclusive conditions, an IF and an ELSE. Sometimes there are many mutual-exclusive conditions, as follows:

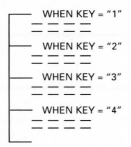

LOOPS

A loop is represented with a repetition bracket with the double line at its top. When many people first start to program, they make mistakes with the point at which they test a loop. Sometimes the test should be made *before* the actions of the loop are performed, and sometimes the test should be made *after*. This difference can be made clear on brackets by drawing the test at either the top or bottom of the bracket:

If the test is at the head of the loop as with a WHILE loop, the actions in the loop may never be executed if the WHILE condition is not satisfied. If the test is at the bottom of the loop, as with an UNTIL loop, the actions in the loop are executed at least once. They will be executed more than once if the condition is fulfilled.

SETS OF DATA

Sometimes a procedure needs to be executed on all of the items in a set of items. It might be applied to all transactions or all records in a file, for example:

```
 ┌══ FOR ALL TRANSACTIONS
 │   ─ ─ ─ ─ ─
 │   ─ ─ ─ ─ ─
 │   ─ ─ ─ ─ ─
 └───────────
```

Action diagrams are used with fourth-generation languages such as NO-MAD, MANTIS, FOCUS, RAMIS, and IDEAL. They are a good tool for teaching end users to work with these languages. Some such languages have a FOR construct with a WHERE clause to qualify the FOR. For example:

SUBPROCEDURES

Sometimes a user needs to add an item to an action diagram, which is itself a procedure that may contain actions. This subprocedure, or subroutine, is drawn with a round-cornered box. A subprocedure might be used in several procedures. It will be exploded into detail, in another chart, showing the actions it contains.

```
    ╭─────────────╮
    │  BACKORDER  │
    │  PROCEDURE  │
    ╰─────────────╯
```

SUBPROCEDURES NOT YET DESIGNED

In some cases the procedure designer has sections of a procedure that are not yet thought out in detail. He can represent this as a box with rounded corners and a right edge made of question marks:

```
    ╭─────────────╮?
    │   ERROR     │?
    │  PROCEDURE  │?
    ╰─────────────╯?
```

COMMON PROCEDURES

Some procedures appear more than once in an action diagram because they are called (or invoked) from more than one place in the logic. These procedures are called *common procedures*. They are indicated by drawing a vertical line down the left-hand side of the procedure box:

```
    │╭────────────╮
    ││   ERROR    │
    ││  PROCEDURE │
    │╰────────────╯
```

The use of procedure boxes enables an action diagrammer to concentrate on those parts of a procedure with which he is familiar. Another person may, perhaps, fill in the details in the boxes. This enables an elusive or complex procedure formation problem to be worked out a stage at a time.

The use of these boxes makes action diagrams a powerful tool for designing procedures at many levels of abstraction. As with other structured techniques, top-down design can be done by first creating a gross structure with such boxes, while remaining vague about the contents of each box. The gross structure can then be broken down into successive levels of detail. Each explosion of a box adds another degree of detail, which might itself contain actions and boxes. Similarly, bottom-up design can be done by specifying small procedures as action diagrams whose names appear as boxes in higher-level action diagrams.

TERMINATIONS

Certain conditions may cause a procedure to be terminated. They may cause the termination of the bracket in which the condition occurs, or they may cause the termination of multiple brackets. Terminations are drawn with an arrow to the left through one or more brackets, as follows:

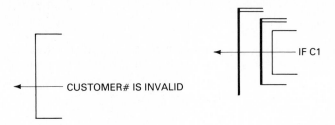

It is important to note than an escape structure allows only a forward skip to the exit point of a bracket. This restriction keeps the structure simple and does not allow action diagrams to degenerate into unstructured "spaghetti" logic.

An escape is different from a GO TO instruction. It represents an orderly close-down of the brackets escaped from. Some fourth-generation languages have an escape construct and no GO TO instruction. The escape command has names such as EXIT, QUIT, and BREAK.

GO TO

When a language has a well-implemented *escape,* there is no need for GO TO instructions. However, some languages have GO TO instructions and no escape. Using good structured design, the GO TO would be employed to emulate an escape. Any attempt to branch to a distant part of the program should be avoided.

It has, nevertheless, been suggested that a GO TO should be included in the action diagram vocabulary. This can be done by using a dashed arrow to replace the solid escape arrow, thus:

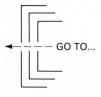

In the interests of structured design we have not included this construct in our recommended list of action diagram features.

NEXT ITERATION

In a repetition bracket a *next-iteration* construct is useful. With this, control skips the remaining instructions in a repetition bracket and goes to the next iteration of the loop. A next-iteration construct (abbreviated "NEXT") is drawn as follows:

The arrow does not break through the bracket as with an escape construct.

FOURTH-GENERATION LANGUAGES

When fourth-generation languages are used the wording on the action diagram may be the wording that is used in coding programs with the language. Examples of this are as follows:

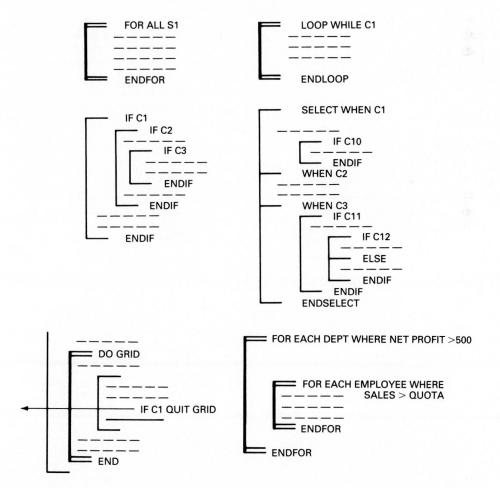

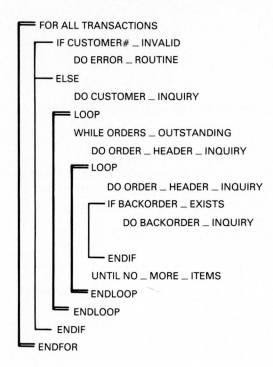

```
━━ FOR ALL TRANSACTIONS
   ┌── IF CUSTOMER# _ INVALID
   │       DO ERROR _ ROUTINE
   └── ELSE
           DO CUSTOMER _ INQUIRY
       ━━ LOOP
           WHILE ORDERS _ OUTSTANDING
               DO ORDER _ HEADER _ INQUIRY
           ━━ LOOP
                   DO ORDER _ HEADER _ INQUIRY
               ┌── IF BACKORDER _ EXISTS
               │       DO BACKORDER _ INQUIRY
               │
               └── ENDIF
               UNTIL NO _ MORE _ ITEMS
           ━━ ENDLOOP
       ━━ ENDLOOP
   └── ENDIF
━━ ENDFOR
```

Figure II.4 Action diagrams can be labeled with the control statement of fourth-generation language and form an excellent way to teach such languages. This example uses statements from the language IDEAL from ADR.

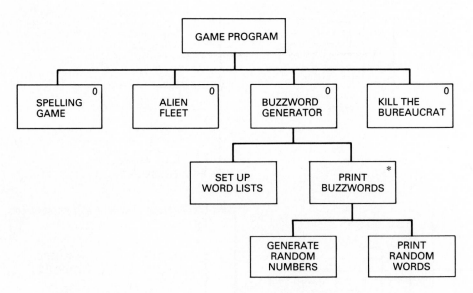

Figure II.5 The "o" and "*" in the top right-hand corner of blocks on charts such as this do not have obvious meaning. The form of the diagram should be selected to make the meaning as obvious as possible to relatively uninitiated readers.

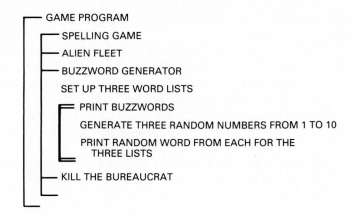

Figure II.6   An action diagram equivalent to the Jackson diagram of Fig. II.5.

Figure II.4 shows an action diagram for a procedure using control statements from the language IDEAL for ADR [1].

DECOMPOSITION TO PROGRAM CODE

Figure II.5 shows a Jackson diagram of a game program. With action diagrams we can decompose this until we have program code. Figure II.6 shows an action diagram equivalent to Figure II.5. The action diagram gives more room for explanation. Instead of saying "PRINT RAN-

```
*  BUZZWORD GENERATOR
   PRINT INSTRUCTION TO OPERATOR
   SET UP ADJECTIVE1 LIST
   SET UP ADJECTIVE2 LIST
   SET UP NOUN LIST
     UNTIL OPERATOR PRESSES "ESC"
       COUNT = 1
         UNTIL COUNT = 22
           GENERATE 3 RANDOM NUMBERS FROM 1 TO 10
           PRINT ADJECTIVE1, ADJECTIVE2, NOUN
           ADD 1 TO COUNT
     WAIT
```

Figure II.7   An expansion of the buzzword generator portion of Fig. II.6.

DOM WORDS'' it says ''PRINT RANDOM WORD FROM EACH OF THE THREE LISTS.''

Figure II.7 decomposes the part of the diagram labeled BUZZWORD GENERATOR. The inner bracket is a repetition bracket that executes 22 times. This is inside a bracket that is terminated by the operator pressing the ESC (escape) key. The last statement in this bracket is WAIT, indicating that the system will wait after executing the remainder of the bracket until the operator presses the ESC key. This gives the operator as much time as he wants to read the printout.

Figure II.8 decomposes the diagram further into an executable program. This program is written in the fourth-generation language MANTIS, from CINCOM INC.†

TITLES VERSUS CODE STRUCTURE At the higher levels of the design process, action diagram brackets represent the *names* of processes and subprocesses. As the designer descends into program-level detail, the brackets become *program constructs:* IF brackets, CASE brackets, LOOP brackets, and so on. To show the difference, different colors may be used. The *name* brackets may be red and the *program-construct* brackets black. If a black-and-white copier or terminal is used, the *name* brackets may be dotted or gray and the *program-construct* brackets black. The program-construct brackets may be labeled with appropriate control words. These may be the control words of a particular programming language or they may be language-independent words.

A bracket that shows a title rather than an action to be implemented, or a program instruction, may be drawn as a dotted or dashed line. It may have a character preceding the title, such as an *, &, or C, to indicate that the title line should be treated as a comment by the compiler. Different compilers use different characters for this purpose.

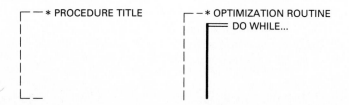

Title brackets may be single ''if else,'' case structure, or repetition brackets.

The designer may use a mix of title brackets and program brackets such that by displaying the title brackets only (with action diagramming software),

†The example in Figs. II.7 and II.8 is adapted from a program in the *MANTIS User's Guide,* Cincom Systems Inc., Cincinnati, Ohio, 1982.

```
┌─ENTER BUZZWORD GENERATOR
│
│   CLEAR
│   SHOW "I WILL GENERATE A SCREEN FULL OF 'BUZZ PHRASES' EVERY "
│   "'TIME YOU HIT 'ENTER'. WHEN YOU WANT TO STOP, HIT 'ESC'.
│
│   TEXT ADJECTIVE1 (10,16), ADJECTIVE2 (10,16), NOUN (10,16)
│
│   ADJECTIVE1 (1) = "INTEGRATED", "TOTAL", "SYSTEMATIZED", "PARALLEL",
│       "'FUNCTIONAL", "RESPONSIVE", "OPTIONAL", "SYNCHRONIXED",
│       "'COMPATIBLE", BALANCED"
│
│   ADJECTIVE2 (1) = "MANAGEMENT", "ORGANIZATIONAL", "MONITORED",
│       "'RECIPROCAL", "DIGITAL", "LOGISTICAL", "TRANSITIONAL",
│       "'INCREMENTAL", "THIRD GENERATION", "POLICY"
│
│   NOUN(1) = "OPTION", "FLEXIBILITY", "CAPABILITY", "MOBILITY",
│       "'PROGRAMMING", "CONCEPT", "TIME PHASE","PROJECTION",
│       "'HARDWARE", "CONTINGENCY"
│
│   SEED
├═─ UNTIL KEY = "ESC"
│   COUNT = 1
│
│  ┌─ UNTIL COUNT = 22
│  │   A = INT(RND(10) + 1)
│  │   B = INT(RND(10) + 1)
│  │   C = INT(RND(10) + 1)
│  │
│  │   SHOW ADJECTIVE1(A) + " " + ADJECTIVE2(B) + " " + NOUN(C)
│  │
│  │   COUNT = COUNT + 1
│  └═ END
│
│      WAIT
└═   END
│
│      CHAIN "GAMES_MENU"
└─   EXIT
```

Figure II.8 An expansion of the action diagram of Fig. II.7 into program code. This is an executable program in the fourth-generation language, MANTIS. Successive decomposition of a diagram until it becomes executable code is called *ultimate decomposition*.

an overview structure of the program is seen. He may also use comments to clarify his design. The comment line starts with an asterisk. The software may be instructed to display or to hide the comments.

Figure II.9 shows the program constructs with language-independent control words. Figure II.10 shows the same constructs with the words of the fourth-generation language IDEAL. It is desirable that any fourth-generation language should have a set of clear words equivalent to Fig. II.9, and it would help if standard words for this existed in the computer industry. In these two illustra-

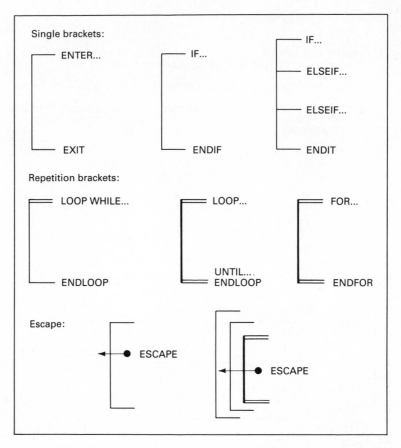

Figure II.9   Program constructs with language-independent control words.

tions, the control words are shown as in bold italic print. The other statements are in normal print.

CONCURRENCY

As discussed in Appendix I, where brackets may be executed concurrently, they are to be joined with a semicircular link:

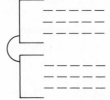

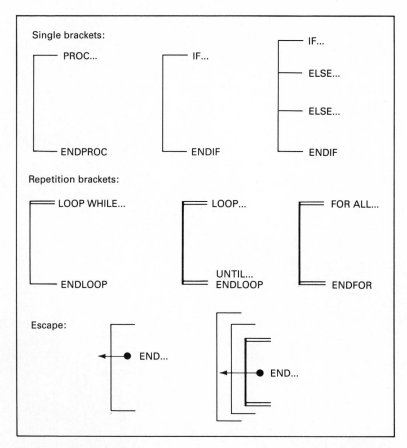

Figure II.10   Program constructs with the control words of the fourth-generation language IDEAL.

INPUT AND
OUTPUT DATA

The brackets of the action diagram are quick and easy to draw. If the user wants to show the data that enters and leaves a process, the bracket is expanded into a rectangle as shown in Fig. II.11. The data entering the process is written at the top right corner of the block. The data leaving is written at the bottom right corner.

This type of functional decomposition is designed for computerized checking to ensure that all the inputs and outputs balance. Figure II.12 shows nested blocks and the arrows represent checks that inputs are used and the outputs come from somewhere. Some CASE tools show the inputs to a bracket at its top and the outputs at its bottom.

A diagramming technique, today, should be designed for both quick manual manipulation and for computerized manipulation. Users and analysts will

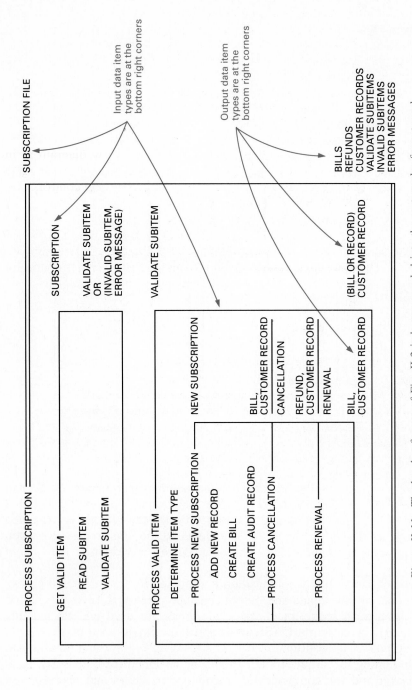

SUBSCRIPTION FILE

Input data item types are at the bottom right corners

Output data item types are at the bottom right corners

PROCESS SUBSCRIPTION

GET VALID ITEM

READ SUBITEM

VALIDATE SUBITEM

SUBSCRIPTION

VALIDATE SUBITEM
OR
(INVALID SUBITEM, ERROR MESSAGE)

PROCESS VALID ITEM

DETERMINE ITEM TYPE

VALIDATE SUBITEM

PROCESS NEW SUBSCRIPTION

ADD NEW RECORD

CREATE BILL

CREATE AUDIT RECORD

NEW SUBSCRIPTION

BILL,
CUSTOMER RECORD

PROCESS CANCELLATION

CANCELLATION

REFUND,
CUSTOMER RECORD

PROCESS RENEWAL

RENEWAL

BILL,
CUSTOMER RECORD

(BILL OR RECORD)
CUSTOMER RECORD

BILLS
REFUNDS
CUSTOMER RECORDS
VALIDATE SUBITEMS
INVALID SUBITEMS
ERROR MESSAGES

Figure II.11   The bracket format of Fig. II.2 is here expanded into the rectangular format used to show the data item types that are input and output to each process. In some CASE tools the inputs are shown at the top and the outputs at the bottom of an action diagram bracket. The computer should perform the checking illustrated in Figure II.12.

want to draw rough sketches on paper or argue at a blackboard using the technique. They will also want to build complex diagrams at a computer screen, using the computer to validate, edit, and maintain the diagrams, possibly linking them to a dictionary, database model, and so on. The tool acts rather like a word processor for diagramming, making it easy for users to modify their diagram. Unlike a word processor, it can perform complex validation and cross-checking on the diagram. In the design of complex specifications the automated correlation of inputs and outputs among program modules is essential if mistakes are to be avoided.

In showing input and output data, Fig. II.11 contains the information on a data flow diagram. It can be converted into a layered data flow diagram as in Fig. II.13. Unlike a data flow diagram, it can be directly extended to show the program structure, including conditions, case constructs, and loop control.

It is highly desirable that a programmer should sketch the structure of programs with action diagram brackets. Often the coder has made a logic error in the use of loops, END statements, CASE structures, EXITs, and so on. When he is taught to draw action diagram brackets and fit the code to them, these structure errors become apparent. Control statements can be automatically placed on brackets by a CASE tool. The CASE tool should do all the cross-checking that is possible.

SIMPLE DATABASE ACTIONS

Most of the action diagrams drawn for commercial data-processing systems relate to databases or on-line files. A common action of these diagrams is the database or file operation. It is desirable that these operations relate to the dictionary and data model employed.

We will distinguish between simple and compound database actions. A simple database action is an operation applied to *one instance of one record type*. There are four types of simple actions:

- CREATE
- READ
- UPDATE
- DELETE

The memorable acronym CRUD is sometimes used to refer to these and to help remember them.

On an action diagram, a simple database action is represented by a rectan-

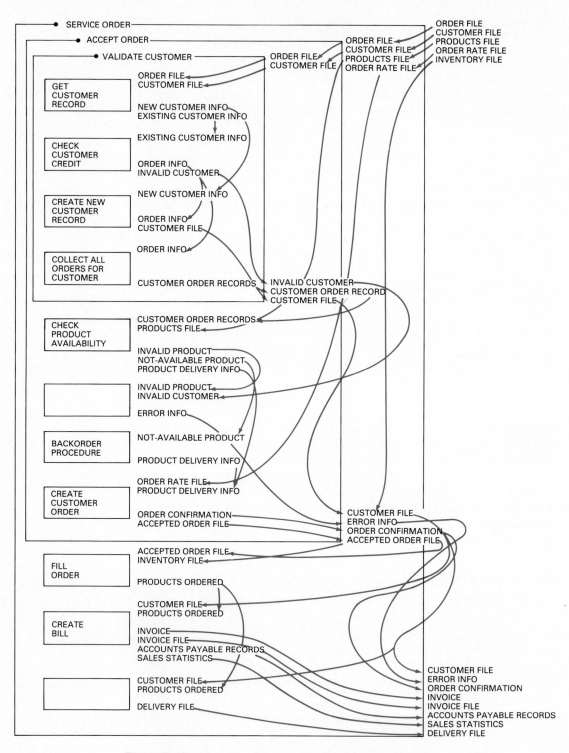

Figure II.12 An action diagram showing inputs and outputs. The arrows indicate a check that the graphics tool should make on the usage of inputs and outputs.

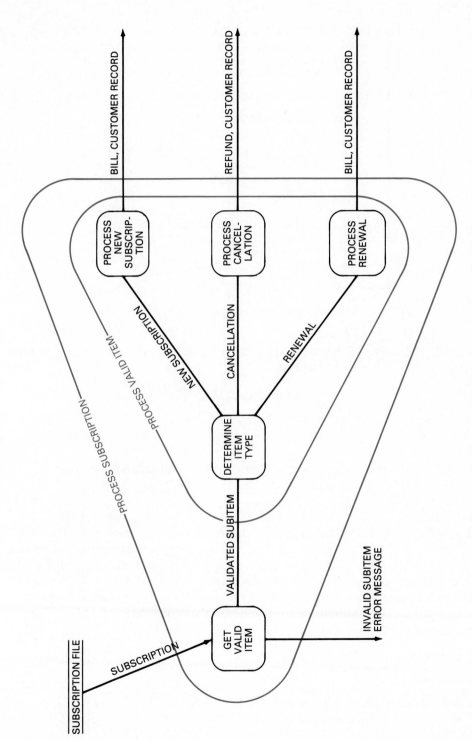

Figure II.13 A data flow diagram corresponding to Fig. II.11.

555

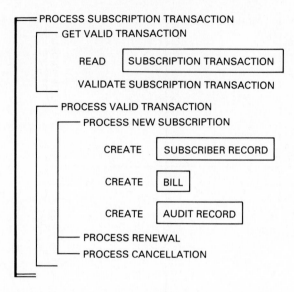

Figure II.14   An action diagram showing four simple database actions.

gular box. The name of the record is written inside the box; the type of action is written on the left side of the box:

Figure II.14 shows an action diagram with several database actions.

COMPOUND DATABASE ACTIONS

A *compound database action* also takes a single action against a database, but the action may use multiple records of the same type and sometimes of more than one type. It may search or sort a logical file. It may be a relational operation that uses an entire relation. It may be a relational operation requiring a join on two or more relations. Fourth-generation languages have instructions for a variety of compound database actions. Examples of such instructions are:

- SEARCH
- SORT
- SELECT certain records from a relation or a file
- JOIN two or more relations or files

- PROJECT a relation or file to obtain a subset of it
- DUPLICATE

CREATE, READ, UPDATE, and DELETE may also be used for compound-database actions. For example, DELETE could be used to delete a whole file.

Most of the database actions in traditional data processing are simple database actions. As relational databases and nonprocedural languages spread, *compound* database actions will become more common. A compound database action is represented as a double rectangular box. The name of the record is written inside the box; the database action is written on the left-hand side of the box:

Often a compound database action needs a qualifying statement associated with it to describe how it is performed. For example:

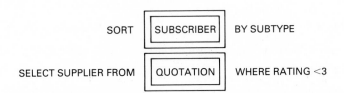

AUTOMATIC NAVIGATION

A compound database action may require automatic navigation by the database management system. Relational databases and a few nonrelational ones have this capability. For a database without automatic navigation, a compiler of a fourth-generation may generate the required sequence of data accesses. With a compound database action, search parameters or conditions are often an integral part of the action itself. They are written inside a bracket containing the access box.

SIMPLE VERSUS COMPOUND DATABASE ACCESSES

There are many procedures that can be done with either simple database accesses or compound accesses. If a traditional DBMS is used, the programmer navigates through the database with simple accesses. If the DBMS or language compiler has automatic navigation, higher-level statements using compound database accesses may be employed.

Suppose, for example, that we want to give a $1000 bonus to all employees who are salespeople in the Southeast region. In IBM's database language SQL, we would write:

```
UPDATE EMPLOYEE
SET SALARY = SALARY + 1000
WHERE JOB = 'SALESMAN'
AND REGION = 'SOUTHEAST'
```

We can diagram this with a compound database action as follows:

With simple actions (no automatic navigation), we can diagram the same procedure as follows:

RELATIONAL JOINS

A relational join merges two relations (logical files or tables) on the basis of a common data item. For example, the EMPLOYEE relation and the REGION relation for a company may look like this:

REGION

REGION-ID	LOCATION	REGION-STATUS	SALES-YTD	
001	NEW YORK	1	198,725	
004	CHICAGO	7	92,615	
006	LA	3	156,230	

EMPLOYEE

SSN	NAME	SALARY	JOBCODE	LOCATION	
337-48-2713	SMITH	42000	07	CHICAGO	
341-25-3340	JOHNSON	39000	15	LA	
391-62-1167	STRATTON	27000	05	LA	

These relations are combined in such a way that the LOCATION data item of the EMPLOYEE relation becomes the same as the LOCATION data item of the REGION relation. We can express this with the statement

REGION.LOCATION = EMPLOYEE.LOCATION

The result is a combined record as follows:

SSN	NAME	SALARY	JOB-CODE	LOCATION	REGION-ID	REGION-STATUS	SALES-YTD
337-48-2713	SMITH	42000	07	CHICAGO	004	7	92,615
341-25-3340	JOHNSON	39000	15	LA	006	3	156,230
391-62-1167	STRATTON	27000	05	LA	006	3	156,230

The database system may not combine them in reality but may join the appropriate data in response to the request. A join is shown on an action diagram by linking the boxes with an access operation applying to the combination:

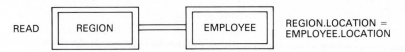

A statement may follow the joined records showing how they are joined. Often this is not necessary because the joined records contain one common data

item which is the basis for the join. For example, the EMPLOYEE record probably contains the data item LOCATION, in which case we can simply show:

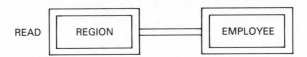

We might, for example, constrain the join operation by asking for employees whose job code is 15, whose salary exceeds $35,000, and whose region status is 3. The result would then be

SSN	NAME	SALARY
341-25-3340	JOHNSON	39000

From the join of EMPLOYEE and REGION, we might say SELECT SSN, NAME, REGION-STATUS, LOCATION. With the data base language SQL from IBM, and others, this operation would be expressed as follows:

```
SELECT SSN, NAME, REGION-STATUS, LOCATION
FROM REGION, EMPLOYEE
WHERE REGION.LOCATION  =  EMPLOYEE.LOCATION
AND JOB-CODE  =  15
AND SALARY  >  35000
```

This can be written on an action diagram as follows:

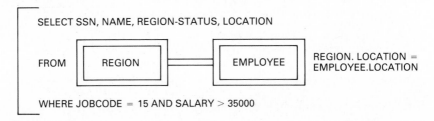

For a simple query such as this, we do not need a diagram representation. The query language itself is clear enough. For a complex operation, we certainly need to diagram the use of compound data actions.

Similarly, a relational join can be represented with either a sequence of single actions or one compound action, as shown in Fig. II.15. In this example, there are multiple projects in an EMPLOYEE PROJECT record showing how employees were rated for their work on each project to which they were assigned. They were given a salary raise if their average rating exceeded 6.

Data used in this example:

EMPLOYEE

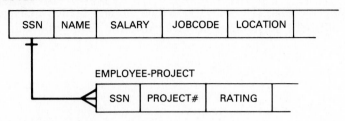

A procedure for giving employees an increase in salary,
using simple database action:

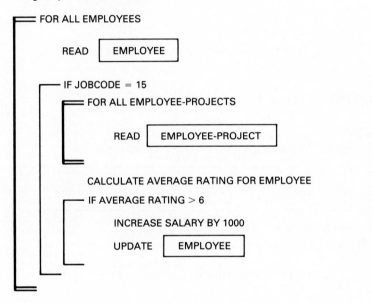

FOR ALL EMPLOYEES

   READ   EMPLOYEE

   IF JOBCODE = 15

      FOR ALL EMPLOYEE-PROJECTS

        READ   EMPLOYEE-PROJECT

      CALCULATE AVERAGE RATING FOR EMPLOYEE

      IF AVERAGE RATING > 6

        INCREASE SALARY BY 1000

        UPDATE   EMPLOYEE

The same procedure using a compound database action:

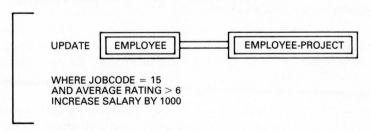

UPDATE   EMPLOYEE   EMPLOYEE-PROJECT

WHERE JOBCODE = 15
AND AVERAGE RATING > 6
INCREASE SALARY BY 1000

Figure II.15 Illustration of a procedure that may be done with either three simple database access commands or one compound access command.

THREE-WAY JOINS   In some cases, three-way joins are useful. Suppose an accountant is concerned that accounts receivable are becoming too high. He wants to telephone any branch manager who has a six-month-old debt outstanding from a customer. The following record structures exist:

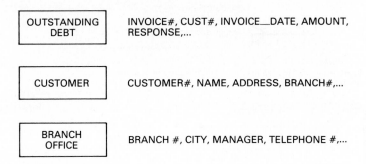

OUTSTANDING DEBT	INVOICE#, CUST#, INVOICE__DATE, AMOUNT, RESPONSE,...
CUSTOMER	CUSTOMER#, NAME, ADDRESS, BRANCH#,...
BRANCH OFFICE	BRANCH #, CITY, MANAGER, TELEPHONE #,...

He enters the following query:

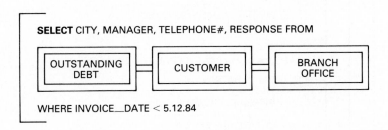

SELECT CITY, MANAGER, TELEPHONE#, RESPONSE FROM

OUTSTANDING DEBT — CUSTOMER — BRANCH OFFICE

WHERE INVOICE__DATE < 5.12.84

The three-way join is shown in a similar fashion to two-way joins.

CONTRACT AND EXPAND   A very useful feature of an action diagram editor is the ability to *contract* large action diagrams, hiding much of the detail. The user selects a bracket and says "CONTRACT." The bracket shrinks so that only its top is seen. Any nested brackets within the contracted bracket disappear. To show the user that information has been hidden, three dots are inserted in front of the text line of the contracted bracket.

In Fig. II.16 the user sets the cursor on a portion of a case structure and says "CONTRACT." The resulting contracted code contains a line beginning with three dots. In Fig. II.17 the user selects this line and says "EXPAND."

"CONTRACT" may be used multiple times to create hierarchies of contraction. "EXPAND" then reveals lines which themselves can be expanded. Contracting and expanding permits large programs to be manipulated with ease.

ACTION DIAGRAM EDITORS AND CASE TOOLS

Action diagram editors exist for personal computers and are also part of most of the good quality CASE tools. The control words of diverse programming languages can be added to the action diagrams by the computer.

The brackets used can be selected from a menu and can be stretched, edited, cut and pasted, and duplicated. The computer can apply a variety of integrity checks. Large programs can be displayed in overview form. Code can be contracted to hide the details and then reexpanded at will.

Experience with action diagram editors has shown that end users can employ them to sketch the systems and procedures they need. When this occurs, action diagrams form a useful communication vehicle between users and systems analysts. The design so created has successively greater detail added to it until it becomes executable code.

AUTOMATIC DERIVATION OF ACTION DIAGRAMS

Action diagrams can be derived automatically from correctly drawn decomposition diagrams, dependency diagrams, decision trees, or state transition diagrams (see Fig. I.5). If a computer algorithm is used for doing this, it needs to check the completeness or integrity of the dependency diagram or navigation diagram. This helps to validate or improve the analyst's design.

CONVERSION OF ACTION DIAGRAMS TO CODE

Different computer languages have different commands relating to the constructs drawn on action diagrams. If the action diagram is being edited on a computer screen, a menu of commands can be provided for any particular language. Using the language IDEAL, for example, the designer might select the word LOOP for the top of a repetition bracket, and the software automatically puts ENDLOOP at the bottom of the bracket and asks the designer for the loop control statement. The designer might select IF and the software creates the following bracket:

The user is asked to specify the IF condition.

Such structures with the commands for a given language may be generated

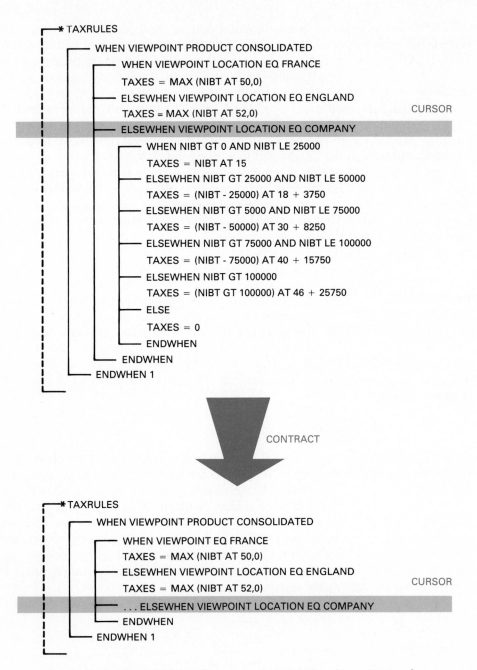

TAXRULES
  WHEN VIEWPOINT PRODUCT CONSOLIDATED
    WHEN VIEWPOINT LOCATION EQ FRANCE
    TAXES = MAX (NIBT AT 50,0)
    ELSEWHEN VIEWPOINT LOCATION EQ ENGLAND
    TAXES = MAX (NIBT AT 52,0)   CURSOR
    ELSEWHEN VIEWPOINT LOCATION EQ COMPANY
      WHEN NIBT GT 0 AND NIBT LE 25000
      TAXES = NIBT AT 15
      ELSEWHEN NIBT GT 25000 AND NIBT LE 50000
      TAXES = (NIBT - 25000) AT 18 + 3750
      ELSEWHEN NIBT GT 5000 AND NIBT LE 75000
      TAXES = (NIBT - 50000) AT 30 + 8250
      ELSEWHEN NIBT GT 75000 AND NIBT LE 100000
      TAXES = (NIBT - 75000) AT 40 + 15750
      ELSEWHEN NIBT GT 100000
      TAXES = (NIBT GT 100000) AT 46 + 25750
      ELSE
      TAXES = 0
      ENDWHEN
    ENDWHEN
  ENDWHEN 1

CONTRACT

TAXRULES
  WHEN VIEWPOINT PRODUCT CONSOLIDATED
    WHEN VIEWPOINT EQ FRANCE
    TAXES = MAX (NIBT AT 50,0)
    ELSEWHEN VIEWPOINT LOCATION EQ ENGLAND
    TAXES = MAX (NIBT AT 52,0)   CURSOR
    . . . ELSEWHEN VIEWPOINT LOCATION EQ COMPANY
    ENDWHEN
  ENDWHEN 1

Figure II.16 The CONTRACT command that hides the contents of a bracket. To show that there is hidden information, three dots are placed at the start of the contracted line.

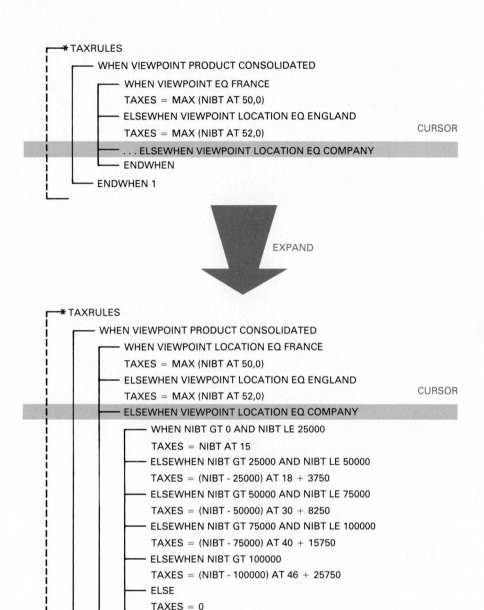

Figure II.17 The EXPAND command can be applied to lines beginning with three dots. It reveals their hidden contents. This and Fig. II.16 show the use of CONTRACT and EXPAND. With these commands, large designs can be reduced to summary form. These commands are very useful in practice.

automatically from a dependency diagram or data navigation diagram. The objective is to speed up as much as possible the task of creating error-free code.

With different menus of commands for different languages, a designer may switch from one language to another if necessary. This facilitates the adoption of different languages in the future.

ACTION DIAGRAMS FOR MANAGEMENT PROCEDURES

Like any other procedure, a management procedure can be represented with an action diagram. It is convenient to represent fourth-generation computer methodologies with action diagrams, because such methodologies are likely to be customized to fit the circumstances in question. A fourth-generation development lifecycle is not a fixed unchangeable lifecycle.

Throughout this book action diagrams are used to represent the methodologies of information engineering. These methodology action diagrams are found in boxes in the chapters that describe the methodology in question. Such procedures can quickly be adjusted with an action diagram editor to fit the circumstances in question.

ADVANTAGES

Action diagrams were designed to solve some of the concerns with other diagramming techniques. They were designed to have the following properties:

1. They are quick and easy to draw and to change.

2. They are good for manual sketching and for computerized editing.

3. A single technique extends from the highest overview down to coding-level detail (ultimate decomposition).

4. They draw all the constructs of traditional structured programming and are more graphic than pseudocode.

5. They are easy to teach to end users; they encourage end users to extend their capability into examination or design of detailed process logic. They are thus designed as an information center tool.

6. They can be printed on normal-width paper rather than wall charts, making them appropriate for design with personal computers.

7. Various types of diagrams, if drawn with precision, can be converted *automatically* into action diagrams.

8. Action diagrams are designed to link to a data model.

BOX II.1 Summary of notation used in action diagrams

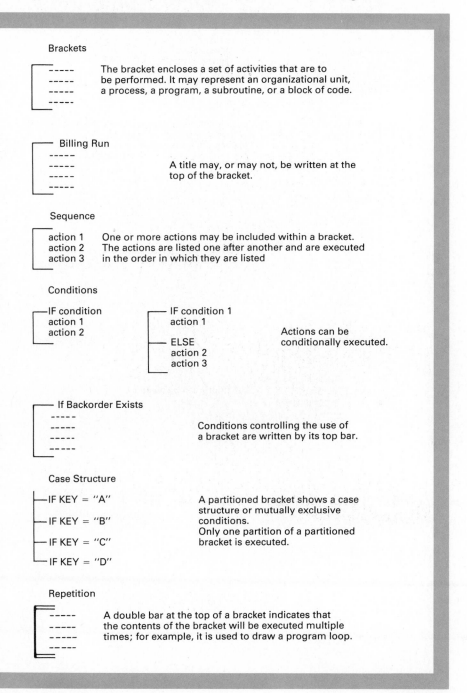

Brackets

```
┌ -----
│ -----
│ -----
│ -----
└
```
The bracket encloses a set of activities that are to
be performed. It may represent an organizational unit,
a process, a program, a subroutine, or a block of code.

```
┌─ Billing Run
│ -----
│ -----
│ -----
│ -----
└
```
A title may, or may not, be written at the
top of the bracket.

Sequence

```
┌ action 1
│ action 2
│ action 3
└
```
One or more actions may be included within a bracket.
The actions are listed one after another and are executed
in the order in which they are listed

Conditions

```
┌─IF condition
│ action 1
│ action 2
└
```

```
┌─ IF condition 1
│  action 1
│
├─ ELSE
│  action 2
│  action 3
└
```
Actions can be
conditionally executed.

```
┌─ If Backorder Exists
│ -----
│ -----
│ -----
│ -----
└
```
Conditions controlling the use of
a bracket are written by its top bar.

Case Structure

```
├─IF KEY = "A"
│
├─ IF KEY = "B"
│
├─ IF KEY = "C"
│
└─ IF KEY = "D"
```
A partitioned bracket shows a case
structure or mutually exclusive
conditions.
Only one partition of a partitioned
bracket is executed.

Repetition

```
╔ -----
║ -----
║ -----
║ -----
╚
```
A double bar at the top of a bracket indicates that
the contents of the bracket will be executed multiple
times; for example, it is used to draw a program loop.

(Continued)

BOX II.1 *(Continued)*

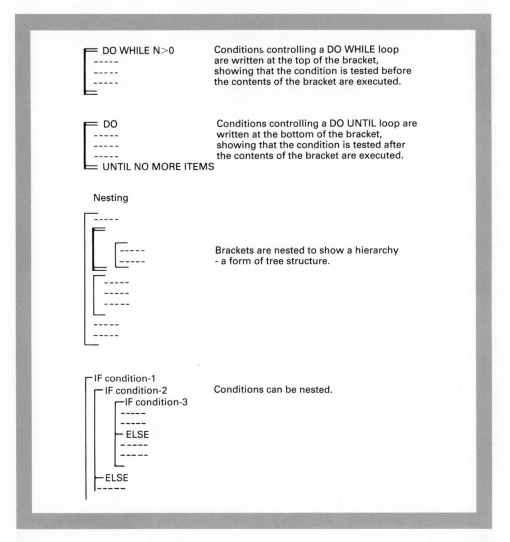

DO WHILE N>0
- - - - -
- - - - -
- - - - -

Conditions controlling a DO WHILE loop are written at the top of the bracket, showing that the condition is tested before the contents of the bracket are executed.

DO
- - - - -
- - - - -
- - - - -
UNTIL NO MORE ITEMS

Conditions controlling a DO UNTIL loop are written at the bottom of the bracket, showing that the condition is tested after the contents of the bracket are executed.

Nesting

- - - - -

- - - - -
- - - - -

Brackets are nested to show a hierarchy - a form of tree structure.

- - - - -
- - - - -
- - - - -

- - - - -
- - - - -

IF condition-1
IF condition-2
IF condition-3
- - - - -
- - - - -
ELSE
- - - - -
- - - - -

ELSE
- - - - -

Conditions can be nested.

BOX II.1   *(Continued)*

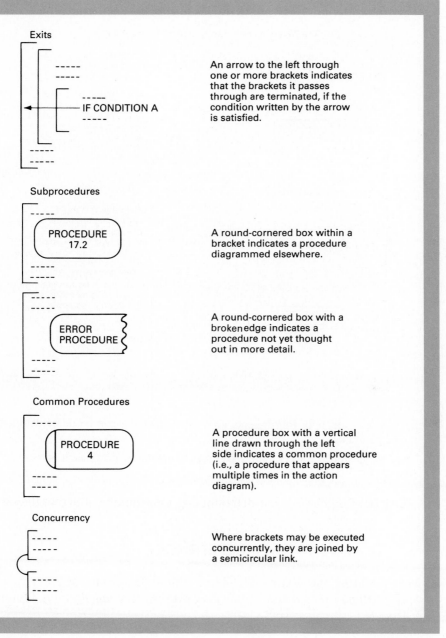

Exits

An arrow to the left through
one or more brackets indicates
that the brackets it passes
through are terminated, if the
condition written by the arrow
is satisfied.

IF CONDITION A

Subprocedures

PROCEDURE
17.2

A round-cornered box within a
bracket indicates a procedure
diagrammed elsewhere.

ERROR
PROCEDURE

A round-cornered box with a
broken edge indicates a
procedure not yet thought
out in more detail.

Common Procedures

PROCEDURE
4

A procedure box with a vertical
line drawn through the left
side indicates a common procedure
(i.e., a procedure that appears
multiple times in the action
diagram).

Concurrency

Where brackets may be executed
concurrently, they are joined by
a semicircular link.

(Continued)

BOX II.1 *(Continued)*

The Following Relate to Database Action Diagrams

Simple Data Action:

```
┌ - - - - -
│ - - - - -
│ READ   │ CUSTOMER │
│
│ - - - - -
└ - - - - -
```

A rectangle containing
the name of a record type
or entity type is preceded
by a simple data access
action: CREATE, READ,
UPDATE, or DELETE.

Compound Data Action:

```
┌ - - - - -
│ - - - - -
│ SELECT SUPPLIER from    ║ QUOTATION ║
│
│ - - - - -
└
```

A double rectangle
containing the name
of a record type or
entity type is preceded
by a compound data access
action, such as SORT,
JOIN, PROJECT, SELECT.
Words of a nonprocedural
language may accompany
the double rectangle.

```
┌ - - - - -
│
│ SORT  ║ CUSTOMER ║  BY SUPPLIER
│
│ - - - - -
└ - - - - -
```

9. They work well with fourth-generation languages and can be tailored to a specific language dialect.

10. They are designed for computerized cross-checking of data usage on complex *specifications*.

Box II.1 summarizes the diagramming conventions of action diagrams.

REFERENCE

1. James Martin and Carma McClure, *Action Diagrams: Clearly Structured Specifications, Programs, and Procedures, Second Edition.* Englewood Cliffs, N.J.: Prentice-Hall, 1989.

GLOSSARY

Note 1: References to Other Entries

Items in **bold** type in the Glossary are defined elsewhere in the Glossary.

Note 2: Types and Instances

Words describing data can either refer to a type of data or an instance (or occurrence) of data. Thus we have:

Entity type	Entity instance (or occurrence)
Attribute type	Attribute instance (or occurrence)
Data item type	Data item instance (or occurrence)
Field type	Field instance (or occurrence)
Association type	Association instance (or occurrence)
Link type	Link instance (or occurrence)
Record type	Record instance (or occurrence)

Type refers to a category of data representation, independent of time or value. *Instance* (or occurrence) refers to a specific example of that data type. The instances of a given type differ from one another in their value. To describe an instance fully, one must provide both the information that defines its type and the values that define this particular instance.

The flight information board at an airport is designed to show certain *types* of data, such as flight number, destination, departure time, and gate. If we look at the board at one instant, it shows values *(instances)* of these data types.

A data model consists exclusively of *type* information. Logical database design is a process of discovering and defining the *types* of entities, attributes, records, associations, and so on. Only when the database is operational are *instances* created (as with the flight information board).

We often refer to data loosely without saying whether we mean a *type* or an *instance*. Thus we say "record," "entity," or "attribute." *Record* is a shorthand word that could mean either *record type* or *record instance*. It might mean employee record (a *type*) or the record for John Jones (an *instance*). This shorthand is useful in that it avoids cluttered descriptions. It should not be used unless that context makes clear whether it refers to *types* or *instances* of data.

Note 3: Items That Are in the Encyclopedia

Some items in this glossary are objects in an IE encyclopedia. These are noted by "(KB)," for knowledge base, at the end of the definition.

ACCEPTANCE TEST. A test, executed by **users** or operators, of the functionality of **procedures** and **programs** against predetermined criteria, to formally accept a new or modified **application system.**

ACCESS. The operation of **seek**ing, reading, or writing **data** on a storage unit.

ACCESS CONTROL SCHEME. A **security technique** by which the use of specific **modules** and **data object types** is restricted to authorized **persons.**

ACCESS MECHANISM. A mechanism for moving one or more reading and writing heads to the position at which certain **data** are to be read or written. Alternatively, the data medium may be moved to the read/write head.

ACCESS METHOD. 1. A **technique** for moving **data** between a computer and its peripheral devices: for example, serial access, **random access, virtual** sequential access method **(VSAM),** hierarchical indexed-sequential access method **(HISAM), access via secondary indices,** and relational accesses such as joins, projects, or other **relational algebra** operations. The word is often used to describe the **type** of file organization that facilitates the accessing technique. 2. A method of retrieving **records** which implies that the records have a particular type of file organization. The word is often used to describe the file organization.

ACCESS TIME. The time that elapses between an instruction being given to **access** some **data** and those data becoming available for use.

ACTION. 1. Something accomplished by a single **program access** command when using the **database.** A *simple action* is a command that creates, reads, updates, or deletes an **instance** of a single **record.** A *compound action* is a command that requires multiple instances of records because it performs a **sort, search,** join, projection, or other relational operation. 2. A **type of activity** by which an **entity** of a given type or a value of a given predicate is involved in some specific way during the execution of a **process,** or by which a record or **linkage** or **field,** is involved in some specific way during the execution of a **procedure.**

ACTION DIAGRAM.   diagram using nested brackets to show a hierarchy or to show the structure of a **program** or specification. An *action diagram* shows loops, **condi-**

tions, case structures, escapes, **database** accesses, subroutine calls, and programming structures in general. Several other types of diagrams can be converted automatically to *action diagrams,* and *action diagrams* can be set to the code of any procedural language. *The use of action diagrams* are the preferred way of representing programming structures and specification structures.

ACTION DIAGRAM EDITOR. A **tool,** usually on a personal computer, with which to build and edit **action diagrams.** The tool helps to enforce good structuring of **programs** and specifications.

ACTION LIST. A selection **list** in which each entry has a defined **action** to be performed upon one or more **objects** in the **encyclopedia.**

ACTION ON ATTRIBUTE. A **type** of **action** performed on a value of an **attribute** during the execution of an action on an **entity** of a given type.

ACTION ON ENTITY TYPE. A **type** of **action** performed on one or more **entities** of an **entity type** at a particular point during the execution of an **elementary process.**

ACTION ON PAIRING. A **type** of **action** on one or more **pairings** of a given **relationship** by an **elementary process** following an action on an **entity.**

ACTION ON PREDICATE. *See* **Action on Attribute; Action on Pairing.**

ACTION STATEMENT. A representation of a minimal unit of a procedural **activity.**

ACTIVITY. 1. Something which is carried out in order to achieve a stated purpose. An *activity* may be a **function, process, procedure,** or **program module.** 2. A collection of **tasks** within the **methodology.**

ACTIVITY ARCHITECTURE. A **model** of the **activities** of the **enterprise** consisting of an **activity decomposition** model and an **activity dependency** model. *See also* **Business Systems Architecture.**

ACTIVITY DECOMPOSITION DIAGRAM. A structure showing the breakdown of **activities** into progressively increasing detail. *See also* **Function Decomposition Diagram; Process Decomposition Diagram; Procedure Decomposition Diagram.**

ACTIVITY RATIO. The percentage of **records** in a file or **data set** which have **activity** (are updated or inspected) in a given period or during a given run.

AD HOC FACILITY. A **set** of **tools** and **techniques** allowing individual **users** to set up their own **systems** and to query databases on a random basis.

ADDRESS. An identification (number, name, **label**) for a **location** in which **data** is stored.

ADDRESSING. The means of assigning **data** to storage **locations,** and subsequently retrieving it, on the basis of the **key** of the data.

AFFINITY. A measure of the strength of the association between two objects.

AFFINITY ANALYSIS. A **technique** for identifying the degree of association between two **objects.**

ALGORITHM. A computational **procedure** containing a finite sequence of steps.

ALTERNATE TRACK. A **track** that is automatically substituted for a damaged track on a disk or other storage device.

ANALYSIS PHASE. A phase of information engineering in which a detailed analysis of business elements is carried out within a defined **business area** in preparation for the design of systems to support that area.

ANTICIPATORY STAGING. The movement of blocks of **data** from one storage device to another device with a shorter **access** time, in anticipation of their being needed by the computer **programs.** This is to be contrasted with **demand staging,** in which the blocks of data are moved *when* programs require them, not *before*.

APPLICATION FLOW DIAGRAM. A schematic representation of the sequence of **application programs.**

APPLICATION PACKAGE. A vendor-supplied, reusable **application system.**

APPLICATION PROGRAM. A **program** included in a specific **application system.** *(KB)*

APPLICATION SYSTEM. The automated and related manual **procedures** within an information system that support a set of **business processes.** One or more applications comprise an information system. *Applications* are defined in the **analysis phase** of the methodology as a result of studying **business area.** *(KB)*

ASSEMBLE. To convert a routine coded in nonmachine language into actual machine language instructions. To perform some or all of the following **functions:** (1) translation of symbolic operation codes into machine codes; (2) allocation of storage, to the extent at least of assigning storage **locations** to successive instructions; (3) computation of absolute or relocatable **addresses** from symbolic addresses; (4) insertion of **library** routines; (5) generation of sequences of symbolic instructions by the insertion of specific parameters into macroinstructions.

ASSOCIATION. A meaningful link between two objects (e.g., **entities,** processes, goals, or **critical success factors**). Associations are used to capture **data** about the relationship between two objects.

ASSOCIATION MATRIX. The summary, in tabular form, of the associations between elements of the same **object type.**

ASSOCIATION RELATION. A **relation** or **record** containing **information** about the association. The association name is sometimes stored. In more advanced forms of **data modeling** information is stored about the *meaning* of the association or the rules which are applied when using the association. *Synonym:* association record.

ASSOCIATIVE ENTITY. An **entity** that exists primarily to interrelate other **entity types.** *See also* **Intersection Entity.**

ASSOCIATIVE STORAGE (MEMORY). Storage that is **addressed** by content rather than by **location,** thus providing a fast way to **search** for **data** having certain contents. (Conventional storage has addresses related to the **physical** location of the data.)

ATTRIBUTE. 1. A **type** of characteristic or property describable in terms of a value that **entities** of a given type possess. *(KB)* 2. A **data item** containing a single piece of **information** about an entity instance. **Records** are composed of *attributes* relating to a given entity. An *attribute* is often atomic; that is, it cannot be broken into parts that have meaning of their own. The term *attribute* is a shorthand meaning of either *attribute type* or *attribute value* (see Note A). All *attributes* of a given type have the same **format,** interpretation, and range of acceptable values. An **instance** of a record has its own (not necessarily unique) value of this *attribute*. 3. A property of an **entity type.** For a specific entity the *attribute* usually has a value that is stored in an **entity record.**

ATTRIBUTE INVOLVEMENT MATRIX. A matrix that shows, for all **attributes** of an **entity type,** the **process**es in which each is involved and by which **actions.**

ATTRIBUTE SOURCE. The categorizing of an **attribute** as to whether its values are basic, derived, or designed. *See also* **Basic Attribute; Derived Attribute; Designed Attribute.**

ATTRIBUTE VALUE. The number, character string, or other element of **information** assigned to a given **attribute** of a given **record instance** at a given time. The name, **format,** interpretation, and range of acceptable values of an attribute are determined by its **attribute type.** Within these constraints, *attribute values* are free to vary from time to time and from one record instance to another. The shorter term ''attribute'' may be used to mean *attribute value,* but only when the context suffices to distinguish it from attribute type. **Attribute instances** can have nulls instead of values. These are of two types: (a) value not yet known (but there can potentially be a value) and (b) value not applicable (the given **entity instance** will *never* have a value for this attribute).

ATTRIBUTIVE ENTITY. An **entity** serving mainly as an **attribute** of another **entity type.**

AUDIT TRAIL. The recording of additions, updates, and deletions to a **data collection,** including time occurred and person responsible.

A means of interaction to transfer **information** between **applications, programs,** or **modules.** *(KB)*

AUTOMATED SYSTEM. A collection of related **programs** performing a routine or repetitive **task.**

AUTOMATIC NAVIGATION. The ability to use high-level **relational algebra** commands, which are automatically executed in the use of a **database,** rather than **accessing records** one at a time.

AVAILABILITY. A measure of system reliability expressed as the fraction of time as agreed. *Availability = time the function is performed as intended/total time during which the function should have been performed.*

BACK UP. The **process** of making copies of files to enable **recovery** of their contents in the event the originals are damaged or lost.

BACKUP COPY. A copy of a **database** or file taken at a known point in time.

BACKUP PROCEDURE. A **procedure** devised to take copies of **data,** transactions, or both to be used in case of loss or corruption of the **database.**

BASIC ATTRIBUTE. An **attribute** whose values cannot be deduced or calculated and hence must be collected during the execution of a **process.**

BATCH PROCESS. A group of **programs** and instructions that accumulates all input before it is run.

BATCH WINDOW. A fixed period of time in which **batch procedures** must be executed.

BEHAVIOR MODEL. The **set** of rules and integrity constraints that determine the combinations of values of **attributes** of different **entity types** in an **information system.**

BEHAVIOR RULE. A rule that must be applied when an **entity, attribute,** or **relationship** is created, **retrieved,** updated, or deleted. It is implemented by invoking a **procedure** that verifies the integrity of the **data structure** and initiates any additional **processing** that may be required. *(KB)*

BENCHMARKING. The execution of a predefined **set** of test cases under **production conditions** in order to evaluate a **system's** performance.

BENEFIT. An effect produced directly or indirectly, by an intervention or **action** upon an **enterprise,** that is helpful, favorable, or profitable to the enterprise. *See also* **Tangible Benefit; Intangible Benefit.**

BENEFIT ANALYSIS. The study of the potential advantages to the **enterprise** resulting from the automation of selected **process**es.

BENEFIT ANALYSIS MATRIX. A matrix containing estimates of the achievable **benefit** from a number of benefit sources resulting from the automation of various **activities.**

"BEST-GUESS" CLUSTERING. A **heuristic** approach to defining **business areas** within an **entity type/process** matrix, based on substantial industry knowledge and experience.

BINARY SEARCH. A method of **search**ing a sequenced **table** or file. The **procedure** involves **select**ing the upper and lower half based on an examination of its midpoint value. The selected portion is then similarly halved, and so on until the required item is found.

BLACK BOX FUNCTION. A reusable **module** developed during the **construction and implementation phase.**

BUFFER. An area of storage that holds **data** temporarily while it is being received, transmitted, read, or written. It is often used to compensate for differences in the speed or timing among devices. *Buffers* are used in terminals, peripheral devices, storage units, and in the CPU.

BUSINESS AREA. A **set** of highly cohesive **process**es and **entity types. Technique**s such as **clustering** or **factor analysis** with an entity type/process matrix are used to identify business areas. A business area is typically the scope of the **analysis phase.**

BUSINESS AREA ANALYSIS. *See* **Analysis Phase.**

BUSINESS AREA ANALYSIS PROJECT. A **project** to analyze a **business area** and produce a **business area information model.** *Synonym:* analysis phase project.

BUSINESS AREA INFORMATION MODEL (BAIM). A product of an **analysis phase.** A *business area information model* is expressed through **data** and **activity models** and represents the **process**es and **information** needed within a **business area** by an organization.

BUSINESS AREA PARTITION. A subdivision of a **business area,** consisting of closely related groups of **process**es and **data** which is created for the purpose of subdividing the effort within an **analysis phase** of a **project.** The **models** pertaining to the **partitions** are progressively consolidated through this **phase.**

BUSINESS EVENT. A significant occurrence, initiated by **external agents** or by the passage of time, which triggers a process that must be recognized and responded to. *(KB)*

BUSINESS FUNCTION. A group of business **activities** which together completely support one aspect of furthering the **mission** of the **enterprise.**

BUSINESS FUNCTION DECOMPOSITION. A **decomposition** of a **business function** into more detailed business functions.

BUSINESS FUNCTION DEPENDENCY. A dependency between two **business functions** which exists because **information** provided by one is required by the other.

BUSINESS PLAN. A high-level, strategic plan used by senior management to direct the **enterprise.** The plan should reference the role of the information systems department within the organization and its expected contribution to business strategies.

BUSINESS PROCESS. A **task** or group of tasks carried out as part of a **business function.**

BUSINESS REQUIREMENT. A formal written statement specifying what the **information system** must do or how it must be structured to support the business.

BUSINESS SEGMENT. A group of **function**s within an organization that provide a family of products or services which relates to a specific market sector. *(KB)*

BUSINESS STRATEGY PLANNING. The **activity** in which the **objective**s and strategies of the **enterprise** are set. This provides prime input to the **information strategy planning stage.**

BUSINESS SYSTEM. *See* **Application System.**

BUSINESS SYSTEM DESIGN (BSD). *See* **Design Phase.**

BUSINESS SYSTEMS ARCHITECTURE. A structure that represents the dependencies between the business **system**s of an **enterprise.**

BUSINESS TRANSACTION. 1. A series of manual steps and computer **process**ing that enables an **elementary process** to be executed successfully. *(KB)* 2. A **logical** unit of work that must be completed as a whole and has a discrete input, defined **procedure,** and specific output or result.

CANDIDATE KEY. A **key** that uniquely identifies **normalized record instance**s of a given **type.** A *candidate key* must have two properties: (a) Each instance of the **record** must have a different value on the key, so that given a key value one can locate a single instance. (b) No **attribute** in the key can be discarded without destroying the property. In a bubble chart, a *candidate key* is a bubble with one or more single-headed arrows leaving it.

CANONICAL MODEL. A **model** of **data** which represents the inherent structure of that data and hence is independent of individual **application**s of the data and also of the software or hardware mechanisms which are employed in representing and using the data. The minimal nonredundant model is a given collection of **data item**s. Neither redundant data items nor redundant associations exist in the *canonical model.* The *canonical model* should correctly represent all **functional dependencies** among the data items in the model. When this is done, the model contains third-normal-form groupings of data items.

CANONICAL SYNTHESIS. The **construction** of a normalized **data model** by integrating separate views of **data** such as inputs, outputs, and **user** views. The views are represented formally and their integration often builds an overall **canonical model.** *Canonical synthesis* is used in conjunction with top-down **entity relationship modeling** to help ensure that a data model is complete.

CARDINALITY. The number of **instance**s of one **object type** associated with an instance of another type. *Cardinality* is a property of an association. *See* **Association.**

CATALOG. A **directory** of all files available to a computer.

CELL. Contiguous storage **location**s referred to as a group in an **addressing** or file **search**ing scheme. The *cell* may be such that it does not cross mechanical boundaries in the storage unit; for example, it could be a **track** or **cylinder.**

CELLULAR CHAINS. **Chain**s that are not permitted to cross **cell** boundaries.

CELLULAR MULTILIST. A form of **multilist organization** in which the **chain**s cannot extend across **cell** boundaries.

CELLULAR SPLITTING. A **technique** for handling **record**s added to a file. The records are organized into **cell**s and a cell is split into two cells when it becomes full.

CHAIN. An organization in which **record**s or other items of **data** are strung together by means of **pointer**s.

CHANNEL. A **subsystem** for input to and output from the computer. **Data** from storage units, for example, flows into the computer via a *channel.*

CHECKPOINT/RESTART. A means of restarting a **program** at some point other than the beginning, used after a failure or interruption has occurred. *Checkpoints* may be used at intervals throughout an **application program;** at these points **record**s are written given enough **information** about the status of the program to permit its being restarted at that point.

CHILD. An **object** in a **decomposition diagram** that is immediately below a specified object.

CIRCULAR FILE. An organization for a file of high volatility, in which new **record**s being added replace the oldest records.

CLUSTER ANALYSIS. A formal **technique** for analyzing the associations of one **object type** to another object type based on their commonality of involvement. Data to activity cluster is specifically used to defining the scope of a phase project. *Synonym:* Clustering.

CODASYL. Conference of Data Systems Languages. The organization that specified the programming language COBOL. It now has specified a **set** of manufacturer-independent, application-independent languages designed to form the basis of **database** management.

COHERENCE. The extent to which components of a **function** or **process** are more closely associated with each other than with components of other functions or processes.

COMMON LOGIC MODULE. A **module** of a **procedure** or **program** that is used in more than one **function** or **process.**

COMMUNICATIONS NETWORK. A **system** that facilitates the transfer of **information** between the components of computer systems. *(KB)*

COMPACTION. A **technique** for reducing the number of bits in **data** without destroying any **information** content.

COMPILER. A computer **program** that in addition to performing the **function**s of an assembler has the following characteristics: (a) it makes use of **information** on the overall **logical** structure of the program to improve the efficiency of the resulting machine program; (b) its language does not parallel the actual form of the machine language, but rather is oriented toward a convenient **problem** or **procedure** statement; (c) it usually generates more than one machine instruction for each symbolic instruction.

COMPOSITE IDENTIFIER. Two or more **attribute**s whose values taken in combination uniquely identify the **entities** of one **type.**

CONCATENATE. To **link** together. A *concatenated* **data set** is a collection of **logically** connected data sets. A *concatenated* **key** is composed of more than one **data item.**

CONCEPTUAL MODEL. The overall **logical** structure of a **database,** which is independent of any software or **data storage structure.** A *conceptual model* often contains data objects not yet implemented in **physical database**s. It gives a formal representation of the **data** needed to run an **enterprise,** even though certain **system**s in the enterprise may not yet conform to the **model.** Some organizations prefer the term *logical model* rather than *conceptual model,* because ''conceptual'' might imply that the model may never be implemented.

CONCEPTUAL SCHEMA. A term used to mean the same as **conceptual model.** The word **schema** often refers to the **logical** representation of **data** which is used by a particular class of **database management systems** (e.g., **CODASYL**). *(James Martin: I recommend that the word* model *be used for software-independent data structures, and schema be used for these linked to a specific class of software.)*

CONDITION. 1. A rule expressed in the form "If *P*, then *Q*," which describes one aspect of the behavior of a business. 2. A specified circumstance that causes a particular set of **actions** to be invoked.

CONDITION EVENT. A specific situation in the **enterprise,** occurrences of which trigger the execution of one or more **process**es.

CONDITION LOGIC. A rule expressed in the form of "If *P*, then *Q*." *P* is known as the **condition.**

CONDITION TABLE. A **table** specifying all the valid combinations of **attribute value**s that constitute the **condition.**

CONDITION TREE. A diagram representing an execution **condition** as a hierarchy of all the valid combinations of **attribute values** that constitute the condition.

CONDITIONAL SUBPROCESS. A **process** whose execution depends on **attribute value**s established by prior processes.

CONNECTIVITY ANALYSIS. A **technique** for checking that all **data flow**s in a **process model** or **procedure** are connected to valid source and destination **object**s.

CONSERVATION ANALYSIS. A **technique** for checking that all references made to the use of **data object**s in a **process** or **procedure** are satisfied by the **data flow model** and that there is no redundancy in this model.

CONSTRUCTION. *See* **Construction and Implementation Phase.**

CONSTRUCTION AND IMPLEMENTATION PHASE. A **phase** of **information engineering.** The period in the **systems** life cycle in which the systems, to support a defined area, are coded and proven according to the detailed design specifications produced during the **design phase.** It is also a **set** of work **activities** that implements the **application system** design. Major products of this phase are the coded and tested system; system documentation **package;** a training package; system operating instructions; an operational **database;** and the installed application system.

CONTINGENCY PLAN. A **set** of provisions to ensure that an application **system function**s when something occurs that interrupts or destroys the **information processing** capability.

CONTINUOUS ATTRIBUTE. An **attribute** whose values cannot be precisely matched against any defined collection. Contrast with **discrete attribute.**

CONTRACT. To contract means to hide **information** and cause **ellipses** to be placed in an item to show that more information is available. It should be possible to *contract* within *contract* within *contract*.

CONTROL REQUIREMENT. A requirement to control the integrity of an **application** (e.g., audit control, **access, security, backup,** and **recovery**). *(KB)*

CONVERSION. The one-time setting up of **data store**s, by transfer of **data** from existing data stores, that will be required by a new **system,** or the translation of existing **program**s to run with new data stores. More generally, it is the **process** of changing **information** from one form of representation to another.

CONVERSION ALGORITHM. A method by which **data** for a field in a current system is transferred to the equivalent field(s) in a new system, and vice versa, for **conversion** and bridging, respectively.

COOPERATING PROCESSES. Two **process**es such that each is dependent on **attribute**s being passed from the other.

COOPERATIVE PROCESSING. A **program** that is split between a personal computer or intelligent workstation and a larger computer to obtain the good human-factoring and low-cost **process**ing of the small machine combined with the power and shared **data** of the large machine.

CORPORATE CULTURE. The collective sense of traditions, conventions, and behavioral **standard**s characteristic of a given **enterprise.** It is determined by **organizational structure** and by formal and informal human resources **policies, procedure**s, and practices.

CORPORATE INFORMATION MODEL. A description of the **entity type**s, **function**s, and **process**es that define an organization and of their inter**relationships.** It consists of a corporate data model, a corporate activity model, and a corporate organizational model.

COURSE ANALYSIS. A **technique** for checking that the paths through a **data flow model** are complete, consistent, and without redundancy.

CRITICAL ASSUMPTIONS. A group of assumptions about a **business segment,** competitor, or industry that supports or validates an organization's **critical success factors.**

CRITICAL DECISIONS. The decisions that must be made by an organization to have an impact on its **critical success factors.**

CRITICAL INFORMATION. The **information** that is required by an organization's operational **system** to enable them to support the organization's **critical success factors.**

CRITICAL SUCCESS FACTOR. An internal or external business-related result that is measurable and that will have a major influence on whether a **business segment** meets its **goals.** *(KB)*

CRITICAL SUCCESS FACTOR ANALYSIS. A **process** for extracting and reconciling **critical success factors.**

CRUD MATRIX. A tabular representation of the **relationship** between **process**es and **entities** with an indication as to whether the type of involvement is created, **re-trieve**d, updated, deleted, or a combination of these.

CULTURAL CHANGES. Changes in the business's **organizational structure, skill** and staffing levels, **job function**s, or **policies** and **procedures.**

CURRENT APPLICATION. *An* **application** *presently in use.*

CURRENT PROCESSING CONFIGURATION. A **process***ing configuration presently in use.*

CYLINDER. That area of a storage unit which can be read without the movement of an **access mechanism.** The term originated with disk files, in which a *cylinder* consisted of one **track** on each disk surface such that each of these tracks could have a read/ write head positioned over it simultaneously.

DASD. *See* **Direct Access Storage Device.**

DATA. Facts or figures from which conclusions can be inferred.

DATA ACCESS DIAGRAM. *See* **Logical Access Map (LAM).**

DATA ADMINISTRATOR. A person with an overview understanding of an organization's **data.** The function is responsible for the most cost-effective organization and use of an **enterprise's** data resources. The *data administrator* is ultimately responsible for designing the **data model** and obtaining agreement about the definitions of data which are maintained in the **data dictionary.**

DATA AGGREGATE. A named collection of **data item**s within a **record.** There are two types: vectors and repeating groups. A vector is a one-dimensional, ordered collection of data items, all of which have identical characteristics. A repeating group is a collection of **data** that occurs an arbitrary number of times within a record occurrence. The collection may consist of data items, vectors, and repeating groups. (CODASYL)

DATA ANALYSIS. A disciplined approach to analyzing the meaning and properties of the **data element**s in existing clerical forms and computer files, independently from the **system**s that produce and use this **data.**

DATA ARCHITECTURE. A structure that **model**s the **data** of the **enterprise.**

DATA BANK. A collection of **online data.** The term **database** is more precise than *data bank. Database* implies the formal **technique**s of database management. *Data bank* refers to any collection of data, whether in the form of files, databases, or an **information retrieval** system.

DATA COLLECTION. A repository of **data** maintained by an **enterprise,** usually in the form of manual or electronic files. *(KB)*

DATA CONSERVATION ANALYSIS. *See* **Conservation Analysis.**

DATA DEPENDENCY. The situation where a **process** creates or modifies some **data,** which is subsequently used by some other process.

DATA DESCRIPTION LANGUAGE. A language for describing **data** (in some software for describing the **logical,** not the **physical,** data; in other software for both).

DATA DICTIONARY. A **catalog** of all **data type**s, giving their names and structures, and **information** about **data** usage. Advanced *data dictionaries* have a **directory**

function that enables them to represent and report on the cross-references between components of data and business **model**s.

DATA DIVISION (COBOL). That division of a COBOL **program** which consists of entries used to define the nature and characteristics of the **data** to be **process**ed by the procedure division of the program.

DATA ELEMENT. The **physical** representation of an **attribute.** A *data element* has a specified size and **format.** The smallest unit of **data** that has meaning in describing information; the smallest unit of named data. *(KB)*

DATA FLOW. The movement of a **data view** between two objects, each being a **process, procedure, data store,** or **external agent.** *(KB)*

DATA FLOW COURSE ANALYSIS. *See* **Course Analysis.**

DATA FLOW DIAGRAM. A diagram of the **data flows** through a set of **process**es or **procedure**s. It shows the **external agent**s that are sources or destinations of data, the **activities** that transform the data, and the **data stores** or **data collections** where the data is held.

DATA FLOW EXPRESSION. A precise definition of the **data** content of a **data flow,** expressed using a formal syntax and notation.

DATA INDEPENDENCE. The property of being able to change the overall **logical** or **physical** structure of the **data** without changing the **application program**'s view of the data.

DATA INDEPENDENCE, LOGICAL. The property of being able to change the overall **logical** structure of the **data** without changing the **application program**'s view of the data.

DATA INDEPENDENCE, PHYSICAL. The property of being able to change the **physical** structure of the **data** without changing the **application program's logical** structure.

DATA ITEM. *See* **Data Element.**

DATA MANAGEMENT. A general term that collectively describes those **function**s of the **system** that provide creation of and **access** to stored **data,** enforce data storage conventions, and regulate the use of input/output devices.

DATA MANIPULATION LANGUAGE. The language that the programmer uses to cause **data** to be transferred between his **program** and the **database.** The *data manipulation language* is not a complete language by itself. It relies on a host programming language to provide a framework for it and to provide the procedural capabilities required to manipulate data.

DATA MODEL. A **logical map** of **data** which represents the inherent properties of the data independently of software, hardware, or machine performance considerations. The **model** shows **data items** grouped into **third-normal-form record**s, and shows the associations among those records. The term *model* may be contrasted with the term **schema.** A schema also shows a logical representation of data, but it is usually related to a type of software representation (e.g., **CODASYL,** hierarchical, or relational). *(James Martin: I recommend that the term* model *be reserved for data representation that are independent of which class of software is used for implementation. The software choice may change, but the model remains a fundamental description of the data.)*

DATA SET. A named collection of **logically** related **data item**s, arranged in a prescribed manner, and described by control **information** to which the programming **system** has access. Also, a part of the storage provided on a storage device, the extent of which is defined in terms of **physical** characteristics of that device and which is used as a container for specific files or parts of files.

DATA SHARING. The situation where one **type** of **data** is used to support more than one **activity.**

DATA STORAGE STRUCTURE. The way in which **data** is organized in storage, which determines the performance of the business **system**s in their use of data, but which is not known to **program**s. **It is a type of data structure. The data storage structures are defined records, relations, and interface files.**

DATA STORE. A repository of **data,** possibly temporary, of which **user**s are aware, and from which data may be read repeatedly and nondestructively. *(KB)*

DATA STRUCTURE. A designed and defined collection of **record types, linkages, field**s, entry points, and **integrity rule**s required to support one or more business **system**s.

DATA STRUCTURE DESIGN. A way of organizing the **data** required to support one or several business **system**s, which assumes the constraints of a given **data management** system.

DATA STRUCTURE DIAGRAM. A representation of a **data structure.**

DATA TYPE. The size and type of a **data element.** An interpretation applied to a string of bits, such as integer, real, or character.

DATA USAGE ANALYSIS. A disciplined approach to documenting the ways and frequencies by which **data element**s are used in each **location** in existing **system**s and will be used in future systems.

DATA USAGE MATRIX. A matrix that shows, for each **record, field** or **linkage type,** the **procedure**s in which it is involved, and by which **action**s.

DATA VIEW. 1 An organized collection of **field**s or layouts that is meaningful to a **procedure,** business **system,** or **organizational unit.** *(KB)* 2. A subset of the **data model** which specifies a grouping of **entities, attributes,** and **relationships** which is used by a **process, procedure, data store,** or **external agent.**

DATABASE. 1. A collection of interrelated **data** stored together with controlled redundancy to serve one or more **application**s; the data is stored so that it is independent of **program**s that use the data; a common and controlled approach is used in adding new data and in modifying and retrieving existing data within a *database.* A **system** is said to contain a collection of *databases* if they are disjoint in structure. *(IE)* 2. A *database* consists of all the **record** occurrences, **set** occurrences, and areas that are controlled by a specific **schema.** If an **installation** has multiple *databases,* there must be a separate schema for each *database.* Furthermore, the content of different *databases* is assumed to be disjoint. (CODASYL)

DATABASE ADMINISTRATOR. A person with an overview of one or more **databases,** who controls the physical design and use of these databases. It is often better to use two people: a **data administrator,** who manages the architecture and logical model, and a database administrator, who designs the **physical** aspects of the database.

DATABASE MANAGEMENT SYSTEM. The collection of software required for using a **database,** and presenting multiple different views of the **data** to the **user**s and programmers. The **system** software manages the database, provides for **logical** and **physical data independence,** controls redundancy, and enforces integrity constraints, privacy, and **security.**

DATA/PROCESS INVOLVEMENT MODEL. A **model** of the associations between **type**s of **data (entities)** and the **process**es that use them, which are constructed as a series of **data views** from the processes.

DB/DC. **Database**/data communication.

DECISION TABLE. A diagram that consists of a **condition table,** together with a list of the **process**es that are executed for each combination of **attribute value** in the **table.**

DECOMPOSITION. The step-by-step breakdown into increasing detail either of **func-tion**s, eventually into **process**es, or of subject areas into subject areas, organizational units.

DECOMPOSITION DIAGRAM. A structure that shows the breakdown of **object**s of a given **type** into progressively increasing detail.

DEFAULT VALUE. The value that represents an **attribute** when no specific value is supplied by the **process**es establishing occurrences of the attribute.

DELIVERABLE. A subset of the **knowledge base** which is presented and approved.

DEMAND STAGING. Blocks of **data** are moved from a storage device to another device with a shorter **access time** (possibly including main memory); when **program**s request them and they are not already in the faster **access** storage. Contrast with **anticipatory staging.**

DEPENDENCY. *See* **Process Dependency; System Dependency; Business Function Dependency; Data Dependency.**

DERIVED ATTRIBUTE. An **attribute** whose values can each be calculated or deduced from the values of other attributes.

DESIGN AREA. A collection of closely related **process**es and **entity types for** which an application system is designed.

DESIGN PHASE. The period in the **systems lifecycle** in which a complete and detailed specification is produced of the **application system** needed to support a defined area within the **enterprise.**

DESIGNED ATTRIBUTE. An **attribute** that has been invented in order to overcome constraints or to simplify the operation of a **system.**

DEVICE/MEDIA CONTROL LANGUAGE. A language for specifying the **physical** layout and organization of **data.**

DIALOG. 1. A generic word for a preplanned human-machine interaction; it encompasses formal programming languages, languages for interrogating **databases,** and innumerable nonformal conversational interchanges, many of which are designed for one specific **application.** *(KB)* 2. A series of exchanges in which a **user,** through the use of **screen** components, either makes an inquiry or provides **information** to an application.

DIALOG FLOW DIAGRAM. A representation of the steps within a **dialog,** their sequence, and the **screen** layouts used by each step.

DICTIONARY. *See* **Data Dictionary.**

DIRECT ACCESS. **Retrieval** or storage of **data** by a reference to its **location** on a **volume,** rather than relative to the previously **retrieved** or stored data. The **access mechanism** goes directly to the data in question, as is normally required with **online** use of data.

DIRECT ACCESS STORAGE DEVICE (DASD). A **data** storage unit on which data can be **access**ed directly at random without having to progress through a serial file such as tape. A disk unit is a *direct access storage device.*

DIRECTORY. A **table** giving the **relationships** between items of **data.** Sometimes a table **(index)** giving the **address**es of data.

DISCRETE ATTRIBUTE. An **attribute** whose values are restricted to a defined collection of values. Contrast with **continuous attribute.**

DISTRIBUTED FREE SPACE. Space left empty at intervals in a **data** layout to permit the possible insertion of new data.

DISTRIBUTION ANALYSIS. A **technique** for assessing the **location** of **data** repositories and **processing systems** across the locations of an **enterprise.**

DL/1. IBM's Data Language/1, for describing **logical** and **physical data structures.**

DOMAIN. 1. The collection of **data items (fields)** of the same **type,** in a **relation (flat file).** 2. A **named set** of values that an **attribute** can assume.

DYNAMIC STORAGE ALLOCATION. The allocation of storage space to a **procedure** based on the instantaneous or actual demand for storage space by the procedure, rather than allocating storage space to a procedure based on its anticipated or predicted demand.

ELEMENTARY PROCESS. The smallest unit of **decomposition** in the **process model** for a **business area.** An *elementary process* is executed in response to a single triggering **event** and consists of a simple sequence of business **procedures.** It is the smallest unit of business **activity** of meaning to a **user,** which when complete leaves the business area in a self-consistent **state.**

ELEMENTARY STEP. A step that is the smallest unit of **activity** within a **procedure** which has meaning to a **user** or operator.

ELLIPSIS. A symbol consisting of three dots (. . .) which indicates that more **information** is available. With **tools** that use this symbol the additional information may be displayed by pointing to the line or block containing the three dots and giving the command **"Expand."**

EMBEDDED POINTERS. **Pointer**s in the **record**s used for addressing the records rather than a directory.

ENCYCLOPEDIA. A repository of knowledge about the **enterprise,** its **goals, entities, records, organizational units, functions, processes, procedure**s, and **application and information systems.** It is populated progressively during each **stage** of **information engineering.** A **dictionary** contains names and descriptions of **data item**s, processes, variables, etc. An *encyclopedia* contains complete coded representations of plans, **model**s, and designs with **tool**s for cross-checking, correlation analysis, and validation. Graphic representations are derived from the *encyclopedia* and are used to update it. The *encyclopedia* contains many rules relating to the knowledge it stores, and employs rule processing, the artificial intelligence **technique,** to help achieve accuracy, integrity, and completeness of the plans, models, and designs. The *encyclopedia* is thus a **knowledge base** which not only stores development **information** but helps to control its accuracy and validity. The *encyclopedia* should be designed to drive a code generator. The toolset helps the **system**s analyst build up in the *encyclopedia* the information necessary for code generation. The *encyclopedia* "understands" the **module**s and designs; a dictionary does not.

ENTERPRISE. An organization that exists to perform a **mission** and to achieve **objectives.** This information is typically stored in the **encyclopedia.** *(KB)*

ENTERPRISE KNOWLEDGE BASE. A formally controlled and approved collection of **information** used to develop, support, maintain, and operate **information systems.**

ENTERPRISE MODEL. A description of the **entity type**s, **function**s, and **process**es that define an **enterprise** and the inter**relationship**s.

ENTERPRISE STRATEGY. A plan or **action** of an **enterprise** to achieve a stated **goal** or **objective.**

ENTITY. 1. A **person,** place, thing or concept that has characteristics of interest to the **enterprise.** *(KB)* 2. An *entity* is something about which we store **data.** Examples of *entities* are: Customer, Part, Employee, Invoice, Machine Tool, Salesperson, Branch Office, Sales TV Area, Warehouse, Warehouse Bin, Shop Order, Shift **Report,** Product, Product Specification, Ledger Account, Payment, Debtor, and Debtor Analysis Record. An *entity* has various **attributes** which we wish to record, such as Color, Size, Monetary Value, Percentage Utilization, or Name. For each **entity type** we have at least one **record type.** Sometimes more than one record type is used to store the data about the *entity* type (because of **normalization**). An *entity* type has one **data item type** or a group of data item types which uniquely identifies it. *Entity* is a shorthand word meaning either *entity type* or *entity instance* (*see* Note A).

ENTITY ANALYSIS. A disciplined approach to understanding and documenting the things of interest to the **enterprise,** independently from the **activities** that take place in the enterprise. *See also* **Data Analysis.**

ENTITY IDENTIFIER. A **key** that uniquely identifies an **entity.**

ENTITY LIFECYCLE. A description of the sets of processes and events that can act on an entity in each of the states that are possible in the lives of the entities of that type. A description of what happens during the lives of entities of one type. The lifecycle is analyzed for the entity from the time it becomes of interest to an enterprise to the time it ceases to be of interest to the enterprise.

ENTITY LIFECYCLE ANALYSIS. A technique for analyzing the transition of an entity between its possible states (defined in terms of changes to the values of its attributes) to identify any missing processes.

ENTITY LIFECYCLE DIAGRAM. A diagram showing all the possible states in the lives of the **entities** of one type and processes that cause changes in their states.

ENTITY LIFECYCLE MATRIX. A matrix showing for each state, applicable to the **entities** of one type, the processes that are valid and those which cause a change in state.

ENTITY MODEL. A **model** of the **entity type**s, their **attribute type**s, and the **relationship** between entity types that represent the kind of **information** needed to **support an enterprise.**

ENTITY-RELATIONSHIP DIAGRAM. A diagram representing **entity type**s and the **relationship**s between them, and certain properties of the relationship, especially its **cardinality** and name.

ENTITY-RELATIONSHIP MODEL. A detailed and structured representation of all the results of **entity analysis.** It contains the diagram and all the released definitions.

ENTITY STATE. A definable, discrete period in the life of an **entity.** *(KB)*

ENTITY STATE MATRIX. A tabular representation of an **entity lifecycle.**

ENTITY STATE TRANSITION DIAGRAM. A pictorial representation of an **entity lifecycle.**

ENTITY SUBTYPE. A collection of **entities** of the same **type** but to which a narrower definition and additional attributes and/or relationships apply.

ENTITY TYPE. *See* **Entity.**

ENTITY-TYPE LIFECYCLE. *See* **Entity Lifecycle.**

ENTITY-TYPE LIFECYCLE ANALYSIS. *See* **Entity Lifecycle Analysis.**

ERROR HANDLING. Computer instructions to detect errors in input **information** and provide a response to a **user** and/or an alternative logic path.

EVENT. *See* **Business Event.**

EVENT MODEL. A diagram illustrating the valid **state**s of a **system** and the **transition**s between states.

EVENT TRIGGER. A value of an **attribute** or a set of attributes that causes a **process** to execute or to cease execution.

EVOLUTION PROPOSAL. A proposal prepared during the end of the **construction and implementation phase** which outlines continued development of **application system**s to meet changes in underlying business needs.

EXECUTION CONTROL SOFTWARE. A **set** of instructions to the computer that control the order of execution of computer **program**s and specify the **data collection**s they will use. *(KB)*

EXISTENCE DEPENDENCY. An **integrity condition** constraining two **attribute**s, such that each value of the first attribute determines whether or not for each **entity** it is meaningful for a value of the second attribute to exist.

EXPAND. A command used to display hidden **information** by pointing to an item containing an **ellipsis** (. . .). It should be possible to *expand* multiple times to reveal successive levels of detail.

EXTENT. A contiguous area of **data** storage.

EXTERNAL AGENT. The persons, **application system**s, or organizations outside the **project scope** with whom a **process** must interact and exchange **information**. *(KB)*

EXTERNAL EVENT. A change in the external environment affecting the area under study. The change is recognized by a flow of incoming **data.**

EXTERNAL SCHEMA. A **user**'s or programmer's view of the **data.** A **set** of similarly constructed **record**s. *Synonym:* **subschema.** *See also* **Data Element.**

FACILITY. A collective term for the accommodation, equipment, services, and supplies necessary to support the development and use of **application system**s. *(KB)*

FACTOR ANALYSIS. A **technique** for defining **business area**s by using a statistical approach to surface correlations between **process**es and **entity types.**

FALLBACK PROCEDURE. A **procedure** that allows business **activities** to continue while a computer **system** is unavailable.

FAN-OUT. The **process** by which a new **system** is first installed in one or a small number of groups of business **user**s and then expanded to involve all potential users within the organization.

FIELD. A physical container for **data elements,** representing part of a screen, report, or form layout.

FILTER. A **select**ion **condition** expressed in terms of values, property **type**s, and **association type**s which restricts a view of **information** from the **encyclopedia.**

FILTERED MODEL. A diagram that represents only those elements **select**ed to be supported by one or more integrated **systems.**

FIXED ATTRIBUTE. An **attribute** whose values, once established for any given **entity,** remain unchanged for the life of that entity.

FIXED CARDINALITY. A type of **cardinality condition** in which the cardinality of a **dependency, relationship,** or subprocess is always the same number.

FIXED EVENT. An event that occurs at fixed time intervals and so is completely predictable.

FLAT FILE. A sequential file of **data elements.**

FLOW EXPRESSION. *See* **Data Flow Expression.**

FOCUS. Arthur Young's strategic management service that is used as a guideline in assisting clients in evaluating their current situation and future developments, developing creative strategies, and implementing their resulting plans through achieving change.

FOREIGN KEY. An **attribute** of an **entity type** that is an **identifier** of a second entity type.

FORM. A pro forma document used for collecting **information** for later storage in a **data collection.** *(KB)*

FORMAT. The way in which the digits and characters are displayed for occurrences of **field.**

FUNCTION. A **logical** collection of **process**es within a **business segment.** *See also* **Business Function.** *(KB)*

FUNCTION ANALYSIS. A disciplined approach to understanding and documenting the detailed **activities** in the **enterprise,** independently from its organization structure.

FUNCTION DECOMPOSITION. 1. The breakdown of the **activities** of an **enterprise** into progressively increasing detail. 2. The breakdown of the **functions** of an enterprise into progressively increasing detail.

FUNCTION DECOMPOSITION DIAGRAM. A structure that shows the breakdown of **functions** into progressively increasing detail.

FUNCTION DEPENDENCY. *See* **Business Function Dependency.**

FUNCTION DEPENDENCY DIAGRAM. A diagram that shows how each **function** depends on other functions.

FUNCTION MODEL. A representation of one or more **activities** that a **system** performs.

FUNCTIONAL DEPENDENCE. 1. **Attribute** B of a **relation** R is *functionally dependent* on attribute A or R if, at every instant in time, each value of A has no more than one value of B associated with in relation R (equivalent to saying that A identifies B). An attribute or collection of attributes, $B,$ of a relation, $R,$ is said to be *fully functionally dependent* on the whole of A but not on any subset of A. 2. A **dependency** between two **field**s, such that the value of the first determines the value of the second.

FUNCTIONAL REQUIREMENT. A functional-level capability or business rule identified by an organization which is necessary to solve a **problem** or achieve an **objective.**

FUNDAMENTAL ENTITY TYPE. An **entity type** whose instances are each not dependent on any other entities for their existence.

GLOBAL MODEL. A diagram that represents all of the **enterprise** or that part of the enterprise so far analyzed.

GOAL. 1. A statement of an organization's medium- to long-term target or direction of development. A *goal* is achieved when all **objective**s relating to it have been achieved. Typically, *goals* do not have exact timetables or achievement measures associated with them. *(KB)* 2. Specific targets that a **business segment** intends to meet within a specified time frame to further the achievement of more general objectives.

HARDWARE COMPONENT. A physical device in a computer **system.** *(KB)*

HASH TOTAL. A total of the values of a certain **field** in a file, maintained for control purposes to ensure that no items are lost or changed invalidly, and thus having no meaning of its own.

HASHING. A **direct access**ing **technique** in which the **key** is converted to a pseudo-random number from which the required **address** is derived.

HEADER RECORD OR HEADER TABLE. A **record** containing common, constant, or identifying **information** for a group of records that follows.

HEURISTIC. Pertaining to trial-and-error methods of obtaining solutions to **problems.**

HIERARCHICAL FILE. A file in which some **record**s are subordinate to others in a **tree structure.**

HIERARCHICAL STORAGE. Storage units **link**ed together to form a storage **subsystem,** in which some forms are fast but small and others are large but slow. Blocks of **data** are moved from the large, slow **level**s to the small, fast levels when required.

HIT RATE. A measure of the number of **record**s in a file which are expected to be **access**ed in a given run. Usually expressed as a percentage: *number of records accessed × 100%/number of records in the file.*

HOME ADDRESS. 1. The **address** of a **physical** storage **location** (e.g., a home bucket) into which a **data record** is assigned; as opposed to **overflow** address. 2. A **field** that contains the physical address of a **track,** recorded at the beginning of a track.

HOMONYM. A name that is used ambiguously to denote two or more different **objects.**

HUFFMAN CODE. A code for **data compaction** in which frequently used characters are encoded with a smaller number of bits than are infrequently used characters.

HYPERCHART. *See* **Hyperdiagram.**

HYPERDIAGRAM. A collection of diagrams relating to a **process** or **procedure** with

logical links and **relationship**s between the diagrams so that they constitute an integrated whole. Changing one of the diagrams that constitute a *hyperdiagram* may result in other diagrams changing automatically in order to preserve consistency among the diagrams. *Synonym:* **hyperchart.**

HYPERVIEW. A **user** view consisting of related diagrams joined into a **hyperdiagram.**

IDENTIFIER. An **attribute** or **relationship** or combination of attributes and relationships that identifies **instances** of an **entity type.**

IMPLEMENTATION AREA. A functional area within the **enterprise** where a new **application,** or parts of it, may be implemented in a coherent fashion. A new application may be phased in over time in a series of *implementation areas.*

INDEPENDENCE, DATA. *See* **Data Independence.**

INDEPENDENCE, DEVICE. **Data** organization that is independent of the device on which the data is stored.

INDEX. A **table** used to determine the **location** of a **record.**

INDEX CHAINS. **Chain**s within an **index.**

INDEX POINT. A hardware reference mark on a disk or drum; used for timing purposes.

INDEX, SECONDARY. *See* **Secondary Index.**

INDEXED-SEQUENTIAL STORAGE. A file structure in which **record**s are stored in ascending sequence by **key. Indices** showing the highest key on a **cylinder, track,** bucket, and so on, are used for the **select**ed **retrieval** of records.

INDICATIVE DATA. **Data** that identify or describe; for example, in a stock file, the product number, description, and pack size. Normally, *indicative data* does not change on a regular, frequent basis during **process**ing (as in, for example, an account balance).

INDIRECT ADDRESSING. Any method of specifying or locating a storage **location** whereby the **key** (directly or through calculation) does not represent an **address:** for example, locating an address through **indices.**

INDUSTRY MODEL. A generic business information model that is applicable to a range of **enterpris**es within a given industry. *Industry models* are maintained (as templates awaiting customizing) in the **information engineering encyclopedia.**

INFORMATION. Any formal, structured **data** that is required to support a business and can be stored in or **retrieve**d from a computer.

INFORMATION ARCHITECTURE. A structure expressed in terms of an **entity-relationship model** and a **function** or **process dependency model,** based on which individual business **system**s can be developed, in the knowledge that these may be readily integrated and share **data** at a future time.

INFORMATION ENGINEER. An **information system**s professional who has been trained in and who practices **information engineering.**

INFORMATION ENGINEERING. 1. An interlocking **set** of formal **technique**s in which business **models**, **data model**s, and **process** models are built up in a comprehensive **knowledge base** and are used to create and maintain **information systems.** 2. An interlocking set of automated techniques which apply structured planning, analysis, and design to the **enterprise** as a whole rather than merely to one **project.** 3. A **methodology** that creates a corporatewide architectural framework for information systems. 4. An interlocking set of computerized techniques in which **enterprise model**s, data models, process models, and system designs are built up in an **encyclopedia** (a knowledge base) and used to create and maintain more effective DP **system**s. 5. An enterprisewide set of disciplines for getting the right **information** to the right people at the right time and providing them with **tool**s to use the information.

INFORMATION ENGINEERING/JOINT SESSION TECHNIQUES (IE/JST). A strategy for rapid product development through end **user** and **system** professional participation in thorough, well-structured group sessions under the control of a facilitator. Ideas are captured in computerized **model**s through automated diagramming **tool**s.

INFORMATION FLOW EVENT. *See* **Business Event.**

INFORMATION MODEL. A high-level **data model,** describing **key** business **entities** and their **relationship**s, but without full **attribute information,** reference, or **intersection** entities.

INFORMATION NEED. A specific **information requirement** of a particular **person** or **organizational unit** to make a decision or complete a **task.** *Information needs* provide an input to **entity modeling.** *(KB)*

INFORMATION REQUIREMENT. *See* **Information Need.**

INFORMATION STRATEGY PLANNING (ISP). The period in the **systems lifecycle** in which an **information architecture,** a **business systems architecture,** and a **technical architecture** are first produced and under which a consistent and integrated set of business systems will be developed. *See also* **Planning Phase.**

INFORMATION SYSTEM. (?) 1. A **system** of **data** and **process**es that can be used to record and maintain **information.** Contrasted with **production system,** to mean a system in which the data stored will be used in ways that are not fully predictable in advance. *(KB)* 2. A **logical partition** of data and processes that can be analyzed independently to collect, store, and **retrieve** information to satisfy a portion of a **business segment**'s **information need**s. **Business area** is often used interchangeably with the **scope** of an *information system.*

INFORMATION SYSTEMS ENVIRONMENT. The technologies, applications portfolio, human resources, and management practices that constitute an organization's **information system**s capability.

INFORMATION SYSTEMS GROUP. A generic name for an enterprise's information systems organizational units.

INFORMATION SYSTEMS REQUIREMENT. A condition or capability that must be met by a **system** or system component to satisfy a contract, standard, specification, or other formal document.

INFORMATION TECHNOLOGY. The merging of computing and high-speed communication **links** carrying **data,** sound, and video.

INFRASTRUCTURE. The basic **installation**s and **facilities** on which continuance and growth of an organization depend.

INHIBITOR. A factor that could prevent the **enterprise** from achieving its **objective**s or **goals.**

INSPECTION. A **technique** of quality control which detects and records defects in **deliverables.**

INSTALLATION. 1. The **process** of making an application's system operative to end users. 2. The process of turning the developed system into a production status.

INSTANCE. See Note A.

INTANGIBLE BENEFIT. A **benefit** to which a direct monetary value cannot be applied. *See also* **Benefit.**

INTEGRATION TEST. A test that is conducted to prove that a group of interfacing modules operates as expected and that the programming language statements (''code'') perform as defined in the module specification. An iterative **process** involving the multiple levels of testing.

INTEGRITY CONDITION. *See* **Integrity Rule.**

INTEGRITY RULE. A rule expressed in terms of **logical data** constructs and/or layouts and/or constants, which states a constraint upon the data values and/or **linkage memberships** of a business **system.**

INTERNAL EVENT. An **event** that results from the execution of some **process** within the **enterprise.**

INTERNAL SCHEMA. The **physical** structure of the **data.** A description of the data described in the **schema** as represented on storage media. *Synonym:* **data storage structure.**

INTERPRETIVE ROUTINE. A routine that decodes instruction written as pseudocodes and immediately executes those instructions, as contrasted with a **compiler,** which decodes the pseudocodes and produces a machine language routine to be executed at a later time.

INTERSECTION. **A form of entity identification requiring of two or more relationship members.**

INTERSECTION DATA. **Data** associated with the conjunction of two or more **entities** or **record type**s, but which has no meaning if associated with only one of them.

INTERSECTION ENTITY. Some characteristics represented in **attributes** belong not to individual **entity instance**s but to specific combinations of two or more entity instances. Such cases require a separate **data** grouping called **intersection data.** The

intersection is represented in a **logical data model** by a **normalized record type** whose **primary key** is the concatenation of the **keys** that identify the entities involved, and whose other attributes represent characteristics belonging to the intersection. Usually, an intersection relates to entities of different types (e.g., Supplier and Part). Less commonly it relates to entities of the same type (e.g., Subassembly and Subassembly, when a product or subassembly contains multiple other subassemblies). *Synonym:* **associative entity.**

INVERTED FILE. A file structure that permits fast spontaneous **search**ing for previous unspecified **information.** Independent **list**s or **indices** are maintained in **record**s **keys** that are accessible according to the values of specific **fields.**

INVERTED LIST. A **list** organized by a **secondary key,** not a **primary key.**

INVOLUTED DEPENDENCY. The situation where the execution of a **process** may lead to a further execution of the same process.

INVOLUTED RELATIONSHIP. A **relationship** in which the two **entities** of every **pairing** are from the same **entity type.**

INVOLVEMENT MATRIX. The summary of the involvement of **process**es with **entity type**s, or **procedure**s with **record types.**

IS FUNCTION. A subtype of **function** specific to IS which provides a service to support **application systems** (e.g., **data** center operations, technical support, data resource management). *(KB)*

IS ORGANIZATIONAL UNIT. A subtype of an **organizational unit** that develops, implements, operates, and maintains **application system**s. *Synonym:* **information systems group.** *(KB)*

IS STRATEGY. A **set** of plans aimed at successful achievement of **goal**s in terms of developing application **systems.** *(KB)*

ISAM. Indexed-sequential **access method.**

ISOLATED ENTITY TYPE. An **entity type** that does not participate in any **relationship.**

JOB. A sequence of one or more **job step**s that is activated as a unit. *Synonyms:* batch job; **run unit.**

JOB FUNCTION. A set of **skill**s of a **person** to fill a role in an organization. *(KB)*

JOB STEP. One main **program** that has (optionally) a hierarchy of one or more subprograms and is activated by an **operating system.** *It is a component of a job.*

JUNCTION. The point at which a **data flow** divides or combines with another flow or crosses a **level** in the data flow **model.**

KEY. A **data item** or combination of data items used to identify or locate a **record instance** (or other **data** groupings).

KEY, CANDIDATE. *See* **Candidate Key.**

KEY COMPRESSION. A **technique** for reducing the number of bits in **key**s; used in making **indices** occupy less space.

KEY, PRIMARY. A **key** that is used to uniquely identify a **record instance** (or other **data** grouping).

KEY, SEARCH. *Synonym:* **secondary key.**

KEY, SECONDARY. An alternative key to the primary key. It is not used to uniquely identify a **record instance;** that is, more than one record instance can have the same key value. A key that contains the value of an **attribute (data item)** other than the unique **identifier.** *Secondary keys* are used to **search** a file or extract subsets of it (e.g., ''all the engineers'' or ''all employees living in Boston''.)

KNOWLEDGE BASE. A **data** repository that contains both **information** and knowledge about applying this information within a particular context. The latter is usually expressed in the form of rules.

KNOWLEDGE COORDINATOR. The portion of the **information engineering** toolkit responsible for applying the rules of information engineering to ensure the consistency and correctness of any **information** that will be saved in the **encyclopedia.**

LABEL. A **set** of symbols used to identify or describe an item, **record,** message, or file. Occasionally, it may be the same as the **address** in storage.

LATENCY. The time taken for a storage **location** to reach the read/write heads on a rotating surface. For general timing purposes, average *latency* is used; this is the time taken by one half-revolution of the surface.

LEVEL. The number of times the **object** of broadest **scope** has been progressively decomposed to arrive at the object being described.

LFU. Least Frequently Used. A replacement **algorithm** in which when new **data** has to replace existing data in an area of storage, the least frequently used items are replaced. Contrast with **LRU.**

LIBRARY. 1. The room in which **volumes** (tapes and disk packs) are stored. 2. An organized collection of **program**s, source statements, or **object module**s maintained on a **direct access storage device** accessible by the **operating system.**

LIFECYCLE ANALYSIS. *See* **Entity Lifecycle Analysis.**

LIFECYCLE DIAGRAM. *See* **Entity Lifecycle Diagram.**

LIFECYCLE MATRIX. *See* **Entity Lifecycle Matrix.**

LINK. An association or **relationship** between **entities** or **records**. A *link* is drawn as a line connecting entities or records on an entity chart or **data model.** The word *link* is more visual than *association* or *relationship* and so is sometimes preferred when referring to such lines drawn on charts. The word *link* sometimes refers to **link relation** or **link record.** A distinction should be made between **link type**s and **link instance**s (see Note A). This is important when the **attribute instance**s associated with a *link* can change as they might in an intelligent **database.**

LINK RELATION OR LINK RECORD. A **relation** or **record** containing **information** about the **link.** *See also* **Association Relation.**

LINKAGE. A connection between two related **records** by which records may be **accessed,** but of which **modules** need have no knowledge.

LINKAGE MEMBERSHIP. The participation of a **record layout** in a **linkage type.**

LINKAGE TYPE. A type of connection between two or more related **record types.**

LIST. An ordered **set** of **data items.** A **chain.**

LOAD MATRIX. A matrix that summarizes the usage of **record type, linkages,** and entry points of the preliminary **data structure** by those **procedures** included within the **design area.**

LOCAL ENCYCLOPEDIA. A subset of the central **encyclopedia** for a **project** together with **information** pertaining to the project but not yet accepted by the central encyclopedia. A *local encyclopedia* is the responsibility of the project leader.

LOCAL MODEL. A diagram that is a subset of a **global model,** which represents a specific view of part of the **enterprise.**

LOCATION. A geographic place where **process**es are performed and/or **data** are recorded or maintained for an organization. *(KB)*

LOCATION MODEL. A representation of **locations.**

LOGICAL. An adjective describing the form of **data** organization, hardware, information systems, or **application system** that is perceived by an analyst, programmer, or **user;** it may be different from the real **(physical)** form. Indicates independence from physical constraints and considerations.

LOGICAL ACCESS MAP (LAM). A chart showing the sequence of **logical access**es to a **data model** used by an **application** system. *LAMs* give guidelines to the designer of the **program** structure which employs the **database.** A collection of *LAMS,* annotated with suitable numbers, form the input to the **physical database** design **process.**

LOGICAL DATABASE. 1. A **database** as perceived by its accessing modules; it may be structured differently from the **physical database** structure. 2. A tree-structured collection of **segments** derived from one or more physical databases by means of **pointer linkages.** (DL/1)

LOGICAL DATABASE DESCRIPTION. A **schema.** A description of the overall logical **database** structure. It is dependent on the database management software.

LOGICAL FILE. A file as perceived by an **application program;** it may be in a completely different form from that which it is stored on the storage unit.

LRU. Least Recently Used. A replacement **algorithm** in which when new **data** has to replace existing data in an area of storage, the least recently used items are replaced. Contrast with **LFU.**

MACHINE INDEPENDENT. An adjective used to indicate that a **procedure** or **program** is conceived, organized, or oriented without specific reference to the **system.** Use of this adjective usually implies that the procedure or program is oriented or organized in terms of the **logical** nature of the **problem** or **process**ing, rather than in terms of the characteristics of the machine used in handling it.

MACROINSTRUCTION. One line of source **program** code which generates a program routine rather than one program instruction.

MAINTENANCE OF A FILE. Periodic reorganization of a file to accommodate, more efficiently, items that have been added or deleted. (Sometimes this term is used to refer to the **process** of updating a file.)

MANAGEMENT, DATABASE. *See* **Database Management System.**

MAPPING. A definition of the way **record**s are associated with one another.

MENU. A type of **screen** used to traverse an online dialog. *(KB)*

METADATA. **Data** about data; that is, the **information** about data which is stored in **data dictionaries, data model**s, **schemas, encyclopedias,** and their computerized representation.

METHODOLOGY. A guideline identifying how to develop an application **system.** A methodology describes the managerial and technical **procedure**s that facilitates development of an application system.

MIGRATION. 1. The **process** whereby an **enterprise** transfers **data** and **procedure**s from an existing **information system** to a new **system** and organizes **business function**s to make best use of the new system. 2. The process of conversion, installation, and transition.

MIGRATION ANALYSIS. The study of how the **business area** is supported by existing systems and how they may be converted or incorporated into new, more comprehensive systems.

MIGRATION DESIGN. The specifying of how existing business systems and files will be gradually replaced by or interfaced with new systems.

MIGRATION PLAN. 1. A **user**-oriented plan for realigning **organizational unit**s, **job** descriptions, and staffing levels to mesh effectively with a new **information system** and to move **data** and **procedure**s to a new **system.** 2. A plan encompassing conversion, installation, and transition.

MILESTONE. A point within the duration of a **project** which is clearly definable and is of interest to management.

MISSION. A general statement of the purpose and nature of the **enterprise.**

MISSION STATEMENT. A broad description of an **enterprise**'s purpose, **policies,** and long-range strategy and vision.

MODEL. A representation for some aspect of an organization. A *model* built using **information engineering technique**s is stored in the **encyclopedia.**

MODELING SOURCE. A **person,** group, or document that provides the **information** used to **model** some aspect of the organization.

MODULE. 1. The section of storage hardware that holds one **volume,** such as one spindle, of disks. *(KB)* 2. A collection of **program** code that can be compiled by itself. 3. A collection of program statements which are designed as reusable and possess four **basic attribute**s: discrete input and output, single **function, standard** mechanics, and internal **data.**

MODULE STRUCTURE DIAGRAM. A diagram which shows the logic of the source code which constitutes the **module.**

MULTILIST ORGANIZATION. A chained file organization in which the **chain**s are divided into fragments and each fragment **indexed,** to permit faster **search**ing.

MULTIPLE ASSOCIATION. An association between two **field**s such that for each value of one field it is possible to know one or more values of the associated field. A type of behavior rule. *Synonym:* **multivalued dependence.**

MULTIPLE-KEY RETRIEVAL. **Retrieval** that requires **search**es of **data** based on the values of several **key field**s (some or all of which may be **secondary keys**).

MULTIVALUED ATTRIBUTE. An **attribute** where more than one value can describe an **entity** at any given time. Not valid in an entity type normalized to first normal.

MULTIVALUED DEPENDENCE. *See* **Multiple Association.**

NATURAL BUSINESS SYSTEM. A collection of **procedure**s which, together, support a particular functional area of an **enterprise.**

NETWORK STRUCTURE. *See* **Plex Structure.**

NONPRIME ATTRIBUTE. An **attribute** that is not part of the **primary key** of a **normalized record.** Attributes that are part of the primary key are called **prime attributes.**

NORMAL FORM, FIRST. **Data** in two-dimensional form, without repeating groups.

NORMAL FORM, SECOND. A **relation** R is in *second normal form* if it is in **first normal form** and every **nonprime attribute** of R is fully **functionally dependent** (q.v.) on each **candidate key** of R *(E.F. Codd's definition).*

NORMAL FORM, THIRD. 1. A **relation** R is in *third normal form* if it is in **second normal form** and every **nonprime attribute** of R is nontransitively dependent on each **candidate key** of R *(E.F. Codd's definition).* 2. A **record, segment,** or **tuple** which is **normalized** (i.e., contains no repeating groups) and in which every **nonprime data item** is nontransitively dependent and fully **functionally dependent** on each candidate key. In other words, the entire **primary key** or candidate key is needed to identify each other **data item** in the tuple, and no data item is identified by a data item that is not in the primary key or candidate key.

NORMALIZATION. The simplification of more complex **data structure**s according to E.F. Codd's rules which are designed to produce simpler, more stable structures. **Third normal form** (q.v.) is usually adequate for stable data structures.

NORMALIZED RECORD. A named **set** of **attributes** representing some or all of the characteristics of some **entity** or **intersection of entities.** One entity is represented by one or more **record**s in **third normal form,** and an **intersection** of two or more entities (if that intersection has **nonprime attributes**) is represented by one *normalized record*. Every *normalized record* has a **primary key. Record** may be used as a shorthand for *normalized record* in contexts where there is no possible confusion with other uses of record that are prevalent in the **field** (e.g., IMS **logical** records or **physical record**s). Moreover, the term *normalized record* is itself a shorthand meaning either *normalized record* **type** or *normalized record* **instance** (see Note 2).

OBJECT. A component of a **logical database description** that represents a real-world **entity** about which **information** is stored.

OBJECTIVE. An end or target **state** that is achieved by accomplishing all **critical success factor**s related to it. *Objectives* are short-term targets (12 to 24 months or less), with defined achievement measures.

ONLINE. An *online* **system** is one in which the input **data** enters the computer directly from the point of origin and/or output data is transmitted directly to where it is used. The intermediate **stage**s, such as punching data, writing tape, loading disks, or offline printings, are avoided.

ONLINE CONVERSATION. A particular path through a set of screens to support a single instance of a **business transaction.** *(KB)*

ONLINE STORAGE. Storage devices, especially the storage media they contain, under the direct control of a computing **system,** not offline or in a **volume library.**

OPERATING SYSTEM. Software that enables a computer to supervise its own operations, automatically calling in **program**s, routines, language, and **data** as needed for continuous throughput of different types of jobs.

OPPORTUNITY/PROBLEM. An identification of the possibilities, constraints, and other factors that assist or hinder an organization's ability to achieve its **goal**s and **critical success factor**s. *(KB)*

OPTIONALITY. The characteristic of an **entity relationship** that describes whether it exists for all occurrences of the **entity type** pair or only for some.

ORGANIZATIONAL ROLE. The primary set of **function**s that an organization performs.

ORGANIZATIONAL STRUCTURE. A representation of the interrelationships between the organization units.

ORGANIZATIONAL UNIT. An administrative subdivision of a **business segment,** which is **partition**ed to reflect reporting lines and which performs one or more **process**es. *(KB)*

ORGANIZATIONAL UNIT TYPE. A classification of **organizational unit** which performs a **standard set** of processes within a **business segment.** *(KB)*

OVERFLOW. The **condition** when a **record** (or **segment**) cannot be stored in its **home address,** that is, the storage **location logically** assigned to it on loading. It may be stored in a special *overflow* location, or in the home address of other records.

PACKAGE. A reusable **program** or collection of programs to be used by more than one business and/or **organizational unit.** *(KB)*

PAGE. A subdivision of a file or program, which is the minimum amount of information that may be transferred from the control of the **operating system** to the control of the **data management** software.

PAGE FAULT. A **program** interruption that occurs when a **page** that is referred to is not in main memory and has to be read in.

PAGING. In **virtual** storage **system**s, the **technique** of making memory appear larger than it is by transferring **pages** of **data** or **program**s into memory from external storage when needed.

PAIRING. Two **entity** instances of one or two **type**s associated by virtue of a defined **relationship.**

PAIRING MEMBERSHIP. The participation of an **entity** in a **pairing.**

PARALLEL DATA ORGANIZATIONS. Data organizations that permit multiple **access** arms to **search,** read, or write **data** simultaneously.

PARALLEL DEPENDENCY. A situation where there is more than one **dependency** between two **process**es, any one of which can apply to a given execution of the processes.

PARALLEL RELATIONSHIPS. Two or more **relationship**s associating two entity types.

PARENT. An **object** in a **decomposition diagram** that is immediately above at least one specified object.

PARTIAL IDENTIFIER. A constituent **attribute** of a composite **identifier.**

PARTITION. *See* **Business Area Partition.**

PARTITIONING. The **technique** for identifying **partitions.**

PERFORMANCE ASSESSMENT. The prediction, within reasonable bounds, of the performance of an application system.

PERFORMANCE MEASURE. An indicator that shows the progress of an **action** against a plan. It indicates to what extent the **goal** has been reached.

PERFORMANCE TEST. An evaluation of how well a **system** performs its **function**s, including speed maximum volume, accuracy, and use of resources such as memory space.

PERSON. An individual who plays a role in an **enterprise.** *(KB)*

PERSPECTIVE. A **user**'s view of an organization or of a portion of one; it is obtained by considering multiple diagrams (e.g., **decomposition** view, **data view,** or **process** view diagrams).

PHASE. A series of **stages** within the **methodology.**

PHYSICAL. An adjective, contrasted with **logical,** which refers to the form in which **data** or **system**s exist in reality. Data is often converted by software from the form in which they are *physically* stored to a form in which a **user** or programmer perceives them.

PHYSICAL DATABASE. A **database** in the form in which it is stored on the storage media, including **pointers** or other means of interconnecting it. Multiple **logical databases** may be derived from one or more *physical databases*.

PHYSICAL RECORD. A collection of bits that are *physically recorded* on the storage medium and which are read or written by one machine input/output instruction.

PLANNING HORIZON. A planning range of the **tactical IS project plan** that can vary from six to nine months to two to three years based on what is being planned (e.g., technology, new applications, organizational changes).

PLANNING PHASE. A **phase** of **information engineering.** A high-level study of an organization (or of a portion of one) that identifies **information needs,** assesses existing **information system**'s capabilities, identifies appropriate technologies and architectures, and defines **business area**s. A **corporate information model,** information needs **report,** existing information systems profile report, and information systems plan (which includes a **tactical IS project plan** and a long-term information systems plan) are produced.

PLEX STRUCTURE. A **relationship** between **record**s (or other groupings) in which a **child record** can have more than one **parent** record. *Synonym:* **network structure.**

POINTER. The **address** of a **record** (or other **data** groupings) contained in another record so that a **program** may **access** the former record when it has **retrieve**d the latter record. The address can be absolute, relative, or symbolic, and hence the *pointer* is referred to as absolute, relative, or symbolic.

POLICY. A principle, plan, or course of **action** pursued by an organization.

PRIMARY KEY   *See* **Key, Primary.**

PRIME ATTRIBUTE. An **attribute** that forms all or part of the **primary key** of a **record.** Other attributes are called **nonprime attributes.**

PROBLEM. An obstacle to achieving a **goal** or **critical success factor;** a situation or issue that presents uncertainty, complication, complexity, or difficulty.

PROBLEMS AND ISSUES LIST. A record of the **problem**s and issues raised during a **structured interview.**

PROCEDURE. 1. A method by which one or more processes may be carried out. Contrast with **process.** *(KB)* 2. A sequence of detailed instructions that performs specific **physical task**s to support a lowest-**level logical** process. *Synonym:* functional primitive.

PROCEDURE ACTION DIAGRAM. A representation of the logic of a **procedure** in terms of the **action**s carried out on each **data object** involved and the **condition**s constraining them.

PROCEDURE CONDITION. A rule expressed in terms of **logical data** constructs and/or layouts and/or constants which constrains the behavior of the business **system.**

PROCEDURE DECOMPOSITION DIAGRAM. A form of **activity decomposition diagram** showing the hierarchical breakdown of **procedure**s.

PROCEDURE DEPENDENCY DIAGRAM. A diagram which shows how for each **procedure,** and execution may depend upon the prior execution of other procedures.

PROCEDURE DESIGN. The **task** of specifying the steps, **data** input and output, and the detailed logic of a **procedure.**

PROCESS. 1. A low-level **activity** that starts and stops, and is executed repeatedly. The execution of the *process* produces a specific kind of effect on **entities** or **information** about entities of a specified **type.** *Processes* are determined by successively decomposing the **business functions.** The word *process* relates to "what" is to be done but not "how" it is done. The word **procedure** relates to "how" something is accomplished. *(KB)* 2. A repetitive, well-defined **set** of **logical task**s that support one **function,** are repeatedly executed in a **business segment,** can be defined in terms of inputs and outputs, and have a definable beginning and end. *Processes* can be decomposed into *processes* and are triggered by an **event** and carried out by a business segment to achieve a stated purpose. A low-level *process* may be replicated across the business segment.

PROCESS ACTION DIAGRAM. A representation of the logic of a **process** in terms of the **action**s carried out on each **entity analysis object** involved and the **condition**s constraining these actions.

PROCESS DECOMPOSITION DIAGRAM. A structure that shows the breakdown of **process**es into progressively increasing detail.

PROCESS DEPENDENCY. An association between **process**es such that an execution of a process produces an **information** view that must be or may be required as input to an execution of another process. The **dependency** may be between executions of the same process.

PROCESS DEPENDENCY ANALYSIS. The analysis of the sequences in which **process**es can be executed and the **attribute**s that are passed from one process to another.

PROCESS DEPENDENCY DIAGRAM. A diagram that shows how each **process** depends on the prior execution of other processes.

PROCESS FILTER. The elimination, prior to the **design phase,** of any **process**es that do not at this time warrant computer support.

PROCESS HIERARCHY. *See* **Process Decomposition Diagram.**

PROCESS LOGIC   An analysis of the inherent logic of a **process** in terms of the **entity type**s, **relationship**s, and **attribute**s involved, the **condition**s constraining the execution of its subprocesses, and the algorithms used.

PROCESS LOGIC DIAGRAM. A diagram showing the inherent logic of a **process,** in terms of the sequence in which **entity type**s and **relationship**s are involved.

PROCESS LOGIC FORM. A pro forma on which all the details from the logic analysis of a **process** are documented.

PROCESS NETWORK DIAGRAM. A diagram that shows the breakdown of **process**es into progressively increasing detail, but such that each process appears only once in the diagram.

PROCESS PURPOSE. The categorization of a **process** according to whether it contributes to the operational, tactical, or strategic **activities** of the **enterprise.**

PROCESS SCHEDULING. The extent to which the timing of the executions of a **process** can be controlled.

PROCESS SELECTION CRITERION. A characteristic of a **process** that is used to judge whether or not a process should be **select**ed for computerization.

PROCESS SELECTION SCORE. A relative value assigned to a **process** according to the degree to which the process meets a **select**ion criterion.

PROCESS STIMULUS. The categorization of a **process** according to whether or not its execution directly follows the execution of some process.

PROCESS-DRIVEN PROCESS. A **process** that follows the completion of some other process.

PROCESSING CYCLE. A period during the **production stage** for a business **system,** which provides a basis for control.

PROCESSOR CONFIGURATION. A combination of the hardware and systems software on which an **application system** is **process**ed. *(KB)*

PRODUCTION. The period in the **systems developed lifecycle** during which application systems provide support to the areas of the **enterprise** for which they were designed.

PRODUCTION SYSTEM. The execution of debugged **program**s that routinely accomplishes its purpose.

PROGRAM GROUP DEPENDENCY DIAGRAM. A diagram that shows the **dependency** of **program** groups on one another for testing purposes.

PROGRAM STRUCTURE DIAGRAM. A diagram that shows the **module**s from which the **program** is constructed and the **field**s by which they communicate.

PROGRESSIVE OVERFLOW. A method of handling **overflow** in a randomly stored file which does not require the use of **pointer**s. An overflow **record** is stored in the first available space and is **retrieve**d by a forward serial **search** from the **home address.**

PROJECT. A related group of work **activities,** organized under the direction of a *project* manager using a *project* plan, which when carried out will allow the *project* **goal**(s) to be achieved. Examples are **analysis phase** *projects,* **infrastructure** *projects,* and **design phase** *projects. (KB)*

PROJECT BASELINE. *See* **Project Knowledge Base.**

PROJECT CHARTER. An approved **project** definition that outlines the purpose, **scope,** and **objective**s of an I.E. project.

PROJECT CONTROL FILE (PCF). The collection of all documentary material from a **project.**

PROJECT KNOWLEDGE BASE. A subset of the **enterprise knowledge base** that is being utilized by an **I.E. project.**

PROJECT MANAGEMENT. The administration of a **project** to ensure enforcement of its **goal**s.

PROJECT SCOPE. A definition of what is and is not included in a **project.** A **business area** is equivalent to an analysis *project scope.*

PROJECT TASK. A unit of work contained within a **project** to be performed by a person to achieve a specific result.

PROTOTYPE. A representation of a **system** that simulates the main **user** interfaces so that users can understand and critique the system. Software **tool**s are used which enable the *prototype* to be built quickly and modified quickly to adapt it to end-user needs. This provides an important means for user needs and capabilities. In some cases tools are used that enable the *prototype* to be successively added to until it becomes the full working system.

PURGE DATE. The date on or after which a **storage area** is available to be overwritten. Used in conjunction with a file **label,** it is a means of protecting file **data** until an agreed release date is reached.

QUALITY ASSURANCE. The development of standards and the formal monitoring to ensure that standards are being enforced.

QUALITY CONTROL. A technique for evaluating the quality of a product being processed, by checking it against a predetermined standard and taking the proper corrective action if the product does not meet the standard.

QUALITY PLAN. A **project management** plan used to indicate key **milestone**s and deliveries in a **project** that will be examined in the quality control review. It is constructed in the preparation **stage** of a project and adjusted during the duration of the project.

RANDOM ACCESS. To obtain **data** directly from any storage **location** regardless of its position with respect to the previously referenced **information.** *Synonym:* **direct access.**

RANDOM ACCESS STORAGE. A storage **technique** in which the time required to obtain **information** is independent of the **location** of the information most recently obtained. This strict definition must be qualified by the observation that we usually mean relatively random. Thus magnetic drums are relatively nonrandom **access** when compared to magnetic cores for main memory, but relatively **random access** when compared to magnetic tapes for file storage.

RANDOMIZING. *See* **Hashing.**

REAL TIME. 1. Pertaining to actual time during which a **physical process** transpires.
2. Pertaining to the performance of a computation during the actual time that the
related physical process transpires so that results of the computation can be used in
guiding the physical process.
3. Pertaining to an **application** in which response to input is fast enough to effect
subsequent input, as when conducting the **dialog**s that take place at terminals on
interactive **system**s.

RECORD. 1. A group of related **data elements** treated as a unit by an **application
program.** *(KB)* 2. A collection of occurrences of **field**s which is read or written as a
single unit, during the execution of a **module.** *(IE)* 3. A named collection of zero,
one, or more data items or **data aggregates.** There may be an arbitrary number of
occurrences in the **database** of each *record* type specified in the **schema** for that
database. For example, there would be one occurrence of the *record* type "payroll
record" for each employee. This distinction between the actual occurrences of a
record and the **type** of *record* is an important one. **(CODASYL)** 4. A **logical database** *record* consists of a named hierarchy (tree) of related **segment**s. There may be
one or more segment types, each of which may have a different length and **format.**
(DL/1)

RECORD LAYOUT. A collection of related **field**s which represent **data** in a structure
visible to both **module**s and the **data management system.**

RECOVERY. The **process** to allow the continuance of **program** execution after a failure.

RECURSION. The dependence of an **activity** or **action** on itself. An activity calling itself.

REDUNDANT ATTRIBUTE. A superfluous **attribute** that already appears elsewhere.

REDUNDANT DEPENDENCY. A **process dependency** that exists only because each of its
processes have a dependency, directly or indirectly, with some third process.

REDUNDANT RELATIONSHIP. A **relationship** where each of its **pairing**s can be derived
from pairings under other, more basic relationships.

RELATION. A two-dimensional array of **data** elements. A file in **normalized** form.

RELATIONAL ALGEBRA. A language providing a **set** of operators for manipulating **relation**s. These include "project," "join," and **"search"** operators.

RELATIONAL CALCULUS. A language in which the **user**s state the result they require
from manipulating a **relational database.**

RELATIONAL DATABASE. A **database** made up of **relation**s (as defined above) that
uses a **database management system** has the capability to recombine the **data item**s
to form different relations, thus giving great flexibility in the usage of **data.** If the
database management system does not provide the **function**s of or equivalent to a
relational algebra, the term *relational database* should not be used.

RELATIONAL VIEW. A representation of part or all of an **enterprise**'s **data architecture** in terms of **relation**s.

RELATIONSHIP. A reason (of relevance to the **enterprise**) why **entities** from one or from two **entity type**s may be associated. *(KB)* A named connection or association between entity types that embodies some relevant **information** of value to an organization.

RELATIONSHIP INVOLVEMENT MATRIX. A matrix which shows for **relationship**s the **process**es in which they are involved and by which **action**s.

RELATIONSHIP MODEL. *See* **Entity-Relationship Diagram.**

RELATIONSHIP ROLE. A business reason whereby **entities** of a specific **type** may participate in groupings under a **relationship,** either as plural members or as single members.

REPORT. A preparation of **information** generated by an **application system** which may be sent to a printer. *(KB)*

RESPONSE TIME. The time taken for a **system** to respond to a **user** input. It is usually measured from the point at which the last character is input at the terminal to the point at which the first character is output.

RETRIEVE. An **action** by which a **record** is made available for use during the execution of a **module.**

REUSABLE COMPONENT. A **construct** developed and used in multiple applications.

RING STRUCTURE. **Data** organized with **chain**s such that the end of the chain points to its beginning, thus forming a ring.

RISK FACTOR. A feature of the environment in which a business **system** is to be developed which can be assessed as contributing to the likely success or failure of the development **project.**

RISK MANAGEMENT PLAN. A plan to address the risks involved in a **project** and the measures to be taken to control and reduce them.

ROLL BACKWARD. A method of **database recovery** in which, after corruption, before images are applied to the database until it is returned to the last known point of consistency.

ROLL FORWARD. A method of **database recovery** in which, after corruption, after-images are applied to a backup copy of the database until it is brought up to the last known point of consistency.

ROOT. The base node of a **tree structure. Data** in the tree may be **access**ed starting at its *root*.

ROOT ENTITY TYPE. An **entity type** that does not participate as the plural entity type in any one-to-many **relationship.**

ROOT FUNCTION. A **function** that is not itself a **subfunction** of any other function.

ROOT IDENTIFIER. The identifying **attribute**s of a **root entity type.**

ROUTINE EVENT. An **event** which occurs with such regularity that the number in a given time period can be estimated but cannot be known precisely.

ROUTINE PROCESS. A **process** which is executed with such regularity that the number in a given time period may be estimated accurately but not precisely.

RUN UNIT. A collection of **batch programs** to be executed as a group based on **processing location**s, processing type (**online** vs. **batch**), and timing. *(KB)*

RUN-TIME INCLUDE. An alternative to copy compile where code is copied into a **program** at *runtime* and then interpreted.

SCHEDULE. A plan for the performance of **task**s within a **project**, detailing the time and resource requirements.

SCHEMA. 1. A **map** of the overall **logical** structure of a **database.** Contrast with **data model.** *(KB)* 2. A *schema* consists of DDL (**data description language**) entries and is a complete description of all the area, **set** occurrences, **record** occurrences, and associated **data item**s and **data aggregate**s as they exist in the database. (CODA-SYL)

SCHEMA LANGUAGE. Logical database description language.

SCOPE. A defined subset of **object**s which are the subject of a specific **project.**

SCREEN. A presentation of **information** generated by an **application system** and sent to a video display device. *(KB)*

SEARCH. To examine a series of items for any that have a desired property or properties.

SEARCH KEY. *See* **Key, Secondary.**

SECONDARY INDEX. An **index** composed of **secondary key**s rather than **primary key**s.

SECONDARY KEY. *See* **Key, Secondary.**

SECONDARY STORAGE. 1. Storage **facilities** forming not an integral part of a computer but directly **link**ed to and controlled by the computer (e.g., disks, magnetic tapes, etc.) The smallest **address** portion of storage on some disk and drum storage units. 2. A hardware product that can be used to store **data** for indefinite periods of time.

SECURITY CLASSIFICATION. The extent to which specific **module**s or **information object type**s need to be protected from unauthorized use.

SECURITY CONTROL. A measure by means of which a form of protection is given to a business **system** or computing environment.

SECURITY SYSTEM. Hardware, software, or control data designed to prevent damage, theft, or corruption of data application.

SEEK. To position the **access mechanism** of a **direct access storage device** at a specified **location.**

SEEK TIME. The time taken to execute a **seek** operation.

SEGMENT. A named fixed-**format** quantum of **data** containing one or more **data items.** A *segment* is the basic quantum of data that is passed to and from the **application program**s when IBM Data Language/1 is used. (DL/1)

SELECT. An **action** by which a value of an **attribute** is used to *select,* or to assist in *selecting,* an **entity** for involvement in the execution of a **process,** or by which a **data** value is used to *select,* or assist in *selecting,* a **record** for use during the execution of a **module.**

SENSITIVITY. A programmer may view only certain of the **data** in a **logical database.** His **program** is said to be *sensitized* to those data.

SEQUENCE SET INDEX. The lowest **level** in a **tree-structured index.** The **entities** in this level are in sequence. **Search**es and other operations may be carried out in the *sequence set index;* those are called *sequence set operations.*

SEQUENTIAL PROCESSING. **Access**ing **record**s in the sequence in which they were stored.

SERIAL ACCESS STORAGE. Storage in which **record**s must be read serially one after the other (e.g., tape).

SERIAL PROCESSING. **Access**ing **record**s in their **physical** sequence. The next record accessed will be the record in the next physical position/**location** in the **field.**

SERVICE-LEVEL BENCHMARK. A point of reference from which measurements can be made.

SERVICE-LEVEL OBJECTIVE. The measurable level of service provided by an **IS organization unit** for an **application system** which has been agreed to with the **user** (e.g., end-user support, **response time,** turnaround). *(KB)*

SET. A *set* is a named collection of **record type**s. As such, it establishes the characteristics of an arbitrary number of occurrences of the named *set.* Each *set* type specified in the **schema** must have one record type declared as its "Owner" and one or more record types declared as its "Member" records. Each occurrence of a *set* must contain one occurrence of its owner record and may contain an arbitrary number of occurrences of each of its member record types. *(CODASYL)*

SET, SINGULAR. A **CODASYL set** without owner **record**s; the owner is declared to be "**System.**" A *singular set* is used to provide simple non**hierarchical file**s such as a file of customer records.

SKELETON PROGRAM. A partially constructed **program** that performs a small but useful subset of the **functions** of the complete program.

SKILL. The ability or proficiency of a **person.** *(KB)*

SKIP-SEARCHED CHAIN. A **chain** having **pointer**s that permit it to be **search**ed by skipping, not examining every **link** in the chain.

SOFTWARE COMPONENT. **Program**s or instructions that tell a computer what to do.

SORT. Arrange a file in the sequence of a specified **key.**

STAGE. A collection of **activities** within the **methodology.**

STAGING. Blocks of **data** are moved from one storage device to another with a shorter **access time,** either before or at the time they are needed.

STAKEHOLDER. A key member of an **organizational unit** who defines and has a personal stake in achieving the **goal** of the unit.

STANDARD. An approved rule and required practice for controlling the technical performance and methods of personnel involved in **system**s development, modification, and maintenance.

STATE. The **condition** of the **system** at a point in time. **Information** about the *state* of a system, together with new **event**s, determines the system's response.

STORAGE AREA. An area that supports a **logical** view of the **physical** storage structures used to hold **data.** *(KB)*

STORAGE HIERARCHY. Storage units **link**ed together to form a storage **subsystem,** in which some are fast but small and others are large but slow. Blocks of **data** are moved (**stage**d) from the large slow **level**s to the small fast levels as required.

STORAGE SCHEMA. *See* **Internal Schema.**

STRATEGIC INFORMATION SYSTEMS PLAN. A plan that sets out the overall **objective**s for **information system**s development over a three- to five-year period.

STRUCTURED ENGLISH. Statements written in a subset of English within a disciplined organization, such that they may be readily translated into a computer language.

STRUCTURED INTERVIEW. An interview session with (normally) a single businessperson which aims to achieve a specific **information**-gathering **objective** through the use of defined, formal **technique**s and a **format** planned in advance.

STRUCTURED WALK-THROUGH. A symbol-by-symbol verbal explanation of a diagram by the analyst or designer responsible, with the **objective** of eliminating errors and inconsistencies.

SUBJECT AREA. A major, high-level classification of **data.** A group of **entity type**s that pertains directly to a **function** or major topic of interest to the **enterprise.** *(KB)*

SUBSCHEMA. A **map** of a **program**'s view of the **data** used. It is derived from the global **logical** view of the data—the **schema.** *(KB)*

SUBSYSTEM. A complete, self-contained subdivision of an **information system** that performs one discrete **function.**

SYSTEM. An interrelated **set** of components that are viewed as a whole. *Synonym:* **application system.**

SYSTEM ARCHITECTURE. The composite of specific components, and the way in which they interact, that form a computer **system.**

SYSTEM DEPENDENCY. An association between two **system**s which exists because **information** originating in one is required by the other.

SYSTEM DEVELOPMENT METHODOLOGY. A defined way of developing a business **system.** *Synonym:* **methodology.**

SYSTEM SOFTWARE COMPONENT. Software other than the **application program**s which is required to operate, maintain, or support the **processor configuration, communications network,** and the **application** (e.g., TP monitor, **operating system**s, utilities, **compiler**s). *(KB)*

SYSTEM STRUCTURE DIAGRAM. A representation of the designed and defined collection of **procedure**s, **data store**s, **data flow**s, **data view**s, and **terminator**s which, when implemented, will make up a **system.**

SYSTEM TEST. A test carried out on a business **system** to verify that as a whole, it **function**s as specified in the **business system design** specification. *Synonym:* **data flow program.**

SYSTEM VARIANT. A business **system** modified for certain **function**s of a specific (**set of**) **location**(s) or **organizational unit**(s). It is based on a business system designed for the functions of another location or organizational unit within the same **business area.**

SYSTEMS LIFECYCLE. The **stage**s and **task**s in the development and productive use of a **system** from its inception to its demise.

TABLE. 1. A collection of **data** suitable for quick reference, each item being uniquely identified either by a **label** or by its relative position. 2. A rectangular grid of data values each identifiable by the labels applied to the rows and columns.

TACTICAL DECISION. A decision concerning changes in the allocation of resources or in the ways in which an **enterprise** operates.

TACTICAL IS PROJECT PLAN. A plan that describes in detail which **project**s are to be carried out in the first one to three years of the **planning horizon.**

TACTICAL PROCESS. A **process** concerned with the allocation and efficient utilization of the resources of an **enterprise.**

TANGIBLE BENEFIT. A **benefit** to which a direct monetary value can be applied.

TASK. A defined, low-level unit of work for one or more **persons** within a **project.**

TASK RESULT. The creation, update, or deletion of a **project** management, **deliverable,** and/or **knowledge base** component.

TECHNICAL ARCHITECTURE. A structure that summarizes the mixture of hardware, system software, and communication **facilities** which supports or will support the information systems within an **enterprise.**

TECHNICAL COMPONENT OR FACILITY. A hardware, systems software, or communication facility object within the **technical architecture.**

TECHNICAL CONTEXT. A subset of the **technical architecture** within the context of which a **design project** will proceed.

TECHNICAL DESIGN. That part of the **design phase** during which a **system** is refined to achieve the most economic and efficient performance using the chosen technology. *Synonym:* internal design.

TECHNICAL REQUIREMENTS. The technological requirements and constraints identified in planning and analysis that will be considered in depth by the design project.

TECHNIQUE. A **set** of interrelated **procedure**s which together describe how a **task** in the **methodology** can be accomplished.

TECHNOLOGY IMPACT ANALYSIS. A **methodology** for the effects or potential of the adoption of new enabling technologies on an organization's business opportunities.

TEMPORAL EVENT. The triggering of one or more **process**es at a predetermined time. These processes use only **data** that has previously been saved within the **system.**

TERMINATION STATE. A final **state** in the life of an **entity.**

TERMINATOR. An **organizational unit,** lying outside the boundary of a **system,** that originates or receives one or more of the system's **data view**s.

TEST. A formally organized execution of **modules**, **program**s, and/or **procedure**s to prove the integrity of part of the business **system.**

TEST CASE. A collection of input **data** and expected output data designed to ascertain whether a **test condition** is met correctly. A **set** of **select**ed **data element** test values and expected results which is used during various types of testing (e.g., unit, integration, performance, acceptance).

TEST CONDITION. A rule that must be tested to ensure the correct operation of a **procedure** step, **action statement,** or statement block.

TEST CYCLE. A collection of **test case**s which are applied in sequence to verify the correct operation of all the **test condition**s tested by the test case.

TEST HARNESS. Software needed to adequately test components of an **application.**

THIRD NORMAL FORM. *See* **Normal Form, Third.**

TIME EVENT. The passage of a specific time period which triggers the execution of one or more **processes.**

TOOL. A software product used by **information systems** personnel to manage and support information systems.

TRACK. The circular recording surface transcribed by a read/write head on a drum, disk, or other rotating mechanism.

TRANSACTION SCREEN. A **screen** that accepts **business transactions** as input to an **application.** *(KB)*

TRANSITION. 1. The period in the **systems lifecycle** in which the new business **systems,** to support a defined area within the **enterprise,** gradually replace or are interfaced to the existing system. 2. The **process** by which a new system is first installed with one or a small number of groups of business **users** and then expanded to involve all potential users within the organization.

TRANSITION ALGORITHM. *See* **Conversion Algorithm.**

TRANSITION ANALYSIS. *See* **Migration Analysis.**

TRANSITION DESIGN. *See* **Migration Design.**

TRANSITIVE DEPENDENCY. A **dependency** between two elements, which is due to the first element being dependent on some other element, which in turn is dependent on the second.

TRANSPARENT DATA. Complexities in the **data structure** are hidden from the programmers or **users** (made transparent to them) by the systems software.

TREE INDEX. An **index** in the form of a **tree structure.**

TREE STRUCTURE. A hierarchy of groups of **data** such that (a) the highest **level** in the hierarchy has only one group, called a **root;** (b) all groups except the root are related to one and only one group on a higher level than themselves. A simple master/detail file is a two-level tree. *Syn:* Hierarchical Structure.

TRIAL RUN. A period in which the **user** can engage the new **system** to perform actual business **procedures** in the working environment, but in which there is still an option to return to the former business system if serious **problems** are encountered when operating the new system.

TUPLE. A group of related **fields.** *N* related fields are called an *N-tuple.*

TYPE. *See* Note 2, p. 445.

UNIT TEST. A test performed on an atomic unit, typically **modules** and **programs,** in order to test detailed logic.

USER. A staff member in a **business area** who will make use of an **information system.**

VIRTUAL. Conceptual or appearing to be, rather than actually being. An adjective which implies that **data,** structures, or hardware appear to the **application** programmer or **user** to be different from what they are in reality, the **conversion** being performed by software.

VIRTUAL MEMORY. Memory that can appear to the **programs** to be larger than it really is because blocks of **data** or program are rapidly moved to or from **secondary storage** when needed.

VOLATILE FILE. A file with a high rate of additions and deletions.

VOLATILE STORAGE. Storage that loses its contents when the power supply is cut off. Solid-state (LSI) storage is volatile; magnetic storage is not.

VOLUME. Demountable tapes, disks, and cartridges are referred to as *volumes.* The word also refers to a nondemountable disk or other storage medium. It has been defined as ''that portion of a single unit of storage medium which is **access**ible to a single read/write mechanism''; however, some devices exist in which a volume is accessible with two or more read/write mechanisms.

VOLUME TABLE OF CONTENTS (VTOC). A **table** associated with a **volume** which describes each file or **data set** on the volume.

VSAM. Virtual Sequential **Access Method.** An IBM **volume**-independent indexed-sequential **access method.**

VTOC. *See* **Volume Table of Contents.**

WORK PLAN. A plan prepared for each **phase** detailing **tasks,** resource estimates, and time **schedules.**

WORKING STORAGE. A portion of storage, usually computer main memory, reserved for the temporary intermediate results of processing.

INDEX

A

Action diagrams, 6–7, 8, 9, 18–19, 59,
   65–67, 72, 73, 514
  adding access data to, 285–92
  advantages of, 566, 570
  automatic derivation of, 563
  automatic navigation, 557
  brackets, 538
  common procedures, 543
  compound database actions, 556–57
  concurrency, 550
  conditions, 540–41
  constructs of, 57, 551
  CONTRACT, 562, 564
  conversion to code, 563, 566
  decomposition to program code,
   547–48
  editors and CASE tools, 563
  of executable code written in C, 84

  of executable code written in IDEAL,
   87
  of executable code written in PL/I,
   85-86
  EXPAND, 562, 565
  for management procedures, 566
  fourth-generation languages, 545–47
  GO TO, 544
  hierarchical dialog structure
   represented as, 72, 75
  input and output data, 551, 553, 554
  loops, 542
  next-iteration construct, 544–45
  overview versus detailed logic
   diagramming, 537
  probabilities on, 292
  procedure for phototyping, 124
  relational joins, 559–61

Information Systems Management and Strategy

AN INFORMATION SYSTEMS MANIFESTO

INFORMATION ENGINEERING (Book I: Introduction)

INFORMATION ENGINEERING (Book II: Planning and Analysis)

STRATEGIC INFORMATION PLANNING METHODOLOGIES (second edition)

SOFTWARE MAINTENANCE: THE PROBLEM AND ITS SOLUTIONS

DESIGN AND STRATEGY FOR DISTRIBUTED DATA PROCESSING

CORPORATE COMMUNICATIONS STRATEGY

Expert Systems

BUILDING EXPERT SYSTEMS: A TUTORIAL

KNOWLEDGE ACQUISITION FOR EXPERT SYSTEMS

Methodologies for Building Systems

STRATEGIC INFORMATION PLANNING METHODOLOGIES (second edition)

INFORMATION ENGINEERING (Book I: Introduction)

INFORMATION ENGINEERING (Book II: Planning and Analysis)

INFORMATION ENGINEERING (Book III: Design and Construction)

STRUCTURED TECHNIQUES: THE BASIS FOR CASE (revised edition)

Diagramming Techniques

DIAGRAMMING TECHNIQUES FOR ANALYSTS AND PROGRAMMERS

RECOMMENDED DIAGRAMMING STANDARDS FOR ANALYSTS AND PROGRAMMERS

ACTION DIAGRAMS: CLEARLY STRUCTURED SPECIFICATIONS, PROGRAMS, AND PROCEDURES (second edition)

Analysis and Design

STRUCTURED TECHNIQUES: THE BASIS FOR CASE (revised edition)

DATABASE ANALYSIS AND DESIGN

DESIGN OF MAN-COMPUTER DIALOGUES

DESIGN OF REAL-TIME COMPUTER SYSTEMS

DATA COMMUNICATIONS DESIGN TECHNIQUES

DESIGN AND STRATEGY FOR DISTRIBUTED DATA PROCESSING

SOFTWARE MAINTENANCE: THE PROBLEM AND ITS SOLUTIONS

SYSTEM DESIGN FROM PROVABLY CORRECT CONSTRUCTS

INFORMATION ENGINEERING (Book II: Planning and Analysis)

INFORMATION ENGINEERING (Book III: Design and Construction)

CASE

STRUCTURED TECHN THE BASIS FOR CA (revised edition)

INFORMATION ENGIN (Book I: Introductio

Languages and Progra

APPLICATION DEVELO WITHOUT PROGRAMM

FOURTH-GENERAT LANGUAGES (Volume I: Principle

FOURTH-GENERAT LANGUAGES (Volume II: Representativ

FOURTH-GENERAT LANGUAGES (Volume III: 4GLs from

ACTION DIAGRAMS: CL STRUCTURED SPECIFIC PROGRAMS, AND PROCE (second edition)